The Cambridge Stravinsky Encyclopedia

Igor Stravinsky is one of a small number of early modernist composers whose music epitomises the stylistic crisis of twentieth-century music, from the Russian nationalist heritage of the early works, to the neo-classical works which anticipate the stylistic diversity of the contemporary musical scene in the early twenty-first century and the integration of serial techniques during his final period. With entries written by more than sixty international contributors from Russian, European and American traditions, *The Cambridge Stravinsky Encyclopedia* presents multiple perspectives on the life, works, writings and aesthetic relationships of this multi-faceted creative artist. This important resource explores Stravinsky's relationships with virtually all the major artistic figures of his time – painters, dramatists, choreographers and producers, as well as musicians – and brings together fresh insights into the life and work of one of the twentieth century's greatest composers.

EDWARD CAMPBELL is Professor of Music at the University of Aberdeen where he specialises in contemporary European art music and aesthetics. His published work includes the books *Boulez, Music and Philosophy* (2010), *Music after Deleuze* (2013) and the co-edited volume *Pierre Boulez Studies* (2016).

PETER O'HAGAN is a pianist and writer specialising in contemporary music. He has given numerous concerts at London's South Bank Centre and Wigmore Hall, as well as at festivals of contemporary music in Europe and the USA.

The Cambridge Stravinsky Encyclopedia

Edited by

EDWARD CAMPBELL
University of Aberdeen

PETER O'HAGAN
Roehampton University, London

CAMBRIDGE
UNIVERSITY PRESS

CAMBRIDGE
UNIVERSITY PRESS

Shaftesbury Road, Cambridge CB2 8EA, United Kingdom

One Liberty Plaza, 20th Floor, New York, NY 10006, USA

477 Williamstown Road, Port Melbourne, VIC 3207, Australia

314–321, 3rd Floor, Plot 3, Splendor Forum, Jasola District Centre, New Delhi – 110025, India

103 Penang Road, #05–06/07, Visioncrest Commercial, Singapore 238467

Cambridge University Press is part of Cambridge University Press & Assessment, a department of the University of Cambridge.

We share the University's mission to contribute to society through the pursuit of education, learning and research at the highest international levels of excellence.

www.cambridge.org
Information on this title: www.cambridge.org/9781316506202

DOI: 10.1017/9781316493205

First published 2021
First paperback edition 2024

A catalogue record for this publication is available from the British Library

Library of Congress Cataloging-in-Publication data
NAMES: Campbell, Edward, 1958– author. | O'Hagan, Peter, author.
TITLE: The Cambridge Stravinsky encyclopedia / edited by Edward Campbell, Peter O'Hagan.
DESCRIPTION: New York : Cambridge University Press, 2020. | Includes bibliographical references and index.
IDENTIFIERS: LCCN 2019038150 (print) | LCCN 2019038151 (ebook) | ISBN 9781107140875 (hardback) | ISBN 9781316493205 (ebook)
SUBJECTS: LCSH: Stravinsky, Igor, 1882–1971 – Encyclopedias.
CLASSIFICATION: LCC ML410.S932 C153 2020 (print) | LCC ML410.S932 (ebook) | DDC 780.92 [B]–dc23
LC record available at https://lccn.loc.gov/2019038150
LC ebook record available at https://lccn.loc.gov/2019038151

ISBN   978-1-107-14087-5   Hardback
ISBN   978-1-316-50620-2   Paperback

Contents

Music Examples

Contributors

Cécile Auzolle	Université de Poitiers
Tatiana Baranova Monighetti	Independent scholar
Nicolas Bell	Trinity College, Cambridge University
Florian Henri Besthorn	Ludwig Maximilian University of Munich
Natalia Braginskaya	Rimsky-Korsakov St Petersburg State Conservatory
Edward Campbell	University of Aberdeen
Matthew Paul Carlson	High Point University, North Carolina
Maureen Carr	Penn State School of Music, Pennsylvania
Jeremy Coleman	University of Malta
Chris Collins	University of Aberdeen
Richard Desinord	Eastman School of Music, Rochester, New York
Valérie Dufour	Free University of Brussels
Ben Earle	University of Birmingham
David Evans	University of St Andrews
Lois Fitch	Royal Conservatory of Scotland, Glasgow
Christoph Flamm	Heidelberg University
Sebastian Forbes	University of Surrey, Guildford
Johanna Frymoyer	University of Notre Dame
Susanne Gärtner	City of Basel Music Academy
Graham Griffiths	City, University of London
Peter Hill	University of Sheffield and Royal Northern College of Music
Millicent Hodson	Choreographer and reconstructor, London
Daniel Jaffé	Independent scholar
Harry Joelson	Winterthur Libraries
Lorin Johnson	California State University, Long Beach
Stephanie Jordan	University of Roehampton
Charles Joseph	Skidmore College, Saratoga Springs, New York
Ihor Junyk	Trent University, Canada
Barbara L. Kelly	Royal Northern College of Music, Manchester
Marie-Pier Leduc	University of Montreal
Katerina Levidou	King's College London
Massimiliano Locanto	University of Salerno
Marina Lupishko	Saarland University Saarbrücken
Mark McFarland	Georgia State University, Atlanta, Georgia
Olga Manulkina	St Petersburg University

Deborah Mawer	Royal Birmingham Conservatoire
Flo Menezes	State University of São Paulo (UNESP)
Marcos Mesquita	Coordinator of the Research Group 'Cogmus: Analytical and Creative Processes and Musical Cognition', São Paulo
Felix Meyer	Paul Sacher Foundation, Basel
Helen Julia Minors	Kingston University, London
Ivan Moody	CESEM, Nova University, Lisbon
Gayle Murchison	College of William and Mary, Williamsburg, Virginia
Christoph Neidhöfer	McGill University, Montreal
Peter O'Hagan	Roehampton University, London
Susanna Pasticci	University of Cassino
Stéphane Pétermann	University of Lausanne
Caroline Potter	Royal Birmingham Conservatoire
Jane Pritchard	Victoria and Albert Museum, London
Kathryn Puffett	Independent scholar, Cambridge
Sophie Redfern	University of Sheffield
Lutero Rodrigues	São Paulo State University (Unesp), Institute of Arts
Lynne Rogers	Mannes School of Music, The New School, New York
Svetlana Savenko	Moscow State Tchaikovsky Conservatory
Joseph Schultz	BBC Music Library, BBC Archives, London
Nigel Simeone	Independent scholar
David Smyth	Louisiana State University, Baton Rouge
Marie Stravinsky	Geneva
Werner Strinz	Strasbourg Conservatory
Barbara Swanson	Dalhousie University, Halifax
Phillip Torbert	Penn State School of Music, Pennsylvania
Don Traut	University of Arizona
Pieter van den Toorn	University of California–Santa Barbara
Elena Vereshchagina	Academy College at the Moscow Conservatory
Tatiana Vereshchagina	Independent scholar
Arnold Whittall	King's College London
Leila Zickgraf	University of Basel

Editors' Preface

Although there have been acclaimed volumes on such leading eighteenth- and nineteenth-century composers as Handel, Mozart, Berlioz, Verdi and Wagner, an encyclopedia devoted to a twentieth-century composer is a new initiative for Cambridge University Press. Igor Stravinsky is one of a small number of early modernist composers whose music epitomises the stylistic crisis of twentieth-century music, and indeed of the arts in general during the last century. In a creative span of some seven decades, he witnessed at first hand the slow decay of the opulent world of post-Wagnerian Romanticism, the advent of serialism, and, finally, the beginning of the era of stylistic pluralism which marked the last three decades of the twentieth century. Indeed, these developments find a parallel in Stravinsky's own evolution, starting from the Russian nationalist heritage of the early works, a world which is irretrievably shattered in the dissonances and rhythmic innovations of *The Rite of Spring*, the seismic shock of which continues to resonate to this day. The subsequent neo-classical works anticipate the stylistic diversity of the contemporary musical scene, the composer's multi-faceted artistic personality finding expression in the adoption of a dazzling and at times bewildering range of identities, culminating in his attempts to integrate serial techniques into a personal style during the final period. Whilst avoiding making exaggerated claims for Stravinsky's artistic legacy, it can be stated with confidence that his position in the history of Western art music is such that he is widely recognised as one of the most imposing musical personalities of his time, and, as such, comparable to Monteverdi, Bach, Beethoven and Wagner.

While it is as a composer that Stravinsky left an indelible mark on the music of the twentieth century, he had two other careers, as writer and performer. Active as both pianist and conductor over many decades, he not only gave the first performances of many of his own works, but in addition left a recorded legacy of considerable historical significance, to the extent that Stravinsky's performances serve as indispensable references for any performer seeking to gain interpretive insights into the music. The composer's writings offer a somewhat more ambiguous legacy. Whilst they cannot be compared in quality or volume with that of the great composer/writers of the previous century already featured in this series – Berlioz and Wagner – they are important sources of information about the composer's life and times. As well as giving trenchant expression to his own views, the writings offer insights into a whole range of his contemporaries across the artistic spectrum and were frequently quoted at face value during the composer's lifetime. It is only in recent years that scholarly research has resulted in a more nuanced view of their status as vehicles for the composer's thoughts.

Stravinsky founded no school of composition and did little formal teaching; however, his influence was enormous, and he exercised a spell over, in turn, his Russian, Parisian and American contemporaries. Indeed, to this day, major living composers acknowledge his importance, and his influence continues to resonate half a century after his death in 1971. During his lifetime, the seemingly unpredictable changes of style provoked considerable controversy, and a critically contentious atmosphere remained, long after many of his works had been accepted as classics of the twentieth century. It is indeed remarkable that the composer of *The Rite of Spring*, the work which produced the most violent audience reaction of any twentieth-century work, was some three decades later being dismissed by the postwar Parisian avant-garde as an irrelevant figure. Only with the perspective of time has the underlying unity and consistency of Stravinsky's oeuvre become increasingly apparent.

The editors of the *Cambridge Stravinsky Encyclopedia* were aware from the outset of the range of critical responses which Stravinsky's music continues to attract, and, moreover, of the distinctive musicological backgrounds in each of the geographical areas in which Stravinsky lived and worked. Hence our desire to involve a wide range of contributors, representing successively Russian, European and American traditions. If this has led to a degree of overlap between entries, and indeed to occasional inconsistency between individual contributors, we have chosen to allow these to remain, in the belief that a pluralistic approach to a figure of such universality is wholly appropriate, and in the end offers the possibility of a richer perspective on this complex artist. It would be beyond the scope of any single-volume reference book to cover every aspect of the composer and the *Cambridge Stravinsky Encyclopedia* makes no attempt to pursue a comprehensive treatment of all the elements which coalesce into producing such a multi-faceted creative artist – to do so would require a study many times longer than the current one. Stravinsky's range of contacts during his career was enormous: indeed, he was personally acquainted with virtually all the major artistic figures of his lifetime – not only musicians, but painters, dramatists, choreographers and producers. Whilst remaining conscious of the *Encyclopedia*'s primary role as a point of reference, the editors have taken the decision to limit the number of short entries on comparatively peripheral figures in Stravinsky's career in order to allow for extended entries on individual works and on those key figures who played a major role in his artistic development. Thus, our intention is to bring together in accessible form a series of concentrated studies in which multiple aspects of Stravinsky's work are examined both within a biographical and historical framework, and in the context of current scholarship. In so doing, it is our hope that readers will benefit from what is undoubtedly a fresh approach to the life and work of one of the greatest composers of the twentieth century.

Acknowledgements

It was in 2014 that Vicki Cooper at Cambridge University Press suggested that we edit an Encyclopedia devoted to Igor Stravinsky. We are grateful to her for her confidence in us, and for her encouragement during the early stages of the project. We are equally grateful to her successor, Kate Brett, and assistant, Eilidh Burrett, who have likewise supported us and given invaluable advice throughout the production of the volume. We would also like to thank our Content Managers at the University Press, Sharon McCann and Sarah Lambert; our copy-editor, Leigh Mueller; and Project Management Executive Sudarsan Siddarthan at Integra Software Services.

We would like to thank all the authors, not only for their distinguished contributions but also for their willingness to respond to requests for alterations and clarification, especially in the case of those authors writing in English as a second language. It would have been impossible for us to produce a volume devoted to such a vast subject without the advice of various specialist colleagues, and we are particularly grateful to Maureen Carr, Valérie Dufour, Charles Joseph and Arnold Whittall. Stephen Walsh, although unable to contribute to the volume, allowed us to consult him on several occasions, and generously offered us the benefit of his peerless knowledge of Stravinsky's life and music. Sadly, two of the originally contracted authors, Ken Gloag and Stuart Campbell, passed away before they were able to complete their texts: we wish to acknowledge their interest in the project, and we are especially grateful to Stuart Campbell for his advice, particularly in the specialist area of Russian transliteration. Christopher Murray was responsible for translating some of the entries from the original French, and we thank him for this work.

Additionally, the editors wish to thank the Paul Sacher Foundation Basel for permission to make reference to original material in its Stravinsky Collection. The curator of the collection, Heidy Zimmermann, dealt with numerous queries with patience and good humour, and offered information about the manuscript sources which was crucial to several entries. Felix Meyer, Director of the Foundation, not only contributed the entry on the Foundation itself, but was a constant source of wisdom and support throughout the project.

Finally, many scholars who have contributed to this volume spent time in Basel as guests at the Metzger family home, and we wish to express our appreciation and thanks to Martin and Ingrid Metzger for their hospitality extending over a period of several decades.

Abbreviations

ASS	Robert Craft, *A Stravinsky Scrapbook 1940–1971* (London: Thames and Hudson, 1983).
Auto	Igor Stravinsky, *Stravinsky: An Autobiography* (New York: Simon and Schuster, 1936).
CASIII	Claude Tappolet (ed.), *Correspondance Ansermet–Strawinsky (1914–1967)*, vol. III (Geneva: Georg, 1992).
Conv	Igor Stravinsky and Robert Craft, *Conversations with Igor Stravinsky* (London: Faber and Faber, 1959).
DB	Robert Craft (ed.), *Dearest Bubushkin: The Correspondence of Vera and Igor Stravinsky, 1921–1954, with Excerpts from Vera Stravinsky's Diaries, 1922–1971*, trans. Lucia Davidova (London: Thames and Hudson, 1985).
Dial	Igor Stravinsky and Robert Craft, *Dialogues and a Diary* (London: Faber and Faber, 1968).
Expo	Igor Stravinsky and Robert Craft, *Expositions and Developments* (London: Faber and Faber, 1962).
ISPS	Viktor Varunts (ed.), *I. Stravinsky: Publitsist i sobesednik* (Moscow: Sovetskiy Kompozitor, 1988).
IVSPA	Vera Stravinsky, Rita McCaffrey and Robert Craft, *Igor and Vera Stravinsky: A Photograph Album, 1921 to 1971* (London: Thames and Hudson, 1982).
M&C	Igor Stravinsky and Robert Craft, *Memories and Commentaries: New One-volume Edition* (London: Faber and Faber, 2002).
Mem	Igor Stravinsky and Robert Craft, *Memories and Commentaries* (London: Faber and Faber, 1960).
Poet	Igor Stravinsky, *Poetics of Music in the Form of Six Lessons*, trans. Arthur Knodel and Ingolf Dahl (Cambridge, Mass.: Harvard University Press, 1947).
PRK	Viktor Varunts (ed.), *I. F. Stravinsky: Perepiska s russkimi korrespondentami. Materiali k biografi*, 3 vols. (Moscow: Kompozitor, 1997, 2000, 2003).
PSS	Paul Sacher Stiftung
SB	K. Yu. Stravinskaya, *O. I. F. Stravinskom i evo blizkikh* (Leningrad: Muzïka, 1978).
SCF (72)	Robert Craft, *Stravinsky: The Chronicle of a Friendship 1948–1971* (London: Gollancz, 1972).

SCF (94)	Robert Craft, *Stravinsky: The Chronicle of a Friendship: Revised and Expanded Edition* (Nashville and London: Vandebilt University Press, 1994).
SCS	Stephen Walsh, *Stravinsky, A Creative Spring: Russia and France 1882–1934* (New York: Knopf, 1999; London: Jonathan Cape, 2000).
SCW	Eric Walter White, *Stravinsky: The Composer and his Works*, 2nd edn (London and Boston: Faber and Faber, 1979).
Sfam	Theodore and Denise Strawinsky, *Stravinsky: A Family Chronicle 1906–1940*, trans. Stephen Walsh (London : Schirmer, 2004); edited translation of T. and D. Strawinsky, *Au cœur du foyer* (Bourg-la-Reine: Zurfluh, 1998), which in turn incorporated a revised text from Theodore Strawinsky, *Catherine & Igor Stravinsky: A Family Album* (London: Boosey & Hawkes, 1973).
SHW	Tamara Levitz (ed.), *Stravinsky and His World* (Princeton University Press, 2013).
SPD	Vera Stravinsky and Robert Craft, *Stravinsky in Pictures and Documents* (New York: Simon and Schuster, 1978).
SRT	Richard Taruskin, *Stravinsky and the Russian Traditions: A Biography of the Works through Mavra*, 2 vols. (Berkeley: University of California Press, 1996).
SSC, I, II, III	Robert Craft (ed.), *Stravinsky: Selected Correspondence*, 3 vols. (London: Faber and Faber, 1982, 1984, 1985).
SSE	Stephen Walsh, *Stravinsky, The Second Exile: France and America 1934–1971* (New York: Knopf, 2006; London: Jonathan Cape, 2006).
T&C	Igor Stravinsky, *Themes and Conclusions* (London: Faber and Faber, 1972)
T&E	Igor Stravinsky and Robert Craft, *Themes and Episodes* (New York: Knopf, 1967).

A

Abraham and Isaac / A Sacred Ballad for Baritone and Chamber Orchestra. Composed 2 August 1962 – 3 March 1963 (according to the sketches). First performance, 23 August 1964, Jerusalem. Conductor, Robert CRAFT. Published 1965, Boosey & Hawkes.

The work was composed on the text in Hebrew taken from the first Book of Moses, Chapter 22, verses 1–19. Originally titled *Cantata*, Stravinsky crossed this out in the first proof of the score and wrote instead: 'Sacred Ballad / Dedicated to the people of the State of Israel'. In the printed score, there are three versions of the biblical text: in Hebrew, Roman alphabet transliteration, and English translation. Nevertheless, the work is to be performed in Hebrew only. According to Stravinsky, 'the syllables, both as accentuation and timbre, are a precisely fixed and principal element of the music' (SCW, 529). His discovery of Hebrew 'as sound' was perhaps stimulated by SCHOENBERG's *De profundis*.

The work based on a biblical text was commissioned in January 1962 by the Israeli Government for The Israel Music Festival (see ISRAEL). Nevertheless, all preliminary negotiations were already conducted at the end of 1961 by Sir Isaiah Berlin, a leading Oxford philosopher and one of the Festival's advisers abroad. He proposed two subjects from the Bible: the Seven Days of the Creation and the Sacrifice of Isaac. The composer chose the story of Abraham and Isaac, which provided a symbolic account of the origin of the Israeli nation (the theological meaning being the unconditional obedience to God and codification of the rejection of human sacrifices). Sir Isaiah read to Stravinsky the passages from the Bible in Hebrew, explaining their pronunciation, supplying a literal translation, and providing Roman alphabet transliteration.

According to the 1962 version of the contract, Stravinsky should have composed a work for choir, soloists and orchestra (20–30 minutes), but the 1963 contract allowed the submission of a composition 'at the composer's own discretion' (15–30 minutes) (PSS). Stravinsky's fee was $15,000.

The work was premièred on 23 August 1964 in Jerusalem, with Ephraim Biran (baritone) and musicians from the Kol Israel Symphony Orchestra and the Haifa City Symphony Orchestra directed by Craft. The concert was repeated the next day in Caesarea. The first European performance came on 22 September 1964 at the Berliner Festwochen with Dietrich Fischer-Dieskau as soloist.

Theodor Kollek asked Stravinsky in his letter (30 March 1965) 'to give the manuscript as a gift to the State of Israel'. Stravinsky replied: 'The enclosed manuscript on transparent paper of my *Abraham and Isaac* full score is my answer to it' (15 July 1965). Today the autograph is located at the Hebrew University of Jerusalem, whilst a copy and the sketches are in the PSS.

The work is based on a TWELVE-NOTE row (F-F♯-E-D-D♯-B-A-G-G♯-A♯-C-C♯), elaborated into two hexachordal rotational arrays (ALPHA, BETA). This technique follows KRENEK's method of rotation together with transposition in his THRENI. Among the sketches in the PSS is Stravinsky's original serial chart (the permutations are transposed in such a way that the first pitch of the original hexachord was retained for each permutation).

Example 1 *Abraham and Isaac*: Stravinsky's serial chart (PSS).

The work begins with G, the eighth note of the row. (That misled some researchers, and they erroneously considered the row G-G♯-A♯-C-C♯-A-B-D♯-D-E-F♯-F as a basic form.)

Stravinsky himself described the structure of the work: 'There are five parts distinguished by changes of tempo and performed without interruption; and nineteen verses comprising ten musical units' (White suggests subdividing it into seven sections – SCW, 530). Stravinsky also writes in his note: 'my setting does not impersonate the protagonist but tells the whole story through the baritone-narrator, underlining a change of speaker by change in dynamics'. In the expressive declamatory vocal line (in the ballad spirit), partly narrative and syllabic, partly melismatic, one can observe the influence of Hebrew cantillations.   TATIANA BARANOVA MONIGHETTI

Abravanel, Maurice (born Salonika (Thessaloniki), 6 January 1903; died Salt Lake City, 22 September 1993). Naturalised American conductor. He studied composition with Kurt WEILL and they remained close. Abravanel conducted the PARIS première of Weill's *Mahagonny-Songspiel* in 1932 and met Stravinsky on that occasion. He moved to America in 1936, and in 1944 conducted the first performances of SCÈNES DE BALLET as part of Billy Rose's revue *The Seven Lively Arts*. It was a fraught experience, with pressure from Rose for cuts and rescoring. Abravanel resisted changes to the scoring, but agreed to cuts (as did a reluctant Stravinsky). Abravanel was chief conductor of the Utah Symphony (1947–79), and with Utah forces he recorded SYMPHONY OF PSALMS, APOLLO, the CONCERTO IN D FOR VIOLIN AND ORCHESTRA (with Tossy Spivakovsky) and BACH–Stravinsky, 'Vom Himmel hoch'.   NIGEL SIMEONE

Adorno, Theodor Wiesengrund (born Frankfurt am Main, 11 September 1903; died Visp, Switzerland, 6 August 1969). German, Frankfurt-School philosopher, sociologist and musicologist. A thinker of profound originality and insight, as well as a composer of merit, who studied with Alban BERG and participated in the life of the SCHOENBERG circle in Vienna from 1925. His writings on music are inherently philosophical and are marked by the integration of technical knowledge and a penetrating critical analysis of the significance of modern music from a dialectical perspective.

In the early essay 'Zur gesellschaflichten Lage der Musik' (1932), Stravinsky's music is given some credit as being dialectical in its relation to society and as resisting commodification in its 'objectivism' and 'surrealism'. The use of FOLK MUSIC for ideological purposes by both fascist and communist regimes sustained Adorno in the conviction that the folkloric and primitivistic elements in Stravinsky's music were symptomatic of a reactionary conservatism, concealing the true state of societal relations within modernity. He was persuaded furthermore of a connection in the 1920s and 1930s linking fascism with 'objectivism' in art, including NEO-CLASSICISM.

While the opposition of Stravinsky and Schoenberg was already significant for Adorno by the mid-1920s, this found its strongest statement in the *Philosophy of New Music* (1949) where the essay 'Stravinsky and the Restoration' (1948) is set in dialectical opposition to the companion essay 'Schoenberg and Progress' (1940–1). For Adorno, all artworks, including musical compositions, contain within themselves in sedimented form truth

3

content that is revelatory of the society in which they are produced, and this is the basis of the analysis in the *Philosophy*.

Adorno compares Stravinsky's pre-World War I music unfavourably to Schoenberg's free atonal works, which later became Adorno's musical ideal in preference to the constraints of the German composer's TWELVE-NOTE works. Beyond musical preference, the music of Stravinsky and Schoenberg is set out as symptomatic of two powerful political oppositions, but where Adorno finds a truthfulness in Schoenbergian dodecaphony as reflective of the various totalitarianisms of the era, aspects of Stravinsky's works are highlighted as harbouring elements of fascism, a particularly uncomfortable parallel given the Russian composer's admiration for MUSSOLINI.

While Schoenberg's music is read as 'an intensification of the survival of the expressive Subject', Stravinsky's continues and exemplifies the Subject's capitulation (Paddison 1993, 256). For Adorno, Stravinsky's The SOLDIER'S TALE illuminates his entire production while featuring a cornucopia of schizophrenic mechanisms, *pace* psychoanalysis, including regression, depersonalisation and alienation (Adorno 2006, 130).

In the essay 'Strawinsky: Ein dialektisches Bild' (1962), Adorno revised his position again, granting once more that the Russian was indeed a dialectical composer and radical on the basis of the surrealistic elements within his music, and his engagement with the music of the past was now recognised as aligning him more with MAHLER than to either WAGNER or DEBUSSY. While remaining wary of the 'detached objectivity' of Stravinsky's music, he nevertheless recognised within it '"a moment of truth" in the way in which the composer manipulates the debris of a culturally exhausted and disintegrating material' (Paddison 1993, 269–70).   EDWARD CAMPBELL

Theodor W. Adorno, *Philosophy of New Music.*, trans., ed. and with an Introduction by Robert Hullot-Kentor (Minneapolis and London: University of Minnesota Press, 2006).
Max Paddison, *Adorno's Aesthetics of Music* (Cambridge University Press, 1993).

Afanasyev, Alexander (Nikolayevich) (born Boguchar, 11 July 1826; died Moscow, 23 October 1871). Russian ethnographer, so popular that his collection of folk tales became the Russian equivalent to the tales of the Brothers Grimm. Stravinsky drew extensively on his work during his Swiss years. His *Russian Folk Tales* were a text source (though not always the sole one) for *Pribaoutki*, *Berceuses du chat*, *Three Children's Tales*, RENARD, The SOLDIER'S TALE and Les NOCES, while there is evidence of some influence on the text of How the Mushrooms Prepared for War too. At the same time, they were among FOKINE's sources for the scenario of The FIREBIRD. Finally, the folklore described in The Slavs' Poetic Outlook on Nature was in all likelihood one of the main literary sources for the scenario of The RITE OF SPRING.   KATERINA LEVIDOU

Agon, BALLET for twelve dancers. Composed 1953–7. First performance, 17 June 1957 (concert performance), LOS ANGELES; staged 1 December 1957, New York (CHOREOGRAPHY by George BALANCHINE). Published 1957, Boosey & Hawkes. 'Dedicated to Lincoln Kirstein and George Balanchine'.

Following the première of ORPHEUS in 1948, Lincoln KIRSTEIN, co-founder with George Balanchine of the NEW YORK CITY BALLET, suggested to Stravinsky that he should write a ballet that would constitute 'a third act' after APOLLO (1927–8) and *Orpheus* (SSC, I, 271). Kirstein proposed various subjects, all of which Stravinsky rejected, but on 31 August 1953 he communicated an idea from Balanchine for a 'competition before the gods' whom 'the dancers re-animate ... by a series of historic dances': 'It is as if time called the tune, and the dances which began quite simply in the sixteenth century took fire in the twentieth and exploded' (SSC, I, 287). With the same letter, Kirstein sent Stravinsky the recent edition of François de Lauze's *Apologie de la danse* (1623), translated with commentary by Joan Wildeblood and additional musical examples from Marin Mersenne's *Harmonie universelle* (1636) (London, 1952).

Having decided not to have a plot, Stravinsky began the composition of the ballet in October 1953 but did not get beyond a draft for the fanfare of the Pas-de-Quatre and a few sketches for the Double Pas-de-Quatre before interrupting work on the score to compose IN MEMORIAM DYLAN THOMAS (1954). Balanchine and Stravinsky established the structural plan of the ballet in July–August 1954, by which time Stravinsky chose the title *Agon* ('Contest', SSC, I, 289). The first six dances up to the First Pas-de-Trois Coda as well as the Prelude, which comprise half the music of *Agon*, were completed between August and December 1954, but then Stravinsky interrupted work on the ballet again, this time for over a year taken up by, among other things, the commission of CANTICUM SACRUM (1955). He resumed work on *Agon* with the Bransle movements in April 1956, completing the final score on 27 April 1957.

Agon features a heterogeneous compilation of materials, ranging from the types of chromatically enriched diatonic texture familiar from Stravinsky's earlier neo-classical works and partially or fully serial, non-dodecaphonic counterpoint similar to that in his more recent compositions, to fully TWELVE-NOTE serial structures (see Table 1). This diversity of technique and style in a single work is unique in Stravinsky's output and has fired the imagination of commentators over the years. (Luciano Berio, for instance, characterised *Agon* as 'the hyper-intelligent parable of a "short history of music" that performs a lucid, but tragic autopsy on itself under the pretext of a game': 1985, 65.) As Susannah Tucker has shown in her analysis of the sketches for *Agon*, the incorporation of different compositional techniques was part and parcel of the initial concept of the ballet and not a by-product of the long interruptions during its genesis. Stravinsky did not, as several authors have claimed, revise some of the earlier movements in 1956 to align them with the serial procedures in the later movements, but employed serial techniques right away in certain of the earlier dances that he completed between August and December 1954.

As laid out in Balanchine and Stravinsky's original plan, the outer sections I and III engage the twelve dancers cumulatively, while each of the three sets of dances that constitute the longer central section II is for a smaller ensemble of three or two dancers respectively (see Table 1). These groups of dances in section II follow the traditional classical ballet format, with the Prelude and Interludes that precede them being choreographed for the entire trio or duo. Demonstrable influences from Stravinsky's reading of the de Lauze / Mersenne edition include the trumpet canon in the Bransle Simple, apparently inspired by an engraving in the treatise showing two trumpeters, as well as the short-short-long-long castanet ostinato rhythm in the Bransle Gay and the complex rhythms of the Bransle Double, which were modelled on patterns described in the manual (Tucker 1992, 166–7).

The serial movements of *Agon* offer a synopsis of Stravinsky's path to twelve-note composition. The Double Pas-de-Quatre and Triple Pas-de-Quatre combine non-dodecaphonic series (i.e. series with fewer than twelve different pitch classes) with non-serial material. The First Pas-de-Trois Coda features the first use of a twelve-note row in Stravinsky's oeuvre, joined by non-serial material (mostly in the solo violin double-stop motions). On the other hand, most of the movements composed in 1956–7 are fully serial, i.e. they contain very little non-serial material, using either non-dodecaphonic or twelve-note series. At the end of Four Trios, a diatonic chord repeated in the horns emerges from the serial structure, leading back to the diatonic world of the ballet's opening.

Agon uses a large orchestra with triple winds (four horns and four trumpets) and including harp, mandolin, piano and xylophone, which for the most part is broken down into smaller ensembles characteristic of individual dances. While no movement uses the full orchestra, larger ensembles are featured in section I, the Prelude and Interludes, and the final Coda.

CHRISTOPH NEIDHÖFER

Table 1 Agon, *Outline*

Sections	Movements	Pitch material	Dancers	
			male	female
I	Pas-de-Quatre	diatonic/modal with some chromaticism	4	
	Double Pas-de-Quatre	chromatic, partially serial (non-dodecaphonic) in second half		8
	Triple Pas-de-Quatre	partially serial (non-dodecaphonic)	4	+ 8
II	Prelude	polytonal	1	+ 2
	First Pas-de-Trois			
	Saraband-Step	tonal with chromaticism	1	
	Gaillarde	tonal/polytonal		2
	Coda	partially 12-note serial, first use of a 12-note row in Stravinsky's oeuvre	1	+ 2
	Interlude	polytonal (same as Prelude with added material)	2	+ 1
	Second Pas-de-Trois			
	Bransle Simple	fully serial (non-dodecaphonic)	2	

Table 1 (*cont.*)

Sections	Movements	Pitch material	Dancers		
			male		female
	Bransle Gay	fully serial (non-dodecaphonic)			1
	Bransle Double	fully serial (12-note)	2	+	1
	Interlude	polytonal (same as first Interlude with added material)	1	+	1
	Pas-de-Deux				
	Adagio	begins with a 12-note row, otherwise non-dodecaphonic serial	1	+	1
	Più mosso	non-dodecaphonic serial	1		
	L'istesso tempo	non-dodecaphonic serial			1
	L'istesso tempo	non-dodecaphonic serial	1		
	Coda	non-dodecaphonic serial	1	+	1
III	Four Duos	12-note serial	4 × (1	+	1)
	Four Trios	12-note serial	4 × (1	+	2)
	Coda	same as opening Pas-de-Quatre with minor changes and starting with a fuller chord	4	+	8

Luciano Berio, *Two Interviews with Rossana Dalmonte and Bálint András Varga*, trans. and ed. David Osmond-Smith (London: Marion Boyars, 1985).
Stephanie Jordan, *Stravinsky Dances: Re-visions Across a Century* (Alton, Hampshire: Dance Books, 2007).
Charles M. Joseph, *Stravinsky's Ballets* (New Haven and London: Yale University Press, 2011).
Julia Randel, 'Dancing with Stravinsky: Balanchine, *Agon, Movements for Piano and Orchestra*, and the language of classical ballet' (Ph.D. dissertation, Harvard University, 2004).
Susannah Tucker, 'Stravinsky and His Sketches: The Composing of *Agon* and Other Serial Works of the 1950s' (D.Phil. dissertation, University of Oxford, 1992).

Akimenko, Fyodor (Stepanovich) (born Kharkov, 8/20 February 1876; died Paris, 3 January 1945). Ukrainian composer and pianist. A former pupil of RIMSKY-KORSAKOV's at the ST PETERSBURG CONSERVATORY, he gave Igor Stravinsky his first harmony lesson (according to Stravinsky's account to TIMOFEYEV) in the summer of 1901. In November, Stravinsky began regular weekly lessons with Akimenko – almost certainly following Rimsky-Korsakov's *Practical Course in Harmony* – costing his father, Fyodor STRAVINSKY, 1 rouble 50 per session. Stravinsky remembered Akimenko as 'a composer of some originality' (SCRIABIN looked upon his music with some favour), but found his teaching 'unsympathetic', ceasing lessons in February. In 1903, Akimenko moved to Nice where he made a living as a pianist, making several visits to PARIS where he published some music; Stravinsky, arriving in Paris for The FIREBIRD, was 'surprised' by several French musicians asking about Akimenko. (DIAGHILEV briefly toyed with the idea of commissioning a ballet from Akimenko, but wrote to BENOIS: 'On closer acquaintance we didn't take to Akimenko – bread and milk, silly and provincial'.)   DANIEL JAFFÉ

American Ballet, The. Ballet company. The American Ballet was the earliest of the George BALANCHINE–Lincoln KIRSTEIN precursors to the NEW YORK CITY BALLET. It grew out of the School of American Ballet (opened 1933), and between 1935 and 1938 was the resident company of the Metropolitan Opera House, New York. In 1937, it staged a Stravinsky Festival for which Stravinsky conducted all performances; JEU DE CARTES was an original commission premièred at the Festival. The company parted ways with the Met. in 1938 and disbanded, though it was briefly reformed as the hybrid American Ballet Caravan in 1941.   SOPHIE REDFERN

Ančerl, Karel (born Tučapy, Bohemia, 11 April 1908; died Toronto, Canada, 3 July 1973). Czech conductor. Ančerl studied conducting with Václav TALICH and Hermann SCHERCHEN. In 1931, he was Scherchen's assistant for the première of Hába's opera The Mother in Munich and probably assisted Scherchen for OEDIPUS REX the same year. On 10 May 1935, Ančerl conducted the Czech première of The SOLDIER'S TALE. He was imprisoned in Theresienstadt in 1942 and sent to Auschwitz in 1944, where his wife and son perished. On 7 April 1948, Ančerl conducted the Czech première of Oedipus Rex. In 1950, he became chief conductor of the Czech Philharmonic. Between 1962 and 1967, he recorded PETRUSHKA, the CONCERTO IN D FOR VIOLIN AND ORCHESTRA (twice, with Ida Haendel and Wolfgang Schneiderhan), The RITE OF SPRING, Les NOCES, Oedipus Rex, SYMPHONY OF PSALMS, MASS and CANTATA.   NIGEL SIMEONE

Andreae, Volkmar (born Bern, 5 July 1879; died Zurich, 18 June 1962). Swiss conductor and composer. From 1906 until 1949, Andreae was chief conductor of the Tonhalle Orchestra in Zurich and also served as director of the Zurich Conservatory (1914–39). At the Tonhalle, he conducted the CONCERTO FOR PIANO AND WIND INSTRUMENTS with Stravinsky as the soloist in November 1925, and on 14 October 1929 he conducted an all-Stravinsky programme including CAPRICCIO (with Stravinsky as the soloist) and the first complete performance in Switzerland of The RITE OF SPRING.   NIGEL SIMEONE

Ansermet, Ernest (born Vevey, 11 November 1883; died Geneva, 20 February 1969). Swiss conductor. Ansermet studied mathematics at Lausanne University and taught there until 1909. He then decided to make music his career, studying composition with Ernest Bloch and taking advice about conducting from Nikisch and Weingartner. From 1910 onwards, he conducted in Lausanne and Montreux, and first met Stravinsky in 1911 or 1912; the composer recalled: 'his appearance – the beard – startled me: he was like an apparition of the Charlatan in Petrushka' (T&C, 229). On 2 April 1914, Ansermet gave the first performance outside Russia of Stravinsky's SYMPHONY IN E♭ MAJOR with the Kursaal orchestra in Montreux, and it was on Stravinsky's recommendation that he was appointed chief conductor of the BALLETS RUSSES in

1915. He went on tour with the company to the UNITED STATES in 1916 (making his first recordings there with the Ballets Russes orchestra) and conducted the first performance of DIAGHILEV's ballet version of FIREWORKS at the Teatro Costanzi, Rome, on 12 April 1917. In 1918, Ansermet founded the Orchestre de la Suisse Romande (OSR), serving as its chief conductor for half a century.

Between 1918 and 1930, Ansermet conducted an extraordinary series of Stravinsky premières – more than any other conductor – including The SOLDIER'S TALE (Lausanne, 28 September 1918, and first performance of the Concert Suite, on 20 June 1920 at the Wigmore Hall in London), The FIREBIRD Suite (Geneva, 12 April 1919; Stravinsky dedicated it to Ansermet and the OSR), The SONG OF THE NIGHTINGALE (Geneva, 6 December 1919), PULCINELLA (Paris, 15 May 1920), the ballet version of The Song of the Nightingale (Paris, 18 May 1920, with sets by Matisse), RENARD (Paris, 18 May 1922), LES NOCES (Paris, 23 June 1923), the CAPRICCIO (Paris, 6 December 1929, with Stravinsky as the soloist) and the SYMPHONY OF PSALMS (Brussels, 13 December 1930, six days before KOUSSEVITZKY gave the American première of the work he had commissioned).

When Ansermet asked Stravinsky to agree to cuts in JEU DE CARTES in 1937, the furious composer refused: 'I have never said to you: take my score and do with it what you wish.' The didactic Ansermet made matters worse by justifying himself on musical grounds, leading Stravinsky to write to Ludwig Strecker at Schott about the conductor's 'strange megalomania'. The result was a rift in their friendship that was to last many years, though there was a reconciliation of sorts in 1966.

In 1948 Ansermet conducted the first performance of the MASS at La Scala, Milan, but he was unsympathetic to the direction Stravinsky's music took in the 1950s, deploring its 'sterile formalism'. Despite this, he continued his energetic advocacy of Stravinsky's earlier music until the end of his life, documented in the extensive series of recordings he made for Decca between 1946 and 1968, mostly with the OSR, including many of the works he had conducted at their premières.   NIGEL SIMEONE

CASIII

Antheil, George (born Trenton, New Jersey, 8 July 1900; died New York City, 12 February 1959). An American composer, known for his avant-garde music and inventions. His Ballet mécanique has a rhythmic drive and energy that brings it close to the Russian composer's LES NOCES and his earlier The RITE OF SPRING. Stravinsky and Antheil shared an interest in expanding the resources of the orchestra, using non-traditional ensembles and stretching the limits of instrumental capacity: for example, the challenging bassoon solo in the upper register at the beginning of Stravinsky's Rite and Antheil's inventions of new musical equipment.

The quasi-mechanical possibilities within music appealed to Stravinsky; his interest, for example, in the mechanical piano which, as Cross suggests, was 'a catalyst to many contemporaries' (Cross, 1998, 12). Antheil's capacity to develop repetition and ostinato by quasi-mechanical means was, nevertheless, far in excess of what Stravinsky had produced in The Rite and elsewhere, without resulting in composition of equal quality.

Travelling to Europe in 1922, Antheil gave a piano recital at the Wigmore Hall, in London, including works by DEBUSSY and Stravinsky, and he first met Stravinsky in Berlin that same year. While Antheil declined Stravinsky's invitation for him to move to PARIS and put on a concert there, he nevertheless arrived in the French capital in 1923 and was present at the première of *Les Noces*. Walsh suggests that, while Antheil's 'Americanness' was the primary source of his appeal to the Russian composer, Stravinsky was also impressed by his energy and knowledge of new music, but above all by his pianism, telling the young American 'you play my music exactly as I wish it to be played' (SCS, 359). Going beyond Antheil's self-promotion, Walsh suggests that Stravinsky was primarily interested in using Antheil's agent, and to this end he strove to endure his many 'irritations'.

Antheil admired Stravinsky greatly and related to friends that the Russian composer likewise supported his work. This was reportedly the source of the rift in their brief relationship. However, as White notes (SCW), Stravinsky invited Antheil to a concert he was giving in Hollywood in 1941.

HELEN JULIA MINORS

Jonathan Cross, *The Stravinsky Legacy* (Cambridge University Press, 1998).
Jonathan Cross (ed.), *The Cambridge Companion to Stravinsky* (Cambridge University Press, 2003).

Anthem ('The Dove Descending'). Composed 1961–2. First performance, 19 February 1962, LOS ANGELES. Conductor, Robert CRAFT. Published 1962, Boosey & Hawkes.

This work for four-part choir, lasting just over 2 minutes, was written in January 1962 as a result of Stravinsky's having been invited by Cambridge University Press to compose a hymn for a new English hymnal. T. S. ELIOT suggested the text, which is Part IV of 'Little Gidding', the last of his *Four Quartets*, and Stravinsky dedicated the resulting setting to him. It was first performed on one of the Monday Evening Concerts in Los Angeles on 19 February 1962.

As the title indicates, this is not a hymn. It is also not a canon, as Roman Vlad has described it, either melodically or rhythmically. The poem is in two stanzas, each consisting of a Sicilian quintain plus a couplet (*ababcc*). However, Stravinsky does not divide the stanzas in this way, but rather into two sections, of four and three lines, the first for two voices, the second for all four. The second stanza is essentially a repetition of the first, though the first section (*abab*) is heard here as a variation or development, consisting of three rather than five rows and moving for the most part in quavers in an almost entirely syllabic setting of the text, whereas in the first stanza this section moved mostly in crotchets with some melismas. The second section is repeated exactly.

The piece is based on a TWELVE-NOTE row, of which only the untransposed prime, inversion and retrograde, and the retrograde inversion at the tritone transposition are used. KATHRYN PUFFETT

Apaches, The. *Les Apaches* was an informal group of artists that formed in PARIS around 1900 to discuss new music, to share new ideas and sources, and to consider how better to represent new developments in the arts, supporting première

performances, and attending repeated performances of works. Loosely translated as 'hooligans', the name derives from the contemporary subculture of
hooligan activity and street gangs that drew the attention of the press, for
example Le Petit Journal (14 August 1904). Pertaining primarily to the celebrated
Native American tribe, the term also signified the group's shared aesthetic
interest in new music (especially that of DEBUSSY and Stravinsky) and other
art. Indeed, the name was coined after a newspaper seller was heard shouting,
'Attention Les Apaches!' (Pasler 2007, 153).

The group included some of the key composers of the era, including Claude
Debussy, Maurice DELAGE, Manuel de FALLA, Maurice RAVEL, Florent Schmitt
and Igor Stravinsky, as well as the painter Paul Sordes, the pianist Ricardo
Viñes, and the critics Michel-Dimitri Calvocoressi and Émile VUILLERMOZ. As
with any new collective, the group came together slowly and was primarily
made up of friendship groups and of those who had studied together: Ravel,
Schmitt and Vuillermoz were members of Fauré's composition class.

The group recognised the achievements of a number of new works
and artists, supporting Debussy's new opera, Pelléas et Mélisande (1902)
and its staging in the face of those critics who did not understand it or
those who did not represent it clearly or favourably. They attended repeat
performances, sitting in the same seats and, as Pasler notes, 'immobilised
the opposition with their enthusiasm' (ibid., 152). Another work they
supported was Ravel's Daphnis et Chloé. As advocates for new music, they
campaigned actively to bring attention to the music they favoured. Meeting
weekly, they were able to plan strategies in advance, plotting how best to
support new works and artists. Despite attending concerts together in small
groups, they never met formally in public or invited non-members to attend
gatherings, their modus operandi resembling that of other 'sects', with no
organising committee or leader, while at the same time supporting mutual
independence.

Beyond the music of Debussy (who never actually attended a meeting) and
Ravel, Les Apaches recognised the potential of Stravinsky's music, and he in turn
joined the group in 1910. The group meetings often included performed
extracts of music which individual members were writing, and it seems clear
that Stravinsky presented parts of PETRUSHKA in this context prior to its
première in 1911. The group met in a private space, a small building rented
by Delage and decorated in oriental style. While Delage was not a founding
member, he accepted responsibility for hosting the members regularly on
Saturday nights, when they shared music and discussed aesthetics. With key
thinkers and critics in their midst, they no doubt discussed how these new
works would be received.

The members shared a respect for one another, which is demonstrated in
Ravel's dedication of new work to particular individuals. The five movements
of Miroirs for piano, for example, are dedicated to Viñes, Léon-Paul Fargue,
Calvocoressi, Sordes and Delage, respectively. Despite their mutual regard and
shared support for Debussy and Russian music, the group were not in agreement on all issues and their meetings undoubtedly included lively debate.
Given that these meetings were private, the descriptions we have of them tell
of an intimate space enabling composers, and performers such as Viñes, to

share work in progress (no doubt as some of them had previously done in Fauré's composition classes).

The members of Les Apaches were also part of a much more extensive Paris network of artists, and they engaged in a wide range of more public artistic organisations, groups and institutions. Sharing poetry and discussing visual art, they were a truly interdisciplinary group whose concerns were drawn from across the arts. As Pasler notes, 'the Apaches help us to understand what is involved when a young generation, impassioned by the innovations of their immediate predecessors, wish to defend those innovations and explore their implications while clearing a space for their own creative experimentation' (2007, 164).   HELEN JULIA MINORS

Jann Pasler, 'A Sociology of the Apaches: "Sacred Battalion for Pelléas"', in Barbara Kelly and Kerry Murphy (eds.), Berlioz and Debussy: Sources, Contexts and Legacies (Aldershot: Ashgate, 2007), 149–66.
SCR

Apollon Musagète (Apollo).   Composed 1927–8. First performance, 27 April 1928. Published 1928, Boosey & Hawkes, Washington, DC. Instrumentation: strings (8.8.6.8.4 suggested by Stravinsky).

Synopsis
First tableau
Prologue: The Birth of Apollo
Second tableau
Variation of Apollo
Pas d'action (Apollo and the Three Muses)
Variation of Calliope (the Alexandrine)
Variation of Polyhymnia
Variation of Terpsichore
Second Variation of Apollo
Pas de deux
Coda
Apotheosis

A ballet choreographed by Adolph BOLM, commissioned by Elizabeth Sprague Coolidge for a festival of new music to be held at the Library of Congress in 1928. Correspondence between Carl Engel, the music chief of the Library of Congress, and Gavriyil Gavrilovich Païchadze, Stravinsky's spokesman for this project, shows that the only restrictions imposed upon Stravinsky had to do with the size of the orchestra and the number of dancers, because of limitations of space. Approximately two months after the US première in Washington DC, the European première took place in PARIS on 12 June 1928 with choreography by George BALANCHINE. It is likely that Balanchine and Stravinsky discussed Apollo before the American première.

Apollo pays tribute to three of the nine muses: Calliope, Polyhymnia and Terpsichore. The choice of subject for this ballet was left up to Stravinsky, and it is possible that he had completed a significant portion of the ballet before he decided on the storyline.

Stravinsky noted that 'Apollo was my largest single line step toward a long-line polyphonic style, and though it has a harmonic and melodic, above all an intervallic character of its own, it nourished many later works as well.' The intervallic character for Apollo flourished within a diatonic framework because Stravinsky focused on tonal triads with added notes. The added notes are dependent upon the diatonic scale, but also allow the tonal triads to become strands in an octatonic web. For example, the chord usually labelled in the literature as the 'chord accompanying the birth of Apollo' is an octatonic sonority. However, most commentators ignore the resolution of this chord – a motion that illustrates Stravinsky's intention to impose a distinctive intervallic character in both horizontal and linear dimensions. The ultimate resolution of this chord takes place at the end of the ballet, where Stravinsky strips away the added notes, leaving only the B minor triad.

Stravinsky also applied techniques of versification found in the *alexandrine* (six iambic feet) to certain musical passages of the ballet. This technique is notably reflected in his unique approach to phrase structure in the section depicting Calliope, the muse of epic poetry. There, Stravinsky uses the *alexandrine* as a prop just as Balanchine's choreography has Calliope receiving a tablet as her prop, brilliantly capturing the poetic meaning of Stravinsky's music.

Stylistically, it is possible to find links between *Apollo* and OEDIPUS REX (1926–7) and also ORPHEUS (1946–7). Furthermore, an excerpt from *Apollo* ('Variation d'Apollon', Rehearsal 22) surfaces a few years later in DUO CONCERTANT (1931–2) after the first statement of the 'Gigue.'   MAUREEN CARR

Dial

Argentina. Stravinsky's music was probably introduced to Argentina on the BALLETS RUSSES' second South American tour in 1917, for which the repertoire included *The* FIREBIRD and PETRUSHKA. (None of Stravinsky's ballets was performed during the 1913 tour.) ANSERMET was the conductor for this tour, and thus began his championing of Stravinsky's music in Buenos Aires, which was to continue through the 1920s in his role as director of the Asociación del Profesorado Orquestal (the precursor of the Argentine National Symphony Orchestra). In 1932, Boris ROMANOV staged *The* RITE OF SPRING at the Teatro Colón in Buenos Aires; Stravinsky's plan to attend with VERA (who was to have designed the costumes) did not come to fruition.

Stravinsky's two visits to Argentina came about through the agency of the writer Victoria OCAMPO. The first of these was from 25 April to 18 May 1936, when he was accompanied not by Vera but by his son Soulima STRAVINSKY. Together they performed CAPRICCIO, the CONCERTO FOR PIANO AND WIND INSTRUMENTS, and the CONCERTO FOR TWO SOLO PIANOS at the Teatro Colón (and the last-named work also in Rosario). In addition, Stravinsky conducted *The Rite*, SYMPHONY OF PSALMS, PULCINELLA, APOLLON MUSAGÈTE and ballet performances of *The Firebird*, *Petrushka* and *The* FAIRY'S KISS. The repertoire was completed by PERSÉPHONE, with Ocampo in the title role. Stravinsky's presence in Buenos Aires was remarked in several polemic newspaper articles, commenting (positively or negatively, depending on editorial viewpoint) on the anti-democratic tone of statements he made on his arrival.

But the critical press did not hesitate to hail the significance of his music, not least in articles by leading composers Juan José Castro, Juan Carlos Paz and Roberto García Morillo.

Among the younger Argentinian composers who declared their debt to Stravinsky were Alberto Ginastera and his pupil Astor Piazzolla. Piazzolla recalled that The Rite of Spring was for many years his 'bedside book': a surprising source of inspiration for a tanguero. Stravinsky's own TANGO for Chamber Orchestra of 1940 was perhaps inspired by his stay in Argentina four years earlier. Stravinsky and Piazzolla became acquainted in New York in 1959, while Ginastera was among the many that he met during his second visit to Argentina the following year.

That 1960 trip was originally planned as a social visit to Ocampo, with expenses to be paid by a film festival; ultimately, the visit was undertaken as part of a wider concert tour of South America. Stravinsky arrived in Buenos Aires with Vera and Robert CRAFT on 25 August, and stayed until 4 September. With Craft, he conducted two concerts at the Teatro Colón. The works in question were those that the Ballets Russes had introduced to Argentina forty-three years earlier: The Firebird and Petrushka.   CHRIS COLLINS

Omar Corrado, 'Stravinsky y la constelación ideológica argentina en 1936', Latin American Music Review, 26. 1 (Spring–Summer 2005), 88–101.
SCF (94)
Colin H. Slim, Stravinsky in the Americas: Transatlantic Tours and Domestic Excursions from Wartime Los Angeles (1925–1945) (Oakland: University of California Press, 2019).
SPD

Artists (visual). Like Felix Mendelssohn, Arnold SCHOENBERG and John Cage, Igor Stravinsky belonged to the synaesthetic class of composers who befriended visual artists, and he maintained a vivid interest in the visual arts throughout his life. In his music he constantly fed himself on different sources of inspiration, of which fine arts – painting, graphic arts, sculpture and architecture – occupied a very significant part.

As Alexandre BENOIS remembered, 'Unlike most musicians who are usually quite indifferent to everything that is not within their sphere, Stravinsky was deeply interested in painting, architecture and sculpture' (cit. in Benois 1947, 302). When Stravinsky was talking about his music, he often drew analogies with art works and art techniques. While discussing PULCINELLA in an interview in 1920, he drew a parallel between the juxtaposition of instrumental timbres and the juxtaposition of the colours red and green (SCS, 312). In Conversations with Igor Stravinsky, the famous credo about the artist who 'must avoid symmetry but may construct in parallelisms' was illustrated by two examples – the Byzantine mosaic of the Last Judgement of Santa Maria Assunta in Torcello, and Piet Mondrian's Blue Façade, Composition 9, of 1914 (Conv, 19). A gifted portraitist himself, Stravinsky was able to make sketches and caricatures of his friends and, since he had very distinctive facial features, he was often portrayed by artists including Pablo PICASSO, Marc CHAGALL, Robert DELAUNAY, Jacques-Émile Blanche, René Auberjonois, Theodore Strawinsky, Alberto Giacometti, Mikhail LARIONOV and Jean COCTEAU. Besides all that, from a young age Stravinsky was an avid art collector, a passion to which he was initiated by Benois. Even before 1914, his collection of paintings numbered several Picassos, all of which disappeared during World War I, when his summer house in USTILUG was plundered.

A son of Fyodor Ignatyevich STRAVINSKY, a famous Russian opera bass singer who made excellent caricatures of himself in different operatic roles, Igor Stravinsky surrounded himself with artists, starting with his immediate family. The composer was married twice, both times to women who were naturally gifted as artists. His first wife, YEKATERINA Gavrilovna Stravinskaya *née* Nosenko (Catherine), the first cousin of the composer and the drawing and painting companion of his summer holidays in Ustilug in the 1890s, was a talented artist who continued drawing and painting *en plein air* while living in SWITZERLAND and being the mother of four. His second wife, Vera Arturovna Sudeykina *née* de Bosset (*see* Vera STRAVINSKY) whom he met in 1921, was previously married to the Symbolist artist, a 'Blue Rose' member, Sergey Sudeykin (1882–1946). She was initiated into art history by Heinrich Woefflin at the University of Berlin and became interested in applied arts under the influence of her husband Sudeykin, the interior decorator of the famous Stray Dog café in ST PETERSBURG. She was on several occasions a costume designer for the BALLETS RUSSES, including productions of *The Soldier's Tale* (1924) and *The Firebird* (1926). After her wedding to Stravinsky in 1940 in the UNITED STATES, Vera Stravinskaya devoted herself to painting and gallery work. During the long period of uncertainty in her private life, which preceded her marriage with Igor Stravinsky, she supported herself financially by running a business in PARIS selling women's clothes, and costumes and accessories for the theatre.

A rare case of a celebrity's offspring who established a solid career of his own, the eldest son of Igor Stravinsky, Theodore Strawinsky (1907–89), became a prominent artist who produced some 1,000 paintings, enjoyed some fifty personal exhibitions, created book illustrations, designed theatre sets and costumes – including the ones for the Brussels production of *Les Noces* (1936) and the Swiss productions of PETRUSHKA (1944) and *The Soldier's Tale* (1945) – and produced stained-glass windows and mosaics for a number of Catholic churches in Switzerland, FRANCE, ITALY, Holland and Belgium. His watercolour, made after the première of *The Soldier's Tale* in September 1918 in Lausanne, when he was only 11, already exhibited a great talent, which flourished during the years the Stravinskys spent in France between the wars. While in France, Theodore studied in the Academy of André Lhote in Paris and took private lessons with George Braque and André Derain. In 1936, Theodore married Denise Guerzoni, the daughter of the Swiss artist Stéphanie Guerzoni. This marriage was the reason why he decided to stay in Switzerland during World War II – the decision that cost him many years of unemployment on account of strict Swiss laws relating to immigration, until 1956 when he was finally granted Swiss citizenship.

In the first half of Stravinsky's life, there were collaborations with Russian artists from the Ballets Russes: with Mikhail Fokine, Alexandre Benois, Léon Bakst and Alexandre Golovine on the libretto, costumes and stage design for *The Firebird* (1910); with Alexandre Benois on the libretto of *Petrushka* (1911) and on the sets and costumes for *Petrushka* (1911) and *The* NIGHTINGALE (1914); with Nicholas ROERICH on the libretto, sets and costumes for *The* RITE OF SPRING (1913); with Mikhail Larionov on sets and costumes for RENARD (1922); and with Natalya GONCHAROVA on sets and costumes for *Les Noces* (1923). There were collaborations with other Russian émigré artists, such as with Léopold Survage on *Mavra* (1922), and with Nicolas REMISOFF, known as 'Ré-Mi', on the Washington production of APOLLO (1928) and on the HOLLYWOOD BOWL production of *The Firebird* (1940); with Sergey Sudeykin on the Metropolitan productions of *Petrushka* (1925), *The Nightingale* (1926) and *Les Noces* (1929); with André Barsacq on the Paris première of PERSÉPHONE (1934); and with Marc Chagall on the New York production of *The Firebird* (1945). With regard to non-Russian artists, worthy of mention are the collaborations with Giacomo BALLA on the non-choreographic light show for FIREWORKS (1917); with Pablo Picasso on *Pulcinella* (1920); with Henri Matisse on the ballet *The* SONG OF THE NIGHTINGALE (1920); with Ewald Dülberg on OEDIPUS REX (1928); with André BAUCHANT and Giorgio de Chirico on APOLLON MUSAGÈTE (1928 and 1947, respectively); with Irene SHARAFF on JEU DE CARTES (1937); and with Isamu Noguchi on ORPHEUS (1948). Only some of these collaborations will be discussed below.

Sergey DIAGHILEV was the initiator of Stravinsky's collaboration with artists – the Wagnerian spirit of *Gesamtkunstwerk* was unshakable in Diaghilev, a theatrical entrepreneur, a prominent art critic and the founder of the *Mir iskusstva* (*World of Art*) journal, which cultivated *art nouveau* aesthetics in RUSSIA and promoted a synthesis of the arts (1898–1904). Diaghilev had a capacity for an acute aesthetic judgement in different artistic domains, a strong temperament and an extraordinary charisma, combined with a flair for networking, and he gathered around himself talented individuals who were sensitive in greater or lesser degrees to different media. The unity of music, CHOREOGRAPHY and visual arts was especially characteristic of Diaghilev's Ballets Russes (1909–29), for which he had engaged the talents of his *World of Art* collaborators including Bakst, Benois and Roerich. Despite the many difficulties in working and communicating with the great impresario, Stravinsky was indebted to Diaghilev not only for his celebrity status in France, but primarily for the fact that, by joining the Ballets Russes, he found a stream of creative energy consonant with his own, and thus was surrounded with like-minded enthusiasts who helped his creativity to flourish fully. For the audiences in Paris, Berlin, London, Rome, Geneva and the UNITED STATES, it was mainly the unconventional stage design and the exotic costumes with a tint of orientalism that became the hallmark of the Ballets Russes style. However, most of Diaghilev's artists came to the theatre from their workshops and did not study stage or costume design professionally. Moreover, like Stravinsky, who never studied at the Conservatory, neither of his co-workers and co-thinkers Benois and Bakst graduated from the Academy of Fine Arts with a diploma. Both artists played a leading role in the first seasons of the Ballets Russes in 1909 and directly contributed to their great success with the French public. For Nicholas Roerich, his collaboration with Stravinsky on *The Rite of Spring* (1913) began in 1910, with the discussion of the initial idea of a ballet on a Stone Age subject. The huge role of Roerich in the very conception and production of this famous ballet, his scientific interest in archaeology and Russian archaic culture, his mysticism and orientalism – all this would be only the beginning of the spiritual quest that would occupy the artist for the rest of his life, bringing him ultimately to India and the Himalayas.

Stravinsky's collaboration with Natalya Goncharova and Mikhail Larionov, the couple to whom he dedicated his vocal cycle *Berceuses du chat* (1915), opens up an interesting question about the impact of the Russian avant-garde on the musical aesthetics of the composer. In 1915, the arrival of Larionov and Goncharova in Switzerland on a permanent contract from Diaghilev contributed to a fresh chapter in the productions of the Ballets Russes, a much-needed one following the forced inactivity of the enterprise at the beginning of World War I. The two painters, who belonged to a younger generation of Russian artists, brought with them a new atmosphere, typical of the futurist environment in Moscow in the 1910s – the atmosphere of burlesque, tomfoolery and nonsense, evident in Larionov's sets and costumes for *Renard*. Goncharova's 1915 sketches for 'Liturgie', Diaghilev's unrealised project for a ballet on biblical subjects, bear the hallmarks of cubism, abstract art, neo-folklorism and neo-primitivism. Both Larionov and Goncharova took their inspiration from unrefined Russian folk art –lubok (pl. lubki, 'popular prints'), peasant dolls, pottery, spoons, commercial signs and peasant costumes. Under Diaghilev's supervision, and with the help of Bronislava Nijinska in the 1920s, Goncharova started to cultivate a certain minimalism in her work, which was a contrast to her designs for RIMSKY-KORSAKOV's *The Golden Cockerel* (1914). The combination of four black pianos, brown peasant costumes and the light empty backdrop of Goncharova's final décor for *Les Noces* (1923) corresponded perfectly well to Stravinsky's final minimalist ORCHESTRATION of this work (four pianos and a percussion ensemble), which also went through at least three revisions. Her backdrop for a new version of *The Firebird* (1926), where Russian churches are planted one on top of the other without any rules of perspective, could be seen as a visual parallel to the 'montage' style of the composer, which came into full maturity during his Swiss period.

After 1916, Diaghilev consciously cultivated a modernist image of his enterprise, and made concrete efforts to engage international avant-garde artists such as Picasso, Matisse, André Derain, Robert and Sonia Delaunay, Georges Braque, Juan Gris, Naum Gabo, Anton Pevzner, Georgy Yakulov, Giorgio de Chirico and Georges Rouault. As a result, Bakst's sketches for at least two productions, including Stravinsky's *Mavra* (1922), were rejected by Diaghilev in favour of avant-garde artists. Picasso befriended Stravinsky in April 1917 in Rome and Naples, where the artist was a guest of Diaghilev, and a participant in the exhibition of futurist paintings. It was during this visit that Picasso met his future wife Olga Khokhlova, a ballerina with the Ballets Russes, and started working on *Parade* (1917) with Erik SATIE, Jean Cocteau and Léonide MASSINE. His collaboration with Stravinsky and Massine on the ballet *Pulcinella* (1920) – in which neo-classical music and traditional COMMEDIA DELL'ARTE costumes contrasted with Picasso's simple dark-blue cubist backdrop depicting a street in Naples and Vesuvius, and Massine's choreography, which introduced Neapolitan folk elements – proved a great success. In fact, the original idea for sets and costume designs, much more elaborate than the final one, was not accepted by Diaghilev, who stamped on Picasso's sketches and left the room (Cooper 1967, 45; Myasin 1997, 161–2), an incident which infuriated Picasso so much that he destroyed some of his sketches for costumes (Kochno 1973, 147). After the première of the ballet, which took place on 15 May 1920 at the Grand Opéra, Stravinsky congratulated Picasso and hailed 'the amazing theatrical flair of this extraordinary man' (Daix 2012, 843). According to Boris Kochno (1973, 148), the violent episode between Diaghilev and Picasso proved to be an exception to the rule: the demanding impresario was usually full of admiration for the famous cubist painter who headed Diaghilev's 'list of ten rare personalities who [as he claimed] know how to see and understand my work' (the other nine names were never mentioned!).

In 1919, Diaghilev proposed to Massine that he should stage a ballet version of the opera The Nightingale of 1914, entitled The Song of the Nightingale, in order to reintroduce Stravinsky's music onto the stage of the Ballets Russes after a period of absence. It was decided to entrust the décor and costumes not to Alexandre Benois, who was in Russia at that time, and not to Fortunato Depero, who was interested in designing a Marinetti-style futurist version of the opera in 1917 (SCS, 276), but to Henri Matisse. Matisse's love for birds and his collection of exotic birds, which included a nightingale with a singing certificate (Myasin 1997, 159–60), helped Diaghilev to obtain the consent of the 50-year-old painter with a well-established reputation as the founder of Fauvism. Although he had never worked for the theatre before, Matisse became interested in the idea of a ballet on a Chinese subject, particularly in the idea of creating two different costumes for the main character – for the real and the mechanical Nightingale. In order to be historically faithful, Matisse looked for inspiration at the Musée Guimet in Paris. The artist opted for bold simplification, rejecting what he called 'the avalanche of colour' in Bakst's pre-war stage designs (Turner and Benjamin 1995, 31). The end result was very impressive from a pictorial point of view: a white backdrop contrasting with Matisse's laconic, brightly coloured costumes, decorated with appliqués of cloud and flower motifs, stripes, circles, triangles, etc. (the technique he would later develop in his famous series of cut-outs, 'Jazz', of 1947). Léonide Massine's work on Pulcinella and The Song of the Nightingale took place simultaneously; in his choreography for the latter, he imitated the reserved dance movements depicted on Chinese silk paintings and lacquer screens. Yet the overall production (Paris, 1920) was not a great success, in particular due to the unconvincing choreography, which attempted to impose on the dancers rhythms somewhat incongruous with those of the music (Kochno 1973, 138–44). Stravinsky's music, on the other hand, pleased public and connoisseurs alike, particularly those who remembered the opera of 1914, and it displeased only conservative critics (SCS, 309–10).

MARINA LUPISHKO

Alexandre Benois, *Reminiscences of the Russian Ballet*, trans. Mary Britnieva (London: Putnam, 1947).

Douglas Cooper, *Picasso et le théâtre* (Paris: Éditions Cercle d'Art, 1967).

Pierre Daix, *Le nouveau dictionnaire Picasso* (Paris: Robert Laffont, 2012).

Boris Kochno, *Diaghilev et les Ballets Russes* (Paris: Fayard, 1973).

Leonid Myasin [Léonide Massine], *Moya zhizn' v balete* ('My Life in Ballet') (Moscow: Artist, Rezhisser, Teatr, 1997).

Caroline Turner and Roger Benjamin (eds.), *Matisse*. Queensland Art Gallery: Art Exhibitions Australia Limited, 1995.

Asafyev, Boris Vladimirovich, pen name Igor Glebov (born St Petersburg, 17 (29) July 1884; died Moscow, 27 January 1949). Composer, musicologist, music critic, pedagogue, public figure and publicist. The author of works devoted to the music of Stravinsky, including the first Russian monograph, as well as various articles and reviews.

Asafyev's *Stravinsky* (1929) (Asafyev 1982) was not only the first Russian monograph on the composer, but also one of the first full-length studies in any language. It is the first comprehensive musicological study of Stravinsky's works up to that time, encompassing both those of the early period and the works of the 1920s up to OEDIPUS REX, APOLLON MUSAGÈTE and The FAIRY'S KISS. He identified key features of Stravinsky's style, such as the irregularity of metric accents and the principle of structural asymmetry; the predominance of laconic motifs (*popevki*) and heterophonic writing; originality of pitch organisation and timbral innovations. Moreover, Asafyev identifed the Russian genesis of Stravinsky's music – specifically, its roots in archaic folklore, peasant polyphony and RUSSIAN ORTHODOX CHURCH liturgy. He highly estimated the work of Stravinsky as a whole, and was convinced that some of his compositions were simply masterpieces.

By the time the monograph was published, Stravinsky already knew the works of Igor Glebov. He subsequently acquired and studied *A Book about Stravinsky* in detail, as evidenced by numerous marginalia in the surviving copy (PSS; Craft 1982; Baranova 2013). Most of them are of a critical nature; the composer's protest was caused by Asafyev's sociological and straightforward materialist interpretations of his music, which primarily concerned *Les Noces*. They served as an incentive for the formulation of his own definition of the work, also detailed in the margins of the book: 'Les Noces is nothing but a symphony of Russian songs and Russian poetic style.'

A Book about Stravinsky is the last major work by Asafyev on the composer. In the 1930s, Stravinsky's music was seldom performed in the USSR, until it almost completely disappeared in the 1940s. In 1948, the composer's work was officially condemned in his homeland as 'bourgeois and formalistic'. Sadly, as a member of the establishment, academician Asafyev also fell in line with the official view. Stravinsky's evaluation of Asafyev's monograph fluctuated throughout his life: a few years after its appearance, in response to an enquiry from PROKOFIEV, he described Asafyev's book as the best of those written about him (*see* Prokofiev's letter to Asafyev, 6 September 1934: PRK, III, 542). Many years later, Pierre SOUVTCHINSKY mentioned a rather less flattering evaluation of the monograph by Stravinsky: 'Asafiev's book [...] contains many true thoughts, but, unfortunately, B.V.A. began later to write extraordinary nonsense ... (I.F.S. himself hates this book by I. Glebov)' (letter to Maria Yudina, 26 April 1960: Yudina 2009, 288).

SVETLANA SAVENKO

Boris Asafyev, *A Book about Stravinsky*, trans. Richard French (Ann Arbor: UMI Research Press, 1982).

Tatiana Baranova, *Stravinsky – chitatel' i bibliofil* ('Stravinsky as Reader and Bibliophile') (Moscow: Nauchnyi vestnik Moskovskoy konservatorii, 2013), no. 1, 5–51.

Robert Craft, 'Asaf'yev and Stravinsky', foreword to Asafyev (1982).

Maria Yudina, *Perepiska 1959–1961* ('Correspondence 1959–1961), ed. Anatoliy Kuznetsov (Moscow: ROSSPEN, 2009).

Auden, W. H. (Wystan Hugh) (born York, 21 February 1907; died Vienna, 29 September 1973). English-American poet, critic, dramatist and librettist. Auden achieved fame in the 1930s as the leading figure in a group of young English writers that also included Stephen SPENDER and Christopher ISHERWOOD. With Isherwood, Auden left England for the UNITED STATES in 1939 and became an American citizen in 1946. In addition to his prolific and varied output as a poet and critic, Auden began writing librettos soon after arriving in New York, collaborating with Stravinsky as well as Benjamin BRITTEN (*Paul Bunyan*), Hans Werner HENZE (*Elegy for Young Lovers* and *The Bassarids*) and Nicolas NABOKOV (*Love's Labour's Lost*).

In September 1947, at the suggestion of Aldous HUXLEY, Stravinsky invited Auden to write the libretto for *The* RAKE'S PROGRESS, which became Auden's best-known operatic text. Although the libretto was co-written with Chester KALLMAN – as were all of his subsequent operatic works – *The Rake's Progress* is permeated throughout with Auden's philosophical, theological and aesthetic ideas. Auden and Kallman proposed further projects to Stravinsky, including a masque-like opera called *Delia*, but these did not come to fruition. Auden did, however, provide the text for ELEGY FOR J. F. K. (1964), and the two men remained close friends. Long after *The Rake's Progress*, the composer continued to speak highly of Auden's artistry: 'we shared the same views not only about opera, but also on the nature of the Beautiful and the Good. Thus, our opera is indeed, and in the highest sense, a collaboration' (T&E 97).

MATTHEW PAUL CARLSON

Audio Recordings. Igor Stravinsky is prominent amongst the first generation of composers whose music is widely recorded (much of it under his own baton) over a CONDUCTING CAREER spanning nearly forty years. Although he was approaching middle age by the time of his first major recordings, the comparison between these and his later conducting output reveals a stark contrast between the less experienced conductor (compared with Pierre MONTEUX or Leopold STOKOWSKI, the former having conducted the première of *The* RITE OF SPRING in 1913 and the latter the first US performance in 1922) and the more confident architect of his later years. Famously, Stravinsky railed against 'interpretation' of the score, exhorting others to 'execute' the music faithfully (Philip 2004, 149). Recording sessions meant that the deputy system that beset French orchestral performances at the time could be circumvented, ensuring continuity on a project for one committed to documenting his pieces 'to serve as guides to all executants of my music' (Philip 2004, 150). Nonetheless, it remains a paradox of Stravinsky's career that his pronouncements and performances should be so at odds: his recordings rarely follow his prescribed tempi and his characteristic rhythmic complexity can (in the earliest recordings) sound slapdash, especially where tempi are notably faster than those in the score. Very late in life, Stravinsky conceded that 'one performance represents only one set of circumstances' (Hill 2000, 137), but this belated reflection must be weighed against a lifetime of exhorting conductors to treat the score (and recordings) as a set of instructions rather than assume primary responsibility for the performance experience. Peter Hill identifies, as the consequence of Stravinsky's dictates, 'a marked loss of character' over time in many recorded performances since (Hill 2000, 138).

There are many potential reasons for this 'loss of character': for one, the increasingly crowded marketplace for new recordings, and simultaneously the greater availability and 'consumption' of recorded exemplars in numerous portable formats, propagating familiarity with the repertoire; a greater number of musicians with experience of Stravinsky's music and that of his peers and successors; standardisation of orchestral instruments; increased international travel and thus the internationalisation of previously national (or even regional) performance styles and preferences; and the opportunities presented by recording technology to edit errors, omissions or simply aspects of performance that are considered worth improving. These are by no means the only reasons, but although Stravinsky praised the opportunity to retake sections of the work in the recording studio, Robert Philip has shown that early recordings of whole pieces comprised as little as two takes, where today a conductor would seize the opportunity to address chaotic ensemble (Philip 2004, 40). Alleging Stravinsky's inexperience is inappropriate here, since the earliest recordings of the Rite by Monteux and Stokowski – both greatly more experienced conductors than Stravinsky at the time – evince the same 'out of control' passages as the composer's own, chiefly the result of too-rapid tempi. Notwithstanding Stravinsky's statements about recordings as 'documents', the inadvertent setting in stone of instrumentalists' struggles bears witness to an immediacy lacking in many recordings today.

Over the course of the twentieth century, the gap between score and performance narrowed: questions of fidelity to the notation superseded and even vitiated the earlier tradition of Romantic 'vitalist' readings. This parallels the increasing rationalisation of compositional techniques, leading to the short-lived but influential experiments with so-called total determination in the early 1950s, and their legacy in subsequent decades. Accustomed as we have become to the blended sound of the present day (to say nothing of enhanced recording techniques), the rawness of early twentieth-century performances is uncomfortable and sonically precarious. The increasing preference for vibrato in strings and winds from the 1930s onwards contrasts with the balder approach in the earliest recordings of works for both large and small ensembles. Furthermore, Philip has shown that it was not untypical for early twentieth-century performers and conductors to subject notated rhythms to localised accelerandos, dotting evenly notated patterns, or curtailing notes at the ends of bars or phrases, or for string players to make audible their position changes as un-notated portamenti, even seeking out opportunities to do so for rhetorical effect (Philip 2004). Such widespread practices, all applied in the name of expression, underlined generally well-understood differences between notated score and performance expression. Their presence in these early recordings (and not all of them early, as Robert Fink shows) can come as a shock, so predisposed are we to think of the Rite as clean cut, and energised by incisive – and accurate! – rhythms (Philip 2004, 137). Fink goes so far as to refer to the 'grimly geometric Rite embalmed in the composer's 1960 Columbia recording' (Fink 1999, 313).

Until World War II, the existence of different European performance traditions could result in significant variation between orchestras' sounds. Philip notes the straight-toned brightness of the metal flute used in pre-war PARIS, comparing it with the Berliners' 'organ-like' wooden flute (Philip 2004, 152). At first, both of these European exemplars contrasted in their turn with the North American preference for smoother-toned, blended timbre, but, over time, the latter became the standard more generally. The temptation is great to reflect only on the perceived deficiencies of older recordings, because typically – and notwithstanding their technological shortcomings – they bring to the fore a pungency that modern technologies (reinforced by familiarity with works and the expectations of conductors and ensembles) are assumed to have overcome.

Even accounting for the disappearance of crackles in early recordings and the prevalence of more sophisticated stereo and digital techniques, their legacy is in the intimacy of performance – not a quality readily associated with the Stravinskian repertoire today.   LOIS FITCH

Robert Fink, '"Rigoroso ($\eighth$ = 126)": "The Rite of Spring" and the forging of a modernist performing style', Journal of the American Musicological Society, 52.2 (1999), 299–362. doi:10.2307/832000.
Peter Hill, Stravinsky: The Rite of Spring (Cambridge University Press, 2000).
Robert Philip, Performing Music in the Age of Recording (New Haven and London: Yale University Press, 2004).

Auric, Georges (born Lodève, Hérault, France, 15 February 1899; died Paris, 23 July 1983). French composer. Auric became involved in Parisian musical and artistic circles from the age of 14, writing his first articles on contemporary music and aesthetics from 1913. He was part of SATIE's and COCTEAU's circles and advised the latter in the so-called manifesto of the future LES SIX: Le Coq et l'arlequin (1918). Auric described the effect of hearing The RITE OF SPRING, conducted by Pierre MONTEUX in 1914 at the Casino de PARIS, as a punch in the face and heart. He was particularly struck by the challenge the work posed for the performers, who were forced to develop new techniques to achieve the difficult registers Stravinsky demanded. Auric became and remained a supporter throughout all of Stravinsky's stylistic and aesthetic phases. He wrote several articles on the composer, most importantly concerning MAVRA and Les NOCES for Les Nouvelles littéraires (6 January and 16 June 1923). For Auric, Mavra represented the start of Stravinsky's new direction, rather than a trivial failure, describing his pride at being one of the few to have supported this work, alongside Satie and the young French school. He was more closely involved with Les Noces as one of the four pianists in the première and was struck by the novel instrumental combinations of pianos, percussion and voices. Auric regarded Stravinsky's failure to be elected to the Institut français in 1936, and subsequent emigration to the UNITED STATES, as a significant loss for French music.   BARBARA L. KELLY

Georges Auric, *Quand j'étais là* (Paris: B. Grasset, 1979).

Colin Roust, 'Auric, Georges (1899–1983): présentation synthétique des écrits', Notice du Dictionnaire des écrits de compositeurs, Dicteco [online], last updated 30 Oct. 2017, https://dicteco.huma-num.fr/person/12143.

Autobiography, An (*Chroniques de ma vie*). In March 1935, at the age of 53, Stravinsky published the first volume of his *Autobiography* with the PUBLISHER Denoël et Steele; the second volume appeared later that year, in December. In publishing his recollections, Stravinsky placed himself in a long line of composer-autobiographers, notably following the model of his professor RIMSKY-KORSAKOV whose *Chronique de ma vie musicale* (1909) bears a similar title. Stravinsky's book is written in a sober, accessible style. His reasons for writing it are clearly enumerated in the preface: to 'dissipate the accumulation of misunderstandings' and present 'a true picture' of himself after having given so many interviews in which his words were 'disfigured'. Of course, Stravinsky had already given many interviews, but he had also published some fifteen articles in the general and specialised press in which his desire to voice his thoughts, often in the form of clarification, was already present.

When writing, Stravinsky often called upon a collaborator to help him formulate his ideas. In the case of *Autobiography*, it was Walter Nouvel (1871–1949), a friend of DIAGHILEV whose biography of the latter was published the same year. Nouvel wrote the text for *Autobiography*, or at least transcribed it from conversations with the composer. A few letters from Nouvel to Stravinsky mention his working stay in Voreppe (FRANCE) during the summer of 1934 to write the autobiography. In this sense, *Autobiography* is a perfect example of a genre described by the literary theorist Philippe Lejeune as 'the autobiography of those who don't write', in the sense that it is an autobiographical account produced by two collaborators (Lejeune 1980, 229). Although the 'hero' of the text does not write, the role of the second actor is not to write, but to transcribe. Unlike the numerous drafts of POETICS OF MUSIC (1939) that allow for a clear understanding of the roles of each co-author, the surviving archives and preparatory texts for *Autobiography* are limited and reveal very little of its genesis. The Stravinsky Collection at the SACHER FOUNDATION in Basel only contains a corrected typescript of the first part and the corrected proofs of the second part. Robert CRAFT has indicated a number of details relative to Walter Nouvel's role in crafting the text, the book's origins, transactions with the editors, financial agreements with the co-author and an early review of the volume.

Despite the composer's supposed exactitude, *Autobiography* contains many approximations and errors. Moreover, temporal indications are often missing, and sometimes false. In general, the composer never seeks to ground his remarks within a historical framework. The half-century that his account covers saw the Russian Revolution, World War I, the rise of communism – all upheavals of political, intellectual and artistic life – yet Stravinsky never refers to them, preferring to concentrate on his personal trajectory. The first part contains three chapters: 'First impressions', 'Adolescence' and 'The period of the Ballets Russes', which takes the reader to the 1920 première of PULCINELLA. The second part is likewise divided in three: 'The postwar years', 'From *Oedipus Rex* to *The Fairy's Kiss*' and 'After the death of Diaghilev'.

In terms of content, the aesthetic ideas found in *Autobiography* were further developed in later publications, notably in *Poetics of Music*. The portraits Stravinsky draws of his collaborators, particularly those still in activity, are often tenuous but kind. The pages devoted to those who influenced him are marked by entrenched opinions, in terms of both taste and distaste, affection-rejection. Notable subjects include his performers, recordings, Wagnerism, TCHAIKOVSKY, BEETHOVEN and musical expression. The composer's obsession with defining the terms for interpreting his works, be that interpretation critical or musical, is present here as much as his other remarks, but in no sense does the composer set forth any sort of aesthetic doctrine or system. Generally speaking, the text, in both its style and chosen episodes, is the reflection of Stravinsky's artistic opinions, as opposed to subjective outpourings and glosses on music. For the most severe critics of the book's early reception, notably Boris de SCHLOEZER and Gabriel Marcel, *Autobiography*, like Stravinsky's most recent music, was cold and emotionless.

Among the ideas set forth in *Autobiography*, that of music's autonomy and absence of signification caused the greatest critical reaction, to the point that it has been dubbed the 'postulate of Stravinsky': 'For I consider that music is, by its very nature, essentially powerless to *express* anything at all, whether a feeling, an attitude of mind, or psychological mood, a phenomenon of nature, etc … *Expression* has never been an inherent property of music.' This idea punctuates Stravinsky's thought at regular intervals, as early as an interview given in 1916 and much later as well ('Music expresses itself" – with Craft in *Expositions and Developments*). It is most often found during the period of the publication of *Autobiography*, and in many other texts written by Stravinsky, such as 'My discussion with Cingria' of March 1935. In passing, it is worth noting that several passages of *Autobiography* were reused word for word in various articles and interviews of 1935 and 1936 (*see* PUBLISHED WRITINGS).

Autobiography quickly circulated in numerous international translations, starting with two English editions in 1936 (*An Autobiography* published in New York, and *Chronicle of my life* published in London), as well as a German edition in 1937 (*Erinnerungen*), partly modified to avoid ruffling Nazi readers and assist in a German rehabilitation of Stravinsky's music. The first Russian edition appeared in 1963.   VALÉRIE DUFOUR

Robert Craft, 'Appendix K: Walter Nouvel and *Chroniques de ma vie*', in *Stravinsky: Selected Correspondence*, vol. II (London: Faber and Faber, 1984), 487–502.

P. Lejeune, *Je est un autre* (Paris: Éditions du Seuil, 1980).

Antoni Piza, 'Stravinsky's *Autobiography* and Stravinsky's authority', in Piza, 'The tradition of autobiography in music' (Ph.D. thesis, City University of New York, 1994), 175–239.

Igor Stravinsky, *Chroniques de ma vie*, 2 vols. (Paris: Denoël et Steele, 1935).

Irina Ya. Vershinina, 'Perechitïvaya knigu Igorya Stravinskogo *Khronika moey zhizni*' ('Re-reading Stravinsky's book *An Autobiography*'), in *Stravinskiy v kontekste vremeni i mesta: Materialï nauchnoy konferentsii. Nauchnïye trudï Moskovskoy gosudarstvennoy konservatorii im. P. I. Chaykovskogo* 57 (Moscow: Gosudarstvennaya Konservatoriya imeni P. I. Chaykovskogo, Kafedra Istorii Zarubezhnoy Muzïki, 2006), 173–85.

Ave Maria (*Bogoroditse Devo*). Composed 4 April 1934. First performance, 18 May 1934, Paris. Conductor, Igor Stravinsky. First published 1934, Édition Russe de Musique (Slavonic); 1949, Boosey & Hawkes (Latin). Text, liturgical.

Written, like the PATER NOSTER (*Otche nash*) for liturgical use, and within the context of Stravinsky's return to the RUSSIAN ORTHODOX CHURCH in 1926, the first version of this piece is a simple four-part setting of the Slavonic version of the *Ave Maria*. It is a harmonisation of a four-note melody (varied metrically) in the Phrygian mode on D, with occasional elements of the Aeolian mode. The transparency of the music and its utter lack of any sentimentality run very much counter to the style of the eighteenth- and nineteenth-century Russian church music with which the composer would have been familiar. The later Latin adaptation is a tone higher, and has the word 'Amen' added at the end.

IVAN MOODY

$$B$$

Babel. Composed 1944. First performance, 18 November 1945, Wilshire Ebell Theater, Los Angeles. Conductor, Werner Janssen. First published 1953, Schott, for Reciter, Male Chorus and Orchestra. Text: from the Book of Genesis.

Babel resulted from a commission funded by Nathaniel Shilkret for a multi-composer work based on the early chapters of Genesis. The other composers who contributed were Schoenberg, Shilkret himself, Tansman, Milhaud, Castelnuovo-Tedesco and Toch. It was the first of Stravinsky's works in the English language. The narrative of *Babel* is given to the narrator, while the voice of God is intoned by the two-part male chorus, by which means the composer avoids 'personalising' God.

Structurally, the work is in one movement with a total duration of between 5 and 7 minutes, a passacaglia that can be divided into four sections. The first is a series of variations on the ground bass theme in E, over which the reciter declaims the first five verses of the text; the second introduces the Voice of God, distant, hieratic and resonantly beautiful, over dense orchestral textures (Walsh speaks of a 'marmoreal calm': SSE, 157). Greatly contrasting is the third section, whose chromatic fugal writing accompanies the scattering of mankind over the earth. The fourth section is a coda, bringing the work to a quiet conclusion on B.

The opening's resemblance to the introduction to The Firebird of thirty-four years earlier has often been remarked upon, and, in spite of similarities later on, in the third section, with the contrapuntal aspects of the Symphony of Psalms, *Babel* in many ways feels like a recasting of elements of the composer's Russian period, paradoxically looking forward not only to the Mass, but to later, similarly austere biblically inspired works, such as The Flood and Threni.

IVAN MOODY

Bach, Johann Sebastian (born Eisenach, 21 Mar. 1685; died Leipzig, 28 July 1750). German composer and keyboardist. 'There is little that interests me in the music of the past. Bach is too remote.' These words of Stravinsky's, reported in a 1913 interview in the London *Daily Mail*, suggest that, by the following decade, his view of Bach had experienced a volte-face ('Bach . . . has all of my veneration', 1924). From the period of his initial turn to a so-called 'neo-classical' style until the end of his life, Bach's music was exemplary of contrapuntal part-writing, fugal devices, rhythmic vigour and unexpected harmonic changes. Stravinsky's relationship to Bach was not without controversy. In his *Three Satires*, op. 28 (1925–6), Schoenberg mocked 'der kleine Modernsky' with the epithet 'Papa Bach', while, in the 1930s, critics including René Leibowitz accused Stravinsky of plagiarising Brandenburg Concerto No. 3 in his CONCERTO IN E♭: 'DUMBARTON OAKS' (1937–8), to which Stravinsky responded by alluding to Bach's own habits of musical borrowing and adaptation. In 1956, he arranged Bach's Five Canonic Chorale-Variations on the Christmas hymn 'Vom Himmel hoch, da komm' ich her', BWV 769, for mixed chorus and orchestra, as a companion piece to CANTICUM SACRUM. His instrumentations of four Preludes and Fugues from The Well-Tempered Clavier, begun in 1969 and continued in hospital, would be his final creative act. JEREMY COLEMAN

Angelo Cantoni, La référence à Bach dans les œuvres néo-classiques de Stravinsky (Hildesheim: Georg Olms, 1998).

Ute Hensler, 'Strawinsky, Igor', in Das Bach-Lexicon (Lilienthal: Laaber Verlag, 2000).

Bakst, Léon, or Lev Bakst, the scenic name of Lev Samoylovich Rosenberg (born Grodno, Belarus, 10 May 1866; died Paris, 27 December 1924). A Russian-Jewish painter, graphic artist, stage and costume designer, fashion and interior designer. In his youth, Bakst was a non-degree student at the Academy of Fine Arts in ST PETERSBURG (1883–7); he also travelled extensively to Europe and North Africa, and studied at various studios in PARIS.

Bakst began his artistic career as an illustrator of teaching brochures; his horizons expanded considerably when he met Alexandre BENOIS and his circle in 1890. Before his emigration to France, Bakst had established himself in RUSSIA as one of the founders of the Mir iskusstva (World of Art) circle and as one of the most remarkable portraitists of his time.

After 1910, Bakst lived permanently in Paris, where he would become one of the most active collaborators of Sergey DIAGHILEV. Following his first two triumphal ballet productions, Cléopâtre (1909) to the music of Arensky and others, and especially RIMSKY-KORSAKOV's Shéhérazade (1910), he became one of the most famous and well-paid theatrical designers, achieving world-wide fame, unimaginable for a Russian artist in Paris. Between 1909 and 1921, Bakst designed a total of sixteen productions for the BALLETS RUSSES, having become Diaghilev's longest Mir iskusstva (World of Art) collaborator. Among his most famous achievements are the sets and costumes for DEBUSSY's L'après-midi d'un faune (1912), as well as the forward-looking minimalist sets and costumes for Jeux (1913). Although he also worked for other celebrities in Paris, including Ida RUBINSTEIN, his name became synonymous with the Ballets Russes until, after a number of incidents with Diaghilev – including that concerning the payment of a penalty for the already finished sets and costumes for Stravinsky's OPERA MAVRA (1922) (which led to a successful court appeal against the impresario) – Bakst broke with Diaghilev and finally left the Ballets Russes (Kochno 1973, 185). His last major production for Diaghilev was his favourite composer TCHAIKOVSKY's BALLET The Sleeping Beauty, staged in 1921.

Bakst was one of the pioneers of modern stage design: he imagined the stage primarily as a three-dimensional space (Bowlt 1991, 24). In his lavish exotic sets, he sought the immediacy of the impression on the viewer, using colour and rhythm in order to achieve a visual integration of vertical and horizontal space with the movement on the stage. As a costume designer, his main preoccupation was the expressiveness of a human body; he created costumes in the forms of tunics, hitons and sandals that would not limit the movement of dancers; he also contributed to choreography by his knowledge of art history. As a painter and stage designer, he was attracted to orientalism, *art nouveau* and, especially, ancient Greece and Egypt, and he used his knowledge of history and archaeology to make costumes and sets that were true to the spirit of the epoch (Golynets 1992, 39).

Stravinsky befriended Bakst and Benois from the very beginning of his involvement with Diaghilev, and remained a close friend of the former up until 1921. The success of Stravinsky's first ballet The FIREBIRD (1910), for which Bakst was one of the co-librettists, was partly due to the decision of Diaghilev and Benois to entrust the commission of the costumes for the two main female characters, the Firebird and the Tsarevna, to Bakst. For a new Ballets Russes production of The *Firebird* in the UNITED STATES in 1916, keeping Golovine's sets, Bakst designed an entirely new set of costumes for all the main characters in a more angular neo-folk style reminiscent of that of Natalya GONCHAROVA (Bespalova 2016, 105).   MARINA LUPISHKO

Elena Bespalova, *Bakst v Parizhe* ('Bakst in Paris') (Moscow: Buksmart, 2016).
John E. Bowlt, *Khudozhniki russkogo teatra 1880–1930: Sobranie Nikity i Niny Lobanovykh-Rostovskikh* ('Artists of the Russian Theatre 1880–1930: The Collection of Nikita and Nina Lobanov-Rostovsky') (Moscow: Iskusstvo, 1991).
Sergey Golynets, *Lev Bakst* (Moscow: Izobrazitel'noe iskusstvo, 1992).
Boris Kochno, *Diaghilev et les Ballets Russes* (Paris: Fayard, 1973).

Balakirev, Mily Alexeyevich (born Nizhny-Novgorod, 21 December 1836 / 2 January 1837; died St Petersburg, 16/29 May 1910). Russian composer, conductor, pianist, founder of the group known as the Moguchaya Kuchka ('Mighty Handful', also known as The FIVE) and, as such, RIMSKY-KORSAKOV's first teacher of composition.

In *Conv* (1959), Stravinsky recalled that, by the first decade of the twentieth century, Balakirev was 'not greatly admired musically at this time ... and, politically, because of his orthodoxy, the liberals considered him a hypocrite'. Certainly, Balakirev's 'anti-establishment' pose ill-matched his neo-nationalism, intolerance of views other than his own, and the religious fanaticism of his final years. Stravinsky, with his self-confessed love of counterpoint, would have found Balakirev's dismissal of Palestrina and BACH deeply uncongenial. His view of Balakirev would also have principally been influenced by Rimsky-Korsakov, who by then had largely fallen out with his former mentor. Though in many respects a brilliant teacher, to whom Rimsky-Korsakov owed – as he acknowledged – a great deal, and highly regarded enough to be offered the post of Director of the Moscow Conservatory in 1881 (which he turned down), Balakirev even in his prime was overbearing, over-prescriptive and yet bigoted against academicism and theoretical knowledge of any kind. Hence, when, in 1871, Rimsky-Korsakov accepted ST PETERSBURG CONSERVATORY's invitation to become Professor of Composition, and subsequently applied himself assiduously to the study of harmony and counterpoint, Balakirev saw this as a betrayal of everything he and the Kuchka stood for.

Matters were hardly improved when Balakirev lost his most talented young protégé, Alexander GLAZUNOV, to Rimsky-Korsakov, immediately after Balakirev had conducted the première of the 16-year-old composer's First Symphony on 17/29 March 1882. Though Rimsky-Korsakov subsequently acted as Balakirev's assistant when the latter was appointed head of the Imperial Capella (Court Chapel) in 1883, he resigned in 1892, citing hopelessly deteriorated relations with Balakirev and candidly admitting that 'serving with Balakirev in the pious and sanctimonious Chapel . . . is unbearable to me'.

Balakirev spent his final years on the fringe of St Petersburg's musical activity, too outspoken and intolerant to find a place in any circle other than his own, although a few musicians, most notably Anatoly LIADOV, remained in favour with both Balakirev and Rimsky-Korsakov. Yet, *pace* Stravinsky, Balakirev's music remained well respected, Leokadiya KASHPEROVA giving the première of his Piano Sonata in 1905, and (with Balakirev's pupil Sergei Lyapunov) of the two-piano version of his Symphony No. 2 in 1909.

DANIEL JAFFÉ

Balanchine, George (orig. Georgi Melitonovich Balanchivadze) (born St Petersburg, 22 January 1904; died 30 April 1983). Stravinsky's collaboration with George Balanchine, the most influential and esteemed ballet choreographer of the twentieth century, is probably the most celebrated example that exists between a composer and choreographer. They were both Russian *émigrés* who, after meeting under the auspices of DIAGHILEV's BALLETS RUSSES, pursued a major part of their careers in the UNITED STATES, and Balanchine set thirty-nine pieces by Stravinsky, a far larger number than by any other composer. In light of this figure, it is perhaps surprising that the actual number of collaborations from scratch is only five – JEU DE CARTES (1937), The *Ballet of the Elephants* (1942, to CIRCUS POLKA), ORPHEUS (1948), AGON (1957) and Noah and the FLOOD (1962) – and, of these, only Agon is considered a major work. Perhaps, indeed, Agon is the most extraordinary meeting of minds of all, the final part of their Greek trilogy, after APOLLO (1927–8) and Orpheus (1948), with twelve dancers in every mathematical combination, in practice leotards, an athletic, leggy, abstract account of the composer's suite of dances, some lightly referencing a seventeenth-century dance manual, some fully fledged serial.

But it is crucial to consider that collaboration for Balanchine (and the norm for ballet CHOREOGRAPHERS during the twentieth century) extends to the arguably more important practice of using existing music – most of it concert scores. Examples of these pieces easily outnumber the commissions, the first being The SONG OF THE NIGHTINGALE (1925) for the Ballets Russes. Some are regarded as top-drawer Stravinsky–Balanchine, such as the ballet Apollo originally choreographed earlier the same year, 1928, by Adolph BOLM. Much later, after Agon, came MOVEMENTS for piano and orchestra (1963), followed by the 1972 Stravinsky Festival with the SYMPHONY IN THREE MOVEMENTS, Concerto for Violin, DUO CONCERTANT and DIVERTIMENTO *from* The FAIRY'S KISS, all of which have remained in the regular repertoire of NEW YORK CITY BALLET and internationally. Balanchine's last work for Stravinsky was the 1982 solo for his current muse Suzanne Farrell, *Variations for Orchestra* (to the VARIATIONS (ALDOUS HUXLEY IN MEMORIAM)). Using existing scores has clear advantages – not only financial, but also the benefit for the choreographer of getting to know and analyse a score in detail prior to making movement, and of

having a clear understanding of a complete score from the start of the choreographic process.

For a choreographer like Balanchine, such score analysis was a natural
part of his methodology, since he was a musician himself, led by music. His
depth and breadth of musical knowledge as a choreographer was unique –
knowledge gained through practice and theory as well as listening, and which
undoubtedly warmed him to Stravinsky. He had trained at the St Petersburg
Conservatory alongside his studies at the Ballet School, in piano, composition and music theory, remained an active pianist throughout his life, able to
play from short scores and to compose the odd song and piano miniature, and
well equipped to discuss with musician colleagues in sophisticated musical
terms. He also made piano transcriptions from orchestral scores for his own
try-outs. The Stravinsky transcriptions include Monumentum Pro Gesualdo, the
Concerto in D for Violin and Orchestra (Aria I), the Choral Variations on
Bach's 'Vom Himmel hoch', and a few pieces that Balanchine never went on to
choreograph.

The ballets that epitomise Stravinsky–Balanchine and are most influential
either are plotless or offer the bare bones of a narrative idea, stemming
from the composer's neo-classical and serial periods, and spare in terms of
design, with dancers dressed in practice clothes. But there are some narrative
exceptions, such as The Flood, Pulcinella (1972) and Perséphone (1982).
Perhaps significantly, Balanchine avoided conventional narrative timing by
using the Firebird Suite (1949), not the full ballet score. Otherwise, Russian-
period Stravinsky held little interest for him.

Much has been written elsewhere about the shared aesthetic belief of
these two artists: in order, precision and economy – all features of the new
classicism, a tendency to play down expressive values, and a practical, no-
nonsense creative approach. Regularly, Balanchine showed deference to music
as the superior art, acknowledging its crucial rhythmic foundation, and, for
him, Stravinsky was 'an architect of time': he especially appreciated the taut-
ness of his pulse drive. For Stravinsky, Balanchine was the choreographer who
best understood his temporal architecture. But both also agreed that there
should be a measure of independence between their media. 'Choreography, as
I conceive it', says Stravinsky, 'must realize its own form ... though measured
to the musical unit', while Balanchine explains to us that 'when I choreograph
Stravinsky's music I am very careful not to hide the music'. Their ballets are, as
a result, full of cross-rhythms, accents and metres, dance moves happening
during silences: the beginning of Agon is a plié for four men in a line (a quick
knee bend) to a musical rest – musical impulses are then left alone to speak for
themselves – and soon the men are striding out on each pulse, unsupported,
the music tracing irregular patterns around them. Balanchine often shows us
the look of the score in outline, the metrical framework of bars and beats.

In a major tribute (through Craft), Stravinsky acknowledged that
Balanchine had revealed to him the detail of his Movements, a ballet that extends
even the boundaries of Agon for charge and intensity: 'To see Balanchine's
choreography of the Movements is to hear the music with one's eyes.... The
choreography emphasizes relationships of which I had hardly been aware ...
and the performance was like a tour of a building for which I had drawn the

plans but never explored the result' (T&E, 24–5). While the younger choreo-grapher was for many years led by the composer twenty-two years his senior, we can now recognise the choreographer's challenge to the composer, which happened in Stravinsky's presence and absence (especially after his death), altering the perspective on his music, even in ways that Stravinsky himself might not have accepted. The composer remained uncertain for many years about having his concert music used for the ballet stage.

Two works demonstrate radical manipulation of the composer's scores. Balanchine removed the Prologue and final ascent to Parnassus in *Apollo* in the late 1970s, beginning the score with the last section of the Prologue as overture and ending the choreography with the fan of arabesques from earlier in the original Apotheosis. The large shape of the music and some of its motivic cross-references disappeared – likewise the sense of loss that came with the protagonists' 'departure' at the end of the ballet.

For DIVERTIMENTO from *The Fairy's Kiss*, which draws from the story ballet *Baiser* (1928, written for Bronislava NIJINSKA), the choreographer went much further and forged his own score arrangement from Stravinsky material, a bold creative musical act after the composer's death, creating a fundamentally unstable work that reflects on its history in an elusive, fragmentary manner. This was Stravinsky's homage to TCHAIKOVSKY, and Balanchine used only 23 minutes or so of the full ballet score and abandoned overt narrative and characters, while adding sections from the *Divertimento* Suite that Stravinsky had extracted and arranged from his ballet score. It represents Balanchine boldly re-shaping a score, in a sense 'composing' it for his own ends. On the surface, it became a typical plotless Balanchine ballet based on the musical score, but deeper scrutiny reveals that it is full of 'ghosts', a telescoped love affair ending in tragedy, with many points of resonance and cross-reference between the early and late ballet.

Balanchine can also be seen to challenge Stravinsky by creating a new balance of power between music and dance. Here, ballet becomes an extension of the musical concert, a no-plot, no-design genre where the dramas, which are structural and intellectual as well as emotional, emerge from choreomusi-cal relations, rather than the other way round.   STEPHANIE JORDAN

Stephanie Jordan, *Moving Music: Dialogues with Music in Twentieth-Century Ballet* (London: Dance Books, 2000).

Stephanie Jordan, *Stravinsky Dances: Re-visions Across a Century* (Alton, Hampshire: Dance Books, 2007).

Charles M. Joseph, *Stravinsky and Balanchine: A Journey of Invention* (New Haven and London: Yale University Press, 2002).

Balla, Giacomo (born Turin, 18 August 1871; died Rome, 1 March 1958). Italian painter, sculptor, stage and decorative designer at the forefront of FUTURISM. Stravinsky met Balla as early as 1915, during a period of exchange and colla-boration between Sergey DIAGHILEV, the BALLETS RUSSES, and the Italian futurists. Stravinsky considered Balla a gifted painter and friend. Together, they chose Stravinsky's FIREWORKS for a futurist BALLET commissioned by Diaghilev in 1916, as it was suitably 'modern' and short enough for the radical experimentation envisioned by Balla. The result was an early exemplar of the light show and the most abstract Ballets Russes production ever staged. Premièred in April 1917, the work featured a complex array of abstract shapes on stage – some translucent, and others painted. Nearly fifty lighting cues created movement and shadow play across the shapes while certain objects radiated light from within, all made possible by the recent introduction of electrical lighting in theatres. By designing a keyboard to implement the lighting cues, Balla extended the futurist appeal of the work to its technical execution, accelerating the possible interplay between Balla's lights and Stravinsky's score. As such, Balla reinvented ballet as a cubo-futurist movement of light over static forms, rendering actual bodies nearly redundant.

BARBARA SWANSON

Ballet. Ballet was a genre that served Stravinsky's artistic demands especially well. Working collaboratively with other artists in weaving together the intersecting elements of music, dance, drama and the plastic arts, ballet offered a complexity that intrigued the composer for the better part of fifty years. From his early ballets developed under the watchful eye of Sergey DIAGHILEV, to his productive partnership with George BALANCHINE in FRANCE and the UNITED STATES, Stravinsky's lifelong attraction to dance inspired a stream of memorable works, many of which staked out important moments in the composer's development. The earth-shattering primitivism of The RITE OF SPRING, the neo-classical elegance of APOLLO, and the athletic élan of the serially constructed AGON – each, in its own way, opens a window on the composer's endlessly evolving interests.

Stravinsky wrote nine of what might be defined as traditional ballets. The early trio of Russian productions mounted by Diaghilev in PARIS remains particularly illuminating in tracking Stravinsky's early trajectory. Successively, they bear witness to the extraordinary distance he travelled as a young composer. They also show him to be an increasingly engaged participant in shaping each work's choreography and scenario. For the rest of his life, Stravinsky would be centrally involved in forging all of a ballet's interlacing layers.

With The FIREBIRD's première on 25 June 1910, Stravinsky suddenly found himself working side by side with a galaxy of Diaghilev's most established artists. Mikhail FOKINE's conception of the fairytale ballet unfolded piecemeal. He submitted section by section to Stravinsky, who then quickly composed the music (although the composer later grumbled that he was forced to write too much music for 'useless pantomime'). While clearly derivative of his teacher RIMSKY-KORSAKOV, the brilliantly orchestrated neonationalist score charmed PARIS. The ballet's triumph catapulted the composer to instant celebrity.

Rushing to capitalise, Diaghilev persuaded Stravinsky to convert the programmatic piano piece upon which he was currently working into a ballet. Fokine, again, created the choreography for PETRUSHKA, premièred on 13 June 1911. Alexandre BENOIS joined Stravinsky in developing a scenario that featured the inestimable Vaslav NIJINSKY. The composer deftly transformed fragments of Russian folk songs, piling them atop one another in amassing a kaleidoscopic jumble of sound. The music's clashing harmonic clusters and unpredictable rhythmic asymmetries were unprecedented. Moreover, Petrushka's scenario outdistances the simplicity of The Firebird with its paradoxical final scene, leaving the audience with more questions than answers. In every way, Petrushka marked a huge leap in Stravinsky's artistic growth as he bid farewell to the canons of nineteenth-century ballet.

Emboldened by success, the composer's The RITE OF SPRING pushed the edges of imagination further. The tumultuous première on 13 May 1913 will forever be seen as a major milepost in the century's cultural history. The scenario by Stravinsky and Nicholas ROERICH recounts a prehistoric pagan ritual culminating with a young girl's sacrificial dance, meant to propitiate the god of spring. The massive score was jolting in its flood of unresolved harmonic dissonances, incessant ostinato patterns, rhythmically disjointed gestures, and the blunt conflation of conflicting contrapuntal lines. The often flat-footed, ungraceful gestures of Nijinsky's choreography seemed defiantly repugnant. Music and dance critics alike quickly condemned The Rite's primal violence as a sacrilegious assault upon the essence of sensibility. No other twentieth-century composition has proven so provocative in forcing a reassessment of the limits of artistic expression.

Fifteen years later, APOLLON MUSAGÈTE's subtlety, restraint and melodic limpidness eschewed any trace of ethnic source materials in making what the composer deemed a 'U-turn'. Inspired by a Hans Christian Andersen story, The FAIRY'S KISS was composed later the same year. The ballet affirmed the composer's admiration of TCHAIKOVSKY, transforming bits and pieces of his short songs and piano pieces as unifying motives in stitching scenes together. The glittering JEU DE CARTES (1937), premièred in New York as part of a Stravinsky Festival, featured Balanchine's recently formed AMERICAN BALLET dancers. While the 1942 DANSES CONCERTANTES was first presented as a work for chamber orchestra, Stravinsky's sketches, including specific choreographic directions, confirm that he planned a ballet from the start. The year 1942 also marked the oddest of the composer's commissions, the CIRCUS POLKA, to be 'danced' by Barnum & Bailey's elephants. It survives in Jerome Robbins' delightful setting for young ballerinas. Stravinsky's only Broadway excursion came in 1944 with his blithesome SCÈNES DE BALLET, written for Billy Rose's revue The Seven Lively Arts. Most of these commercially designed dance diversions – all dating from the composer's early American years – were summarily dismissed as fluff. In diametric contrast, Stravinsky and Balanchine's next two collaborations, ORPHEUS (1948) and AGON (1957), reveal two artists working as one in constructing completely integrated artistic conceptions. The synthesis achieved was unlike any other in twentieth-century classical ballet.

Ranging over five decades, these ballets tell only part of the story. The composer also fashioned several unorthodox, unclassifiable works that include dance but clearly defy categorisation as traditional ballet. Throughout his career, Stravinsky resisted adopting conventional – and, to his way of thinking, prescriptive – paradigms. What he wished to express musically would determine the form, not the other way around. Nowhere is this more evident than in his multi-faceted works for theatre. Six such creations, perhaps best understood as dance hybrids, are among his most inventive compositions.

The moralistic dramas of RENARD (1915–16) and The SOLDIER'S TALE (1918) rely upon dance to help tell their cautionary tales. And while each work employed chamber-sized performing forces – given wartime constraints – Stravinsky resumed writing more formidable dance undertakings once the armistice was agreed. The Diaghilev-produced PULCINELLA (1920) is very much a ballet supplemented by mime and song. The protracted development of Les NOCES, begun in 1914, finally reached a conclusion in 1923, when it was premièred. These 'Russian choreographic scenes with song and music' (as the composer described them in attempting to explain the work's formal design) incorporate the stark beauty of Bronislava NIJINSKA's choreography, complemented by the arrestingly brittle sound of Stravinsky's four pianos and percussion. The composer described his lyrical PERSÉPHONE (1934) as 'a masque or dance-pantomime coordinated with a sung or spoken text'. Written for tenor, narrator, chorus, children's choir and orchestra, it was one of the composer's most artistically ambitious projects. The serially structured The FLOOD (1961–2), conceived for television, was a mismatch from the start. The fragmented, quasi-operatic work enfolded two dance sequences choreographed by Balanchine. Intended as a contemporary commentary on what were then the current perils of nuclear war, the work failed to resonate with American television audiences more interested in being entertained than lectured.

Given Stravinsky's childhood immersion in dance, his attraction to ballet is not all that surprising. The Imperial Ballet held forth in the nearby Mariinsky Theatre, where he attended performances of the Golden Age ballets of the 1890s featuring the very artists with whom he would soon collaborate. But Tchaikovsky's and Petipa's productions aside, ballet scores were frequently relegated to propping up formulaic choreography meant to dazzle audiences. While Stravinsky's affinity for ballet developed during his formative years, the thought of actually writing for dance was wholly unappetising. The genre had become a blind alley for aspiring young composers. Why risk the stigma of manufacturing humdrum accompaniments comprised of stale harmonic progressions lumbering through one dull repetition after another?

The truth is, Stravinsky, arguably the preeminent ballet composer of the twentieth century, came to write for dance by sheer happenstance. When several established composers declined Diaghilev's request to compose The Firebird's score, the impresario turned to the inexperienced Stravinsky. The virtually unknown composer had produced little of substance before the orchestral SCHERZO FANTASTIQUE and FIREWORKS of 1908. The instrumental flair of the Scherzo, which Diaghilev happened to hear in early 1909, unlocked the door to Stravinsky's future. The unforeseen invitation to work within the ambitious world of the BALLETS RUSSES easily outweighed whatever qualms he may have harboured. For the next twenty years, Diaghilev's cutting-edge company blended a modernistic mix of classicism and innovation in confronting crystal-lised conventions. Stravinsky's ballets would become pivotal in fuelling the direction of a new age.

In placing his ballets in perspective, Stravinsky's instrumental writing rises foremost. The young composer's 'orchestral wizardry', as André Levinson observed, quickly became apparent. The openings of his three Russian ballets, for example, immediately elevate the music to a plateau far more germane than unobtrusive accompaniments. The string writing in The Firebird's 'Introduction' produced a powerful impact. The lugubrious sounding muted lower strings contrasted with the bird-like chirping of the Firebird's dance, mimicked by strings squealing in their highest register (through the use of glissando natural harmonics). The composer's ORCHESTRATION evocatively painted Fokine's picture of a magical kingdom. Similarly, Petrushka's opening bars command one's attention well before the curtain is raised 33 bars later. Stravinsky's expanded orchestra conjures up a whirl of sound in replicating the hubbub of the Shrovetide Fair. Competing orchestral colours fade in and out of focus as the composer achieves a balance in highlighting individual instrumental choirs within the overall orchestral landscape. The notorious bassoon solo that opens The Rite of Spring tests the instrument's upper range. Its otherworldly sound seems to seep out of the earth, ushering in a procession of other woodwinds entering one-by-one, and surely meant to portray the gradual budding of spring. Indeed, the solo's idiosyncrasy foreshadows the many startling effects the composer pulls out of his orchestra in the service of the ballet's mythic scenario.

While the resourceful composer could adeptly tap any instrument's inherent capabilities, he was also not averse to writing against its grain, or featuring it in ingenious ways. The piano, for example, takes on the role of a protagonist in depicting Petrushka's character. The ballet's second tableau is largely built around the piano's juxtaposition of contrasting black and white keys in a torrent of cascading figurations symbolising the imprisoned puppet's frenzied helplessness. In many of his ballets and hybrids, the composer exploited an array of keyboard instruments that might provide the distinctive colour he needed. While he initially planned either a piano or harp for Renard, he ultimately enlisted the cimbalom in attempting to 'imitate the cries of animals'. Les Noces was to have employed two cimbaloms, or a harmonium, or a pianola, before the composer eventually settled on the score's quartet of pianos. More idiomatically, the harp intones the fragile opening of Orpheus – a logical substitute for the god's mystical lyre. Sketches for Apollo divulge Stravinsky's original intention to use both a piano and harp. But when informed that the orchestra pit for the ballet's première at The Library of Congress could not accommodate the bulky instruments, he reassigned their parts for divisi strings.

The vibrancy of his orchestral palette was pronounced. A litany of well-known ballet passages is representative: the jarring force of the imposing percussion battery in The Firebird's 'Infernal Dance'; the brilliant flute and cornet solos in the Third Tableau of Petrushka; the suspense of The Rite's simmering bass clarinets leading into the explosive 'Danse sacrale'; the violin's diabolic fiddling in The Soldier's Tale; the satirical trombone and contrabassoon pairing in the Vivo (VII) of Pulcinella; the diaphanous string writing throughout Apollo; the blaring brass section's recurring fanfares initiating each of the three deals of Jeu de cartes; and the canonic trumpets of Agon's 'Bransle simple'.

35

Indeed, one of the most distinguishing features of Stravinsky's dance music is the uncommonly wide spectrum of colours employed. His ballet scores embrace a robust instrumental vocabulary more often found in the symphonic literature.

Ever the pragmatist, Stravinsky understood that his ballet scores would be programmed more often by orchestras than staged by ballet companies. As he confessed to Georges AURIC in a 1938 conversation, Petrushka's music was conceived symphonically, adding that concert performances of his ballet suites were as important to him as the ballets themselves. The composer's correspondence reveals that the congenial score of Jeu de cartes was expressly written with an eye towards a broad acceptance in the concert halls of Europe as much as ballet performances in America.

The premium Stravinsky placed on his scores as freestanding orchestral works did nothing to deter him from actively shaping a ballet's scenario and staging. With Perséphone, he voiced opinions on everything from the rhythmic flow of André GIDE's text setting to Ida RUBINSTEIN's choice of choreographer and set designer. For Jeu de cartes, he took it upon himself to determine the ballet's length, stage design and the number of dancers. Not only do his compositional sketches disclose his choreographic suggestions, but Lincoln KIRSTEIN remembers Stravinsky physically demonstrating his ideas to Balanchine's dancers. Robert CRAFT recalled that, during a rehearsal for Renard's 1947 revival, Stravinsky commandeered the stage to demonstrate specific gestures and movements he envisioned.

While he adamantly rejected Diaghilev's own directives to cut or alter parts of his scores towards highlighting a dancer's strengths, Stravinsky was in fact open to adapting completed passages to accommodate choreographic or dramatic needs. The piano reduction of Jeu de cartes reveals that he added and relocated music even at the last moment during rehearsals. Adjustments are also evident in sketches and rehearsal scores of earlier ballets. The piano reduction of The Firebird discloses newly composed and reordered passages in the 'Infernal Dance', doubtlessly made to comply with Fokine's vision. Such on-the-spot alterations confirm the young composer's agility. In one instance, Stravinsky composed eight new bars (leading to Rehearsal 104) on a separate scrap of paper, taping it into the score with the direction 'insert'. Similar modifications are found throughout Orpheus, as in the final bars (bb. 67–84) of the 'Pas de deux', where Balanchine prevailed upon the composer to extend the climactic passage in emphasising the overall arc of the choreography's pacing.

Few CHOREOGRAPHERS eluded his criticism. In Balanchine, however, Stravinsky found a kindred spirit. They initially worked together in 1925, preparing a new staging of the 1920 The SONG OF THE NIGHTINGALE. The production provided a crucible in which their deep-seated artistic bond first took root. Although not a true collaboration, the two men interacted closely. Stravinsky often played for rehearsals while the young Balanchine nimbly adjusted his choreography in deference to the composer's wishes. In later years, Balanchine, whose musicianship Stravinsky repeatedly acknowledged, professed the unthinkable upside-down view that ballet must never masquerade the primacy of the music: 'When too much goes on on stage, you don't hear the music', Balanchine proclaimed. For many ballet aficionados, it was blasphemy; but for both the composer and choreographer, it stood as a cornerstone belief.

The two artists also shared similar abstract views on order, boundaries, space and time. They insisted on temporal precision in both musical and choreographic movements. The composer's sketches for *The Fairy's Kiss*, *Jeu de cartes*, *Orpheus* and *Agon* stand in evidence. On every page, Stravinsky clocked exacting durations of individual passages that Balanchine would then choreograph: 1 minute 15 seconds here, 37 seconds there. In choreographing *Agon*, Balanchine took his task as assembling a symbiotic complement to Stravinsky's score, and not a redundant illustration. Theirs was a counterpoint of minds in which music and dance melded in a cohesive, artistic equipoise that distinguished their ballets.

Acknowledging the synergistic relationship of music and dance was fundamental. But also pertinent in understanding the composer's ballets as a whole was his reliance upon a rich assortment of pre-compositional musical and literary sources. Anthologised folk materials served as models in his earliest ballets. Quoting a few folk songs in *The Firebird* morphed into fragmenting and transforming Russian melodies in *Petrushka*. In *The Rite*, the pervasive transmogrification of melodic material drawn from several folk song collections was so thoroughly embedded in the ballet's fabric as to have escaped recognition by scholars until rather recently. In subsequent ballets and hybrids, the composer turned to a diversity of poets, authors, painters and philosophers in catalysing his scenarios. The poetry and texts of Hans Christian Andersen, Nicolas Boileau, T. S. ELIOT, Jean de La Fontaine, Homer and Ovid were all influential in jumpstarting his thinking. In some instances, they did much more than that.

For example, the composer's ardent interest in versification found a direct, applicable use in *Apollo*. The music's rhythmic flow unequivocally owes to the composer's adoption of Greek prosody. Stravinsky made no secret of structuring the ballet's musical syntax upon the fundamental precepts of prosody as an overarching grammatical device. Most explicitly, the metre of poetic verse furnished the template for specific rhythmic figurations, as in the 'Variation de Calliope' where Stravinsky appropriated one poetically meaningful alexandrine, syllable by syllable, from Boileau's 1674 treatise, *L'Art poétique* – a work that espoused the same inviolable tenets of classicism very much on Stravinsky's mind while composing his ballet.

Such source reliance is even more transparent in *Agon*. Stravinsky's wholesale implementation of seventeenth-century dance models runs to the ballet's core. Its origins are attributable to the composer's detailed study of his profusely inscribed copy of François de Lauze's 1623 treatise, *Apologie de la danse*. Stylised dance forms, including a Sarabande, Galliard and three Bransles, exhibit formal designs and rhythmic traits closely emulating their models (as does Balanchine's choreography). Several of the dance manual's illustrative plates manifestly inspired the score's instrumentation. One plate, in which a woman is snapping her fingers, finds its orchestral counterpart in the 'Bransle Gay' with the snapping of castanets. Another, in which two antiphonal trumpets play from separate balconies, undoubtedly inspired the ballet's opening fanfare, as well as the canonic trumpets of the 'Bransle simple'. The modestly sized ensemble's inclusion of a mandolin speaks further to Stravinsky's indebtedness to his Renaissance models.

In his final years, Stravinsky turned most of his attention to vocal and orchestral works. Although, time and again, he contended that his concert works should not be danced, during the 1960s Balanchine's NEW YORK CITY BALLET did just that. A year after the composer's death, the choreographer helped stage the 1972 Stravinsky Festival at the Lincoln Center wherein thirty of the composer's ballets, hybrids and recently converted concert works were presented. Several of Balanchine's new ballets became staples, including: *Stravinsky Violin Concerto* (originally choreographed by Balanchine in 1941 as *Balustrade*), DUO CONCERTANT and SYMPHONY IN THREE MOVEMENTS.

Beyond Balanchine's devotion, Stravinsky's ballets have perennially drawn the favour of hundreds of choreographers with notably diverse styles, from Frederick Ashton's 1948 treatment of the plotless *Scènes de ballet*, through Martha Graham's 1984 haunting vision of *The Rite of Spring*, to Justin Peck's 2016 elegant setting of the 1908 *Scherzo fantastique* – the very piece that first caught Diaghilev's ear. Remarkably, of Stravinsky's roughly 100 compositions and arrangements, almost 90 per cent have been set to dance. Such magnetism is traceable to a variety of contributing factors. Stravinsky understood dance from the inside out. The fragile intersecting of ballet's multiple layers in precisely the right proportion was paramount. Instinctually, his musical imagination seemed perfectly in sync with his eye for physical movement. His sense of temporal architecture, in which events arose and receded at just the right moment, surely lent itself to limitless choreographic visions. In his hands, the orchestra acted as a forceful agent in advancing a ballet's story without sacrificing its own musical autonomy. And perhaps chief among his ballets' distinctive qualities stands the rhythmic intensity of every score, sometimes subtly expressed, sometimes befittingly predominant. In every case, it is the ebullience of Stravinsky's music – its elemental, relentless pulse that draws us in – while calling out to be danced. CHARLES M. JOSEPH

Stephanie Jordan, *Stravinsky Dances: Re-visions Across a Century* (Alton, Hampshire: Dance Books Ltd, 2007).
Charles M. Joseph, *Stravinsky's Ballets* (New Haven and London: Yale University Press, 2011).

Ballet Collaborations. Each of Stravinsky's stage works involved intricate relations with directors, producers and theatre managers, score copyists and music publishers, as well as creative personalities responsible for scenarios, choreography, costumes and décor, and, of course, performers – the orchestras, dancers and, in some cases, singers. His collaboration with conductors, who link all aspects of a performance, is another aspect of Stravinsky's role as a theatrical team player. Because he often conducted his own work, he was particularly aware of the risks and obligations of the maestro's art. To truly understand Stravinsky as a collaborator would require a look at all these factors to see how he held them in balance and how, in each case, he preserved his musical score.

The RITE OF SPRING (1913). Stravinsky reconfigured fragments of Slavic folk song and RITUAL chants for his ground-breaking score, working with the

scenarist and designer Nicholas ROERICH – who was also an erudite archae-
ologist – and the choreographer Vaslav NIJINSKY. From the outset of his career,
Stravinsky was a commanding presence. He declared what he wanted, for
example, in the timing and phrasing of movement. His visits to rehearsals
with Nijinsky for The Rite of Spring were stormy. Both artists imagined archaic
mass movement but disagreed on how to achieve it. Nijinsky sought to reveal
the ritual roots of dance, breaking academic rules with inverted postures and
angular gestures. The complex architecture of Stravinsky's score he magnified,
by contrasting tight groups and animating successive planes of the stage: all
these initiatives were difficult for dancers in 1913, and Nijinsky could not guide
them through the complications as fast as Stravinsky wished.

Legendary battles ensued, especially over issues of tempi. By 1920, Roerich
was based in England, and Nijinsky committed to a Swiss mental institution.
When Coco CHANEL wrote Diaghilev a cheque in connection with a proposal
for a revival of The Rite, he asked current choreographer Léonide MASSINE for
a remake. Less complex and uncontroversial, 'le deuxième Sacre' made some
critics revise their earlier views and endorse the Nijinsky original, which
Kenneth Archer and Millicent Hodson reconstructed in 1987 with the Joffrey
Ballet in the UNITED STATES. By the end of the twentieth century, The Rite had
become a choreographic rite of passage with some 200 versions documented
on a world database.

The NIGHTINGALE Project (1908–25). Stravinsky's trio of Russian ethnic works
for the BALLETS RUSSES launched a life-long pattern of work with partners in
dance, design and text. He was always inclined more to ballet than OPERA but
pushed the definitions of both, engaging with authors of lyrics and libretti as
vigorously as with CHOREOGRAPHERS and designers. In the aftermath of The Rite
of Spring, he returned to work on his first opera, based on the Hans Christian
Andersen story of a nightingale whose song saves the life of an ailing Chinese
emperor. The composer worked on the score for a decade, with a variety of
collaborators. Hence, the Nightingale project is a case study of Stravinsky as
team player.

He conceived the scenario as early as 1908 with his ST PETERSBURG
CONSERVATORY mentor, Nikolay RIMSKY-KORSAKOV, and librettist Vladimir
Belsky. The sung text by Stravinsky's fellow student and pianist Stepan
MITUSOV made the composer realise that 'words not meaning' were what
liberated his music, a view that troubled a few later collaborators. Progress
on the opera was interrupted by an invitation to compose The Firebird for the
Ballets Russes. Thus, The Nightingale was begun before and completed after
Stravinsky's early trilogy of Russian ballets for Diaghilev. The composer later
said of it: 'I wrote it in the Firebird period (what can I say?) I was on some kind of
ornithological streak.'

Stravinsky had completed a single scene of the story in 1908, which he then
extended in 1913 at the urging of Alexander Sanin, the director who had staged
all Diaghilev's operas. The composer seized on this expansion as a way to
obtain much-needed funds for himself and his family from Sanin, founder and
Director of the new Moscow Free Theatre, which wanted exclusive rights for
presenting the opera to the Russian public.

Diaghilev had established the idea of the triple bill for BALLET programmes, and so Stravinsky was accustomed to scores lasting half an hour or less. *The Nightingale* is short by operatic standards – under an hour – but a big spectacle with props and supernumeraries. After several twists of fate, the Moscow Free Theatre closed, and Diaghilev took the project for a 1914 première with designs by Alexandre BENOIS. During a Ballets Russes tour, the Benois décors and costumes were lost at sea. Diaghilev then asked Stravinsky to prepare a ballet suite from the opera, which he finished in 1917 and named *The* SONG OF THE NIGHTINGALE. Not until 1920, after the end of the war, was Diaghilev able to stage the ballet, for which he commissioned designs by Henri Matisse and choreography by Léonide Massine.

Meanwhile, Stravinsky's dream of staging *The Nightingale* opera at the Mariinsky had come true. Because he appreciated the vibrant chinoiserie of the lost 1914 production, he proposed that Benois join the team with avant-garde theatre director Vsevelod Meyerhold. However, the Mariinsky had already engaged Golovine, so the standing rivalry between the two designers became an outright battle. The design was done by Golovine, but, due to the effects of World War I and the Russian Revolution, *The Nightingale* was performed only once. The singers, seated on Constructivist benches across the stage, were surrounded by a large ensemble of dancers and extras. Among them was the young Soviet dancer George BALANCHINE. By 1925, when he and several members of his Young Ballet troupe came west on tour, they unexpectedly joined the Ballets Russes and never went home. Diaghilev immediately commissioned Balanchine to revise *The Song of the Nightingale*, the choreographer's first encounter with Stravinsky, whose *The Rite of Spring* he had attempted to stage at the Mariinsky in 1923 – but the directorate refused. The 1920 version of *The Song of the Nightingale* had clung to operatic props and staging effects which, by instinct, Balanchine deleted in 1925. At the London première of the latest Nightingale project, the *Observer* critic noted that 'simplification of the stage mechanism is carried considerably further'. The young choreographer had never heard of Matisse, but his Soviet reduction of means finally made the master painter's modernised Ming designs visible to audience and critics.

Between the Wars in Europe. Stravinsky continued to collaborate with the BALLETS RUSSES until DIAGHILEV's death in 1929. PULCINELLA (1920), choreographed by MASSINE and designed by Pablo PICASSO, is regarded as his first venture into NEO-CLASSICISM. However, Stravinsky's theatrical masterpiece after World War I was *Les* NOCES (1923), a ballet-cantata with his own libretto based on music for Russian peasant weddings and choreographed by Bronislava NIJINSKA. It was designed by Natalya GONCHAROVA, who proposed modernist exaggerations of folk décor and costumes. Nijinska heralded the stripped-down aesthetic of mid-twenties MODERNISM with her insistence on simple, monochromatic designs. Her choreography, too, though classically based, pared down and blunted the steps to match Stravinsky's austere manipulations of peasant songs and melodies. Nijinska also choreographed RENARD (1922), a song-and-dance burlesque. In 1928, both the composer and the choreographer decamped from the Ballets Russes to create *The* FAIRY'S KISS for Ida RUBINSTEIN's company, a direct rival of Diaghilev, right on his Parisian doorstep.

APOLLON MUSAGÈTE (1927–8). The year 1928 was kaleidoscopic for Stravinsky collaborations, with not only the première of *The Fairy's Kiss* for Rubinstein in Paris but also *Apollon Musagète* in Washington DC, with choreography by the Russian émigré Adolf BOLM. Stravinsky took little interest in the American production, and later the same year joined forces again with Diaghilev and George BALANCHINE to stage the version that became iconic. Eventually entitled just *Apollo*, it was the turning point at which Balanchine recalibrated his work from post-Mariinsky narrative into pure dance, updating the academic vocabulary with his own contemporary irony and clarity. In this period, Stravinsky used traditional forms, predominantly from the eighteenth century, and it was the model of this music, the choreographer later maintained, that urged him to limit expression, developing a single idea for each of his ballets. Balanchine's style was soon labelled neo-classicism and became the dominant aesthetic in ballet world-wide.

With *The Song of the Nightingale*, Balanchine, as a rank beginner in the West, had entered into the relationship of disciple and master with Stravinsky, who was already well established. But now they forged a more equal partnership that would maximise the talents of both over the next half-century. Stravinsky and Balanchine returned to *Apollo* numerous times, adjusting the choreography and even the music. The mise-en-scène changed radically. BAUCHANT's tutus and belted tunic of 1928 were redesigned the year after the première by Chanel, and his backdrop abandoned. In 1928, a Constructivist staircase in Meyerhold's Soviet style enabled the ascent to Olympus in the finale by the god of music with his muses. Several times over the years, this finale was cut and then reinstated. Apollo remains an emblem of the combined theatrical genius of Stravinsky and Balanchine.

PERSÉPHONE (1934). After Diaghilev's death in 1929 and the reorganisation of the Ballets Russes under various directors, Stravinsky returned to Rubinstein's company in 1934 to create the melodrama *Perséphone*, a dance piece by Kurt Jooss with sung text written by André GIDE. For the singers, Stravinsky broke the French text into rhythmic syllables which had nothing to do with how Gide intended it to sound. The rift between the collaborators became a national issue in FRANCE, with Gide defending the language, and Stravinsky, just as he was to become a citizen of the country, standing firm on the need to treat words of any language as pure sound. To support his case, he cited the Latinate tradition of variable stress for sacred music. Despite acclaim for performances of *Perséphone* on several continents, the scansion scandal left this creative team in disarray. Gide never saw a performance of their work and the conflict was never resolved.

From Europe to the United States. Through the patronage of the balletomane and dance scholar, Lincoln KIRSTEIN, Balanchine began working in the United States in 1934. Stravinsky, although still a French citizen until 1939, frequently took part in American events and tours. During this period, critics complained that Balanchine was too Russian, and Stravinsky, whose Diaghilev ballets they still preferred, was not Russian enough. Undeterred, Balanchine in 1937 decided to stage an all-Stravinsky Festival for his AMERICAN BALLET, the company founded with Kirstein which was resident at New York's Metropolitan Opera. The 1937 festival included their creation of *Jeu de cartes* with designs by Irene SHARAFF, a new version by Balanchine of *Le Baiser de la fée* (which they would revise together as *The Fairy's Kiss* in 1950) and their iconic collaboration *Apollon Musagète* from the Ballets Russes repertoire. Although their US debut as an émigré team was a success, both artists continued to struggle with critical resistance throughout the thirties and forties. With ingenuity and perseverance, they began to assimilate, catching the populist American spirit, for example, in CIRCUS POLKA, their ballet for Barnum & Bailey's elephants (1942).

ORPHEUS (1948). The breakthrough for the Stravinsky–Balanchine partnership came with *Orpheus* in 1948, which had sets and costumes by sculptor Isamu Noguchi, famed for his collaborations with Martha Graham. The choreographer worked directly with the composer on the music, taking their collaboration to a new level, as they transformed the Orpheus tradition into twentieth-century neo-classicism. When the score was ready, Stravinsky took part in rehearsals to keep their mutual ideas intact. Keeping up a regime of physical training all his life, he did not hesitate to dance passages of his scores to show Balanchine and the dancers his ideas.

AGON (1957). The title of the ballet indicates a competition. Young contestants break barriers to astonish each other, but with no resolution in win or loss. Virtuosity is its own reward. Balanchine, who called *Agon* a 'quintessential contemporary ballet', had supplanted costumes and décor with rehearsal dress by this point. Stravinsky's score marked his move towards TWELVE-NOTE technique, and, coincidentally, Balanchine used twelve dancers for the choreography, arranging duets, trios and quartets that are constantly in flux. Although the music and dance are based on seventeenth-century French court dances such as the sarabande, galliard and bransle, Balanchine created jazzy, up-to-date versions. The ballet contrasts sporty, athletic encounters with the sensuous intimacy of the now famous love duet, startling at the time for its slow, sprung positions and entanglements. Without an agenda as such, the pairing of a black male soloist, Arthur Mitchell, with a white ballerina, Diana Adams, also spoke to issues of race and segregation in the United States of the fifties.

Balanchine used for ballets many of Stravinsky's compositions not originally intended for dance, setting a standard for countless CHOREOGRAPHERS all over the world. These adaptations were virtual collaborations, as he remained close to Stravinsky until the end of his life. In 1972, a year after the composer's death, Balanchine produced his second Stravinsky Festival, choreographing many new ballets himself, such as the SYMPHONY IN THREE MOVEMENTS and CONCERTO IN D FOR VIOLIN AND ORCHESTRA, and commissioning others, urging use of the composer's lesser-known music, an inestimable service to the theatre-going public. In 1982, just one year before Balanchine's death, he directed the Stravinsky Centennial Celebration, presenting NEW YORK CITY BALLET in twenty-five of his own ballets created to music by Stravinsky.

MILLICENT HODSON

Ballet Companies. If one understands BALLET in general, and that of Stravinsky in particular, as an interaction as equals between music and dance (and perhaps also stage design), and thus disregards the hybrid stage works RENARD (1916), *The* SOLDIER'S TALE (1917), PULCINELLA (1920), *Les* NOCES (1923), PERSÉPHONE (1934) and *The* FLOOD (1961–2) (which also include dance), the majority of Stravinsky's ballets were produced with the two subsequently most well-known ballet companies of the twentieth century: the Russian impresario Sergey DIAGHILEV's BALLETS RUSSES (*The* FIREBIRD, 1910; PETRUSHKA, 1911; *The* RITE OF SPRING, 1913), and the NEW YORK CITY BALLET (AGON, 1957) and its precursor institutions the School of American Ballet (1934–46; JEU DE CARTES, 1937) and the Ballet Society (1946–8; ORPHEUS, 1948), all of which were initiated by the American author and creative artist Lincoln KIRSTEIN and the Russian dancer and choreographer George BALANCHINE. Only four ballets by Stravinsky were produced – at least initially – independently of these institutions: (1) APOLLON MUSAGÈTE, 1928; (2) *The* FAIRY'S KISS, 1928; (3) CIRCUS POLKA (the original title of which was *The Ballet of the Elephants*, 1942); and (4) SCÈNES DE BALLET, 1944.

(1) *Apollon Musagète* was commissioned by the American composer, pianist and patron of chamber music Elisabeth Sprague Coolidge for the 1925 opening of the Coolidge Auditorium at the Library of Congress in Washington, DC, and first performed there on 27 April 1928 with choreography by Adolph BOLM (Adolph Bolm, Apollo; Elise Reiman, Calliope; Ruth PAGE, Terpsichore; Berenice HOLMES, Polyhymnia; Hans KINDLER. Conductor; Nicolas REMISOFF, scenography). Although this was – as the American music critic Olin Downes put it in the 6 May 1928 issue of the *New York Times* – 'the first time in history a major ballet work [meaning a major ballet work by a European composer] had its world premier in America', *Apollon Musagète* was shown with the cast and in the form of its première only on this one evening. The more well-known European première by the Ballets Russes was held just less than two months later, on 12 June 1928, at the THÉÂTRE SARAH BERNHARDT in PARIS. This time, however, it was staged with a (different) choreography by George Balanchine (Serge LIFAR, Apollo; Alice Nikitina and Alexandra Danilova, Terpsichore; Lubov Tchernicheva, Calliope; Felia Doubrovska, Polyhymnia; Igor Stravinsky, conductor; André BAUCHANT, scenography). Carl Engel, then Director of the Music Division of the Library of Congress, and Elisabeth Sprague Coolidge had already arranged in November 1926 for Adolph Bolm to direct the choreography for a dance and pantomime programme for the Coolidge Festival in 1928. Stravinsky, on the other hand, was only their third choice for a composer: it was not until Manuel de FALLA and Ottorino Respighi had turned down invitations that Coolidge and Engel approached him. Despite limitations to the size of the orchestra and the number of dancers due to a lack of space, Stravinsky accepted the invitation in June 1927. Before doing so, however, he negotiated permission to perform the ballet in Europe and South America immediately after the American première. His correspondence with the organisers from Washington reveals that Stravinsky attempted to dictate every detail of the production from afar – from

the staging and choreography to the costumes. It is very likely that Stravinsky had discussed these details previously with Diaghilev and Balanchine. After all, he had already rehearsed entire parts of the ballet with Balanchine even before having the scenario and score sent to Bolm.

(2) The wealthy former Ballets Russes dancer and actress Ida RUBINSTEIN commissioned Stravinsky to write her an entirely new ballet inspired by TCHAIKOVSKY, The Fairy's Kiss (1928), shortly after she had asked him unsuccessfully in December 1927 for permission to perform Apollon Musagète, which was being prepared for Washington at the time, with Ballets Ida Rubinstein, the company she had founded one year previously in Paris. After Stravinsky had worked on the composition between July and October 1928 and given her numerous instructions concerning the production in advance, some of which are documented in the score and piano reduction, the ballet was performed for the first time at the Théâtre National de l'Opéra on 27 November 1928 with a choreography by Bronislava NIJINSKA and a set design by Alexandre BENOIS. Stravinsky received $6,000 dollars for this work, six times more than the fee he received for Coolidge's Washington production. In addition – as Stravinsky himself claimed – Diaghilev supposedly never forgave him for accepting this engagement. The latter had seen Rubinstein's own productions, which were put on independently of the Ballets Russes and were always equipped with a large budget, as competition from the beginning. As the ballet did not meet with any real success at the première, Rubinstein had The Fairy's Kiss performed a total of only five times (twice in Paris and once each in Brussels, Monte Carlo and Milan) before removing it from the company's repertoire. The Fairy's Kiss attracted more attention through George Balanchine, who first presented it with his School of American Ballet in New York on 27 April 1937 – during the first Stravinsky Festival at the Metropolitan Opera, and with the composer himself on the conductor's podium.

(3) As far as the Circus Polka is concerned (the original title was The Ballet of the Elephants, 1942), Stravinsky received, with the help of Balanchine, a commission from the American circus company Ringling Bros. and Barnum & Bailey Circus, founded in 1919, to write the music for a performance of 'Fifty Elephants and Fifty Beautiful Girls in an Original Choreographic Tour de Force' choreographed by Balanchine. The show premièred on 9 April 1942 at Madison Square Garden with a total of fifty fully grown elephants and fifty female dancers – all of them dressed up in pink-coloured tutus and led by the ballet dancer and actress Vera Zorina and the oldest elephant, Modoc – and was performed more than 400 times. Unlike in the previously described productions, Stravinsky supplied only the music here, and left all responsibility for scenario and production to Balanchine.

(4) After Kurt WEILL had declined an invitation from the show manager, song writer and nightclub owner Billy Rose to write the music for a ballet number for his planned Broadway revue The Seven Lively Arts, Rose contacted Stravinsky and asked him to write the music for Scènes de ballet (1944), which was intended as part of the production. The former Ballets Russes dancer Anton DOLIN was

responsible for the choreography, which he was then to dance together with his former Ballets Russes colleague Alicia Markova. Following a pre-Broadway run in the form of public rehearsals at the Forrest Theatre in Philadelphia starting on 27 November 1944 and several telegrams and telephone calls between Dolin, Rose, Maurice Abravanel, who had conducted the Philadelphia run, and Stravinsky, the approximately 17-minute-long composition was cut to around 10 minutes and the ORCHESTRATION reduced. As a result, the show finally opened on 7 December 1944 at Ziegfeld Theater in New York City containing only excerpts from Stravinsky's *Scènes de ballet*.

Apart from Ballets Ida Rubinstein, the clients who commissioned the ballets not produced in connection with the Ballets Russes or the New York City Ballet were therefore not ballet companies in the proper sense. Rather, they were entertainment industry ventures from the New World that had little to do with ballet, or were even foreign to the classical cultural canon – coming from chamber music (Coolidge), circus (Ringling Bros. and Barnum & Bailey Circus), show business (Billy Rose) – and that approached the European ballet composer par excellence to engage his services for their purposes.   LEILA ZICKGRAF

Charles M. Joseph, *Stravinsky & Balanchine: A Journey of Invention* (New Haven and London: Yale University Press, 2002).

Charles M. Joseph, *Stravinsky Inside Out* (New Haven and London: Yale University Press, 2001).

Charles M. Joseph, *Stravinsky's Ballets* (New Haven and London: Yale University Press, 2011).

Jacques Depaulis, *Ida Rubinstein. Une inconnue jadis célèbre* (Paris: Honoré Champion, 1995).

Charles S. Mayer, 'Ida Rubinstein: a twentieth-century Cleopatra', *Dance Research Journal*, 20.2 (1988), 33–51.

John Schuster-Craig, 'Stravinsky's "Scènes de ballet" and Billy Rose's "The seven lively arts": the Abravanel account', in Susan Parisi (ed.), with collaboration of Ernest Harriss II and Calvin M. Bower, *Music in the Theater, Church, and Villa: Essays in Honor of Robert Lamar Weaver and Norma Wright Weaver* (Michigan: Harmonie Park Press, 2000), 285–9.

Exp; SSE

Ballet Dancing. Stravinsky's name is synonymous with BALLET. It was in ballet that his international career was launched, and it would be for ballet that he would write some of his most important scores. It was an enduring interest, and he returned to dance at a number of points in his life (though his involvement with ballet was always dependent on companies, impresarios and CHOREOGRAPHERS). As for the dancing itself, his input and connection to the choreography for the original ballets he worked on varied depending on the project, though his scores have had an extraordinary independent life as music for dance. During his lifetime and since his death, his music – whether conceived for ballet or not – has been used for dance in all its forms. Stravinsky and ballet is therefore an expansive topic, encompassing his early acquaintance with dance, original BALLET COLLABORATIONS, ballets he was involved in to existing scores, broader theatrical works featuring dance, and the hundreds of dance works created to his music. Also relevant are the composer's reported views on the relationship between music and dance: often changing, contradictory or simply at odds with the evidence of his own collaborations, they provide a curious record of his views, biases and ever-changing personal relationships.

Born into the theatrical world of ST PETERSBURG, Stravinsky had a strong understanding of ballet and dance from his youth. His exposure was unusually rich: he saw the first productions of the Tchaikovsky–Petipa ballets (Petipa himself was a friend of Stravinsky's father), watched Anna Pavlova at the Mariinsky Theatre, became familiar with the stories of the major ballets, and learnt the basics of classical technique. He remembered how ballet was 'an important part of our culture and a familiar subject to me from my earliest childhood' (*Mem*, 31). As such, by the time he was approached by Sergey Diaghilev about working for the Ballets Russes, Stravinsky had extensive knowledge of the history of ballet, its latest developments, and the art of dancing itself.

The first of his music used for dance was not an original commission, however. In 1909, Diaghilev commissioned Stravinsky to orchestrate Chopin's Nocturne in A♭, op. 32, No. 2, and Grand Valse brillante, op. 18, for inclusion in *Les Sylphides* (formerly *Chopiniana*), part of the Ballets Russes' first Paris season. The choreographer was Mikhail Fokine, an innovator who wanted to unify the arts and reflect the setting, music and style of a ballet in the movement (i.e. realism within the onstage world). His aim was to release ballet from the strictures of set forms and adopt a naturalistic approach to story-telling; Lynn Garafola refers to his 'liberating aesthetic' in *Diaghilev's Ballets Russes* (Garafola 1989, 3–49). This was the approach he took as the choreographer of Stravinsky's first two original ballet scores, The Firebird (1910) and Petrushka (1911). For Fokine, movement was dictated by character or emotion, and so, in terms of dance style, traditional classical ballet was only included when deemed appropriate. For example, in *The Firebird*, the human Princesses perform simple folk-like dances barefoot, while the mythical and enchanting Firebird has solos featuring virtuosic leaps and is en pointe (her style of movement therefore highlighting her magical otherworldliness and flightiness as a bird). In *Petrushka*, while the Ballerina is the archetypal classical ballerina in pointe shoes (albeit a particularly clipped version since she is a ballerina doll), the other female dancers take the roles of peasants, nurses and other visitors to the Shrovetide Fair, and so move like (and don the footwear of) these types of characters. This was Fokine's naturalism.

Stravinsky would later heavily criticise Fokine's *Firebird* choreography, claiming it was 'complicated and overburdened with plastic detail', but he recognised the skill of the dancers (*Auto*, 30). The press at the time had few qualms: '[L'Oiseau] heralds an entirely new direction in the art of dancing', declared a critic for *Le Figaro* (Beaumont 1945, 68). As for *Petrushka*, Fokine struggled to understand Stravinsky's music and turmoil engulfed rehearsals – Stravinsky wrote of Fokine's 'capriciousness and despotism' and 'lack of sensitivity' (SCS, 162), while Fokine considered Stravinsky's music unnecessarily difficult (Fokine 1961, 188). On reflection, Stravinsky believed the choreographer neglected aspects, but admitted that the solo dances and those of the coachmen, nurses and mummers 'must be regarded as Fokine's finest creations' (*Auto*, 62). All accounts agree on one thing: Vaslav Nijinsky transformed himself into the tragic figure of the puppet in a manner unmatched by later interpretations.

The dancing of Stravinsky's next ballet was to be quite different. The Rite of Spring (1913) was choreographed by Nijinsky, who responded to the ancient Slavic rite and Stravinsky's radical score by rejecting classical ballet's most central tenets. The arabesques and jetés Nijinsky himself was so famous for were replaced by stamping, hunching, shaking and turned-in feet. Jumps were performed 'flat-footed and straight-legged', with dancers remembering how 'with every leap we landed heavily enough to jar every organ in us' (Joseph 2011, 91). Over the course of 100 rehearsals, Nijinsky attempted to visualise the score and set each musical component. He drew on the eurhythmics of Émile Jaques-DALCROZE and the help of Marie RAMBERT (dubbed 'Rhythmitchka'), but his ideas were fundamentally at odds with Stravinsky's own. Still, Stravinsky was happy with what was presented on stage at the première and defended Nijinsky immediately afterwards. Conflicting views were subsequently recorded: from the 1930s he disparaged Nijinsky's choreography in print, but there are reports he later privately claimed it the finest of all he'd seen.

In the years following World War I, the choreographer Léonide MASSINE was Stravinsky's principal ballet collaborator (he succeeded Fokine and Nijinsky at the Ballets Russes). Massine would set THE SONG OF THE NIGHTINGALE (1920) and PULCINELLA (1920), and the first production of the Rite since its 1913 première (working closely with Stravinsky). Through the use of gesture, mime, acrobatics and spectacle, he brought a greater sense of theatre, and of the artificiality of theatre, to the staging of Stravinsky's scores. For The Song of the Nightingale, Massine drew inspiration from Chinese objects and the work of the ballet's designer, Henri Matisse. The vivid but simple designs created a striking visual feast, and Massine's dances were similarly stylistically bold. Stravinsky's role was negligible, due to the score being drawn from his earlier NIGHTINGALE.

In Pulcinella, a highly original ballet-hybrid featuring mime and song, Italy's rich cultural and artistic heritage would provide the impetus for all the collaborators: Stravinsky, Massine and PICASSO (also Diaghilev, who oversaw all aspects). For Massine, COMMEDIA DELL' ARTE, Neapolitan folk dance, classical ballet and gesture were key to the staging. Massine himself performed the demanding dancer-actor title role, and, with Pulcinella wearing a mask (precluding facial expressions), his gestural movements were his sole method of conveying character and story. Though the collaboration was challenging, the result was, according to Alexandre BENOIS, 'outstandingly successful' – Benois also referred to the 'transparent design of Massine's dances' (Benois 1947, 379 n.1). The cumulative effect of the choreography, music and design signalled a new direction, and Stravinsky considered it one of Massine's best, 'so fully has he assimilated the spirit of the Neapolitan theatre' (Auto, 142).

After Massine, Stravinsky collaborated with Bronislava NIJINSKA, who brought her experiences in the Ballets Russes and immersion in the experimental art of the early Soviet Union to her choreography. She created the dances in two Stravinsky music theatre works in 1922, the raucous Russian burlesque RENARD and the one-act opera MAVRA, and would later set The FAIRY'S KISS (1928) for Ida RUBINSTEIN (Stravinsky had little oversight on The Fairy's Kiss and disliked some of Nijinska's production). Nevertheless, it is for the stark collective ceremony of Les NOCES (1923) that she is most celebrated. The austerity and elemental bleakness of the resulting balletic RITUAL she staged was imposed by her (she rejected GONCHAROVA's original colourful designs as at odds with her own ideas). Responding to Stravinsky's percussive score, she modified classical technique to her own end rather than abandoning it, and was particularly innovative in the way the dancers were grouped on stage: Cyril Beaumont described them being 'moved and massed in a manner which is part geometrical, part architectural in conception' (Beaumont 1938, 658). Unlike with most of his other Ballets Russes collaborators, and despite her approach to Noces not being what he envisaged, Stravinsky never distanced himself from Nijinska or their work together: he later claimed that 'her choreography for the original productions' of Renard and Les Noces 'pleased me more than any other works of mine interpreted by the Diaghilev troupe' (Mem, 40).

While the nature of Stravinsky's personal relationship with ballet dancing ebbed and flowed depending on the collaboration, in 1925 the composer met choreographer and dancer George BALANCHINE. The CHOREOGRAPHER'S distilled approach would go on to define NEO-CLASSICISM in dance, but this style evolved over time (often with Stravinsky). In 1925, Balanchine re-set The Song of the Nightingale in a Ballets Russes production featuring a very young Alicia MARKOVA and a form of modern choreography quite distant from the classicism he later pioneered. Following this was APOLLON MUSAGÈTE (1928), a ballet now almost exclusively associated with Balanchine, but which was not an original Balanchine–Stravinsky commission. The first production was for the Coolidge Festival at the Library of Congress, Washington, DC, and was choreographed by Adolph BOLM (Bolm's contribution was praised but Stravinsky's music was considered banal by the press in the UNITED STATES). Stravinsky, however, concentrated on the Ballets Russes production mounted in Paris by Balanchine six weeks later, and Balanchine's choreography was to prove a major turning point. Through the series of tableaux depicting Apollo's birth and education by three muses, Balanchine presented a vision of the pure and clear classicism that would open a new direction in dancing. Classical dance was extended in pursuit of balance and beauty in Balanchine's ancient Greece, and it was his style and approach, more than any other, that would be linked with Stravinsky for the remainder of the composer's life.

Following the death of Diaghilev in 1929 and the subsequent dismantling of the Ballets Russes, there was an inevitable rupture in Stravinsky's relationship with dance. In America, he formed relationships with the often newly established ballet companies – many involving former Ballets Russes artists – who mounted revivals or new versions of his works. But there would be only five new original scores for dance from 1937 until his death, of which four were for Balanchine: JEU DE CARTES (1937), The Ballet of the Elephants (1942, later CIRCUS POLKA), ORPHEUS (1947) and AGON (1957). The lone exception was SCÈNES DE BALLET (1944), a segment in a Billy Rose Broadway revue choreographed by Anton DOLIN and imagined as a classical-inspired divertissement.

Stravinsky was inevitably (by dint of age, experience and status) the dominant partner in his collaboration with Balanchine; Lincoln KIRSTEIN referred to the choreographer as the 'junior assistant', and Joseph writes of Balanchine's acquiesence being the reason they worked so well together (Joseph 2002, 147–8). This had an impact on the resulting works. Balanchine's choreography for Jeu de cartes was apparently altered by Stravinsky, while dancer Maria

Tallchief remembered the composer 'always making suggestions' during the creation of *Orpheus* (Joseph 2002, 205). In response, Balanchine told Stravinsky: 'You compose the music. I will do the dancing' (Taper 1984, 222). Whatever the relationship, Balanchine's restriction of form and shape in favour of single lines (echoed in Isamu Noguchi's sculptural designs) were recognised by dance critic John Martin, who referred to the 'ordered gesture in highly abstracted form' and the ballet's supreme simplicity (*New York Times*, 16 May 1948).

For *Agon*, Stravinsky and Balanchine worked with different resources: a seventeenth-century dance suite provided the framework and inspiration for Stravinsky's rhythmically vibrant TWELVE-NOTE score and Balanchine's corresponding choreography for twelve dancers. As elsewhere, Stravinsky had paid close attention to choreographic needs (he always focused intently on timings when preparing his dance scores), and Balanchine responded with an intricate rendering of the score through dance. Its compact and dense form was packed with the 'energy of fifty dancers' according to Edwin Denby, who also noted how the dancing is constantly counter – counter-accent, counterrhythm – to the score (Denby 2007, 459–65). Joseph has since called the ballet a 'counterpoint of minds' (2011 167–96) and it is regarded by many, including Balanchine, as their finest work together. Stravinsky's only new score featuring dance after *Agon* was the 1962 THE FLOOD (Balanchine choreography). Balanchine would, however, constantly return to Stravinsky's scores, setting over thirty of them to dance and mounting three Stravinsky festivals. As such, in the decades after the Ballets Russes, the relationship between Stravinsky and ballet dancing was defined by one style: that of Balanchine.

Stravinsky regularly wrote about ballet and dancing, not only to assess ballets and individual contributions, but to reflect on the relationship between music, dance and himself. In 1911, he declared the importance of classical dance: 'I love ballet and am more interested in it than in anything else. And this is not just an idle enthusiasm, but a serious and profound enjoyment of scenic spectacle – of the art of animated form' (SRT, 973). Often, he stressed the independence of music. In 1921, he claimed to 'have never tried, in my stage works, to make the music illustrate the action, or the action the music' (*Observer*, 3 July) – a comment against his earliest ballets – and in 1934 he referred to how music and dance should be 'a partnership, not a dictatorship of one over the other' (*Manchester Guardian*, 22 February). The following year, he refused to consider what united or separated the arts: 'Let us speak, on the contrary, of the struggle between music and choreography' (SPD, 200). When, later, this was put to Balanchine, the choreographer responded, 'Absolutely! Struggle means to be together' (Cott 2002, 133). (For more, see Joseph's discussion: 2002, 1–29.)

Stravinsky's name and music are central to twentieth-century dance, with new ballets and dances, covering an extraordinary range of choreographic approaches and styles, constantly being created to his scores. The online database 'Stravinsky the Global Dancer', compiled by Stephanie Jordan and Larraine Nicholas, records 1,200 new dances to 99 different Stravinsky scores by upwards of 680 choreographers as of 2007. It is a fascinating resource, and, among other things, Jordan has highlighted how it reveals the extent to which a production becomes the ballet: while there are 185 new versions of The Rite of Spring, there are but 10 productions of Agon recorded (and none between 1967 and 1992) (analysis in Jordan 2004). Ultimately, as Jordan explains, the scores, 'once out of the hands of their composer, acquired a life of their own, with new connotations, styles and political implications' (Jordan 2004, 58). More than to any other twentieth-century composer, choreographers and dancers have been, and continue to be, drawn to Stravinsky's music. And so, whether in revivals, reconstructions, reimaginings or wholly original new productions, the relationship between Stravinsky and ballet dancing remains dynamic and vital to this day. SOPHIE REDFERN

Cyril W. Beaumont, Complete Book of Ballets: A Guide to the Principal Ballets of the Nineteenth and Twentieth Centuries (New York: Putnam, 1938).

Cyril W. Beaumont, Michel Fokine and His Ballets (London: Wyman & Sons, 1935; repr. 1945).

Jonathan Cott, Back to a Shadow in the Night: Music Writings and Interviews, 1968–2001 (Milwaukee: Hal Leonard, 2002).

Edwin Denby, Dance Writings, ed. Robert Cornfield and William MacKay (Gainesville: University of Florida Press, 2007).

Michel Fokine, Fokine: Memoirs of a Ballet Master, trans. Vitale Fokine, ed. Anatole Chujoy (London: Constable, 1961).

Lynn Garafola, Diaghilev's Ballets Russes (New York: Oxford University Press, 1989).

Stephanie Jordan, 'The Demons in a Database: Interrogating "Stravinsky the Global Dancer"', Dance Research: Journal of the Society for Dance Research, 22.1 (Summer 2004), 57–83.

Charles M. Joseph, Stravinsky and Balanchine: A Journey of Invention (New Haven and London: Yale University Press, 2002).

Charles M. Joseph, Stravinsky's Ballets (New Haven and London: Yale University Press, 2011).

Bernard Taper, Balanchine: A Biography (Berkeley and Los Angeles: University of California Press, 1984).

Ballets Ida Rubinstein. BALLET company founded in 1927 by Russian dancer, actor and producer Ida RUBINSTEIN. The Paris-based Ballets Ida Rubinstein, which staged a number of hybrid theatrical works as well as ballets, remained active until 1935 and engaged many ex-BALLETS RUSSES artists (Bronislava NIJINSKA was its first chief CHOREOGRAPHER). As it was a rival to the Ballets Russes, Stravinsky created a rift with DIAGHILEV when he completed two commissions for the company: the 1928 ballet The FAIRY'S KISS (music after TCHAIKOVSKY), and the 1934 'melodrama' PERSÉPHONE (words by André GIDE). Rubinstein starred in both. SOPHIE REDFERN

Ballets Russes, The. The Ballets Russes, established by Sergey DIAGHILEV between 1911 and his death in 1929, was a hugely influential company playing a central role in the development of the performing arts for the twentieth century. It drew on the BALLET of nineteenth-century RUSSIA, modified to meet and challenge the tastes of its audience as ballet for export. The company never performed in Russia. PARIS, recognised as the cultural heart of Europe, was the city in which ballets were premièred, and the response – whether ecstatic or controversial – could be used to promote the company. Monte Carlo became the company's winter and spring-time base (both in 1911–14 and 1923–9), with rehearsal facilities in which to create new productions. Significantly, the Ballets Russes revitalised the art form in western Europe and the UNITED STATES. Through the work of Diaghilev, ballet became accepted as a stand-alone art, rather than part of OPERA or popular entertainments.

Although the company toured extensively in North and South America as well as Europe, it was in Paris, London, Monaco and Berlin that the more controversial ballets were presented. Elsewhere, the focus was on more traditional works. The Polovtsian Dances from *Prince Igor* were performed at a quarter of all performances, closely followed by the romantic *Les Sylphides*. The exotic *Shéhérazade* was in demand, given its subject matter of sex and violence in a harem and stunning designs by Léon BAKST, and the lively tale of toys coming to life in *La Boutique fantasque* was the most frequently performed of the later works.

The history of the company may be divided into four sections. Firstly, there were the pre-company seasons of 1909 and 1910 when ballet was first presented as the principal feature of Diaghilev's *Saison Russe*. It was essentially a pick-up company of dancers available to perform during their summer break from the Imperial Theatres of ST PETERSBURG, Moscow and Warsaw. For the first season, the ballets were essentially reworkings of short ballets from the Imperial Ballet repertoire revitalised with new designs and modified scores. The Parisian audiences were stunned by the quality of the productions and dancing, at a time when ballet in Paris appeared in decline, with few talented CHOREOGRAPHERS available. Stars of the first seasons were Léon Bakst with his bejewelled pallete and exotic costumes, and virtuoso dancer Vaslav NIJINSKY, who had the ability to transform himself to become each role he danced. The choreographer for the first season was Mikhail FOKINE, who did away with lengthy mime and processional scenes to convey his narrative through dance. He ensured movement and costumes fitted his subject matter evoking a multiplicity of 'worlds' and, from the second season, with the première of *The FIREBIRD*, entirely new ballets were created.

In 1910, the Ballets Russes was seen in Berlin and Brussels in addition to Paris, and impresarios from around the globe were vying to sign up the star dancers for their own theatres and tours. Diaghilev realised that, if he was to proceed, he would have to put dancers under long-term contracts and establish a year-round touring company. Nijinsky's dismissal from the Imperial Theatre over his inappropriate costume for *Giselle* played into Diaghilev's hands and, having secured his star, he was able to lure many dancers from their secure work with the Imperial Ballet. He always employed the finest available dancers (hiding their nationality under Russian names if necessary).

Establishing the company led to the second period, 1911–14, when the peripatetic company consolidated its early successes and productions became more radical, particularly with Nijinsky as choreographer. Nijinsky sought a different style of movement for each production and choreographed the more controversial works: *L'Après-midi d'un faune* and *The RITE OF SPRING*. The year 1914 also saw a change in design with the introduction of Natalya GONCHAROVA and her partner Mikhail LARIONOV, who broke with Bakst's *art nouveau* flowing designs and introduced Russian modernism and a more acidic pallete. Many of the summer seasons were given in conjunction with Russian opera, calling on singers from Moscow to join the dancers during the pre-war years.

Thirdly, there were the years 1915–22, in which the company operated against the background of the Great War and Revolution. This was a period of radical experimentation and workshopping ideas when proposed ballets such as 'Liturgie' and a trilogy of Spanish ballets failed to reach the stage, although others, including *Fireworks*, *Parade* and *Chout*, eventually materialised. It was also the period in which the company seemed most conservative on tours to America, Spain and ITALY. Character works choreographed by Léonide MASSINE dominated the creative repertory and, after his dismissal, Diaghilev presented Marius Petipa's costly but influential *Sleeping Princess* in London.

In the final period, the remainder of the 1920s, Diaghilev commissioned a wide range of artists and composers in a constant search for novelty. With choreographers Bronislava NIJINSKA and George BALANCHINE, academic ballet technique came back into focus, albeit often used in novel ways. Key ballets included the masterpieces *Les* NOCES and APOLLON MUSAGÈTE.

Igor Stravinsky was involved with the company during all periods and collaborated with all of Diaghilev's choreographers. He was involved with fourteen distinct productions, including commissions, adaptations and works Diaghilev acquired. Three ballets were staged in two different productions and six were vocal works: the opera-ballet *The* NIGHTINGALE, opera MAVRA and oratorio OEDIPUS REX, with ballets PULCINELLA, RENARD and *Les Noces* incorporating a significant vocal element.

The Company was notable for its collaborative creations, with choreographers, designers and composers responding to one another's contributions. If not a true *Gesamtkunstwerk*, the productions needed to be sufficiently adaptable to tour, and Diaghilev's directorial eye ensured quality was maintained. Along with parallel work by Anna Pavlova's Company, audiences internationally accepted ballet as a stand-alone art and, thanks to Nijinsky, Massine and Serge LIFAR, the public's perception of the male dancers was transformed. The lasting impact of the Ballets Russes was enormous. For the next four decades, successor Ballet Russe companies toured. Artists who had been employed by Diaghilev led companies world-wide, and fine artists and leading composers maintained an interest in working with dance. The world of fashion continues to be inspired by Diaghilev's designers, and excitement is generated when productions created for the Ballets Russes are revived or reconstructed.   JANE PRITCHARD

Balmont, Konstantin (Dmitrevich) (born Shuya, Vladimir province, 3/15 June 1867; died PARIS, 23 December 1942). Russian symbolist poet and translator. He emigrated to FRANCE in 1920. It seems that Stravinsky never met him, although he mentioned he saw him at one concert in ST PETERSBURG. He set to music three of his poems, from the collection 'The Green Garden': 'The Forget-Me-Not' and 'The Dove' for voice and piano, under the title *Two Poems of Balmont*; and 'Star-Face', usually known as *Le Roi des étoiles* (KING OF THE STARS), for male-voice chorus and orchestra. Stravinsky, commenting on his setting of the latter, emphasised his attraction to the words *per se*, rather than the meaning of the poem, an approach that largely characterises his setting of the two other poems as well.   KATERINA LEVIDOU

Mem; SCS; SRT

Bartók, Béla (Viktor János) (born Nagyszentmiklós, Hungary (now Sînnicolau Mare, Romania), 25 Mar. 1881; died New York City, 26 Sept. 1945). Hungarian composer, ethnomusicologist and pianist. Stravinsky was perhaps the single most important contemporary composer for Bartók, and many of the latter's works have apparent Stravinskian models which predate them by a few years – for example *The Wooden Prince*, 1914–17 (*see* The FIREBIRD, PETRUSHKA), *The Miraculous Mandarin*, 1918–19 (*see* THE RITE OF SPRING) and Bartók's Piano Concertos Nos. 1 and 2, 1926 and 1931 respectively (*see* Stravinsky's CONCERTO FOR PIANO AND WIND INSTRUMENTS) (*see* Schneider 1995). The two encountered each other a few times in April 1922 while in PARIS, but never became closely acquainted. On one occasion (8 April), Bartók played in a private performance of his Sonata No. 1 for Violin and Piano at the home of the French musicologist Henry Prunières which was 'attended by half the "leading composers of the world"', including Stravinsky (Bartók's letter to his mother, 15 April 1922). While Bartók's admiration for Stravinsky was never really reciprocated, the latter's professed scepticism towards Bartók's passion for native folklore probably served to disguise his own debt to Russian folk traditions (*see* SRT). JEREMY COLEMAN

David E. Schneider, 'Bartók and Stravinsky: respect, competition, influence, and the Hungarian reaction to modernism in the 1920s', in Peter Laki (ed.), *Bartók and His World* (Princeton University Press, 1995), 172–99.

Bauchant, André (born Château Renault, FRANCE, 24 April 1873; died Montoire-sur-le-Loir, France, 12 August 1958). Professional gardener turned self-taught painter, celebrated in 1920s PARIS for his primitive treatment of landscape, myth, flowers and country scenes. Despite Stravinsky's preference for the classicist Giorgio de Chirico, Sergey DIAGHILEV invited Bauchant to design the 1928 Paris production of Stravinsky's APOLLON MUSAGÈTE, capitalising on Bauchant's recent popularity in the press. Merging folk-infused classicism with spectacle, Bauchant's designs featured an oversized vase of flowers for the front-cloth, a large central rock from which Apollo emerged in scene 1, and an airborne horse-drawn chariot in the final scene. Stravinsky appreciated aspects of Bauchant's designs, but preferred the more streamlined costumes created by Coco CHANEL for a later restaging of the work. BARBARA SWANSON

Beckett, Samuel (born Foxrock, Ireland, 13 April 1906; died PARIS, 22 December 1989). Irish avant-garde playwright, novelist and poet who wrote in both English and French, winning the Nobel Prize for Literature in 1969. Beckett lived most of his adult life in Paris, explaining that he chose to write in French because the process helped him to write 'without style', and his work tests the limits of linguistic expression, gesturing towards either a plenitude, or a void, of meaning beyond it. His plays, like those of Ionesco and GENET, explore the medium of theatre itself, often bleak in tone but with much dark humour, giving the unsettling impression of an endless, irresolvable search for sense. Stravinsky was intrigued by the slow pace and long silences of Beckett's plays, and as early as 1956 hinted at the possibility of a collaboration. When he met the playwright in May 1962, Stravinsky told him he would be 'honoured to compose music for any opera that Beckett might wish to write', although no such collaboration came to pass. In Beckett's radio play *Words and Music*, written in late 1961 and broadcast on the BBC in November 1962 with music written independently by his cousin John Beckett, Words and Music appear as two performers attempting to work together, despite their problematic and challenging relationship. At Beckett's suggestion, Morton Feldman wrote the music for the American radio production in 1987. Fittingly, Feldman went about his composition without reading the text from start to finish, supplying musical fragments which articulate an unending longing wholly in keeping with the tone of the play.   DAVID EVANS

Beethoven, Ludwig van (born Bonn, bap. 17 Dec. 1770; died Vienna, 26 Mar. 1827). German composer and pianist. As a young man, Stravinsky expressed hostility towards Beethoven's music. Around 1924, he began intensive study of the works, particularly of the late Piano Sonatas (*Auto*), which provided models of formal procedure that directly influenced his compositions, such as the PIANO SONATA and the CONCERTO FOR PIANO AND WIND INSTRUMENTS. The first movement of Stravinsky's SYMPHONY IN C is only one of the more explicit homages to Beethoven's use of rhythmic motives (*see* Hyde 2003). Comparison with Beethoven had been a feature of Stravinsky's press reception as early as the 1910s, with the *Guardian* newspaper, for example, stating in a 1913 review of the FIREBIRD Suite that 'in this department [rhythm] he is the greatest master that has arisen since Beethoven'. Stravinsky renewed his appreciation of Beethoven once again in his old age (*Dial*), professing admiration for the Eighth Symphony and describing the string quartet movement *Grosse Fuge*, op. 133, as 'pure interval music' and as an 'absolutely contemporary piece of music that will be contemporary forever'.   JEREMY COLEMAN

Martha M. Hyde, 'Stravinsky's neoclassicism', in Jonathan Cross (ed.), *The Cambridge Companion to Stravinsky* (Cambridge University Press, 2003), 98–136.

Belyayev, Mitrofan Petrovich (born ST PETERSBURG, 10/22 February 1836; died St Petersburg, 22 December 1903 / 4 January 1904). Russian music publisher and patron. The première of GLAZUNOV's First Symphony inspired him to set up in 1885 a publishing house, Edition M. P. Belaieff, in Leipzig (to secure international copyright), to promote Russian music; Nikolay RIMSKY-KORSAKOV, Glazunov and Anatoly LIADOV became the firm's music advisers. In that same year, with Rimsky-Korsakov's encouragement, Belyayev launched, under his own sponsorship, the RUSSIAN SYMPHONY CONCERTS (RSC), exclusively devoted to Russian music – in practice, works by Rimsky-Korsakov and his pupils – held annually until 1918. Stravinsky recalled going in his adolescence to several RSC performances and would also have accompanied Rimsky-Korsakov, as his student, to RSC rehearsals. Stravinsky's first publication, *The Faun and the Shepherdess*, was with Edition Belaieff in 1908, thanks to Rimsky-Korsakov's intervention when the work was rejected by the publisher Julius Zimmerman – Rimsky-Korsakov furthermore insisting that it should be programmed in the next RSC season. Though hugely grateful, Stravinsky felt increasingly that Belyayev's circle – the Belyayevtsï – was fundamentally reactionary. Stravinsky also received a Glinka Prize in 1909 (for SCHERZO FANTASTIQUE), the annual award established by the terms of Belyayev's will following his death.   DANIEL JAFFÉ

Mem; SCS; SRT

Benois, Alexandre (Aleksandr Nikolayevich Benua) (born St Petersburg, 3 May 1870; died PARIS, 9 February 1960), a Russian painter, graphic artist, stage designer, art critic, BALLET and theatre critic, art historian and museum curator. Alexandre Benois came from a famous ST PETERSBURG dynasty of architects, sculptors, composers and artists of Franco-Italian origin. He graduated from the Faculty of Law, ST PETERSBURG UNIVERSITY (1890–4). Although he briefly attended the Academy of Fine Arts (1887–8) and studied in various private studios in FRANCE, including that of James Whistler (1896), he considered himself largely a self-taught artist. In RUSSIA, Benois was respected by his contemporaries for his exquisite (although somewhat conservative) taste and for an extensive knowledge in all areas of the arts, including music, theatre and choreography.

A man of great organisational talent, Benois started some important initiatives in Russian culture at the turn of the century, including the magazine *Mir iskusstva* (*World of Art*) (1898–1904, together with Sergey DIAGHILEV, Dmitry Filosofov, Léon BAKST, Konstantin Somov, Eugène Lanceray and Walter Nouvel), of which he was the second Principal Editor after Diaghilev. Benois also co-founded with Diaghilev the Russian Seasons (1906–8) and the BALLETS RUSSES (1909–29), and was Artistic Director there (1908–11), as well as a stage designer and a librettist or co-librettist for numerous productions. It was mainly Benois' concept of the ballet as 'one of the most consistent and complete expressions of the idea of the *Gesamtkunstwerk*, the idea for which our circle was ready to give its soul' (Benois 1947, 370–1), which inspired the synaesthetic format of the Ballets Russes. Benois was the ideological inspirer and the brain centre of the enterprise, next to the practical organiser, driving force and indefatigable impresario Diaghilev. The relation with Diaghilev, however, did not always go smoothly: it was very upsetting for Benois to learn, for instance, that Diaghilev publicly attributed the authorship of the libretto of the ballet *Shéhérazade*, staged in 1910, to Léon Bakst. The subsequent quarrel with Diaghilev, an incident with an injured hand and the inactivity that followed, threatened to suspend Benois' career as an artist but, in order to make amends for the incident, Diaghilev entrusted to him the libretto, sets and costumes of Stravinsky's ballet PETRUSHKA (1911). The collaboration with Stravinsky and the choreographer Mikhail FOKINE on *Petrushka* was the pinnacle of Benois' career as a stage designer, which embodied for him his ideal of a post-Wagnerian type of *Gesamtkunstwerk* (Roberts 2011, 156). The correspondence of 1910–14 between the composer and the painter reveals that the relationship was truly synaesthetic and mutually inspirational: Stravinsky composed under Benois' guidance, while Benois often chose his colours and décor after having played Stravinsky's music on his piano. In *An* AUTOBIOGRAPHY, Stravinsky praised Benois' stage designs, keeping practically silent about his work as a co-librettist, but their correspondence during the winter of 1910–11 reveals Benois' profound influence on the whole concept, the final set of characters, the narrative plot and even the music of the ballet (Smirnov 1973, 155–62).

At the beginning of the twentieth century, Benois was one of the most respected art critics in Russia. In this role, he was quite conservative in his tastes, and he often disliked avant-garde art and abstract art. At the same time, Benois appreciated avant-garde music (in particular, that of his friend Stravinsky), and he also launched the international career of Natalya GONCHAROVA as a theatrical artist, delegating to her the stage designs for the 1914 Parisian production of RIMSKY-KORSAKOV's opera The Golden Cockerel.

The favourite topics of Benois the painter were the Russian balagan or folk street art – the principal subject of Petrushka – the epoch of Louis XIV and Versailles, the history of St Petersburg, as well as Chinese Art, the subject of the stage designs for Stravinsky's OPERA The NIGHTINGALE (1914). Originally, it was Nicholas ROERICH who was supposed to make sets and costumes for The Nightingale, but in a letter to Benois, dated 30 July 1913, Stravinsky expressed his doubts about Roerich's suitability for the project, thus marking the beginning of a new fruitful collaboration with Benois (D'yachkova and Yarustovsky 1973, 475). After 1917, Benois remained in Russia, working as Curator of one of the departments of the Hermitage Museum. After his permanent departure from the USSR to France in 1926, he resumed his career as a book illustrator and a stage designer (e.g., he designed sets and costumes for Stravinsky's ballet The FAIRY'S KISS, produced by Ida RUBINSTEIN's company in 1928), continued his painting and drawing, and published two books of personal memoirs.   MARINA LUPISHKO

Alexandre Benois, Reminiscences of the Russian Ballet, trans. Mary Britnieva (London: Putnam, 1947).
Alexandre Benois, Zhizn' khudozhnika: Vospominaniya ('An Artist's Life: Memoirs'). 2 vols. (New York: Chekhov Publishing House, 1955) (Engl. trans. M. Budberg as Memoirs, 2 vols., London: Chatto & Windus, 1960–4).
Lyudmila D'yachkova and Boris Yarustovsky (eds.), I. F. Stravinsky: Stat'i i materialy ('I. F. Stravinsky: Articles and Materials') (Moscow: Sovetsky Kompozitor, 1973).
Boris Kochno, Diaghilev et les Ballets Russes (Paris: Fayard, 1973).
David Roberts, The Total Work of Art in European Modernism (Ithaca, NY: Cornell University Press, 2011).
Valery Smirnov, 'Benua – librettist "Petrushki"' ('Benois, the librettist of Petrushka'), in L. D'yachkova and B. Yarustovsky (1973), 155–69.

Berg, Alban (Albano Maria Johannes) (born Vienna, 9 February 1885; died Vienna, 24 December 1935). Stravinsky may have met both Berg and WEBERN for the first time in 1926, at a reception in Vienna after he played his CONCERTO FOR PIANO AND WIND INSTRUMENTS at the Musikverein, though such a meeting is not mentioned in any correspondence. It is certain, however, that he met Berg in September 1934, in the green room of the TEATRO LA FENICE after a performance of his CAPRICCIO and Berg's Der Wein (which Stravinsky is said to have described as 'two pieces as different as Eros and Agape') at the VENICE Biennale.

Stravinsky came to admire Berg's music, although this appreciation was not immediate. CRAFT quotes Pierre SOUVTCHINSKY in 1956:

> Not long ago Poulenc told me that the mere suggestion by anyone of his group that the music of Schoenberg or Berg might be worth examining would automatically have made them traitors in Stravinsky's eyes. At that time Stravinsky was dismissing Wozzeck, which he had not heard, as une musique boche, and Mahler, of whom he knew nothing, as 'Malheur'.

It is not clear exactly when 'that time' was, but Stravinsky's opinion of *Wozzeck* and of Berg in general had definitely changed by the 1950s. In April 1952 Stravinsky flew to Paris from Geneva after attending a performance of *The Rake's Progress* there, in order to see the Vienna Opera company's production of *Wozzeck* at the Théâtre des Champs-Elysées later that month. According to Craft, Stravinsky and Camus shared a loge in the Théâtre des Champs-Elysées for a performance of *Wozzeck* in May 1952, which, if correct, would mean that he attended at least two performances of *Wozzeck* on that occasion. Craft quotes him as saying that the greatest achievement of *Wozzeck* was that Berg succeeded in creating what the audience perceived as something 'totally spontaneous' from a score 'compounded of strict formal devices'. When he was asked in 1964 what he considered to be the masterpieces of contemporary opera, he answered: '*Wozzeck, Lulu, Erwartung, Moses und Aron*, and even perhaps my *Rake* and my *Rex*'.

It was not only *Wozzeck* that Stravinsky admired. He was also particularly impressed by Berg's 'Reigen', the second of *Three Pieces for Orchestra*: 'Berg's orchestral imagination and orchestral skill are phenomenal, especially in creating orchestral blocks, by which I mean balancing the whole orchestra in several polyphonic planes. One of the most remarkable noises he ever imagined is at bar 89 in 'Reigen', but there are many other striking sonorous inventions.' Bruce Archibald quotes him as saying in 1959:

If I were able to penetrate the barrier of style (Berg's radically alien emotional climate) I suspect he would appear to me as the most gifted constructor in form of the composers of this century.... Berg's forms are thematic (in which respect, as in most others, he is Webern's opposite) ... However complex, however 'mathematical'..., they are always 'free' thematic forms born of 'pure feeling' and 'expression'. The perfect work in which to study this and, I think, the essential work, with *Wozzeck*, for the study of all of his music – is the *Three Pieces for Orchestra*, op. 6. Berg's personality is mature in these pieces, and they seem to me a richer and freer expression of his talent than the twelve-note serial pieces. When one considers their early date – 1914; Berg was twenty-nine – they are something of a miracle. KATHRYN PUFFETT

Berger, Arthur Victor (born New York, 15 May 1912; died Boston, Mass., 7 October 2003). American composer and critic who attended New York University (BS, 1934) and Harvard University (MA Musicology 1936). He later studied with Nadia Boulanger in Paris (1937–9) and Darius Milhaud at Mills College. He taught at Mills (1939–42), Brooklyn College (1942–3), Brandeis University (1953–78) and the New England Conservatory (1979–98). In 1962, Berger and Benjamin Boretz co-founded the journal *Perspectives of New Music* (Editor, 1962–4).

Berger's most significant contribution was as a music critic and scholar of contemporary music. His 1953 *Aaron Copland* (Oxford University Press) was the first major analytical study of Copland's music and linked him to the European modernists (Schoenberg, Stravinsky, Bartók, Milhaud). His germinal 1963 *Perspectives of New Music* article 'Problems of pitch organization in Stravinsky' introduced two important analytical concepts: octatonicism and pitch centricity, and rejected 'bitonality'. Previously, critics had used this term, overly relying on the 'Petrushka' chord. The second tableau of PETRUSHKA (originally a Konzertstück for piano) begins with superimposed C major and F♯ major triads, a tritone, which led to the early interpretation of Stravinsky's music as 'bitonal' or even 'pantonal'. Berger debunked this notion by showing how Stravinsky established stable tonal centres through the use of pedal points, and the importance of third relations as structural devices. He went on to demonstrate how these are properties of octatonicism and Stravinsky's compositional technique. Further, he located Stravinsky in the context of the ST PETERSBURG group of composers, a historical tradition from MUSSORGSKY to RIMSKY-KORSAKOV. Later Stravinsky scholars are indebted to his work. GAYLE MURCHISON

Berman, Eugene (born St Petersburg, 4 November 1899; died Rome, 14 December 1972). Stravinsky and fellow Russian émigré Berman (an artist and stage designer who became a US citizen in LOS ANGELES in 1944) were friends and collaborators throughout the composer's life. Berman even married his wife (the actress Ona Munson) in the Stravinskys' living room in Hollywood. Considered a neo-Romantic artist and fondly referred to as an 'Italophile' by Stravinsky (Conv, 97), Berman achieved acclaim as a theatrical designer in the 1930s–1940s. In 1944, Stravinsky and choreographer George BALANCHINE collaborated with Berman on DANSES CONCERTANTES. Though the designer's first sketches for Danses were not to Stravinsky's liking, upon revision he was satisfied and later remarked in T&E that 'though I liked the décors, by Eugene Berman, the ballet is not among my Balanchine favorites'. Following Stravinsky's passing, Berman wistfully designed PULCINELLA for the NEW YORK CITY BALLET's 1972 Stravinsky Festival at the New York State Theater. CRAFT records that it was Berman who suggested Manzù (Italian artist Giacomo Manzoni) as the designer of Stravinsky's tombstone (SCF (94)). LORIN JOHNSON

Berners, Lord (born Apley Park, nr Bridgnorth, 18 September 1883; died Faringdon, 19 April 1950). British composer. In Memories and Commentaries, Stravinsky recounted meeting Berners in 1911 – then Gerald Tyrwhitt, and studying with CASELLA in Rome. They met regularly after that and Stravinsky states 'I was a guest of his on each of my English visits' between the wars. Stravinsky also advised Berners on his compositions – 'though I considered him an amateur ... I would not call him amateurish' – and found 'his Wedding Bouquet and his [The triumph of] Neptune as good as the French works of that kind produced by Diaghilev, though whether or not this could be construed as a compliment I cannot say' (Mem, 83). ARNOLD WHITTALL

Bernhardt, Sarah (born Paris, 22 or 23 October 1844; died Paris, 26 March 1923). A celebrated French actress who from 1899 leased the Théâtre des Nations on Place du Châtelet, producing the THÉÂTRE SARAH BERNHARDT. She produced works here for two decades, and collaborated with the BALLETS RUSSES to stage a number of their new works at her theatre.

She attended the première of The FIREBIRD, as had DEBUSSY, and recognised the quality of the music. It was the summer after this première that Bernhardt met with Stravinsky. It is then, perhaps, no surprise she should support the staging of Stravinsky's APOLLON MUSAGÈTE at her theatre on 12 June 1928 as part of the Ballets Russes season. HELEN JULIA MINORS

Bernstein, Leonard (born Lawrence, Mass., 25 August 1918; died New York City, 14 October 1990). American composer and conductor. A protégé of Sergey KOUSSEVITZKY and a pupil of Fritz REINER, and one of the most charismatic conductors of the twentieth century, Bernstein became assistant conductor of the New York Philharmonic in 1943, and with them he conducted the FIREBIRD Suite (1919) in 1944 and The RITE OF SPRING in 1951 – both works that he performed on many subsequent occasions with the orchestra, of which he became Music Director in 1957. He conducted many other works by Stravinsky in New York, London, Boston, ISRAEL and elsewhere, many of which he recorded for Columbia (now Sony Classical) and Deutsche Grammophon, including PETRUSHKA, LES NOCES, OEDIPUS REX, SYMPHONY OF PSALMS (which he described in 1972 as 'undoubtedly the greatest musical celebration of the religious spirit to have been written in our [20th] century'), SYMPHONY IN C, SYMPHONY IN THREE MOVEMENTS, CONCERTO FOR PIANO AND WIND INSTRUMENTS and MASS. On the whole, Bernstein did not conduct Stravinsky's later works, though he included AGON on the same 1968 programme as the world première of Berio's Sinfonia. One of his earliest recordings, made for RCA in 1947, included the suite from The SOLDIER'S TALE and the OCTET FOR WIND INSTRUMENTS, performed by members of the Boston Symphony. His deep admiration for Stravinsky's music was something he declared publicly on a number of occasions, including one of his Young People's Concerts in 1962, in celebration of the composer's eightieth birthday, much of which was devoted to a discussion and performance of *Petrushka*. In his 1973 Harvard lectures, 'The Unanswered Question', Bernstein ended the series with a complete performance of *Oedipus Rex*.

As a composer, Bernstein freely admitted the influence of Stravinsky on his music, and this can be heard in parts of *West Side Story*, the *Jeremiah Symphony* and other works, though Stravinsky himself had a low opinion of Bernstein as a composer. As for his view of Bernstein the conductor, his occasionally disparaging remarks were partly a result of resentment at Bernstein's large record sales (they both recorded for the same company, Columbia), and some of his reported comments may have stemmed from CRAFT rather than Stravinsky himself. 'Wow!', Stravinsky's famous one-word reaction to hearing Bernstein's 1958 recording of *The Rite of Spring* suggests that he was impressed by some of Bernstein's performances of his music (the best of them are marked by extraordinary rhythmic energy), and, in a late interview (published in 1971), Stravinsky also acknowledged Bernstein's personal kindness towards him: 'Mr Bernstein was as thoughtful and attentive to me as any of my musician friends during my illnesses last year and the year before.' For Bernstein, who was ambivalent about some directions in modern music (notably serialism), Stravinsky was a pivotal figure whose stylistic changes he likened to PICASSO's in the visual arts, and several of his works (including *The Rite*, *Les*

Noces and the Symphony of Psalms) he considered to be the very greatest works of the twentieth century. NIGEL SIMEONE

Nigel Simeone, The Leonard Bernstein Letters (London and New Haven: Yale University Press, 2013).
T&C

Biography: Stravinsky, Igor Fyodorovich (born ORANIENBAUM, near ST PETERSBURG, 5/17 June 1882; died New York, 6 April 1971). Russian composer, the third son of Fyodor STRAVINSKY, the leading bass-baritone singer of the Mariinsky Theatre. In later life, Stravinsky claimed that his parents failed to recognise his musical talent, particularly his aspiration to become a composer; yet Fyodor secured one of RUSSIA's leading young pianists, Leokadiya KASHPEROVA, to teach Igor, and arranged private tuition in the basics of composition from two talented young graduates from the ST PETERSBURG CONSERVATORY, AKIMENKO and KALAFATI, while Igor – at his father's insistence – studied law at ST PETERSBURG UNIVERSITY. After Fyodor's death in 1902, Igor asked his mother, Anna, to be released from his legal studies to devote himself to music, which Anna refused. Though Igor eventually gave in, from that point onwards there was a mutual and almost constant – if low-key – antagonism between mother and son.

The summer before his father's death, Stravinsky met Nikolay RIMSKY-KORSAKOV, under whom, from the following year, he studied composition. A friend, Ivan POKROVSKY, introduced Stravinsky to EVENINGS OF CONTEMPORARY MUSIC, and his early SONATA IN F♯ MINOR for piano became his first music heard in public when performed under its auspices. With Rimsky-Korsakov's tutelage, Stravinsky's skill as a composer developed rapidly, his mastery of instrumental colour evident in his first orchestral work, SYMPHONY IN E♭ MAJOR (1905–7), followed by SCHERZO FANTASTIQUE (1907–8) and FIREWORKS (1908), both latter works championed by St Petersburg's leading conductor Alexander ZILOTI. Sergey DIAGHILEV, who attended Ziloti's première of Scherzo fantastique, subsequently gave Stravinsky his first commission for the BALLETS RUSSES: to orchestrate two Chopin pieces for a production of Les Sylphides in PARIS.

In 1906, Stravinsky married his first cousin, Yekaterina ('Katya', later known as CATHERINE) Nosenko; she remained over the next two decades his most constant source of support, both practically and in her faith in his talent. Their first two children – Theodore (Fyodor) in 1907; Lyudmila (Mika) in 1908 – were born while they were living with Anna in the Stravinsky family home at 66 Kryukov Canal. Although they moved into their own St Petersburg apartment in 1909, Katya's delicate health (eventually she was diagnosed as suffering from tuberculosis) meant they spent more time in the warmer climes of USTILUG, the West Ukrainian estate owned by Katya's family: in 1907, they moved into a country house designed by Stravinsky, where they spent part of each summer until 1913. Stravinsky composed several of his early works there, including part of The RITE OF SPRING.

With Rimsky-Korsakov's death in 1908, Stravinsky's position on St Petersburg's music scene appeared precarious as he struggled to find an orchestra willing to programme FUNERAL SONG (written in his teacher's memory). Less than two years later, thanks to Diaghilev's shrewd assessment of the young composer's potential, Stravinsky was catapulted to celebrity in Paris with the première of his first ballet, The FIREBIRD (1910). The contrast between that experience and his humbling ordeal with Funeral Song certainly led to Stravinsky's increasing resentment towards St Petersburg's musical establishment, including several of his erstwhile colleagues, such as Maximilian STEINBERG. In Paris, by contrast, even before Firebird's première, Diaghilev let it be known that he had a new composing star, and several of the Ballets Russes' most important financial backers became Stravinsky's patrons. In his next two ballets – PETRUSHKA and, most particularly, The Rite of Spring – Stravinsky struck out on his own distinctive and innovative path. Though The Rite of Spring's notoriety was largely fuelled by the scandal caused by Vaslav NIJINSKY's radical choreography, the music's triumph when subsequently given its first concert performance in Paris by Pierre MONTEUX on 5 April 1914 was absolute. Both ballets not only won the delighted admiration of FRANCE's leading composers DEBUSSY and RAVEL, but soon had a widespread international impact, influencing composers well beyond the borders of France and (more belatedly) Russia.

Following Firebird's first night, Stravinsky collected Katya and their Ustilug household to witness the ballet's triumph in Paris. With Katya by then heavily pregnant, they awaited her confinement in SWITZERLAND, and their second son, Svyatoslav ('Soulima' STRAVINSKY), was born in Lausanne. Their fourth and final child, Milène, was born at the same clinic in 1914. Ordered to rest after the birth, Katya went with Igor to a health resort in the Vaud Alps. World War I found them still in Switzerland, where they remained for the family's safety (Stravinsky being unfit to enlist). Stravinsky began composing Les NOCES ('The Wedding') in CLARENS while staying in a villa sub-let from Ernest ANSERMET. In preparation, he wrote several short experimental works, including Pribaoutki, in which he 'discovered' an unorthodox approach to word setting, subsequently used for virtually every text he set through the rest of his career.

In 1915, after a year or so of itinerant living, the Stravinskys settled in MORGES, where Igor became close friends with the novelist Charles Ferdinand RAMUZ. Together they created The SOLDIER'S TALE: intended to be an inexpensive, easy-to-stage dramatic work to generate income quickly, Stravinsky's inability to restrain his fecund creativity resulted in music for an ensemble of virtuosic musicians requiring extensive rehearsal and a conductor. (Despite his reputation for driving a hard bargain, Stravinsky showed little business sense: witness his revision of the 'Sacrificial Dance' of The Rite of Spring in 1943.)

Stravinsky's involvement with both the Ballets Russes and Paris' music scene resumed after the war with PULCINELLA (1919–20). This heralded a new creative phase often identified as NEO-CLASSICISM – a term first applied to his music by Boris de SCHLOEZER in reference to his SYMPHONIES OF WIND INSTRUMENTS (1920), so implying a far broader aesthetic than simply a reference to past musical styles. After briefly considering Rome, Stravinsky and his family moved to France to be closer to the activities of the Ballets Russes. Gabrielle 'Coco' CHANEL, who generously sponsored the 1920 revival of The Rite of Spring, became one of Stravinsky's several lovers before his far more consequential involvement with Vera Sudeykina (later Vera STRAVINSKY), introduced to him by Diaghilev early in 1921. Both Vera and Stravinsky became involved with Diaghilev's full-scale revival of TCHAIKOVSKY's *Sleeping Beauty*, for which Stravinsky orchestrated two numbers. Inspired by this to reconsider his Russian heritage, Stravinsky then composed MAVRA (1921–2), an opera buffa that displeased critics and even some of his friends, such as Ravel, but was embraced wholeheartedly by a new generation of French composers, notably by two members of LES SIX – AURIC and POULENC – as well as the group's sometime mentor Jean COCTEAU.

In 1921, while Stravinsky's family settled in Biarritz, he gained a Paris studio, courtesy of Maison Pleyel. His professional need to be in Paris was also a convenient alibi for seeing Vera. Matters were further complicated by the arrival from Petrograd of his mother, Anna, whom Igor collected in Berlin and brought back to Biarritz. While in Berlin, Stravinsky met another new arrival from Russia, Pierre SOUVTCHINSKY, whose aesthetic theories were later reworked by Stravinsky's ghost writers – principally Walter Nouvel and ROLAND-MANUEL – as the composer's own. Arthur LOURIÉ, another émigré from the Soviet Union, became another sometime ghost writer, who, together with Cocteau, also encouraged Stravinsky's turn to religion and his engagement with Jacques MARITAIN's aesthetic theories.

Notwithstanding the huge success enjoyed by Les NOCES when finally staged in 1923, Stravinsky now had to support his mother (whom he kept in ignorance about Vera), the Belyankins (the family of Katya's sister, Lyudmila, who, having escaped civil war in Russia, joined his family in 1918), his wife and children, as well as his mistress. With that in mind, Stravinsky composed several works for himself to perform: a CONCERTO FOR PIANO AND WIND INSTRUMENTS (1923–4), a PIANO SONATA (1924) and his SERENADE IN A (1925). As well as touring as a pianist, Stravinsky increasingly conducted his own music: after almost ten years conducting single items in various concerts, on 7 November 1923 in Paris he conducted for the first time an entire programme of his music. Other engagements followed, making Stravinsky as familiar a figure on the podium and in the recording studio (eventually recording, with some assistance from Robert CRAFT at the latter end of his career, all his major works involving orchestra or instrumental ensemble) as at the keyboard.

In 1926, the year he returned to the RUSSIAN ORTHODOX CHURCH, Stravinsky wrote his first overtly religious composition, *Our Father* (*Otche nash*). SYMPHONY OF PSALMS (1930), his most public confession of his faith, was composed to a commission from Sergey KOUSSEVITZKY to celebrate the fiftieth anniversary of the Boston Symphony Orchestra; other religious works such as the MASS (1944–8) followed after he had emigrated to the UNITED STATES. There is perhaps a religious sensibility, too, in OEDIPUS REX (1926–7), created with Cocteau.

A severe blow came with Diaghilev's death in 1929: although they had had a public falling out, the impresario had not only raised Stravinsky to international significance, but had several times given crucial nudges to his creative imagination – notably with *Petrushka* and *Pulcinella*. Among many artists and creative talents Diaghilev had introduced him to was the choreographer George BALANCHINE, with whom Stravinsky enjoyed a long-standing creative partnership, starting with the 1925 revival of The SONG OF THE NIGHTINGALE and confirmed by the seminal APOLLON MUSAGÈTE in June 1928.

From Biarritz, Stravinsky's family moved first to Nice in 1924; then, in 1931, to Voreppe near Grenoble, the latter a compromise move closer to Paris made necessary by Soulima's developing career as a pianist (studying under Isidor Philipp, and taking lessons in harmony and counterpoint under Nadia BOULANGER), while at the same time keeping a decent distance between Igor's family (most specifically his mother) and his mistress. Yet, with Stravinsky's children now young adults, and their mother's poor health increasingly requiring the kind of specialist treatment only a major city could offer, their move to Paris could not be resisted. They moved to the capital in October 1933, as Stravinsky worked on his first major French-language work, PERSÉPHONE. In June 1934, Stravinsky was granted French citizenship; yet, when he sought election to the Institut de France in the following year, he received only five of a possible thirty-two votes. Meanwhile, he enjoyed increasing fame and success in the United States with many major commissions, his championship by such conductors as Koussevitzky and Monteux, and his own successful visits: first in January 1925, when he was feted by the American public and press as he toured the east coast as pianist and conductor; then, in 1935, he toured with the violinist Samuel DUSHKIN; a third tour in 1937 culminated in his conducting the première of the ballet JEU DE CARTES at New York's Metropolitan Opera.

Late in 1938, his eldest daughter Lyudmila died of tuberculosis; Catherine and Anna died soon afterwards early in 1939, just months before the outbreak of World War II. Stravinsky himself had to spend five months in a sanatorium to recover his health. Eager to escape the chaos of impending war, he accepted an invitation (secured by Boulanger) to deliver the Charles Eliot Norton Lectures at Harvard University (published as The POETICS OF MUSIC, 1942), sailing for America in September 1939. Vera followed in January, and they were married in March 1940. They settled in Hollywood, California, Stravinsky having found that its warm, clean air eased the symptoms of his lung condition. After completing his SYMPHONY IN C (1938–40), Stravinsky then composed SYMPHONY IN THREE MOVEMENTS (1942–5), its successful 1946 première revitalising his reputation. Prior to this, Stravinsky had suffered a severe fall in income as the PUBLISHERS of most of his music were based in Nazi-occupied Europe. To mitigate this, he had attempted several times to secure work as a FILM composer, arranged what he vainly hoped might become the 'authorised' version of 'The Star-Spangled Banner', and even composed a CIRCUS POLKA for Barnum & Bailey's circus elephants.

An old friend of Stravinsky's, Nicolas NABOKOV, became a key promoter of Stravinsky and his work after the war, organising several festivals in his honour in Europe. Nabokov also secured the VENICE première of Stravinsky's only full-length OPERA, The RAKE'S PROGRESS (1947–51), his last major 'neo-classical' work. Making his first visit to Europe since 1939 to conduct its première, Stravinsky became aware that his European reputation was apparently on the wane. In France and GERMANY particularly, a new generation of composers had rejected neo-classicism, embracing instead the TWELVE-NOTE serial method of the SECOND VIENNESE SCHOOL (founded by Arnold SCHOENBERG), and the works of WEBERN especially. Stravinsky, though a near neighbour of Schoenberg's in Hollywood, avoided both the man and his music.

Shortly after Schoenberg's death in 1951, Stravinsky suffered a creative crisis, whereupon the young conductor Robert Craft, who from 1948 effectively became Stravinsky's business and artistic associate, encouraged him to begin experimenting in serial techniques. The CANTATA (1951–2), SEPTET (1952–3) and IN MEMORIAM DYLAN THOMAS (1954) were all steps in this process leading to his first works to make partial use of 12-note rows: CANTICUM SACRUM (1955), and the ballet AGON (1953–7). Then followed his first entirely twelve-note serial composition, THRENI (1957–8). Notwithstanding a stroke late in 1956, Stravinsky regained his characteristic voice in MOVEMENTS for piano and orchestra (1958–9) and his orchestral VARIATIONS (1964), culminating in his final masterpiece, REQUIEM CANTICLES (1966).

He continued to tour and conduct – including a legendary return visit to Russia, when, despite his long-standing hostility to the Soviet regime, he was persuaded to accept an invitation from Tikhon KHRENNIKOV to visit during his eightieth birthday year in 1962. Stravinsky's last conducting engagement was *Pulcinella* in Toronto, 1967. The Stravinskys moved to New York in 1969 to be near the necessary medical care for the increasingly ailing composer. He died in that city. After the funeral, his body was flown at Vera's request to Venice, then buried in the island cemetery of San Michele near to Diaghilev's grave.

DANIEL JAFFÉ

Jonathan Cross, *Igor Stravinsky* (London: Reaktion Books, 2015).
Auto; Mem; SCS; Sfam; SSE

Blok, Alexander (Alexandrovich) (born St Petersburg, 16/28 November 1880; died Petrograd, 7 August 1921). Russian poet, eminent representative of Russian Symbolism. Stravinsky never set any of his works to music, nor, apparently, did he ever meet him. Yet Blok's exaltation of the 'elemental spontaneity' of the people (versus the intelligentsia's 'culture') in his essay 'The Poetry of Magic and Spells' is thought to have prepared the ground for the primitivism encountered in The RITE OF SPRING. Moreover, the Pierrotic element of the poems 'The Little Showbooth' (1905) and 'The Showbooth' (1906) is believed to have inspired BENOIS for the plot of PETRUSHKA.   KATERINA LEVIDOU

SRT

Bolm, Adolph Rudolphovich (born St Petersburg, 25 September 1884; died Hollywood, 16 April 1951). Russian-American dancer and CHOREOGRAPHER. Bolm was a principal dancer with the BALLETS RUSSES between 1909 and 1917 (roles included Ivan Tsarevich in The FIREBIRD and the Moor in PETRUSHKA). He settled in the UNITED STATES after the company's second American tour and went on to choreograph, and dance the title role in, the first production of APOLLON MUSAGÈTE (Washington, DC, 1928); Stravinsky did not attend. Bolm later choreographed productions of The Firebird and *Petrushka*. His 1940 HOLLYWOOD BOWL *Firebird*, to the 1919 concert suite, was conducted by Stravinsky (in exchange for Bolm writing in support of the composer's application for American citizenship). He was also the first to choreograph the 1945 *Firebird* ballet suite (Ballet Theatre, Metropolitan Opera House, New York, 1945). Stravinsky did not always like Bolm's stagings, but the two were friends and the composer was a regular visitor to Bolm's Hollywood home.

SOPHIE REDFERN

Borodin, Alexander Porfir'yevich (born St Petersburg, 31 October / 12 November 1833; died St Petersburg, 15/27 February 1887). Russian composer and organic chemist, a member of BALAKIREV's circle of amateur composers, known as the Moguchaya Kuchka ('The Mighty Handful'), which included MUSSORGSKY, RIMSKY-KORSAKOV and CUI.

Stravinsky's father, Fyodor STRAVINSKY, had a close association with Borodin, and particularly his opera *Prince Igor*; even while still unfinished (it was eventually 'completed' posthumously by GLAZUNOV and Rimsky-Korsakov), Borodin orchestrated two of its bass arias, which Fyodor performed widely. Fyodor sang one of those, Galitsky's aria, in Moscow just six days before the birth of his third son and future composer; as Richard Taruskin suggests, it was probably in honour of Borodin's opera that Fyodor chose such an un-Christian first name for his son.

Igor Stravinsky grew up hearing his father singing Borodin's music, and, aged 5, after Borodin's sudden death from a heart attack, apparently requested picture postcards from GLINKA's sister, Lyudmila Shestakova, of her famous brother and of Borodin (both are visibly on display in a photo of Stravinsky's room taken in his late teens). Borodin's music inevitably informed several of Stravinsky's earliest works: *How the Mushrooms Prepared for War* (1904) includes *Prince Igor*-style declamation, including what Taruskin identifies as 'a literal quotation of a phrase that occurs repeatedly, and very prominently, in Skula's part [a role Fyodor was famed for] in the final scene'. Borodin's influence is also evident in Stravinsky's SYMPHONY IN E♭ MAJOR (1905), particularly in the scherzo movement (placed second in the symphony's four-movement scheme, following the precedent established by Borodin's two symphonies); Borodin's influence also surfaces in the finale, most obviously in Stravinsky's earliest sketches before the music was reworked under Rimsky-Korsakov's instruction.

Yet, by his maturity, Stravinsky had mostly rejected Borodin's legacy. First, the Russian symphonic style substantially established by Borodin, particularly its use of themes 'in the style of' Russian FOLK MUSIC made malleable for symphonic development, was the antithesis of Stravinsky's abrupt juxtapositions and use of 'raw' folk material from PETRUSHKA onwards. Furthermore, while setting Russian folk or popular verse in *Pribaoutki*, Stravinsky 'discovered' that, when such verse is traditionally sung, the accents that would naturally occur when it is spoken are simply ignored or made irrelevant by the priorities of the music. Embracing this principle, Stravinsky jettisoned Borodin's 'naturalistic' style of word setting, as exemplified by Skula's prosody in *Prince Igor*.

Arguably, though, Borodin's enterprising ORCHESTRATION (his pioneering woodwind writing, in particular, inspired Rimsky-Korsakov as well as such non-Russian composers as RAVEL) was an enduring heritage of Russian music

which Stravinsky continued to evolve in such works as the Symphonies of Wind
Instruments.   DANIEL JAFFÉ

SRT

Boulanger, Nadia (born Paris, 16 September 1887; died Paris, 22 October 1979).
French composer, conductor and teacher. Boulanger was a loyal supporter of
Stravinsky's music from her first encounter with it at the première of The
Firebird (1910) onwards. They began to exchange music in 1923 when
Stravinsky 'sent "Mademoiselle Nadia Boulanger" an autographed version of
his re-orchestrated Firebird, following this in 1924 with 'the organ arrangement
of his "Ronde des princesses" and "Berceuse et Finale"' from the same work
(Francis 2009, 146). Fifty-two texts in all were exchanged. The composer
entrusted Boulanger in 1929 with overseeing the music education of his son
(Soulima Stravinsky), from which point they were in regular communication
until the composer's death in 1971. Stravinsky also charged her with revising,
performing and conducting his compositions, to the extent that she was 'a
central influence on his career during the 1930s and 1940s' (Francis 2009, 138).
Despite this, as Kimberly Francis noted in 2009, 'Boulanger's voice has all but
been erased from the literature on the composer', and to this point very little
had been published on their interaction. Between 1929 and 1979, various
members of the Stravinsky family sent no less than 389 letters to Boulanger,
124 of them from Igor, the latter revealing how their relationship developed
from a working partnership to one of 'deep friendship' (Francis 2009, 140).
She also mediated 'between Stravinsky and her students, friends, and colleagues', as well as performing, editing, lecturing on and commissioning works
by him (Francis 2009, 141).

Boulanger was responsible in 1931 for the pre-publication edits to the
revisions Stravinsky had integrated into the piano/vocal reduction of the
Symphony of Psalms. She organised the private première performance of
Perséphone (1934) at the Opéra in Paris and edited the vocal score. She was
influential in securing the commission for the Concerto in E♭ in 1937,
conducting the first performance on 8 May 1938 in Stravinsky's absence, and
she was also active in securing patronage for the Symphony in C, a work which
she spent a great deal of time editing. As a result of her recommendation,
Stravinsky was hired as a co-professor in her composition class at the École
normale in 1936, and her large network of contacts was of great importance to
him in the late 1930s. Boulanger followed Stravinsky to the United States in
1940, and remained there until the beginning of 1946 when she returned to
Paris. During the war years, they 'collaborated on scores, lectures, books,
performances and commissions' (Francis 2009, 149) and, during her visits to
Los Angeles, they 'read through scores, analyzed them, and admired them'
(Francis 2009, 151). While she continued to edit his scores, this is much less
the case from 1941 onwards and, with her return to France in 1946, the nature
of the relationship changed once again, though they continued to exchange
scores. She became highly active on Stravinsky's behalf in Europe, writing
reviews, giving lectures and organising concerts, and she was influential in
securing performances of The Rake's Progress. However, she felt unable to
follow Stravinsky wholeheartedly along the serial path he pursued at this time,

and the presence of Robert CRAFT at Stravinsky's side was a further barrier. Despite the waning of their personal relationship, Stravinsky's works retained their primacy in Boulanger's affections and pedagogy, and she continued to support his music enthusiastically. As a teacher, performer (conductor) and composer, Boulanger taught a great number of important composers, particularly those who were neo-classical in orientation, including Aaron COPLAND, Joseph Horovitz, Walter Piston and (at the time) Elliott CARTER.   HELEN JULIA MINORS

Charles M. Joseph, *Stravinsky's Ballets* (New Haven and London: Yale University Press, 2011).
Kimberley A. Francis, 'Nadia Boulanger and Igor Stravinsky: documents of the Bibliothèque nationale de France', *Revue de Musicologie*, 95.1 (2009), 137–56.
Kimberley A. Francis, *Nadia Boulanger and the Stravinskys: A Selected Correspondence* (University of Rochester Press, 2018).
Kimberley A. Francis, *Teaching Stravinsky: Nadia Boulanger and the Consecration of a Modernist Icon* (New York: Oxford University Press, 2015).

Boulez, Pierre (born Montbrison/Loire, 26 March 1925; died Baden-Baden, 5 January 2016). French composer and conductor. It was The SONG OF THE NIGHTINGALE that first awakened Boulez's interest in Stravinsky. In 1942, while a student of mathematics in Lyon, he heard a radio transmission of the piece, which deeply surprised and attracted him. A year later, the promising pianist decided to choose music as the centre of his life, moved to the capital, and applied to the PARIS Conservatory. In the autumn of 1944, Boulez was admitted to the advanced harmony class of Olivier MESSIAEN and was amongst the chosen ones who attended Messiaen's private analysis courses. These meetings aroused his desire to compose and confronted him with key works of the early twentieth century, including Stravinsky's PETRUSHKA, Les NOCES and The RITE OF SPRING. Concurrently, René LEIBOWITZ introduced Boulez and a group of fellow students to TWELVE-NOTE technique and the music of SCHOENBERG, BERG and WEBERN. The students shared Leibowitz' rejection of Stravinsky's neo-classical period and furiously disrupted two concerts during the Parisian Stravinsky festival in the spring of 1945. By whistling at DANSES CONCERTANTES and interrupting the FOUR NORWEGIAN MOODS, they provoked a public controversy.

When Pierre Boulez had the opportunity to engage in the current music debates, he defined his credentials as a composer by sharply criticising his predecessors. In articles such as 'Propositions' (1948), 'Trajectoires: Ravel, Stravinsky, Schönberg' (1949) and 'Moment de Jean-Sébastien Bach' (1951), he praised Stravinsky's great rhythmic achievements, particularly the technique of independent rhythmic cells, but pointed out fundamental harmonic and contrapuntal shortcomings in Stravinsky's language. After Boulez had distanced himself from Schoenberg in 'Schönberg is Dead' (1952), he proceeded to pass judgement on Stravinsky's oeuvre in 'Stravinsky demeure'. Whereas he observed an atrophy of every element, even rhythm, after Les Noces, he assigned the early works an admitted importance and singled out the lasting significance of The Rite. In his view, the best-known work of modern times had so far remained without offspring. With extended and detailed analyses of The Rite, Boulez illustrated the rhythmic potential, which now should be combined with the morphologically and syntactically complex vocabulary perfected by Webern.

The writing of 'Stravinsky demeure' was already completed, but not yet published, when Stravinsky and Boulez met personally for the first time. They were invited to a dinner party at Virgil THOMSON's in December 1952, when Boulez was in New York as Musical Director of the Renaud-Barrault Theatre Company. Stravinsky was unaware of Boulez's past polemics and curious to get to know the young composer whose *Polyphonie X* and *Structures Ia* he had heard. They talked for hours and left mutually enchanted. Therefore, Stravinsky was all the more bewildered when Boulez's article appeared the following year in Pierre SOUVTCHINSKY's *Musique russe*.

It was Boulez who, three years later, re-established contact by engaging Robert CRAFT to conduct a Stravinsky–Webern concert within his recently founded series Domaine Musical. In November 1956, when Craft was in Paris, Boulez arranged a meeting with Souvtchinsky and thus opened the way to a reconciliation between the two Russian friends after a break of more than seventeen years. He even flew to Munich and, together with STOCKHAUSEN and Nono, visited Stravinsky when he was recovering from a stroke in the Red Cross Hospital. Two years of close contact followed. In March 1957, when Boulez went to LOS ANGELES to prepare a performance of *Le marteau sans maître*, he stayed in Hollywood near Stravinsky and impressed the latter again through his musicianship and intelligence. Stravinsky therefore agreed to conduct the European première of AGON in the Domaine Musical series in October 1957. This concert, well prepared by Hans ROSBAUD and the Südwestfunk orchestra, was highly successful. However, the renewed collaboration with THRENI in November 1958 ended up in a complete disaster. This time, Boulez had engaged local musicians and he himself didn't take part in the preparations, being too preoccupied with his own *Poésie pour pouvoir* for Donaueschingen. The performance of *Threni* turned out so chaotic that Stravinsky, deeply humiliated, left the audience without a bow and swore never to conduct in Paris again, a vow that he kept.

In addition to this traumatic event, relations between Boulez and Stravinsky were further strained by commentaries in Antoine Goléa's *Rencontres avec Pierre Boulez* (1958) and a derisive review of the *Threni* concert by the same author in the *Neue Zeitschrift für Musik*. While Souvtchinsky was playing the role of a double agent in the background, Stravinsky demanded from Boulez a public reparation, which, with several corrections and quite a delay, finally appeared in October 1959. Boulez, who in the meantime had moved to Baden-Baden and was starting his career as a conductor, had been hoping for renewed collaboration. However, the following Parisian concerts in honour of Stravinsky took place without the latter's presence: a chamber concert by the Domaine Musical in November 1961 in anticipation of Stravinsky's eightieth birthday, and the fiftieth anniversary performance of the *Rite* in June 1963. In addition to these concerts, and bearing in mind Stravinsky's expressed interest in *Pli selon pli*, Boulez created out of fragments of this work a short homage titled *Domaine-Épigraphe-Texte-Dédicace*, dated it '18 June 1962' and presented it to Stravinsky as 'testimony of amity from the founders and friends of the Domaine Musical'.

Relations appeared to have been restored when Boulez conducted the première of Éclat in Los Angeles in March 1965. Stravinsky, having already praised Le marteau as the only significant work of the postwar period of exploration, declared Éclat another small masterpiece. But new tensions arose. During his stay, Boulez was invited for lunch to Wetherly Drive and was filmed by Rolf Liebermann and Richard Leacock persuading Stravinsky to expunge a supposedly superfluous bar of silence on the last page of Les Noces. Later in the year, Stravinsky restored the bar, but the scene remained in the film. Then, in 1966, Boulez's early essays reappeared, as Relevés d'apprenti collected by Paule Thévenin, and Stravinsky for the first time read all that Boulez had written on him. An interview, published in Melos in 1967, in which Boulez again judged Stravinsky's neo-classical period as rather weak, and the recent VARIATIONS from 1964 as falling short of Webern, led Stravinsky, now marked by age and illness, to distance himself for the final time.

After Stravinsky's death in 1971, when asked by the periodical Tempo for a contribution to a memorial issue, Boulez presented ... explosante-fixe ..., an open-form-work-model with instructions for realisation. He himself developed several different versions of the work, but only authorised the last one, a 40-minute concerto for MIDI-flute, live electronics and chamber orchestra, written between 1991 and 1994. In 2010, in one of his last appearances as a conductor, Boulez combined this personal homage with Stravinsky's THE NIGHTINGALE, whose masterly and colourful instrumentation had been the start of a lifetime's fascination.

Boulez remained true to his early judgements. It was the first period of Stravinsky which he held in esteem. These works had influenced his own musical language, and their performances and recordings established him later as a star conductor. Stravinsky didn't appreciate Boulez's interpretations and never got rid of the suspicion that he was being used by his younger colleague for the publicity value of his name. He recognised in the Frenchman, however, the leading figure of the European avant-garde. For Stravinsky, contact with Boulez meant keeping up with the times.   SUSANNE GÄRTNER

Pierre Boulez, Stocktakings from an Apprenticeship, trans. Stephen Walsh (Oxford University Press, 1991).
Pierre Boulez, 'Stravinsky and the century: style or idea?' Saturday Review (May 1971), 39–41 and 58–9.
Pierre Boulez and Igor Stravinsky, 'Correspondence'. PSS.
Antoine Goléa, Rencontres avec Pierre Boulez (Paris: René Julliard, 1958; new edn 1982).
Igor Stravinsky, Letter to the Music Editor of the Los Angeles Times (23 June 1970); reprinted in T&E, 214–17.

Brasseur, Pierre (orig. Pierre-Albert Espinasse) (born Paris, 22 December 1905; died Brunico/Bruneck, Italy, 14 August 1972). French actor. Brasseur created the role of the Speaker in OEDIPUS REX. He performed the part under Stravinsky's baton for the private first performance in the home of the Princess de Polignac (29 May 1927), and for the public concert première the following night at the THÉÂTRE SARAH BERNHARDT, Paris. According to the composer, the 'very handsome, very young' Brasseur was 'deliberately chosen to be the speaker ... and this was certainly to spite [Jean] Cocteau, who, when composing the play must have thought of that part for himself' (Dial, 25).   SOPHIE REDFERN

Brazil. Stravinsky visited Brazil on two occasions, first of all in 1936 and then, over a quarter of a century later, in 1963. In 1936, the sixth year of the dictatorship of Getúlio Dornelles Vargas, the Argentinean socialite and writer Victoria OCAMPO organised a South American tour for Stravinsky to the cities of Buenos Aires, Montevideo and Rio de Janeiro. The negotiations in Rio were handled by Silvio Piergilli, the artistic director of the firm Empreza Artística Theatral Limitada, which leased the Theatro Municipal in Rio between 1933 and 1937. From March 1936 onwards, the newspapers in Rio included regular notifications of the forthcoming concerts featuring Stravinsky and his son Soulima (*see* Soulima STRAVINSKY). The Stravinskys duly arrived in Rio on 31 May, travelling from Buenos Aires aboard the British ship *Almanzora*. All three concerts in 1936 were given in the Theatro Municipal. The programme for the opening concert on 6 June, which Stravinsky conducted, featured the DIVERTIMENTO from The FAIRY'S KISS, CAPRICCIO FOR PIANO AND ORCHESTRA (soloist Soulima Stravinsky) and PERSÉPHONE (Victoria Ocampo; Eumolpe, George James, the Symphonic Orchestra and Choir of the Theatro Municipal, with Chorus Director Santiago Guerra). In the second concert, on 8 June, Soulima Stravinsky played a *Sonata* in D Major by Haydn, a *Partita* by Bach, and Debussy's *Children's Corner*. Victoria Ocampo declaimed three *Sonnets pour Hélène* by Pierre de Ronsard and three poems by Charles Baudelaire (*Le Balcon*, *Recueillement* and *Moesta et Errabunda*), and Soulima and his father together played the CONCERTO FOR TWO SOLO PIANOS, preceded by a talk from the composer. The third concert, which took place on 10 June with the same performers as in the first concert, featured *Perséphone*, the CONCERTO FOR PIANO AND WIND INSTRUMENTS and three scenes from PETRUSHKA – The Magic Trick and Russian Dance; Petrushka's Cell; and a third scene which was named Carnival and its Dances. A fourth concert which was planned for 12 June, and for which tickets were on sale at popular prices, was cancelled for 'technical reasons'. The following day, the Stravinskys travelled back to Europe aboard the German ocean liner *Cap Arcona*.

Stravinsky's second visit to Brazil, in 1963, took place in the context of a series of cultural events that was planned with the intention of stimulating tourism in the country beyond the Carnival season. In this context, the offices of culture and tourism, with the assistance of the private firms Empresa Viggiani and Conciertos Associados, organised the Festival Internacional de Música e Danças, which took place between 18 August and 12 September 1963, and of which Oscar Alcazar was the general coordinator. Among the international attractions at the festival in 1963 were Claudio Arrau, John Barbirolli (conducting the London Philharmonia Orchestra), Carlos CHÁVEZ, Aaron COPLAND, Hans Werner HENZE, Eugene Ormandy (conducting the Philadelphia Orchestra), Robert CRAFT and Igor Stravinsky.

Stravinsky arrived in Rio by air from New York on 30 June with his wife Vera de Bosset STRAVINSKY and Robert Craft, and he participated in two concerts. The first, on 3 September, which featured the London Philharmonia Orchestra, was held at the Theatro Municipal, and comprised his FIREWORKS, op. 4, and the SYMPHONY IN THREE MOVEMENTS, both conducted by Craft, and Stravinsky conducted The Fairy's Kiss. The second concert, which took place on 8 September, was held in the Igreja da Candelária (Candelária Church) and

included the Symphonies of Wind Instruments conducted by Craft, and the Mass, announced as being in praise of Pope St John xxiii, which Stravinsky himself conducted. The performers were members of the Orquestra Sinfônica Nacional and the Associação de Canto Coral (Chorus Master: Cleofe Person de Mattos). Craft provides an account of this second visit to Rio (SCF (94), 369–75).
MARCOS MESQUITA AND LUTERO RODRIGUES

Brelet, Gisèle (born Fontenay-le-Compte, Vendée, 6 March 1916; died La Tranche-sur-Mer, Vendée, 21 June 1973). Studied piano with Lazare Lévy at the Paris Conservatory, also pursuing training in biology and later philosophy at the Sorbonne. In her philosophical work on experiencing music, she is a clear disciple of Pierre Souvtchinsky. In preparation for her doctoral dissertation (defended in 1949), exchanges with Souvtchinsky led Brelet to adopt ideas that the Russian philosopher and musicologist had developed in his publications of the 1920s and 1930s. During this period (between 1947 and 1952), Brelet also wrote five letters to Stravinsky in which she declared her faith in his art: 'No body of work is as rich in teachings for the philosopher as yours. Not only does it contain the fundamental truths of musical aesthetics laid bare in their essence, but an entire moral system, an entire philosophy' (letter from Brelet to Stravinsky, dated June 1947). Robert Craft spoke of the influence that Brelet might have had on Stravinsky during this period, notably through her article 'Chances de la musique atonale' published in 1946–7. Brelet authored three books that can be considered an organised demonstration of Stravinsky's artistic excellence. In the first, *Esthétique et création musicale* (1947), Brelet expresses the necessity of associating the creator's aesthetics with their psychology and of considering art along with the human character of the artist, studying the conditions of musical creativity for Stravinsky, Schoenberg and Hindemith. In her second book, *Le temps musical* (1949), based partly on Bergsonian philosophy, Brelet elaborates a typology of creators and an immanent philosophy of music based on the fundamental dimension of time. In *L'interprétation créatrice* (1951), Brelet takes up and distances herself from the opposition of *performance vs. interpretation* so important to Stravinsky, returning a certain degree of creativity to the interpreter. Exchanges between Stravinsky and Brelet seem to have come to an end after this publication. In all of these texts, one finds many of Souvtchinsky's ideas relayed by Brelet in building a favorable discourse on Stravinsky after 1945.
VALÉRIE DUFOUR
Translated from French by Christopher Murray

British Library. Although the Paul Sacher Stiftung (Foundation) in Basel is the primary repository of Stravinsky's manuscripts, a significant body of material has also been assembled at the British Library in London. As well as a near-complete collection of Stravinsky's lifetime publications, and several thousand published and unpublished recordings of his music, the Library holds a good number of original manuscript sources. Collectively, these provide examples of Stravinsky's work from all the major periods of his career, and from each stage of his compositional process. The first manuscript acquisition arrived shortly after the composer's death: the full score of the Capriccio for Piano and Orchestra, marked up for performance and subsequently used as the engraver's copy for its publication by the Édition Russe in 1930, was presented in memory of Stravinsky's PUBLISHER Ernst Roth by his widow. In 1986, the Library was presented with the remarkable collection of musical, literary and historical autographs assembled by Stefan Zweig and developed by his heirs after his death. Zweig himself had been able to buy only an album-leaf quotation from The FIREBIRD, but his heirs had the good fortune to acquire the attractive sketchbook in which Stravinsky drafted his first ideas for PULCINELLA between September 1919 and April 1920. This was almost certainly the notebook Stravinsky gave to PICASSO in June 1920, and provides elegant evidence of his skill in arranging and adapting the transcriptions of PERGOLESI and others which DIAGHILEV had provided for him. Manuscripts of some fifteen pieces have been placed on loan at the British Library by Chester Music. These include the vocal scores of Les Noces and Pulcinella, smaller pieces including Quatre chants russes and PIANO-RAG-MUSIC, and the original calligraphic score of the Four Russian Peasant Songs (1914–17), which came to light only in 2014. A dossier relating to the Four Russian Songs (1953–4) charts the various stages from the adaptation of earlier pieces to the transliteration and translation of the texts for publication. More recent bequests to the Library have shed light on the close attention Stravinsky paid to the production of his published scores, and continue to present vital information for the preparation of new editions. The musicologist Alan Tyson presented a copyist's score, probably in the hand of Catherine STRAVINSKY, of the orchestral version of the Étude for PIANOLA, with corrections by the composer, some of which were not incorporated into either of the published scores. Sir William Glock bequeathed a printed proof of MOVEMENTS for piano and orchestra with autograph corrections, as well as his correspondence with the composer, and other letters from Stravinsky are preserved among the papers of John Amis, Edward Clark, Eugene GOOSSENS, Donald Mitchell and Malcolm Smith. Oliver Neighbour, Music Librarian of the British Library, was responsible for filling most of the gaps in the published holdings of Stravinsky's works, while also buying two Stravinsky manuscripts for his own private collection of musical autographs, which he later presented to the Library. One of these, a single leaf from the draft score of the VARIATIONS (ALDOUS HUXLEY IN MEMORIAM) demonstrates a further aspect of Stravinsky's compositional process in the later period: it is written in pencil on transparent paper, from which a reprographic copy was printed on which the composer made further changes prior to performance and publication. The other is a notebook dating from 1913, containing the vocal score of Stravinsky's completion of the final chorus of MUSSORGSKY's KHOVANSHCHINA, written in ink but substantially revised and annotated in pencil thereafter. This manuscript was presented by Stravinsky to the music critic M. D. Calvocoressi, along with the printed vocal score of Khovanshchina in which Diaghilev and Stravinsky had planned their 'restoration' of the OPERA. Two large archives recently acquired by the British Library provide further layers of information as yet awaiting fuller scrutiny: the written archives of Boosey & Hawkes chart many of the negotiations over copyright and royalty payments for Stravinsky's works, while the papers of the music dealer Otto Haas and his successor Albi

Rosenthal tell the story of the convoluted discussions which led to the purchase of the Stravinsky manuscripts by Paul SACHER.   NICOLAS BELL

Britten, Benjamin (Lord Britten of Aldeburgh) (born Lowestoft, 22 November 1913; died Aldeburgh, 4 December 1976). British composer. Britten and Stravinsky shared a publisher for many years, but there was little sign that the older composer thought highly of his junior contemporary. In 1966, Stravinsky observed that his 'original title' for REQUIEM CANTICLES was '*Sinfonia da Requiem*, and I did not use it only because I seem to have shared too many titles with Mr Britten already' (T&C, 98). While Stravinsky did not discuss the differences between The FLOOD and ABRAHAM AND ISAAC and Britten's *Noye's Fludde* and *Canticle 2*, he made some particularly acidic remarks about *War Requiem*'s need for 'Kleenex at the ready' (T&C, 26). By contrast, Britten was an early admirer, declaring in 1936 that '*Oedipus Rex* demonstrated Stravinsky's remarkable sense of style in drawing inspiration from every age of music' ('Soviet opera at BBC', in Kildea 2003, 17), though a few years later he expressed a preference for Les NOCES over The RITE OF SPRING: in the later work, 'Stravinsky is far more controlled and the harmonies are closely related to the tunes. In this fine work he breaks up his folk-themes into small phrases, and is consequently freer to develop the form' ('England and the folk-art problem' (1941), in Kildea 2003, 33). In 1963, confronting what seemed to him a regrettable enthusiasm for the latest in TWELVE-NOTE technique, Britten described Stravinsky as 'a great man' and 'a great composer', but – in comparison with *Noye's Fludde* – his music in The Flood was 'frightfully difficult' ('Address to Kesgrave School, Ipswich', in Kildea 2003, 242).

Britten's partner Peter Pears sang Stravinsky's Oedipus on two occasions, the first in Cologne in 1951 with the composer conducting. As Pears told Britten in a letter, 'he wants accents all the time, spitting out words.... The old boy couldn't be nicer to me, though, I'm sure I'm no Oedipus' (Stroeher, Clark and Grimmer 2016, 182). Britten would doubtless have agreed.

ARNOLD WHITTALL

Paul Kildea (ed.), *Britten on Music* (Oxford University Press, 2003).
Vicki P. Stroeher, Nicholas Clark and Jude Grimmer (eds.), *My Beloved Man: The Letters of Benjamin Britten and Peter Pears* (Woodbridge: The Boydell Press, 2016)

$$\boxed{C}$$

Camus, Albert (born Dréan, Algeria, 7 November 1913; died Villeblevin, France, 4 January 1960). Novelist, playwright and essayist who explored a dualistic conception of the human predicament, examining the tension between an indifferent universe and the human desire for meaning. His groundbreaking novel *L'Étranger* and the influential essay *Le Mythe de Sisyphe* both appeared in 1942, and by 1945 Camus was a major figure in French public life, editing *Combat*, a Resistance newspaper with national circulation. Frequently seen as a close intellectual relation of Jean-Paul Sartre, Camus carefully distanced himself from Sartre's existentialism. He received the Nobel Prize for Literature in 1957. Stravinsky met Camus in April 1952 at a PARIS performance of *Wozzeck* by the Vienna State Opera. They shared a box together before dining afterwards, during which Camus revealed he had no ear for music. In the summer of that year, he tried to interest Stravinsky in a ballet scenario by René Char, to no avail. Stravinsky did appreciate Camus's writing, especially the novel *L'Homme révolté* and its critique of the Stalinist wing of the French socialists, but there the attraction ended, as he told Robert CRAFT: 'He is the only person in France who can stand up to Sartre, who has a very powerful brain, but for whom, unfortunately, I have absolutely no sympathy.'   DAVID EVANS

Canon for Two Horns. Composed and completed in 1917, this piece has never been published and remains 'lost'. There is no evidence of a performance having taken place. The manuscript was presented to a certain Dr Roux, a medical doctor in Geneva. According to Robert CRAFT (1957), whose account is all that survives of the circumstances surrounding this piece, Stravinsky's 9-year-old daughter Lyudmila (Mika) 'was in grave danger from an appendix and was saved by a Swiss doctor who would take no payment from Stravinsky but music. The doctor was a horn player and Stravinsky sent him a set of canons for two horns, which one may hope still exists with the family of Dr. Roux, somewhere in the neighbourhood of Geneva.' It is one of the first signs of the composer's interest in a compositional technique that would dominate much of his later style (*see* Watkins 1986).   JEREMY COLEMAN

Robert Craft, 'A personal preface', *The Score*, 20 (1957), 7–13.
Glenn Watkins, 'The canon and Stravinsky's late style', in Jann Pasler (ed.), *Confronting Stravinsky: Man, Musician, and Modernist* (Berkeley and Los Angeles: University of California Press, 1986), 217–46.

Canon on a Russian Popular Tune. Otherwise known as: Canon for Concert Introduction or Encore. Composed in 1965 for full orchestra and dedicated to the memory of the conductor Pierre MONTEUX, who had died in July 1964. First performance, 16 December 1965, Toronto, Canadian Broadcasting Corporation Symphony Orchestra (CBCSO). Conductor, Robert CRAFT. Published 1973, Boosey & Hawkes. The 'Russian popular tune' is namely the 'Coronation' theme at the close of Stravinsky's 1910 ballet The FIREBIRD. Ironically, The Firebird was one of the few early stage works of Stravinsky's which Monteux did not conduct in its first performance, and it has been suggested that Stravinsky 'wrote the piece first and only then decided to represent it as an in memoriam' (SSE, 515). Barely a minute long in performance, the piece is in C major and marked *fortissimo e moderato*, the canon theme appearing simultaneously in (rhythmic) augmentation, inversion and augmented inversion.

JEREMY COLEMAN

Cantata for soprano, tenor, female chorus, 2 flutes, oboe, cor anglais (doubling oboe 2), violoncello. Composed 1951–2. First performance, 11 November 1952, LOS ANGELES. Conductor, Igor Stravinsky. Published 1952, Boosey & Hawkes. Dedicated to Los Angeles Symphony Society. Anonymous fifteenth- and sixteenth-century English lyrics. A Lyke-Wake Dirge (Versus I: Prelude), Ricercar I, A Lyke-Wake Dirge (Versus II: 1st Interlude), Ricercar II, A Lyke-Wake Dirge (Versus III: 2nd Interlude), Westron Wind, A Lyke-Wake Dirge (Versus IV: Postlude).

For this secular cantata, Stravinsky chose four anonymous fifteenth- and sixteenth-century lyrics, three of which are semi-sacred, from the anthology *Poets of the English Language* edited by W. H. AUDEN and N. H. Pearson (1950), a copy of which Auden had gifted to the composer (SSC, I, 315). Stravinsky began with the composition of Ricercar I ('The maidens came'), not yet titled as such, for soprano, two flutes and violoncello in April 1951, the same month he completed The RAKE'S PROGRESS. The remaining movements and a revised version of Ricercar I were composed in 1952, by which time Stravinsky had developed a keen interest in SCHOENBERG's and WEBERN's serial music. The impact of this is most evident in Ricercar II ('To-morrow shall be my dancing day') where Stravinsky uses an eleven-note series, heard at the beginning in its four basic forms in the solo tenor (original, retrograde, inversion and retrograde-inversion). Unlike a TWELVE-NOTE series, Stravinsky's row is largely diatonic using the five 'white-key' notes between B and F plus one chromatic note E♭ (E-C-D-E-F-E♭-D-E-C-D-B), which in inversion around the first two notes elegantly preserves the 'white-key' notes, replacing chromatic E♭ by C♯ (C-E-D-C-B-C♯-D-C-E-D-F). Following an introductory bar, the tenor sings throughout this longest of the seven movements, which tells the life of Christ in the first person. Except in the eleven non-serial ritornellos, the tenor line is built entirely from different forms of the series, once (at 'Where Barabbas had deliverance') transformed into a purely diatonic version. The first, third and fifth section, each marked 'Cantus cancrizans' with reference to the serial palindromes in the tenor, are in recitative style and, like the intervening two ritornellos, mostly centred on C. The remainder of the movement alternates partially serial canonic sections (accompanied by oboes and violoncello only) that modulate to various keys, often starting out on A, with an altered version of the ritornello that now always ends on a B major sonority (the dominant to the following Interlude).

Stravinsky revised Ricercar I, and gave it its full title, in 1952, mostly thickening the original instrumental accompaniment with additional counterpoint, including further canons, and adding oboe and cor anglais. While the counterpoint remains non-serial here, Stravinsky's revisions clearly show the impact of his developing serial thinking. The movement uses mainly the minor keys of D, G and eventually A, concluding with a recitative ('Right mighty and famus Elizabeth'), prayer, and plagal cadence on G ('Amen').

The lively C minor vocal duet 'Westron Wind', on a love poem, does away with canon but sustains a contrapuntal flavour through imitation of motives by their contour rather than their exact intervals and rhythms, particularly audible in the imitative vocal phrases.

Stravinsky wrote the Prelude, two Interludes and Postlude last, distributing the poem on the passage of the soul from earth to purgatory ('A Lyke-Wake Dirge') over four movements of roughly the same non-serial music. Each opens with a short instrumental introduction 'in the Phrygian mode' (Stravinsky), with a melody modelled on a traditional tune, and ends with a cadence on the tonic of the following movement. The Postlude surprisingly concludes on a bright A major triad (in second inversion), a final tonic not shared by any previous movement. Overall, the Cantata is striking for its combination of large- and small-scale cyclic form.   CHRISTOPH NEIDHÖFER

Christoph Neidhöfer, 'A case of cross-fertilization: serial and non-serial counterpoint in Stravinsky's Cantata (1951–52)', Tijdschrift voor Muziektheorie, 9.2 (2004), 87–104.
Joseph N. Straus, Stravinsky's Late Music (Cambridge University Press, 2001).
Igor Stravinsky, programme note for the Cantata, in SCW, 469–71.

Canticum sacrum. Composed 1955. First performance, 13 September 1956, St Mark's Basilica VENICE. Conductor Igor Stravinsky. Published 1956, Boosey & Hawkes. 'Dedicated to the City of Venice, in praise of its Patron Saint, the Blessed Mark, Apostle'.

Venice always held a special place in Stravinsky's heart. By the mid-1950s, four of his works had been performed at the Biennale Festivals: his PIANO SONATA in 1925, his CAPRICCIO in 1934, JEU DE CARTES in 1937 and The RAKE'S PROGRESS in 1951. And his recomposed Gesualdo madrigals would be performed there in 1960, The OWL AND THE PUSSY-CAT in 1967.

Thus, a commission from Venice in 1954 was warmly welcomed. In the spring of that year, Alessandro Piovesan, the new Director of the Venice Biennale, wrote to Stravinsky suggesting a choral work of 30 or 40 minutes, to be performed in ST MARK'S BASILICA in a programme that would begin with music by Gabrieli. This was to result in the Canticum sacrum ad honorem Sancti Marci nominis, a work of just over 15 minutes for chorus, tenor and baritone soloists, organ and an ensemble of mostly wind instruments, on texts taken from the Vulgate. It was composed in a very short time in the summer and autumn of 1955 and first performed in St Mark's Basilica on 13 September 1956, along with Stravinsky's instrumental arrangement of BACH's 'Vom Himmel hoch da komm' ich her' (rather than the Gabrieli of Piovesan's original plan), as a part of the nineteenth International Society of Contemporary Music (ISCM) Festival.

The work begins with an eight-bar prelude for tenor and baritone soloists and three trombones, the text of which comprises the dedication (in Latin): 'To the City of Venice, in praise of its Patron Saint, the Blessed Mark, Apostle'. This is followed by five movements, mirroring the five domes of the Basilica. The symmetry of the cathedral is reflected in the first and fifth movements, 'Euntes in mundum' and 'Illi autem profecti', which set texts from the Gospel of St Mark – in the first, 'Go ye into all the world, and preach the gospel to every creature', and in the fifth, 'And they went forth, and preached everywhere . . .' – the fifth movement being a retrograde of the first. Both of these movements consist of five sections, *ababa*, *a* for chorus, organ and all the instruments, *b* played by only three bassoons and organ. This symmetry is not continued in the second and fourth movements, which use texts from, respectively, the Song of Solomon and the Gospel of St Mark. The second movement, 'Surge, aquilo', a tenor aria on carnal love, is Stravinsky's first piece to be written entirely on a TWELVE-NOTE row. The fourth, 'Brevis motus cantilenae', a baritone aria with chorus and instruments, is based on a second twelve-note row, which is used also for the central movement. This movement, 'Ad tres virtutes hortationes', which corresponds to the large central dome, is in three sections, 'Caritas', 'Spes' and 'Fides' (Charity, Hope and Faith, reversing their familiar order), and incorporates a mixture of styles and techniques: passacaglia, canon; inversion, augmentation and diminution. Vlad calls this movement a 'little three-part cantata' and both White and CRAFT have written of it as a 'cantata within a cantata'.

KATHRYN PUFFETT

Capriccio, for piano and orchestra. Composed 1928–9 and completed 1929, in Nice; rev. 1949. First performance, 6 December 1929, Orchestre Symphonique de Paris, Salle Pleyel, PARIS. Conductor, Ernest ANSERMET with Stravinsky at the piano. Full score published 1930, revised score published 1952 (both Édition Russe de Musique). In three movements (*attacca*): (I) Presto; (II) Andante rapsodico; (III) Allegro capriccioso ma tempo giusto. Stravinsky drafted the movements of the work in reverse order, beginning with the third movement (Allegro capriccioso) in late December 1928. The work was conceived partly as a vehicle to showcase Stravinsky's own piano playing, which might earn him money through multiple concert appearances. Stravinsky also appeared as the soloist in a commercial recording made in Paris, May 1930, with the Walther STRARAM Concerts Orchestra conducted once again by Ansermet. The style of piano writing retains the percussive use of the instrument exemplified in previous works such as the CONCERTO FOR PIANO AND WIND INSTRUMENTS (1923–4), but now mixed with a greater profusion of Romantic figurations. From around the mid-1930s, Stravinsky's son Svyatoslav (Soulima STRAVINSKY) typically performed the solo part under the composer's baton. The work integrates the piano into the orchestral sound more than is typical of generic concertos, as Ezra Pound once noted (following a performance in VENICE, 11 September 1934): 'there the piano and the orchestra are as two shells of a walnut' (quoted in SPD). Subsequently, the score was repurposed as BALLET music, notably by George BALANCHINE in his 1968 production *Jewels* at the NEW YORK CITY BALLET.

JEREMY COLEMAN

Carpenter, John Alden (born Park Ridge, Illinois, 28 February 1876; died Chicago, 26 April 1951). One of the first American composers to be influenced by Stravinsky; he first came into contact with Stravinsky's music when the BALLETS RUSSES visited Chicago in 1916 to perform *The* FIREBIRD and PETRUSHKA. Through the tour, Carpenter met Adolph BOLM, Ernest ANSERMET and others and, as Howard Pollack speculates (1995), eventually Stravinsky. Stravinsky and Carpenter became quite good friends, spending a great deal of time together when the Russian composer visited Chicago in 1925, 1935 and 1940.

EDWARD CAMPBELL

Howard Pollack, *Skyscraper Lullaby: The Life and Music of John Alden Carpenter* (Washington and London: Smithsonian Institution Press, 1995).

Carter, Elliott (born New York City, 11 December 1908; died New York City, 5 November 2012). One of the leading composers in the UNITED STATES in the twentieth century, Carter was present at the American première of Stravinsky's *The* RITE OF SPRING on 31 January 1924, an event which quickened his decision to become a composer and ignited his lifelong passion for the Russian master's music.

Living in PARIS from 1932 to 1935, Carter studied for two years with Nadia BOULANGER, a passionate advocate of Stravinsky's music, and it was at this time that he first met the Russian composer. Some of Carter's neo-classical compositions, such as the ballet *Pocahontas* (1936–9) and the Piano Sonata (1945–6) contain reminiscences of Stravinsky's music. In the late 1940s, Carter abandoned NEO-CLASSICISM and began to rethink the compositional foundations of his music, abandoning functional harmony, regular rhythm, thematic and motivic development and traditional forms. The first composition of his fully modernist period, the Sonata for Cello and Piano (1947–8), contains his earliest experiments with what Franko Goldman termed 'metrical modulation', and Carter noted that his thinking concerning 'the structural possibilities of tempo relationships' had benefitted from his exposure to medieval music, non-Western music, and the music of Stravinsky, SCRIABIN, Ives, Cowell and Chopin (Meyer and Shreffler 2008, 92).

Carter's writings contain many references to Stravinsky and, while he acknowledged his importance in helping awaken American music 'from its provincial lethargy', he judged that, by the end of the 1940s and the beginning of the 1950s, American composers had begun to find their own way (Carter in Meyer and Shreffler 2008, 112–13). According to Robert CRAFT, the Carters were 'the closest long-standing friends of the Stravinskys in the American musical world, especially during the last years of the older composer's life, after his move from California to New York' (Meyer and Shreffler 2008, 325). In *Dialogues*, Stravinsky named Carter's Double Concerto (1959–61) as the recent composition by an American-born composer that had most attracted him, praising its 'mood' ('full of new-found good spirits'), something he failed to find in the quartets. Carter in turn dedicated his *Piano Concerto* (1961–5) to Stravinsky on his eighty-fifth birthday. Following Stravinsky's death in 1971, Carter contributed one of a number of short 'in memoriam' pieces (Canon for 3) to the English music journal *Tempo* (*Tempo*, 98 (1972)).

Carter was a well-placed figure to understand Stravinsky's musical meta-morphosis, sharing with him a neo-classical past, a Constructivist present and a commitment to renewing the rhythmical idea in music.   EDWARD CAMPBELL

Felix Meyer and Anne C. Shreffler (eds.), *Elliott Carter: A Centennial Portrait in Letters and Documents* (Woodbridge, Suffolk: The Boydell Press, 2008).

Casella, Alfredo (born Turin, 25 July 1883; died Rome, 5 March 1947). Italian composer, pianist, conductor, editor, teacher, writer on music and concert organiser, the leading figure in Italian musical MODERNISM in the first half of the twentieth century. He left ITALY at 13 for PARIS, where he trained as a pianist at the Conservatoire (1896–1902), remaining in the city until 1915. It was in Paris that he became friendly with Stravinsky (the two men had first met in ST PETERSBURG in 1907). Back in Italy, Casella remained a vigorous promo-ter of Stravinsky's music, conducting local premières and publishing two monographs: the minuscule *Igor Strawinski* (1926) and normal-sized *Strawinski* (1947). His own compositions, especially those of the period 1913–26, track Stravinsky's stylistic evolution, at times almost too faithfully.

BEN EARLE

Alfredo Casella, *Music in My Time*, trans. and ed. Spencer Norton (Norman: University of Oklahoma Press, 1955).

Cecchetti, Enrico (born Rome, 21 June 1850; died Milan, 13 November 1928). Italian dancer, BALLET master and teacher. Cecchetti became ballet master of DIAGHILEV's BALLETS RUSSES in 1911. His principal role was to ensure a high standard of dancing, but he was also famed as a mime: he created two character roles in Stravinsky ballets – the Showman in PETRUSHKA (1911) and the Doctor in PULCINELLA (1920) – and was a noted interpreter of Kostchei in *The* FIREBIRD. Traditional in outlook, after seeing a rehearsal of NIJINSKY's *The* RITE OF SPRING, Cecchetti is reported to have told Diaghilev, 'the whole thing has been done by four idiots' (Beaumont 1929, 34).   SOPHIE REDFERN

Cyril W. Beaumont, *Enrico Cecchetti: A Memoir* (London: Wyman & Sons, 1929).

Chagall, Marc (born Moishe Zakharovich Shagal) (born Vitebsk, 7 July 1887; died St Paul-de-Vence, 28 March 1985). The relationship between Stravinsky and the Jewish-Belarusian painter Marc Chagall is one defined by both proximity and distance.

In many ways, Stravinsky and Chagall were the products of very different worlds. A Russian Orthodox Christian from the bourgeois milieu of ST PETERSBURG, Stravinsky's experiences were distant from those of Chagall – the son of a poor Jewish family from the Pale of Settlement. However, as they matured and developed, both artists grew ever closer in terms of life experience and sensibility. Both lived lives marked by the tumultuous political events of the twentieth century. Both experienced exile and displacement – initially to FRANCE and subsequently, as a consequence of World War II, to the UNITED STATES.

There is also an uncanny similarity in the themes that came to preoccupy the artistic lives of both men. Both were intensely interested in religion (Orthodox Christianity in Stravinsky's case, primarily Judaism in Chagall's, although the painter occasionally tackled Christian subjects as well). Whether it is The SYMPHONY OF PSALMS (1930) or The FLOOD (1961–2) for Stravinsky, or Jacob's Dream (1963), The Sabbath (1909) or Return From the Synagogue (1926) for Chagall, religious subjects have pride of place in the oeuvres of both artists.

Both men were also drawn to folklore and popular culture. This was true, in the first instance, of the folk tales and cultural practices of eastern Europe, but extended as well to sites such as the COMMEDIA DELL' ARTE and the circus. Finally, although certainly not exhaustively, one might also point to a shared interest in classical culture. Both artists turned time and again to the myths and texts of Greco-Roman antiquity for subject matter.

There is also a surprising resonance between the two artists in terms of the strategies and styles they deploy in their work. Annetta Floirat has argued that an intense spirit of self-reflexivity, bordering on artifice or theatricality, stands at the very heart of both Chagall's visual art and Stravinsky's music (Floirat, 1–6). We can see this in the prevalence of masquerade in Chagall's work or in the heavily stylised and artificial settings of paintings such as Birth (1911–12). This finds a correlate in the self-reflexive artifice of such works as PULCINELLA – with its theme of carnivalesque masquerade in both the music and stage action – or The RAKE'S PROGRESS, which features an epilogue in which the characters appear out of costume to discuss the moral of the story. One might also point to the importance of a kind of 'primitivism' for both artists and to their tendency to engage in pastiche (what Stravinsky once referred to as his 'kleptomania').

These connections should have made them ideal artistic partners, but of three proposed collaborations only one came to fruition. It is difficult not to look at this history of missed connections as a series of lost opportunities for twentieth-century art.

Stravinsky had heard of Chagall from Mikhail Larionov and met the painter personally in New York City. He wanted Chagall to create the sets for the 1929 revival of RENARD, but the painter declined the commission. The composer disliked the revival that was staged and felt that '[it] was ruined chiefly by some jugglers Diaghilev had borrowed from a circus' (Mem, 40). 'I regret very much that he refused', Stravinsky lamented, noting that 'I still hope [Chagall] will one day do Renard and Les Noces; no one could be more perfect for them' (Conv, 102).

The two artists did manage a collaboration of sorts on the re-staging of Stravinsky's ballet The FIREBIRD. Chagall was engaged to re-envision the stage curtain, sets, and costumes for the BALLET, which debuted at the Metropolitan Opera House in New York on 24 October 1945. Chagall's elaborate designs emphasised the whimsy and fantasy of the piece, and the production was so successful that it continues to be staged today. Stravinsky noted that it was a 'very flamboyant exhibition' and that Chagall 'made an ink portrait of me and presented it to me as a memento of our collaboration' (Conv, 115).

But this success did not facilitate further collaboration and the relationship between the two artists ended with not a bang, but a whimper. In 1960, attempts were made to arrange a meeting between Stravinsky and Chagall, in the hope of facilitating a collaboration for the staging of the composer's musical play, The Flood. On the date in question, Chagall arrived at

Stravinsky's PARIS apartment to be told that the composer was drunk and unconscious and unable to meet. No follow-up meeting ever took place and the collaboration did not proceed. All that is left to students of the arts is to imagine what might have been.   IHOR JUNYK

Annetta Floirat, 'Chagall and Stravinsky, different arts and similar solutions to twentieth-century challenges', www.academia.edu/12290198/Chagall_and_Stravinsky_different_ar ts_and_similar_solutions_to_twentieth-century_challenges.

Chaliapin, Fyodor (Ivanovich) (born near Kazan, 1/13 Feb. 1873; died Paris, 12 April 1938). Russian bass, considered as the great successor of Stravinsky's father. Stravinsky recalled that in his early twenties he frequently saw Chaliapin at RIMSKY-KORSAKOV's home and witnessed his story-telling talent. In 1909, the great bass performed Stravinsky's song arrangements of Mephistopheles' 'Song of the Flea' by BEETHOVEN and MUSSORGSKY. He recorded the Mussorgsky song in Stravinsky's ORCHESTRATION on multiple occasions. In 1912, Chaliapin suggested to the young composer a collaboration with the writer Maxim Gorky on an opera about the Novgorod epic hero Vasiliy Buslayev, but he declined. In 1913, Stravinsky's and Chaliapin's routes crossed again, during DIAGHILEV's restoration of KHOVANSHCHINA, for which, however, the bass sang Stravinsky's music only in the final chorus.   KATERINA LEVIDOU

SRT

Chamber Music. As in the case of the composer's orchestral music, it is sometimes difficult to state with absolute confidence which works of Stravinsky fall into the category of chamber compositions. Some of the pieces discussed in the following account are arguably not chamber works as the term is generally understood, but at the same time do not sit comfortably in alternative genre classifications. In any case, Stravinsky's chamber oeuvre has received substantially less attention than his orchestral and dramatic works. Although chamber compositions appear at a consistent rate throughout his career – from the THREE PIECES FOR STRING QUARTET (1914) up to the FANFARE FOR A NEW THEATRE (1964) – the proportion of works written for such an ensemble is small, and many are under 5 minutes in length. Nevertheless, several of these works contain music of considerable originality and inventiveness, and a handful are among the composer's most important creations.

The first original, true chamber work by Stravinsky that is extant (not counting the *Three Japanese Lyrics* for high voice and piano or chamber orchestra (1912–13)) is the Three Pieces for String Quartet (1914; rev. 1918). This opening foray into chamber composition is significant, as it displays a number of musical approaches which the composer was subsequently to explore after The RITE OF SPRING (1913): rustic nationalism (through the use of repetition and drone-like pedal points in the first movement); chromaticism bordering on atonality (in the second, a movement which the composer himself noted was influenced by the movements of the great clown 'Little Tich'); and block chordal writing (in the third) which, as André Boucourechliev indicates, anticipates the SYMPHONIES OF WIND INSTRUMENTS (1920; rev. 1947). (A comparable combination of folk-influenced music and homophony is likewise perceivable in the fleeting Duet for Two Bassoons (1918).) While some commentators have noted the influence of WEBERN and SCHOENBERG in these instrumental miniatures (especially in the second movement), Stravinsky denied having knowledge of his Viennese contemporaries at this time (except for *Pierrot lunaire*), and instead insisted that the *Three Pieces* in fact anticipated his neo-classical period via the THREE EASY PIECES for piano duet (1915). An arguably less successful contribution to the string quartet medium was the later CONCERTINO (1920), a work in a free sonata allegro form with what the composer described as 'a definitely *concertante* part' for the first violin. As Eric Walter White explains, the violin part is the most successful feature of this 'unsatisfying' work (SCW, 291). Stravinsky decided to re-orchestrate it in 1952 for flute, oboe, cor anglais, clarinet in A, 2 bassoons, 2 trumpets in B♭, tenor trombone, bass trombone, and violin and cello obligati, believing a larger ensemble to be more appropriate for the musical content.

Barring piano works, the THREE PIECES FOR SOLO CLARINET (1919) is Stravinsky's first real attempt to write a stand-alone piece for solo instrument (the earlier POUR PABLO PICASSO (1917), also for solo clarinet, is inconsequential). The originality of the second movement is readily apparent, 'written without barlines in an improvisatory vein with fast-flowing arpeggios and arabesques' (SCW, 282). Stravinsky was later to compose another work for unaccompanied solo instrument, the ELEGY for solo viola (or violin)(1944, also playable a fifth higher on solo violin). This piece in ternary form combines elements of chant, two-part invention, and fugal writing, and the soloist plays *con sordino* throughout.

The Three Pieces were written for Werner Reinhart, a keen amateur clarinettist who had been instrumental in financing the first production of the stage work The SOLDIER'S TALE (1918). As is well known, financial circumstances often influenced Stravinsky's compositional projects: it has been suggested that *The Soldier's Tale* – later turned into a concert suite for chamber ensemble, as well as a suite for violin, clarinet, and piano, again written to please Reinhart – was at least partially scored for its ensemble of clarinet, bassoon, cornet à pistons, trombone, violin, double bass, and percussionist to secure more performances. Securing royalties in the wartime period was challenging, and the work was written to be 'frequently performed, if necessary under adverse circumstances, with minimal scenery and few players'. Indeed, many of the chamber works that Stravinsky wrote in his 'neo-classical' period were reworkings or arrangements of earlier compositions: the three SUITE ITALIENNE arrangements (1925, 1932, 1933), for instance, were transcriptions of material from various movements of PULCINELLA (the first titled *Suite for violin and piano, after themes, fragments and pieces by Giambattista Pergolesi*, rather than *Suite Italienne*). Likewise, Stravinsky made two chamber arrangements of the early PASTORALE (1907) in 1933 – one for violin and piano in collaboration with the violinist Samuel DUSHKIN, and the other for violin, oboe, cor anglais, clarinet and bassoon. It appears that these works were written, at least partially, for financial reasons. Stravinsky explained composing the DUO CONCERTANT (1932), a work in five movements for violin and piano, as an attempt to 'reconcile' himself to the combination of 'strings struck in the piano with strings set in vibration with the bow ... The mating of these [two] instruments seems much clearer than the combination of a piano with several stringed instruments, which tends to confusion with the orchestra.' However, White (SCW, 374) argues instead that:

> Another reason that had led to the composition of the *Duo Concertant* was Stravinsky's wish to open up a wider field for his music through chamber music performances. He found such concerts 'much easier to arrange as they do not require large orchestras of high quality, which are costly and so rarely to be found except in big cities' ... The *Duo Concertant* was to form the kernel of such a programme. Between them Dushkin and Stravinsky planned to make new arrangements of the Pergolesi and Chaikovsky material from *Pulcinella* and *The Fairy's Kiss* under the titles *Suite Italienne* and *Divertimento*; and they also prepared transcriptions of the early *Pastorale*, the 'Chinese March' and 'Nightingale's Songs' from *The Nightingale*, the Scherzo ('Dance of the Firebird') and 'Lullaby' from *The Firebird*, and the 'Russian Dance' from *Petrushka*. With this programme they toured Europe during the 1932/33 and 1933/34 seasons.

JAZZ was a notable, if occasional, influence on Stravinsky's compositional style, and is apparent in a handful of works from both the so-called 'Russian' and 'neo-classical' periods. RAGTIME, for eleven players (1918), makes use of the genre's characteristic rhythmic features, especially syncopation. (The use of a cimbalom in this work should also be noted as a striking addition to the instrumental palette.) Similarly, *The Soldier's Tale* features a rag; as Paul Griffiths states, 'the 4/8 metre is persistently being jolted by added or subtracted beats and by small-scale repetitions as well as by syncopation, but the violin assures continuity' (1992, 59). It also appears that Stravinsky's new enthusiasm for jazz was reflected in the prominent use of percussion in the work. The composer's penchant for jazz was also to resurface in the short PRAELUDIUM, for JAZZ ensemble (1936/7), and especially in the EBONY CONCERTO (1945). In the latter work, Stravinsky attempted to 'produce a jazz equivalent of a *concerto grosso*, with a blues slow movement' (SCW, 437), as well as a theme and variations finale. While Eric Walter White hailed the *Ebony Concerto* as the 'most ambitious and most successful of his various flirtations with jazz' (SCW, 437), it is known that the composer found writing in this new medium challenging (the work was a commission by the Woody Herman band). According to White, 'He studied recordings of the [Woody Herman] band ... and enlisted the services of a saxophonist to demonstrate fingerings'. Nevertheless, in the end, Stravinsky 'managed to solve the problem of writing for a jazz-band without abdicating any part of his own artistic integrity, and at the same time exacted the maximum discipline from the players, refusing to make allowance for any improvisatory element in the performance'.

Stravinsky wrote relatively few original neo-classical chamber works, especially when it is taken into account that this period spanned over thirty years of his compositional output. Nevertheless, two works of the 1920s are generally considered to stand among his finest. The SYMPHONIES OF WIND INSTRUMENTS (1920; rev. 1947) straddles the Russian and neo-classical periods, and can be regarded as 'a kind of symphonic summary of some of the musical ideas that had been fermenting in his mind during the previous six years'. At the same time, its dry wind sonorities also pre-empt the unquestionably neo-classical

OCTET FOR WIND INSTRUMENTS (1923), and it has even been claimed that the *Symphonies* 'have the stronger claim as the earliest convincing demonstration of radical thought'; indeed, it appears that Stravinsky thought of the *Symphonies* as the first of his 'so-called classical works'. Although the title suggests a composition of symphonic proportions, the composer used the term 'symphony' in the original sense of 'sounding together'. The musical material – which is arranged in contrasting blocks – is divided into three sections, each with a different fundamental tempo. As he did with the Concertino, Stravinsky was to rework the *Symphonies* in the 1940s. He altered the instrumentation slightly, which consequently led to various musical modifications, and re-barred the work, as was his later practice.

The Octet is scored for flute, clarinet in B♭, two bassoons, trumpet in C, trumpet in A, tenor trombone, and bass trombone, and is one of the composer's earliest works in the neo-classical style. It 'marks his rediscovery of sonata form', a process utilised in the first movement (of three) alongside functional tonality and modulation. The second movement is a theme and variations, employing fugato procedures. Indeed, counterpoint is an important neo-classical feature of the Octet; as Stravinsky explained: 'Form, in my music, derives from counterpoint. I consider counterpoint as the only means through which the attention of the composer is concentrated on purely musical questions. Its elements also lend themselves perfectly to an architectural construction.' The revised version of the Octet (1952) features only minimal changes.

Stravinsky's first serial chamber composition, and one of the first works in which he experimented with this new compositional method, was the SEPTET (1952–3). The composition, in three movements, was influenced by various twelve-note works by Schoenberg, such as the Wind Quintet (1924) and Suite for Septet (1926). The first movement is in sonata form, and the second movement, *Passacaglia*, is densely contrapuntal, a set of variations featuring imitation at the inversion, retrograde, and retrograde inversion. The final *Gigue* movement features multiple fugati. The short EPITAPHIUM (1959) is likewise based on dodecaphonic principles, although it seems that Stravinsky only decided to write in this manner after realising the work's serial potential about halfway through the compositional process. Originally written for two flutes, the second flute was later replaced by a clarinet, apparently when Stravinsky became aware that the work was to be performed in a programme alongside Webern's *Geistliche Lieder*, which uses this instrumental combination.

Many of the chamber works that Stravinsky composed in his late period are relatively brief; the DOUBLE CANON ('Raoul Dufy in Memoriam') for string quartet (1959), for instance, is under a minute and a half in length. This piece, which features strict canonical writing and a variety of manipulations of the basic series, was originally written for flute and clarinet duet. Similarly, the *Fanfare for a New Theatre* for two trumpets (1964) lasts under a minute; despite this, White notes that the work is successful because of its 'remarkable' series, in which 'each group of three consecutive notes is so arranged that it explores the interval of a second, and these groups follow each other in an ascending order'.

The preceding overview of Stravinsky's chamber oeuvre reveals that these works, though frequently brief in duration, clearly trace the same broad evolutionary path as the composer's other compositions, with no less variety or originality than in more familiar genres such as orchestral music. Regardless of the period in which they were written, each chamber work displays Stravinsky's distinctive compositional characteristics, and deserves as much critical attention as the remainder of his output.   JOSEPH SCHULTZ

Paul Griffiths, *Stravinsky* (London: J. M. Dent & Sons Ltd, 1992).

Chanel, Gabrielle 'Coco' (born Saumur, 19 August 1883; died Paris, 10 January 1971). In her early years, Chanel had wanted to be a music hall star but developed her work in fashion, sewing and then designing new fashions. She continued her interest in music, attending performances and artistic events: the connection between Stravinsky and Chanel began when she attended the Parisian première of The RITE OF SPRING (May 1913). In 1919, DIAGHILEV wanted to reprise the activity of the BALLETS RUSSES and to restage The *Rite* with the original costumes. The cost of this was underwritten by Chanel, who by this point had been part of the clique following the troupe (Davis 2006, 348). It was rumoured that Chanel and Stravinsky had an affair: this rumour was the basis of a fictional novel (*Coco and Igor*, by Chris Greenhalgh, 2002) and, latterly, a film based on the novel (*Coco Chanel and Igor Stravinsky*, 2009, directed by Jan Kounen). Chanel's reminiscence of the 1920s does refer to her affair with Stravinsky, recalling notably how it affected them both: 'it transformed him from a self-effacing and timid man … into a strong and monocled man, from the conquered to the conqueror' (cited in Davis). Stravinsky's wife Vera (*see* Vera STRAVINSKY), and his colleague Robert CRAFT, both rejected the claims.

NEO-CLASSICISM and the clean chic of Chanel's fashions link both artists aesthetically, as do their connections to colleagues and friends aligned to the Ballets Russes. Their families were also connected: Stravinsky's family went to stay with Chanel in her villa just outside Paris in the summer of 1920. Davis has outlined how they came to land at her doorstep: post-Russian Revolution, many Russians in Europe were state-less, and so stayed with friends while they worked through their future plans. In this way, Chanel supported Stravinsky in providing financial backing for his work, and accommodation for a short time during 1920.   HELEN JULIA MINORS

Lisa Chaney, *Chanel: An Intimate Life* (London: Penguin, 2012).
Mary Davis, 'Chanel, Stravinsky and musical chic', *Fashion Theory*, 10.4 (2006), 431–60.

Charitable Activities. Stravinsky's charity is less known than his great interest in earning money. Nevertheless, he provided considerable financial support to various projects and individuals throughout his life: he donated to different charitable organisations; being close to the RUSSIAN ORTHODOX CHURCH in exile, he participated in charitable actions, made donations to various parishes, priests and needy Russian *émigrés*; he took part in benefit concerts; he provided his works for publication in charitable editions; he established scholarships – for example, the ASCAP Stravinsky Award; he donated the manuscripts of his works to various institutions (for example, the manuscript of ABRAHAM AND ISAAC to the State of ISRAEL and of REQUIEM CANTICLES to the library of Princeton University).

Stravinsky provided particularly generous financial support to his family members and close friends. Despite his own difficult situation after World War I and the 1917 Russian Revolution, he financed the emigration from Russia of the family of his sister-in-law Ludmila Belyankin. In 1928, Stravinsky sent money to his cousin Sergej Jelachich, who emigrated to Harbin, and also to his mother in Leningrad. In the same period, PROKOFIEV helped to transmit money to Stravinsky's brother Yury in Leningrad. Igor also paid for living expenses and tuition in PARIS for Tatiana Stravinsky (Yury's daughter).

For a very long time, Stravinsky was forced to support his adult children and their families, and his relatives not infrequently borrowed money from him. During the German occupation of FRANCE, Stravinsky sent money from the UNITED STATES to his children, Madubo (the children's elderly nanny), Vera STRAVINSKY's friend Olga Sallard, Ira Beliankin, Kitty Mandelstam and the Nosenko sisters. In 1957, he sent a cheque to the great Russian writer Aleksey REMIZOV, who died in poverty in Paris that year. Letters expressing gratitude from different people are preserved in the PSS.   TATIANA BARANOVA MONIGHETTI

Chase, Lucia (born Waterbury, Connecticut, 24 March 1897; died New York City, 9 January 1986). American dancer and company director. Chase was founder, co-director and sometime chief financer of Ballet Theatre (established 1939, later American Ballet Theatre). She had sporadic dealings with Stravinsky through the BALLET company: in 1941, he arranged TCHAIKOVSKY's Act 3 'Bluebird Pas de Deux' from *The Sleeping Beauty* for Ballet Theatre, and he was an occasional guest conductor. Chase also secured the 1945 FIREBIRD *Suite* for first presentation as a ballet by the company. Despite Chase's efforts, Stravinsky never composed an original ballet score for Ballet Theatre.

SOPHIE REDFERN

Chávez (Ramírez), Carlos (Antonio de Padua) (born Mexico City, 13 June 1899; died Mexico City, 2 August 1978). Composer, conductor, writer and administrator. Largely self-taught as a musician, Chávez began to champion Stravinsky's music in Mexico in the mid-1920s, following periods of self-discovery in Europe and the UNITED STATES. From 1928 to 1949, he was the principal conductor of the Orquesta Sinfónica de México (OSM). In that role, and later with the Orquesta Sinfónica Nacional, he programmed Stravinsky's music frequently. In 1940, he invited Stravinsky to Mexico City to conduct the OSM in four concerts; Stravinsky returned to give more concerts the following year, and subsequently on several occasions until 1961. Chávez acted as the official host for Stravinsky's visits to Mexico, and the two men became friends, also meeting frequently in the United States. Stravinsky was an admirer of Chávez's conducting (SSC, III, 317).

As in some of Stravinsky's early Russian-period works, Chávez sought to develop a primitivist aesthetic through allusion to vernacular music, though by his own admission Chávez's source material – music of pre-Cortesian Mexico – was lost, and had to be reimagined; a key work in this respect is *Xochipilli* (1940). From the early 1930s onwards, both composers shared a predilection for classical genres, not least the concerto. However, Chávez's manner of working was otherwise very different from Stravinsky's: he presided over government-sponsored institutions at various stages in his career, and much of his output has explicitly nationalist aspirations.   CHRIS COLLINS

Tamara Levitz, 'Igor the Angeleno: the Mexican connection', in SHW, 141–76.
Robert L. Parker, *Carlos Chávez: Mexico's Modern-Day Orpheus* (Boston, Mass.: Twayne, 1983).

Choral Music. Choral music was a mainstay of Stravinsky's compositional output throughout his career. Though he, regrettably, did not compose for chorus quite as prolifically as he did for instrumental ensembles, the evolution of his choral works follows the same path as that of his more abstract instrumental works and his balletic and operatic collaborations.

As Stravinsky was celebrating the success of his three great Russian ballets (1910–13), he was also experimenting with uncommon combinations of instrumental and vocal forces in *Zvezdoliki* (1911–12). Better known by its French title, *Le Roi des Étoiles* (KING OF THE STARS), this setting for male choir and an orchestra with its fascinatingly experimental musical language and oversized wind section (the score calls for eight French horns) lasts just over 5 minutes, which unfortunately makes its performance rare. Stravinsky, while clearly imitating DEBUSSY, incorporated the same kind of musical framework that he was using in the concurrently composed *The* RITE OF SPRING. This structure enabled him to create blocks of sound that helped define the musical texture of *Zvezdoliki* and supported a musical dialogue between the text by Russian symbolist poet Konstantin Dmitriyevich BALMONT and the accompanying instrumental parts. In many ways, Balmont's text (translated into French by Michel-Dimitri Calvocoressi) served as a backdrop for Stravinsky as he echoed Debussy's technique of planing (streaming chords in parallel motion) and his quartal harmonisation (harmonic intervals based on perfect fourths instead of the more customary thirds) while simultaneously continuing to create static harmonies in musical sound blocks. Also heard in this brief work are some of the sounds that he would later revisit in the SYMPHONIES OF WIND INSTRUMENTS (1920, rev. 1947), another work with a Debussy connection – this time dedicated to his memory after his death in 1918.

Between 1914 and 1917, just a few years after *Zvezdoliki*, Stravinsky completed the *Four Russian Peasant Songs* (*Saucers*) for unaccompanied female voices, a work he would revise in 1954 by adding four horns that provide both fanfare-like flourishes before each song and brief instrumental interludes throughout all four songs. The choral forces were also changed in the revised version from exclusively female voices to four equal voices, but the choral parts were otherwise altered minimally, the changes consisting mainly of re-barring, though with the notable addition of a *da capo* repeat in the first song and the transposition of the second song up a major third. With the addition of the instrumental framework, Stravinsky was able not only to incorporate contrapuntal techniques that he was experimenting with in his other works, but also to include echoes of the choruses of CANTATA (1951–2), also for female voices.

On returning to communion with the RUSSIAN ORTHODOX CHURCH in 1926, Stravinsky produced his first sacred *a cappella* mixed choral work, *Otche nash* (PATER NOSTER), which would undergo significant revision in 1949. On the surface level, one can easily see the influence of the traditional Russian Orthodox chant from Stravinsky's childhood. However, instead of leaving the music unmetered, Stravinsky dictates the musical motion by means of multimetric phrasing, which by this time had become one of his familiar compositional devices.

When he was commissioned by Sergey Koussevitzky and the Boston Symphony Orchestra to compose a new work celebrating the orchestra's fiftieth anniversary in 1930, the orchestra requested that he write something symphonic, while his publisher was looking for something popular. Stravinsky responded with the Symphony of Psalms (1929–30), the first of his mixed works for chorus and orchestra, for a concert hall setting. Interestingly, the work was premièred in Brussels by Ernest Ansermet and the Société Philharmonique de Bruxelles on 13 December 1930, with the American première in Boston on 19 December.

There is a purity and directness in the *Symphony of Psalms*, which appears to derive from the sincerity of the psalm texts themselves – the first two consisting of pleas for mercy and deliverance, and the third, the most joyous of all the psalms, praising the Lord without reservation. Stravinsky did not obscure the text with dense ORCHESTRATION or merely double the choral and instrumental parts; rather, he lays it bare for the listener to experience in both its soulful stillness and spiritual grandeur. This is heard clearly in the closing words of Psalm 150, which conclude the final movement: 'Alleluia Laudate Dominum' which evoke an unmistakable sense of awe in the listener, regardless of religious belief.

The *Symphony of Psalms* is a clear manifestation of Stravinsky's neo-classical aesthetic, with three movements that evoke aspects of the music of Haydn and Mozart, while avoiding any kind of word painting and conveying the text without emotional pretence. Also to be found is a remarkable motivic unity, both within and across all three movements. The middle movement includes a spectacular double fugue in which the first subject is overtly reminiscent of J. S. Bach's *Musical Offering*. The melodic and harmonic combination of two minor thirds separated by a half-step (e.g. C + E♭, B + D) operates not only as the fugue subject but appears in all three movements as a defining melodic and harmonic feature – in the first movement as an ostinato figure, and in the third as stacked harmonic thirds. Along with other works of the late 1920s, such as the oratorio Oedipus Rex (1926–7), Stravinsky's proclivity for motivic unification is one of the features that looked both backward and forward, reflecting the structures of his earlier compositions while simultaneously foreshadowing the motivic unification of the later works.

The 1930s saw just two works for unaccompanied voices: Simvol' veri (Credo) in 1932, revised in 1949, and Bogoroditse Devo (Ave Maria) in 1934. Stravinsky intended these works, along with *Otche nash*, to be performed not in a concert setting, but as part of the traditional mass; hence there was some practicality in his writing. Gone is the multimetric writing that prevailed in *Otche nash* in favour of a more traditional chant-like unbarred *Credo*. The nature of the text of the Nicene Creed must have had some bearing on Stravinsky's reliance on a repetitive tonic sonority as the words must be clearly understood for this profession of faith. We are consequently presented with declamatory choral writing with triadic sonorities, a quick pulse and uncomplicated cadences. The text of *Bogoroditse Devo (Ave Maria)*, however, not being a necessary part of the liturgy, is free of the requirements that might have constrained Stravinsky with the *Credo*. Here he introduces more melismatic writing and turns once again to multimetre, in keeping with traditional chant phrasing.

Stravinsky received a commission for a section of the *Genesis Suite* in 1944, the brainchild of the Hollywood music director Nathaniel Shilkret, who persuaded several prominent composers to contribute, including Arnold SCHOENBERG and Darius MILHAUD. The text for the seven movements was drawn from the first eleven chapters of the Book of Genesis, with Stravinsky setting the last movement based on the well-known story of the tower of Babel (Genesis 11:1–9). In BABEL (1944), for narrator, male chorus and orchestra, the text from the American King James Version of the Bible is spoken by a narrator, except for the words of God, which are sung by the male chorus. The chorus parts representing the voice of God are set in a chant-like two-part contrapuntal texture, superimposed against a harmonic block sounded by strings (including harp) with some repetition of harmonies in triplets. Stravinsky combines all of these elements to create a feeling of stasis, symbolic of the divine confounding of humankind's language. The use of harmonic and melodic blocks to construct the form is a notable evolution of the blocks found in his early BALLET works (particularly PETRUSHKA and *The Rite of Spring*).

As with Stravinsky's earlier *a cappella* sacred vocal works, the MASS (1944–8) was also intended to be performed in a church and not a concert hall. Nevertheless, he leaves his unmistakable musical stamp on the mass setting, distributing homophonic and polyphonic textures among the five sections (Kyrie, Gloria, Credo, Sanctus, Agnus Dei) to create an overall symmetry: the first and fifth sections are homophonic, the second and fourth are polyphonic, with the third and central section containing a chant-like declamatory choral style, reminiscent of his previous Credo setting from 1932. Stravinsky's thumbprint is overtly present in the block of sound that appears at the beginning of the Sanctus – each of the three appearances of the word 'Sanctus', symbolising the Holy Trinity, begins with a melodic block of two melismatic vocal lines in a free imitative texture, and ends with a block of harmonies with full chorus and ensemble. Soon after completing the *Mass*, Stravinsky revisited his earlier sacred works with Slavonic texts and re-set them with Latin versions: *Pater Noster* (1949) from the earlier *Otche nash* (1926), and *Ave Maria* (1949) from the earlier *Bogoroditse Devo* (1934).

Cantata was composed in 1951–2, immediately after *The* RAKE'S PROGRESS. In the programme note for the première, Stravinsky wrote that he

> was persuaded by a strong desire to compose another work in which the problems of setting English words to music would reappear, but this time in a pure, non-dramatic form ... I selected four popular anonymous lyrics of the fifteenth and sixteenth centuries, verses which attracted me not only for their great beauty and their compelling syllabification, but for their construction which suggested musical construction.

The four choral sections ('versus I–IV') use text from the 'Lyke-Wake Dirge', a popular traditional English song dating from at least the early seventeenth century that tells of the soul's journey from earth to purgatory. These sections alternate with a solo soprano ricercar with the text 'A maiden came', a solo tenor ricercar with 'Tomorrow shall be my dancing day', and finally a soprano and tenor duet with text from the oft-used song 'Westron Wind' (the *cantus firmus* source for mass settings by English Renaissance composers John Taverner, Christopher Tye and John Sheppard). Each of the choral sections consist of almost identical homophonic material, serving as repetitive blocks in the overall structure of the work: prelude, two interludes, and postlude.

The eleven-year period from 1955–66 saw almost as many new choral compositions as the prior forty-four years since *Zvezdoliki*. Premièred at the VENICE Biennale Festival in 1956 and 1958, respectively, CANTICUM SACRUM (1955) and THRENI (1957–8), both with sacred texts, came near the beginning of Stravinsky's serial period. Stravinsky created a musical symmetry in *Canticum sacrum* that reflects the architectural design of ST MARK'S BASILICA, as well as a compositional process that combines eighteenth-century contrapuntal textures with twentieth-century TWELVE-NOTE techniques. While this was the first of his works to contain a movement based entirely on a tone row, diatonic passages nevertheless remain present, as does evidence of the influence of Gregorian chant. Robert CRAFT notes in 'A concert for Saint Mark' (*The Score*, December 1956) that the influence of WEBERN is also evident, particularly in relation to 'the structure of a canon such as the one in "Caritas" which ends like the last movement of Webern's opus 31, and which resembles a canon in the Webern *Variations for Orchestra* in that each entrance is at the semitone'.

During this time, Stravinsky also transcribed Bach's organ work *Canonic Variations on 'Vom Himmel hoch da komm' ich her'* for chorus and orchestra. The forces for the *Chorale Variations on 'Vom Himmel hoch da komm' ich her'* (1956) are almost identical to those for *Canticum sacrum*, as it was conceived as a companion piece for the concert in which *Canticum sacrum* was premièred. The accompanying instrumental canons are of far greater interest than the choral element in this work, as the voices merely sing the unharmonised chorale melody.

Threni: id est lamentationes Jeremiae prophetae (1957–8), which was premièred at the next Biennale in the hall of the Scuola grande di San Rocco, and dedicated to the memory of Alessandro Piovesan, is the first and most substantial of Stravinsky's works written entirely with the twelve-note system, and using Ernst KRENEK's technique of hexachordal rotation. The principal tone row in *Threni* is nevertheless harmonically malleable, full of tonal and diatonic possibilities, and is employed freely to create a dodecaphonic work with an unmistakable Stravinskian stamp.

Around the same time, according to Stephen Walsh (SSE, 362), Robert Craft persuaded Stravinsky to supply the missing parts for a score that Craft was piecing together from motets of Carlo Gesualdo's *Sacrae cantiones* (completed in Naples in 1603). Instead of endeavouring to recreate accurately Gesualdo's enigmatic musical style, which may have presented its own challenges, Stravinsky once again put his own thumbprint on the centuries-old motets, producing *Tres sacrae cantiones* (1959). As he recalled in *Conversations*, 'the existing material was only my starting point: from it I recomposed the whole'.

Commissioned by (and also dedicated to) Paul SACHER, A SERMON, A NARRATIVE AND A PRAYER (1960–1) appears to serve as a New Testament counterpart to *Threni*, Stravinsky's Old Testament cantata, and it received its first performance in Basel in February 1962. In October 1961, T. S. ELIOT and Stravinsky met in London to discuss a proposal from Cambridge University Press that Stravinsky 'set to music two lyrical stanzas' from *Little Gidding*, but Eliot was quick to doubt that the stanzas could be set to music (*Dial*, 176). Nevertheless, Stravinsky went ahead and completed ANTHEM (1961–2), setting text from Part IV of Eliot's *Little Gidding*: 'The dove descending breaks the air'. Inspired by twelve-note technique, *Anthem* is characterised by contrapuntal devices that include the imitation between soprano and alto at the opening of the work, and rhythmic diminution and augmentation.

When T. S. Eliot passed away in 1965, Stravinsky responded that same year by writing INTROITUS (T. S. ELIOT IN MEMORIAM), once again featuring a male chorus. This work is illustrative of Stravinsky's use of SERIALISM for expressive purposes: the combination of twelve-note technique and the unusual instrumentation creates a heart-wrenching effect. He writes that 'the only novelty in serial treatment is in chord structure – the chant is punctuated by fragments of a chordal dirge' (T&C, 66). This results in a texture that echoes the use of harmonic stasis as accompaniment to chant-like melodies. A performance of *Introitus* by the choir of Westminster Abbey was part of the 'Homage to T. S. Eliot' that took place at the Globe Theatre in London on 14 June 1965.

REQUIEM CANTICLES (1965–6) was commissioned by Princeton University in honour of a major university benefactor in 1965, and Claudio SPIES was instrumental in coordinating the details of the first performance at Princeton in 1966. Documents in the Claudio Spies collection at the Library of Congress confirm that he was in close communication with both Craft and Stravinsky concerning the serial analysis of the work, and he published a detailed analysis the following year, illuminating both the inter- and intra-symmetry of its nine sections.

Stravinsky himself would pass away just five years after the première of *Requiem Canticles*. A performance of this work, conducted by Robert Craft, at San Giovanni e Paolo in Venice before the composer's body was taken to its final resting place at San Michele, made for a fitting musical epitaph. *Requiem Canticles* is written in the same Stravinskian language as his prior works, merely using a different vocabulary, tying together elements of all his stylistic periods and all of his characteristic instrumental and choral tendencies into a singular work of great brevity, yet packed with religious piety and intense emotion.

Throughout his various stylistic periods, the choral medium served Stravinsky's compositional evolution well, and his choral works stretch from his early Russian period through his neo-classical, contrapuntal compositions to his serial experimentations. He treats the chorus as an equal partner in his combined works and accords text equal status within the musical narrative. The influence of poetic versification is evident in many of his instrumental works, particularly those from his neo-classical and serial periods. His text sources are wide-ranging, encompassing Russian poetry (though not always in its original language), Slavonic and Latin biblical and liturgical texts, and poetry spanning from late medieval England to contemporary works by T. S. Eliot. Even so, his choral music should not be viewed in isolation from the rest of his work, but as an integral part of his compositional output and as always representative of his developing preoccupations.

MAUREEN CARR AND PHILLIP TORBERT

Robert Craft, 'A concert for Saint Mark', *The Score*, 8 (1956), 35, 44–5.
Expo; SCW

Chorale. Composed 1918–20 (*Symphonies d'instruments à vent*). First published December 1920 in the *Revue musicale* (PARIS) – supplement: 'Tombeau de Claude Debussy' – as 'Fragment des Symphonies pour [*sic*] instruments à vent a la mémoire de C. A. Debussy' ('Copyright 1920 by J. & W. Chester and Co'.), 1926 (ed. Arthur Lourié: London, Boosey & Hawkes). Dedicated 'à la mémoire de Claude Achille Debussy'.

Stravinsky initiated composition of *Chorale*, later to become the final section of SYMPHONIES OF WIND INSTRUMENTS, on 26 March 1918 upon hearing of the death of DEBUSSY. Taruskin (1997) makes the correlation between this funereal 'rite' and the conclusion of the Russian Orthodox *panikhida* service, particularly its three-fold presentation of *Vechnaya pamyat'* ('Eternal remembrance'). Yet the work's understated dignity, enhanced by characteristically Stravinskian chord-spacings, also qualifies *Chorale* as an ur neo-classical statement: devoid of agogic markings, demonstratively non-expressive and 'objective'. In anticipation of the conclusion to the SYMPHONY OF PSALMS, to borrow from ANSERMET, it admirably 'expresses the religiosity of others'.   GRAHAM GRIFFITHS

Graham Griffiths, *Stravinsky's Piano: Genesis of a Musical Language* (Cambridge University Press, 2013).
Richard Taruskin, *Defining Russia Musically* (Princeton University Press, 1997).

Choreographers, Choreography and Dancers. A list of Stravinsky's choreographers reads as both a 'who's who' of early- to mid-twentieth-century classical dance and a brief history of some of its most notable developments. Intricately linked with the comings and goings of DIAGHILEV'S BALLETS RUSSES – for whom all bar two of Stravinsky's BALLET scores between 1910 and 1929 were composed – the artists he collaborated with during his early career were those with the company and in favour with Diaghilev. His earliest ballets, The FIREBIRD (1910) and PETRUSHKA (1911), were created by then chief choreographer Mikhail FOKINE, who had set out to reform the stolid and formulaic classical style comprising of an endless stream of *divertissements*, pas de deux, variations and set pieces for the corps de ballet. He instead pursued a naturalistic choreographic approach – i.e. the look and style of a dance reflected the context, character and narrative – and greater integration of the arts. He was able to realize his ideas fully within the fertile environment of the Ballets Russes.

Fokine found Stravinsky's music for both The Firebird and Petrushka challenging, and so it seems fitting that the musical revolution of The RITE OF SPRING (1913) was choreographed by Vaslav NIJINSKY, whose own reforms made Fokine's appear dated and quaint. Nijinsky's brief choreographic career saw him rejecting the most fundamental tenets of ballet; he experimented with its very foundations. For The Rite, the traditional classical turnout was inverted (giving the appearance of 'pigeon toes') while prized qualities such as lightness and a long line were banished in favour of a round-shouldered inward body shape, heavy stamping and flat-footed jumps. But, just as Stravinsky's music soon turned away from The Rite's barbaric sound world, so Nijinsky's approach remained a one-off. Stravinsky's next ballets would be in a very different style.

The immediate postwar ballets (mostly conceived during the war) saw Stravinsky work closely with Léonide Massine, who would become known for his vivid and stylised characterisations and dynamic use of movement. He choreographed the first productions of The Song of the Nightingale (1920) and Pulcinella (1920), and in these he synthesised a wide range of dance styles and often used gesture and mime in addition to dance. In the same year, he re-set The Rite for its first presentation since Nijinsky left the company, and the contrast with his predecessor became evident: Nijinsky had set every beat, while Massine stressed he was working in counterpoint to Stravinsky's score. Lydia Sokolova, who danced in both versions, remarked also on the sadness that permeated Nijinsky's, which was quite different from Massine's.

A different aesthetic was brought in when Bronislava Nijinska became chief choreographer. Inspired by the pioneering work of her brother (Nijinsky) and the major artistic developments happening in the newly founded Soviet Union (she was based there 1914–21), Nijinska choreographed three Stravinsky works, of which the ballet Les Noces (1923) stands as a remarkable statement of intent. The austere, collective ceremony she staged (it was criticised as being 'Marxist') was enhanced by the powerful and muted visual design eventually produced by Natalya Goncharova (Nijinska had refused to choreograph to the original colourful designs approved by Diaghilev and Stravinsky).

It is at this point that the Diaghilev–Stravinsky link becomes more fractured, with Apollon Musagète (1928) and The Fairy's Kiss (1928), both commissioned by wealthy female patrons: Apollo by Elizabeth Sprague Coolidge for her festival at the Library of Congress, Washington, DC; and The Fairy's Kiss by Ida Rubinstein for her new company. The Diaghilev connection between artists is ever present, however: ex-Diaghilev dancer Adolph Bolm, by then based in the United States, choreographed the first production of Apollo, while Nijinska created The Fairy's Kiss. Significantly, though Apollo was an American commission, Stravinsky distanced himself from the production and did not attend the première, instead focusing his attentions on the Ballets Russes production (presented six weeks later) which was choreographed by the company's last chief choreographer, George Balanchine.

Stravinsky's neo-classical turn found its supreme interpreter in Balanchine, whose choreographic vocabulary drew so strongly on ballet's classical heritage but was imbued with a new sense of purpose. Through their work together for the Ballets Russes (Balanchine had also created a version of Chant for the company in 1925), they established a relationship that continued to develop after Diaghilev's death in 1929. Both made America their home – not insignificantly, Balanchine founded various companies, including, ultimately, the New York City Ballet – and the result was that, of the five new ballet scores Stravinsky composed over the rest of his lifetime, Balanchine choreographed four of them: Jeu de cartes (1937), The Ballet of the Elephants (1942, later Circus Polka), Orpheus (1948) and Agon (1957). Throughout his career, Balanchine also extensively choreographed new ballets to existing Stravinsky scores, and re-set Stravinsky ballets originally created by others. The one new ballet

Balanchine was not involved in during this period was SCÈNES DE BALLET (1944), a segment in a Billy Rose Broadway revue which was choreographed by Anton DOLIN, another former Ballets Russes dancer.

Outside of ballet, choreographers collaborated with Stravinsky on an array of other theatrical works. In many cases, there was a crossover in artistic personnel because Diaghilev produced them, but on other occasions Stravinsky worked with choreographers he otherwise did not encounter. Boris ROMANOV choreographed The NIGHTINGALE (1914), George and Ludmilla PITOËFF directed and staged The SOLDIER'S TALE (1918) (including the dance elements), Nijinska created RENARD and MAVRA (both 1922), and Kurt Jooss was responsible for PERSÉPHONE (1934). The 1962 made-for-television The FLOOD had choreography by Balanchine; it was Stravinsky's final new work featuring dance.

As for the dancers involved in Stravinsky premières, this was largely dictated by who was then with the commissioning ballet companies and who was supported or deemed suitable for the roles by the choreographer (or others). The first seasons of the Ballets Russes were dominated by Russian-trained dancers, but over time the company became increasingly international (even if the Russianified names belie this). Of the dancers particularly associated with Stravinsky, Tamara KARSAVINA starred in both Fokine–Stravinsky works (as the title role in The Firebird and the Ballerina in Petrushka) and created principal roles for Massine in Chant and Pulcinella. Lydia Sokolova danced in multiple productions of the same ballets: both Rites (creating the Chosen One in Massine's version), both Chants (as Death), and in the première of The Nightingale. Stanislas Idzikowski was another regular in the early 1920s, creating roles in The Song of the Nightingale, Pulcinella and Renard.

The choreographers themselves also often starred: Fokine and his wife, Vera Fokina, danced Ivan Tsarevich and Tsarevna in the first The Firebird; Massine created the title role in Pulcinella to great acclaim; Nijinska danced as the Fox in Renard (and, not insignificantly, also danced in the premières of The Firebird and Petrushka); and Balanchine performed as the Mechanical Nightingale in his own Chant. The exception was Nijinsky, who created the iconic puppet Petrushka for Fokine but did not dance in The Rite (it was the only ballet he choreographed but didn't feature in).

Other notable dancers from Stravinsky's earlier ballet premières include the ballet master Enrico CECCHETTI, who created character roles in Petrushka and Pulcinella; Maria PILTZ, who was Nijinsky's Chosen One (The Rite); Ida Rubinstein, who led both theatrical works Stravinsky composed for her; Felia Doubrovska and Léon Wozikowsky, who were the Bride and Groom in Les Noces; Adolph Bolm, Ruth PAGE, Elise REIMAN and Berenice HOLMES who danced Apollo and his muses for the première of Apollon Musagète; and Serge LIFAR, Alice Nikitina, Lubov Tchernicheva and Doubrovska who presented Balanchine's Ballets Russes version soon after.

The US Balanchine–Stravinsky ballets featured some of the choreographer's most renowned interpreters, with William Dollar as the Joker in Jeu de cartes, and a cast for Orpheus that included Nicholas Magallanes (Orpheus), Francisco Moncion (Dark Angel), Maria Tallchief (Eurydice), Beatrice Tompkins (Leader of the Furies) and Tanaquil LeClerq (Leader of the

Bacchanates). The première of *Agon* by New York City Ballet had roles for Todd Bolender, Melissa Hayden, Diana Adams and Arthur Mitchell, while, for *The Flood*, Balanchine drew on the talents of Jacques d'Amboise, Jilliana, Edward Villela and Ramon Segarra. Nevertheless, perhaps Stravinsky's most unique interpreter was Miss Modoc the elephant, the star of the Ringling Brothers and Barnum & Bailey Circus, who, along with forty-nine other elephants and fifty dancers (including Vera Zorina) premièred the Balanchine–Stravinsky *Ballet of the Elephants*.   SOPHIE REDFERN

Lynn Garafola, *Diaghilev's Ballets Russes* (New York: Oxford University Press, 1989).

Stephanie Jordan and Larraine Nicholas, *Stravinsky the Global Dancer: A Chronology of Choreography to the Music of Igor Stravinsky*, online database, University of Roehampton, London: http://urweb.roehampton.ac.uk/stravinsky/index.asp.

Charles M. Joseph, *Stravinsky and Balanchine: A Journey of Invention* (New Haven and London: Yale University Press, 2002).

Cingria, Charles-Albert   (born Geneva, 10 February 1883; died Geneva, 1 August 1954). A Swiss writer, musician and musicologist who profoundly influenced Stravinsky's compositional process through his friendship and his diverse intellectual explorations.

Towards the end of 1932, Cingria gave a copy of his newly published *Pétrarque* to Stravinsky, with an inscription comparing it to Stravinsky's own Duo Concertant. In this copy, housed at the Paul Sacher Stiftung (Foundation), Stravinsky underlined a passage regarding the need to observe rules in poetry, commenting in the margin that this remark could be generalised for other forms of art. Cingria also included a French translation of the original text *Dialogue between Joy and Reason* (from 1366) that inspired Stravinsky to experiment with some musical ideas for a setting of part of the text that he never finished, though a fragment surfaced in the music for Perséphone (1933–4).

Cingria had some input into Stravinsky's article 'Igor Strawinsky nous parle de "Perséphone"', which appeared in *Excelsior* on 29 April 1934, shortly before the première of *Perséphone*. This article is often referred to as Stravinsky's 'manifesto' and several parallels can be drawn between it, Nietzsche's 'musical mood' and Cingria's 'l'ivresse musicale'. The statement 'music is, by its very nature, essentially powerless to *express* anything at all, whether a feeling, an attitude of mind, a psychological mood, a phenomenon of nature', shows the influence of Nietzsche on Stravinsky, or perhaps on Walter Nouvel, Stravinsky's ghost writer for An Autobiography. As Nietzsche put it: 'The will itself and feelings ... are totally incapable of representing feelings or having feelings for its subject, the will being its only subject'. Some of these sentiments are shared in a published interview for Radio Paris co-authored by Stravinsky and Cingria.

It is clear that Cingria and Stravinsky were loyal friends from their first meeting in 1914 until Cingria's death. The magnitude of Cingria's influence on Stravinsky is evident from the volume of their correspondence – fifty-four letters, according to Stéphane Pétermann, Maryke de Courten and Alessio Christen of the Cingria Archive at the University of Lausanne. His importance is also manifest through Stravinsky's interest in *Pétrarque* and other Cingria writings, through Cingria's writings about and reviews of performances by

Stravinsky (sixteen texts appear in Cingria's *Œuvres complètes*), through Cingria's collaboration with Stravinsky in writing the article in *Excelsior* (1934), in the interview for Radio Paris (1936), and in their possible intellectual collaboration for passages in the *Autobiography* (*Chroniques de ma vie*) and POETICS.

A number of documents, including correspondence from Stravinsky to Cingria, can be found at the Archive of the Centre de recherches sur les lettres romandes (CRLR) at the University of Lausanne. Doris Jakkubec's Introduction to the first volume of the current Cingria edition provides a brilliant overview of his written works that takes into account his remarkable life, filled with travel and adventure.   MAUREEN CARR

Maureen A. Carr, *Multiple Masks: Neoclassicism in Stravinsky's Works on Greek Subjects* (Lincoln: University of Nebraska Press, 2002), xxii.

Charles-Albert Cingria, *Complete Works of Charles-Albert Cingria*, 2nd edn (Lausanne: Éditions L'Âge d'Homme, 2013–).

Cinq Doigts, Les – 8 Easy Pieces for Piano. Composed 1921, Garches. First performance, 15 December 1921, Salle des Agriculteurs, Paris; piano, Jean Wiener. Published 1922, J. & W. Chester, London. Order of movements: (I) Andante (II) Allegro (III) Allegretto (IV) Larghetto (V) Moderato (VI) Lento (VII) Vivo (VIII) Pesante.

Transcription: For player piano: *Rondeaux* (1922) – Pleyela/Odéola: 8448–8449.

Arrangement: *Eight Instrumental Miniatures for Fifteen Players* (1962). First performance (Mvts. 1–4), 26 March 1962, LOS ANGELES (Monday Evening Concerts). Conductor, Robert CRAFT. First complete performance, 29 April 1962, Toronto (Massey Hall). Conductor, Igor Stravinsky. Published 1963, J. & W. Chester, London. Dedication: Lawrence Morton. Order of movements: (I) Andantino (II) Vivace (III) Lento (IV) Allegretto (V) Moderato alla breve (VI) Tempo di Marcia (VII) Larghetto (VIII) Tempo di Tango.

Demonstrating Stravinsky's consistent interest in didactic piano literature (e.g. THREE EASY PIECES, FIVE EASY PIECES and, for professionals, the FOUR STUDIES), *Les Cinq Doigts* ('The Five Fingers') is another collection of appealing miniatures originally intended for his children. Their musical discourse helpfully revolves around a constant play of limited options disguised under a varied and colourful mantle that refers stylistically to both Russian and neo-classical models (e.g. *Pribaoutki*, The SOLDIER'S TALE, PULCINELLA). The suite presents a set of gently 'progressive studies' with regard to notation and technique: for example, the final movement develops independence in the third and fourth fingers of the left hand. The underlying pedagogic intent of *Les Cinq Doigts* can best be observed through the restriction of the right hand to a single five-note position, its fingering indicated at the head of each movement. Throughout, the musical syntax reflects that technical aspect so characteristic of Stravinsky's early neo-classical idiom, the pieces resembling a pack of construction kits designed for eager young fingers to assemble step-by-step. Grounded in the processes of trial and error, *Les Cinq Doigts* is based upon those patterns of varied repetition that epitomise the evolutionary process of musical development. It was a dialectic that appealed to the neo-classical Stravinsky for its balance between construction, de(con)struction, and re-construction. The arrangement for ensemble, as *Eight Instrumental Miniatures*, re-orders and re-titles some movements with occasional canonic re-composition.

GRAHAM GRIFFITHS

Circus Polka. Subtitled: 'for a young elephant'. Commissioned by the Ringling Bros. and Barnum & Bailey Circus for a circus BALLET featuring fifty tutu-clad elephants and fifty human ballet dancers, and first performed in a band arrangement by David Raksin under M. Evans at Madison Square Garden, New York City, on 9 April 1942. Raksin's arrangement was published in 1948 (Associated Music Press). The circus reportedly ran for no fewer than 425 performances (*SCW*, 414). The work was originally written for piano in 1941–2, completed in its piano version on 5 February 1942, and published by Associated Music Press later that year. Stravinsky made his own instrumentation of the work, dated 5 October 1942 but not performed until 13 January 1944, in Cambridge, Mass., by the Boston Symphony Orchestra under the composer, and published in the same year (Associated Music Press and Schott). The work's curious subtitle was an allusion to Stravinsky's response to the initial pitch made over the phone by George BALANCHINE who was choreographing the show: the composer agreed to the commission on the sole condition that the performing elephants be 'very young'.

JEREMY COLEMAN

Clarens. Clarens is a small village in south-west SWITZERLAND, at the north-east side of Lake Geneva and part of an area often known as the Swiss Riviera, which also attracted Maurice RAVEL, and the conductor, Ernest ANSERMET. Stravinsky recalled that Ansermet 'introduced himself to me in a street in Clarens one day in 1911', having moved there the previous year in search of a climate conducive to his wife's health (*T&C*, 229). They became very good friends and Ansermet later worked on Stravinsky's music in the 1920s. Two significant works, both for DIAGHILEV's BALLETS RUSSES, were largely composed here: The RITE OF SPRING (staged 1913) and PULCINELLA (staged 1920). Stravinsky composed a significant portion of *The Rite of Spring* at their family pension in Clarens, where most of the score was finished by spring 1912. Stravinsky later described the room in which he worked when composing *The Rite*, noting that the 'only furniture was a small upright piano which I kept muted (I always worked at a muted piano), a table, and two chairs' (*Expo*, 141). This reference provides an important insight into his compositional process, particularly in relation to the role the piano played in the creation of the work. The manuscript sketches are dated, and page 88 includes the message 'Today, 4/II 1912, Sunday, with an unbearable toothache I finished the music of the *Sacre*. I. Stravinsky, Clarens, Châtelard Hotel' (Hill 2000, 24). Stravinsky returned to Clarens at times to compose and to experience the healthier climate, notably moving there in the winter of 1913–14. Published family albums include photographs of the composer at Hôtel du Châtalard (*Sfam*). It was at Clarens that Stravinsky played Diaghilev extracts of two new works – 'Russian Dance' and 'Petrushka's Cry' – following which Diaghilev suggested the creation of another ballet

(Scheijen 2009, 213). The open air in Clarens seemed conducive to his
work.   HELEN JULIA MINORS

Peter Hill, Stravinsky, The Rite of Spring (Cambridge University Press, 2000).
Sjeng Scheijen, Diaghilev: A Life, trans. Jane Hedley-Prôle and S. J. Leinbach (London: Profile
   Books, 2009).

Claudel, Paul   (born Villeneuve-sur-Fère, France, 6 August 1868; died Paris,
23 February 1955). French Catholic dramatist and poet, known as
a reactionary in his religious and political ideas, but also as an innovator in
both verse form and theatrical production. The so-called verset claudélien, as
featured in Cinq Grandes Odes (1911), is a form of unrhymed free verse of widely
varying lengths, written for declamation and based on the structural techniques
of Latin psalms. Claudel's plays, which were long believed to be unstageable
thanks to their great length, explore the conflict between morality and passion,
presenting extreme forms of suffering as part of a divine plan, as in Le Partage de
midi (1911) and L'Annonce faite à Marie (1912). Le Soulier de Satin (1929), his best-
known play, is eleven hours long, and was influenced by avant-garde European
drama and Japanese Noh theatre, using music and a cinema screen to create
a multimedia experience. Claudel enjoyed a long career as a diplomat (1893–
1935), and, during his posting in Rio de Janeiro from 1917 to 1919, Darius
MILHAUD served as his secretary. Milhaud was heavily influenced by Claudel's
ideas on music, and composed music for several of his works. Stravinsky first
met Claudel before World War I at a performance by the BALLETS RUSSES, and
from the outset there was little personal sympathy between them. Stravinsky
disliked Claudel's intellectual dogmatism and moralising tendency, and
disagreed vehemently with his article of 1938 'Le Poison wagnérien' (The
Wagnerian poison). Yet, when he attended a concert of SERENADE later
that year, Claudel had something of a revelation, writing to the composer:

> What an Elysian language you make music speak! What perfection! What
> sovereign elegance! The concentration of the entire soul in what is heard
> obviates the need for words, ideas, even feelings, leaving attention only for
> the divine voices, which make music together, and separate only in order to
> recombine. But how to introduce a foreign element into this superior and
> self-sufficient world? The chief impression that I retain from yesterday
> evening, one of the most beautiful in my artistic life, is one of intimidation.

When Ida RUBINSTEIN approached the pair hoping to commission
a large-scale stage work with choir and speaking roles, Stravinsky suggested the story of Prometheus, another Homeric myth along the lines of
PERSÉPHONE. Claudel, however, proceeded instead to write a version of the
biblical story of Tobit, to which Stravinsky was on principle opposed,
leaving Claudel to remark, 'We were not meant to collaborate. You are too
great a musician, and we could never have penetrated each other's minds.'

                                                                    DAVID EVANS

Coates, Albert   (born St Petersburg, 23 April 1882; died Cape Town, South Africa,
11 December 1953). British conductor. Coates spent his early childhood in
RUSSIA before attending school and university in England. He returned to

Russia where he studied composition with RIMSKY-KORSAKOV before going to the Leipzig Conservatory, where his teachers included Julius Klengel (cello) and Arthur Nikisch (conducting). After working at opera houses in Elberfeld, Dresden and Mannheim, he started conducting at the Mariinsky Theatre in St Petersburg in 1910, where he was appointed Principal Conductor of the company then known as the Imperial Mariinsky Theatre. After the 1917 Revolution, Coates was appointed 'President of all Opera Houses' in the USSR, but in April 1919 he left Russia and settled in England where he worked regularly at Covent Garden and with the London Symphony Orchestra (whose chief conductor he was from 1919 to 1922).

On 31 March 1915, Coates and Alexander ZILOTI played a private performance of The NIGHTINGALE (on piano four hands) for the committee of the Imperial Theatres, and Coates subsequently conducted the work's Russian première in May 1918. In October 1924, Coates recorded a slightly abridged version of the 1911 Suite from The FIREBIRD and, between October 1927 and February 1928, he made a complete recording of PETRUSHKA with the London Symphony Orchestra. This is a notable landmark in the Stravinsky discography: the work's earliest electric recording (its only predecessor was an acoustic recording conducted by Goossens), and a performance of remarkable assurance, brilliant colour and rhythmic energy.   NIGEL SIMEONE

SCS; SRT, I

Cocteau, Jean (born Maisons-Laffitte, near Paris, 5 July 1889; died Milly-la-forêt, near Paris, 11 October 1963). A multi-disciplinary creator, over the course of his career Cocteau worked as a poet, novelist, playwright, filmmaker, aesthetic philosopher and visual artist. Equal parts avant-garde innovator and shameless self-promoter, he holds an ambiguous position in histories of MODERNISM. There is also ambivalence in his relationship with Stravinsky. Although at times the two men worked closely together, their relationship was equally characterised by periods of distance and moments of pique, suspicion and jealousy.

Having achieved a modicum of fame as the author of witty and precious verses, Cocteau attached himself to Sergey DIAGHILEV and the BALLETS RUSSES. Hoping to enhance his position by associating with the most popular and scandalous company in pre-war Paris, Cocteau penned the libretto for Le Diable Bleu. This work premièred in 1912 with music by Reynaldo Hahn, but was mediocre and poorly received and led to Diaghilev's exasperated exhortation for Cocteau to 'Astound me!'

It wasn't until the explosive première of Stravinsky's The RITE OF SPRING in 1913 that Cocteau fully understood what Diaghilev was asking for. Having first met the composer in 1910, Cocteau approached him after the première of the Rite with a proposal for a BALLET based on carnival and circus themes. Although David (as the ballet was to be called) was never realised (it would ultimately turn into Parade, Cocteau's 1917 collaboration with PICASSO and SATIE), the proposed partnership initiated a long series of interactions between the two men that would profoundly affect the lives and careers of both.

The next stage of interaction, however, was not particularly positive. With the commencement of World War I, Parisian culture took a conservative turn, and Cocteau unexpectedly emerged as a key representative of the so-called 'return to order'. In his aesthetic treatise *The Cock and the Harlequin* (1918), he argued for the restoration of clarity and sobriety to art, qualities he associated with the French national character. Even though he had previously travelled in cosmopolitan circles, he now vilified the foreign influence on French art. Stravinsky was one of the artists he singled out for attack. 'Wagner, Stravinsky, and even Debussy are first-rate octopuses', he wrote; 'Whoever goes near them is sore put to it to escape from their tentacles.' Stravinsky's foreign music surrounded and smothered the auditor, blurring boundaries and threatening critical, rational autonomy. What was needed was a bracing dose of clear, objective, Gallic art: 'The music I want must be French', he wrote, 'of France' (Cocteau 1926, 17–18).

Interestingly, this attack on Stravinsky's foreignness corresponds with a change in the composer's music. Whether this change was influenced by Cocteau or by the general wartime atmosphere and Stravinsky's experiences is difficult to say. But, from about 1917, the Russian composer entered into a neo-classical phase whose characteristics of order, clarity and engagement with tradition have significant connections to the aesthetic elaborated by Cocteau.

By the mid-1920s, the two men had re-established regular contact. This was a difficult period for Stravinsky. Cut off from his homeland by the war and the Russian Revolution, his financial situation was parlous, in addition to which he found that his increasing estrangement from the Russian language made the composition of large-scale vocal works impossible. In the summer of 1925, he began to see Cocteau frequently. The poet was staying in Villefranche in the south of FRANCE, just 2 kilometres from Stravinsky's home. Cocteau had undergone another transformation since the two artists had last been in contact. Thrown into a terrible depression by the death of his lover, Raymond Radiguet, Cocteau had sought comfort and solace from the conservative theologian Jacques MARITAIN, and by the mid-1920s had returned to Catholicism. In the wake of his conversations with Cocteau, Stravinsky made his own religious turn. During Russian Holy Week in 1926, he returned to the RUSSIAN ORTHODOX CHURCH and shortly afterwards invited an Orthodox priest to live with his family. In June of 1926, the composer met Maritain in person.

Stravinsky's turn to religion would have a powerful impact on his music as well. Inspired by a biography of St Francis of Assisi (which he read as part of his immersion in religious literature), he decided to turn away from quotidian language and to compose his next major vocal work – the opera-oratorio OEDIPUS REX – in Latin. Shortly after returning from ITALY (where he experienced the 'miraculous' healing of an infected finger prior to a concert), Stravinsky invited Cocteau to write the libretto for *Oedipus*. Cocteau's influence seems to be present in the content of this work as well. In contrast to works such as PULCINELLA, that deal with the classical past in a playful and ironic fashion, *Oedipus* is characterised by its static and monumental nature and the radical depersonalisation of its masked staging. It calls to mind both Cocteau's obsession with the order and clarity of the French classical tradition, and Maritain's call for 'the deindividualization of personal expression' in art, and a 'return to a quasi-medieval ideal of humility and anonymity, and a divine concept of order' (SCS, 499).

Stravinsky and Cocteau would never work so closely again. Both would continue to metamorphose as artists and individuals in ways that would put distance between them. With the outbreak of World War II, Stravinsky would emigrate to the UNITED STATES, and eventually embrace SERIALISM, while Cocteau would remain in Paris and, after somewhat ambivalent behaviour during the Occupation, become a Surrealist-inspired filmmaker. However, in spite of both geographical and artistic difference, a bond of closeness remained. More than 70 years old and terribly ill, Cocteau dedicated poetry in his final collection, Requiem, to the Russian composer. While Stravinsky refused to record a get-well message for Cocteau, stating that 'Cocteau can't die without making publicity out of it', he nevertheless broke down in tears when the poet did actually die. Robert CRAFT, who was present when the composer received news of the deaths of other friends, remembered that he had never seen him so distressed.   IHOR JUNYK

Commedia dell'arte. A form of Italian popular culture in the street-theatre tradition, the commedia dell'arte first emerged in Rome in the sixteenth century. It featured performances improvised around stock plots and recurring, often grotesque, masked characters – the clownish Harlequin, the pompous Il Dottore, the greedy Pantalone, etc. Almost immediately, it spread to northern ITALY and other European nations. It was especially beloved in FRANCE where its popularity eclipsed even its status in its country of origin.

From early in its history, the commedia dell'arte also exerted a profound influence on élite culture. Jean-Antoine Watteau (1684–1721) and Jean-Honoré Fragonard (1732–1806) both frequently painted stock commedia dell'arte characters, while the plot conventions of the commedia can be seen in such diverse works as the plays of Molière and the Italian operatic tradition of Rossini, VERDI and Puccini.

The commedia dell'arte was an object of long-standing fascination for Stravinsky. Its influence can be seen in PETRUSHKA, a 1910 BALLET COLLABORATION between the composer and Alexandre BENOIS. The scenario melds motifs from Russian folk puppetry with the commedia dell'arte. The artists reimagine Petrushka (a comic jester puppet character) as a kind of Slavic Pierrot and re-stage the classic story of Pierrot, Harlequin and Columbina as the tragic love triangle of Petrushka, the Moor and the Ballerina. Many of the classic commedia dell'arte elements are present, but exoticised and Russified.

Stravinsky's most intense engagement with the commedia dell'arte was to come a few years later. He encountered the commedia firsthand during his famous trip to Italy with PICASSO and COCTEAU in 1917. In his Conversations with Robert CRAFT, he notes that he and Picasso 'were both much impressed with the commedia dell'arte, which we saw in a crowded little room reeking of garlic. The Pulcinella was a great drunken lout whose every gesture, and probably every word if I had understood, was obscene' (Conv, 104–5).

After this trip, commedia dell'arte motifs began to appear in the works of all the participants. For Picasso, this was most evident in the neo-classical drop curtain he painted for the BALLETS RUSSES production Parade. But references to stock commedia dell'arte characters also emerged in numerous works of the interwar period, in both neo-classical and cubist styles. Cocteau followed suit, titling his influential work of interwar aesthetic theory (a key work in the so-called *rappel à l'ordre*) *The Cock and the Harlequin*.

As for Stravinsky, in the period immediately following the Italian journey, he collaborated with Picasso and Léonide MASSINE on the Ballets Russes production PULCINELLA. Massine transformed the *commedia dell'arte* play *The Four Identical Pulcinellas* (1700) that he found in the Naples Public Library into a BALLET scenario, while Stravinsky provided the music by developing, arranging and orchestrating a series of fragments attributed to the eighteenth-century Neapolitan composer Giovanni Battista PERGOLESI.

Critics have been sharply divided over the meaning and significance of the *commedia dell'arte* in Stravinsky's work and in interwar MODERNISM more generally. In a very influential interpretation, the critic Kenneth Silver has seen the fascination with the *commedia dell'arte* as part of a more general rightward drift in modernism during and immediately after World War I (Silver 1989, 119). At a time of increased nationalism and chauvinism, the *commedia dell'arte* was appealing because it signified a distinctly 'Latin' tradition. In *The Cock and the Harlequin* (mentioned above), Cocteau is at pains to emphasise the rationality and clarity of French *latinité* and to distinguish it from the irrationality and Romanticism of the Germanic and Slavic national characters. For artists such as Stravinsky who stood outside of the French national tradition and participated in the cosmopolitan avant-garde community of PARIS, the invocation of the *commedia dell'arte* was a way of appeasing the French nationalists, of signifying an allegiance to French values, of throwing his lot in on the French side.

But there are difficulties with this interpretation. As we have seen, Stravinsky's interest in the *commedia dell'arte* preceded the war. Further, it is possible to see Stravinsky's interwar use of the *commedia dell'arte* in very different terms from those elaborated by Silver. Arguably, the *commedia dell'arte* is an odd form to use as a signifier of cultural purity. With its emphasis on burlesque, satire, disguise and reversal, it seems closer to the subversive and anti-authoritarian sensibility that Mikhail Bakhtin called the 'carnivalesque'. Understood in this way, Stravinsky's use of the *commedia dell'arte* (as well as Picasso's) might be seen as a complex negotiation of wartime nationalist pressures: a superficial nod to Latin tradition that rehabilitates, at a deeper level, a modernist commitment to fluidity, hybridity and unstable identity.

Consider, for example, Stravinsky's contribution to the *Pulcinella* collaboration. While utilising the music of Western classicism, Stravinsky distorts the 'Pergolesi' fragments in significant ways. Both Robert Craft and Richard Taruskin have identified this distortion as stemming in part from the introduction of eastern European harmonies, rhythms and arrangements (Craft quoted in Whittall 1977, 51; SRT, 1502). The music, then, not only enacts precisely the carnivalesque masquerade of the plot (in which Pulcinella frequently appears in disguise), but also undermines the purity of Latin classicism in favour of cosmopolitan hybridity. In this, *Pulcinella* might be seen as the inverse of *Petrushka*. While the latter work expanded Russian popular culture by putting it into contact with the *commedia dell'arte*, the former problematises a purely Latin *commedia* by showing (in Richard Taruskin's words) that 'beady Scythian eyes seem to glint behind the mask of European urbanity' (SRT, 1505).

It is notable that Stravinsky would return to these *commedia dell'arte* themes and motifs in the Suite Italienne of the 1930s – a time even more radically committed to the idea of cultural purity.   IHOR JUNYK

Jean Cocteau, *A Call to Order*, trans. Rollo Myers (London: Faber and Gwyer, 1926).
Kenneth Silver, *Esprit de Corps: The Art of the Parisian Avant-Garde and the First World War*, 1914–1925 (Princeton University Press, 1989).
Arnold Whittall, *Music Since the First World War* (New York: St Martin's Press, 1977).

Compositional Process. For a composer whose work spans three relatively clear and different periods, Stravinsky's compositional process remained remarkably consistent throughout his life. From the setting he preferred, to the materials he used, the tools of his trade were relatively fixed. When it came time to compose, some very specific musical idea almost always served as a point of departure. This idea was then placed in a context of rules and limits that forced creativity. As ideas developed, they formed larger passages of material, which then were arranged and rearranged. It was this bottom-up approach – beginning with something very specific and building larger passages from it – that served him so well throughout his career.

Almost every creative person has an ideal atmosphere for working; Stravinsky was no exception. Stravinsky himself and those around him have left us with a pretty clear picture of what the Russian master required if focused work was to get done. While he did not demand a large room, it did need to be secluded to minimise interruptions. It needed to be as soundproof as possible. (He could not tolerate the idea of his unfinished musings being heard by others.) Second, he required a piano. Again, it need not be large, nor even perfectly in tune. An upright grand often sufficed, especially considering he most often muted the piano anyway. Third, he needed a large desk, not only for his manuscript paper (which would eventually be bound into portable notebooks), but also for his many pencils, sharpeners, inks, and, of course, his Stravigor, the special tool he designed for drawing musical staves. Indeed, more than one source described his tools and workspace as akin 'to those of a surgeon'. If space permitted, a small table was reserved for cigarettes, an ashtray, whisky and a deck of playing cards.

When it came time to actually generate new material, Stravinsky worked primarily bottom-up, starting with a very specific idea in mind that was subjected to various developments. In The Rite of Spring, for example, there is the famous 'Augurs' chord, consisting of an E♭ dominant seventh combined with E major. In the 'Grand chorale' from The Soldier's Tale, there is the melody from 'A mighty fortress is Our God' and the two intervalically equivalent tetrachords (D-C♯-B-A and G-F♯-E-D) extracted from it. In the Concerto for Piano and Wind Instruments, there is the Baroque theme he scribbled on a page torn from a small pocket calendar several weeks before composing began in earnest. From the Symphony of Psalms, there is the 'Psalms' chord and the more vague idea of 'two minor thirds joined by a major third'. For the Violin Concerto, there is the recurring and widely spaced chord d1-e2-a3 that appears at the start of each movement. In Memoriam Dylan Thomas and other late works feature very precise motivic ideas constructed within a major third.

These specific ideas seem to have been crucial starting points for most of his work.

Stravinsky believed in imposing limits on himself while composing. For him, 'the more controlled the art, the more free'. In the same way as we can find specific musical ideas at the core of each piece, so too can we discover the other compositional constraints he placed on himself. In the early Russian pieces, the constraint was often one of story, be it one of the big ballets, Song of the Volga Boatmen, or The SOLDIER'S TALE. In the neo-classical works, the constraints of course were supplied by the earlier epochs of musical style and genre on which he was commenting and from which he was borrowing. And in the late serial pieces, the constraints most often came in the form of a sacred text he had chosen and/or a specific tone row he had developed. In each case, the limits he placed on himself forced creativity.

Having decided on and explored the transformational potential of a specific motive or motivic cell, Stravinsky most often moved next to composing discrete 'chunks' of music that he could later arrange, like tiles in a mosaic. These musical 'blocks', as they are often called, form the trademark discontinuity so closely associated with Stravinsky. The motive itself will be subject to rhythmic displacement, here beginning on a strong beat, there beginning on a weak beat. In some cases, an unchanging part against a changing part is heard until all possible combinations occur, forming a sort of 'cycle'. In other places, he composed in phrases, starting with the beginning, then composing the ending, then filling in the intervening material.

Among the final steps for Stravinsky was arranging the discrete blocks of material into order. Time after time, we read how this was among the final steps. In the Rite, after composing the Augurs section, he finished the remainder of Part 1, then wrote the famous Introduction for it. In the Grand chorale, discrete phrases are reordered compared to his initial draft, and sometimes even transposed from their initial pitch level (and an entirely new final phrase is added at virtually the last minute). In the Piano Concerto, the primary piano solo is worked out first, then placed in a context of the Allegro. A slow introduction is the final step. In the third movement of that piece, the sketchbook shows discrete chunks of music composed on different types of paper and literally cut and pasted into place among the rest of the sketches, suggesting they were composed while on the move, and out of order. All of this points to a very non-linear style of construction. Indeed, it was only quite late in the game that he paid much attention to or began to formulate and envision what the piece would sound like from start to finish as a whole. Again, this is not surprising for a composer whose works are described as a series of disjunct 'moments' or 'blocks'. That seems to be part of the goal, and his working method made it easy to achieve.   DON TRAUT

Gretchen Horlacher, 'Running in place: sketches and superimposition in Stravinsky's music', Music Theory Spectrum, 23.2 (Autumn 2001), 196–216.
Joseph N. Straus, Stravinsky's Late Music (Cambridge University Press, 2001).
SCW

Concertino. Composed 1920; revised 1952. First performance of the revised version, 11 November 1952, Los Angeles Chamber Symphony Orchestra. Revised version published 1953, Wilhelm Hansen, Copenhagen.

The Concertino was originally written for string quartet in 1920 and was dedicated to the Flonzaley Quartet and to André de Caplet. The piece consists of one movement and was characterised by Stravinsky as a 'free sonata *allegro* with a definitely *concertante* part for the first violin' (*Auto*). The reference to the term 'sonata' is however to be treated with caution, the title 'concertino' may be misleading and no influence of the Baroque concerto grosso is to be found. The title is instead justified by the fact that the first violin plays an essentially soloistic part in the work.

The first part of the work is characterised by several changes of metre and shifts of stress, resulting in a rather harsh and impetuous-sounding sonic language. A contrasting Andante takes over at rehearsal figure 10 where the first violin develops material from the first part in a sprawling cadenza, with double stopping throughout – this segment (Figures 10–14) providing a tranquil episode between the two related Allegro sections.

Stravinsky recast the work in 1952, orchestrating it for twelve instruments: violin and cello, both obbligato, accompanied by ten wind players (flute, oboe, cor anglais, clarinet, 2 bassoons, 2 trumpets, tenor trombone, bass trombone). For the revised version, Stravinsky rebarred the work 'rather extensively' and clarified certain elements of harmony and phrasing. Bars are often contracted, single beats added, or downbeats omitted (cf. Figures 7–9). While the fast sections are now characterised by the sound of the winds, the violin cadenza from the string quartet original remains almost untouched and occupies a third of the length of the revised version. While both versions are based on the same material, they are distinguished by their distinctive instrumentation, and the version for twelve instruments is rather JAZZ-like in effect.

FLORIAN HENRI BESTHORN

Concerto for Piano and Wind Instruments. Composed 1923–4. First performance, 22 May 1924, Concerts Koussevitzky, Opera House, PARIS. Published 1924 (two-piano reduction), 1936 (full score), Édition Russe de Musique (Russischer Musikverlag). Copyright assigned in 1947 to Boosey & Hawkes who also published an edition incorporating revisions by the composer in 1960. Dedicated to Madame Natalie Koussevitzky.

Stravinsky began work on the Concerto for Piano and Wind Instruments in the summer of 1923 and completed it on 13 April 1924. The première was on 22 May 1924 at the Paris Opera House with the composer as featured soloist. (A performance for two pianos was given one week earlier at the residence of Princess de Polignac, an important supporter of Stravinsky and other artists of the time.) Indeed, with the Concerto, Stravinsky launched his career as a concert pianist, playing his own compositions for financial gain. He followed the Concerto with the SERENADE IN A, the PIANO SONATA, and the CAPRICCIO, all of which he alone was allowed to perform for several years after their composition. The extensive tours he launched – including his first trip to the UNITED STATES – ensured that the Concerto was among the first truly original compositions many heard in his new neo-classical style. Because of this, the piece has received more negative criticism than usual, including relatively extensive attention from such famous critics as Heinrich Schenker, Constant Lambert and Theodor ADORNO.

To be sure, the Piano Concerto exemplifies many of the traits commonly associated with Stravinsky's NEO-CLASSICISM. It is scored for solo piano – played primarily in a dry percussive manner – and wind instruments (with the addition of double bass). Further, as do many of his compositions from the 1920s, the Piano Concerto draws heavily on earlier styles, especially the Baroque. Its three movements conform to the 'fast-slow-fast' arrangement typical of a seventeenth-century concerto. The first movement, Allegro, begins and ends with a framing slow section featuring dotted rhythms reminiscent of a Handelian overture. Once underway, the Allegro portion conforms loosely to sonata form, featuring melodic ideas and textures similar to BACH inventions and clear quotations from Bach's *Musical Offering*. Indeed, the Piano Concerto is central to the 'back to Bach' fervour surrounding Stravinsky during this time. The second movement, Largo, is ternary, but with two extensive cadenzas separating each of the primary episodes. The full ensemble texture and a dash of rare rubato and virtuosity in the cadenzas give this movement an almost Romantic character. The third movement is something of a pastiche, moving easily from contrapuntal material to sections of JAZZ-influenced syncopation, to a surprising fugato. A return to the first-movement slow introduction ties the piece together prior to a last exciting presto flourish to the end.

While the pitch content of the Concerto defies simple categorisation, there are sufficient clear tonal references to argue that tonal pitch centres hold the piece together. Indeed, a recurring stepwise pattern emerges in each movement. Based on the A-B-C♯ motion of the bass line in the very first bar, this pattern is replicated as the Allegro gets under way, and the primary theme is heard first centred on A, then on B, before a forceful cadence on C. In the second movement, the pattern reverses as C major moves to A minor before return to C major. In the finale, clearly established tonal centres on C, D and E♭ precede the fugato in A♭, prior to the ending on C major. As a whole, then, the Concerto moves from A to C, but, taken all together, the key centres lend the piece an octatonic element as well: A♭-A-B-C-D-E♭. DON TRAUT

Donald G. Traut, *Stravinsky's 'Great Passacaglia': Recurring Elements in the Concerto for Piano and Wind Instruments* (University of Rochester Press, 2016).
Robert Morgan, 'Stravinsky: Concerto for piano and winds (first movement)', in *Anthology of Twentieth-Century Music* (New York: W. W. Norton, 1992), 138–73.

Concerto in D ('Basler Concerto'). Composed 1932, 1935. First performance, 21 November 1935, Salle Gaveau (Université des Annales), PARIS. The composer with (Svyatoslav) Soulima STRAVINSKY. First published 1936, Edition Schott. Order of movements: (I) Con moto (II) Notturno (Adagietto) (III) Quattro variazioni (IV) Preludio e Fuga.

During his pre-concert talk at the first performance of the Concerto for Two Solo Pianos, Stravinsky clarified his understanding of the concerto genre in terms of *l'ancienne formule* ('the ancient formula'). His declared affinity with the *concerto grosso* enabled him to justify his conception of his new Concerto as a sparring between equal rivals where the absence of an accompanying role, i.e. the omnipresence of two solo performers, called for a composition of essentially contrapuntal nature. For, as the composer made clear to his audience, the term *concerto* 'derives from the Italian word *concertare* which means to compete [that is] to participate in a contest, in a match'. This fascination with *le concours concertant* would eventually lead Stravinsky to transfer his instrumental formula to the stage in AGON (1953–7) via a combination of French courtly dance and ancient Greek competition. (I) Con moto: The moto(r)-energy of this opening movement, which Cortot described as an 'oeuvre athlétique', communicates most aptly the composer's desire to portray a virtuosic, even combative, rhetoric (quoted in Goubault 1991, 248). The performers are driven to ever-greater feats of strength and agility by the composer's instructions to play *marcato più forte*, *marcatissimo*, *forte e brillante* and *martelé* (*sempre*) via a clangorous evocation of Brandenburgian models. (II) The Notturno reveals some of the most beautiful slow music that Stravinsky composed, elegant and controlled, yet whose elaborate and most original traceries of ornamentation barely conceal an intense, if repressed, emotionalism. It rivals Stravinsky's other memorable *adagiettos* in SONATA FOR PIANO and CAPRICCIO in its 'floating' quality, achieved here by the neo-classically appropriate absence of the sustaining pedal to reveal the music's complex yet fragile textures. Paraphrasing the composer, 'Notturno' does not refer to those 'dreamy miniatures for piano' by Field and Chopin, but to the instrumental *Nachtmusik* of the eighteenth-century cassation whose many different moods Stravinsky wished to condense into this one pianistic essay. (III) Quattro variazioni: When the composition of this Concerto was complete, Stravinsky inverted the order of the last two movements. Thus, the listener hears the theme upon which these four variations are based only *after* savouring their ingenuities and sensing the shape and rhythmic character of the fugal material, until now only heard subliminally. Consistent with examples in all four movements of the Concerto, the expressive impact of the Variations' calculated virtuosity is considerably negated by the pervasive use of rapidly repeating notes which act as a highly effective guarantor of neo-classical objectivity, as emotionless energy. (IV) Preludio e Fuga: The final challenge for the two combatants is a technical *and* a compositional tour de force: to perform at speed a four-part fugue whose threads are exchanged across the two instruments and the four hands. After a brief interlude recalling material from the lento Preludio, the impressive feat is repeated – this time, *nell'inversione*. It is as if, by creating his own 'Contrapunctus inversus a 4', Stravinsky wished to share with us an act of homage to *The Art of Fugue*, BACH's own testimonial to the musical/cerebral rigours of a past era. GRAHAM GRIFFITHS

Christian Goubault, *Igor Stravinsky* (Paris: Librairie Honore Champion, 1991).

Graham Griffiths, *Stravinsky's Piano: Genesis of a Musical Language* (Cambridge University Press, 2013).

Pierre-Olivier Walzer (ed.), *Charles-Albert Cingria: Correspondance avec Igor Strawinsky* (Lausanne: Éditions L'Age d'Homme, 2001).

Eric Walter White, *Stravinsky: A Critical Survey* (London: John Lehmann, 1947).

Auto

Concerto in D ('Basler Concerto'). For String Orchestra. Composed 1946. First performance, 27 (or 21) January 1947, Basel, Basler Kammerorchester.

Conductor, Paul SACHER. Published 1947, London: Boosey & Hawkes. Dedicated to 'the Basel Chamber Orchestra and its conductor Paul Sacher'.

The Concerto in D for String Orchestra (8.8.6.6.4) was commissioned by Paul Sacher for his Basel Chamber orchestra and was premièred as part of the festivities for the orchestra's twentieth anniversary in Basel in January 1947. The three-movement work is consequently often referred to simply as the 'Basle Concerto'. As the first European commission Stravinsky had received in more than ten years, it was also the first composition he completed after becoming a naturalised American citizen and, furthermore, the first of his works to be published by his new PUBLISHER, Boosey & Hawkes. While Stravinsky claimed that it draws on the tradition of the Baroque *Concerto grosso* – and he mentioned BACH's *Brandenburg Concerto* – it is in fact more closely linked to the chamber concertos of the early classical era, the interplay of soloists and string orchestra occurring only occasionally.

The first movement begins with a Vivace passage in D major, which moves steadily onward, despite various disruptions to the flow, in six-eight time. A Moderato section, played 'dolce cantando', begins finally, after 130 bars, a contrast that is amplified by the modulation of the key by a minor second. Indeed, this interval, which is found already in the opening bars, characterises the structure of the entire movement. The melody, with which the Moderato passage begins, and which is incessantly punctuated by pauses, is unable to establish itself and the section is superseded finally by a rigorous, rhythmical and harsh Con *moto* segment. Both the Vivace and the Moderato passages return towards the end of the movement, but without any real potential for development: on the contrary, after a brief coda, the second movement begins *attacca*.

The slow Arioso of the second movement flows gently with expressive duets in B♭ major, the melody once again taking up the characteristic minor second of the first movement, though amplified here to a major seventh and to the related interval of a minor ninth. Even if this second movement seems at first to be very different from the first in its design, a subtle irony underpins the complete work. The allusion to the 'endless melodies' of Romantic opera is broken by two marcato interruptions – both isolated cadences – in the low strings. The third movement, Rondo, providing further contrast, begins *attacca* and is a tour de force, an exuberant jamboree. Various soloists appear over the fast-flowing, accompanying figures, and the formative element is once again the minor second. Shortly after the première, Stravinsky revised the entire composition, making substantial changes to this last movement in particular.

The concerto has been choreographed several times as a BALLET: while the first production was Dore Hoyer's *Vision* at the Hamburg Staatsoper in 1950, the most noted ballet version is *The Cage*, a psychoanalytic dance performance with the NEW YORK CITY BALLET by Jerome Robbins, in 1951.

FLORIAN HENRI BESTHORN

Concerto in D for Violin and Orchestra. Composed 1931. First performance, 23 October 1931, Berlin Funkorchester, Berlin. Published 1931, B. Schott's Söhne. Copyright renewed 1959, Schott's.

Stravinsky composed his Concerto in D for Violin and Orchestra during the spring and summer of 1931, which places it just after SYMPHONY OF PSALMS

(1930) and just prior to DUO CONCERTANT (1931/2). Samuel DUSHKIN was the soloist in the première on 23 October 1931, with the composer conducting the Berlin Radio Orchestra. Due to his relative lack of experience in composing for solo violin (the String Quartet and THE SOLDIER'S TALE notwithstanding), Stravinsky conferred with Dushkin during the compositional process (the two would collaborate again on Duo Concertant). Indeed, the piece would be very different were it not for this collaboration. The Concerto in D for Violin and Orchestra is thus part of the small group of concertante works for solo and ensemble, including the CONCERTO FOR PIANO AND WIND INSTRUMENTS (1923/4), CAPRICCIO (1928/9), CONCERTO IN E♭: 'DUMBARTON OAKS' (1937/8) and the late MOVEMENTS (1958/9). Not surprisingly, given the potential problems of textural balance, Stravinsky assigns each orchestral part a specific number of instruments. Furthermore, since it is only rarely that all instruments are used at once, the effect is more of a chamber piece than a true concerto, with a running time of around 20 minutes.

In terms of style and form, the Violin Concerto exemplifies Stravinsky's neo-classical style. As with many pieces from this period, the piece evokes the spirit of BACH and is more neo-Baroque than neo-classical. The four movements are entitled Toccata, Aria I, Aria II and Capriccio. Indeed, it follows the familiar Baroque concerto pattern of fast-slow-fast movements (as did the Piano Concerto and the Capriccio), aside from the middle slow movement being split into two arias. The composer himself admitted that Bach's Concerto for Two Violins was in his mind while composing, which is most evident during the many duets between the solo violin and other instruments during the finale. In general, each of the four movements comprises a typical 'statement – contrast – restatement' formal layout. In the opening Toccata, each of the three parts begins with the same primary material, heard at rehearsal numbers 1, 16, and 36. The same holds true in the two arias, the second of which represents the only extended time away from the D centricity featured in the rest of the piece. In the finale, multiple statements of primary material comprise a rondo-like form, with faster and faster tempo markings creating the drama.

Like his other neo-classical works, Stravinsky's Concerto in D for Violin and Orchestra plays with the conventions of tonality. The piece is somewhat unusual in that it employs key signatures throughout. And while these do reinforce the suggested tonal centres, such as D major, D minor and F♯ minor, the tonal centres themselves are rarely marked by clear cadence points. Indeed, multiple stratified layers, each with their own characteristics, form a sort of dissociated counterpoint that eventually leads to a cadence. Even these points, however, leave a sense of tonal ambiguity, as each movement ends on a non-triadic sonority, thereby reflecting the most prominent pitch structure in the piece, the widely spaced d1-e2-a3 chord that begins each movement.   DON TRAUT

Lynne Rogers, 'Stravinsky's eleventh-hour revision of the Third Movement of his Violin Concerto', The Journal of Musicology, 17.2 (Spring 1999), 272–303.
SCW

Concerto in E♭: 'Dumbarton Oaks'.   Composed 1937–8. First performance, 8 May 1938, Dumbarton Oaks Estate (Washington, DC). Conductor, Nadia BOULANGER. Published in 1938 by B. Schott's Söhne, Mainz. Instrumentation:

Flute, Clarinet in B♭, Bassoon, 2 Horns in F, 3 Violins, 3 Violas, 2 Cellos, 2 Double Basses. Order of movements: (I) Tempo giusto (II) Allegretto (III) Con moto (performed without a break).

The Concerto in E♭: 'Dumbarton Oaks' was commissioned by Robert Woods Bliss and his wife, Mildred Barnes Bliss, in honour of their thirtieth wedding anniversary. The Blisses were major art collectors and philanthropists, in addition to founding the Dumbarton Oaks Research Library and Collection, later gifted to Harvard University. According to Jeanice Brooks, Stravinsky had become acquainted with the Blisses prior to the commission, most likely through their mutual relationship with Samuel DUSHKIN, who was the adopted son of one of Mildred Bliss' good friends, Blair Fairchild. Nadia Boulanger was influential in securing the commission, and she agreed to conduct the first performance, due to Stravinsky's hospitalisation with tuberculosis in Europe. The programme also included Stravinsky's DUO CONCERTANT (1931–2), performed by Samuel Dushkin (violin) and Beveridge Webster (piano), as well as pieces by J. S. BACH. The European première, conducted by Stravinsky, took place on 8 June 1938, at the Salle Gaveau in Paris, and he conducted the Concerto at Dumbarton Oaks on two occasions: on 25 April 1947, in observance of the tenth anniversary of the composition, a few days before the first recording of the work (Reeves Beaux Arts Studios in New York City for the Keynote label, according to James Carder), and on 8 May 1958 for the Bliss' fiftieth wedding anniversary.

Several reviewers in the French press were 'distracted' by an allusion in the Dumbarton Oaks Concerto to a theme from Bach's Third Brandenburg Concerto. While René LEIBOWITZ did not identify the exact source of Stravinsky's Bach influence, he wrote in Ésprit (1 July 1938) that 'the essential impression that emerges here is that of complete creative impotence. An insolent borrowing from one of Bach's themes, an episode riddled by revolting academicism, little melodies of an accomplished bad taste, a dull and boring orchestration, all of this crafted in the manner of an "ultra-pompous" Tschaikowski.' Rebutting the points raised by Leibowitz, André SCHAEFFNER described it as 'a report in the form of a postcard', and identified the source of the so-called 'Bach theme', clarifying that Stravinsky only focused on a motive that is 'an element borrowed from the theme and repeated on the successive degrees of a chord'. Schaeffner further explained that, while Stravinsky was composing 'Dumbarton Oaks', he was asked about what he was working on and had answered that 'he was writing a little concerto in the genre of the Brandenberg Concertos. If he really had thought of them, wouldn't he have been absolutely allowed to refer to this supposed model and to insolently borrow – ten notes?' Stravinsky echoed this sentiment, saying that he was 'much censured for these resemblances, but I do not think that Bach himself would have begrudged me the use of his examples, as he frequently borrowed in this way himself' (T&C, 47).

Whether Stravinsky consciously or unconsciously borrowed a theme from the third Brandenburg Concerto, he inarguably moulded it to his style. Stravinsky's neo-classical style is apparent in this chamber work in the appearance of block form, even using the Bachian motive as one of the elements in the construction. It is possible that the Bach reference was a way of looking simultaneously both backward and forward – the Brandenburg borrowing became the basis for a musical texture that, while neo-classical overall, was also futuristic, and even whimsical in places. Perhaps this is what inspired Émile VUILLERMOZ to write, in an article in *Candide* titled 'Igor-le-Terrible' (16 June 1938), that 'The *Dumbarton Oaks Concerto* is written in the neo-classical style of a devil that is entertaining himself playing hermit by pastiching certain Bach formulas by using some short fugal entries and by giving the shape of an old knick-knack to a musical material that is quite ill-fitting to this usage'.

The first and last movements centre on E♭ and the middle movement on B♭. At the end of the first two movements, Stravinsky uses a chorale-like texture in the form of a block that creates a feeling of stasis at the end of these movements – both used, perhaps paradoxically, as propulsion devices into the next movement. Elliott CARTER referred to this compositional technique, regarding its use in ORPHEUS (1947), as cross-cutting. Stravinsky's deliberate use of block form can be clearly discerned by examination of his earliest sketches for the work, housed at the Dumbarton Oaks Library (with a single page at the Paul SACHER STIFTUNG (Foundation)), which show several melodic and contrapuntal ideas in a mosaic style, typical of block form in his other works.

MAUREEN CARR

Jeanice Brooks, *The Musical Work of Nadia Boulanger: Performing Past and Future between the Wars* (Cambridge University Press, 2013).

James N. Carder, 'Dumbarton Oaks Concerto'. *From the Archives. Dumbarton Oaks Research Library and Collection*, 26 September 2017: www.doaks.org/research/library-archives/dumbarton-oaks-archives/historical-records/from-the-archives/dumbarton-oaks-concerto.

René Leibowitz, 'Review, "Sérénade: Festival Strawinsky"', *Ésprit*, 6/70 (1 July 1938), 587.

André Schaeffner, 'Critique et thématique', *La Revue Musicale* [dedicated to Stravinsky], 191 (1939), 241–54.

Conducting Career. Stravinsky's conducting career spanned a period of over half a century. The first time Stravinsky conducted one of his own works appears to have been on the morning of 30 March 1914 when he attended ANSERMET's rehearsal for the SYMPHONY IN E♭ MAJOR at the Kursaal in Montreux and led one movement of the work, although he did not conduct any of the actual concert on 2 April. However, the Scherzo was repeated by popular demand on 16 April (again in the Kursaal) and Stravinsky made his first public appearance as a conductor on this occasion. On 20 December 1915, Stravinsky conducted a suite from The FIREBIRD at the Grand Théâtre in Geneva, as part of a DIAGHILEV gala. In March 1921, when the BALLETS RUSSES was on tour in Madrid, he conducted PETRUSHKA for the first time. Stravinsky conducted the première of the OCTET FOR WIND INSTRUMENTS at the PARIS Opéra on 18 October 1923: the first time he had directed a new work in public. A private recording was made a few days later, marking Stravinsky's conducting debut in the studio.

On 8 and 9 January 1925, Stravinsky appeared with the New York Philharmonic at Carnegie Hall. The programme describes the occasion as 'Mr Stravinsky's first appearance in America' and he conducted the *Song of the Volga Boatmen*, FIREWORKS, SCHERZO FANTASTIQUE, The SONG OF THE NIGHTINGALE and suites from PULCINELLA and *The Firebird*. On 10 January, he repeated this programme but replaced *The Firebird* with a suite from *Petrushka*. On 25 January at the Aeolian Hall, Stravinsky conducted an ensemble from the orchestra in the Octet, RAGTIME and RENARD.

Stravinsky's commercial recording career as a conductor began with a suite from Petrushka made for UK Columbia with an unnamed 'Symphony Orchestra' in London on 27–28 June 1928. Later that year, he recorded the 1911 suite from Firebird and excerpts from Pulcinella with the Straram Orchestra in Paris, and in May 1929 he made his first recording of The RITE OF SPRING with the same orchestra. On 17–18 February 1931, Stravinsky conducted the first recording of the SYMPHONY OF PSALMS with the Straram Orchestra and the Alexis Vlassov Choir. The first composer-conducted recordings of the Octet and a suite from The SOLDIER'S TALE were made in Paris in May 1932, and, on 10 July 1934, Stravinsky conducted the first recording of Les NOCES (sung in English) at the Abbey Road Studios in London. Two more important recordings were made in the 1930s: the CONCERTO IN D FOR VIOLIN AND ORCHESTRA with Samuel DUSHKIN and the Lamoureux Orchestra in October 1935, and JEU DE CARTES with the Berlin Philharmonic on 21 February 1938.

When Stravinsky returned to the New York Philharmonic for a series of concerts in January 1937, the programmes included his own works alongside GLINKA's Ruslan and Lyudmila overture, RIMSKY-KORSAKOV's Sadko, TCHAIKOVSKY's Third Symphony, Weber's Turandot and Mozart's Piano Concerto in G K453 (with Beveridge Webster). With the same orchestra in January 1940, he conducted an all-Tchaikovsky programme comprising the 'Little Russian' Symphony (a work he repeated in 1945 and later conducted in Boston and LOS ANGELES), the Violin Concerto (with Erica Morini) and the Nutcracker Suite. On 6, 7 and 8 April 1940, Stravinsky conducted a programme comprising Petrushka (complete), The Firebird (1919 suite) and The Rite. Columbia recorded The Rite and a suite from Petrushka on 4 April, just before these concerts, and this marked the start of a long and sometimes querulous relationship with Columbia Records. The result was an extraordinary series of recordings of Stravinsky conducting his own works produced and overseen by Goddard LIEBERSON. In 1945, Stravinsky recorded SCÈNES DE BALLET, FOUR NORWEGIAN MOODS, ODE and CIRCUS POLKA with the New York Philharmonic, following this in January 1946 with the 1945 FIREBIRD SUITE, Fireworks and SYMPHONY IN THREE MOVEMENTS. A second recording of the Symphony of Psalms followed in December 1946. Dissatisfaction with Columbia led Stravinsky to defect to RCA Victor between 1947 and 1950, for which he recorded DANSES CONCERTANTES, DIVERTIMENTO from The FAIRY'S KISS, ORPHEUS, MASS, CONCERTO FOR PIANO AND WIND INSTRUMENTS (with Soulima STRAVINSKY), the CONCERTO IN D and APOLLO. He returned to Columbia in 1951, recording OEDIPUS REX and the SYMPHONIES OF WIND INSTRUMENTS in Cologne. In 1952, he recorded the complete Pulcinella and Symphony in C in Cleveland, and the CANTATA in New York. The first recording of The RAKE'S PROGRESS was made with Metropolitan Opera forces in March 1953. PERSÉPHONE was recorded (in mono) in January 1957. Stravinsky's first stereo recordings for Columbia were of AGON and CANTICUM SACRUM (June 1957), followed by THRENI and Les Noces in 1959. The advent of stereo marked the start of a new series of recordings conducted by the composer, including The Rite and Petrushka in 1960; The Firebird (complete), Symphony in Three Movements and Concerto in D for Violin and Orchestra (with Isaac Stern) in 1961; *Oedipus Rex*, *Renard* and CONCERTO IN Eb: 'DUMBARTON OAKS' in 1962; and numerous shorter pieces in 1962–3. The last recording Stravinsky made was the 1945 FIREBIRD *Suite* in January 1967. The involvement of Robert CRAFT with the preparation of many Stravinsky later recordings has cast some doubt on their status as composer-conducted performances, since it is impossible to establish from Columbia's studio logs whether Stravinsky or Craft conducted a particular published take. However, extracts from the rehearsals for sessions in 1962–5 of works such as *Apollo*, the Concerto for Piano and Wind Instruments, *Pulcinella* and the Symphony in C reveal Stravinsky firmly in command on the podium, and there is little doubt that the finished recordings were conducted by him too.

From the late 1920s onwards, Stravinsky often conducted the world premières of his own works, including *The Fairy's Kiss* (Paris, 27 November 1928), the Concerto in D for Violin and Orchestra (Berlin, 23 October 1931), *Perséphone* (Paris, 30 April 1934), *Jeu de cartes* (New York, 27 April 1937), Symphony in C (Chicago, 7 November 1940), Symphony in Three Movements (New York, 24 January 1946), *Orpheus* (New York, 28 April 1948), *The Rake's Progress* (VENICE, 11 September 1951), Cantata (LOS ANGELES, 11 November 1952), SEPTET (Washington, DC, 23 January 1954) and *Canticum sacrum* (Venice, 13 September 1956). The last première Stravinsky conducted himself was MOVEMENTS (New York, 10 January 1960). In the 1960s, his concert appearances gradually became fewer and he restricted himself to old favourites. He conducted *The Rite* in New York in January 1960 (prior to the recording). In 1961, he conducted *The Rite* in Mexico City (his last performances of the work), *Oedipus Rex* in Santa Fe, *Perséphone* in Berlin and London, and *The Soldier's Tale* in Zurich; 1962 saw him conducting *Oedipus Rex* in Washington, DC, the FIREBIRD *Suite* at the inaugural concert of the Seattle World's Fair, and *Apollo* in Hamburg. The following year, he conducted the *Symphony of Psalms* at Oberlin, and *Oedipus Rex* in Hamburg. Concerts in 1964 included appearances with the Philadelphia and Cleveland orchestras, and the *Symphony of Psalms* in Oxford. His last appearance in England was to conduct the 1945 *Firebird Suite* with the New Philharmonia Orchestra at the Royal Festival Hall on 14 September 1965. Despite increasing frailty, in 1966 Stravinsky conducted *Perséphone* in Los Angeles, *Oedipus Rex* in Lisbon, and *Symphony of Psalms* in New York. In March 1967, his performance of *The Soldier's Tale* was described by Craft as 'erratic', and his final appearance on a concert platform was on 17 May, when he conducted the PULCINELLA SUITE in Toronto.

Live performances of Stravinsky conducting from the 1930s onwards survive in sound archives in Washington, London and elsewhere, and many have been published. Video of Stravinsky conducting includes the 1945 *Firebird Suite* at the Osaka Festival (1 May 1959) and in London (14 September 1965), extracts from *The Firebird* with the New York Philharmonic (January 1960), rehearsals for the 1954 Columbia recording of the suite from *The Soldier's Tale*, rehearsals for the *Symphony of Psalms* in Toronto, and extracts from the rehearsal and concert of Stravinsky's final appearance in Toronto in May 1967.   NIGEL SIMEONE

SCS, SCW, SSE

Conversations with Robert Craft. In 1957, Stravinsky and Robert CRAFT began compiling a list of questions and answers that eventually led to what became known as their conversation books. The co-authors set out to fill in the many blanks of Stravinsky's heretofore-sketchy BIOGRAPHY, while also enunciating the composer's opinions on an array of historical and contemporary issues. Unlike his earlier ghosted writings, the more casual tone of these give-and-take exchanges (akin to 'fireside chats', as one reviewer dubbed them) would carry the appeal of hearing directly from the composer, thus precluding any chance of misinterpretation. Over the ensuing decade six books were published: *Conversations with Igor Stravinsky* (1959), *Memories and Commentaries* (1960), *Expositions and Developments* (1962), *Dialogues and a Diary* (1963), *Themes and Episodes* (1966) and *Retrospectives and Conclusions* (1969). As the series gained exposure, Stravinsky's British and American publishers released separate, substantially modified versions of these same titles, often with differing deletions, expansions and new materials. Some of the original six books were conflated into single volumes, as with the posthumously published 1972 *Themes and Conclusions*. Readers seeking a complete record of the series' unabridged contents must consult all printings.

Stravinsky was besieged by constant requests for press interviews. Not only did such time-consuming sessions encroach upon composing, but the same predictable questions grew wearisome. How many times could Stravinsky be coaxed into recounting the infamous riot at the première of *The* RITE OF SPRING, or made to explain his proclamation that music expressed nothing at all? Responding to Craft's pre-ordained questions, and doing so within the limits of the composer's tight schedule, would surely be more productive. Such dialogues could be carried out whenever an unintrusive opportunity presented itself, while travelling on concert tours, or during more leisurely after-dinner talks at the composer's Hollywood home. Rather than responding to random questions extemporaneously, Stravinsky welcomed some measure of control in setting straight the often-misinformed record of criticisms and erroneous assumptions that dogged him. The widely disseminated 1957 publication of Stravinsky and Craft's 'Answers to thirty-six questions' served as a successful trial balloon, subsequently leading to their co-authored six conversation books

The first three volumes covered a hodgepodge of topics, ranging from the composer's earliest memories of Imperial RUSSIA to his opinions on the shortcomings of electronic music. As one reviewer remarked, Stravinsky expounded his views 'with unimpaired acuity'. Readers revelled in the sometimes contrarian, sometimes sardonic bantering of the witty septuagenarian, while the scholarly community was buoyed by the indisputability of Stravinsky's replies as expressed, supposedly, through the composer's own precisely chosen words. 'How beautifully Stravinsky writes', observed the *New York Times* – and with remarkable 'linguistic and literary gifts', added the *New Statesman*. Nonetheless, scepticism immediately surfaced. Was the artfully honed prose of Stravinsky's lucid answers a tad too lucid? Was the grandiloquence of 'ten dollar words', as another reviewer wondered, that of the interrogator rather than the interrogated? Craft argued that Stravinsky's inadequate English necessitated his assistance, adding candidly that he enfolded some of his own independent contributions along the way. By the time

Expositions and Developments appeared in 1962, Paul Henry Lang's review surmised that Stravinsky's statements might have been coloured by 'the intrusion of Mr. Craft's own ideas'.

Stravinsky was perfectly aware of his collaborator's increasingly dominant presence in each successive book, nor did he express any qualms. On the contrary, his 1958 letter to Columbia Records' Deborah Ishlon (reprinted in SPD), explicitly acknowledges Craft's authorship of *Conversations with Igor Stravinsky*: 'it is his language, his presentation, his imagination, and his memory'. And, further, 'It's not a question simply of ghost writing but of somebody who is to a large extent creating me.' So just how involved was Stravinsky? A willing participant on the outside, archival documents confirm that Stravinsky carefully revised typescripts he himself wrote (sometimes in Russian with his own English translation), as well as editing remarks that Craft, on his own initiative, had first drafted. For example, while touring in VENICE, Stravinsky penned his initial thoughts about MUSSORGSKY (also reproduced in SPD) on hotel stationery. The printed version reflects Craft's grammatical emendations while still preserving the substance of the composer's comments. In *Memories and Commentaries*, Craft's rhetorical flair turned more robust. The composer's nondescript mentioning of the childhood bedroom shared with his brother was ultimately more evocatively inflated by Craft as a room reminiscent of '*Petrouchka's* cell'.

Stephen Walsh, whose meticulous study of archival documents prompted judicious criticisms of Craft's editing, enumerates multiple passages marred by frequent inaccuracies. In many instances, as Walsh observes, Stravinsky was quick to correct 'crude errors and sheer inventions'. Walsh also settles the long-standing suspicion that Craft alone authored several of the published texts. As the series progressed, Craft assumed a larger role in framing both questions and answers. Stravinsky's original description of *The* FLOOD, for instance, varies significantly from the altered version appearing in *Expositions and Developments*. The composer's lengthy description of APOLLO, appearing in *Dialogues and a Diary*, was cobbled together by Craft from Stravinsky's rather skimpy notes. Gradually, the slippery slope of editorial licence gave way to a number of misleading interpretations. A survey of the appertaining typescripts held by the Sacher Stiftung reveals that, among the hundreds of surviving pages, only a fraction are in the composer's hand.

Stravinsky's active involvement in the series steadily faded to where his voice virtually vanished. By the time *Themes and Episodes* and *Retrospectives and Conclusions* appeared in the late 1960s, Craft substantially 'padded' (his own word) the contents. A considerable distance separates his original assertion that Stravinsky 'wrote or dictated' everything in the six books from his later admission that the collection ultimately 'deteriorated' into his own writing. With publishers eager to extend the series, Craft resorted to inserting his own diary excerpts; programme notes for several Stravinsky works; earlier published interviews (many having first appeared in the *New York Review of Books*); and several piercing newspaper editorials, including one that Stravinsky – though it is hard to imagine – authored and signed only a few weeks before his death.

Exactly where do Stravinsky's words and thoughts begin and Craft's end? Long after the composer's death, his co-author asserted in *Stravinsky: Discoveries and Memories* (2013) that, despite substituting his own words, assembling 'an alloyed Stravinsky would be preferable to no Stravinsky'. Arguably so, but the resulting quandary resides in determining just how 'alloyed' the pieced-together composer had been. In smoothing out Stravinsky's grammar and vocabulary, Craft surely hoped to avoid muddling the message itself. Improving textual fluency here and there by swapping one word for another seems defensible. Even the injection of an occasional linguistic flourish might be overlooked, although in fact Stravinsky inserted exclamation points in typescripts wherever Craft's embellishments struck him as excessive. Still, given the pervasiveness of both minor tweaks and more crucial alterations, doubts about textual reliability accrue. In an expurgated film clip from Tony Palmer's 1982 Stravinsky documentary, the composer's friend Alexei Haieff worried that the conversation books depicted Stravinsky as a 'much more erudite man than he actually was'. Consequently, a somewhat mythologised composer emerges, and one whose responses are often cast in the same distinctively literate voice as Craft's own eloquent writings.

Dismissing the series out of hand seems ill considered. Initially hailed as invaluable in deepening our understanding of the composer, the series is perhaps now most benignly viewed as an engaging but flawed historical document. Particularly within the pages of the first four volumes – and owing primarily to recent archival research – the conversations' once promising disclosures may now be either more assuredly verified or disproven. Still, while at times illuminating, the collection is too often compromised by concerns over authorial interpretation. Moreover, and far beyond the reach of Craft's intercession, Stravinsky's own distortions and faulty memories add another obfuscating layer in untangling fact from fiction. Over half a century after the first book appeared, we are left with a caveat emptor: readers should resist indiscriminately accepting Stravinsky's and Craft's statements, while scholars hoping to corroborate their own theses upon the strength of the books' purported truths would be wise to proceed cautiously. CHARLES M. JOSEPH

Robert Craft, 'Conversations with Stravinsky', in *Present Perspectives* (New York: Alfred A. Knopf, 1984), 265–75.
SSE

Copland, Aaron   (born Brooklyn, New York, 14 November 1900; died North Tarrytown (now Sleepy Hollow), New York, 2 December 1990) was extensively influenced by Igor Stravinsky. He embraced early twentieth-century European MODERNISM, combining modernist compositional techniques with American idioms such as JAZZ and FOLK MUSIC to create a populist, accessible style in works from the late 1930s into the 1950s. As a critic, Copland promoted Stravinsky to a broad American public.

Copland's interest in modern music began in his teens. While studying composition in high school in New York, he independently discovered modern music, studying scores and attending concerts, including a performance of Stravinsky's FIREBIRD and PETRUSHKA by the BALLETS RUSSES at the Metropolitan Opera. In June 1921, Copland departed for FRANCE, where he studied at the new

American summer school of music and art at Fontainebleau. His primary teacher there was Nadia BOULANGER. He later became her private student in PARIS after the summer programme ended.

Copland matured during these Paris years, 1921–4. Boulanger inculcated an appreciation for Stravinsky among her students: she regularly featured his works in her Wednesday afternoon analysis class, and he was sometimes a guest at her afternoon teas. Copland's earliest compositions had already shown the influence of DEBUSSY and SCRIABIN. Studying with Boulanger, Copland further mastered many Stravinskian techniques, as seen in his first published work, Scherzo humoristique (The Cat and the Mouse), begun in 1920 in New York, but completed and published in 1921 in Paris. Highly dissonant, this work explores several scales. Copland's use of pentatonic and whole tone scales reflects the influence of Debussy. He also uses octatonicism, ostinato and other techniques suggestive of Stravinsky's Petrushka. Copland continued to use octatonicism in other 1920s works: 'Rondino' from Two Pieces for String Quartet (1923–8), Symphony for Organ and Orchestra (1924) and the jazz-inflected Music for the Theatre (1925). Interlocking poly-rhythmic layers further characterise all three, tonal centers that lie a tritone apart, rhythmic ostinati and juxtaposed blocks of contrasting material. Thus, like Stravinsky, Copland had learned to integrate octatonicism melodically, harmonically and structurally. In his approach to rhythm, Copland found a way to blend both jazz and Stravinskian techniques, as is evident in Dance Symphony (1925, which contains part of a BALLET composed in Paris: Grohg) and Music for the Theatre. In these works, Copland explores rhythm, both jazz and Stravinskian, odd and constantly shifting metres and metrical accents.

After establishing himself as a brash young modernist, Copland came to be associated with 'Americana', i.e., works that somehow evoked 'Americanness', or that appealed to a broad audience that resulted from his new accessible style and use of folk tunes. Following his return to the UNITED STATES in 1924, Copland relied on fellowships, commissions and the patronage of wealthy individuals, which became scarce during the Great Depression. As the economic crisis deepened, Copland became concerned about the relationship between composer and audience. Interested in leftist politics, he was an informal mentor for the Young Composers' Collective. Wedding politics to his music, Copland briefly explored workers' music. Ultimately embracing an accessible populist style, he eventually turned to folk music. Again, he took Stravinsky as a model, noting the elder composer's approach. Copland like-wise segmented his folk tunes, used them as ostinati and juxtaposed densely polyrhythmic passages as he had done in his earlier works. Leaving behind octatonicism, he devised a diatonic harmonic style built on nonfunctional tonal centres. We first see this in El Salón México (1936) and in his best-known works such as Billy the Kid (1938), Rodeo (1942) and Appalachian Spring (1944). (The latter three are ballet collaborations with American modern-dance choreographers Lincoln KIRSTEIN, Agnes de Mille and Martha Graham). These, and patriotic works such as Fanfare for the Common Man (1942), Lincoln Portrait (1942) and Third Symphony (1944–6), cemented Copland's reputation as a composer of 'Americana' with broad populist appeal. These techniques are also used in his film music, such as *Of Mice and Men* (1939), *Our Town* (1940), *The Heiress* (1948) and *The Red Pony* (1948).

Other European composers also influenced Copland during the 1920s. In his teens, he had been influenced by Debussy and MILHAUD. While in Europe, he had heard the music of SCHOENBERG and Alois Hába, and had limitedly experimented with both TWELVE-NOTE composition (though adapted to his own use, as seen in Poet's Song (1927, text by e.e. cummings), *Symphonic Ode* (1929) and *Piano Variations* (1930)) and quarter-tones (*Vitebsk* (1929)). In the 1950s and 1960s, however, Copland decisively turned towards serialism, then the avant-garde (as did Stravinsky, to a degree). His serial works include: Piano Quartet (1950), *Piano Fantasy* (1957), *Connotations* (1961) and *Inscape* (1967). Some Copland scholars have drawn a connection between his turn towards serialism and the investigation of Copland as a communist by the House Committee on Un-American Activities (HUAC), in 1953–5 (HUAC called Copland in to testify in May and June 1953). His serialism is seen as a way in which he might have distanced himself from the Popular Front and other leftist activities of the 1930s. By 1973, Copland had ceased composing and turned his attention to conducting.

In addition to conducting (in his later years), Copland's activities also extended to writing and teaching. In these ways, Copland served as a prominent spokesperson for both modern European and American music. He began writing for both music and general-interest publications in the mid-1920s. He occasionally lectured on contemporary music at the New School for Social Research (1927–30 and 1935–8) and Harvard (the prestigious Charles Eliot Norton Professorship lectures, 1951–2). These provided the basis for his books: *What to Listen for in Music* (1939, reprinted 1957), *Our New Music* (1941, revised in 1968 as *The New Music: 1900–1960*) and *Music and Imagination* (1952). Several articles were anthologised as *Copland on Music* (1960), which included a full chapter on Stravinsky. His two-volume autobiography, *Copland: 1900 Through 1942* (1984) and *Copland Since 1943* (1989), was co-written with his friend, pioneering American music scholar Vivian Perlis.   GAYLE MURCHISON

Gayle Murchison, *The American Stravinsky: The Style and Aesthetics of Copland's New American Music, the Early Works, 1921–1938* (Ann Arbor: University of Michigan Press, 2012).
Howard Pollack, *Aaron Copland: The Life and Work of an Uncommon Man* (Urbana: University of Illinois Press, 1999).

Correspondence. Throughout his long life, Stravinsky maintained an intensive correspondence with a wide circle of people. As a composer, conductor, pianist and literary man, he came into contact with concert bureaux and orchestras, painters and writers, as well as philosophers and public figures. People of assorted professions from different countries were drawn by his fame, wit, joviality and breadth of interests. Due to the composer's constant travels, his correspondence with family members was also very intensive. He kept everything, even documents of little importance, such as water and electricity bills. Thousands of letters have been preserved both in archives (the most extensive collection is housed in the PSS) and privately, so that documents of exceptional value, which were hitherto unknown, emerge from time to time. They shed light on the cultural and spiritual life of several generations, historical events of the epoch, the composer's psychology and aesthetic credo, and his vivid personality with its striking contradictions.

Stravinsky's letters in his native language written between the 1890s and 1910s are the most direct, emotional (passionate, even) and stylistically vivid. This was the heady period of his early creativity and studies with Nikolay RIMSKY-KORSAKOV, of his close friendships with Maximilian STEINBERG and Andrey and Vladimir Rimsky-Korsakov, of his first major successes, as well as the time when he was heatedly discussing his artistic plans and advocating new aesthetic views. Letters of the 1910s tell of Stravinsky's distress at the rejection of his early work for DIAGHILEV by what one might call 'the Rimsky-Korsakov faction' amongst Russian musicians. Stravinsky's correspondence with Diaghilev, as well as with BENOIS, ROERICH, BAKST and MITUSOV (the librettists and designers of his works in the 1910s) is invaluable. The contacts with Russian music publishing houses (Bessel, Jurgenson, BELYAYEV, Édition Russe de Musique) were also intensive.

Stravinsky was fluent enough in French to communicate in that language with his colleagues, managers, and sometimes his own children. His cordial artistic contacts with DEBUSSY, RAVEL, RAMUZ, CINGRIA, LOURIÉ, Nadia BOULANGER, as well as with such sponsors as Misia Sert, Ida RUBINSTEIN, and Coco CHANEL, are reflected in the correspondence (in French and in Russian) from his period of residence in SWITZERLAND and FRANCE. Some letters reveal to us the secrets of Stravinsky's collaboration with his ghost-writers (Walter Nouvel, Pierre SOUVTCHINSKY and Yuri MANDELSTAM). Moreover, the letters of that period tell about the composer's religious quest and the tragedy that befell almost all the members of his family, who spent months at a sanatorium for consumptives.

After 1939, when the composer moved to the UNITED STATES, his secretaries helped him to conduct his correspondence in English, and Robert CRAFT, Stravinsky's *alter ego*, emerged in his life at the end of the 1940s. Although old friendships with Souvtchinsky, NABOKOV, KOUSSEVITZKY, BOLM, BALANCHINE, DUSHKIN, MILHAUD and Nadia Boulanger continued, the volume of correspondence in Russian and in French gradually lessened. American orchestras, managers, musicians and writers appeared among the composer's new addressees (AUDEN, ISHERWOOD, HUXLEY, BERNSTEIN, KIRSTEIN, Victor Babin, Lilian Libmann, Sol Hurok, Arthur Sachs *et al.*). In the 1960s, renewed contacts with Soviet RUSSIA became possible after Stalin's death, and especially after Stravinsky's visit to Moscow and Leningrad in 1962. Maria Yudina, a Soviet pianist, was the first who began to send the most interesting lengthy Russian letters and books as gifts to Igor Fyodorovich.

Stravinsky's countless addressees can be divided into the following groups:

Various Organisations: such as orchestras, theatres, festivals, publishing houses, copyright agencies, recording companies, concert bureaux and charitable organisations.

VIPs: US President John F. Kennedy; President of the USSR, Nikita Khrushchev; Israeli President, Ben Zvi; Elisabeth, Queen of Belgium; Italian Prime Minister, Benito Mussolini; Mayor of West Berlin, Willy Brandt; France's first Minister of Cultural Affairs, André Malraux.

Patrons: in Europe – Princess de Polignac, Compte Étienne de Beaumont, Baroness Catherine Erlanger, Lady Gladys Ripon, Comtesse Lily Pastré, Eugenia Errázuriz, Paul Fromm, Paul SACHER; in the UNITED STATES – Elizabeth Sprague Coolidge, Arthur Sachs, Robert and Mildred Bliss (et al.).

Managers, Impresarios, Intendants: Russian émigrés – Diaghilev, Prince Alexei Zereteli, Vladimir Napravnik; agents in various European countries – Charles Kiesgen, Lina Lalandi, Rolf Liebermann, Salomon Bottenheim; in the USA – Alexander Merovitch, Otto Kahn, Lilian Libmann, Sol Hurok, Lincoln Kirstein (et al.).

Composers: of Russian origin – Rimsky-Korsakov, Steinberg, SCRIABIN, Tcherepnin, PROKOFIEV, Aram and Karen KHACHATURIAN; in Europe – KRENEK, DELAGE, HONEGGER, MESSIAEN, POULENC, SATIE, CASELLA, de FALLA, TANSMAN, Luciano Berio, Paul Hindemith, Luigi Dallapiccola, Francesco Malipiero, Vittorio Rieti, Mario Castelnuovo-Tedesco et al.); in the USA – COPLAND, CARTER, Victor Babin, Samuel Barber, Leonard Bernstein, Harold Shapero, Franz Waxman; in South America – CHAVEZ, Alberto Ginastera (et al.).

Conductors: of Russian origin – Koussevitzky, ZILOTI, MARKEVITCH, Igor Blazhkov, Nikolai Malko; in Europe – MONTEUX, ANSERMET, FURTWÄNGLER, KLEMPERER, ROSBAUD, MENGELBERG, SCHERCHEN, WALTER, DÉSORMIÈRE, Karl Maria Zwissler, Charles Munch, Gilbert Amy; in England and the USA – STOKOWSKI, MITROPOULOS, Malcolm Sargent, Rafael Kubelik, Erich Leinsdorf, Lorin Maazel, Eugene Ormandy, Arthur Rodzinski, George Szell (et al.).

Choral Conductors: Vasily (Basile) Kibaltchich, Gregg Smith.

Philosophers: Jacques MARITAIN.

Clerics: Nikolai Podossenov, Seraphim (Archbishop), Sister Edward Blackwell.

Writers: Russian – KOCHNO, REMISOFF, Mitusov; European – MAETERLINCK, CLAUDEL, ROLLAND, GIDE, VALÉRY, CAMUS, T. S. ELIOT, Dylan THOMAS, Cingria, Ramuz, Blais Cendrars, Saint-John Perse (Alexis Léger), Samuel BECKETT; USA – W. H. Auden, Christopher Isherwood, Paul Horgan, Aldous Huxley; Argentinean – Victoria OCAMPO (et al.).

Painters, Designers, Photographers: of Russian origin – Benois, Roerich, Bakst, GONCHAROVA, CHAGALL, Sonia DELAUNAY-TERK, BERMAN, TCHELITCHEFF, Sergei Soudeikin; in Europe – PICASSO, Max Ernst, Henri Matisse, René Auberjonois, Alberto Giacometti, Giorgio Morandi; in the USA – Man Ray, Noémi Raymond (et al.).

Dancers and Choreographers: of Russian origin – FOKINE, NIJINSKY, LIFAR, MASSINE, Balanchine, Bolm, DOLIN; in the USA – Jerome Robbins (et al.).

Musicologists, Editors and Critics: of Russian origin – Souvtchinsky, de SCHLOEZER, Vladimir Derjanosky, Walter Nouvel; in France – BRELET, LALOY, LEIBOWITZ, SCHAEFFNER, VUILLERMOZ, Henry Prunières, Jacques Rivière; in Italy – Domenico de Paoli, Roman Vlad; in England – Michel-Dimitri Calvocoressi, Edwin Evans, Eric Walter White; in GERMANY – Heinrich Lindlar, Walter Panofsky, Leo Schrade, Heinrich Strobel, Hans Heinz Stuckenschmidt; in Switzerland – Jacques Handschin, Alexander Truslit; in the USA – Edward Lowinsky, Lawrence MORTON, Glenn Watkins, Robert Tangemann. (et al.)

Performers: pianists – Shura Cherkassky, Artur RUBINSTEIN, Maria Yudina, Margrit Weber, Beveridge Webster, Ingolf DAHL; violonists – Samuel Dushkin, Sol Babitz, Alma Moodie, Erika Morini, Yehudi Menuhin, Pawel

Kochansky, Eudice Shapiro; *violists* – Germain Prévost; *cellists* – Grigori Piatigorsky; *vocal* – Cathy Berberian; JAZZ – Woody Herman; *lute, guitar* – Julian Bream; *Cimbalom* – Aládar Rácz; *harp* – Carlos Salzedo (*et al.*).

Lawyers: William Montapert, Aaron Sapiro.

Doctors (many different doctors in the Europe and USA)

Intellectuals, Professors: Edward Forbes, Sir Isaiah Berlin, Lord BERNERS (*et al.*).

Actors, Stage Directors: Alexander Sanin, Ludmilla PITOËFF, Marlene Dietrich, Jean-Louis Barrault, Ingmar Bergman (*et al.*).

Relatives: Igor's parents, wife Catherine STRAVINSKY, children, cousins etc

Friends: Henriette Hirshmann, Alexis Kall, Nikita Malayev, Lucia Davidova, Mikhail Semionov, family Sokolov (*et al.*).

Strangers: fans, collectors of autographs, requests for financial assistance or for recommendation, curious offerings of synopses and scenarios for the future works, etc.

With some of his addressees, Stravinsky confined himself to the exchange of greeting cards or brief messages, whereas he kept up communication with others for many years. Throughout virtually his entire professional life, the composer conducted written negotiations with Édition Russe de Musique through its directors Nikolai Struve, Ernest Oeberg and Gavriyil Païchadze, and later with Boosey & Hawkes. Of Russian *émigrés*, his friendships with Nabokov and Souvtchinsky were the most long-lasting. His correspondence with the latter, who had a profound understanding of the composer's oeuvre and personality, was particularly frank. Nadia Boulanger remained a faithful and like-minded friend. The long-term correspondences with Cingria, Ansermet, Monteux, Willy Strecker (including letters from the Nazi period) and W. H. Auden (librettist of *The Rake's Progress*) contains hundreds of extremely interesting documents.

Some of Stravinsky's letters are exceptionally courteous and warm, such as those addressed to the Soviet officials Tikhon Khrennikov and Karen KHACHATURIAN. Naturally, researchers should avoid excessively literal interpretations of these materials without due consideration of their context. Conversely, the sharp tone of other letters reveals the composer's hot temper and authoritarian character. Some correspondence was either wound down or interrupted on Stravinsky's initiative.

Stravinsky's correspondence with his wife Catherine STRAVINSKY, who died in 1939, and with Vera Sudeykina, at first his lover and, subsequently, his second wife (*see* Vera STRAVINSKY), was exceptionally intensive. Unfortunately, with few exceptions, only both women's sides of the correspondence have been preserved. According to Craft's testimony, Vera obeyed Igor Fyodorovich's request and destroyed the letters that he sent to her prior to her departure for the United States in 1939. Then, after Stravinsky's death, she also destroyed his letters to Catherine, as the composer expressed this wish shortly before he died, although it was not stipulated in his will (Craft 2013, 122). Fortunately, Stravinsky's children preserved their mother's letters to their father. Later, Fyodor and Denise Stravinsky passed them to the PSS.

Publications. Paradoxical as it may seem, the first scholarly publications of Stravinsky's correspondence were made in the USSR, where his oeuvre had long been banned. They became possible after the composer's visit to his fatherland in 1962 and his rehabilitation by Soviet officialdom (letters from Stravinsky to Roerich published by Irina Vershinina in *Sovetskaya Muzïka*, 8 (1966), and Stravinsky's sixty-two Russian letters published by Igor Blazhkov (in D'yachkova and Yarustovsky 1973). An almost complete collection of Stravinsky's Russian correspondence between 1882 and 1939, in chronological order, was published in three massive tomes a quarter of a century later (PRK). Varunts adduced and annotated hundreds of extremely interesting documents, and added citations from the diaries and letters of Stravinsky's Russian contemporaries. The shortcomings of this publication resulted from the extraordinary difficulty of the task for a lone scholar of working through such a vast quantity of material. In addition to small inaccuracies, the edition contains numerous unwarranted cuts, erroneous dates and unidentified French sources. Importantly, some Russian letters in which the handwriting was hard to read were often wrongly deciphered: some of Benois's and Lourié's letters suffered the most in this respect and undoubtedly need to be republished.

An English translation of some of Stravinsky's correspondence was published by Robert Craft during the composer's lifetime (for example, letters by Ravel, Debussy, Rivière, etc., in *Conv, Mem*). However, the three-volume edition *Stravinsky: Selected Correspondence* prepared by Craft (SSC) became the main source of information for Western readers in the 1980s. This contained extensive and valuable material from 1911 to 1968. Craft's long-standing connection with Stravinsky's family helped him to annotate the material. Yet this edition often falls short of modern standards of scholarship. Suffice it to mention that he only reproduced letters from Nadia Boulanger if they were typewritten, approximately an eighth of the total, ignoring all her handwritten letters. In addition, one finds tacit omissions, erroneous dates, and fragments of text transposed from one letter to another. In other chapters, Craft often departs from the principle of publishing a document in full, replacing it with a free narration of the material interspersed with fragmentary quotations from letters. As a result, the reader receives either an incomplete or, sometimes, tendentious picture of the composer's relations with his correspondents. The portrayal of Stravinsky's first wife is distorted in an especially unfortunate way in the chapter *Igor, Catherina and God* (SSC, I). Here Craft manipulates the quotations, avoids publishing the full texts of the letters and interprets them out of context, often in a negative light. Craft also indulges in much editorial arbitrariness in the book DB.

Stravinsky's letters to his Swiss addressees enjoyed the best fortune. The chronicle of the creation of The SOLDIER'S TALE is documented in detail by the epistolary materials in the book *C. F. Ramuz – Igor Stravinsky 'Histoire du soldat'. Chronique d'une naissance* (Gerard and Rochat 2007). Separate editions are dedicated to each of the main addressees, such as Cingria (2001) and Ansermet (CASIII). These publications meet contemporary scholarly criteria, and the same can be said of the edition of Stravinsky's correspondence with Koussevitzky published by Victor Yuzefovich (2002), and of the book *Nadia Boulanger and the Stravinskys: A Selected Correspondence*, edited by Kimberly A. Francis in 2018.   TATIANA BARANOVA MONIGHETTI

Charles Albert Cingria, *Correspondance avec Igor Strawinsky*, ed. Pierre-Olivier Walzer (Lausanne: L'Age d'homme, 2001).

Robert Craft, *Stravinsky: Discoveries and Memories* (Naxos Books, 2013).

L. D'yachkova and B. Yarustovsky (eds.), *I. F. Stravinsky. Stat'i i materialy* ('I. F. Stravinsky: Articles and Materials') (Moscow: Sovetsky kompozitor, 1973).

Kimberly A. Francis (eds.), *Nadia Boulanger and the Stravinskys: A Selected Correspondence* (Rochester University Press, 2018).

Philippe Gerard and Alain Rochat (eds.), *C. F. Ramuz – Igor Stravinsky 'Histoire du soldat'. Chronique d'une naissance* (Geneva: Édition Slatkine, 2007).

Victor Yuzefovich (ed.), 'Chronicle of a non-friendship: letters of Stravinsky and Koussevitzky', intro. and annot. Yuzefovich, *The Musical Quarterly*, 86.4 (2002), 750–885.

Cosmopolitan Identity. Formed from the Greek words *kosmos* ('world', 'universe' or 'cosmos') and *politês* ('citizen', 'member of a city'), cosmopolitanism has come to mean 'citizenship of the world'. This identification beyond the nation has been valorised and derided in equal measure over the course of the modern period. For some (often on the political Left), cosmopolitanism has been a mark of worldliness, sophistication, cultural complexity and humanism. While for others (often on the Right, although a similar discourse was also prevalent in the Soviet Union under Stalin), cosmopolitanism has been associated with sterile deracination, cultural decline and even Jewish conspiracies against the nation.

The early twentieth century was a time of great cosmopolitanism. Improved transportation technology facilitated mass migrations of people looking for improved economic opportunities or in flight from war or political persecution. This was true of artists as well, who often gravitated to perceived cultural capitals such as PARIS or Berlin (and later New York) in order to advance their careers both spiritually and materially. Relocated in foreign cultural and national contexts, many of these artists began to explore new forms of self-understanding and identification. Igor Stravinsky was one of these artists.

From 1910 onwards, Stravinsky divided his time between various locations in the Russian Empire (ST PETERSBURG, USTILUG – now in Ukraine) and the West (SWITZERLAND, FRANCE). Stravinsky returned to Switzerland just before the outbreak of World War I, and due to the war and the subsequent Russian Revolution he was unable to return to his homeland. Not only did this enforced exile make the composer's life difficult materially – RUSSIA and the USSR did not adhere to the Berne Convention and Stravinsky had difficulty collecting royalties for the performances of his works – it also precipitated a crisis of identity. A student of the arch-nationalist Nikolay RIMSKY-KORSAKOV, Stravinsky's early work was profoundly rooted in RUSSIAN MYTH, folk traditions and musical elements. Cut off from the wellspring of his creativity, he began to look for new sources of inspiration.

The key moment in this transformation was his work on the BALLETS RUSSES production PULCINELLA. Stravinsky was strongly connected to the cosmopolitan avant-garde community in Paris and was engaged by Sergey DIAGHILEV to orchestrate a series of fragments attributed to the eighteenth-century Neapolitan composer Giovanni Battista PERGOLESI. While he initially bristled against a task that he thought of as beneath him, he quickly grew to love the work and subsequently saw it as crucial for his artistic development and sense of self. '*Pulcinella* was my discovery of the past', wrote Stravinsky in his *Expositions*, 'the epiphany through which the whole of my late work became possible. It was a backward look, of course – the first of many love affairs in that direction – but it was a look in the mirror, too' (*Expo*, 113). The first portion of this quotation indicates that an engagement with the past allowed Stravinsky to reconceive his musical identity – allowing him to transform himself from a 'Russian' composer to a cosmopolitan one whose musical inspiration came out of an ironic and playful engagement with the classical past. But the second portion of the quote – the 'look in the mirror' – suggests that this was an even more profound experience, having to do with personal identity as well. Given the carnivalesque character of *Pulcinella* – its focus on masquerade, metamorphosis and transformation – it may indicate that this work showed Stravinsky a path from the Russian essentialism of his youth to an acceptance of a more fluid and unstable self.

Many of these same themes are also present in a work taken up shortly after *Pulcinella* – the opera-oratorio OEDIPUS REX – although with a considerably different valence. From the time of his exile, the composer had been 'unable to resolve the language problem in my future vocal works. Russian, the exiled language of my heart had become musically impracticable, and French, German, and Italian were temperamentally alien' (*Dial*, 22). For Stravinsky, whose work in musical theatre was 'set in motion by the sounds and rhythms of the syllables', the loss of his country and his mother tongue had rendered him mute. Here, once again, an abandonment of Russian essentialism and embrace of the classical past offered a way out. In a biography of St Francis of Assisi, he read about how the Saint wrote in Provençal rather than quotidian Italian, and this gave him the idea that it might be possible to work 'by translation backwards, so to speak, from a secular to a sacred language'. The move from Russian to Ciceronian Latin gave the composer his voice back and allowed him to compose the opera. But *Oedipus Rex* is a tense and conflicted work very different from *Pulcinella*. While the latter celebrates instability and self-invention, the former seems desperate to reassert rootedness and stability. From the monumental and static staging and composition to the conception of Latin as a 'medium not dead, but turned to stone', the opera can perhaps be seen as an anxious reaction against the fluidity of cosmopolitan identity and shows the composer in conflict with himself.

With World War II, Stravinsky encountered yet another reshuffling of the self. He moved to the UNITED STATES, settling in LOS ANGELES, and became a naturalised US citizen in 1945. By all accounts, Stravinsky embraced this cosmopolitan identity. He did not see himself as an exile, cut off from his homeland, as did some other Europeans in the United States. 'I'm finished with leaving for Europe', he wrote to Victoria OCAMPO in 1941; 'And anyway, everybody is coming here, which is why you can't find an affordable place to live.' He moved in cosmopolitan artistic circles – associating with German *émigrés*, former dancers of the Ballets Russes (including Adolph BOLM) and British writers, particularly Aldous HUXLEY with whom he spoke French. He was also inspired by the diversity of cultural life in Los Angeles, including the JAZZ clubs of Central Avenue and the Latin music scene. In a discussion with a writer from the *Los Angeles Times* in 1950, he argued that historically some of the greatest art had been made by emigrants, such as Poussin, Handel, Chopin, Gogol and PICASSO, showing his increasing identification with artistic migrants. It is interesting to consider whether his turn to SERIALISM at this time might be connected to his latest experiences with emigration. The formalism of Stravinsky's late work might be seen as yet another form of cosmopolitanism – a purely musical language beyond all ethnic and national identifications.

The question of whether Stravinsky's music should be considered cosmopolitan or whether it remained somehow essentially Russian has continued to be controversial in musicological circles. Arthur BERGER and Pieter van den Toorn argued that much of Stravinsky's music, across the entirety of his oeuvre, was rooted in the octatonic scale. Richard Taruskin extended this analysis by arguing that the octatonic scale was used extensively in Russian music, where it was named after Stravinsky's teacher and known as the Rimsky-Korsakov scale. For Taruskin, then, in spite of Stravinsky's actual geographical displacements, and his identification with other cultures (or the condition of cultural migration itself), he remained at heart a Russian composer, deeply connected to Russian musical idioms. Other scholars, including Berger and van den Toorn, have challenged these conclusions. Kofi Agawu has expressed scepticism that 'Russianness is definable as a set of essential characteristics.' For Agawu, Taruskin's 'claim that the extensive use of the octatonic scale indexes a Russian compositional sensibility' is impossible to establish conclusively, and has 'the effect of depriving Stravinsky of what might be called his hard-won cosmopolitanism'.

IHOR JUNYK

Kofi Agawu, Review of 'Music Theory and the Exploration of the Past' by Christopher Hatch and David W. Bernstein, *Music Theory Spectrum* 17.2 (Autumn 1995), 268–74.
Arthur Berger, 'Problems of pitch organization in Stravinsky,' *Perspectives of New Music*, 2.1 (1963), 11–42.
Richard Taruskin, 'Catching up with Rimsky-Korsakov,' *Music Theory Spectrum*, 33.2 (Fall 2011), 169–85.
Pieter Van den Toorn, *The Music of Igor Stravinsky* (New Haven: Yale University Press, 1983).

Costume Design for Stravinsky's Ballets. Just as hundreds of CHOREOGRAPHERS have been stimulated by the opportunity to create new ballets to Stravinsky's music, so artists and theatre designers have welcomed the opportunity to design these ballets. In respect of costumes, these fall into three main categories. First, there are productions that evoke a traditional RUSSIA. Second, many ballets have costumes which, although carefully designed, are minimal. Third, there are the more traditional costumes for BALLET and dance, from folk-inspired outfits to tutus. Stravinsky's scores have attracted many of the greatest designers of the last century to costume visually stunning ballets: Alexandre BENOIS' PETRUSHKA (1911) portraying visitors to the nineteenth-century Butterweek fairs of ST PETERSBURG; the bejewelled *Balustrade* (1941), designed by Pavel TCHELITCHEFF; the playful, story-book styles of Bruce McLean for The SOLDIER'S TALE (1988); the utter simplicity of the uncredited DUO CONCERTANT (1972).

Many factors come into play when designing for dance: while the designer of the set needs to provide the space for the performance, the costume designer needs to ensure the dancers are comfortable as they move. The costume designer must ask questions. Should the costume reveal or conceal movement? Do the costumes need to convey character as is clearly seen in ballets including

Petrushka and PULCINELLA (1920), evoke a community as in *Les* NOCES (1923), or a mood as with André Beaurepaire's chic hats and pearls to accessorise the tutus of Frederick Ashton's SCÈNES DE BALLET (1948)? Or should the costumes simply enhance the audience's focus on the movement as in George BALANCHINE'S AGON (1957)?

Stravinsky's first ballet, *The* FIREBIRD (1910) reveals some of those challenges. The experienced artist-designer Alexander Golovine designed it specifically for the stage of the PARIS Opéra; it was not thought of as a touring production. For his production, many of the monstrous creatures of the train of Koschei wore elaborate masks, which were discarded when Natalya GONCHAROVA re-designed the ballet in 1926. For the Firebird herself, Golovine created an oriental-inspired outfit with harem pants and modest head-dress cap with protruding feathers, but this seems to have been rarely used in performance. Instead, a costume designed by Léon BAKST for KARSAVINA's 'Firebird' role in the *Le Festin divertissement* (1909), a heavy feathered tutu with an elaborate plumed headdress, was preferred. This was further adapted in 1916, simplifying the layered dress; however, photographs of Lydia LOPOKOVA show a very high, slim plume. In 1926, Goncharova designed new costumes to suit the individual dancers. Lopokova wore trousers, while the taller, slimmer Felia Doubovska had the short tutu and feathered headdress which became the basic template for most of her successor Firebirds. The Russian-ness was deliberately presented in the T-shaped tunics (with gusseted underarms to enable free movement) used in both *Firebird* and *The* RITE OF SPRING (1913). In *The Firebird*, the princesses wear these tunics; Golovine decorated them with *fin-de-siècle* geometric motifs in blue, pink and green, while Goncharova used bold, gold-painted organic decorations outlined with gold braid. Her revised costumes for The Royal Ballet (1954) used rather weaker silver decoration. *The Firebird*, with its elements of Russian folklore, has attracted many artists, including Marc CHAGALL who designed a production for the American Ballet Theater in 1945. These costumes were taken over by NEW YORK CITY BALLET from 1949, and used for a succession of colourful Balanchine/Robbins productions.

In *The Rite of Spring*, all the dancers wear tunics: white flannel for the men and fine wool for the women. These are colourfully dyed, hand-painted and stencilled with circular motifs, so that Valentine Gross' 1913 pastels show blocks of red, turquoise and white costumes against the bright green country-side of the set. The costumes designed by Nicholas ROERICH both evoked contemporary rural dress and suggested primitive tribes of the Steppes. The tunics made by Caffi in ST PETERSBURG were accessorised with belts, pendants, combs and daggers inspired by archaeological finds. The patterning continued into the painting of the shoes and leg bindings and Roerich incorporated silver strands into the women's plaits, which would have picked up the light as they span.

Goncharova established her credentials as a designer for dance with colour-ful portrayals of Russia. Her initial designs for *Les Noces* were typically folkloric, but once Bronislava NIJINSKA was commissioned to choreograph it, she insisted on simple pinafores over blouses for the women, and breeches and shirts for the men. Goncharova chose a colour scheme of dark blue and cream, but Nijinska wanted earth-brown. George Skibine did create a version of the ballet in 1962 using Goncharova's colourful first thoughts but many designers, including Patricia Zipprodt for Jerome Robbins, have essentially followed the Nijinska–Goncharova approach.

In effect, Nijinska stripped down the ballet, as also occurred with Balanchine's production of APOLLON MUSAGÈTE – although in this case a year after the 1928 première. André BAUCHANT's ugly, pale mauve tutus with uneven hems for the Muses were quickly discarded in favour of Coco CHANEL's knitted tunics fastened with ties, which reflected rehearsal outfits of the late 1920s. Obvious stripping down of the costumes can be seen in Maurice Béjart's productions, including The Rite of Spring for Brussels in 1959, when Pierre Caille dressed the company in leotards. Thereafter, close-fitting costumes have often been used. For Kenneth MacMillan's 1962 production, Sidney Nolan evoked Australian aboriginal art, picking up colours of the Australian desert and decorating the body tights with patterns of handprints. The simple sculptural quality of Isamu Noguchi's post-Tchelitchevian set for ORPHEUS (1948) was reflected in his 3D decoration of unitards.

Designs for Agon followed a 1950s trend in New York City Ballet productions for dressing the women in black leotards or tunics and the men in black tights and what looks like a white T-shirt, often described as 'practice clothes'. However, it might be noted that, after 1951, when designer Lucinda Ballard put Marlon Brando in such a fitted T-shirt for the film A Streetcar named Desire, it became a uniform of male virility. At a time when the role of men in tights was being questioned, this simple garment sent out a contrasting message.

Evocation of place and period costumes by Benois (1914), Henri Matisse (1920) and David Hockney (1981) reveal their individual interpretations of Japan for The NIGHTINGALE. Matisse became so fascinated by his costumes that he appears to have painted the designs on silk tunics and appliquéd the chevrons to the gowns for the mourners, thus giving him a first taste of collage work. Hockney for the Metropolitan Opera was inspired by blue-and-white porcelain. Pablo PICASSO's costumes for Pulcinella are his interpretation of COMMEDIA DELL' ARTE costumes, including an extraordinary mask with a flat face and Cyranoesque nose for Pulcinella himself. Other artists who have created colourful personal commedia worlds for Pulcinella include Giorgio de Chirico, Gino Severini, Barry Kay, Eugene BERMAN, Rouben Ter-Arutunian and Howard Hodgkin. The latter also designed the fabrics used for the costumes.

Tutus of varying styles have been designed for a range of ballets. JEU DE CARTES, whether designed by Irene SHARAFF for George Balanchine at American Ballet in 1937, or Dorothee Zippel for John Cranko at Stuttgart Ballet (1965), is usually presented with the women in short tutus and the men in unitards, all decorated by playing-card symbols. For The FAIRY'S KISS, the costumes have a folk element and, like the setting, may reflect the passing of the seasons. Benois (1928), George Kirsta (1934) and Alice Halicka (1937) designed costumes for successive productions by Nijinska, and other designers include Sophie Fedorovitch (1935), Kenneth Rowell (1960) and John Macfarlane (2008), all of whom use colour and mood to enhance the productions. JANE PRITCHARD

Craft, Robert (Lawson) (born Kingston, New York, 20 October 1923; died Gulf Stream, Florida, 10 November 2015). Although his own independent accomplishments as a conductor and prolific author were significant, history will most likely remember Robert Craft as Stravinsky's erstwhile associate. His recordings and writings helped define Stravinsky's image during the composer's lifetime and after his death. While Craft's parents introduced him to performances at the Metropolitan Opera and New York Philharmonic, by his own admission his early musical training was unremarkable. His initial interests in composition and conducting eventually led him to the Juilliard School in 1941. Craft wrote to Stravinsky in 1947 requesting his help in obtaining the score and parts for the SYMPHONIES OF WIND INSTRUMENTS. The composer's cordial response proved fateful. They first met in the spring of 1948 in Washington, DC. A year later, at Stravinsky's invitation, Craft moved to LOS ANGELES, where he assisted the composer with daily business-related matters. The historical bond they quickly forged would endure over the final twenty-three years of the composer's life.

Attempting to encapsulate Craft's presence in Stravinsky's life is challenging. Factotum; amanuensis; negotiator; rehearsal conductor; editor of books, film documentaries and recordings; ghostwriter; family friend; global travelling companion; perhaps even surrogate son – all are among a litany of roles he fulfilled. Craft's position in the Stravinsky household grew exponentially as he earned both the composer's confidence and his affection. He moved from proofing letters to writing them; from screening possible concert engagements to deciding which to choose, nudging Stravinsky to decline certain commissions in favour of accepting others judged more worthwhile. Some commentators have likened him to Boswell, others to Svengali. Whatever the comparison, Stravinsky trusted Craft implicitly, seldom objecting to the younger man's suggestions and decisions.

The generational gap, which might have distanced the two, in fact provided a bridge to unexplored possibilities. Stravinsky appreciated Craft's literacy, his crisp thinking and his bent for erudition. Although the composer was already casually acquainted with the Hollywood literati during his early years in Los Angeles, it was Craft who pressed him to cultivate a more meaningful fellowship with what became a coterie of intellectually vigorous friends: Isaiah Berlin, T. S. ELIOT, Gerald Heard, Aldous HUXLEY, Christopher ISHERWOOD, Dylan THOMAS, Stephen SPENDER and others. Craft's youthful exuberance in exploring unfamiliar pathways clearly meshed with Stravinsky's own instinctual curiosity. He regularly brought new books, scores and recordings into the composer's library. And while Stravinsky had already exhibited an interest in pre-Baroque literature, Craft stoked the composer's fervency all the more with the addition of music by Machaut, Josquin, Gesualdo, and other pre-tonal composers whose fundamental techniques later found their way into the composer's post-tonal music.

It was, in fact, Craft's steadfast dedication to contemporary post-tonal music that provided an unforeseen gateway for the composer. He encouraged Stravinsky to study the literature of the SECOND VIENNESE SCHOOL – a once unfathomable notion. Moreover, Craft's suggestion came just at the right moment. The lukewarm reception that met The RAKE'S PROGRESS in 1951 had profoundly dispirited the composer. He seemed unsure of his path forward, and feared a growing obsolescence in the eyes of younger composers whose interests had turned elsewhere. Astonishingly, Stravinsky reversed himself, fully embracing SERIALISM's rigorous principles – principles he had previously denigrated as 'slavish'. His archives reveal a number of copiously annotated serial scores, particularly those of Anton WEBERN. The economically pointillistic, clean sound of Webern's music intrigued him. Further, Stravinsky accompanied Craft to rehearsal sessions of Webern's music, attentively listening to compositions conducted by Craft and eventually preserved in Craft's own pioneering recordings. Stravinsky's startling turnabout proved revitalising in extending his productivity another fifteen years. Craft had led Stravinsky to a place he otherwise would never have gone. Without his timely intercession, it is unlikely that masterworks such as AGON and REQUIEM CANTICLES would have been written.

Craft's accomplishments include a large discography compiled over sixty-four years. He released dozens of recordings, ranging from Renaissance madrigals to several landmark works by BOULEZ and STOCKHAUSEN. His readings of virtually all of Stravinsky's music evince a deep bar-by-bar knowledge of the composer's original manuscripts. With the notable exception of varying tempi, Craft seldom strayed far from the score. While criticised by those seeking more personalised, flashier interpretations, Craft's fidelity to Stravinsky's scores held firm. Consequently, his readings surely come closest to delivering an accurate historical record of the composer's intentions.

The compass of Craft's recordings is easily matched by his inexhaustible energy as an author. Countless articles, reviews, miscellaneous essays, as well as dozens of books, appeared over six decades. The once thought-to-be-reliable 'conversation' volumes began appearing in 1959. In the wake of Stravinsky's death in 1971, Craft produced an avalanche of books. Among the most illuminating was his 1972 diary, Stravinsky: Chronicle of a Friendship (SCF (72)). The sumptuously illustrated Stravinsky in Pictures and Documents (SPD), featuring a treasure trove of unpublished manuscripts, followed in 1978. In 1982, Craft published the first of three collections of the composer's letters, Stravinsky: Selected Correspondence (SSC). These compilations, however, generated considerable criticism. Numerous expurgations evident in Craft's liberal editing seemed aimed at protecting Stravinsky from his own impolitic views and biases. Readers are left with a filtered and sometimes skewed record of the composer's important exchanges. In 2002, Craft released An Improbable Life, in effect a memoir that cast an even brighter light on his association with Stravinsky. Nor was his writing restricted to this recurring theme. Throughout several more wide-ranging books, Craft's perspicacious views on broader historical, philosophical and political issues were elucidated with cogency, humour and eloquence.

An eyewitness for over two decades, Craft rightly professed to knowing Stravinsky better than anyone. Such closeness, he readily avowed, disqualified him as an objective biographer. Nonetheless, his unparalleled knowledge of the composer could be fiercely asserted in rebuffing opinions that ran contrary to his own. Craft became a vigilant gatekeeper and tenacious defender of the composer's legacy. But with the long-awaited release of Stravinsky's private papers came a turning of the tide. An emerging wave of source-based studies challenged inherited assumptions. Several scholars disputed many of Craft's statements. He was quick to respond, sometimes caustically, with point-by-point rebuttals. All the while, Craft remained undeterred in proposing his own new hypotheses about Stravinsky's life. As late as 2013, in a controversial essay entitled 'Amorous augmentations' (Craft 1983), Craft pried open the history of Stravinsky's sexual orientation, implying his bisexuality. A consensus of scholars, however, dismissed the claim as unsubstantiated supposition.

Given his prominence over the last quarter of Stravinsky's life, Craft was acutely aware he would be judged as a flashpoint. For the forty years following the composer's death, Craft repeatedly tried to explain the chemistry he and Stravinsky shared. As he confessed in his self-reflective essay 'Influence or assistance' (Craft 1984), he worried that indeed he 'had directed and controlled' one of the century's most iconic figures. Yet it was Stravinsky who welcomed Craft's intercession, encouraging him to act as his advocate in procuring the composer's best interests. The responsibility was enormous – and, by his own analysis, fraught with anxiety. Craft's fate became that of walking a precariously thin line. Armed with the composer's archives as a guide, scholars have now begun to realise just how thin it was. In assessing Craft's inextricably intertwined life with Stravinsky, history must now sort through an entangled web of interactions, disclosures, distortions, influences and other shaping forces – all of which sum to a uniquely complex relationship in the annals of twentieth-century music. CHARLES M. JOSEPH

Robert Craft, 'Amorous augmentations', in *Stravinsky: Discoveries and Memories* (Franklin, Tenn.: Naxos Books, 1983), 163–87.
Robert Craft, *An Improbable Life* (Nashville: Vanderbilt University Press, 2002).
Robert Craft, 'Influence or assistance', in *Present Perspectives* (New York: Alfred A. Knopf, 1984), 246–74.

Credo (Simvol' verĭ). Composed 1932. First performance, ? First published 1933, Édition Russe de Musique (Slavonic); 1964, Boosey & Hawkes (Latin). Text: Nicene Creed.

The third in the group of pieces sometimes collectively called Three Sacred Choruses, the *Credo* shares with the PATER NOSTER and AVE MARIA a simplicity and severity intended to counteract what the composer perceived as the sentimentality of the repertoire he heard at the RUSSIAN ORTHODOX CHURCH in Nice. Initially written in Slavonic, a Latin adaptation was made later. The music of the *Credo* is plain and syllabic, as settings of this text in the Russian tradition generally are, and in this it is also stylistically of a piece with the other two works in the group, a result of Stravinsky's return to his ancestral Orthodox faith in 1926. It resembles a *fauxbourdon*, and is in harmonic terms essentially modal; it has a descendant in the Credo of the later MASS (1944–8). The Latin version includes the word *Filioque* ('and from the Son') reflecting the different theological positions on the procession of the Holy Spirit in the Orthodox and Roman Catholic Churches. IVAN MOODY

Cui, César Antonovich (born Vilnius, 6/18 January 1835; died Petrograd, 26 March 1918). Russian composer and critic, of French and Lithuanian descent. Though a member of BALAKIREV's Moguchaya Kuchka ('The Mighty

Handful' / THE FIVE), he was more notable as a waspish music critic for journals including the *Sanktpeteburgskiye vedomosti* (1864–77), *Novoye vremya* (1876–80, 1917) and *Nedelya* (1884–90). As an admirer of Stravinsky's father, Fyodor STRAVINSKY, Cui was for the young Stravinsky a familiar, if rather distant, figure: in *Memories and Commentaries* (Mem.), Stravinsky recalls delivering an invitation to Cui (or, at least, to Cui's home) for his father's jubilee performance as Holofernes in Serov's *Judith*. In later years, Stravinsky claimed to have had little time for the 'orientalism' of Cui's music, yet appreciated his writings on Alexander Dargomïzhsky's operas, since they drew Stravinsky's attention to 'the remarkable quality of the recitatives' of *The Stone Guest*, which in turn 'had an influence on my subsequent operatic thinking'; this is most evident in Stravinsky's *The* NIGHTINGALE, most particularly Act III composed in 1914. Cui, for his part, had little time for Stravinsky's 'monotonous and unbearable ... pursuit of sonorities and orchestral effects'. DANIEL JAFFÉ

D

Dahl, Ingolf (born Hamburg, 9 June 1912; died Frutigen, Switzerland, 6 August 1970). German-American composer, pianist, conductor and educator. After studies in GERMANY and SWITZERLAND, Dahl visited the UNITED STATES in 1935 to study with Nadia BOULANGER and, in view of the dire political situation in Europe, decided to stay, settling in LOS ANGELES. Stravinsky first got to know him through his performances as conductor and pianist at the EVENINGS ON THE ROOF concerts, which began in 1939, and the Russian composer took Dahl on as a musical assistant, delegating to him the task of translating his Harvard lectures, The POETICS, into English. Dahl also worked with Stravinsky on the piano reduction of his DANSES CONCERTANTES. Influenced first by the contrapuntal music of Hindemith, Dahl's own compositions eventually displayed aspects of Stravinsky's NEO-CLASSICISM. He was part of Stravinsky's circle and one of his closest musician friends in Los Angeles.   EDWARD CAMPBELL

Dalcroze Eurhythmics. Stravinsky's estimation of Émile Jaques-Dalcroze (1865–1950) and his system of eurhythmics remains elusive, but the composer's relative silence may hold the key. Well documented is the 1912 visit of Sergey DIAGHILEV and his protégé Vaslav NIJINSKY to the Dalcroze school in Hellarau (Stravinsky did not attend) – an attempt by Diaghilev to help the young choreographer disentangle the complex rhythms of Stravinsky's The RITE OF SPRING. Though Stravinsky had his own misgivings about Nijinsky's musical abilities – stating in his AUTOBIOGRAPHY that 'the poor boy knew nothing of music' – he never suggests Dalcroze as a remedy. Rather, Stravinsky hardly praises the Swiss pedagogue in Expositions and Developments when he describes Léonide MASSINE's 1921 version of The Rite as 'too gymnastic and Dalcrozean to please me'. In contrast, correspondence from Dalcroze to Stravinsky (brought to light by Robert CRAFT and published in Dance Magazine) reveals that Dalcroze was an avid fan of the composer's music. It appears the two had met on at least a couple of occasions, and Dalcroze writes how he 'was overwhelmed with joy, emotion, and human pride' when attending a concert of Stravinsky's music in 1915. Yet, according to Craft, there is not 'a single word the other way around' originating from Stravinsky. Despite numerous invitations from Dalcroze to host Stravinsky at his institute, letters suggest the composer managed to avoid such a reunion. Perhaps Stravinsky's attitude toward eurhythmics can be at least partially discerned from statements he made in Craft's conversation books: 'Choreography, as I see it, must realize its own form, independent of the musical form, but measured to the musical units . . . it must not seek merely to duplicate the line and beat of the music'.　　　　　　　LORIN JOHNSON

Danses concertantes. Composed 1939–42. First performance, 8 February 1942, LOS ANGELES, The Werner Janssen Orchestra of Los Angeles. Conductor, Igor Stravinsky. Published 1943, New York: Associate Music Publishers.

This concert work, written for a chamber orchestra of twenty-four players and lasting about 20 minutes, was commissioned by the Werner Janssen Orchestra of Los Angeles. Although Stravinsky wrote 'Concerto for Small Orchestra' on the original manuscript (this was deleted before publication), it is obvious from the titles of the movements that he also thought of it as music that could be used as an abstract (themeless) BALLET, and so it was performed in New York in 1944 by the Ballet Russe de Monte Carlo, choreographed by BALANCHINE with designs by Eugene BERMAN.

It is usually said that the work, which was finished on 13 January 1942, was composed in 1940–2, but, according to Stravinsky, the beginnings of the work in fact predate 1940. In *Themes and Conclusions*, he says that about half of the music had been composed before he received the commission from Janssen, that 'the music began in the first theme of the final *Allegro* [*Tempo giusto alla breve*] of the *Symphony in C*', and that he composed the 'Pas d'Action', which he says 'is simply a variant of the Symphony theme', on 19 October 1939, while still sketching the earlier work.

Danses concertantes is in five movements: 'Marche-Introduction', 'Pas d'Action', 'Thème Varié', 'Pas de Deux' and 'Marche-Conclusion', and, in a ballet performance, the two marches serve as points of entry and exit for the dancers. The final march recapitulates the first twenty-three bars of the opening one, before going into a seventeen-bar conclusion. These two movements are quite clearly in B♭ major, with rhythmic melodies in staccato quavers and semiquavers that conform to the opening 2/4 metre, eschewing, except in the second section, the syncopation that becomes so characteristic of some of the later movements. The first march comes to a very quiet end, with a bar and a half of quasi-diatonic descending semiquavers in the violins and continued *staccatissimo* in the bassoon under a descending chromatic scale in the clarinet: a moment's silence is followed by a *piano* first-inversion B♭ major triad in the woodwind and brass affirming the tonal centre of the movement.

The second movement, 'Pas d'Action', is in C major and is marked *Con moto*. The metre alternates between 3/4 and 2/4, with the principal sections of a strongly rhythmic character, and the melodic phrases based on a clearly defined pulse. The melody at Rehearsal No. 24 acts as a refrain, recurring at Nos. 29, 48, 49, 52 and 61; these sections are punctuated by sudden *sff* tutti chords, giving the movement a rondo-like structure. In the slower *legato* B section at 34–48 melodies in the violins are always accompanied by constant pairs of semiquavers, and in the C section, at No. 53, by repeated notes in quavers in the strings, then by repeated four-semiquaver figures at 57–9. The reduced scoring of the B section sets it apart from the rest of the movement. These interludes are followed by a final return of the A section, beginning at No. 61, and end with four tutti chords played *ff*, most of which are a combination of tonic and dominant triads.

A single sustained high G in the clarinet acts as a link into the central movement, which is cast in the form of a theme and variations and is by far the longest movement with the most variation of tempos. Stravinsky described his variation technique as follows: 'In writing variations my method is to remain faithful to the theme as a *melody* – never mind the rest! I regard the theme as a melodic skeleton and am very strict in exposing it in the variations.' In spite of his avowed 'strictness' and his 'faithfulness to the melody', one is often hard put to hear melodic similarities in these variations, as the 'skeletons' are treated in various ways to make them unrecognisable, especially on first hearing: octave displacements that produce extremely jagged melodies with adjacent notes sometimes in different instruments and octaves apart, complete changes of rhythm, addition of rests and syncopations. The effect is of a series of contrasting character pieces. What is traditional here is the change of tempo and character in successive variations, which differ in length from 42 to 74 bars. The theme, marked *Lento*, is in G, with the variations rising in semitones – *Allegretto* in A♭, *Scherzando* in A, *Andantino* in A and *Tempo giusto* in B♭. The fourth variation is in 6/8 and thus stands apart from the rest of the work, which exploits various crotchet metres.

Again, the ending of the variations flows seamlessly into the succeeding 'Pas de Deux', where the sustained melodic phrases on the oboe would have an almost romantic character were it not for the spiky accompaniment on the strings, which introduces elements of bitonality. These opening and concluding sections are separated by abrupt changes of mood and tempo, featuring a soloistic treatment of the woodwind. The quasi-narrative character of the writing is a reminder of the dance-like conception of the work as a whole, which is rounded off by an extended restatement of the opening Marche.

KATHRYN PUFFETT

Debussy, (Achille-) Claude (born St-Germain-en-Laye, 22 August 1862; died Paris, 25 March 1918). Innovative French composer whose colouristic approach to harmony and ORCHESTRATION proved highly influential. Debussy and Stravinsky first met in PARIS in 1910 – the older composer invited Stravinsky for dinner after the première of FIREBIRD on 25 June – and, given the importance of Russian music to Debussy in his formative years, they must have had much to discuss. As a student at the Paris Conservatory, Debussy had visited RUSSIA during the summers of 1880–2 as an employee of TCHAIKOVSKY's patron Madame von Meck: he was the house pianist and part of a piano trio. In Russia, he got to know the music of Tchaikovsky, and Stravinsky said that Debussy discovered MUSSORGSKY in Russia in 1881, during his second summer spent with the von Meck family, though most other reports suggest Debussy first encountered Mussorgsky's music in Paris. Mussorgsky's *Boris Godunov* in particular had a strong impact on Debussy's opera *Pelléas et Mélisande*.

Russian music appealed to Debussy for its evocative and colourful qualities, and in this sense Stravinsky's teacher RIMSKY-KORSAKOV was a key influence. For his part Rimsky, according to many reports, did not want to listen too much to Debussy because he might have ended up liking it ... In technical terms, Debussy's use of systematic duplication, ostinato patterns, modalism and sung conversation bear witness to the Russian influence – though, unlike many of his Russian forebears, Debussy tends to vary a musical motif when it is immediately repeated. Later works by Debussy, for instance his second book of *Préludes* (1910–13), feature some octatonic harmony, though, as is usual in Debussy's musical language, he fuses modal and tonal elements in this collection.

Firebird launched the 28-year-old Stravinsky as one of the most exciting composers on the Paris scene and ensured his artistic identity in this period was bound up with the early picturesque style of DIAGHILEV's BALLETS RUSSES. Debussy was at the première: he considered the ballet 'not perfect but in many ways it is nevertheless very fine because music is not subservient to the dance'. He was, however, an unreserved admirer of PETRUSHKA, telling Stravinsky that it had 'an orchestral infallibility that I have found only in *Parsifal*'. Debussy wrote to his close friend Robert Godet on 18 December 1911 of Stravinsky's 'instinctive genius for colour and rhythm', praising his music because it 'doesn't "show off"! It's made of real orchestral stuff, directly, in a way which concerns itself only with the events of its own emotion. There is neither caution nor pretension. It's childlike and untamed. Yet the execution is extremely delicate. If you get a chance to meet him, don't hesitate.'

Debussy played Part I of the piano duet version of The RITE OF SPRING with Stravinsky at the critic Louis LALOY's home on 9 June 1912, a year before the première (Debussy played the secondo part). 'I still preserve the memory of the performance of your *Sacre du printemps* at Laloy's', Debussy wrote to Stravinsky on 5 November; 'It haunts me like a beautiful nightmare and I try in vain to retrieve the terrifying impression it made. For which reason I look forward to its production like a greedy child who has been promised sweets.' The ambiguous tone of this letter is surely that of an older composer who knows he is about to be overshadowed. Debussy's relationship with the Ballets Russes was more difficult than Stravinsky's: his own BALLET commission *Jeux* was premièred on 15 May 1913 at the THÉÂTRE DES CHAMPS-ELYSÉES, two weeks before the cataclysm that was *The Rite of Spring* which ensured Debussy's ballet was overlooked by critics. (Stravinsky, for his part, considered *Jeux* 'Debussy's freshest, most youthful work of recent years'.) And a few days after the première of *The Rite of Spring*, Stravinsky was present at the first performance of NIJINSKY's choreographed version of *Prélude à L'après-midi d'un faune* on 29 May 1913, with its scandalous concluding scene in which the frustrated faun masturbates with a nymph's discarded scarf. Debussy was not amused by this explicit visualisation of what was only suggested in Mallarmé's poem.

Stravinsky's dedication of KING OF THE STARS (1911–12) to Debussy is testament to his admiration for the French composer. While Debussy thought the work was 'extraordinary', he wrote to Stravinsky on 18 August 1913 that he 'could only envisage a possible performance of this "cantata for planets" on Sirius or Aldebaran'! If Debussy was suggesting that the combination of the huge orchestral and choral forces required and its 5-minute duration would limit performance opportunities for this work, he was right. By 1915, Debussy had refined his opinion of Stravinsky, writing to his friend Robert Godet on 14 October: 'Stravinsky himself is leaning dangerously in the direction of Schoenberg, but nevertheless remains the most wonderful orchestral technician of our time.' Nine days later, he wrote to Stravinsky himself that 'you are a great artist! Be above all a great Russian artist! It's such a fine thing to be from

one's country, to be attached to the earth like the most humble peasant!'
Debussy's remarks reveal at least as much about his own preoccupations as
a 'musicien français' in wartime as they do about Stravinsky. And a month after
an unsuccessful operation for the rectal cancer that would kill him two years
later, Debussy expressed a caustic view of Stravinsky to Godet, calling him 'a
spoilt child who sometimes dabbles in music' who 'pretends to be my friend,
because I helped him climb the ladder from the top of which he now throws
bombs which don't all explode. But I'll say it again, he's unbelievable.'

Stravinsky's SYMPHONIES OF WIND INSTRUMENTS (1920) is dedicated to the
memory of Debussy, though Stravinsky said in his AUTOBIOGRAPHY (*Chroniques
de ma vie*) that he believed Debussy 'would have been rather disconcerted by my
musical idiom' in this work. *Symphonies of Wind Instruments* represented
a turning point in Stravinsky's music and became a key work of the twentieth
century for later generations of composers, notably Harrison Birtwistle and
Pierre BOULEZ.   CAROLINE POTTER

Claude Debussy, *Correspondance 1884–1918*, ed. François Lesure (Paris: Hermann, 1993).

Delage, Maurice (born Paris, 13 November 1879; died Paris, 19 September 1961).
French composer who studied composition with RAVEL, and who was a fellow
member of the APACHES. He is known for his *poèmes symphoniques* (including *Les
Bâtisseurs de ponts*, 1913) and his *mélodies* (including *Sobre las Olas*, 1924, which set
a poem by Jean COCTEAU). Stravinsky was clearly very fond of Delage, noting in
his AUTOBIOGRAPHY: 'Maurice Delage was with me constantly. I was greatly
attracted by his buoyant disposition' (*Auto*, 50). He refers to Delage often in
his letters, they travelled at times together, and it is clear that Delage was
a trusted friend who introduced Stravinsky to others in his social network.
Stravinsky stayed with Delage at his home in PARIS in 1911, and Delage in turn
visited Stravinsky at CLARENS. The artistic group of *Les Apaches* was a helpful
support for Stravinsky, and it was in a shared box with Delage, Ravel and
Schmitt that he heard FOKINE's production of Ravel's *Daphnis et Chloé* in 1912.

Delage had travelled to India and Japan towards the end of 1911 and early in
1912, and drew on his experience, integrating his ideas of the 'exotic' within
several of his compositions, notably the *Quatre poèmes hindous* (1912), *Ragmalika*
(1915) and the *Sept haï-kaïs* for soprano and chamber orchestra (1923).
Stravinsky's 'exoticism', in contrast, arguably derives from his own personal
circumstances of living and working in RUSSIA, FRANCE and, latterly, the
UNITED STATES, though obviously 'exotic' elements, redolent of the East, are
found in The NIGHTINGALE, The SONG OF THE NIGHTINGALE and the *Three Japanese
Lyrics* (1914). Japanese prints held pride of place on Stravinsky's walls, some of
which may have been bought for him by Delage. That Stravinsky dedicated the
first of the *Japanese Lyrics* to Delage is perhaps unsurprising since Delage had
organised the meetings at the Pavilion, the little cottage where *Les Apaches* met –
in effect, a little Japanese retreat decorated in oriental style. Delage visited
Stravinsky at Clarens in order to translate the Japanese lyrics into French, and
in this way participated in the creation of the work. The Japanese songs were
premièred by the Société Musicale Indépendante, in Salle Erard, in a concert
arranged by Ravel on 14 January 1914.   HELEN JULIA MINORS

Charles N. Joseph, *Stravinsky's Ballets* (New Haven and London: Yale University Press, 2011).
SCS

Delaunay, Robert (born Paris, 12 April 1885; died Montpellier, 25 October 1941). French painter, printmaker and writer who co-founded 'simultanism', an abstract style featuring bold use of colour and geometric form. Although Delaunay was active in the Parisian art scene prior to World War I, he and Stravinsky became friends in Spain where Robert lived during and after the war and where the BALLETS RUSSES performed frequently between 1916 and 1918. During these years, Stravinsky described himself, Delaunay and Sergey DIAGHILEV as inseparable. Although Stravinsky claimed to tire of Delaunay's constant conversation about modern art, Delaunay had interesting ideas regarding art and music, including colour as a quasi-musical element and recurring visual motifs as a correlate of musical variation.

While Stravinsky frequently collaborated with artist-friends, Stravinsky and Delaunay never worked together on a theatrical project. Delaunay, however, painted an oil portrait of Stravinsky in 1918 (New Art Gallery Walsall) that brought visual and musical modernism into more subtle dialogue. Using colour to convey Stravinsky's form loosely, Delaunay's portrait revealed his overarching interest in colour and light. Notably, the painting was reproduced in a 1922 issue of *Vanity Fair* for an article by Tristan Tzara extolling modernism. Various sources claim that Delaunay also completed a rendering in charcoal of Stravinsky composing The SOLDIER'S TALE.   BARBARA SWANSON

Delaunay-Terk, Sonia (born Gradizhsk, Ukraine, 14 November 1885; died Paris, 5 December 1979). Painter, printmaker, fashion and costume designer at the forefront of abstraction and the Parisian avant-garde. Delaunay-Terk met Stravinsky during one of the BALLETS RUSSES' Spanish tours and while herself a wartime resident of Spain. Back in FRANCE, their work frequently intersected. Delaunay-Terk chose the première of Stravinsky's MAVRA to wear her newly designed *robe à poème* – evidence of Stravinsky's importance to Parisian art and taste-making. In 1968, Delaunay-Terk designed the BALLET adaptation of Stravinsky's DANSES CONCERTANTES (Ballet-Théâtre Contemporain Amiens). A related series of lithographs entitled *Hommage à Stravinsky* and *Danses concertantes* (1968–71) features boldly coloured interlocking circles, suggesting a resonance between Stravinsky's music and the elements of visual abstraction.

BARBARA SWANSON

Désormière, Roger (born Vichy, 13 September 1898; died Paris, 25 October 1963). French conductor. His principal study at the Paris Conservatory was the flute, which he was taught by Philippe Gaubert. He first met Stravinsky when he became a conductor for DIAGHILEV's BALLETS RUSSES in 1925. In a tribute to Désormière written after his death, Stravinsky described him as 'an exceptional musician. A remarkable flautist, he abandoned his solo career to become a conductor ... I will never forget his attitude to *Apollon Musagète* (which so annoyed the musical *avant-garde* in Paris) ... Until the end of my days I will have admiration and infinite gratitude for everything he succeeded in doing for the music of our time.' Désormière conducted the *Three Japanese Lyrics* in 1922 and several performances of The SOLDIER'S TALE in 1925. He first conducted

Petrushka with the Ballets Russes in 1925, and between 1926 and 1929 he conducted multiple performances of Pulcinella, Les Noces, The Firebird, Oedipus Rex, The Song of the Nightingale, The Rite of Spring, Apollo and Renard. In the 1930s, he performed Stravinsky regularly, adding Symphony of Psalms and the Octet for Wind Instruments to his repertoire. He conducted the European premières of Scènes de ballet (7 December 1945) and the Symphony in Three Movements (21 November 1946). In 1948, he conducted the Symphony in C and Orpheus, and gave a concert performance of The Nightingale the following year. In 1950, Désormière conducted a broadcast of the Concerto in D, his only Stravinsky performance to be published on disc (by INA Mémoire vive). In March 1952, Désormière suffered a catastrophic stroke which ended his career. NIGEL SIMEONE

Nicolas Guillot: 'Roger Désormière (1898–1963)': https://sites.google.com/site/rogerdesormiere18981963.
Denise Meyer and Pierre Souvtchinsky (eds.), Roger Désormière et son temps: textes en hommage (Monaco: Éditions du Rocher, 1966).

Diaghilev, Sergey (born near Novgorod, Russia, 19/31 March 1872; died Venice, 19 August 1929). Although not a recognisable artist, musician or performer in his own right, Sergey Diaghilev changed the face of European culture in the first third of the twentieth century by bringing together the finest artists of the day to collaborate on projects. When asked by King Alfonso of Spain what he did, Diaghilev responded: 'I am like you, Your Majesty, I do nothing, but I am indispensable.' Asked by others about his role, he simply claimed, 'I supervise the lighting.' While there is truth in these statements, they are far from the whole truth. Diaghilev did light the ballets at a time when electric theatre lighting was becoming more sophisticated, but he also supervised every aspect of productions mounted by his company so that they met his high standards. Diaghilev was an animator in the truest sense of the word, an impresario, an artistic director of vision who commissioned choreography, musical scores and designs from the finest creative talent, and a fundraiser who kept his unsubsidised company afloat for almost two decades, until his death in 1929.

Sergey Diaghilev was born near Novgorod, Russia, but raised from his tenth year in Perm in the Urals, where Europe and Asia meet. The family owned a large house in town and a country estate, Bikbarda, about 300 kilometres away, with their income derived from the vodka monopoly for the region. Sergey's mother had died three months after his birth, but he had a happy relationship with his stepmother, Yelena, who encouraged his interest in the arts and instilled in him the will to succeed. Perm had an active opera house and Yelena employed a German teacher, Eduard Dennebaum, to educate Sergey and his two younger step-brothers. Significantly, this included training as a pianist and Diaghilev became a competent musician, which would stand him in good stead when editing the music of those he commissioned, including Stravinsky, Debussy and Prokofiev, and when searching for forgotten scores in Italian archives.

Diaghilev's family failed to adapt to modern life and the reforms of the 1860s and 1870s, thus, in 1890, when Sergey was aged 18, the family was declared bankrupt. At this time, Diaghilev, with his cousin (also lover for twelve years), Dmitry Filosofov, was travelling in Europe seeking out celebrities, developing his philosophy and coming to terms with his homosexuality (which he never hid). On his return, Diaghilev settled in St Petersburg to read law and, as he was the only family member with funds, having directly inherited from his birth-mother, Diaghilev assumed responsibility for his two siblings. He aspired to being a composer but, after consulting Rimsky-Korsakov, was advised to find an alternative career.

In St Petersburg, Diaghilev was introduced by Filosofov to a group of artists, led by Alexandre Benois, who were looking to expand their artistic horizons. Where Diaghilev was well informed about music, his new friends introduced him to fine, applied and theatre arts, and quickly he took the lead in promoting all these areas. As he wrote to Leo Tolstoy in 1893, 'The dream and purpose of my life is to work on the field of art.' In late 1898, Diaghilev and Benois founded Mir iskusstva (World of Art), Russia's first lavishly illustrated periodical that promoted both west European and contemporary Russian art. In addition, the group promoted a series of concerts of Russian music and exhibitions which culminated in the enormous immersive Exhibition of Russian Historical Portraits at the Tauride Palace in 1905. Before this, in 1899, Diaghilev had been employed by the Imperial Theatres for special assignments, including editing the theatre's Year Book. He tried to seize the opportunity to produce ballets, planning a production of Delibes's Sylvia to be designed by his friends, but before this was realised he was dismissed.

Diaghilev was aware that, with the disastrous Russo-Japanese War (1904–5), the ongoing disturbances and strikes, and his widely known homosexuality, St Petersburg in the early 1900s was not the place to fulfil his ambitions, so he turned to western Europe. Russia was economically reliant on France, and the French were increasingly fascinated by Russian arts, encouraging Diaghilev to mount a major exhibition, 'Two Centuries of Russian Painting and Sculpture', within the Parisian Salon d'Automne in 1906. During the planning of this exhibition, Diaghilev met many key figures in the French art world, notably the wealthy Comtesse Greffuhle who offered to support a series of Russian concerts at the Paris Opéra in May 1907. Thereafter, although always experiencing a peripatetic existence, Paris provided the principal platform for his work. The renowned Russian bass Fyodor Chaliapin had been a great success at the concerts, and in 1908 Diaghilev presented him as Boris Godunov at the Opéra. This experience introduced Diaghilev to the full range of the challenges of theatrical production and, for the remainder of his life, he would be responsible for productions of first-class ballets and operas for the international stage.

Diaghilev's 1909 Saison Russe of opera and ballet showed he had absorbed his step-mother's determination to succeed. In March, the Tsar had suddenly withdrawn financial support for Diaghilev's programme. Rather than give up, he refocused his season to include single scenes from operas, placing emphasis on one-act ballets. Although he overreached himself financially, with adroit negotiation he avoided disaster and thereafter the presentation of innovative ballet became his focus. Diaghilev loved opera, but he realised it was expensive to promote, and Russian opera and music had been revitalised at the end of the nineteenth century. Standards of dance were higher in Russia than elsewhere, where there was a creative vacuum he could fill. After two seasons in which he depended on the availability of dancers during their summer vacation, he recognised the need to establish his own company to ensure their year-round services.

Once his company was extant, from 1911, Diaghilev's life took on a regular pattern, although that was interrupted by the impact of war and revolution, which completely cut him off from his homeland. Regular short seasons were presented in Paris in early summer, during which most ballets would be premièred. Monte Carlo became the place for winter rehearsals and performances during the fashionable 'season'. Post-war, the company also served as the opera-ballet. Longer performance seasons were presented in London, where patrons and commercially successful seasons were important to the survival of Diaghilev's company. Diaghilev would often find time in the summer to relax with visits to Bayreuth and VENICE.

Diaghilev quickly understood his audiences' tastes and he would combine more accessible works with more controversial productions. For his first performances in Paris, he included such homages to French culture as the Louis XIV-style *Le Pavilon d'Armide* and *Les Sylphides*, for Berlin he added *Carnaval* evoking the Biedermeier style, and it was for London that he produced narrative classics: *Swan Lake* in 1911 and *The Sleeping Princess* in 1921. The more avant-garde ballets were reserved for Paris, London, Monte Carlo and Berlin, although ballets such as *Parade* were occasionally presented in Madrid at the special request of the King of Spain. For other cities, the focus was on the popular ballets which appealed to theatre managers and audiences, and whose scores could be tackled by theatre orchestras. Diaghilev was never averse to controversy, and as a publicist knew how to turn this to his advantage.

He recognised the West's interest in Russia and the diverse cultures within the Russian Empire, ranging from those of cities and the steppes to Asia, as well as drawing on Russian folk tales. Beginning with the Polovtsian Dances from *Prince Igor*, *The* FIREBIRD and PETRUSHKA, he presented aspects of Russia, which would continue with *The* RITE OF SPRING, *Chout*, *Les* NOCES and *Pas d'Acier*. Many of the Russian ballets had original scores by Igor Stravinsky or Sergey Prokofiev, the two composers he most frequently turned to, and who were so important for him that he referred to them as his sons.

Stravinsky's collaborations with Diaghilev's BALLETS RUSSES enabled him to be quickly recognised internationally as a major talent. He was unusual in that he collaborated with Diaghilev throughout the history of the Ballets Russes, from contributing to the arrangement of Chopin's music for *Les Sylphides* in 1909 through to agreeing that his score APOLLON MUSAGÈTE (1927–8), although commissioned for the Washington Library of Congress, would receive its European première with Diaghilev's company. He received his real break with the score for *The Firebird* in 1910. The music Diaghilev commissioned is the most enduring aspect of his creative work. Over half the scores for Diaghilev's ballets were original creations and many continue to inspire CHOREOGRAPHERS. The impressive range of composers who contributed to the Ballets Russes also includes Nikolay Tcherepnin, Reynaldo Hahn, Claude Debussy, Richard STRAUSS, Erik SATIE, Ottorino Respighi, Manuel de FALLA,

Francis POULENC, Georges AURIC, Darius MILHAUD, Vladimir Dukelsky (Vernon Duke), Vittorio Rieti, Constant Lambert, Lord BERNERS, Henri Sauguet and Nicolas NABOKOV.

A similarly impressive list of artist designers could be presented. Initially, Diaghilev depended heavily on Alexandre Benois with his love of history, and Léon BAKST with his bursts of jewel-like colour and exoticism. Russian artists dominated in the early years, with Natalya GONCHAROVA and Mikhail LARIONOV bringing a modern dynamism and more acidic palette. José-Maria Sert became the first non-Russian to design a production, although Jean COCTEAU was contributing ideas and poster images from the birth of the company in 1911. From 1917, Diaghilev increasingly drew on European fine artists, and it was a proud moment when the company returned to Paris after the war with new productions designed by the three artists recognised as the greatest of the time: Pablo PICASSO with *The Three-Cornered Hat*, André Derain with *La Boutique fantasque* and Henri Matisse with *The* SONG OF THE NIGHTINGALE. Matisse was typical of many collaborators who were reluctant to be commissioned, but Diaghilev had the ability to charm individuals to get his own way. For many of the designers, like the composers, being commissioned by Diaghilev launched them on continuing careers of involvement with the theatre.

Although the first ballets Diaghilev presented were reworkings of Mikhail FOKINE's creations for the Imperial Ballet, he went on to present mainly original choreography. For Fokine, Bronislava NIJINSKA and George BALANCHINE, he provided the platform for them to develop their choreography; for Vaslav NIJINSKY and Léonide MASSINE, he nurtured their choreographic careers. The bisexual Nijinsky and Massine were also Diaghilev's lovers, and major personal and company crises arose when they deserted him for marriage. Diaghilev controlled the company's productions, but he always worked with a committee of advisers, an inner circle, whose make-up changed from one year to the next. While his informal committee made suggestions about collaborators, and themes, oversaw costumes (Coco CHANEL was part of the group in the 1920s) and assisted with fund-raising, Diaghilev's own decisions dominated. He had no qualms about suggesting Picasso re-think designs or Prokofiev re-write a score. Diaghilev understood what worked on stage and expected his artists to follow his vision. His success was such that ballet became recognised as an art form to be taken seriously. He encouraged audiences to accept whole evenings of dance and returned the male dancer to a central role.

Diaghilev was a man of contradictions. While at heart he appears to have been conservative, his determination to be at the cutting edge of the avant-garde enabled him to embrace more radical ventures. He was a large man with distinctive appearance and quiff of white hair who would always be noticed. He embraced the modern world but was highly superstitious. A gypsy had told him he would die on water, making even crossing the Channel alarming, and the Atlantic a nightmare. In a 1902 letter to his stepmother, he predicted he would 'manage to act like Wagner and will come to Venice to die'. In the summer of 1929, ill because of diabetes, he dragged himself back to the city he loved, for him a place of escape, relaxation and renewal, to fulfil this last ambition. He had transformed European arts and theatre and continues to inspire new generations. Indeed, as the composer Sergey Prokofiev claimed, he was 'a giant, undoubtedly the only one whose dimensions increase the more he recedes into the distance'.   JANE PRITCHARD

Divertimento. Suite in four movements ((I) Sinfonia (II) Danses suisses (III) Scherzo [Au Moulin] (IV) Pas de deux: Adagio, Variation, Coda) from Stravinsky's one-act BALLET The FAIRY'S KISS (1928). Stravinsky authorised the performance of concert extracts from The Fairy's Kiss as early as 1931 but only undertook the arrangement of the work as a 'Suite symphonique' in 1934, first performed under the composer at the Salle Pleyel, PARIS, on 4 November the same year, and published in full orchestral score in 1938 (Édition Russe de Musique). According to Craft (SSC, II), Stravinsky worked on the violin–piano transcription of the Suite together with Samuel DUSHKIN at Fontainebleau in autumn 1933, although this chronology has been disputed (SCS). The transcription formed part of the duo's touring repertoire, receiving its first performance in Strasbourg on 12 December 1934. All four movements of the violin–piano transcription were published in 1934 (Édition Russe de Musique). Dushkin made his own arrangement of the 'Ballade', which Stravinsky approved but ultimately excluded from the published Suite.   JEREMY COLEMAN

Stephanie Jordan, 'Divertimento from Le Baiser de la fée: ghost stories', Dance Chronicle, 29.1 (2006), 1–16.

Dolin, (Sir) Anton (orig. Sydney Francis Patrick Chippendall Healey-Kay) (born Slinfold, England, 27 July 1904; died Paris, 25 November 1983). British dancer, CHOREOGRAPHER and director. Dolin first saw Stravinsky during rehearsals for the BALLETS RUSSES' 1921 production of the Sleeping Princess (featuring Stravinsky orchestrations of TCHAIKOVSKY), and he subsequently joined the company and met the composer. Twenty-three years later, they collaborated on SCÈNES DE BALLET (1944), a BALLET segment in Billy Rose's Broadway revue The Seven Lively Arts. The two devised the scenario and Dolin choreographed, and starred in, the production (alongside his regular partner Alicia MARKOVA). Although mostly a successful collaboration, there were minor frictions: Stravinsky refused Dolin's requests for rescoring. Dolin later described Stravinsky's score as 'more than unsuitable' (Dolin 1973, 242). SOPHIE REDFERN

Anton Dolin, Markova: Her Life and Art (London: White Lion, 1973).

Double Canon for String Quartet. Composed late November 1959. First performance, 20 December 1959, New York. Published 1960, Boosey & Hawkes. Dedication: 'Raoul Dufy in Memoriam'. The Quartet began life as a two-part canon for flute and clarinet using a TWELVE-NOTE series, sketched while Stravinsky was staying in VENICE in October 1959. It was then expanded as a double canon for string quartet, one canon theme between violins 1 and 2 and a second theme (also a twelve-note row) between viola and 'cello. The two violins frame the piece, opening it with the first canon and concluding it with an inversion of the second canon. The canonic imitation takes place alternately at the whole tone and at the unison. This piece was intended from the start as a response to a commission: Marcelle Oury was preparing an edition of her correspondence with the French Fauvist painter Raoul Dufy, who had died in

March 1959, and inquired whether Stravinsky might contribute a piece. After some vacillation, he accepted the commission, despite the fact that he never knew Dufy.   JEREMY COLEMAN

Duet for Two Bassoons, 'Lied ohne Name'. Composed 1916–18, and completed 1918. In July 1949, Stravinsky added a German title 'Lied ohne Name [sic] für zwei Fagotten' ('Song without a Name, for Two Bassoons'). (This was a grammatical error on Stravinsky's part. 'Name' is a weak masculine noun which takes an 'n' in the accusative case, and the title should therefore read: 'Lied ohne Namen'.) First performance, 30 October 1979, London. The surviving sketch, dated December 1916, and the autograph manuscript were both published in 1982 (SSC, I); and the score by Boosey & Hawkes, 1997. Robert CRAFT claimed that Stravinsky reworked the piece as a song, which in turn provided the basis of his THREE PIECES FOR SOLO CLARINET (1919) (SSC, I). More significantly, the scoring 'reflects Stravinsky's increasing confidence in wind instruments to provide an ideally cold and "less vague" sonority for his emerging objective idiom', and, indeed, anticipates his OCTET FOR WIND INSTRUMENTS (first performed in 1923), a work in which the two bassoons assume a prominent role throughout (Griffiths 2013).   JEREMY COLEMAN

Graham Griffiths, *Stravinsky's Piano: Genesis of a Musical Language* (Cambridge University Press, 2013).

Dukas, Paul (born Paris, 1 October 1865; died Paris, 17 May 1935). Composer known for his orchestral vibrancy, a prolific critic and essayist, as well as a teacher who ended his career as Professor of Composition at the PARIS Conservatory. He has been given credit for influencing Stravinsky's FIREBIRD (1911) (Joseph 2011, 25), as Stravinsky's first BALLET score goes beyond the orchestral tones and timbres of the Russian school. Dukas taught ORCHESTRATION and composition at the Paris Conservatory from 1927 until his death, and his best-known work, *The Sorcerer's Apprentice* (1897), explores a wide range of orchestral colours. The opening of *The Sorcerer's Apprentice* has been compared to the slower music in Stravinsky's FIREWORKS (Pople 2003, 67) and the influence of the new French school, with its clearer textures and an interest in mythology, can be seen in Stravinsky's earlier piece, *The Faun and the Shepherdess*, op. 2 (1906–7) (Vlad 1967, 5). It is likely that Stravinsky first heard the music of Dukas, alongside that of DEBUSSY, RAVEL and D'Indy, in the course of the concert series EVENINGS OF CONTEMPORARY MUSIC in ST PETERSBURG, a series held between 1901 and 1912 (Routh 1975, 4), as part of which Stravinsky's first orchestral performances took place, with the support of the conductor Alexander ZILOTI. Having become a French citizen on 10 June 1934, Stravinsky applied in 1935 to replace the recently deceased Dukas as a member of the Institut de France, but unfortunately he lost out to fellow composer Florent Schmitt.

HELEN JULIA MINORS

Charles M. Joseph, *Stravinsky's Ballets* (New Haven and London: Yale University Press, 2011).
Anthony Pople, 'Early Stravinsky', in Jonathan Cross (ed.), *The Cambridge Companion to Stravinsky* (Cambridge University Press, 2003), 58–78.
Francis Routh, *The Master Musicians: Stravinsky* (London: J. M. Dent and Sons Ltd, 1975).
Roman Vlad, *Stravinsky*, trans. Frederick and Ann Fuller (New York: Oxford University Press, 1967).

Duo Concertant, for violin and piano. Composed 1931–2. Published 1933, Édition Russe de Musique (Russischer Musikverlag); 1947, Boosey & Hawkes. First performance, 28 October 1932, Berlin, Funkhaus. First public performance, 2 November 1932, Gdansk, Poland.

(I) Cantilène (II) Eglogue I (III) Eglogue II (IV) Gigue (V) Dithyrambe.

As an aesthetic statement, Duo Concertant reflects the composer's affinity with the ideas expressed by the Vaudois writer Charles-Albert CINGRIA (1883–1954) in Pétrarque (1932), his study of the great Italian poet and scholar. Cingria's book was published just after Duo Concertant was completed, yet Stravinsky gained great satisfaction from finding his own neo-classical views reflected in it 'with the utmost appropriateness'. Most relevant of these for being quoted in Stravinsky's AUTOBIOGRAPHY (1936) is 'Lyricism cannot exist without rules' (Auto, 170). Lyrical art, therefore, must be constructed via craft and be 'ingenious [astucieux] and difficult', an apt description of Duo Concertant's rich and challenging rhetoric. 'Cantilène' opens with a striking effect, the piano imitating the bisbigliando tremolo of a harp or, in anticipation perhaps of ORPHEUS (1947), the lyre. 'Eglogue' (a misreading for 'eclogue', corrected in the second movement of ODE, 1944) was a poetic form associated with Virgil, later with Dante, Boccaccio and Petrarch. 'Dithyrambe' refers to the ancient Greek choric hymn performed with mime. It was originally a wild dance in honour of Dionysius, though here it brings the work to a sombre conclusion, sorrowful yet also dignified and graceful. Structurally, and in performance, Duo Concertant is dominated by the amaranthine 'Gigue'; this is a veritable tour-de-force for both players – a particularly fierce test for the pianist – clear evidence that Stravinsky, with this work, had resolved previously expressed concerns about blending 'strings struck in the piano with strings set in vibration by the bow'. The equally concertante violin part was elaborated, as the score makes clear, 'with the collaboration of [Stravinsky's duo partner] Samuel DUSHKIN'.

GRAHAM GRIFFITHS

Charles-Albert Cingria, Pétrarque (Lausanne: Éditions L'Age d'Homme, 2003 [1932]).
Graham Griffiths, Stravinsky's Piano: Genesis of a Musical Language (Cambridge University Press, 2013).

Duparc, Henri (born Paris, 12 January 1848; died Mont-de-Marsan, 12 February 1933). French composer who studied with César Franck and was a close friend of the Breton composer Jean Cras. In his retirement, Duparc lived in an apartment in CLARENS, the Swiss village where Stravinsky composed most of The RITE OF SPRING. Stravinsky recalled meeting the conductor Ernest ANSERMET at Duparc's home. Recalling Duparc years later, Stravinsky noted that he was 'a morose old gentleman' and a 'chanson composer' (T&C, 229).   HELEN JULIA MINORS

Dushkin, Samuel (born Suwałki, 13 December 1891; died New York, 24 June 1976). Polish-American violinist, composer and teacher of Jewish origin. Dushkin studied at the Conservatory in PARIS, and in New York City with Leopold Auer and Fritz Kreisler. When Willy Strecker suggested in 1930 that Stravinsky should write a violin concerto for publication by Schott, he invited Dushkin to dine with them in Wiesbaden to discuss the proposal. The composer and violinist got on very well together from the outset; Stravinsky began to note down ideas for the piece the following day and Dushkin was charged with advising him regarding the technical aspects of solo writing for violin. As Dushkin noted later, 'Stravinsky's music is so original and so personal that it constantly posed new problems of technique and sound for the violin. These problems often touched the very core of the composition itself and led to most of our discussions' (cited in SCS, 507). As Walsh notes, Dushkin's 'task was unenviable. He had to make effective bravura out of ideas that might lie awkwardly for the violin, but without compromising the ideas themselves.' Dushkin gave the world and US premières of the work and performed with the composer for the first recording of the piece. Beyond the concerto, Stravinsky composed the DUO CONCERTANT and DIVERTIMENTO to play in concert with Dushkin, and they also worked together on transcriptions of other pieces such as the SUITE ITALIENNE from PULCINELLA.   EDWARD CAMPBELL

Samuel Dushkin, 'Working with Stravinsky', in Edwin Corle (ed.), *A Merle Armitage Book: Igor Stravinsky* (New York: Duell Sloan & Pearce, 1949), 179–92.

E

Ebony Concerto, for clarinet and jazz ensemble. Completed 1 December 1945. First performance, 25 March 1946, New York. Published 1946, Charling Music Corporation, New York; reissued 1954 by Edwin H. Morris & Co., London. Order of movements: (I) Allegro moderato (II) Andante (III) Moderato (Con Moto).

Stravinsky's final JAZZ-inspired foray, the *Ebony Concerto* (*c.* 11 minutes' duration), was commissioned by the clarinettist/bandleader Woody Herman, who premièred it in Carnegie Hall and recorded it. Later, in April 1965, Stravinsky recorded it with Benny GOODMAN and the Columbia Jazz Ensemble. The title supposedly reflects Stravinsky's admiration for African-American jazz musicians – including Charlie Parker, as related in George Russell's *A Bird in Igor's Yard* (1949) – and blues culture, as much as the assumed reference to Woody's clarinet. 'Concerto', meanwhile, incorporates aspects of Baroque *concerto grosso*.

The work is scored for solo clarinet in B♭ and large jazz ensemble: saxophones (altos, tenors, baritone), clarinets (3 in B♭, plus bass), horn, trumpets, trombones, piano, harp (!), guitar, double bass, percussion and drums. Its opening movement (B♭ major) adopts a neo-classical sonata-allegro form, with repeat marks. Layered syncopations – interspersed by fleeting jazz 'breaks' – lead to and accompany the bluesy clarinet melody (Figure 10, with hints of the 'Ragtime' from The SOLDIER'S TALE and PETRUSHKA), like a barrel organ. The 'Andante' (F minor–major) explores a lugubrious blues theme (saxophones), together with mechanised 'clockwork' figurations on brass (Figure 4). Unusually, the finale blends variation and rondo-like forms, featuring riffs, swung triplets and brass glissandi, then showcasing the clarinettist's virtuosity ('Vivo', Figure 24). As Stephen Walsh (1993, 186) has noted, the piece 'merely uses conventions from ... [concerto] tradition as a framing device for a study in jazz idioms', albeit highly stylised, abstracted and gestural in treatment.

Like much Stravinsky, this work has been explored choreographically: notably in 1960, by John Taras and the NEW YORK CITY BALLET.

DEBORAH MAWER

Stephen Walsh, *The Music of Stravinsky* (London: Routledge, 1988).

Eight Instrumental Miniatures for 15 players. Composed 1921; 1961–2. First (integral) performance, 29 April 1962, Toronto. Published 1962, London: J. & W. Chester. Dedication: 'To Lawrence Morton'.

The *Eight Instrumental Miniatures* are a reworking of *Les* CINQ DOIGTS (1921), an early piano composition, which contains eight 'very easy melodies on 5 notes'. The revision is not only a new instrumentation of the earlier pieces for ensemble (2.2.2.2. – 1.0.0.0. – 2.2.2.0) but also a rethinking of the musical material, including, as Stravinsky put it, 'rhythmic rewriting, phrase regrouping', 'canonic elaboration' and 'new modulation'. He also changed the keys of number II (from F major to A major) and number VI (from C major to B major) (SCW, 300). The outer movements are retained for the most part unchanged, in both their material and their positioning. Stravinsky nevertheless elaborated all of the movements contrapuntally, which can be seen, for example, in the canonical development of the third section of the first movement. Numbers IV and V were lengthened slightly. Apart from pieces I, V and VIII, which remained in place, all of the others have new positions in the suite and were arranged and enhanced by extrapolated material. The concluding piece (VIII) was originally written for twelve musicians in 1961, performed with Robert CRAFT conducting, and then withdrawn. Stravinsky re-composed the complete suite shortly afterwards. The composition is dedicated to Lawrence MORTON, director of the Monday Evening Concerts in LOS ANGELES, as part of which numbers I–IV were premièred on 26 March 1962, again conducted by Craft. The first performance of all eight miniatures was conducted by the composer and took place at Massey Hall, Toronto, on 29 April 1962.   FLORIAN HENRI BESTHORN

Elegy for J. F. K. For medium voice (baritone or mezzo-soprano) and three clarinets (clarinets 1 and 2 in B♭, clarinet 3 in E♭ alto), setting an English text by W. H. AUDEN. Composed late March 1964. First performance (in the baritone version), 6 April 1964, in a Monday Evening Concert, LOS ANGELES. Conductor, Robert CRAFT. Published 1964, Boosey & Hawkes. The first performance with mezzo-soprano took place on 6 December 1964, at the Philharmonic Hall, New York City, conducted by the composer. This twelve-note serialist miniature was written to commemorate the death of President John F. Kennedy following his assassination (22 November 1963), and both the poem and Stravinsky's setting are dedicated to Kennedy. The idea of the piece dates to January 1964 during an evening Stravinsky spent in Auden's company. The first performance was prepared with all due haste but reportedly turned out well. The concert series director Lawrence MORTON had requested that there be no applause, and Stravinsky noted that the performance 'was very dignifying'.

                                                                        JEREMY COLEMAN

SSE

Elegy for solo viola (or violin). Composed 1944. First performance, 26 January 1945. Published 1945, New York: Chappell. Dedication: 'composée à l'intention de *Germain Prévost*, pour être jouée à la mémoire de *Alphonse Onnou* fondateur de *Quatuor Pro Arte*'.

The *Elegy* for solo viola was composed in memory of Alphonse Onnou, the founder of the Pro Arte Quartet, and was commissioned by Germain Prévost. It can also be performed a fifth higher on the violin. A two-part invention in three sections, the elegy is written without any time signature and should be played *con sordino* throughout. In the first section of fifteen bars, what White described as 'a kind of chant' is 'played above a simple flowing accompaniment' (SCW, 427).

The middle segment (twenty-nine bars) is an expressive fugue, while the third section repeats the first eleven bars of the piece before ending with a short four-bar coda.   FLORIAN HENRI BESTHORN

Eliot, T. S. (Thomas Stearns) (born St Louis, 26 September 1888; died London, 4 January 1965). American-British poet, dramatist and literary critic. One of the most influential and widely studied poets of the twentieth century, Eliot's best-known poems include 'The Love Song of J. Alfred Prufrock' (1915), *The Waste Land* (1922) and *Four Quartets* (1943). Eliot immigrated to England in 1914 and became a British citizen in 1927. He expressed an appreciation for Stravinsky's music as early as 1921, but they did not meet in person until 1956, when Stephen SPENDER introduced them in London. Given their remarkably similar views on artistic innovation within the context of tradition, it is not surprising that Stravinsky sought out opportunities to collaborate with the Nobel Prize-winning poet. Most notably, the composer hoped Eliot would provide a text for a dramatic work based on the story of Noah, which would eventually become *The* FLOOD. Instead of an original text by Eliot, however, Robert CRAFT compiled quotations from Genesis and the Chester mystery plays.

Although these two giants of MODERNISM never formally collaborated, Stravinsky did use the fourth section of 'Little Gidding', the last of Eliot's *Four Quartets*, as the text for his 1961–2 ANTHEM ('The dove descending breaks the air'). After meeting in 1956, the two men corresponded and socialised on a regular basis, and when Eliot died of emphysema in 1965, Stravinsky dedicated his INTROITUS to his friend's memory.   MATTHEW PAUL CARLSON

T. S. Eliot, 'London letter', *The Dial*, 71 (October 1921), 452–5.
SPD; SSE

Epitaphium. Subtitled: 'für das Grabmal des Prinzen Max Egon zu Fürstenberg'. Composed between mid-April and early June 1959, in commemoration of Prince Max Egon von Fürstenberg who had died on 6 April. First performance, 17 October 1959, Donaueschingen Music Festival. Conductor, Pierre BOULEZ. Published 1959, the Boosey & Hawkes. The work was commissioned by Heinrich Strobel alongside other new works intended as funeral music. Stravinsky had been a guest of the Prince at the Festival in 1957 and 1958. The work is scored for harp, flute and clarinet, the instrumentation having been partly determined by the decision to programme the work with Anton WEBERN's 5 *Geistliche Lieder*, op. 15 (which uses those instruments as well as soprano voice, violin/viola and trumpet). An aphoristic piece (seven bars long), the harmony is based on a TWELVE-NOTE row but uses it in such a way that no two forms of the row ever appear simultaneously; rather, the different permutations alternate between harp (bass) and winds (descant) in a responsorial manner. Stravinsky later gave a revealing account of the compositional process of the work (M&C).   JEREMY COLEMAN

Evenings of Contemporary Music. A musical section of *Mir iskusstva*, active between 1901 and 1912, founded in ST PETERSBURG by Alfred Nurok (1863–1919) and Walter Nouvel (1871–1949). An official at the Naval Ministry by vocation, Nurok was one of the founding members of *Mir iskusstva*, the head of its music division and its main musical chronicler. Notorious for his sarcastic wit, he was a man of immense intelligence and education, profound kindness and no ambition at all. A professed bibliophile, an ardent fan of Hoffmann, Baudelaire and Verlaine, himself a Hoffmannesque figure, he stood for everything ultramodern and iconoclastic in art, and was the first to acquaint the Miriskusnik artists with the drawings of Aubrey Beardsley, which influenced them greatly, and to introduce RAVEL to a Russian audience. Walter ('Valechka') Nouvel, a special duty officer at the Ministry of Court and an amateur composer, was one of the driving forces of Mir iskusstva. Emigrating in 1919, he remained one of the closest associates of DIAGHILEV until his death, and wrote his first biography, unpublished but used as a source by Arnold Haskell for his book, Diaghileff: His Artistic and Private Life. Later, Nouvel ghostwrote for Stravinsky his AUTOBIOGRAPHY (1935) (Chronique de ma vie ('Chronicle of My Life')). Nurok and Nouvel formed the EVENINGS OF CONTEMPORARY MUSIC (EOCM) Committee together with the music critic Vyacheslav KARATÏGIN (1875–1925), the composer Ivan Kryzhanovsky (1867–1924) and the pianist Alexander Medem (1871–1927).

The inaugural concert of the EOCM took place on 31 March 1902 (O.S.) at the Small Hall of the ST PETERSBURG CONSERVATORY and featured RACHMANINOV, GLAZUNOV, Kryzhanovsky and Nouvel himself. The EOCM aimed at promoting 'nothing but novelties' (according to Nurok); however, its criteria for MODERNISM were arbitrary and based on the personal taste of the Committee. Besides the above-mentioned Rachmaninov, the EOCM performed works by DEBUSSY, D'Indy, DUKAS, Tcherepnin, GNESIN, STEINBERG and others, and had evenings dedicated to César Franck, Max Reger, Maurice Ravel and Alexander SCRIABIN. PROKOFIEV and Myaskovsky both had their debut at EOCM on 18 December 1908 (O.S.). The Moscow branch, led by music critic and publisher Vladimir Derzhanovsky (1881–1942), was active between 1909 and 1915.

Stravinsky's debut at the EOCM took place on 27 December 1907 (O.S.), when his songs Vesna (Monastyrskya) and PASTORALE were both sung by Elizaveta Petrenko (dedicatee of the songs and the first interpreter of The Faun and the Shepherdess), accompanied by Mladen Iovanovich (the house EOCM pianist at the time). His songs were also on the programme of the EOCM on 24 February 1909 and 13 January 1911 (O.S.). At the Moscow branch of EOCM, Stravinsky's Three Japanese Lyrics were given their Russian première on 23 January 1914 (O.S.), performed together with the songs Vesna and Forget-Me-Not Flower by soprano Yekaterina Koposova (Derzhanovsky's wife). She was accompanied by Konstantin Saradzhev, at the time the Chief Conductor of the Free Theatre, and co-founder of the Moscow EOCM branch.

ELENA VERESHCHAGINA AND TATIANA VERESHCHAGINA

Evenings on the Roof. Founded in 1939, the LOS ANGELES concert series Evenings on the Roof (later Monday Evening Concerts) was attended by Stravinsky from March 1944, after he heard of them from fellow musicians Sol Babitz and Ingolf DAHL. Pioneered in bohemian fashion by Peter Yates and his wife Frances Mullen at their loft in Silverlake, the Roof concerts promised affordable access to contemporary music with, in Stephen Walsh's words, 'a minimum of ostentation'. Though early audiences were modest in size, participation grew to the hundreds by the mid-1940s. Stravinsky affectionately related how they reminded him of the EVENINGS OF CONTEMPORARY MUSIC he had frequented in St Petersburg – the origin of his public debut as a composer in 1907. He notes in *Memories and Commentaries* (*M&C*) that the LA series, similar to the St Petersburg concerts, 'tried to match the new with the old. This was important and rare.' Stravinsky designed certain arrangements specifically for the concerts, such as a re-orchestrated version of his Tango for Chamber Orchestra and updated instrumentation for *Podblyudniye*. In spring 1964, the composer wrote Elegy for J. F. K. and then asked to have it included in the programme to honour the fallen president. During Stravinsky's twenty-nine years in residence in Los Angeles, the Monday Evening Concerts included seventy-two performances covering fifty-eight of his compositions, including world premières such as In Memoriam Dylan Thomas, which was first performed in September 1954, with Aldous Huxley providing a dedicatory address at the start of the concert.   LORIN JOHNSON

$$\boxed{\text{F}}$$

The Fairy's Kiss (Le Baiser de la fée). Allegorical BALLET in four tableaux based on a tale, *The Ice Maiden*, by Hans Christian Andersen. Composed April to 17 October 1928, Nice. First performance, 27 November 1928, PARIS Opéra, Ballets de Madame Rubinstein. Conductor, Igor Stravinsky. Published 1928, Édition Russe, piano score; 1952, Boosey & Hawkes (full score).

Dedication: 'To the memory of Pyotr Il'ich Tchaikovsky. The ballet has an allegorical meaning, since Tchaikovsky's Muse, like the Fairy, marked the artist with her fatal kiss, the mysterious seal of which was imprinted on all creations of this great artist.'

Synopsis: a woman with her baby is struggling through a snowstorm; the sprites from the Fairy's troop pursue her, separate her from the child and take the child to the Fairy, who bestows her kiss on his forehead and leaves. The boy, named Rudi, is found by peasants and grows up as an orphan in a village in the Alps. On his wedding night with a local girl, Babette, the Fairy comes to claim him for herself. At a village fête, the Fairy appears as a Gipsy, dances with the boy and tells his fortune. At the mill, Babette plays with the other girls, and then leaves to prepare for the wedding. The Fairy comes, dressed in a wedding veil, and Rudi, taking her for Babette, declares his love to her. The Fairy transfers him to the land beyond time and space. She again bestows her kiss on him, this time on his heel.

The work was commissioned by Ida RUBINSTEIN, who in 1927 founded a ballet company of her own, recruiting Alexandre BENOIS as her main artistic adviser and chief designer, and Bronislava NIJINSKA as principal CHOREOGRAPHER. It was Benois who approached Stravinsky on Rubinstein's behalf, proposing 'to do something to Uncle Petya's music' and citing a list of carefully chosen works by TCHAIKOVSKY which amounted to fifteen piano pieces (op. 19, 37a, 40, 51), the main condition being that the sources were not initially orchestrated by Tchaikovsky himself. Stravinsky used more than half of Benois's suggestions, adding to them several songs at key points of the story: 'Lullaby in a storm', op. 54/10, with the other related song, 'Winter evening', op. 54/7, encompassing the first scene; the love lyrics, op. 6/3, at the end of the village fête; op. 63/6 in *Pas de deux* at the mill; and 'None but the lonely heart', op. 6/6, in the masterly scene that follows. 'Lullaby in a storm' returns in the final part of the ballet as the lullaby beyond time and space. The intimate tone, lyrical substance and downplayed pathos of the sources defined Stravinsky's approach to the work, which he described as his 'heartfelt homage to Tchaikovsky's wonderful talent' (*Auto*, 146). The composer himself listed the borrowings in his programme notes to the recording with the Cleveland

Orchestra, and later, in expanded form, discussed them with Robert CRAFT (Expo, 84–5), differentiating between exact quotation ('Lullaby in a storm' in the first tableau), imitation (Entr'acte symphonique from The Sleeping Beauty at the beginning of the third tableau) and his own music. Lawrence MORTON (1963), and later Richard Taruskin, further elaborated the list of sources (for a full and updated list, see: SRT, 1611–12).

Stravinsky himself chose the title of the ballet, but it was most likely Benois who proposed the Andersen tale as a literary base: Andersen formed a link to his previous collaboration with Stravinsky, The NIGHTINGALE, and nostalgically evoked the 1900s, when Russian culture was extremely susceptible to Andersen's influence.

Stravinsky preserved only 'a skeleton' of Andersen's story in a libretto of his own, as he claimed in a letter to Gavriyil Païchadze (26 October 1928), with neither sets nor choreography necessarily tied 'to the precise details and exigencies of the place and time of the action' (Stravinsky to Benois, 12 August 1928). He was mainly interested in the artistic initiation, which formed the substance of the story for him, as revealed in the same letter and stated in the Dedication. The moment of poetic consecration is marked as the moment of rapture, passing from seasonal time to the eternal land beyond time and space, a symbolic death: dying for the profane world, the poet is born anew for his poetic and prophetic calling.

For Stravinsky, Tchaikovsky stood for Europeanised RUSSIA, that of ST PETERSBURG (as opposed to Moscow), with its cultivated aristocracy and great literature so dear to his heart, of the Imperial Russian style par excellence. He avowed an umbilical connection to that 'Latin-Slav' – that is, Europeanised – stratum of Russian culture, many times, most famously in an open letter to DIAGHILEV dated 1 October 1921, at the time of the latter's The Sleeping Beauty project in London. That is why his treatment of Tchaikovsky's material is so different from his treatment of PERGOLESI in PULCINELLA – more like a homage than an ironical manipulation. He borrowed not only melodies: the ORCHESTRATION is a carefully studied imitation of Tchaikovsky (most notable examples – Panorama; Entr'acte Symphonique from The Sleeping Beauty), the harmony is unequivocally tonal, and the overall structure is striking for the almost total absence of his trademark ostinati.

The reception of the ballet was a mixed one, with the most acid review by Diaghilev in his letter to LIFAR after the première and later in public (in the émigré paper Vozrozhdenije, 18 December 1928; Stravinsky read and commented on this article). Famously jealous of Stravinsky for his collaboration with Rubinstein, Diaghilev criticised the overall performance: Ida's haggard looks, hunched back, bent knees and lack of professional ballet skills; the under-schooled corps de ballet; the hapless décor by Benois; 'dull and lachry-mose' music by Tchaikovsky; and 'overall lack of vitality' in Stravinsky's arrangement (Diaghilev to Serge Lifar, 28 November 1928). After The Fairy's Kiss, Stravinsky's relations with Diaghilev came virtually to a standstill. Other critics were more benevolent. André Levinson hailed Stravinsky's return to the classical ballet tradition, finding in the music 'a concentrated extract of what was at its apogee the ballet d'action' (Levinson 1928, 2). Stravinsky confessed that Nijinska's choreography 'left him cold' (Auto, 149), but was enthusiastic about his own music, as revealed in his 1929 New Year greeting card to ANSERMET: 'this year, with *Apollo* and *Fée*, was one of the most fruitful ones in my life, where my work is concerned, and one of the most significant in terms of development' (cited in SRT, 1617).

ELENA VERESHCHAGINA AND TATIANA VERESHCHAGINA

André Levinson, 'La Chorégraphie', *Comoedia*, 1 December 1928, 2.

Falla (y Matheu), Manuel (María de los Dolores) de (born Cádiz, 23 November 1876; died Córdoba, Argentina, 14 November 1946). Composer. Intensely religious and private as a person, Falla is remembered for writing highly colourful and sensual music. This juxtaposition is evident in his close friendship with Stravinsky, evinced in their extensive correspondence and numerous handwritten dedications of scores, whose style, by turns sarcastic and devotional, demonstrates considerable intimacy. Stravinsky told Robert CRAFT that Falla was 'the most devoted of all my musical friends' (*Mem*, 81).

The two first met in PARIS in 1910; both were occasional members of the APACHES. On his return to Madrid at the outbreak of war, Falla became Stravinsky's most prominent apologist in Spain. He positioned his music as a shining example to Spanish composers, not least in a 1916 article tellingly entitled 'El gran músico de nuestro tiempo', written to herald Stravinsky's visit to Madrid with the BALLETS RUSSES. The two met a further ten times between 1920 and 1930, and corresponded intermittently until 1945.

In the aforementioned article, Falla especially commends two aspects of Stravinsky's music. One is the 'national character of its rhythms and melodies'; it is significant that early works by both composers rework folk song material without abstracting its original meaning. The other is 'the conquest of new sonorities'. Falla and Stravinsky began experiments with smaller instrumental forces around the same time: *El amor brujo*, originally for an ensemble of fifteen instrumentalists, dates from 1915, while Stravinsky played an early version of *Les* NOCES privately for his friend in 1916. Falla took further steps in this direction with his puppet-OPERA *El retablo de Maese Pedro* (first performed in the Princess de Polignac's salon just two weeks after the first performance of *Les Noces* in the same locale) and his Concerto for harpsichord and five solo instruments, the latter perhaps influenced by his close study of Stravinsky's CONCERTO FOR PIANO AND WIND INSTRUMENTS. (Stravinsky conducted a performance of Falla's Concerto at Dumbarton Oaks in 1947.) Other shared attributes can be traced to innovations by one composer or the other. The rhythmic drive and complexity of *The* RITE OF SPRING undoubtedly influenced the ritual spirit of *El amor brujo*, while Falla's adoption of eighteenth-century mannerisms in his DIAGHILEV BALLET *El sombrero de tres picos* ('The Three-Cornered Hat') (an early version of which he played for Stravinsky in 1916) predated PULCINELLA by four years.

CHRIS COLLINS

C. G. Collins, 'Manuel de Falla and his European contemporaries: encounters, relationships and influences' (Ph.D. thesis, University of Wales, Bangor, 2002), 463–537.

Manuel de Falla, *Escritos sobre música y músicos*, 4th edn. (Madrid: Espasa-Calpe, 1988).

SSC, II, 160–76.

Fanfare for a New Theatre. Composed 23 March 1964 for two trumpets. First performance, 20 April 1964 by Robert Nagel and Theodore Weiss at a private gala for the opening of the New York State Theater, Lincoln Center for the Performing Arts, New York City, then the new home of the NEW YORK CITY BALLET. The first public performance took place at the official opening night of the City Ballet on 24 April 1964. Published in 1968 (Boosey & Hawkes). Dedicated 'To Lincoln and George': Lincoln KIRSTEIN, the Theater's administrator, who commissioned the Fanfare in early March, and CHOREOGRAPHER George BALANCHINE. Stravinsky used a TWELVE-NOTE series employing all the main forms of the row (prime, retrograde, inversion, retrograde inversion). The piece opens with a generic fanfare in unison on A♯, after which the two parts diverge to present the same form of the row in canon. The harmonic and rhythmic character is mostly dissonant and both parts use wide tonal intervals.

JEREMY COLEMAN

Film. Stravinsky never completed an original film score. However, his compositions have often been used in films, both during his lifetime and subsequently. Throughout his life, he had innumerable failed negotiations with the film industry, some of which gave rise to music that was later reused for other purposes. Cinema (and later television) occupied rather more than a negligible portion of his activity and also played an important role in the reception of his works and in the creation of the 'myth' surrounding him.

According to Stravinsky's memoirs, his first encounter with moving pictures dates back to 1904, when he was a student in ST PETERSBURG. Following his move from RUSSIA, his interest in film greatly increased, and throughout the Swiss and French years he was an enthusiastic cinema-goer, with a strong predilection for Buster Keaton and Charlie Chaplin. His first professional contacts with the world of film go back to the years of the silent movies. In October 1919, he was asked by Blaise Cendrars to write music for a film about *Don Quixote* directed by Abel Gance. Stravinsky showed interest in the proposal but questioned whether the subject might conform to his ideas on the role of music in cinematographic spectacle. This early episode demonstrates that he had already contemplated the possibility of writing film music and had formulated a personal view of filmmaking's relationship to music (see below).

Other examples of aborted collaborations in film productions date back to the early years of the sound movie. According to Luis Buñuel's memoirs, in 1930 the aristocratic patron of the arts, Charles de Noailles, was about to commission the former to make a film for which Stravinsky would compose the music. However, Buñuel refused to work with 'someone who's always falling to his knees and beating his breast'. An ORCHESTRATION of the *Three Little Songs: Recollections of my Childhood* (1906–13), which Stravinsky worked on from December 1929 to January 1930 seems to have been originally meant for a French film which was never released. A further failed project occurred in April 1932, when the German Tonfilm company asked him for twenty minutes of music from PETRUSHKA to be used as a soundtrack. It was in those years that the film industry also started turning its attention to theatrical and concert performance of Stravinsky's music as possible subject matter for films.

Stravinsky's subsequent contacts with the film industry in the 1930s were occasioned by his US tours. In 1935, he visited the MGM studios in Culver City, guided by the studio's senior composer Herbert Stothart. On that occasion, he gave a short speech in German in the presence of all the members of the MGM music department and had a meeting with Louis B. Mayer. During this tour, he also had dinner with Chaplin, in the course of which the two artists set out ideas for a possible collaboration on a film based on a subject that Chaplin sketched out on the spot. However, Chaplin never returned to the proposal, either in their next meeting in 1937, or in reply to the composer's queries on the subject.

During his third US tour in 1937, Stravinsky made contact with Boris Morros, head of the music department at Paramount Pictures. On this occasion, a contract was signed according to which Paramount would suggest to Stravinsky a number of possible scenarios, for one of which he would provide music, in exchange for a payment of $25,000. In the end, even this project collapsed, probably due to Stravinsky's idea that 'the story and the setting and all the rest will be written around the music' (as some interviews and advertising of the day reported), which did not correspond to the producer's intentions.

All this notwithstanding, Stravinsky persevered in negotiations with the world of film. After his move to the UNITED STATES in September 1939, he realised that writing for the cinema could be a lifeline at a time when he had lost the royalties on his music in Europe and, as he was not yet sufficiently familiar with the new American environment, could expect no important commissions from there. At this time, he reached an agreement with Disney over what would remain the best-known use of one of his not-originally-for-film scores in a movie: that of The RITE OF SPRING in Walt Disney's animation film Fantasia (1940). The contract, signed in New York in January 1939, stated that, in exchange for just $6,000 (Disney only needed Stravinsky's permission for distribution in countries under the Berne Convention on copyright, since all music by foreign composers was in the public domain in the United States), the composer allowed the producer to use the score as he pleased, either cutting parts of it or arranging them in the order that he deemed most appropriate. Therefore, when Stravinsky saw the pre-screening of the film in Hollywood in December 1939, and then again in the October of the following year, he was not at all surprised or disappointed (as he maintained twenty years later he had been (Expo, 145–6)) at Leopold STOKOWSKI's changes to the score, nor did he voice any complaint about them. Stravinsky's relationship with Disney certainly remained friendly, at least until October 1940, when he signed a new contract with Disney for the use of FIREWORKS, RENARD or The FIREBIRD. It was only after Fantasia's release, when the work was not so enthusiastically received by the audience as other Disney productions, that the composer started distancing himself from the project. Finally, in 1960, Stravinsky publicly expressed total disapproval of both Stokowski's rearrangements and his orchestral conducting, and questioned the whole artistic value of the production as a 'dangerous misunderstanding' of his music, thus leading to a quarrel with Disney.

During the war years, Stravinsky's financial needs compelled him to embark on film projects related to wartime anti-Nazi American propaganda. In March 1941, he signed a contract with MGM to provide music for a film about the invasion of Norway – The Commandos Strike at Dawn (1942, directed by John Farrow). The music written for the occasion, based on Norwegian folk tunes he found in a nineteenth-century collection, was later turned into an orchestral suite entitled FOUR NORWEGIAN MOODS. In 1942–3, he was then asked to write a score for a film about the Nazi invasion of Russia, The North Star (1943; written by Lillian Hellman; directed by Lewis Milestone). When contract negotiations failed – the score was finally provided by Aaron COPLAND – Stravinsky converted the music he had drafted up to that point into a piece for Paul WHITEMAN's famous big band: SCHERZO À LA RUSSE (1944). Two other film projects from those years also resulted in music for the concert halls: a film adaptation of Charlotte Brontë's Jane Eyre, produced by 20th Century Fox and directed by Robert Stevenson, with Orson Welles as Rochester; and The Song of Bernadette, a 1943 film based on Franz Werfel's novel of the same title. The music composed for a 'hunting scene' in Jane Eyre was transformed into the central movement (Eclogue) of his ODE (1943), commissioned by the conductor Sergey KOUSSEVITZKY in memory of his wife. The music drafted for the 'Apparition of the Virgin' scene in The Song of Bernadette was recycled in the second movement of his SYMPHONY IN THREE MOVEMENTS (1942–5).

There is evidence of several other failed projects in the following years. In early 1952, a suggestion came from the English film writer Simon Harcourt-Smith to write music for a film about the Odyssey. This proposal was later reiterated by Michael Powell, who was thinking of the film as a sort of Masque, for which Stravinsky would write the music and Dylan THOMAS the verses. In April 1964, an agreement was almost reached with the Italian film producer Dino De Laurentiis to provide music for the film entitled The Bible (1966). Both projects, however, collapsed, probably for financial reasons. The only occasion when Stravinsky succeeded in writing the music for a movie was in 1963, with Joseph Strick's film adaptation of Jean GENET's play The Balcony. However, he did not write an original score but simply adapted some excerpts from his OCTET FOR WIND INSTRUMENTS and The SOLDIER'S TALE. Moreover, there is some evidence that the adaptation was made by Robert CRAFT.

When all is said and done, the only original work that Stravinsky conceived and completed entirely for the screen was not the soundtrack of a film but the music of a television OPERA: The FLOOD, produced by Robert Graff and first (and last) broadcast by CBS on 14 June 1962. While reflecting an essentially theatrical (operatic) conception, the film made use of many visual effects impossible to achieve on the stage, most of which were partially envisaged by Stravinsky, George BALANCHINE and Robert Craft. However, the decisive contribution to the visual component of the opera came from the director Kirk Browning, who traduced their ideas into fascinating visual effects achieved by the technology of television. In his writings, Stravinsky insisted that in The Flood he had tried to create a new artistic form appropriate for this electronic medium. Stravinsky dedicated himself to this work with great diligence, and with the hope of increasing his popularity with the American television audience, following his repeated failure with cinema. However, his hopes were again to be dashed: in terms of audience, the telecast was judged to be 'an inglorious flop'.

It is difficult to say whether Stravinsky's failures in negotiation with cinema owe more to his excessive financial demands, to the incompatibility of his compositional practices with the labour organisation of the studios, or to his aesthetic convictions. Stravinsky was capable of writing music very quickly when he wished to do so, but his compositional routines did not lend themselves to the flexibility required by such a process, and nor would his authoritarian view of the composer's complete control over all aspects of the musical production have allowed him to negotiate the final form of his music with any studio's music department.

As for Stravinsky's aesthetic ideas about film music, their role in his difficulties with studios should not be over-estimated, since they were not always as negative as in his best-known published views on the subject. An example of the latter occurs in a short article in the form of a discussion with Ingolf DAHL, which was published in the Musical Digest in September 1946 (then followed in 1948 by a rebuttal by the film composer David Raksin, entitled Hollywood Strikes Back). Here, Stravinsky gave a totally negative assessment of film music, recognising as its only role that of providing a 'background' to the images, bridging the 'holes' and filling 'the emptiness of the screen ... with more or less pleasant sounds'. The basic premises to this conclusion were, firstly, his well-known rejection of the expressive function of music – i.e. the conviction that music is unable 'to express ... to explain, to narrate or to underline something' – and, secondly, the idea that, in addition to not being related by any content, each art should construct its own form independently from others – an idea he had originally formulated in relation to BALLET. Both concepts were applied by Stravinsky to the genre of film music in various statements dating from 1919 – when he wrote a letter to E. ANSERMET dealing en passant with film music – to the early 1930s. However, on these occasions, Stravinsky had contemplated the possibility that, in the cinema too, music could relate to moving images according to the 'principle of independence' (as he stated in 1932 in an unpublished reply to a journalist for the weekly Candide), exactly as it did in ballet and, more generally, in theatre. If cinema was conceived 'as a separate art form', music would have 'a most important part to play in [this] art' (from an interview with the Manchester Guardian, 22 February 1934). It was only with the 1946 article that Stravinsky seemed to deny film music any possibility of 'independence'. This shift can be interpreted as an angry reaction by the composer against Hollywood after the long series of failed attempts at working together, as well as a consequence of the general climate of condemnation of mass culture which characterised postwar American intellectual debates. The main target of Stravinsky's critique in that article, in fact, is not so much film music as such, but rather film music as used in mass culture, together with 'film people' who had 'a primitive and childish concept of music', and whom he '[found] it impossible to talk [to] about music because we [had] no common meeting ground'.

As for the possible impact of cinema on Stravinsky's musical language and compositional technique, many scholars and critics have sensed a link between Stravinsky's conception of musical form as something resulting from a 'sum of the parts' (an element, dubbed *drobnost'* by Richard Taruskin, which reflects Stravinsky's Russian roots and is radically opposed to the organicism of the Austro-German tradition) and the technique of montage, in particular as practised and theorised by Sergei Eisenstein around 1923–5. The analogy is particularly evident in compositions such as SYMPHONIES OF WIND INSTRUMENTS (1920), where short, non-developing blocks of different musical materials continuously return, brusquely alternating one to the other, giving rise to a discontinuous and splintered form. However, more than to a direct influence of cinema, this characteristic can be ascribed, rather, to the close connections of Stravinsky's music with theatre and ballet. In fact, it is clearly announced in the first and fourth tableaux of *Petrushka* (1911), where the abrupt succession of the different melodic fragments corresponds to a theatrical situation characterised by a multiplicity of contrasting events that take place simultaneously or in rapid succession on the stage. In fact, by the early 1910s, 'montage' had become a sort of general principle that invested all the arts, and theatre was a compelling force in this respect. Also, Eisenstein's ideas on montage – and on cinema in general – were developed on the basis of his previous theatrical experiences.   MASSIMILIANO LOCANTO

Financial Situation.   World War I and the 1917 Russian Revolution deprived Stravinsky of his property in USTILUG, which was 'the largest single source' of his income. From that time, Stravinsky earned his living composing, conducting and performing his own piano music. His income consisted of: composer's fees (commissions and selling the copyright to the publishers); fees for performances (as conductor and pianist), broadcasts, recordings; royalties – a sum paid to the composer for copies of the printed editions sold, for the rental or hire of materials (scores, parts, chorus parts), for mechanical reproduction of his works, for their performances; fees and royalties for literary works, music for cinema, arrangements.

At the outset of his composing career, Stravinsky was forced to be satisfied with modest fees. For example, his SCHERZO FANTASTIQUE, op. 3, was sold to Jurgenson in 1908 for 100 roubles (approximately $50 at that time). His growing celebrity resulted in the increasing of his fee, and in 1911 Jurgenson paid him 1,500 roubles ($750) for THE FIREBIRD, and 2,000 for PETRUSHKA. The RITE OF SPRING was commissioned by DIAGHILEV for 4,000 roubles and the composer planned to ask for the same honorarium from ERM (Édition Russe de Musique) (PRK II, 298). Generally, in the early 1910s, Stravinsky received an annual income of 4,000 roubles from ERM (PRK II, 438): in comparison, his father [Fyodor STRAVINSKY], soloist for the MARIINSKY THEATRE, earned 8,000 roubles a year.

After the Russian Revolution, Stravinsky's finances were becoming precarious while his family expenses were high. Some patrons and friends helped Stravinsky to survive this hard time by giving him money or commissioning works: Misia Sert, Princess de Polignac, Coco CHANEL, Werner Reinhart, Artur RUBINSTEIN. Leopold STOKOWSKI offered the composer a gift of $6,000 on behalf of a lady who wished to remain anonymous.

The situation improved in the mid-1920s to early 1930s when Stravinsky established himself as an international concert performer. In this period, his average fee as conductor and pianist was $500 for a concert, and his 1925

American tour brought him $1,000 for each concert (a contract with S. Bottenheim). To prevent pirate performances of his work, he joined the French copyright agencies SACEM and EDIFO.

In 1927, Stravinsky could afford to work on OEDIPUS REX 'without the least hope of material gain' (the performance should have been a part of the celebration of the twentieth anniversary of Diaghilev's theatrical activity). The first American commission came from Elizabeth Sprague Coolidge with a fee of $1,000 dollars for APOLLO (1928), whilst in 1938 the CONCERTO IN E♭: 'DUMBARTON OAKS' brought him $2,500 (SSE, 66). In this context, the fee of $6,000, which was offered by Ida RUBINSTEIN for The FAIRY'S KISS in 1928, seemed especially lucrative, and Stravinsky duly signed a contract, though aware of the risk of a potential conflict with Diaghilev. For PERSÉPHONE (1934), Ida Rubinstein paid a sum of 75,000 French francs (approximately $3,500 at that time) (SSC III, 190).

In the mid-1930s, the financial crisis in Europe, with the resultant cancellation of concerts and reduction of fees, negatively affected Stravinsky's budget. And the expenses increased: the adult children earned little, his wife Catherine STRAVINSKY spent almost the entire time in a tuberculosis sanatorium, and the other family members who were ill likewise needed very expensive treatment. In this situation, the tours to the UNITED STATES (1935, 1937) and South America (1936) were especially important.

Stravinsky moved to the USA, where he was already well known, in 1939, and signed a one-year contract to lecture at Harvard University at a salary of $9,000. Nevertheless, in the early 1940s, he had only a few conducting engagements with American orchestras and received some commissions – for example, from KOUSSEVITZKY for ODE (1943) ($1,000), or from the Orchestra of Los Angeles for DANSES CONCERTANTES (1942, $1,500). Stravinsky also sold to Disney for $6,000 the right to use the music from The Rite of Spring in Disney's film Fantasia. In the mid-1940s, joining the ASCAP and signing a contract with Boosey & Hawkes for the publication of new versions of his old works were very important for him from the point of view of copyright.

After the war, Stravinsky's conducting fees increased constantly. In Europe, he received either $1,500–2,000 or $3,000 for a concert. In the USA, his earnings could be higher: for example, in May 1964 he received $7,500 for a performance with the Philadelphia Orchestra in Ann Arbor (contract in the PSS). In his final years, splitting the conducting at concerts with Robert CRAFT, Stravinsky generally shared with him approximately a third of his fees.

Stravinsky's fee for commissions also increased: he received the sum of $20,000 for A SERMON, A NARRATIVE AND A PRAYER (1961), $15,000 for MOVEMENTS (1960), $15,000 for ABRAHAM AND ISAAC (1963), $25,000 for REQUIEM CANTICLES (1964). In the 1960s, Stravinsky's income was so high that he relates he had to pay a tax rate of 90 per cent to the state (SB, 127).

TATIANA BARANOVA MONIGHETTI

Firebird, The (Zhar-ptitsa; L'Oiseau de feu). Composed November 1909 to 18 May 1910; autograph orchestral score dated 1/14 April to 5/18 May 1910; autograph piano reduction dated 21 March / 3 April 1910. First performance, 25 June 1910, PARIS Opera. Conductor, Gabriel Pierné. Choreography Mikhail FOKINE. Stage design and costumes by Alexander Golovine, partially Léon BAKST (Firebird, Tsarevna). Firebird: Tamara Karsavina; Tsarevna: Vera Fokina; Ivan-Tsarevich: Mikhail Fokine; Kashchey: Alexis Bulgakov. Published 1911 (score and piano reduction), 1912 (parts), Jurgenson.

Orchestral Suites: I. 'Suite 1911': first performance, 23 October / 5 November 1910, ST PETERSBURG; first published 1912, Jurgenson. II. 'Suite 1919': first performance, 12 April 1919, Geneva; first published 1920, J. & W. Chester. III. 'Suite 1945': first performance, 24 October 1945, New York; first published 1946, Leeds Music Corporation.

'Mark him well, he is a man on the eve of celebrity.' The oft cited phrase of DIAGHILEV, launched during the rehearsals for the first production of The Firebird, was cleverly disseminated to goad the expectations of music and BALLET lovers. It was Diaghilev who recognised the future potential of that late developer, known as the son of a recently deceased famous OPERA singer rather than for his own works. Having heard the repetitive and schematic SCHERZO FANTASTIQUE under ZILOTI in early 1909, he commissioned from Stravinsky the ORCHESTRATION of two Chopin pieces for Les Sylphides, to be staged the same year in Paris. As it turned out, Stravinsky was the ideal man for Diaghilev who, after the spectacular but ruinous Boris Godunov season of 1908, had abandoned opera and switched to ballet productions. The Saison russe of 1909 consisted of a handful of one-act ballets, mostly imaginatively reshaped standard pastiches of the Russian Imperial ballet; it established the BALLETS RUSSES as a novelty, highly acclaimed for their lavish productions which aimed at rejuvenating ballet traditions. For the next season, Diaghilev was in search of new material which would satisfy the Parisian need for exotic entertainment and erotic excitement, a trend he had fuelled himself with the barbaric masculinity of the Polovtsian Dances in Nicholas ROERICH's atavistic design of steppe, warriors and yurts, and above all with the hypertrophic striptease-and-cohabitation plot of Cléopâtre, taking place against a background of BAKST's sumptuous Egyptian scenery and audaciously revealing costumes. Both demands would be accommodated in 1910, first with Shéhérazade, taking RIMSKY-KORSAKOV's symphonic suite as a pretext for unleashed sensuality to the point of an onstage group orgy with final mass slaughter. But Diaghilev was looking for more than arbitrary orientalism, erroneously classified as 'Russian' in the eyes of the western European audiences. He wanted to produce a ballet which would bear the signature of the Russian neonationalist arts, to export contemporary Russian artistic identity, not directed at Russian audiences, but tailored to the needs of the Paris public. 'I need a ballet, and a Russian one – the first Russian ballet. There is Russian opera, Russian symphony, Russian song, Russian dance, Russian rhythm – but no Russian ballet. And it is precisely such a thing that I need' (cited after Taruskin, SRT, 576). Diaghilev's diagnosis, in a letter to Anatoly LIADOV in September 1909, was correct: nineteenth-century folkloristic devices in Russian arts had often taken a social or curious standpoint towards peasantry, such as is the case with the peredvizhniki painters or MUSSORGSKY and STASOV, whereas the use of folkloristic material or folklore images for purely artistic purposes – i.e. the neonationalist tendency – had certainly entered Rimsky-Korsakov's fairytale operas and Liadov's orchestral miniatures, but not ballet. The Firebird was going to demonstrate the application of the neonationalistic principle to all elements of a ballet, as a newly conceived artwork of collaborating professionals in all the related fields of art. For this reason alone, even without considering the specific quality of the result, The Firebird should be considered a landmark in ballet history. Stravinsky was chosen only after Liadov had failed to deliver, Nikolay Tcherepnin had lost interest (his symphonic sketch Le Royaume enchanté, a spin-off of the abandoned ballet score, was published and premièred in 1910), and others such as GLAZUNOV were deemed inappropriate for setting new paths. Stravinsky had already started composing on his own in the autumn, realising that it was futile to continue work on The NIGHTINGALE, and anticipating a possible collaboration with Diaghilev. Having consulted other Petersburg musicians, Diaghilev finally commissioned the young composer to write the music for Firebird. Potential collaborators, above all FOKINE, were partially reassured of Stravinsky's capabilities as a result of hearing FIREWORKS in early 1910; still, the risk Diaghilev was running was exceptionally high. As a newcomer, Stravinsky had to follow precisely the instructions given by Fokine, who had elaborated (with a range of collaborators, including the writer Nicolas REMISOFF) the scenario out of several Russian fairytales, most of them to be found in the legendary collection by AFANASYEV, with several of them enjoying particular popularity in recent lavish editions with illustrations by Ivan Bilibin. The story and its characters were, from a Russian perspective, a rather saucy mixture, yet specifically designed for the French audience in its combination of supernatural forces both good and evil, with a Russian Prince Charming as hero and a dozen beautiful Russian princesses. Diaghilev himself took over the lighting, not only crucial for the changes of Day to Night, but elevated to a dramaturgical means when directing the spotlight onto the gauze which covered the illuminated legs of the Firebird. Alexander Golovine devised the fantastic scenery of the enchanted kingdom as a carpet-like, almost pointillistic vision of speckled colours devoid of clear perspective; his costumes for the princesses and warriors were based on traditional costumes of northern RUSSIA. Bakst's design for the Firebird costume, however, emphasised not only bird-like elements such as peacock feathers or overlong pigtails, but the eroticism of semi-transparent tissues and oriental harem pants: thus, the main character was presented as the embodiment of liberated sensuality. The Tsarevna and the other princesses personified the principle of moral decency and, in the final wedding ceremony, of dynastic continuity, whereas Kashchey stood for an evil threat from the East, an anti-Russian force to be defeated, and its Russian territories (captives) freed. From this perspective, the supernatural Firebird represented ultimately Russia's own immense power, an embryonic version of Eurasianist dreams to come.

Except for several closed dance numbers (e.g. the Dance of the Firebird, the Princesses' Game with the Golden Apples and Round Dance), the most innovative aspect of the ballet's overall structure was its continuous pantomimic action, resulting in a sort of gigantic orchestral recitative. Stravinsky accommodated his musical imagination directly to Fokine's model acting, inventing fitting motivic material to mimic the specific movements and actions of the characters. Fokine developed his ideas of choreographic renewal much further, abandoning classic postures and gestures in the barefoot dance of the princesses, in the ethereal toe-dance of the flying Firebird with his floating arms, and in the bizarre moves of the monsters, squatting, jumping and crawling like grotesque animals. Further, he dismissed the traditional repertoire of pantomimic gestures which symbolically explained acts of communication, introducing alternatives similar to normal body language. The overall construction of the ballet followed models laid out above all by Rimsky-Korsakov's fairytale operas: accordingly, the corresponding musical fabric was split into chromaticism (i.e. octatonicism) for the evil sorcerer Kashchey and the magic Firebird, and 'natural', folk-like diatonicism for the humans Ivan Tsarevich and the Princesses. For a long time, the many structural, harmonic and orchestral ties linking Stravinsky's score to those of his teacher Rimsky-Korsakov and his disciples – in some instances, bordering on plagiarism – had been overlooked until Richard Taruskin revealed them. Yet the questions are, first, to what extent did Stravinsky merely follow known formulas, where did he extend them, and where did he strive for new approaches? – and, second (as always), are conservatism and innovation suitable indicators of aesthetic quality? Stravinsky's indebtedness to Rimsky-Korsakov, both in the fantastic and the folk-like elements, is no less important than it is to Glazunov – e.g. in the Apple Games – but there is an aspiration to reach the extreme limits of his models and to transcend them. In analytical commentaries made for a recording on piano rolls in 1927, the composer characterised his germinal material as equivalent to the operatic *leitmotif,* now on the level of harmonic structures. This is only partially correct: Kashchey's music is indeed vertically oriented, based on alternating minor and major thirds which create octatonic chains, whereby Stravinsky exceeds the span of an octave – which for Rimsky had set the limit – and almost completely exhausts the available twenty-four thirds in the circle (twenty-two thirds in the dialogue between the sorcerer and Ivan). On the other hand, the Firebird's music is horizontally conceived of as a short melodic phrase treated like a small tone row, i.e. inverted and retrograded, monumentally resounding in the brass fanfare of the final bars. Stravinsky ingeniously exploits the possibilities of this material in ever new combinations, e.g. when depicting the magic carillon of Kashchey's castle as a swelling of polyrhythmic octatonic layers up to monstrous cacophony, or developing the famous melody of the 'Infernal Dance' (adopted from Rimsky's *Night on Mount Triglav*) out of a diminished seventh chord – the skeleton of octatonicism – as a prolation canon. Just how venturesome Stravinsky was can be seen in the passage leading to the 'Infernal Dance' at [131]: here, the superimposition of a sequence of fifths covering the whole circle of twelve, with a sequence of twelve thirds covering half of the complete octatonic chain – i.e. of two completely different harmonic procedures, as if it were two gigantic parts in a hybrid contrapuntal structure – leads to a chaotic, and indeed atonal, result, foretasting the layer structures of later works. Stravinsky was innovative as well in handling the other, folklore-based, human sphere: when citing a real folk melody (already ennobled by Rimsky-Korsakov in his *Symphoniette sur des thèmes russes,* op. 31) at [76], he starts first in the manner of epic byline singing with harp (lyre) accompaniment, as if looking back to the time of the Kuchka (the FIVE). However, he adds an afterplay with characteristic *podgoloski* (imitative counterpoints) which opens the harmony to the supertonic, thus matching folk practice and idioms much more than Rimsky. Then, the melody of Ivan is modelled after the *protyazhnaya* (stretched-out) type of Russian folk song, but, picking up the suggestion of Fokine to introduce the hero step by step, it is ultimately treated like a series of building blocks in diverse succession, especially after [75]. Finally, the structure of the apotheosis at the end of the ballet was the one idea which goes back not to Fokine but to the composer himself. Instead of a conventional series of dances, choreographically effective but musically dull, Stravinsky created a step-by-step climax based on the descant ostinato ('changing background') technique, going back to GLINKA's *Kamarinskaya*, and thus transformed the original folk melody to an overwhelming triumphal effect. In other words, Stravinsky made use of a vast gamut of Russian national music traditions, synthesising them and extending the constructive aspects of the musical material. He even was attentive enough to benefit from SCRIABIN's recent *Poem of Ecstasy*, the then state of the art of orchestral brilliance, for depicting the flight-dance of the Firebird. But the Achilles' heel of the ballet remained its rootedness in mimesis as the leading artistic principle: all elements were in the minutest details related to each other, so that the overall impression was beautifully enhanced, but not the slightest change conceivable. This proved problematic when Fokine's idea of having real horses on stage for the symbolical figures of the Black and White Horsemen (Night and Day) proved impractical after the first performances: Stravinsky had composed not only the spatially separated signals for the white rider [89], but the sinister hoofbeat of the trotting Black Rider at [2], vaguely recalling Mussorgsky's *Bydło* oxcart. Now that there were no more horses to be seen, the music lost its direct meaning and was simply another scary element within the eerie soundscape of Kashchey's garden. No wonder that Stravinsky soon preferred his orchestral suites to the original ballet score which, willy-nilly, bore witness to the extent of his reliance on the contribution of others.   CHRISTOPH FLAMM

Fireworks (Feyerverk; Feu d'artifice). Fantasia for large symphony orchestra, op. 4, Con fuoco. Composed April–June 1908, ST PETERSBURG – USTILUG, rev. May 1909. First performance, 9/22 January 1910, St Petersburg. Conductor, Alexander ZILOTI. Published 1910, Schott. 'Dedicated to Nadezhda and Maximilian Steinberg'.

'Petersburg has been caught by a monstrous musical fire', Vyacheslav KARATÏGIN wrote in 1911 (*Apollon*, 9 (1911)), mentioning the performances in the Ziloti Concerts series of SCRIABIN's *Prometheus: The Poem of Fire*, RAVEL's *Daphnis et Chloé* with its piracy torches, as well as the self-immolation fire in MUSSORGSKY's KHOVANSHCHINA premièred in the MARIINSKY THEATRE. Meanwhile, the first spark of this 'fire' was produced by Igor Stravinsky with his symphonic work *Fireworks*, which he conceived in 1908 immediately after finishing SCHERZO FANTASTIQUE. Perhaps the idea of *Fireworks* formed in Stravinsky's mind under the impression of 'the elements of fire' embodied in DEBUSSY's *Fêtes* (*Nocturnes* No. 2) performed in Ziloti's Concerts in December 1907.

In April 1908, before his departure from St Petersburg to Ustilug, Stravinsky managed to discuss his new work with RIMSKY-KORSAKOV. The piece was completed in about six weeks, by the time of the wedding of Rimsky-Korsakov's daughter Nadezhda to Maximilian STEINBERG in Lyubensk on 4/17 June, four days before Rimsky's death. 'Igor had composed the *Fireworks* fantasy for large orchestra – something like a march in ¾ – and sent the score (thirty pages) here', Steinberg wrote to Mikhail GNESIN on 1/ 14 July 1908; 'It is scored brilliantly if only it's possible to play it, for it's incredibly difficult' (PRK, I, 191). In May 1909, Stravinsky undertook a 'rescoring' of *Fireworks*. The première in the winter of 1910 was conducted by Alexander Ziloti and the Imperial Russian OPERA orchestra in the fifth Ziloti Concert at the Assembly of Nobility. Approving reviews were written by Alfred Nurok (*Apollon*, 4 (1910)) and Vyacheslav Karatïgin. Other critics competed in mordacity, being perplexed as to why such an 'empty' and 'scanty' thing needed 'such a complex apparatus as an orchestra' (Victor Walter, *Rech'*, 10/23 January 1910).

After the lightly scored *Scherzo fantastique*, Stravinsky reverted to a full orchestra in *Fireworks*. Despite employing such massive resources, in *Fireworks* (which is three times shorter than *Scherzo fantastique*), an aphoristic scherzo-like souvenir marking the celebratory occasion, Stravinsky moulds the principal thematic segment of the main section into a festive-fanfare diatonic melody, akin to a glorious toast, while the refined chromaticism of the middle section (Lento) brings to mind the fragile arioso of Rimsky-Korsakov's *Snow Maiden*.

Fireworks is constructed on a kaleidoscope of fire images – now slightly phosphorescing in *pp* ostinato figurations, then blowing up into dazzling sheaves of *fff* chords. Thus, Stravinsky develops the impressionistic colouristic style of *Scherzo fantastique*, and, at the same time, the technique of the micro-thematic score becomes even more sophisticated and detailed. It is symbolic that the première of *Fireworks* in 1910 became a sort of 'Bickford fuse' which led directly to the next Stravinsky work, crucial for the subsequent development of his career – the BALLET, *The* FIREBIRD. NATALIA BRAGINSKAYA

SCS

Fitelberg, Grzegorz (born Dyneburg (now Daugavpils, Latvia), 18 October 1879; died Katowice, 10 June 1953). Polish conductor and composer. In 1905, he co-founded the Young Poland group along with Szymanowski, whose works he promoted tirelessly throughout his career. In 1914–21, Fitelberg conducted in RUSSIA, and in 1921 he moved to PARIS and became a conductor for DIAGHILEV's BALLETS RUSSES, with which he conducted the world première of MAVRA on 3 June 1922. He returned to Poland in 1923, conducting the Warsaw Philharmonic and founding the Polish Radio Symphony Orchestra (1935). On 30 October 1924, Fitelberg conducted the CONCERTO FOR PIANO AND WIND INSTRUMENTS in Warsaw, with Stravinsky as the soloist. Fitelberg fled Warsaw in 1939, working in FRANCE and Britain before moving to the UNITED

STATES. After the war, he was a regular guest conductor in London, and in 1947 he became director of the radio orchestra in Katowice.   NIGEL SIMEONE

The Five. Also referred to as 'The Mighty Handful', 'The Mighty Five', Moguchaya Kuchka, the Balakirev Circle, and, as a stylistic movement, *kuchkism* or the New Russian School. A loosely affiliated group of composers in ST PETERSBURG, headed by Mily BALAKIREV, that also included Alexander BORODIN, César CUI, Modest MUSSORGSKY and Nikolay RIMSKY-KORSAKOV. Music critic Vladimir STASOV first used the term 'Moguchaya Kuchka' in a review dated 12/24 May 1867 to describe composers in an all-Russian concert under the direction of Balakirev. Later, the term came to refer more specifically to the five composers listed here. Though these composers differed with regard to preferred genres, style and output, they were united in their opposition to foreign influence as represented by formalised training in theory and counterpoint (training which none of the five composers had received in RUSSIA). Wary that German-style tuition would cloud the innovative spirit and unique style of Russian composition, the group adamantly opposed a conservatory in St Petersburg. (The ST PETERSBURG CONSERVATORY nonetheless opened in 1862 under the direction of Anton Rubinstein.)

Several compositional features characterise the aesthetic outlook known as *kuchkism* associated with the group. Above all, the group was fiercely nationalist and viewed themselves as the inheritors of a musical tradition established by GLINKA and Dargomïzhsky. In operatic composition, Rimsky-Korsakov, Mussorgsky, Borodin and, to a lesser extent, Cui sought to extend the two distinct national paths established by Glinka in the operas *A Life for a Tsar* and *Ruslan and Lyudmila*, by composing operas on historical and nationalist themes, source material from PUSHKIN, and folk and magic tales. Symphonic composition also formed a large body of the iconic works associated with the circle, influenced by the programmatic and harmonic innovations of Berlioz, Liszt and WAGNER. The use of symmetrical scales (whole-tone and octatonic), often to depict supernatural episodes and settings, can be found throughout the Five's operas and programme symphonies, with precedents traced to Schubert, Glinka, Liszt and Wagner. Exoticism also played an important role in the programmatic and stylistic features of the Five (and would become synonymous with 'Russianness' for DIAGHILEV's Parisian audiences in the early twentieth century). The Russian fascination with exoticism was shaped in part by ongoing military campaigns in the nineteenth century in the Crimea and Caucasus and the geo-political intrigue with Great Britain in Central Asia during the so-called 'Great Game'. Musically, the Five adopted features of exoticism well established in Europe, such as *alla turca* style, drones, percussive effects and augmented seconds, but also prominent in Russian exoticism is a chromatic pass between the fifth and sixth scale degrees, often embedded within an undulating melody.

By the 1880s, the Five had lost its cohesiveness. The death of Mussorgsky in 1881 signalled a major blow to one of the group's most charismatic members. But, even earlier, with the appointment of Rimsky-Korsakov as a professor at the St Petersburg Conservatory in 1871, the group's aesthetic agenda shifted away from its anti-institutional stance. Another important development in the

1880s was the patronage of the wealthy timber merchant and music publisher Mitrofan Petrovich BELYAYEV. While Rimsky-Korsakov remained the compositional patriarch, under Belyayev's direction CHAMBER MUSIC, rather than programmatic symphonies and nationalist or fairytale operas, became the favoured genre, with increasingly formalist and even pedantic characteristics. Upon Belyayev's death in 1903, Rimsky-Korsakov and his students LIADOV and GLAZUNOV became the trustees of Belyayev's publishing house and concert series. By this point, the consensus among Russian music critics was that the 'New Russian School' begun with the Five had lost its vitality. Taruskin emphatically describes a 'cloistered, sectarian, moribund musical world' into which Stravinsky entered when he began attending Rimsky-Korsakov's musical gatherings (SRT, 71).

It is therefore not surprising that Stravinsky's relationship to the original composers and inheritors of the New Russian School is complex. In his youth, Stravinsky was eager to be accepted into this circle; after permanently emigrating to the West, he went to great lengths to distance himself from the group, and especially Rimsky-Korsakov. Recent historiographic re-evaluation of Stravinsky's music, however, points to deep indebtedness to the Five, particularly during his early and 'Russian' stylistic phases. His early ballets on folk and magic themes reveal obvious topical links. Distinctive block and stratified textures in Stravinsky's music find precedent in Mussorgsky's striking harmonic juxtapositions and the 'changing background' procedures inherited from Glinka and honed by the Five. Non-conventional harmonies, characterised by superimposed chords and symmetrical scale types, are easily traced to the harmonic language of Rimsky-Korsakov and Mussorgsky. In his later years, Stravinsky adamantly denied using folk sources in his music, an important stylistic feature of the Five's nationalist agenda; yet recent studies reveal extensive borrowing from FOLK MUSIC collections in Stravinsky's music – even, at times, borrowing from Rimsky-Korsakov's own collected editions.

Indeed, we do observe a shift with Stravinsky's so-called NEO-CLASSICAL period, in which connections to his immediate Russian roots become less obvious. Nonetheless, the basic compositional procedures – juxtapositions, non-traditional scales and harmonies, Russian folklore, RITUAL and song – remain evident here as well and confirm the composer's indebtedness to his predecessors.   JOHANNA FRYMOYER

Five Easy Pieces for Piano Duet 'Right Hand Easy'. Composed 4 January to 3 April 1917, Morges. First (public) performance 22 April 1918, Lausanne, Conservatoire. N. Rossi and Ernest ANSERMET (with the THREE EASY PIECES). 8 November 1919, Lausanne. José Iturbi and the composer. Published 1917, Geneva: Ad. Henn; London: J. & W. Chester.

Dedication: 'A Madame Eugenia Errazuriz – hommage très respectueux'. Order of movements: (I) Andante (II) Española (III) Balalaïka (IV) Napolitana (V) Galop.

Three of the Five Easy Pieces require considerably greater dexterity than Stravinsky's earlier set of so-called 'easy' duets: 'Española', composed after Stravinsky's first visit to Spain in 1916; 'Napolitana', written following his return from Naples in 1917; and 'Galop'. The sketches for 'Española' reveal

didactic fingerings in the manner of Les CINQ DOIGTS. This would support the
view that, in the years after The RITE OF SPRING, Stravinsky was re-evaluating the
essentials of performance, possibly, even, modelling the Easy Pieces on Russian
four-hand literature by Dargomïzhsky (and others) within a deliberate process
of 'simplification' – whilst reviewing his own creative direction en route to
NEO-CLASSICISM.   GRAHAM GRIFFITHS

Graham Griffiths, Stravinsky's Piano: Genesis of a Musical Language (Cambridge University Press,
   2013).

Flood, The. A Musical Play in six parts. Composed between 1961 and 1962. First
   performance, 14 June 1962 on the CBS Television Network, USA. First stage
   performance Staatsoper, 30 April 1963, Hamburg. Conductor, Robert CRAFT.
   Published 1963, Boosey & Hawkes.
   Completed in early 1962, this 24-minute work was written expressly for
   television. The serially composed score calls for a tenor (Lucifer/Satan), two
   basses (God), chorus, orchestra, dancers, and includes spoken dialogue for
   the parts of Noah, his wife, their sons, a Narrator and Caller. The dramatic
   action is divided into two groups: the celestials who sing, and the terrestrials
   who provide the spoken dialogue. The libretto lays out the biblical story of
   Adam and Eve's banishment from Eden – a sinful transgression that ultimately
   precipitated God's purging flood. Noah's building of an ark, which would
   allow life to spring anew, serves as the drama's centrepiece. Programmed as
   part of the CBS Television Network's Golden Showcase, Noah and the Flood, as the
   première was originally entitled, reached several million viewers on
   14 June 1962. The first full operatic staging was mounted at the Hamburg
   Staatsoper on 30 April 1963. Robert Craft conducted both versions, as well as
   the original Columbia Masterworks recording released in 1962. This 'dance
   drama' (the composer's preferred description) appeared as Stravinsky was
   marking his eightieth birthday.
   Produced by Robert Graff, designed by Rouben Ter-Arutunian, and directed
   by Kirk Browning, the telecast featured such notables as Laurence Harvey as
   the Narrator and Sebastian Cabot as Noah. Harvey also delivered the telecast's
   introductory commentary – an ominous homily warning of the pending catastrophe of the current nuclear age. The similarities between Stravinsky's The
   Flood and 'The Bomb' were deliberate. George BALANCHINE, outspokenly
   suspicious of the shortcomings of televised dance, nonetheless agreed to
   choreograph the two extended dance sequences for 'The Building of the Ark'
   and 'The Flood'. Although Graff suggested W. H. AUDEN as the librettist,
   Stravinsky tried to entice T. S. ELIOT to become his collaborator as early as
   1959. Initially sympathetic, Eliot urged the composer to study the Everyman and
   Medieval Miracle Plays as a starting point. But when Eliot's enthusiasm waned,
   Stravinsky turned to Robert Craft to furnish the text.
   Initially relying upon Eliot's Everyman source, Craft consulted the Chester
   and York pageants, blending passages he determined suitable. Yet, far beyond
   his role as librettist, Craft's guiding influence was never more evident. Their
   famous 'Working Notes for The Flood' methodically tracks the composer and
   Balanchine's thinking as it developed in the spring of 1962. All three collaborators, led by Craft who suggested specific musical models, joined in

shaping the production's design, including the plotting of specific camera angles, entrances and exits, and the timing of virtually every segment of the complexly structured drama.

Throughout the work's evolution, a sense of hurriedness progressively conspired against the première's success. A prescient Stravinsky wrote to Goddard LIEBERSON, 'I hope The Flood will not be A Flop.' The producers mistakenly wagered that Stravinsky's vaulted status would hold sway with a populist audience. It did not. Fractured by intervening commercials, interruptive documentary clips and irrelevant interviews, the telecast was roundly denounced. Despite Stravinsky's imaginative score and colourful ORCHESTRATION, television was unprepared for what many saw as a sanctimonious message set to the composer's unmelodic, fragmented serial music. Twenty years later, Balanchine and Jacques d'Amboise restaged the work for the 1982 Stravinsky Festival at the Lincoln Center in New York. Subsequent productions in several OPERA houses, as well as a few American and European telecasts, have done little to elevate The Flood to the prominence enjoyed by many of Stravinsky's other theatrical works.   CHARLES M. JOSEPH

Charles M. Joseph, 'Television and The Flood: anatomy of an "inglorious Flop"', in Stravinsky Inside Out (New Haven and London: Yale University Press, 2001), 132–61.
Igor Stravinsky and Robert Craft, 'Working notes for The Flood', in Dial, 89–98.

Fokine, Mikhail Mikhailovich (self-styled as Michel in the West) (born St Petersburg, 13/25 April 1880; died New York City, 22 August 1942). Russian dancer, CHOREOGRAPHER and teacher. Fokine trained in ST PETERSBURG (Platon Karsavin, father of Tamara KARSAVINA, was a teacher) and graduated into the Mariinsky as a dancer in 1898. He choreographed his first student BALLET in 1905 (the same year he set the Dying Swan), and created his first major work in 1907. A reformer, Fokine sought to revitalise ballet, pushing for greater integration between the arts and a naturalistic approach to movement. In 1909, he was engaged by DIAGHILEV to choreograph the first season of Russian ballet in Paris, and he remained with the BALLETS RUSSES until 1912 (brief return 1914); his approach defined the early style of the company.

Fokine was the first choreographer Stravinsky worked with and the two original ballets they created for the Ballets Russes, The FIREBIRD (1910) and PETRUSHKA (1911), launched Stravinsky onto the international scene. Stravinsky had orchestrated two Chopin works for a 1909 production of Les Sylphides (formerly Chopiniana) choreographed by Fokine, but their first collaboration was The Firebird, and the scenario (credited to Fokine, but with input by others) was largely complete when Stravinsky was commissioned; the composer added the final coronation scene. Stravinsky therefore wrote music to order – something he later balked at – but the two worked together closely. Stravinsky attended rehearsals, and Fokine claimed it was his closest collaboration with a composer (1961, 161). At the première, Fokine created the role of Ivan Tsarevich while his wife Vera Fokina danced Tsarevna.

After The Firebird, the next new production discussed was what would become The RITE OF SPRING (1913), though it would be Petrushka that made it to the stage. In contrast to The Firebird, the Petrushka scenario (by Stravinsky and Alexandre BENOIS) and score were complete when Fokine became involved.

Stravinsky again attended rehearsals, though they proved challenging: time was short, Fokine and the dancers struggled with the rhythms, and final preparations featured battles over tempi. Two months after the première, Stravinsky wrote of how Fokine's 'capriciousness and despotism' affected the work's creation (SCS, 162). Fokine went on to criticise Stravinsky's music as unnecessarily complicated, and even referred to its 'nondanceability' (1961, 188). The two did not collaborate again, and relations soured irreparably. When Fokine was briefly mooted as a potential choreographer for the Ida RUBINSTEIN production PERSÉPHONE (1934), Stravinsky stressed that it would be 'extremely painful' to work with him (SCS, 530).

Later in life, Fokine reflected on Stravinsky's output and, unsurprisingly, focused on the two ballets he was involved in: 'Stravinsky wrote many ballets, but none of them so great as The Firebird. In Petrushka there is power, expression, character, and originality. In The Firebird there is poetry and beauty' (Fokine 1961, 179). For his part, Stravinsky found little to recommend Fokine in print. The composer acknowledged Fokine had created the occasional nice gesture and fine movement but largely pushed a narrative claiming to have never liked his choreography. By Memories and Commentaries, published eighteen years after the choreographer's death, Stravinsky made a damning final appraisal of his former collaborator: 'Fokine was easily the most disagreeable man I have ever worked with. In fact, with Glazunov, he was the most disagreeable man I have ever met' (Mem, 34).   SOPHIE REDFERN

Cyril W. Beaumont, Michel Fokine and His Ballets (London: Wyman & Sons, 1935; repr. 1945). Michel Fokine, Fokine: Memoirs of a Ballet Master, trans. Vitale Fokine, ed. Anatole Chujoy (London: Constable, 1961).

Folk Music. Stravinsky was formed in an environment where folk art was an important part of the cultural soil and was absorbed naturally from the earliest years, like the native language itself. In the years of his childhood and youth, despite the rapid development of industry, RUSSIA continued to remain predominantly an agrarian country, where peasants accounted for about 80 per cent of the population. Accordingly, the traditional rural culture, including its archaic forms, was preserved: folk songs could be heard everywhere, in the village and on the street, in the city, at home and in public places. Folk music was well known also in cultivated forms. Stravinsky later recalled the collections of TCHAIKOVSKY, Anatoly LIADOV and RIMSKY-KORSAKOV. He was also acquainted with other publications, for example, that of Mily BALAKIREV, as well as a completely new collection by Yevgenia Linyova, who used a phonograph for her recordings. Stravinsky's preference for authentic recordings demonstrated an interest in genuine folklore – a fascination which he shared with other progressive musicians of the time.

Nevertheless, Stravinsky began his compositional career using traditional arrangements. The FIREBIRD (1910) contains two folklore citations, both of which are borrowed from the collection of Stravinsky's teacher Rimsky-Korsakov, One Hundred Russian Folk Songs (1877). Whilst retaining the essential characteristics of both melodies, Stravinsky created his own versions, especially so in the second song, which became the basis of the final solemn procession accompanied by the chimes of bells.

In Petrushka (1911), the number of folk excerpts is greater, and they are more diverse and colourful in character. Some of the material is based on popular tunes, which even include compositions by living authors – for example, Emil Spencer's song 'Elle avait une jambe de bois' ('She had a wooden leg'), about the famous actress Sarah Bernhardt. As for Russian folk tunes, there were only three old peasant songs in Petrushka. All other quotations belong to the category of tunes and sounds associated with the Russian city street, and these were usually considered second-rate in comparison with old peasant songs. Petrushka was very shocking to traditional musicians, including the family of the late Rimsky-Korsakov. His son, Igor's friend Andrey Rimsky-Korsakov, referred to Petrushka as 'a mixture of Russian vodka ("folk scenes") with French perfumes ("puppet comedy")', and Stravinsky retained a lifelong memory of these words (Mem, 46).

The scandalous première of The Rite of Spring followed a year later (1913). Stravinsky claimed in his later memoirs that he quoted only one folk theme in The Rite of Spring – the famous initial high bassoon solo, the melody of which he borrowed from a collection of Lithuanian folk songs (the Jusckiewicz collection). However, Lawrence Morton discovered three more songs in the same publication which were included in the ballet (Morton 1979). At the same time, Stravinsky chose a quotation that was close to his own melodic style. Indeed, there are melodies in The Rite, along with explicit borrowings, which are very similar to folk tunes, yet are not quotations. As quotations, they are all related to the ancient Russian calendar and ritual songs, and fully correspond to the plot of the ballet. It is evident that, during the composition of The Rite of Spring, Stravinsky could already dispense with direct quotations, since he himself was able to create material akin to folk music, as a true 'master of popular speech' (Asafyev [Glebov] 1977, 20). At the heart of the music of The Rite were popevki (short diatonic melodies of a small range), which the composer developed according to the principle of variant, an innate characteristic of Russian folk music. After all, a folk singer never repeats a song literally, and if you ask him to sing a song anew, it will not sound exactly like the previous time. In Stravinsky's music, the principle of variation manifested itself in refined compositional techniques: variations of melodic contours and length, irregular rhythmic accents, and the method of 'scissors' (montage juxtaposition). Folk material, authentic or composed, dominated absolutely in The Rite of Spring, which is fundamentally different in this respect from The Firebird and Petrushka.

The unique Stravinskian technique was forged in The Rite of Spring on folkloric soil, developed in his subsequent 'Russian' works, and it served him without fail throughout his creative evolution, in both the neo-classical and serial periods. Many innovations of Stravinsky's neo-folkloristic style resonated not only with folk sources, but with contemporary music more generally. He did not feel the need to differentiate folklore from other sources: on the contrary, his artistic goal was to unite and reconcile them.

In a general survey of the folk influences in Stravinsky's music, the sounds of the Russian Orthodox service must be considered as an integral element of his early environment. They appeared first as instrumental imitations of choral singing: one of the first examples occurs in 'Evocation of the Ancestors' in The

Rite of Spring. Stravinsky reproduced here the typical antiphonal syllabic chant of the Russian liturgy, in the manner of a litany. Instruments imitated the juxtaposition of mixed and male choirs; the composer used here the old *obikhodnyi lad* ('church scale') which had a non-octave structure. A similar fragment, but this time vocal, can be found in Les Noces, consisting of a two-part episode in the second tableau, 'Boslovite, otech' s mater'u' (Rehearsal No. 50), imitating the old church psalmody. In the modern church service, Stravinsky would not have heard anything of the sort. Hence, such an archaic heterophony could well have been imagined, recreated intuitively thanks to the 'ability to imitate', which the composer himself noted. A little later, Stravinsky turned to the specific genre of the Orthodox liturgy and wrote three choruses on religious texts: *Otche nash* (1926), *Veruyu* (1932) and *Bogoroditse Devo* (1934). Stravinsky composed them for church use, following the strict rules and traditions of his time, and therefore they differ noticeably from the 'portraits' of ancient ritual singing, recreated in *The Rite of Spring* and Les Noces. All three choruses were subsequently adapted to Latin versions: Pater Noster, Credo and Ave Maria (1949).

In the summer of 1914, just before the outbreak of World War I, Stravinsky travelled from Switzerland to Kiev and Ustilug (as it turned out, for the last time) and brought back many 'interesting books', as he wrote to Alexandre Benois on 14 July 1914 (PRK, II, 272). At the time, Stravinsky was looking for suitable texts for Les Noces, and was pleased that his search was crowned with success. Moreover, the collection of Russian folk texts he selected from the publications of Ivan Sakharov, Pyotr Kireyevsky, Alexander Afanasyev, as well as from the *Explanatory Dictionary of the Living Great Russian Language* by Vladimir Dahl and other similar sources, became the basis of most of Stravinsky's works of the 1910s, from *Pribaoutki* (1914) to Les Noces (1923). (For a collection of textual sources, see Vershinina 1967; Taruskin; SRT; Baranova 2013.) So, in the music of Stravinsky at this time, there appeared another genuine folk ingredient: poetic and prose texts taken from various genres of Russian people's art. Of course, we cannot say that this was unfamiliar territory for the composer, but for the first time he faced the problem of finding an appropriate musical interpretation. Subsequently, Stravinsky testified that, most of all, he was attracted by the pure sound of folk texts, which is equivalent to music in its effect. Indeed, the phonetics of a word in Stravinsky's music often came to the fore. One of the best-known examples is the choral refrain at the beginning of Les Noces: 'Chesu, pochesu Nastas'inu kosu' ('I am combing, I shall comb Nastasia's braids') (Kireyevsky's collection), where, thanks to the interplay of consonants *ch-s-t*, the phrase is perceived as a single almost indivisible sound complex – as 'phonemic music', as the composer himself put it. Often, the dialectal vernacular which Stravinsky usually added to the texts derived from phonetics, as though returning published sources to their oral, spoken sound (*see* Russian vocal music).

The other side of the interpretation of the folk word was related to prosody, to the interplay of accents. It was folk verse that gave Stravinsky the opportunity to discover a vocal treatment which was adequate to his already existing instrumental style. In fact, in Russian poetic folklore, he heard irregular accents and variable stresses, paralleling those of his own works, including

Petrushka and especially *The Rite of Spring.* 'One important characteristic of Russian popular verse is that the accents of the spoken verse are ignored when the verse is sung. The recognition of the musical possibilities inherent in this fact was one of the most rejoicing discoveries of my life' (*Expo*, 138). The composer's delight at this conjunction is understandable: folklore itself confirmed the 'correctness' of his style.

Finally, with folk texts came specific genres and genre forms. Stravinsky's three major theatrical opuses of the 1910s (RENARD, The SOLDIER'S TALE and *Les Noces*), represented three varieties of synthetic theatre, composed of music, word (vocal or speech) and choreography. The composer himself found it difficult to define these works in the usual terms, and, as a result, each of them received a specific genre designation. However, the prototypes of all three in Russian folk art are unquestionable and obvious. *Renard* is a 'cheerful performance' of *skomorokhi* (wandering minstrels) in animal masks; *The Soldier's Tale* is a fair theatre with stable roles and favourite subjects; *Les Noces* is a Russian peasant rite (Karlinsky 1983). In *Pribaoutki*, *Three Children's Tales*, *Berceuses du chat* and other pieces, we can also observe theatrical features: they are generally characteristic of folk singers who, according to the village language, do not *sing* the song, but *act* it.

There are practically no musical borrowings in Stravinsky's works incorporating folk texts, except for the quotation in 'Kornilo' from *Pribaoutki* (SRT, 1167–8), as well as the melody in the final section of *Les Noces* – the lyrical song 'Ne vesyolaya da kanpan'itsa' from the collection of Fyodor Istomin and Georgy Dutsch. Stravinsky no longer felt the need for such quotations, since melodies, like folk tunes, were naturally born from folk texts – they had become their own language. That said, there are occasional reminiscences of the use of direct references to folk music in the later works, a good example occurring in the SONATA FOR TWO PIANOS (1943–4), which dates from some thirty years after *The Firebird* and *Petrushka*. Here, the theme of the variations which form the second movement, together with the material of the middle section in the finale, were borrowed from the collection *Songs of the Russian People in the Harmonisation of M. Bernard*, published by Jurgenson in 1886. In his choice of source material, Stravinsky seems to return to the academic style typical of early Russian music. It is evident that, by that time, the degree of authenticity of borrowed material was of no great importance for the composer.

In general, we can conclude that Stravinsky's attitude towards folk art was deeply serious in a philosophical sense. Borrowing and imitating, he developed his own style on the basis of folklore, translating into the art of the twentieth century a national culture founded on distinctive ethical and aesthetic views. They are not correlated with the individual and his values, but with other, transpersonal forces – with the power of flesh and blood, with ritual and tradition. Hence the ethical ambivalence of the archetypal motifs of Stravinsky's art, where there is no place for personal compassion for the fate of the Chosen One or the Bride. Undoubtedly, the great range and power of the folk influence on Stravinsky's work demonstrated the significance of the phenomenon itself – an unprecedented embodiment of the spirit and substance of Russian folk art, transformed by the power of genius into a summit of world culture. SVETLANA SAVENKO

Boris Asafyev [Igor Glebov], *A Book about Stravinsky*, trans. Richard French (Ann Arbor: UMI Research Press, 1982).

Tatiana Baranova, *Stravinsky – chitatel' i bibliofil* ('Stravinsky as Reader and Bibliophile') (Moscow: Nauchnyi vestnik Moskovskoy konservatorii, 2013).

Simon Karlinsky, 'Stravinsky and Russian pre-literate theatre', *Nineteenth-Century Music*, 16.3 (1983), 232–40.

Lawrence Morton, 'Footnotes to Stravinsky Studies: Le Sacre du Printemps', *Tempo*, 128 (1979), 9–16.

Irina Vershinina, *Ranniye balety Stravinskogo* ('Stravinsky: The Early Ballets') (Moscow: Nauka, 1967).

Form. One of Stravinsky's most frequently cited statements refers to form. 'In borrowing a form already established and consecrated, the creative artist is not in the least restricting the manifestations of his personality. On the contrary, it is more detached, and stands out better, when it moves within the limits of a convention' (*Auto*, 132). Included in the ghost-written AUTOBIOGRAPHY published in the mid-1930s, this would appear to proclaim an unambiguously neo-classical commitment to the kind of musical structures that could be designated 'profoundly traditional, both as to cultural outlook and as to musical technique' (SRT, 847). Yet, in linking this observation directly to The RITE OF SPRING, rather than to OEDIPUS REX or the SYMPHONY IN C, Richard Taruskin dramatises the paradoxical role of compositional conventions and traditions in the development of a composer consistently acclaimed for his originality and radicalism.

The personality that is embodied in Stravinsky's distinctive musical materials ensures that the formal designs implied by generic, structural and – to some extent – textural traditions become what Taruskin terms 'a magnificent extension' of those traditional manifestations, and 'moving within the limits of a convention' invariably highlights the distancing from the original character of those conventions (as found in earlier Baroque, classical and Romantic styles) which Stravinsky's own compositions display. In other words, it is in its treatment of both material and form that Stravinsky's music reveals its essential and inexhaustible MODERNISM.

Where musical form is concerned, Stravinsky appears to make a fairly dogmatic distinction in his conversations with CRAFT when he declares that:

> composers and painters are not conceptual thinkers … The composer works through a perceptual, not a conceptual process. He perceives, he selects, he combines, and he is not in the least aware at what point meanings of a different sort and significance grow into his work. All he knows or cares about is his apprehension of the contour of the form, for the form is everything. (*Expo*, 102–3)

From this, the compositional process appears to involve the perception, selection and combination of materials so that the listener can in turn perceive some degree of connection to 'tradition' as something which 'is not the relic of a past irretrievably gone' but 'a living force that animates and informs the present' (*Poet*, 58). Most of Stravinsky's work titles identify vocal or instrumental genres, for concert hall or theatre, with long histories, and it is when these familiar templates are 'extended', or otherwise challenged, that radical intent is most directly signalled.

For example, Symphonies of Wind Instruments has attracted extensive scholarly attention on the grounds that 'the limits of a convention', relating to symphonic form, are far from obvious. Rather than attempt to force this short single-movement design into the straitjacket of symphonic tradition, Edward T. Cone proposed replacing the classic 'exposition, development, recapitulation' formal scheme with 'stratification, interlock, and synthesis', suggesting a process of evolution from separate to more fully integrated textural layers (Cone 1962, 19). Allusions to traditional harmonic as well as formal elements within any of these stages might be possible, but they are not essential to music embodying the modernist principles of emancipated dissonance and extended – or even suspended – tonality by way of manipulations of pitch materials often illustrating Stravinsky's interest in hexatonic and octatonic modal constructs.

Stravinsky's modernistic flexibility in the use of traditional generic titles is confirmed in that, whereas Symphony of Psalms likewise has little to do with classical symphonic conventions, Symphony in C is a virtuoso demonstration of 'magnificent extension'. Given that the most basic formal and procedural polarity applicable to modernist music is connection and separation, studies like Gretchen Horlacher's *Building Blocks: Repetition and Continuity in the Music of Stravinsky* (Oxford University Press, 2011) can illustrate in depth how the traditional, classical aesthetic and technical principles of interconnectedness at all levels of structure can be offset by more strongly asserted distinctions between separate blocks of material than such classical principles can usually accommodate. The modernist potential within the looser, more suite-like designs of pre-1900 oratorios, cantatas, operas and ballets brings particular interest to comparisons between Mozart's *Don Giovanni* and Stravinsky's The Rake's Progress, or between Tchaikovsky's *Sleeping Beauty* and Stravinsky's The Fairy's Kiss. Obviously enough, an extended vocal composition for the stage need not include clearly detached arias, recitatives and choruses in order to be labelled an 'opera', and an orchestral score for the theatre need not include sections labelled 'waltz', 'pas de deux' or 'entr'acte' in order to function as a ballet. But Stravinsky seems to have relished the challenge of preserving these specifics, these conventions, even after the major shift of technical thinking that came with his adoption of twelve-note techniques after 1950.

It seems undeniable that 'moving within the limits of a convention' in order to achieve magnificent extensions of traditional forms is less explicit after 1950 than it was before. One consequence of Stravinsky's awareness of the initiatives of Webern, and his younger devotees Boulez and Stockhausen, was an apparent acknowledgement that all but the most attenuated allusions to tonality should be avoided. However, with his increasing reliance on smaller-scale, ritualised threnodies, with their religious, even liturgical associations, it seemed appropriate to use formal categories, and also compositional strategies, that could retain at least some elements of those hierarchies made possible by the invariant focusing on single pitches in relation to the twelve-note rotational schemes used in works like A Sermon, a Narrative and a Prayer and Requiem Canticles. For all their stylistic novelty, the conventions and traditions associated with liturgies and other forms of sacred music ensured that Stravinsky intensified his modernist reshapings of time-honoured musical genres and formal templates in his serial compositions. Extended neo-Baroque manifestations of canon and fugue were avoided, but the austere counterpoint of Renaissance motets and instrumental canzonas resonate behind the twelve-note textures of THRENI and VARIATIONS (ALDOUS HUXLEY IN MEMORIAM). ARNOLD WHITTALL

Edward T. Cone, 'The progress of a method', *Perspectives of New Music*, 1.1 (1962), 18–26.

Foss, Lukas (originally Lukas Fuchs) (born Berlin, 15 August 1922; died New York City, 1 February 2009). German-American composer, pianist and conductor, often considered part of the Boston School of composers. He studied with Sergey KOUSSEVITZKY (1939–43), was a special composition student with Paul Hindemith at Yale (1939–40) and was described by his friend Leonard BERNSTEIN as an 'authentic genius'. Foss was one of four leading American composers (along with Barber, Sessions and COPLAND) who participated as pianists in a concert performance of *Les Noces* given at the Town Hall in New York on 20 December 1960. He organised an enticing Stravinsky Festival at the Lincoln Center, New York, in 1966 with the participation of the conductors Bernstein, Kondrashin, ANSERMET, and Stravinsky himself for the final concert. Indeed, Foss provided Stravinsky with an honorarium of $1,000 for his attendance at the opening concert, during which Bernstein conducted The RITE OF SPRING (SSE, 518–19). As part of the festival, Foss conducted a performance of The SOLDIER'S TALE with Aaron Copland as the Narrator, Elliott CARTER as the Soldier, and John Cage, mischievously, as the Devil. All of this was in spite of the stinging criticism Stravinsky had made of Foss's composition *Time Cycle* in the American edition of *Dialogues and a Diary*, comments that were deleted from subsequent editions.

EDWARD CAMPBELL

Four Norwegian Moods for orchestra. Composed 1942. First performance, 13 January 1944, Sanders Theatre, Cambridge, Mass. Boston Symphony Orchestra. Conductor, Igor Stravinsky. Published 1944, New York: Associated Music Publishers. Order of movements: (I) Intrada (II) Song (III) Wedding Dance (IV) Cortège.

After Stravinsky's emigration to the UNITED STATES, he had to write a number of shorter commissioned pieces due to serious financial difficulties. In this situation, he even considered composing FILM music – however, none of the music he drafted for the purpose ever reached the stage of studio production (*Mem*, 108). Nonetheless, the *Four Norwegian Moods* are characterised by the setting and theme of the film for which they were originally intended, namely the Nazi invasion of Norway. As Eric Walter White notes, Stravinsky 'borrowed the themes he needed from a collection of Norwegian folk music his wife had just picked up in a second-hand bookshop in Los Angeles (*Mem*)' (*SCW*, 414–15), the 'Norges Melodier' (Kraemer). The material for the first movement, Intrada, originates from a Norwegian folk-tune ('Brurelaat') and the other pieces – (II) Song, (III) Wedding Dance and (IV) Cortège – take up melodies from the same anthology and follow the episodic structure of the Intrada. The *Four Norwegian Moods* for orchestra (2.2.2.2 – 4.2.2.1 – timpani – strings) are original work and not merely 'transcriptions' since Stravinsky used the source material only as melodic and rhythmic starting points for composition. The musical quotations are treated freely, with Stravinsky emphasising that the work is without aspirations to ethnological authenticity and that the 'moods' of the title should not be thought of as 'impressions' of Norway. He consequently proposed to rename the work 'Quatre pièces à la norvegienne'.   FLORIAN HENRI BESTHORN

Uwe Kraemer, '"Four Norwegian Moods" von Igor Strawinsky', *Melos*, 39.2 (1972), 80–4.

Four Songs. For voice, flute, harp and guitar. (1) 'The Drake' (2) 'A Russian Spiritual' (3) 'Geese and Swans' (4) 'Tilimbom'. Arranged 1953–4. First performance, at one of the Monday Evening Concerts, 21 February 1955, LOS ANGELES. Conductor, Robert CRAFT. Published 1955, J. & W. Chester. This collection of songs consisted of a re-instrumentation of Nos. 1 and 4 of his *Four Russian Songs* (1919) and Nos. 2 and 1 of *Three Children's Tales* (1917). Stravinsky sent the first two songs to Douglas Gibson at Chester's on 15 June 1954, and it wasn't until the middle of August that he announced his decision to add two more songs to make a set of four. Stravinsky produced a transliteration of the Russian texts, and these were printed together with English translations by Craft (Nos. 1–3) and by Rosa Newmarch (No. 4).   JEREMY COLEMAN

Four Studies for orchestra. In four movements: (I) Danse (Con moto) (II) Excentrique (Moderato) (III) Cantique (Largo) (IV) Madrid (Allegro con moto). Arranged 1928–9, revised 1952. First performance: No. 4 alone, 16 November 1928, PARIS; complete set, 7 November 1930, Berlin. Conductor, Ernest ANSERMET. Published 1930, Édition Russe de Musique, Boosey & Hawkes. The first three movements were orchestrated from Stravinsky's THREE PIECES FOR STRING QUARTET (1914), and the fourth movement was taken from his *Étude for Pianola* (1921). He had actually been working on an ORCHESTRATION of the Three Pieces for String Quartet between 1914 and 1918. The instrumentation of the *Four Studies* highlights affinities between the Three Pieces and orchestral works from that period, such as PETRUSHKA.   JEREMY COLEMAN

Four Studies, op. 7, for piano. Composed May–September 1908, USTILUG. First performance, autumn 1908, ST PETERSBURG, by the composer. Published 1910, Moscow: Jurgenson; subsequent editions by Martin Frey (1925), Isidor Philipp (1953), Moscow: Musïka (1968), and ed. Soulima STRAVINSKY (1977, Boosey & Hawkes). Dedication: (I) Stepan MITUSOV (II) Nicholas Richter (III) Andrey Rimsky-Korsakov (IV) Vladimir Rimsky-Korsakov. Order of movements: *Con moto; Allegro brillante; Andantino; Vivo.*

   The *Four Studies* were Stravinsky's last piano works written under the guidance of RIMSKY-KORSAKOV, and they reveal an extraordinary advance, both compositionally and as 'piano instrumentation', upon his previous compositional project for piano, the SONATA IN F♯ MINOR. The sophisticated textures of the *Four Studies* are clearly modelled upon the didactic literature of Russian pianism and its traditional emphasis on virtuosity. Furthermore, the set is Stravinsky's most important testimony, together with KING OF THE STARS (1911–12), to a transitory yet intense interest in the music of SCRIABIN. Paradoxically, and significantly, the Studies also anticipate several eighteenth-century tropes more characteristic of Stravinsky's later neo-classical idiom: for example, in No. 1 (*Con moto*) the simultaneous presentation of legato in one hand and staccato in the other – an effect inverted in No. 2, Allegro brillante; in No. 3 (Andantino), the obsessive use of index-finger-over-thumb overlap; and in Nos. 2 and 4 (Vivo) the tendency for extreme tempi which, besides augmenting the technical difficulty of the music, also convey an apparently excessive 'test of stamina' and, to borrow Bronislava Nijinska's term, muscular drive. The greater value of the Four Studies may be revealed in the manner with which, under Rimsky-Korsakov's tutelage, Stravinsky's early music acquired textural sophistication, technical assurance and, in these miniatures especially, extreme rhythmic complexity. Their appeal may be limited to virtuosi but, by 1931, André Schaeffner could write that 'the F♯ major study [No. 4] is included in the repertoire of a good many pianists'.

GRAHAM GRIFFITHS

Igor Glebov, 'Pathways into the future', in Melos, Book II (Petrograd, 1918), in Stuart Campbell (ed. and trans.), Russians on Russian Music, 1880–1917: An Anthology (Cambridge University Press, 2003).
Graham Griffiths, Stravinsky's Piano: Genesis of a Musical Language (Cambridge University Press, 2013).
André Schaeffner, Strawinsky (Paris: Les Editions Rieder, 1931).

France. Stravinsky's relationship with France is complex. Many of his works, notably his early ballets, were premièred there in the second decade of the twentieth century, as he collaborated with Sergey Diaghilev, Léon Bakst and others. But, beyond this, he found friends and colleagues in France with whom he maintained contact throughout his life. Stravinsky was brought to Paris to work on his first three ballets for Diaghilev, and visited the city repeatedly from 1910 to 1913. The première of The Firebird on 25 June 1910 gives a lively flavour of the milieu within which Stravinsky was now operating. Beyond the usual Parisian well-heeled and socially dominant operatic audience, Stravinsky claimed to have met Marcel Proust, Saint-John Perse, Paul Claudel and Sarah Bernhardt, while Debussy congratulated him on his success in person at the end of the performance and issued an invitation to dinner; they maintained contact until the French composer's death in 1918. Stephen Walsh speculates that Stravinsky 'may also have met – or have already met' the composers Maurice Ravel, Satie, Falla, Maurice Delage, Florent Schmitt, Reynaldo Hahn, the writers Jean Cocteau, André Gide and Gabriele d'Annunzio, as well as various important patrons including the Princess de Polignac (SCS, 142). Living for a time in Delage's home in Paris in 1911, he regularly came into contact with the Apaches where, in addition to those already mentioned, he got to know the painter Paul Sordes, the pianist Ricardo Viñes, and the critics Michel-Dimitri Calvocoressi and Émile Vuillermoz. His contact with Ravel was also significant: he heard, for example, fragments of Ravel's Daphnis and viewed the première from the French composer's box (Pasler 1982, 405).

Stravinsky returned to the capital often, but lived over time in various parts of the country. Moving to Brittany in northwest France in 1920, he developed new relationships with a number of creative people, including Coco Chanel. In 1921, he moved to Anglet in the southwest, and commuted between there and Paris. In 1924, he bought a house in Nice, Villa des Roses, and he lived also in Grenoble, Southeastern France, from 1931 to 1933. He employed Nadia

BOULANGER in Paris as a piano teacher for his son, Soulima STRAVINSKY, from 1929, also developing a strong professional relationship with her.

As a composer working in France (and elsewhere), Stravinsky's Russian identity remained of great importance to him, most obviously in the numerous Russian musical references in his early works. It was also significant for audiences, for whom, as a Russian musician working in France and SWITZERLAND, he represented Otherness, a quality which was one of the most immediately striking elements in his three great works for Diaghilev's BALLETS RUSSES (Firebird, 1910; PETRUSHKA, 1911; The RITE OF SPRING, 1913). The French capital was in many ways the platform from which his international career was launched in 1910 with The Firebird.

Many have referred to Stravinsky as a magpie-like composer, able to bring together elements from his Russian heritage, local influences and progressive ideas. Perhaps the diversity of his musical output offers evidence of his emigré status, through his use of FOLK MUSIC, Russian nationalism and the new approaches he formulated after leaving Russia. As Tamara Levitz notes, his embrace of NEO-CLASSICISM represents his 'desire to assimilate' and to 'translate his life into French after his emigration' (Levitz 2012, 312). While working in several culturally distinctive environments gave Stravinsky an intercultural perspective on music, his Russian upbringing and musical heritage, as it manifested itself in his three great Russian ballets from 1910 to 1913, could appear exotic to French – specifically Parisian – audiences.

Jonathan Cross refers to Stravinsky's 'concerted effort at assimilation' (Cross 2013, 16), illustrated practically in the unambiguously neo-classical OCTET FOR WIND INSTRUMENTS (1923), which, with its contrapuntal passages, has been interpreted as simultaneously anti-Debussyist and aligning itself with the musical direction of LES SIX. Nadia Boulanger noted its 'precise, simple, and classic lines' (Boulanger 1924, 25). In engaging with the critical discourse surrounding neo-classicism, writing an essay on the Octet after its première, Stravinsky behaved as other French composers had done (DEBUSSY and DUKAS produced essays on their operas), and published his ideas for his French audience. As Levitz and Cross highlight, if he was indeed assimilating Frenchness, then the Octet and the subsequent essay can be seen as a clear iteration of that process.

The creative collaboration of diverse artistic personalities in Paris' theatres, together with the rich music education available at the Paris Conservatory and the Schola Cantorum, made for an active and stimulating environment for this Russian immigrant. The inevitable cultural differences at times made for conflict, and for some of his early works to be viewed at times as exotic. The scandal created by The RITE OF SPRING, arguably occasioned by the choreography as much as the music, was a significant artistic event in the city, with different aesthetic attitudes and opinions being exchanged in the press. As Roman Vlad noted: 'Stravinsky was out to be the arch-revolutionary, an iconoclast out to destroy all the most sacred canons of musical aesthetics and grammar' (Vlad 1967, 28). Despite this reaction, and the BALLET dropping out of the repertoire rather quickly, Stravinsky's music became a concert staple, with the first concert performances of The Rite and Petrushka taking place in the French capital in April 1914, conducted by Pierre MONTEUX.

Beyond the early period of the Russian ballets, Stravinsky had many other Parisian premières, notably a concert performance of OEDIPUS REX at the THÉÂTRE SARAH BERNHARDT in 1927. In 1935, together with his son Soulima, he premièred the CONCERTO FOR TWO SOLO PIANOS at the Salle Gaveau in Paris. Indeed, simply following the succession of Stravinsky's Parisian premières during this period is instructive of his continuing development. PULCINELLA, a reworking of music that had been attributed to PERGOLESI, but which was in fact composed by others including Gallo and Monza, was also staged in Paris, again for Diaghilev, at the Paris Opera on 15 May 1920. His balletic work in France continued with PERSÉPHONE which was staged at the Paris Opera on 30 April 1934, following a complex collaboration with André GIDE and Ida RUBINSTEIN. In the 1950s, a performance of THRENI in Paris (1958), conducted by the composer, went badly wrong and there were arguments between BOULEZ, CRAFT and Stravinsky concerning the amount of rehearsal time and the quality of the preparation for the performance.

Stravinsky's time in Paris, and more generally in France, was undoubtedly crucial for his musical development, not least for the exposure and experience it afforded him of the great artistic developments that were taking place there with cubism, FUTURISM and so on, and with which he was able to engage in terms of music. Certainly, at a time when ballet was declining in his own country, new and progressive balletic works were being staged in the French capital.   HELEN JULIA MINORS

Nadia Boulanger, 'L'Octuor de Stravinsky, Le monde musicale', La revue Pleyel, 1 (1924), 25.
Jonathan Cross, 'Stravinsky in exile', in SHW, 3–19.
Tamara Levitz, Modernist Mysteries: Perséphone (New York: Oxford University Press, 2012).
Jann Pasler, 'Stravinsky and the Apaches', The Musical Times, 123.1672 (1982), 403–7.
Roman Vlad, Stravinsky, trans. Frederick Fuller and Ann Fuller (New York: Oxford University Press, 1967).
Eric Walter White, 'Stravinsky and Debussy', Tempo, 61.62 (Spring–Summer, 1962), 2–5.

Funeral Song (Pogrebal'naya pesnya) for large orchestra, op. 5, Largo assai. Composed 1908, USTILUG. First performance, 17/30 January 1909, ST PETERSBURG. Conductor, Felix Blumenfeld. Published 2017, Boosey & Hawkes.

For many decades, in all of the Stravinsky work-lists, the title Funeral Song was accompanied by the mysterious note, 'unpublished, lost'. It was not until a miraculous find in 2015, in Stravinsky's native city of St Petersburg, that the piece was finally restored to existence.

Funeral Song was written by the then unknown, 26-year-old Igor Stravinsky as a tribute to the memory of his adored teacher, the leading professor at the ST PETERSBURG CONSERVATORY, Nikolay RIMSKY-KORSAKOV, who passed away on 8/21 June 1908. 'Orchestral piece on the death of Nikolay Andreyevich', as Stravinsky named the work in his summer letters to the Rimsky-Korsakov family, appears to have been completely 'scored' already by 28 July / 10 August 1908 (PRK, I, 193–4). Then the orphaned disciple had to mobilise huge efforts in order for the work to be included in one of the memorial concerts, which began in the Russian capital in autumn 1908. In the end, Stravinsky scarcely succeeded in his endeavour: his piece was eventually performed in the January programme of the RUSSIAN SYMPHONY CONCERTS series.

The final title of the piece (*Pogrebal'naya pesnya*) was mentioned for the first time by Stravinsky in his letter of 30 December / 12 January addressed to the officer of the 'Russian Symphony Concerts', Fyodor Gruss (PRK, I, 200). In this letter, Stravinsky discusses the pre-rehearsal corrections in the handwritten orchestral parts of *Funeral Song*. The concert presentation itself took place in the Great Hall of the St Petersburg Conservatory, with the Orchestra of Count Sheremetev under Felix Blumenfeld, and was destined to remain the only one in Stravinsky's lifetime. Despite a sceptical critical response to *Funeral Song*, the author himself highly estimated it even at the end of the 1950s: 'I remember the piece as the best of my works before *The Firebird* and the most advanced in chromatic harmony' (*Conv*). *Funeral Song* became his first independent experience, realised without any of the assistance generously supplied by Rimsky-Korsakov in his previous works. The piece symbolised not only the deep love of a devoted pupil – while composing it, the ambitious author had to prove both his professional abilities and his right to take a significant place in Russian music.

Very soon afterwards, Stravinsky was commissioned by Sergey DIAGHILEV to orchestrate two Chopin pieces for the Paris ballet *Les Sylphides*. Being absorbed by new, spectacular projects, the composer did not care about publishing *Funeral Song* since its role had already been fulfilled. The score 'unfortunately disappeared in Russia during the Revolution', Stravinsky stated in the AUTOBIOGRAPHY. Nevertheless, during his late years, the composer anticipated the recent discovery, asserting that 'the orchestral parts [of *Funeral Song*] must have been preserved in one of the St Petersburg orchestral libraries' (*Conv*).

Stravinsky was right. The orchestral parts of *Funeral Song* awaited their time in the St Petersburg Conservatory music library, where they reposed among old, uncatalogued items. For decades, they remained invisible until a time of relocation, when in the early spring of 2015, the entire historic building of the Conservatory was closed for general renovation – for the first time since 1896. At this point, the full set of fifty-eight orchestral parts was discovered by the author of this entry in collaboration with a librarian, Irina Sidorenko.

Never being able to recollect that lost music, Stravinsky only kept in mind a general programmatic idea of the piece, 'which was that all the solo instruments of the orchestra filed past the tomb of the master in succession, each laying down its own melody as its wreath against a deep background of tremolo murmurings simulating the vibrations of bass voices singing in chorus' (*Auto*, 24). Really, *Funeral Song* is a kind of slow procession (Largo assai, 6/4) of about 12 minutes' duration, in which different instruments and groups of orchestra transfer to one another a single leading melody, on the first occasion presented by solo horn. Cast in a free strophic form with a middle section which serves as development, the principal theme, diatonic at the beginning, intensively absorbs fissured chromatic lines, passing through several climaxes before vanishing in a *ppp morendo* at the end. The lamentations of *Funeral Song* are remarkable in their strongly Romantic character: this genuine musical tragedy demonstrates a unique experiment of assimilating a Wagnerian idiom, whilst combining it with some of Rimsky-Korsakov's, TCHAIKOVSKY's and Stravinsky's own stylistic elements. As a result, due to its passionate tone, *Funeral Song* became an extraordinary example of emotional expressiveness in Stravinsky's output. Whilst rooted in past traditions, this early Stravinsky piece also points in the direction of future stylistic developments: its opening has similarities to the opening of *The Firebird*, while one chromatic phrase (see Trumpet I, bar 21 onwards), evolving formally from the trumpet signals of the second movement of Rimsky-Korsakov's *Scheherazade*, anticipates the finale of The RITE OF SPRING. Being the first threnody in Stravinsky's oeuvre, *Funeral Song* at the same time established a whole genre of such 'songs', in various languages, extending throughout his career up to the final works, such as the REQUIEM CANTICLES and the instrumentation of *Lieder* by Hugo Wolf.

The new birth of the rediscovered *Funeral Song* took place in St Petersburg on 2 December 2016 with the Mariinsky orchestra under Valery Gergiev, based on the score reconstructed at the St Petersburg Rimsky-Korsakov State Conservatory. During 2017, it was performed by great orchestras and outstanding conductors of the world, among them Charles Dutoit, Esa-Pekka Salonen, Riccardo Chailly and Sir Simon Rattle, who called the piece 'Stravinsky's early *chef-d'oeuvre*'. Over a century after its composition, a long-lost Stravinsky work has finally entered the concert repertoire.

NATALIA BRAGINSKAYA

Natalia Braginskaya, 'New light on the fate of some early works of Stravinsky: the *Funeral Song* re-discovery', trans. Stephen Walsh, *Acta Musicologica*, 87.2 (December 2015), 133–51.
Natalia Braginskaya, 'Predilection', trans. Stephen Walsh, in Igor Stravinsky, *Funeral Song Score* (Boosey & Hawkes, 2017), v–vi.

Furtwängler, Wilhelm (born Schöneberg, Berlin, 25 January 1886; died Baden-Baden, 30 November 1954). German conductor. He was principal conductor of the Berlin Philharmonic 1922–45, and the Leipzig Gewandhaus Orchestra 1922–6. He conducted The RITE OF SPRING in Leipzig (1923), Berlin (1924 and 1930), and with the New York Philharmonic (1925). With Stravinsky as soloist, he conducted the CONCERTO FOR PIANO AND WIND INSTRUMENTS in December 1924. Stravinsky claimed that Furtwängler 'conducted it wretchedly, even worse than Koussevitzky at the première' (T&C, 226). Between 1929 and 1939, Furtwängler gave more than forty performances of The FIREBIRD with the Berlin Philharmonic throughout Europe. His pre-war repertoire also included PETRUSHKA, SCHERZO FANTASTIQUE, Suite No. 1 and The FAIRY'S KISS. At the Salzburg Festival, he conducted the 1947 version of *Petrushka* (1948) and the SYMPHONY IN THREE MOVEMENTS (1950) with the Vienna Philharmonic. Live recordings survive of *The Fairy's Kiss* (1953) and Symphony in Three Movements (1950). NIGEL SIMEONE

Société Wilhelm Furtwängler, 'Liste des concerts': http://furtwangler.fr/liste-des-concerts.

Futurism. 'Some of the drollest hours of my life were spent in [Balla's] and his fellow Futurists' company' (*Conv*, 92). In his CONVERSATIONS WITH ROBERT CRAFT, Stravinsky recounts that his meetings with the futurists took place in an atmosphere of amusement and friendship: 'they were absurd but sympathetically so, and they were infinitely less pretentious than some of the later movements that borrowed from them ... The Futurists were not the aeroplanes they wanted to be but they were at any rate a pack of very nice, noisy Vespas' (*Conv*,

94). This image of aeroplanes evoked by Stravinsky effectively sums up the most relevant traits of the poetics of futurism – theorised by Filippo Tommaso Marinetti in The Foundation and Manifesto of Futurism in 1909 – which praises the dynamism of modern life and technological progress to promote a new conception of Art based on the idea of 'the beauty of speed'.

The myth of technology also conditions futurist research in the field of music. In the manifesto The Art of Noises, published in 1913, Luigi Russolo affirms that the only possible evolution of music – in a society dominated by the noise of machines – is 'the addition and substitution of noises for sounds' (Russolo 1986, 28). In order to achieve this objective, Russolo invented and constructed a series of musical instruments, the intonarumori ('noise machines'), that permitted the creation and control in pitch and dynamic of different kinds of noises: whistlers, buzzers, exploders, murmurers, gurglers, clackers, rattlers, thunderers, roarers and so on.

Stravinsky heard a 'Grand Futurist Concert of Noises' for the first time on 15 June 1914 at the London Coliseum, where an orchestra of eighteen noise machines performed A Meeting of Motor-car and Aeroplanes and other pieces by Russolo, whilst Marinetti read the manifesto The Art of Noises. DIAGHILEV, who also attended the concert, developed a strong interest in the experiments of the futurists and – in a telegram to Stravinsky in January 1915 – urged him to form an 'alliance with Marinetti'. On 13 February, Stravinsky and Diaghilev met Marinetti, the painters Giacomo Balla, Fortunato Depero, Umberto Boccioni and the composer Francesco Balilla Pratella, in Rome. The following day, Alfredo CASELLA conducted the first Italian performance of PETRUSHKA and, at the end of the concert, Marinetti shouted 'Down with Wagner! Long live Stravinsky!' According to a review published in the Russian World, 'Stravinsky had an enormous success … The ovation was somewhat spoiled by Marinetti who wanted to get in on Stravinsky's triumph.' However, the interference of the futurists did not displease Stravinsky, who wrote to his mother: 'there were continued lengthy demonstrations in the corridors. All the Italian Futurists were present and saluted me noisily.'

In the following weeks, Diaghilev continued to put pressure on Stravinsky to begin an artistic collaboration with the futurists and, in a letter dated 8 March 1915, he proposed that Stravinsky work with them on the ballet 'Liturgie'. Diaghilev explained that he had abandoned the original project to have the performers dance without musical accompaniment and to limit the music to short interludes. His new idea was that the 'dance action must be supported not by music but by sounds' produced by noise machines, and he urged the composer to join the futurists in Milan, to 'discuss matters with the orchestra's representatives and to examine all of their instruments'.

The meeting, which took place at Marinetti's house one evening in April 1915, is documented in various, rather contradictory, reports. According to the futurist Francesco Cangiullo: 'Those gentlemen were enchanted and declared the new instruments to be the most original orchestral discovery.' Stravinsky, in his Conversations with Craft, affirmed, however, that he only 'pretended to be enthusiastic'; in fact, he never used Russolo's instruments and he did not produce a score for 'Liturgie'. Nevertheless, it was a memorable evening and the disruptive vitality of the futurists influenced all who were present. As PROKOFIEV, who played some of Stravinsky's four-hand piano pieces with the composer, recalls: 'Stravinsky, always small and anaemic, during the playing boiled, became bloodshot, sweated, sang hoarsely and so comfortably gave the rhythm that we played with a stunning effect.'

In autumn 1916, Diaghilev settled in Rome where he decided to involve the futurists in two new productions with Stravinsky. His interest was focused on the work of Balla and Depero who, in the manifesto *Futurist Reconstruction of the Universe* (1915), had proclaimed the necessity of performance conceived as 'a fully dynamic stage space'. Balla was asked to design a set with scenery and lighting for FIREWORKS, while Depero was commissioned to provide scenery and costumes for the BALLET The SONG OF THE NIGHTINGALE, with choreography by MASSINE. Stravinsky was constantly informed as to how the works were progressing. In a letter of 14 March 1917, Gerald Tyrwhitt (BERNERS) announced that 'A great Deperesque work is also being prepared for your *Nightingale*: I saw the sets and costumes which are very, very pretty. Balla is working for you as well and has already made some gigantic constructions.'

Balla's work bears a strong avant-garde and visionary imprint: on the stage, there was only a play of lights which emphasised the details of the set design, composed of abstract forms and geometric shapes. The staging of *Fireworks* was presented in Rome on 12 April 1917, with the orchestra directed by Stravinsky, whilst the production of The *Song of the Nightingale* was in the end withdrawn by Diaghilev. He had great expectations for this venture – 'Depero is brilliant', he wrote to Stravinsky on 3 December 1916 – and the composer completed the score on 4 April 1917. For the set, Depero had created a 'gigantic mechanical tropical flora', but the costumes (rigid, geometrised space suits that concealed body, hands and faces) turned out to be unusable. Diaghilev had already expressed certain reservations in a letter to Stravinsky's wife (17 December 1916): 'The Futurists are working a great deal and, so far, very amusingly. I do not know how people are going to move around in Futuristic costumes, but, in any case, the *quality* of their movements must change totally, i.e., movement must be renewed.'

All of Stravinsky's collaborations with the futurists were therefore solicited by Diaghilev, who wanted to give a strong modernist slant to the new productions of the BALLETS RUSSES. If the concrete results of this collaboration were very limited, it was perhaps because the avant-garde trajectory of the futurists was really too visionary and too much ahead of its time.   SUSANNA PASTICCI

Giovanni Lista, 'Stravinsky et les futuristes', in François Lesure (ed.), *Igor Stravinsky: la carrière européenne* (Paris: Musée d'Art Moderne de la Ville de Paris, 1980), 54–6.
Luigi Russolo, *The Art of Noises*, trans. Barclay Brown (New York: Pendragon Press, 1986).

G

Gagnebin, Elie (born Liège, Belgium, 4 February 1891; died Zurich, 16 July 1949). Belgian-born Swiss geologist. In addition to pursuing a scientific career at the University of Lausanne, Gagnebin was immersed in the artistic and intellectual life of the Canton of Vaud. His connections, and renown as a public speaker, led to him performing the role of the Narrator at the première of The Soldier's Tale (Lausanne, 1918). Theodore Strawinsky remembered his performance: 'I must mention Elie Gagnebin's unforgettable reading of the Narrator's part, a masterpiece of acting that delighted us all. His long friendship with all our family was to date from The Soldier's Tale' (Sfam, n.p.).   SOPHIE REDFERN

Genet, Jean (born Paris, 19 December 1910; died Paris, 15 April 1986). French playwright and novelist who courted scandal throughout his life. Championed by Sartre early on, he emerged as a powerful and innovative dramatist in the 1950s, with his ambitious dismantling of stage conventions similar to that of Antonin Artaud. After a meeting in early 1963, Stravinsky agreed to provide music for director Joseph Strick's film adaptation of Genet's play The Balcony, adapting his Octet for Wind Instruments and parts of The Soldier's Tale for the project. After their meeting, Genet commented that Stravinsky's voice reminded him of 'the sound of the percussion instruments in Histoire du Soldat'.   DAVID EVANS

Germany. From World War I onwards, Stravinsky openly distanced himself from the heritage of German music, which for him could mean either tubthumping bombast or the intimate spaces of heightened subjectivity and expression. Given the influence on him of various German composers and works throughout his career, from Johann Sebastian Bach's contrapuntal invention to Beethovenian formal procedures and rhythmic innovation, his ostentatious anti-Teutonic stance was arguably more political than aesthetic. On 20 September 1914, a few months after the German declarations of war on Russia and on France, Stravinsky wrote to his colleague at the Ballets Russes Léon Bakst: 'My hatred of Germans grows not by the day but by the hour.' The following year, he wrote the solo piano piece Souvenir d'une marche boche ('Souvenir of a "Kraut" march') which featured in Edith Wharton's Le Livre des sans-foyer ('The book of the homeless'), a gift book in aid of Belgian war orphans.

Following the end of the war, Stravinsky visited Germany sporadically for the rest of his life, usually on concert tours. In November 1912, The Firebird and Petrushka were performed at Berlin's Neues Operntheater (subsequently the Kroll Theatre) with the composer in attendance. He spent over a month in

Berlin in autumn 1922 to meet his mother Anna off the boat from ST PETERSBURG in Stettin (Berlin's Baltic port), narrowly missing the first German performance of The RITE OF SPRING in late November, also in Berlin, conducted by Ernest ANSERMET. The concert was met by scandal reminiscent of the legendary 1913 PARIS première, although, in the event, audience reception was overwhelmingly positive.

The single most important work for Stravinsky's reception in Weimar Germany was The SOLDIER'S TALE, whose first German performance took place at the Schauspielhaus, Frankfurt, on 20 June 1923 under Hermann SCHERCHEN. (The performance was reviewed in the Neue Zeitschrift für Musik by a 19-year-old Theodor Wiesengrund-ADORNO.) That performance was repeated on 19 August in Weimar, as part of the Bauhaus Exhibition week, this time attended by the composer and by many of the foremost avant-garde artists and thinkers of the day. This genre-defying chamber piece of music theatre – translated as Die Geschichte vom Soldaten by Werner Reinhart and his brother Hans – left an indelible impression on composers as different as Kurt WEILL, Karl Amadeus HARTMANN and Ferruccio Busoni. Thereafter, Scherchen became a force for the promotion and performance of Stravinsky's works in Germany generally, a highlight being his Stravinsky Festival in Frankfurt (24–25 November 1925), although many of his plans for Stravinsky performances never materialised.

Still more authoritative as a conductor and all-round interpreter of Stravinsky's music in Weimar Germany was Otto KLEMPERER, whose professional relationship with Stravinsky began in earnest in November 1925 with a Wiesbaden performance of the CONCERTO FOR PIANO AND WIND INSTRUMENTS and the PULCINELLA SUITE (see Heyworth 1983). This association continued at the Kroll Theatre, Berlin, which saw the first staged production of OEDIPUS REX on 25 February 1928 (two days after the première in Vienna), and more or less ended with the theatre's untimely closure in November 1930, marked by a valedictory performance of The Soldier's Tale. Stravinsky was quoted in Tempo (12 November 1930): 'In no other city have I and my works met with such interest and understanding as in Berlin, and for that I have above all to thank Otto Klemperer and the Kroll Opera.'

In a review of Stravinsky's Oedipus Rex (November 1928), Weill observed astutely that the 'oratorio form makes [the work] suitable for radio'. Not only did the work provide a direct model for Weill's own radio cantatas, but, for the next few years, the Berlin and Frankfurt radio stations took a central role in the dissemination of Stravinsky's music in Germany, culminating in a pair of concerts broadcast nationally in honour of Stravinsky's semicentennial birthday in June 1932. Hans ROSBAUD, conductor of the Frankfurt Radio Symphony Orchestra from October 1929, was a key figure in this respect, as was his German publisher Willy Strecker (B. Schott's Söhne, Mainz). It was Strecker who facilitated commissions with German radio – for example, the CONCERTO FOR VIOLIN conceived in collaboration with Samuel DUSHKIN and first performed in a live radio broadcast from the Berlin Philharmonie on 23 October 1931. By this point, there was growing fascist disapproval of Stravinsky's works, such as that of Fritz Stege who pronounced the Concerto a 'desecration of Bach' in a review that foreshadowed the cultural politics of Stravinsky's German reception during the Third Reich.

Performances of Stravinsky in Germany continued well into the late 1930s, with his ballet JEU DE CARTES receiving its first staged European performance at the Dresden Staatsoper on 13 October 1937. Only in 1940 were his works banned under the Nazi regime, and then on account of his French citizenship (see Evans 2003). It was as a 'Brechtian' work of the Weimar era that The Soldier's Tale featured alongside Stravinsky's AUTOBIOGRAPHY in the notorious 'Entartete Musik' ('Degenerate Music') Exhibition in Düsseldorf in 1938. He responded with a letter denying charges that he was Jewish or communist. The defamations did not stop the party from roundly approving Stravinsky as a 'pure Aryan' and 'nationalist', such statements being no less tendentious than erstwhile attempts to brand him as a cultural Bolshevik who wrote 'peasant ballet' music (e.g. Alfred Heuss, December 1923).

In the postwar era, Stravinsky returned to Germany several times throughout the 1950s, attending performances of his works at festivals including Hartmann's Munich-based Musica Viva concert series, often in the capacity of conductor. Meanwhile, his music was scarcely heard in East Germany, compared with its reception in the West, largely because it continued to be denounced as 'formalist' by Soviet critics (see Calico 2008). A landmark performance in the German Democratic Republic, however, was the fully staged production of PETRUSHKA at the Komische Oper, Berlin, in 1957, choreographed by Gertrud Steinweg. In many ways inspired by Stravinsky's The Rite of Spring, Wolfgang Rihm's ballet Tutuguri: Poème dansé (1982), setting the poem by Antonin Artaud subtitled 'le rite du soleil noir' ('The rite of the black sun'), is one of surprisingly few musical compositions to emerge from late twentieth-century Germany with an apparent Stravinskian model.   JEREMY COLEMAN

Joy H. Calico, Brecht at the Opera (Berkeley: University of California Press, 2008).
Joan Evans, 'Stravinsky's Music in Hitler's Germany', Journal of the American Musicological Society, 56.3 (Fall 2003), 525–94.
Peter Heyworth, Otto Klemperer: His Life and Times, vol. I: 1885–1933 (Cambridge University Press, 1983).

Gide, André (born Paris, 22 November 1869; died Paris, 19 February 1951). French novelist, critic, essayist and translator, a leading light on the French intellectual scene from the early 1900s who won the Nobel Prize for Literature in 1947. Gide's hallmark was the récit, an ironic first-person narrative through which he explored the tensions between gratification of the instincts and self-denial. He produced carefully structured texts, with formal symmetries, as in some of his best-known works Les Caves du Vatican (1914), La Symphonie pastorale (1919) and Les Faux-monnayeurs (1926). Stravinsky met Gide in 1910, and a few months after the première of The RITE OF SPRING, Gide asked him for some incidental music for his translation of Anthony and Cleopatra, but nothing came of the idea since they disagreed on both musical and visual style, the author favouring period costume and the composer modern dress.

In 1933, at the request of Ida RUBINSTEIN, and for a $7,500 fee, the pair began work on a stage version of Gide's early melodrama PERSÉPHONE, adapted from the Homeric hymn to Demeter in which the sense of 'extraordinary exaltation' thrilled the French author. This was not strictly a collaboration, since Gide had written his first version of the text before 1914, full of rich rhyme and romantic phrasing, Christianising the myth by making Persephone's sacrifice a voluntary one. The early signs were promising: Gide visited Stravinsky in Wiesbaden, where they read the text together, agreed on the device of a speaker – requested by Rubinstein – and a tripartite form, such that the author noted in his diary that evening, 'Entente parfaite'. Indeed, his letters to Stravinsky at the start of the process were very positive – 'You understand the subject as the celebration of a mystery', he wrote – and Gide made major revisions to his original text, telling him, 'I consider the text as definitive only in so far as it suits you.' He agreed to Stravinsky's request to remove the episodic *divertissements*, and offered to add an extra scene 'if the text seems to you too short for the musical development'. In a letter of 8 August 1933, there is some discussion of scansion, Gide altering the text to fit the requirements of the music. Yet the collaboration soon turned sour, and, according to Stravinsky, when Gide first heard the piece during a run-through with Rubinstein, he commented only, 'C'est curieux, c'est très curieux', and promptly left. Furthermore, he attended neither rehearsals nor any of the three performances. He was, however, present at a private audition at the home of Princess Edmond de Polignac, with the composer at the piano, and Stravinsky later described him 'bridling more noticeably with each phrase'. Stravinsky speculated that Gide took a dislike to his musical treatment of the text, or that 'he could not follow my musical speech'. While the music is exceptionally rich, Stravinsky did not synchronise Rubinstein's speaking role – commissioned as such, since she was not a trained singer – with the music. Moreover, Gide's text features mostly regular alexandrine lines, which Stravinsky set in extremely idiosyncratic and unnatural ways. VALÉRY attempted to persuade Gide of music's right to independence, and, such was the potential for critical outrage, Stravinsky published a defence of his work in *Excelsior* on 29 April 1934, the eve of the première at the PARIS Opera House. In this article, he claims: 'For *Perséphone* I wanted only syllables, beautiful, strong syllables and a plot. As such, I count myself lucky to have met Gide, whose highly poetic text, with its liberal jolts, was to furnish me with an excellent syllabic structure.' Later, in *Memories and Commentaries (Mem)*, he elaborates:

> Words combined with music lose some of the rhythmic and sonorous relationships that obtained when they were words only; or, rather, they exchange these relationships for new ones – for, in fact, a new 'music'. They no doubt *mean* the same things; but they are magical as well as meaningful and their magic is transformed when they are combined with music.

The problem, he complains, was that 'Gide understood nothing whatever about music … He had expected the *Perséphone* text to be sung with exactly the same stresses he would use to recite it. He believed my musical purpose should be to imitate or underline the verbal pattern … he was only horrified by the discrepancies between my music and his', and he concludes by asking: 'But what kind of music did Gide expect of me?' Despite not having seen him since that ill-fated run-through, Stravinsky was very moved upon learning of Gide's death.   DAVID EVANS

Glazunov, Alexander Konstantinovich (born St. Petersburg, 29 July / 10 August 1865; died Paris, 21 March 1936). Russian/Soviet composer. Glazunov was one of

RIMSKY-KORSAKOV's most successful pupils; his first symphony and string quartet, both premièred in 1882, earned the young composer early acclaim. These premières drew the attention of the wealthy patron Mitrofan BELYAYEV, who, for the next two decades, provided financial backing for performances and publication of the composer's music. Upon Belyayev's death in 1903, Glazunov, along with Rimsky-Korsakov and LIADOV, was appointed to the board of trustees to oversee Belyayev's publishing house and concert series. With his additional election as Director of the ST PETERSBURG CONSERVATORY in 1905, Glazunov was the most visible heir to Rimsky-Korsakov's musical legacy and thus an important stylistic influence on Stravinsky, eighteen years his junior, when the latter entered Rimsky-Korsakov's intimate circle in 1902. This influence can be heard in the formal balance of Stravinsky's SONATA IN F♯ MINOR (1903–4) and SYMPHONY IN E♭ MAJOR (1905–7). Though Glazunov was supportive of Stravinsky initially, Maximilian STEINBERG emerged as the more promising member of the younger generation. By the death of Rimsky-Korsakov in 1908, Stravinsky's waning presence is evident in Glazunov's conspicuous omission of Stravinsky's name among Rimsky-Korsakov's pupils in a memorial interview. The animosity between the composers intensified as Stravinsky, overlooked in his homeland, gained in reputation abroad. Glazunov particularly disparaged Stravinsky's lack of conservatory training and 'poor ear' (see MUSICAL EDUCATION). While Stravinsky occasionally acknowledged his early admiration of Glazunov's command of form and counterpoint, after the death of Glazunov Stravinsky distanced himself from the composer's 'academicism'.   JOHANNA FRYMOYER

Glinka, Mikhail Ivanovich   (born Novospasskoye, Smolensk District, 20 May / 1 June 1804; died Berlin, 3/15 February 1857). Russian composer. Reception history typically paints Glinka as the 'father' of Russian music, to whom many 'firsts' are attributed: through-sung and internationally acclaimed operas, unique synthesis of Western and Russian musical idioms, use of Russian FOLK MUSIC, etc. Current historiographic revaluation of OPERA before Glinka cautions against such narratives; however, there is no doubt that Glinka profoundly shaped later generations of Russian composers. His operas A Life for the Tsar (1836) and Ruslan and Lyudmila (1842) present two distinct directions for Russian opera. The former is a celebration of Russian nationalist ideals of 'Autocracy, Orthodoxy and Nationality'. Praised for its use of Russian and Polish musical idioms and innovative text setting, the opera served as a model of operatic realism and historical drama. On the other hand, Ruslan presented a very different direction in 'magic opera', taking as its subject PUSHKIN's epic poem on a Russian folk tale. Though the opera perplexed critics at its première, its novel use of musical exoticism and chromatic harmonies to establish place and ethnic difference of the opera's varied characters formed an important model for THE FIVE's fascination with the fantastic and exotic. Nonetheless, the cool reception of Ruslan led Glinka to redirect his later compositional efforts to programme music.

During his childhood, Stravinsky became well acquainted with Glinka's music through his father's performances, particularly as Farlaf in Ruslan, at the MARIINSKY THEATRE. During his Russian period, Stravinsky built on many of Glinka's precedents, with dramatic plots rooted in the folk and fantastic, the use of whole-tone sonorities to depict the supernatural, and the incorporation of Russian folk melodies. Though Glinka was not the first Russian composer to experiment with the latter, the distinctive 'changing background' technique found in works such as *Kamarinskaya* (1848), in which a melody is repeated exactly amidst changing texture and ORCHESTRATION, is evident in Stravinsky's music as well, notably the finale of FIREBIRD (1910). The most obvious homage to Glinka is found in Stravinsky's MAVRA (1922), a short one-act *buffa* piece dedicated to Pushkin, Glinka and TCHAIKOVSKY. In particular, Parasha's florid vocal lines and the Mother's aria find models in Glinka's romances and folk stylisations.

JOHANNA FRYMOYER

Gnesin, Mikhail Fabianovich (born Rostov-on-the-Don, 21 January / 2 February 1883; died Moscow, 5 May 1957). Russian composer, musicologist and teacher of Jewish heritage. In 1905, expelled from the ST PETERSBURG CONSERVATORY for taking part in a revolutionary student strike, Gnesin continued lessons privately at Nikolay RIMSKY-KORSAKOV's home. Alongside Stravinsky and Maximilian STEINBERG, Gnesin was considered one of the most talented of Rimsky's young students; Stravinsky recalled him as 'the liveliest and most openminded spirit of the Rimsky group'.

Gnesin's involvement with EVENINGS OF CONTEMPORARY MUSIC (ECM) and his harmonically adventurous settings of symbolist poetry gave him a reputation as an enterprising MODERNIST. Richard Taruskin suggests that Gnesin, as 'the only person among Stravinsky's acquaintances ... who was a genuine insider ... to the very loosely defined network of artistic "decadents" normally so abhorrent to the Rimsky set', was most likely to have introduced Stravinsky to 'the more advanced artistic circles in St Petersburg'. One of Stravinsky's earliest exposures as a composer to a paying audience was at an ECM concert, held on 27 December 1907 / 9 January 1908, in which his GORODETSKY setting 'Vesna' was heard alongside other settings of symbolist poetry by Gnessin and Steinberg.

Gnesin's surviving correspondence with Steinberg reflects the growing astonishment and scepticism the Rimsky-Korsakov family and their circle felt at Stravinsky's sudden success with FIREBIRD. Gnesin's later articles and reminiscences about Rimsky-Korsakov, SCRIABIN's 1909 visit to the Rimsky-Korsakov home, and more generally concerning Stravinsky's St Petersburg years have offered vivid and valuable insights for Stravinsky biographers.

DANIEL JAFFÉ

Dial; SCS; SRT

Golschmann, Vladimir (born Paris, 16 December 1893; died New York City, 1 March 1972). French conductor. After working as a violinist, he began to conduct in 1919, giving the première of MILHAUD's *Le Boeuf sur le toit* (21 February 1920). For the BALLETS RUSSES PARIS season in December 1920, he shared the conducting with ANSERMET, performing *The* RITE OF SPRING, PETRUSHKA and PULCINELLA. From 1931 until 1958, Golschmann was Music Director of the St Louis Symphony and remained on friendly terms with

Stravinsky. In April 1943, he conducted the New York première of DANSES CONCERTANTES at the Museum of Modern Art, after Stravinsky spent 'many hours coaching him in the work' (SSE, 147). Golschmann had an outstanding private art collection, including important works by PICASSO, Braque and Modigliani.   NIGEL SIMEONE

Goncharova, Natalya Sergeyevna (born Nagaevo, Tula Province, 16 June 1881; died Paris, 17 October 1962). Russian painter, stage designer, graphic artist, print-maker and illustrator. She was the lifelong companion and wife of the Russian painter, stage designer and graphic artist Mikhail Fyodorovich LARIONOV. At the turn of the century, Goncharova and Larionov both entered the Moscow School of Painting, Sculpture and Architecture, and it was Larionov who suggested that she switch her focus of study from sculpture to painting. Goncharova's early works (mainly pastels) were shown at Sergey DIAGHILEV's Russian Art Exhibition at the Salon D'Automne in PARIS in 1906. Although their purely easel-painting careers lasted only about a decade (they left RUSSIA permanently in 1915 to work for Diaghilev's BALLETS RUSSES), they became the leading avant-garde artists in Russia in the 1910s and prominent figures in the École de Paris in the 1920s.

As was the case with other Russian avant-garde artists of their generation, Goncharova and Larionov became acquainted with modernist French art mainly through the exhibitions of Sergey Shchukin's collection of French art, held in his mansion in Moscow from 1909 onwards. During the early 1910s, both artists experimented with post-impressionism, Italian FUTURISM, Fauvism and cubism, and exhibited in Russia and abroad; their other influences included Byzantine art, Russian icons and the Russian folk-art lubok (pl. lubki, Russian popular prints). In 1912, Larionov became the founder of the Russian version of non-objective art called luchizm (le rayonnisme), while Goncharova was the driving force and theoretician behind this achievement of her husband (Sharp 2006, 14 n.36). In 1913, Goncharova enjoyed a one-woman exhibition of over 700 works in Moscow and ST PETERSBURG. For this exhibition she published a manifesto, in which she stated her intention to turn away aesthetically from the West towards the East.

Ironic as it may be, in 1914 Goncharova made her reputation in Paris for her sets and costumes for Diaghilev's production of RIMSKY-KORSAKOV's OPERA *The Golden Cockerel*, which started her international career as a stage designer and which eventually resulted in her and Larionov's permanent emigration to the West. In his memoirs, Alexandre BENOIS attributes to himself the idea for the spatial separation between singers and actors in *The Golden Cockerel*, yet it seems that the original idea belonged to Goncharova (Sharp 2006, 260 n.6). The same configuration was later repeated in Stravinsky's RENARD, for which Larionov was the stage designer in 1922 and 1929 (with choreography, respectively, by Bronislava NIJINSKA and Serge LIFAR).

As a couple, they were somewhat unusual; the daring extrovert Larionov did not seem to fit to the introvert Goncharova, whose seriousness, hard work and modesty were mentioned by many. As artists, they were different: Larionov was a great colourist (his early impressionist works of 1906–9 stand out as the most striking example of this style in Russia), while Goncharova's main preoccupation was the organisation of the pictorial space. At the request of Diaghilev, who was always eager to pour new Russian blood into his progeny, the Ballets Russes, Goncharova and Larionov left Russia for SWITZERLAND in 1915, staying first with Diaghilev near Lake Geneva, then travelling to ITALY and Spain, before eventually settling in Paris in 1919 (in 1938, they were both granted French citizenship, but it was only in 1955 that they were, at last, officially married). In the summer of 1915, Goncharova worked with Stravinsky and the choreographer Léonide MASSINE on the unfinished ballet 'Liturgie', from which sixteen costumes survive, while Larionov (who, like many of Diaghilev's artists, also served as a CHOREOGRAPHER) was designing the BALLET Soleil de nuit to the music of Rimsky-Korsakov; his other projects included LIADOV 's Kikimora (1916) and Contes russes (1917), and PROKOFIEV's Chout (1921). The pinnacle of Goncharova's career as a stage designer was her minimalist monochromatic final sets and costumes for Stravinsky's LES NOCES (1923, with choreography by Bronislava Nijinska) – which captured well the severity and the drama of the peasant wedding ritual – as well as her coloured cubist designs for a new version of The FIREBIRD (1926).   MARINA LUPISHKO

John E. Bowlt, Khudozhniki russkogo teatra 1880–1930: Sobranie Nikity i Niny Lobanovykh-Rostovskikh ('Artists of the Russian Theatre 1880–1930: The Collection of Nikita and Nina Lobanov-Rostovsky') (Moscow: Iskusstvo, 1991).

Natalia Goncharova, 'The metamorphoses of the ballet "Les Noces"', Leonardo, 12 (1979), 137–43.

Natalie Goncharova and Michel Larionov and Pierre Vorms, Les Ballets Russes (Paris: Belves, 1955).

Jane A. Sharp, Russian Modernism between East and West: Natalia Goncharova and the Moscow Avant-garde (Cambridge University Press, 2006).

Goodman, Benjamin David ('Benny') (born Chicago, 30 May 1909; died New York City, 13 June 1986). Born into a Jewish immigrant family of small means, Benny Goodman rose to prominence as a clarinettist and bandleader of racially integrated bands during the interwar years. Dubbed the 'King of Swing', he achieved widespread fame with, arguably, the first JAZZ concert to be held at Carnegie Hall in January 1938. Acting defiantly within a period of continuing racial segregation, Goodman featured guest musicians from Count Basie's and Duke Ellington's bands. He also maintained a strong interest in both classical and contemporary musics: from Mozart, through to POULENC and COPLAND. Goodman was associated with Stravinsky as the soloist for the EBONY CONCERTO, in a recording made on 27 April 1965 with the Columbia Jazz Ensemble. As with Leonard BERNSTEIN's Prelude, Fugue, and Riffs, although the Concerto was commissioned by Woody Herman, it was Goodman who was best placed to respond to the stylistic and technical demands of Stravinsky's classical–jazz mélange.   DEBORAH MAWER

Goossens, Eugene   (born London, 26 May 1893; died Hillingdon, Middlesex, 13 June 1962). British conductor. After studying at the Royal College of Music, Goossens became an orchestral violinist, and later recalled playing PETRUSHKA under MONTEUX during the 1913 BALLETS RUSSES season at Covent Garden. On 7 June 1921, he gave the London concert première of The RITE OF SPRING, which was attended by Stravinsky, who told Edwin Evans that it had 'never sounded so well before', a view echoed in *The Times* (11 June 1921) which hailed a 'wonderful performance'. DIAGHILEV immediately engaged Goossens as a conductor for the Ballets Russes, where he worked alongside ANSERMET and FITELBERG until 1924. In 1923–4, Goossens made the first ever recording of *Petrushka* with the Royal Albert Hall Orchestra for HMV. Stravinsky later described him as 'a natural musician … and a master of orchestral technique. I recall his performance of *Le Sacre*, in London in 1921, with pleasure' (T&C, 231).

NIGEL SIMEONE

Gorodetsky, Sergey (Mitrofanovich) (born St Petersburg, 5/17 January 1884; died Obnisk, 8 June 1967). Russian poet, co-founder of Acmeism. A great part of his poetry was inspired by Slavic mythology and Russian folklore, although after the Revolution he developed a Soviet voice. Stravinsky set to music two of his songs under the title *Two Songs (Romances)* for mezzo and piano: 'Spring' and 'A Song of the Dew' – the latter dedicated to the poet. Apparently, he knew Gorodetsky well at the time he was composing these songs, and the poet confessed to him that, although he liked the music, Stravinsky had not rendered the text accurately. His collection of poems *Yar'* was part of the cultural background that inspired The RITE OF SPRING.

KATERINA LEVIDOU

Mem; SRT

Greeting Prelude for orchestra. Composed 1950, 1955. First performance, 4 April 1955, Boston. Conductor, Charles Munch. Published 1956, London: Boosey & Hawkes. Dedication: 'for the 80th birthday of Pierre Monteux'.

The *Greeting Prelude* for full orchestra, a felicitation composed for the eightieth birthday of conductor Pierre MONTEUX in 1955, consists of only thirty-two bars and has a duration of around 45 seconds. While the diatonic material for this miniature is based on the well-known tune 'Happy birthday to you', Stravinsky extracted a row of intervals from the melody, which is subjected to serial processes (transposition, inversion, retrograde and vertical setting). In *Memories and Commentaries*, Stravinsky mentions that, while he had already sketched out the work in 1950, the composition was only brought to fruition in 1955.

FLORIAN HENRI BESTHORN

Grigoriev, Sergey (born Tichvin, 5 October 1883; died London, 28 June 1968) was impresario Sergey DIAGHILEV's manager (1909–29). Known as the *régisseur* of the BALLETS RUSSES, Grigoriev made copious notes and kept a series of record books outlining the repertoire and recording details of every performance of the company from 1909 to 1929, and subsequently for the Ballets Russes de Monte Carlo from 1932 to 1952. These records, which are part of the Harvard Theatre Collection, give detailed insight into the activities of the companies, including what happened in rehearsal. Alicia MARKOVA, a member of the Ballets Russes, recalled of LES NOCES that Grigoriev documented the process, noting down all the dance counts, while also intervening during rehearsals to pin the counts to the dancers (Jordan 2007, 345). When Léonide MASSINE choreographed a re-interpretation of The RITE OF SPRING, Grigoriev recorded Massine's choices in great detail, remarking on the counterpoint he perceived in the choreography: 'It was as if Massine paid greater heed to the complicated rhythms than to meaning. The result was something mechanical' (cited in Jordan 2007, 441).   HELEN JULIA MINORS

Stephanie Jordan, *Stravinsky Dances: Re-visions across a Century* (Alton, Hampshire: Dance Books, 2007).

Haieff, Alexei (born Blagoveshchensk, Siberia, 25 August 1914; died Rome, 1 March 1994). Russian-American composer. After Juilliard School (1934–8), he studied with Nadia BOULANGER at Gerry's Landing in Cambridge, Mass. (1938–9), then at her home in Gargenville near PARIS in the summer of 1939, where he first met Stravinsky. That October, he re-encountered Stravinsky at a reception in Cambridge held after the composer had given his Charles Eliot Norton public lectures (POETICS OF MUSIC).

In November 1943, Boulanger hired Haieff to correct the score of Stravinsky's SYMPHONY IN C for publication by Associated Music Publishers. Haieff never quite completed this project, yet Stravinsky was impressed by his work; their close friendship – sustained both by Haieff's enthusiasm for and understanding of Stravinsky's music, and by their shared Russian heritage – was reinforced in 1945 when Haieff successfully prepared and rehearsed the EBONY CONCERTO with Woody Herman's players prior to its première the following year. Stravinsky subsequently provided Haieff a reference for a Guggenheim Fellowship, which he received in 1946. Haieff conducted further performances of *Ebony Concerto* in Baltimore and Boston, and in the late summer of 1946 prepared the band in LOS ANGELES for Stravinsky's recording of the work. While based in New York, Haieff often assisted Igor and Vera STRAVINSKY by booking hotels for their visits. Robert CRAFT recalled that Haieff facilitated his relationship with the Stravinskys, helping to 'cover up for my gaucheness and inadequacies'. DANIEL JAFFÉ

Hartmann, Karl Amadeus (born Munich, 2 August 1905; died Munich, 5 December 1963). German composer. Studied at Munich's Akademie der Tonkunst from 1924 and remained in GERMANY during the Third Reich, entering a so-called 'inner emigration'. His chamber OPERA *Simplicius simplicissimus* (1934–5) was inspired in large part by The SOLDIER'S TALE, a work he first heard in performance under his mentor Hermann SCHERCHEN in 1930 at the Munich Vereinigung für Zeitgenössische Musik. After the war, Hartmann returned to Munich to co-found the Musica Viva concert series of international contemporary music, which he directed until his death. Stravinsky's PIANO SONATA (1924) was programmed with Hartmann's own *Concerto funèbre* (1939) in the second-ever concert of the Musica Viva series (October 1945). Between 1945 and 1958, there were up to forty-four performances of Stravinsky's music, more than for any other composer. JEREMY COLEMAN

Renata Wagner (ed.), *Karl Amadeus Hartmann und die Musica Viva* (Munich: R. Piper & Co., 1980).

Health. Stravinsky lived a long life, but, from his childhood onwards, he struggled with various – including some very serious – illnesses. He was consumptive, often had gastric troubles and neuralgia, survived a stroke, suffered thrombosis and polycythaemia. Doctors, tests, diets, X-rays, bloodlettings, blood transfusion, phlebotomy, etc., were a feature of a large part of his life.

Stravinsky's illnesses are well documented through family correspondence and Igor's, Vera STRAVINSKY's and Robert CRAFT's diaries. These documents demonstrate his unwavering vital energy, the resilience of his creative spirit and its triumph over bodily frailty. 'Stravinsky's medical life ... was a social and philosophical, as well as strictly clinical, phenomenon' (SSE, 380).

Igor was a tiny, fragile child who was considered too frail to participate in any sports or games. In 1886, he survived scarlet fever, and the first symptoms of tuberculosis appeared when he was 13 (this disease, which was typical in the climate of ST PETERSBURG, was endemic in his family). For health reasons, he was exempted from military service. Yet, almost all his life, he paid much attention to calisthenics and was proud of his muscular build.

On 3 June 1913, a few days after the première of The RITE OF SPRING, he was admitted to a Parisian hospital with typhoid fever. In 1918, soon after the première of The SOLDIER'S TALE, he survived Spanish influenza. In March 1911, he was forced to interrupt his work on PETRUSHKA because of intercostal neuralgia, caused by nicotine poisoning, and he was afflicted once again with neuralgia in December 1917, during his work on LES NOCES.

In 1939, after the death of his wife Catherine and daughter Lyudmila, his tuberculosis recurred, and he was forced to spend six months in the sanatorium in Sancellemoz (from 12 March). Though ill, he worked here on the SYMPHONY IN C and the Harvard lectures. On 2 September, Igor was discharged from Sancellemoz, and twenty days later sailed to the UNITED STATES.

The Californian climate was favourable for Stravinsky's health and he was able to forget about his tuberculosis for several years. But, on 2 October 1956, during a concert in Berlin, he blacked out on the rostrum. He refused to see a doctor and went to Munich, where, on 5 October, Professor Diehl diagnosed a stroke, and he spent more than five weeks in hospital. Nevertheless, on 29 November, he conducted CANTICUM SACRUM in Rome. On 4 December, he arrived in London, where the great neurologist Sir Charles Symonds diagnosed a basilar stenosis and polycythaemia, advising him that he had only 'a fair chance' of surviving more than six months. Yet Stravinsky continued working intensely, creating one or two compositions a year until 1966. He also performed regularly as a conductor, usually sharing the programmes with Craft.

In September 1964, his polycythaemia became dangerously aggravated, and he became much slower in movement and speech. Nevertheless, in 1964–5, he undertook some concert tours (ISRAEL, Berlin, Warsaw, etc.), and in 1966 he created his final two works – REQUIEM CANTICLES and The OWL AND THE PUSSY-CAT. In 1967, he gave his last concert in Toronto, and in April 1969 he appeared for the final time in public, attending a *Homage to Stravinsky* concert at New York State University.

For the final four years of his life, Stravinsky was under constant medical supervision, increasingly in need of nursing. Mentally, he remained sharp and aware and continued listening to music, playing the piano and trying to compose or to orchestrate. In May 1968, he was taken into hospital with an embolism of the left leg. 'He sits in a wheelchair and hardly speaks' (Milène's letter, December 1969). In 1969, he was twice in hospital with respiratory troubles – his tuberculosis had resurfaced. On 6 April 1970, he was taken into intensive care with pneumonia and symptoms of heart failure, but in June Dr Henry Lax gave him permission to travel to Evian. On 18 March 1971, Stravinsky entered New York hospital with pulmonary edema and stayed there until 29 March. On 4 April, symptoms of edema recurred. The following day, Dr Lax visited Stravinsky and reported: 'It is not 100 percent hopeless. His strength is incredible, and he is man of surprises' (SCF 1994, 544). The next day, at 5.20 p.m., the composer died – according to the death certificate, of heart failure.   TATIANA BARANOVA MONIGHETTI

Henze, Hans Werner (born Gütersloh, 1 July 1926; died Dresden, 27 October 2012). German composer; emigrated to ITALY in 1953. Stravinsky's works were a formative influence on the ever-eclectic Henze even during his student years in Darmstadt, and continued to influence him into his later career (see Henze, *Die englische Katze*). Henze's first fully fledged OPERA *Boulevard Solitude* (1952), a reworking of Abbé Prévost's Manon Lescaut story, was inspired by *The* RAKE'S PROGRESS (1951) with its early-eighteenth-century subject matter and stylistic urbanity. Henze first met Stravinsky in Rome in early April 1954, a few days before the première performance of *Boulevard Solitude*. Stravinsky quizzed Henze about the latter's already well-established use of serial technique around the time Stravinsky was thinking of adopting it himself. The day of the première was marked by a bizarre fracas at the theatre door (related vividly by Henze in his autobiography) in which Stravinsky and Robert CRAFT were refused entry on grounds that they hadn't observed the dress code. (They were successfully admitted to the second performance a few days later.) Stravinsky was the dedicatee of Henze's opera *The Prince of Homburg* (1958) in a clear acknowledgement of a creative relationship.

                                                                                JEREMY COLEMAN

Hans Werner Henze, *Bohemian Fifths: An Autobiography*, trans. Stewart Spencer (Princeton University Press, 1999).
Hans Werner Henze, *Die englische Katze: ein Arbeitstagebuch 1978–82* (Frankfurt: Fischer, 1983).

Hollywood Bowl. The Hollywood Bowl opened in 1922, its name coined by conductor Hugo Kirchhofer to match its shape in the natural surroundings. Bowl audiences were first introduced to Stravinsky's FIREBIRD *Suite* in 1925, and *The* RITE OF SPRING shook the amphitheatre in 1928 (though neither were conducted by Stravinsky). When settling in Hollywood, Stravinsky was asked by former BALLETS RUSSES star dancer Adolph BOLM to conduct his production of *Firebird* in 1940, to which he agreed, on condition that Bolm would be his guarantor for citizenship. This debut led to an on-going relationship with the Bowl and repeated appearances there with the LA Philharmonic – a mutual fondness reflected in the celebration of his eightieth birthday there in 1962 (featuring selections from *Firebird*). Rarely satisfied by performances of his work, in 1957 Stravinsky was observed shaking his head in disappointment during a performance at the Bowl. According to Robert CRAFT, at the conclusion of the piece an elderly lady tapped him on the shoulder, assuring him that with perseverance he may learn to appreciate contemporary music. Without missing a beat, Stravinsky replied: 'I'll try it, if it kills me.'   LORIN JOHNSON

Holmes, Berenice (born Illinois, 4 February 1905; died Chicago, 3 April 1982). American dancer, CHOREOGRAPHER and teacher. Holmes was part of the burgeoning BALLET scene in Chicago. She danced in companies led by ex-BALLETS RUSSES star Adolph BOLM, directed and founded her own company (Palette Ballet), and had a long career as a teacher (Gene Kelly was a pupil). In 1928, she created the role of Polyhymnia in the first production of APOLLON MUSAGÈTE at the Library of Congress, Washington, DC (choreography by Bolm). Stravinsky did not attend the première and there is no evidence Holmes ever met the composer.   SOPHIE REDFERN

Honegger, Arthur (born Le Havre, 10 March 1892; died Paris, 27 November 1955). Swiss-French composer. Honegger was the member of Les SIX least drawn to Stravinsky's music and aesthetics. He acknowledged the importance of works such as The RITE OF SPRING, which he described as following a 'perceptible progression', despite its 'roughness'. He admitted somewhat controversially to Bernard Gavoty that the real danger in works such as The Rite of Spring 'is the boredom which is a consequence of so many clumsy improvisations' (Honegger 1966, 23). Unlike other members of Les Six, Honegger was not drawn to Stravinsky's NEO-CLASSICISM. He was, however, indebted to Stravinsky and Ernest ANSERMET for recommending him to the poet René Morax who commissioned him to write the music for his first critical success, Le Roi David (1921). Stravinsky helped again when Honegger was unsure how to write for a large chorus and a very restricted instrumental ensemble, advising: 'Go ahead as if you had chosen this ensemble and compose for a hundred singers and seventeen instrumentalists.' For Honegger, this was 'a splendid lesson in composition' (Halbreich 1999, 74).

Critics have detected Stravinsky's influence in a number of Honegger's works. His experimental war-time BALLET, Le Dit des jeux du monde, which was performed at the Théâtre du Vieux-Colombier, PARIS, in December 1918, is a case in point. While the rhythmic scenes for percussion instruments are more indebted to MILHAUD than to Stravinsky, they share a contemporary fascination with primitivism and origin stories. Halbreich detects Stravinsky's influence in fleeting moments in works such as the third of the Trois Chansons de la petite sirène ('Three songs of the little siren') (1926), the first movement of the Fourth Symphony (1946), the Orchestral Suite from Phaedra (1926) and the allusion to TCHAIKOVSKY in L'Appel de la montagne (1945). In 1942, Honegger identified the element that made him fundamentally distinct from Stravinsky: 'my essential aim is not to astonish or even to charm: it is to move people' (Halbreich 1999, 605).   BARBARA L. KELLY

Harry Halbreich, Arthur Honegger, trans. Roger Nichols (Portland, Oreg.: Amadeus Press, 1999).
Arthur Honegger, I am a Composer, trans. Wilson O. Clough and Allan Willman (London: Faber, 1966).

Horenstein, Jascha (born Kiev, 6/24 May 1898; died London, 2 April 1973). Russian–Austrian conductor, naturalised American. He studied in Vienna with Adolf Busch (violin) and Franz Schreker (composition) before becoming Wilhelm FURTWÄNGLER's assistant in Berlin. He became chief conductor of Düsseldorf Opera in 1928, where he conducted BERG's *Wozzeck*, supervised by the composer. He fled to the UNITED STATES in 1933. Horenstein conducted the première of the 1945 *Firebird Suite* first heard in a production choreographed by Adolf BOLM with sets by Marc CHAGALL at the Metropolitan Opera on 24 October 1945. Horenstein sent a despairing telegram to Stravinsky the next day, describing the Leeds Music orchestral parts as 'simply horrible, manuscripts done by non-professional copyists, worse than anything ever experienced'. Horenstein's recordings include the 1919 *Firebird Suite*, The RITE OF SPRING, SYMPHONY OF PSALMS and SYMPHONY IN THREE MOVEMENTS.   NIGEL SIMEONE

Horne, Marilyn (born Bradford, Pennsylvania, 16 January 1934). American mezzo-soprano. Stravinsky thought highly of Horne's voice, and he was the source of her first major break in the music profession, inviting her to perform as part of the VENICE FESTIVAL in 1956. Walsh suggests that Stravinsky may have first heard Horne perform as part of Robert CRAFT's vocal ensemble for his Gesualdo recordings (SSE, 325–6). She was also cast as Jocasta for a recording of Stravinsky's OEDIPUS REX for Columbia Records in 1967. Her career moved from Europe to America, and she sang at the inauguration of President Bill Clinton in 1993.   HELEN JULIA MINORS

Marilyn Horne, 'Marilyn Horne' (n.d.), www.marilynhorne.org/marilynhorne.html.
Lillian Libman, *And Music at the Close: Stravinsky's Last Years* (London: Macmillan, 1972).

Huxley, Aldous (Leonard) (born Godalming, nr London, 26 July 1894; died Los Angeles, 22 November 1963). English writer. Perhaps best known for his dystopian novel *Brave New World*, Huxley originally met Stravinsky in 1934 in London, but they did not become close friends until the late 1940s in southern California. The composer regularly consulted him on many cultural and intellectual matters; it was Huxley, for instance, who suggested W. H. AUDEN as an appropriate librettist for The RAKE'S PROGRESS. After Huxley's death – on the same day as John F. Kennedy's assassination – Stravinsky dedicated his final orchestral composition, VARIATIONS, to the writer's memory.
                                                    MATTHEW PAUL CARLSON

Dial

In Memoriam Dylan Thomas – Dirge-canons and song for tenor, string quartet, four trombones. Composed 1954. First performance, 20 September 1954, Los Angeles. Conductor, Robert Craft. Published 1954, Boosey & Hawkes. Poem by Dylan Thomas.

Order of movements: Dirge-Canons (Prelude), Song, Dirge-Canons (Postlude).

Stravinsky and Dylan Thomas were in the early planning stages of an opera project when the latter died suddenly in November 1953. In Thomas' memory, Stravinsky set the writer's famous poem 'Do not go gentle into that good night' in a song for tenor and string quartet, framed by a Prelude and Postlude for four trombones and string quartet.

Stravinsky explains in his prefatory notes to the score that 'Here my music is entirely canonic.' For the most part, canonic imitation involves only pitch, not rhythm, in the form of serial counterpoint built entirely from a five-note series and its derivations (transposition, inversion, retrograde, retrograde-inversion). This series, labelled 'theme' in the Prelude and first heard as e_1-$e\flat_1$-c_1-$c\sharp_1$-d_1, can be thought of as a condensed cambiata: it can thus be seen as an allusion to the use of this figure in some of the Renaissance and Baroque works which also featured on the programme of the première (likewise involving a trombone quartet).

Thomas' poem (published 1951), addressed to his father whose health was failing, is in the form of a villanelle. Stravinsky sets the two refrains (first and third line from the first tercet repeated alternately on the third line of the following four tercets, and on the third and fourth line, respectively, of the concluding quatrain) as two distinct melodies in the tenor, both of which, however, end with the same retrograde of the series on a soft high e_1 ($f\flat_1$), underlining the rhyme between 'night' and 'light'. The quiet accompaniment to the first refrain ('Do not go gentle into that good night') is varied each time, while the frustration portrayed in the second ('Rage, rage against the dying of the light') is always coupled with the same accented falling gesture followed by softer rising legato lines in the string quartet. The song opens with a short ritornello in the strings that features the original 'theme' in the first violin (as $f\flat_2$-$e\flat_2$-c_2-$c\sharp_2$-d_1). The ritornello recurs six more times with changed rhythms and, in the final bars, with rearranged instrumental lines in a lower register.

The Prelude and Postlude are, as Stravinsky describes them, 'antiphonal canons' between the trombone quartet and string quartet. The five-note series not only provides the motivic material for the imitative counterpoint, clearly audible in the trombone canons, but also supplies the anchor pitches for the beginnings and endings of phrases. In the Prelude, phrases start on E, D or C, and end with harmonies on E or C, with reference to the three 'white-key' notes in the 'theme'. In the Postlude, Stravinsky rotates the order of the canons (beginning on the second, omitting the last and returning to the second), swaps the instrumentation, and transposes the original string canons (now in trombones) down an octave, and the trombone canons (now in strings) up a minor seventh, with phrases now starting and ending on pitches, or harmonies on, D and C only.   CHRISTOPH NEIDHÖFER

Christoph Neidhöfer, 'An approach to interrelating counterpoint and serialism in the music of Igor Stravinsky, focusing on the principal diatonic works of his transitional period' (Ph.D. dissertation, Harvard University, 1999).
Joseph N. Straus, *Stravinsky's Late Music* (Cambridge University Press, 2001).
Stephen Walsh, *The Music of Stravinsky* (London: Routledge, 1988).

Introitus (T. S. Eliot in memoriam). Composed 1965. First performance, 17 April 1965, Chicago. Published 1965, Boosey & Hawkes. Text: Introit from the Latin Mass for the Dead.

Scored for tenors, basses, harp, piano, 2 timpani, 2 tam-tams, solo viola and double basses, *Introitus* was written in Hollywood in response to the death of T. S. ELIOT on 4 January 1965. Stravinsky had not been a close collaborator of Eliot's, having only set his words in ANTHEM ('The dove descending') (1961–2), but felt the need to memorialise the poet, beginning work in LOS ANGELES in February of that year.

It is a solemn, hieratic memorial cast in a straightforward strophic form, each of the three verses made up of a TWELVE-NOTE row and its retrograde. The first two are followed by rhythmic chanting with the indication *parlando sotto voce* (Stephen Walsh notes that the work is essentially a monody: SSE, 498–9), and the third by an instrumental section, and all three are preceded by and interspersed with what White calls 'cadences' for harp, piano and tam-tams (SCW, 538). A particularly characteristic colour is given by the use of the sextuplets played by the timpani.

Walsh points out that the work's harmony is not only derived inconsistently from his charts of note rows, but that the charts contain mistakes, thus allowing Stravinsky to arrive at chords that would otherwise have been impossible (Walsh 1988, 271). The work's ritual character is emphasised by the consistency that this facilitates, as well as the music's rhythmic regularity.

                                                                IVAN MOODY

Stephen Walsh, *The Music of Stravinsky* (London: Routledge, 1988).

Isherwood, Christopher (born High Lane, nr Manchester, 26 August 1904; died Santa Monica, 4 January 1986). English-American novelist. A close friend and early collaborator of the poet W. H. AUDEN, Isherwood is best known for his 1939 novella *Goodbye to Berlin*, a story set in Weimar GERMANY that inspired the 1951 play *I Am a Camera* and the 1966 musical *Cabaret*. Stravinsky met Isherwood in 1949, and the writer quickly became a regular and beloved member of the Stravinskys' social circle of émigré artists in southern California, which also included Isherwood's friend Aldous HUXLEY.   MATTHEW PAUL CARLSON

Israel. Like many Russian émigrés of his time, Stravinsky was not free of anti-Semitic prejudice. Nevertheless, he had many Jewish friends and collaborators, and gave his blessing for the marriage of his daughter Mika and Yuri Mandelstam, a Jewish poet who emigrated from RUSSIA. Moreover, his attitude towards the Jewish people evolved over the course of his long life. He was undoubtedly influenced by his friendship with Jacques MARITAIN, his later life in the UNITED STATES, the international response to the Holocaust, and the positive developments in Jewish-Christian relations fostered by POPE ST JOHN XXIII, whom Stravinsky highly esteemed. His close contacts with the Jewish world in the early 1960s were not a coincidence.

In January 1962, Stravinsky accepted an invitation from the Israeli government (represented by Theodor Kollek, Director of the General Prime Minister's Office) to participate in the Second Israel Music and Drama Festival (director Aaron Propes). Just fifteen years after the founding of the State of Israel, participation in the Festival signalled recognition and support of the new state's identity. The Festival was held under the aegis of the Government Tourist Corporation and in cooperation with the American–Israel Cultural Foundation. The Honorary Committee included the Minister for Foreign Affairs (Golda Meir, Honorary Chairman), Minister of Education, etc. Before his visit, Stravinsky made a public statement: 'It will be a historical event for me and it is one I have hoped for ever since the founding of the Israel Nation' (Programme Book of the Festival).

Stravinsky's first visit to Israel lasted from 29 August to 7 September 1962. On 2 September, he conducted The FIREBIRD in Haifa, then in Jerusalem (in the presence of President Ben Zvi) and Tel Aviv, whilst Robert CRAFT conducted MOVEMENTS and the CONCERTO IN D FOR VIOLIN AND ORCHESTRA, with the Israel Philharmonic Orchestra, and Zvi Zeitlin as soloist. An exhibition of Vera STRAVINSKY'S paintings was also organised in Tel Aviv. When Ben Zvi died in 1963, Stravinsky sent a warm letter of condolence to his widow (PSS).

Also in 1962, Stravinsky accepted an invitation from the American–Israel Music Alliance to cooperate on a project 'designed to contribute to the promotion of mutual understanding and brotherhood through music between the United States and Israel'. At the same time, Stravinsky received a commission to create a work on a biblical text in Hebrew (ABRAHAM AND ISAAC). The 80-year-old composer announced at a press conference: 'I am learning to pronounce Hebrew words and letters correctly . . . and I find its sound wonderful' (PSS).

Stravinsky's second visit to Israel in 1964 (20–25 August) began dramatically: on the eve of his departure, doctors forbade him to travel. Aaron Propes cabled: 'The whole Festival is around you and your composition . . . We have sent hundreds of invitations to leading personalities all over the world . . . There is tremendous expectation about your arrival' (PSS). Stravinsky arrived and conducted The SYMPHONY OF PSALMS and 'Vom Himmel hoch' sung in Hebrew, not Latin and German (a unique case in Stravinsky's performance practice), in Jerusalem (on 23 September) and in Caesarea (the following day). In the same concerts, Craft directed CAPRICCIO and the première of Abraham and Isaac. In Caesarea, the new President of Israel, Zalman Shazar, awarded Stravinsky a gold medal, and the composer conducted the Israel Hymn.

TATIANA BARANOVA MONIGHETTI

Italy. Stravinsky liked being in Italy. He could be disparaging about Italian orchestral playing, and had his share of tussles with the local bureaucracy, but he appreciated the quality of life offered by the major cities – Rome and VENICE especially – and went sightseeing all over the country. More than once, he considered moving there permanently. The Italian public responded with enthusiasm to his music, which was frequently performed and broadcast from the 1920s onwards. Younger Italian composers of the interwar period took Stravinsky as their principal stylistic model. By the late 1950s, he was a national celebrity. Stravinsky's numerous visits to Italy over more than half a century fall into three periods. The first is dominated by his relationship with the BALLETS RUSSES, and above all DIAGHILEV, who regularly summoned Stravinsky south to discuss future productions and meet potential collaborators. In the Albergo d'Italia in Rome in May 1911, Stravinsky completed the score of PETRUSHKA; in the Grand Hotel in Venice in September 1912, he played Diaghilev The RITE OF SPRING. In 1915, he met the futurists (see FUTURISM). The tumultuous Roman première of Petrushka in February was greeted by F. T. Marinetti's shouts of 'Down with Wagner! Long live Stravinsky!'; in Milan in April, Stravinsky listened to Luigi Russolo's intonarumori, or noise-intoners. The climax of Stravinsky's futurist involvement came in Rome in April 1917, when FIREWORKS was staged as a light show designed by Giacomo Balla. On this trip, Stravinsky also met Pablo PICASSO for the first time. Stravinsky's second Italian period featured the composer as performer. In April 1925, he was the soloist in his CONCERTO FOR PIANO AND WIND INSTRUMENTS in Rome, and in September of the same year he played his PIANO SONATA in Venice. In May 1926, Stravinsky conducted Petrushka and The NIGHTINGALE at La Scala, Milan, replacing an indisposed Toscanini, and in April 1928, The Nightingale at the Teatro dell'Opera in Rome. He returned frequently to Italy, either to play or conduct, right up until 1939 – visits that were appreciated at the highest level. Stravinsky appears to have had three audiences with Benito MUSSOLINI, in 1930, 1933 and 1935; the composer's contemporary statements of admiration for the Duce and his regime are notorious. Following Stravinsky's move to the UNITED STATES in September 1939, he did not return to Italy until 1951. In September that year, he conducted the première of The RAKE'S PROGRESS in Venice. This glittering occasion launched Stravinsky's final Italian period, which saw three further premières in Venice, along with conducting appearances in other Italian cities. With the exception of 1961, Stravinsky was in Italy every year between 1954 and 1963. He not only conducted, dined and went sightseeing – installed in the cellar nightclub of the Hotel Bauer-Grünewald in Venice, he also composed, working there on AGON, THRENI, A SERMON, A NARRATIVE AND A PRAYER and ABRAHAM AND ISAAC. Stravinsky's final trip to Italy in 1965, when he attended a performance of the SYMPHONY OF PSALMS in the Vatican, was in a sense not his last, for in April 1971, amid a media circus, his funeral and burial were held in Venice – not the composer's idea, but an appropriate choice, given his affection for the city.   BEN EARLE

Tamara Levitz, Modernist Mysteries: Perséphone (New York: Oxford University Press, 2012), 334–6.
Harvey Sachs, Music in Fascist Italy (London: Weidenfeld and Nicolson, 1987), 167–9.
SCS; SPD; SSE

Janacópulos, Vera (born Pétropolis, 20 December 1886; died Rio de Janeiro, 5 December 1955). Brazilian soprano. Stravinsky wrote to Janacópulos on 6 August 1924 asking her to learn his orchestral song cycle *The Faun and the Shepherdess*, which he had composed in 1906. She was living in PARIS at the time with her husband, the lawyer Alexey Fyodorovich Staal. Colin Slim outlines how Stravinsky had hoped that he would perform this work with her during a tour of the UNITED STATES in 1925 (Slim 2019, 16). As Stravinsky's first published work, in 1907, it was also the first to be acknowledged in reviews outside RUSSIA. It had its first public performance on 16 Feburary 1908 in ST PETERSBURG, as part of the BELYAYEV Concerts, conducted by Felix Blumenfeld.

HELEN JULIA MINORS

H. Colin Slim, *Stravinsky in the Americas: Transatlantic Tours and Domestic Excursions from Wartime Los Angeles (1925–1945)* (Oakland: University of California Press, 2019).

Jazz. Although the title of this entry may sound something of an anomaly in relation to Stravinsky, 'jazz' was a term employed much more loosely in its early years, around the end of World War I. It also offers a useful shorthand to encompass Stravinsky's wartime fascination with what was primarily ragtime and cake-walk, but which also brought in popular Latin dance references, boogie-woogie and even hints of the blues. For Stravinsky studies, the notion in fact cues two distinct clusters of compositions: the first, main cluster from c. 1917 to 1919 consists of the 'Ragtime' from The SOLDIER'S TALE (1918); the contemporaneous RAGTIME, for eleven instruments (1917–18); THREE PIECES FOR SOLO CLARINET (1918); and the PIANO-RAG-MUSIC (1919). The second group, emerging around World War II after a substantial gap, takes in PRAELUDIUM, for jazz ensemble (1936–7); the SCHERZO À LA RUSSE for jazz band (1943–4) and the EBONY CONCERTO for clarinet and jazz ensemble (1945).

There are various ambiguities, even 'fictions', associated with the first repertoire of pieces, occasioned by Stravinsky's often contradictory recollections and accounts across his many autobiographical volumes, co-authored with Robert CRAFT. One issue concerns the exact compositional chronology of the two 'Ragtime' items. In *Dialogues* (54), Stravinsky states: 'I composed the *Ragtime* in *Histoire du soldat*, and, after completing *Histoire*, the *Ragtime* for eleven instruments.' However, it may well be that the second, which was begun earlier, was largely completed before the first. Other ambiguities involve exactly when, within his period of enforced exile from PARIS during World War I, Stravinsky was sent a bundle of ragtime sheet music by Ernest ANSERMET; and whether or not he had also heard early jazz and music-hall items to supplement his visual notational knowledge by the time he composed *The Soldier's Tale* (see SRT, 1310).

Whatever the reality, these pieces, as expressed in AUTOBIOGRAPHY (p. 78), constituted for their composer 'a composite portrait of this new dance music', and so the precise sequence of events is perhaps less consequential. The 'composite portrait' idea is pursued below in this main entry (and within other entries on individual works), but it is worth drawing attention first to Stravinsky's claim about a 'new dance music'. While ragtime remained popular through this period, as attested to by Maurice RAVEL's interpretation of the genre in *L'Enfant et les sortilèges* (1920–5), it was certainly not 'new'. Indeed, the ultimate exponent of the classic piano rag, from the late 1890s onwards, was the incomparable Scott Joplin ('King of Ragtime') who died in 1917. Similarly, Joplin's rags – from which emerged the notion of 'ragged-time' – were not intended as 'dance music', but rather as serious art music.

Stravinsky's 'composite portrait' played with the notion of a broadly regular metric-rhythmic background against which to set syncopation, elaborations and closely related thematic material across the ragtime pieces. At times, to exploit the compositional potential, this basic concept was tested to its breaking point, as in *Piano-Rag-Music*. Although these pieces invoke a wider set of cultural references than the profoundly Russian pre-war works, they do not sever that native connection. And even Stravinsky acknowledged in his *Dialogues* (Dial, 54) that: 'The snapshot … must always have seemed to Americans like very alien corn'.

While the truest representation of ragtime is undoubtedly found in *Ragtime*, for eleven instruments, the focus here as a kind of 'source' or model is on the smaller-scaled 'Ragtime' from *The Soldier's Tale*. For Taruskin (SRT, 1305–6), the instrumentation – violin, double bass, clarinet, bassoon, percussion, cornet and trombone – owes most to east European klezmer bands, though Barbara Heyman (1982, 551) argues for similarities to Irving Berlin's band line-ups. This East–West interplay continues (see, too, Mawer 2014, 87–9).

Stravinsky's 'Ragtime' adapts its formal scheme from that of a classic rag, such as Joplin's *Maple Leaf Rag* (1899), in terms of a ternary form plus trio: aa¹bb¹aa¹, cd, aa¹ (a brief reprise-cum-coda). Morphing from the 3/4 waltz time into 2/4 metre, the violin's syncopated tune is set against a more regular bass. This double-stopped, bluesy melody (reworked elsewhere) operates in a flexible D major that explores modal 'mixture' at the third and fifth: F♯–A, E♯–G♯, F♯–A. Stravinsky's playing upon the blues third (F♯–F♮) and seventh (C♯–C♮) of the D-scale becomes more apparent in the return of this main theme on violin (c. Figures 31–3.) Also notable is an off-beat dotted, descending and then ascending, rag-like 'head' motive – with hints of diverse rags including Joplin's *Magnetic Rag* – first sounded by clarinet and bassoon, and later supported by trombone glissandi.

Conversely, in the contrasting 'B' section (Figures 26–31), the intricate bassoon figuration, use of repeated sonic cells, and stuttering rhythmic disintegration amid irregular metre are strongly reminiscent of *The* RITE OF SPRING. More generally, such Russian and east European association is reinforced by the percussive articulation of tambourine, triangle and bass drum, combined with a notably 'dark' timbral palette.

Meanwhile, the THREE PIECES FOR SOLO CLARINET mediate between the two sets of 'jazz'-related compositions, linking loosely back to 'Ragtime' in the accented, reiterated thematic material of the finale, while looking forward via the solo clarinet focus to the EBONY CONCERTO. This second cluster of works is characterised by its connection with jazz performers, including the clarinettist-bandleaders Woody Herman and Benny GOODMAN, as well as Paul WHITEMAN, with his more old-fashioned, commercialised product. Consequently, Stravinsky's output of the mid-1930s to mid-1940s is scored for big-band-type forces and is more contemporaneous in its style than his early ragtime oeuvre. Francis POULENC (Buckland and Chimènes 1999, 369) nicely articulated the difference: 'How interesting it is to compare the Ebony Concerto with the Ragtime for 11 instruments of 1918. The latter ... is a portrait of jazz. The Ebony Concerto is the lesson learnt from jazz by an artist of genius.' Nonetheless, both sets of pieces thrive on an eclectic mix of classical–jazz techniques and sonorities, which contribute to Stravinsky's long-term compositional development.   DEBORAH MAWER

Sidney Buckland and Myriam Chimènes (eds.), Francis Poulenc: Music, Art and Literature (Aldershot: Ashgate, 1999).

Barbara Heyman, 'Stravinsky and ragtime', Musical Quarterly, 68.4 (October 1982), 543–62.

Deborah Mawer, French Music and Jazz in Conversation: From Debussy to Brubeck (Cambridge University Press, 2014, repr. paperback, 2016).

Jeu de cartes. Composed 1936. First performance, 27 April 1937, Metropolitan Opera House, New York. Published 1937, B. Schott's Söhne. Copyright renewed 1965, Schott's.

Jeu de cartes is a comic BALLET that Stravinsky composed for the AMERICAN BALLET company in 1936, placing it just after the CONCERTO FOR TWO SOLO PIANOS, and just prior to CONCERTO IN E♭: 'DUMBARTON OAKS'. George BALANCHINE choreographed the première performance, which took place on 27 April 1937, at a festival devoted to Stravinsky held at the New York Metropolitan Opera House. The ballet's story – conceived by the composer – revolves around several characters depicted as playing cards. Indeed, playing card games was one of Stravinsky's favourite pastimes. The action unfolds in three 'deals', with the Joker – who believes he is invincible – playing a central and disruptive role in each. After the first and second deals, the Joker is finally defeated in the third deal by a Royal Flush (of hearts). According to Balanchine, the story, music and dancing all reflect how sometimes seemingly powerful figures are mere silhouettes that can be defeated by the pure of heart. While the action divides into three parts, which are labelled in the score, the music is continuous throughout. Unlike the earlier Russian ballets, there are no section names (e.g., 'Augurs of Spring'), but Stravinsky's stage directions and programme notes outline clear subdivisions. In terms of instrumental forces, Jeu de cartes calls for a small orchestra (with no percussion), aligning it more with APOLLON MUSAGÈTE (1927–8) than with PETRUSHKA or The RITE OF SPRING.

Throughout the piece, many of the hallmark techniques of Stravinsky's neoclassical style provide structure and interest. Clear tonal centres (including key signatures) form the structural basis of the piece. Each of the three deals begins with a loud fanfare in B♭ major. Subsequent keys relate to B♭ primarily by thirds (D and D♭ in the 'First Deal'), chromatic half-step (A and A♭ in the 'Second Deal'), or some combination of those two (C, E♭, E and G in the 'Third Deal'). Obvious allusions to established genres abound as well, including marches, waltzes, minuets and variations. Finally, allusions to and explicit quotations from specific earlier pieces are sprinkled throughout. A prominent flute melody in D♭ major recalls the middle section of DEBUSSY's *Prélude à l'après-midi d'un faune*. Other sections have echoes of RAVEL's *La Valse* or Johann Strauss' *Die Fledermaus*. In the 'Third Deal', a clear quotation from Rossini's *Barber of Seville* comes seemingly out of nowhere. All this combined with his usual rhythmic gestures and flair for orchestral sonorities create a whimsical and enjoyable piece. That said, it is the combination of these very traits that caused more than one critic to discount *Jeu de cartes* as too derivative and too focused on pleasing an American audience.   DON TRAUT

SCW

Kalafati, Vasily Pavlovich (born Yevpatoriya, 29 January / 10 February 1869; died Leningrad, 30 January 1942). Russian composer and pedagogue of Greek descent. He studied composition under RIMSKY-KORSAKOV at the ST PETERSBURG CONSERVATORY, graduating in 1899. From March/April 1902, Stravinsky took private lessons in counterpoint from Kalafati, essentially learning the basics of compositional technique – chorale harmonisation, species counterpoint, writing in two and three parts, and fugue. Though Stravinsky found Kalafati no less pedantic than his predecessor, AKIMENKO, and later described his feedback as monosyllabic – Kalafati insisting that Stravinsky should develop his musical ear to refine his exercises – they clearly had a warmer and more productive relationship: by the end of two years' tuition, Stravinsky referred to his teacher as 'Uncle Vanya' and used the intimate 'ty' form of address. For a number of Kalafati's counterpoint lessons, Stravinsky was joined by a fellow student, Stepan MITUSOV, who became a long-standing friend and future librettist of his opera The NIGHTINGALE.

DANIEL JAFFÉ

Nicolas Slonimsky, 'Kalafati, Vasili (Pavlovich)', in Laura Kuhn (ed.), *Baker's Biographical Dictionary of Twentieth-Century Classical Musicians* (New York: Schirmer Books, 1997), 655.
SCS

Kallman, Chester (Simon) (born Brooklyn, 7 January 1921; died Athens, 18 January 1975). American poet and librettist. A poet in his own right, Kallman is best known for his operatic collaborations with W. H. AUDEN, particularly their libretto for The RAKE'S PROGRESS. He had no hand in devising the thoroughly Audenesque scenario, but he was ultimately responsible for writing some of the libretto's most memorable numbers, including Anne's famous aria at the end of the first act. Stravinsky did not initially approve of Kallman's involvement; however, after they met in April 1948, the composer quickly came to appreciate his contributions, and the two men remained lifelong friends.

MATTHEW PAUL CARLSON

W. H. Auden and Chester Kallman, *Libretti and Other Dramatic Writings by W. H. Auden: 1939–1973*, ed. Edward Mendelson (Princeton University Press, 1993).

Karatïgin, Vyacheslav Gavrilovich (born Pavlovsk, 5/17 September 1875; died Leningrad, 23 October 1925). Music critic, musicologist, historian and composer. A key organiser of the EVENINGS OF CONTEMPORARY MUSIC, he championed Alexander SCRIABIN, Arnold SCHOENBERG and Sergey PROKOFIEV, and as music critic in various journals wrote some of the most perceptive articles on Stravinsky's music published prior to the Russian Revolution. Karatïgin's two major articles on The RITE OF SPRING – 'Vesna svyashchennaya' (published in Rech', 16 February / 1 March 1914) and 'Muzïka staraya i novaya' (published in Teatr i iskusstvo, 9 (1914)) – not only demonstrate his extraordinary understanding of Stravinsky's use of polytonality, but also include his uncannily prophetic statement that such art will inspire 'a deliberate return to simplicity', anticipating Stravinsky's turn to NEO-CLASSICISM in the 1920s. Yet, by describing Stravinsky's Rite as 'a flawed monument to the impressionist phase of Russian music', Karatïgin earned Stravinsky's enmity. In 1915, Karatïgin joined the editorial board of a new journal Muzïkal'nïy sovremennik (the Musical Contemporary), edited by Andrey Rimsky-Korsakov, which from its launch in September was overtly hostile to Stravinsky; Karatïgin contributed regularly, including snide footnotes which closely echoed comments hostile to Stravinsky from the journal's editor, until the journal folded in 1917 shortly after the defection at the end of 1916 of Boris ASAFYEV and the journal's patron Pierre SOUVTCHINSKY. Karatïgin's earlier and remarkably perceptive writings on Stravinsky nonetheless remained an important foundation for Asafyev's scholarly writings on the composer.   DANIEL JAFFÉ

SRT

Karsavina, Tamara Platonova (born St Petersburg, 25 February / 9 March 1885; died Beaconsfield, England, 26 May 1978). Russian-British dancer and teacher. Karsavina danced as a principal artist with the BALLETS RUSSES intermittently from its first season. Known to Stravinsky in ST PETERSBURG (she lived in the apartment above the family), she created roles in four Stravinsky ballets: the title character in The FIREBIRD (1910), the Ballerina in PETRUSHKA (1911), the Nightingale in The SONG OF THE NIGHTINGALE (1920) and Pimpinella in PULCINELLA (1920). She fondly remembered the composer helping her learn The Firebird, and in later life wrote of how her musical education 'began with the Firebird and progressed with each subsequent association with Strawinsky's music' (Karsavina 1948, 7). Stravinsky referred to her as his 'faithful interpreter' (Auto, 34).   SOPHIE REDFERN

Tamara Karsavina, 'A recollection of Strawinsky', Tempo, 8 (1948), 7–9.

Kashperova, Leokadiya Alexandrovna (born Lyubim, Yaroslavl district, 4/16 May 1872; died Moscow, 3 December 1940). Russian pianist, composer and pedagogue. A former star pupil of Anton Rubinstein (1888–91), in 1899 she was engaged by Stravinsky's parents to give their son piano lessons. Kashperova – as he recalled – made him learn principally sonatas by Clementi and Mozart (which may have seemed a regressive step to a young student who had already been learning piano for seven or so years), with occasional excursions to Schumann, Mendelssohn's Piano Concerto No. 1 and RIMSKY-KORSAKOV's operas. Though he chafed under Kashperova's restrictive regime – he was forbidden to use the pedals (an unexceptional form of training for virtuoso pianists to improve fingerwork: indeed, he later imposed the same restriction when teaching his children) and was banned from playing Chopin – Stravinsky allows in his AUTOBIOGRAPHY that her two years of tuition gave 'a new impetus to my piano playing and to the development of my technique'.

Kashperova was herself quite adventurous in her repertoire, giving several premières, including of Glazunov's Piano Sonata No. 2 at the first Evening of Contemporary Music held on 31 March / 13 April 1902; she may have secured Stravinsky's first appearance in Evenings of Contemporary Music as a pianist sometime in the 1902–3 season. Kashperova may also – however unconsciously – have been something of a role model for Stravinsky, combining as she did the career of virtuoso pianist and composer. Notwithstanding all this, Stravinsky gives her short shrift in both his autobiography and his reminiscences with Robert Craft. DANIEL JAFFÉ

Graham Griffiths, Stravinsky's Piano: Genesis of a Musical Language. (Cambridge University Press, 2013).

Graham Griffiths, Kadja Grönke and Luisa Klaus, 'Kaschperowa', in Europäische Instrumentalistinnen des 18. und 19. Jahrhunderts, Sophie Drinker Institut: www.sophie-drinker-institut.de/kaschperowa-leokadia.

SCS; SRT

Khachaturian, Aram Il'ich (born Tbilisi, 24 May / 6 June 1903; died Moscow, 1 May 1978). Georgian/Armenian composer, conductor and teacher. As a prominent member of the Union of Soviet Composers, Khachaturian played a central role during Stravinsky's visit to the USSR in 1962. We are informed by Robert Craft that a number of important Soviet composers were present at a 'very animated' evening reception given by Yekaterina Furtseva, the Soviet Minister of Culture, on 1 October 1962, including Khachaturian, Shostakovich, Kara Karayev and Khrennikov. During this meeting, Khachaturian toasted Stravinsky, asserting that, even though he had been a legend to him all his life, 'now that I have seen the man I am greatly moved by his sincerity'. Indeed, despite Craft's reservations about the genuineness of this proclamation, Stravinsky's harmonic and orchestral vocabulary was almost certainly an influence on a number of works by Khachaturian, especially the Piano Concerto (1936). At the same party, Stravinsky told Khachaturian that he desired to know more of his music, a statement Craft believed to be untrue. Khachaturian (and Khrennikov) bade Stravinsky farewell from the USSR on 10 October, 'laden with farewell gifts of samovars, gold spoons, gold tea-glass holders, inscribed scores'. JOSEPH SCHULTZ

Khachaturian, Karen (born Moscow, 19 September 1920; died Moscow, 19 July 2011). Soviet Armenian composer, nephew of Aram Khachaturian. His studies at the Moscow Conservatory were interrupted by the war, when he became librarian of the NKVD Ensemble of Song and Dance. From 1943, he studied composition at the Moscow Conservatory under Shebalin, Shostakovich and Myaskovsky, graduating in 1949. When Igor and Vera Stravinsky, accompanied by Robert Craft, visited the Soviet Union in 1962, Karen Khachaturian, by then a secretary of the Union of Soviet Composers, was appointed their guide by Khrennikov. Most of the practicalities of the Stravinskys' visit – such as ordering food, arranging passes, transport and, not least, interpreting for Robert Craft – in fact fell to the official interpreter, Alexandra Alexandrovna Afonina. It appears Khachaturian's main job (evident from Craft's diary) was to act as a guide and political commentator, introducing the Stravinskys to the glories of Soviet Russia, though this did not preclude their visiting, at Vera

Stravinsky's insistence (however reluctantly on Afonina and Khachaturian's part), the Novodevichy Monastery in Moscow. Any chance of further rapport between the two composers was further diluted by the appearance of Stravinsky's niece from Leningrad – Xenya – whose presence Stravinsky warmly welcomed and with whom he spent much time during his Soviet visit, catching up with family history. After the collapse of the Soviet Union, Karen Khachaturian provided intriguing memoirs published in Russian – not only concerning the visit itself, but some of the machinations behind it on the Soviet side. His recollections, published in English by Elizabeth Wilson, appear, unfortunately, less than reliable, several details being contradicted by both Craft's and Xenya Stravinskaya's diaries.   DANIEL JAFFÉ

Khovanshchina. OPERA by Modest MUSSORGSKY, revised and completed by Stravinsky. Mussorgsky left his five-act opera incomplete on his death in 1881, and RIMSKY-KORSAKOV made various cuts and alterations when orchestrating and preparing the work for its first performance in 1886. Its subject of the clash between the Old Believers and the introduction of Western ideas by Peter the Great would soon gain a new topicality which inevitably appealed to DIAGHILEV, and by 1910 he had already begun to make plans for staging the ST PETERSBURG première. In 1911, CHALIAPIN usurped these plans by directing a performance at the Mariinsky (in which he also took the role of Dosifey), but in a version with further substantial cuts from the Rimsky-Korsakov edition. Diaghilev became sufficiently concerned at the ways in which the opera had been curtailed that he commissioned Stravinsky to restore the missing scenes, with the plan of staging the opera with his company in PARIS and London. A printed vocal score of the Rimsky-Korsakov edition now preserved in the British Library was annotated in 1912 with details of the work required of Stravinsky in inserting deleted sections and re-orchestrating passages where the earlier edition had ventured too far from Mussorgsky's intentions. As it turned out, Stravinsky was too occupied with completing *The* RITE OF SPRING to begin work on *Khovanshchina* until the end of March 1913. Diaghilev therefore summoned the help of RAVEL, who undertook much of the work of orchestrating while Stravinsky completed a new setting of the final chorus and self-immolation of the Old Believers. One unexpected consequence of this collaboration was the opportunity it afforded for Stravinsky and Ravel to discuss other music of the time, especially that of SCHOENBERG, a conversation which led Ravel to dedicate his setting of Mallarmé's *Soupir* to Stravinsky. In the end, ironically, Diaghilev made rather more substantial cuts to the opera than even Rimsky-Korsakov had done, including the whole of the second act. Some of these were part of a complex negotiation to prevent Chaliapin from withdrawing from the production, which would have decimated ticket sales. Moreover, there had been much consternation in the press at the idea of Rimsky-Korsakov's work being supplanted by that of the composer of the *Rite*, and so Diaghilev at the last minute replaced Stravinsky's final chorus with the Rimsky-Korsakov version for the first performance, on 5 June 1913. It was only at a performance a fortnight later that the Stravinsky chorus was substituted. Stravinsky's final chorus was published the following year (in an edition which is now exceptionally rare), but never achieved common currency;

since 1959, the comprehensive revision by SHOSTAKOVICH has generally been used. The Stravinsky chorus ingeniously combines a chant of the Old Believers which Mussorgsky had already planned to use with two other melodies from earlier in the opera, also associated with the Old Believers. Its harmonic style begins within the idiom of Mussorgsky but soon extends some way beyond, ending the opera on an unresolved ninth chord.   NICOLAS BELL

Khrennikov, Tikhon Nikolayevich (born Yelets, 28 May / 10 June 1913; died Moscow, 14 August 2007). Russian composer and teacher. Secretary General of the Union of Soviet Composers (1948); First Secretary (1957). After several attempts to entice Stravinsky to visit the USSR, Khrennikov personally invited him there in June 1961 to conduct a concert of Stravinsky's own music. Khrennikov met Stravinsky upon arrival and the pair socialised throughout the trip, including at a meeting with Khrushchev (11 October). Although they appeared disdainful of each other's music, and Stravinsky described Khrennikov as 'a servant of the old regime . . . of Stalin', they were on amicable terms, remaining in touch and discussing an unrealised second visit to the USSR.   JOSEPH SCHULTZ

Kindler, Hans (born Rotterdam, 8 January 1882; died Watch Hill, Rhode Island, 30 August 1949). Dutch cellist and conductor. After a successful career as a cellist, Kindler turned to conducting in 1927, making his debut that year with the Philadelphia Orchestra (in which he had played from 1914 to 1920). On 27 April 1928, Kindler conducted twenty-five members of the Philadelphia Orchestra in the world première of APOLLO, given in the Coolidge Auditorium at the Library of Congress, Washington, DC. Stravinsky was not present. In 1931, Kindler founded the National Symphony Orchestra, which he conducted until his retirement in 1948.   NIGEL SIMEONE

King of the Stars, The (*Zvezdolikiy; Le Roi des étoiles*). Cantata for male chorus and orchestra, words by Konstantin BALMONT, French translation by M. D. Calvocoressi. Composed 1911–12, USTILUG. First performance, 19 April 1939, Brussels. Conductor, Franz André. Published 1913, Jurgenson. Dedicated to Claude DEBUSSY.

Subsumed under the genre of cantata, *The King of the Stars*, for four male chorus and orchestra, remains in the shadow of the Russian ballets, because of the musical difficulties and the contrast between its duration – scarcely 6 minutes – and the large-scale instrumental forces required. As a consequence, the first performance only took place over a quarter of a century after the work was completed, in the concerts of the Institut Nationale de Radiodiffusion Belge.

Like the *Two Poems* for soprano and piano, dating from the same period, the text of *The King of the Stars* is taken from a collection of poems by Konstantin Balmont, *The Green Garden*. The poem is found in a part of Balmont's oeuvre which draws together symbolist elements and subjects anchored in the complexity of Russian religiosity: the heavenly King of the title can be identified as the Messianic figure awaited by the Coptic sect which was founded in the eighteenth century, and which associated the concept of purity of the soul with the absolute rejection of physical love outside of reproduction, going as far as ritual castration. Coming at the time of his preparatory researches for The Rite of Spring, the choice of a poem rooted in Russian spirituality is certainly significant, even if, later on, Stravinsky chose to downplay its importance: 'The King of the Stars is obscure as poetry and as mysticism, but its words are good, and words were what I needed, not meanings. I couldn't tell you even now exactly what the poem means' (M&C, 83).

If the symbolic elements of the text, the association of fire and resurrection, recall Prometheus – Poem of Fire, the characteristic harmonies of the cantata have scarcely any relationship with the researches of Alexander Scriabin during this period. The octatonic scales in The King of the Stars are incomplete and arise from the chromatic expansion of superimposed major and minor thirds in a single harmonic complex first heard in the opening vocal section. This acts as a point of reference for the composition as a whole.

Stravinsky employs the large-scale orchestral forces in such a way as to differentiate the complex stratifications by means of a wide variety of instrumental combinations, in particular exploiting the full range of the eight horns, which are superimposed and combined with other groups of wind instruments.

In thanks, the dedicatee, Claude Debussy, acknowledged that 'only in Sirius or Aldébaran would there be a possible performance of this Cantata' – leaving no doubt that he had perfectly understood the significance of the gesture of friendship and trust shown by the gift of a score which the author considered his 'most radical and difficult' composition (Conv, 54).   WERNER STRINZ

Kirstein, Lincoln (born Rochester, New York, 4 May 1907; died New York City, 5 January 1996). American writer, impresario and cultural patron. Kirstein was an instrumental figure in American BALLET: with Choreographer George Balanchine he co-founded the School of American Ballet and the New York City Ballet (plus earlier short-lived companies). Kirstein met Stravinsky on 10 March 1935 – he described the composer as 'a strange little rat-like man' (Duberman 2008, 287) – and they went on to have various ballet and Balanchine-related dealings over the years. Kirstein was involved in commissioning Jeu de cartes (1937) for The American Ballet, Orpheus (1948) for Ballet Society, and Agon (1957) for the New York City Ballet.   SOPHIE REDFERN

Martin Duberman, The Worlds of Lincoln Kirstein (Evanston, Ill.: Northwestern University Press, 2008).

Klemperer, Otto (born Breslau (Wrocław), 14 May 1885; died Zurich, 6 July 1973). German conductor. He first met Stravinsky in Paris after a performance of Petrushka in 1914. In the early 1920s, Klemperer conducted The Soldier's Tale and the Pulcinella Suite in Wiesbaden. Stravinsky appeared there as soloist in the Concerto for Piano and Wind Instruments conducted by Klemperer on 17 November 1925, and this evidently impressed the composer: when Klemperer invited him to play the work again, Stravinsky wrote 'With you I am always happy to play my concerto.' At the Berlin Kroll Opera on 25 February 1928, Stravinsky attended Klemperer's performance of Oedipus Rex on a triple bill with Mavra and Petrushka, and, at the Kroll on 17 June 1929, Klemperer conducted an all-Stravinsky programme including Apollo, the Piano Concerto (with Stravinsky as soloist) and Les Noces, with George Szell and Fritz Zweig among the pianists. Klemperer continued to conduct Stravinsky's works into old age: in the early 1960s, he recorded the SYMPHONY IN THREE MOVEMENTS and *Pulcinella Suite* with the Philharmonia Orchestra for EMI, and in 1967 he recorded *Petrushka* (1947 version) with the New Philharmonia, which was only released in 1999, by Testament.

NIGEL SIMEONE

Peter Heyworth, *Otto Klemperer: His Life and Times*, 2 vols. (Cambridge University Press, 1983 and 1996).

Koch, Caspar (born Cologne, 1889; died Cologne, 5 December 1952). An operatic tenor and a significant figure in the operatic world in GERMANY, Koch performed regularly at the Opera House in Cologne from 1917 to 1926 before moving to the Opera House in Düsseldorf for the 1927–8 season. During this time, he also performed in WAGNER's *Das Rheingold* at both the Bayreuth Festival and at the Berlin Kroll Opera in 1927–8. Following this success, he was cast in the title role of Stravinsky's OEDIPUS REX for its German première in Berlin in 1928. The reviews of this production show that the original flavour of Stravinsky's work was retained in the set and re-staging (Walsh 1993, 71). Stravinsky noted that the performance was 'well-prepared' (SCS, 464), but the Berlin director noted negatively that 'Koch again sang Oedipus! And as badly as at the première.'

HELEN JULIA MINORS

Stephen Walsh, *Oedipus Rex*, Cambridge Music Handbook (Cambridge University Press, 1993).

Kochno, Boris (Evgenievich) (born Moscow, 3/16 January 1904; died Paris, 9 December 1990). Russian librettist, poet, artistic adviser and director. He served as DIAGHILEV's secretary from 1921 until the impresario's death in 1929. In this capacity, and through Diaghilev, he had the privilege of frequent contact with Stravinsky. Being a friend of the Sudeykins – and having feelings for Sergey himself – Kochno facilitated Igor's communication by letter with Vera Sudeykina (*see* Vera STRAVINSKY) at the early stages of their affair. Kochno was the librettist of MAVRA. Stravinsky greatly appreciated his literary gifts and enjoyed working with him, as he found his Russian verse text 'musical'.

KATERINA LEVIDOU

Auto; Expo; SCS

Kosloff, Theodore (Fyodor) (born Moscow, 22 January 1882; died Los Angeles, 22 November 1956). A dancer with the Imperial Russian Ballet, Kosloff most likely first met Stravinsky when appearing in the debut season of the BALLETS RUSSES in 1909. Kosloff came to New York in 1911 for the *Saison des Ballets Russes* and settled in LOS ANGELES, where he appeared in Hollywood films, choreographed, and directed a BALLET school. Kosloff began corresponding with Stravinsky for a 1937 LA production of PETRUSHKA and was first to meet the composer at the train station when he arrived during his third US tour. According to Naima Prevots, since the composer was required to travel during preparations for *Petrushka*, Kosloff ensured the dancers understood proper tempi by calling rehearsals during live radio broadcasts of Stravinsky conducting (*Dancing in the Sun: Hollywood Choreographers 1915–1937*, 127). Though

Stravinsky claimed to remember nothing about Kosloff's production, a photograph exists showing the composer in the Shrine Auditorium sporting a fedora and wrapped in a bath towel to keep out the chill. The composer was diagnosed with tuberculosis shortly thereafter. LORIN JOHNSON

Koussevitzky, Sergey (born Vyshny Volochyok, 14/26 July 1874; died Boston, Mass., 4 June 1951). Russian conductor and publisher. Koussevitzky was an important figure in the dissemination of Stravinsky's music, as both publisher and conductor. His company Édition Russe de Musique published many of Stravinsky's major works, from PETRUSHKA and The RITE OF SPRING up to PERSÉPHONE in 1934, with a hiatus during and just after World War I (*see* PUBLISHERS). At the same time, Koussevitzky conducted a number of these works. He gave the Russian première of extracts from *Petrushka* at a concert in ST PETERSBURG on 23 January / 5 February 1913, and again in Moscow one week later. A year later, Koussevitzky conducted the Russian première of *The Rite of Spring* (a concert performance) in February 1914. It is hard to imagine what this performance would have been like since, in the early 1920s (according to Nicolas Slonimsky), Koussevitzky did not have the technical skills required to conduct the work, a view confirmed by Myaskovsky, who wrote of the 1914 performances that 'Koussevitzky did not have command of *Le Sacre du printemps*, but let's not blame him for that: at least he performed it.' Stravinsky was generally critical of Koussevitzky's conducting (in later life, Vera said he was 'contemptuous' of it), and he doesn't seem to have had any affection for Koussevitzky either, despite his energetic advocacy of Stravinsky's music at a time when few others were prepared to take on such difficult scores.

Koussevitzky emigrated from RUSSIA in 1920, and the first time Stravinsky is known to have seen him conducting one of his works was the London première of the SYMPHONIES OF WIND INSTRUMENTS on 10 June 1921, a shambolic affair by all accounts. By 1923, Koussevitzky seemed to have mastered the difficulties of *The Rite* (helped by Nicolas Slonimsky's rebarring of the 'Danse sacrale') and he performed it regularly in PARIS and Boston, and never lost his passionate enthusiasm for the work, writing in 1933 that '*Le Sacre* is not outdated – on the contrary, it sounds like it was written yesterday. Having created a work of such super-genius, Stravinsky can be forgiven for many things.' One of the things for which he had to be forgiven was his consistently dismissive attitude to Koussevitzky, partly motivated by his own conducting ambitions, partly by his low opinion of Koussevitzky's talent. On 24 February 1928, Koussevitzky conducted the American première of OEDIPUS REX in Boston and, the same year, gave several performances of APOLLO, writing to the composer that 'everyone here is ecstatic about Stravinsky's music'. On 19 December 1930, he led the American première of the CAPRICCIO (with Jesus-Maria Sanromá as the soloist).

By this time, Stravinsky had accepted the commission from the Boston Symphony Orchestra for the SYMPHONY OF PSALMS. Koussevitzky was denied the world première of the work he had commissioned when Stravinsky gave it to ANSERMET (in Brussels) but he led the American première six days later, on 19 December 1930, and went on to conduct it many times. While the Boston commission for the *Symphony of Psalms* was in progress (a work that Koussevitzky's firm also published), Stravinsky was looking for a more lucrative publishing agreement and sold the CONCERTO IN D FOR VIOLIN AND ORCHESTRA to Schott in Mainz. In his correspondence with Stravinsky, Koussevitzky managed not to show how hurt and offended he was by this, though in private he was furious, writing to Païchadze at Édition Russe that:

> Stravinsky's action provoked the deepest disgust in Natalia Konstantinovna and myself. He certainly must have realized that in the light of his relationship with our firm, what he did was appalling.... We do not expect anything good from Stravinsky or Prokofiev. We know that they are callous egoists who think only about themselves and relate to people merely when it is profitable.

In the same letter, Koussevitzky urged tact and restraint in direct dealings with Stravinsky. When Koussevitzky's wife, Natalia, died in 1942, Stravinsky sent a genuinely heartfelt letter of condolence, though most of their correspondence from the period was connected with financial matters. In 1943, Stravinsky composed his ODE in memory of Natalia, and Koussevitzky conducted the world première with the Boston Symphony on 8 October 1943. Stravinsky became a regular visitor to the orchestra to conduct his own works, and Koussevitzky continued to programme Stravinsky's music until he relinquished his directorship of the orchestra through ill health in 1949. Their relationship was never easy or particularly close, but, thanks to Koussevitzky's determined (and often selfless) efforts to promote Stravinsky's music, it was a fruitful one.   NIGEL SIMEONE

Victor Yuzefovich and Marina Kostalevsky, 'Chronicle of a non-friendship: letters of Stravinsky and Koussevitzky', *Musical Quarterly*, 86.4 (Winter 2002), 750–885.
SCS; SSE

Krenek, Ernst   (born Vienna, 23 August 1900; died Palm Springs, Calif., 22 December 1991). Austrian composer; also music theorist and writer. One of the most prolific and eclectic composers of the twentieth century, he emigrated to the UNITED STATES in 1938 and gained citizenship in 1945. While in PARIS, he encountered the music of 'LES SIX' as well as Stravinsky's earliest neo-classical works, e.g., the PULCINELLA SUITE (1922), which Krenek emulated in his *Concerto Grosso, No. 2* (1924). Krenek first met Stravinsky in late November 1924 at the Swiss villa of their mutual patron, Werner Reinhart. Krenek attended the first performance of Stravinsky's CONCERTO FOR PIANO AND WIND INSTRUMENTS, which made an 'almost terrifying, astonishing, and elementary impression' (Krenek's letter to Paul Bekker, 14 December 1924). The two reconnected in 1950s LOS ANGELES and now the influence went the other way: Stravinsky held Krenek in high esteem as both a composer and an authority on SERIALISM, musical antiquarianism (particularly Josquin) and even Latin. Most significantly, Krenek was a direct source for Stravinsky's pursuit of twelve-note composition (*see* Hogan 1982; Straus 2001), with his *Lamentatio Jeremiae prophetae*, op. 93 (written 1941–2 but only published in 1957) providing a model for Stravinsky's first fully twelve-note work THRENI: *id est Lamentationes Jeremiae Prophetae* (1957–8).   JEREMY COLEMAN

Clare Hogan, 'Threni: Stravinsky's "debt" to Krenek', *Tempo*, 141 (1982), 22–29.
John L. Stewart, *Ernst Krenek: The Man and His Music* (Berkeley: University of California Press, 1991).
Joseph N. Straus, *Stravinsky's Late Music* (Cambridge University Press, 2001).

Kurtz, Efrem (born St Petersburg, 7 November 1900; died London, 27 June 1995). Russian conductor. He studied with GLAZUNOV in ST PETERSBURG and with Nikisch in Leipzig. Between 1928 and 1931, he conducted for Pavlova, then became chief conductor of the Ballet Russe de Monte Carlo until 1942, conducting several Stravinsky ballets including PETRUSHKA, The FAIRY'S KISS and JEU DE CARTES. He was music director of the Kansas City Philharmonic 1943–8, and in that capacity approached Stravinsky to write a cello concerto in 1944 (Stravinsky declined). The 1946 edition of *Current Biography* described Kurtz as 'a consistent advocate of Igor Stravinsky, whom he has known for many years'. In 1957, he recorded *Petrushka* and the two Suites for small orchestra with the Philharmonia Orchestra in London.   NIGEL SIMEONE

L

Laloy, Louis (born Gray, France, 18 February 1874; died Dole, France, 4 March 1944). Music critic and musicologist. Laloy graduated from the École normale supérieure and gained his doctorate in musicology from the Sorbonne in 1904. He rose to prominence from 1902 as an advocate for DEBUSSY. He got to know Stravinsky's work from 1912, when Debussy and Stravinsky performed a piano-duet version of The RITE OF SPRING. His reviews of The Rite emphasise the superhuman qualities of the work, primitivism and Stravinsky's ability to transpose noise into music. He was quick to blame NIJINSKY's choreography for the scandalous première of the BALLET, arguing that the music did not require a programme. In this respect, he bolsters Stravinsky's move to a more formalist, neo-classical position; his review of Léonide MASSINE's revised choreography in Comœdia (16 December 1920) emphasised its abstract and purely musical qualities. Laloy showed a certain independence for backing apparently minor or failed works, particularly The NIGHTINGALE and the more controversial MAVRA, which he described as a 'tour de force'. In contrast, Laloy showed his reservations about the highly successful Les NOCES because of its 'austere set purpose' and 'reaction against charm'. He commented on a range of Stravinsky's neo-classical works, noting that, whatever restriction the composer imposed on himself, 'he would always be a master musician'. BARBARA L. KELLY

Louis Laloy, La Musique retrouvée, 1902–1928 (Paris: Plon, 1928).
Deborah Priest, Louis Laloy (1874–1944) on Debussy, Ravel and Stravinsky (Aldershot: Ashgate, 1999).

Larionov, Mikhail (born Tiraspol, Kherson Province, now Moldova, 22 May / 3 June 1881; died Fontenay-aux-Roses, France, 10 May 1964). Russian avant-garde painter, printmaker and stage designer, associated early in his career with Neo-Primitivism, FUTURISM and Rayism. Larionov and Stravinsky met as early as 1914, when Larionov and his partner Natalya GONCHAROVA travelled to PARIS to execute her stage designs for the BALLETS RUSSES production of The Golden Cockerel. In 1915, Larionov and Goncharova moved to SWITZERLAND at the invitation of Sergey DIAGHILEV, where they interacted regularly with Stravinsky as well as other Ballets Russes collaborators. During this period, Larionov completed numerous sketches of Stravinsky, both alone and with Ballets Russes colleagues, including impromptu renderings on paper tablecloths. Stravinsky completed his Berceuses du chat during this same period, dedicating it to Goncharova and Larionov.

Given Larionov's reputation as a leader of the Russian avant-garde, Stravinsky may have been familiar with his work before 1914. Known especially for his nationalist-modernist interpretation of Slavic folk material, Larionov's work resonated with Stravinsky's experiments with Russian folk melody as realised in The RITE OF SPRING. This resonance between their work came to productive fruition in 1922 when Stravinsky and Larionov worked together on RENARD for the Ballets Russes. Interestingly, Larionov's designs used a more muted palette than his previous Ballets Russes work (*Soleil de nuit*, *Kikimora*, *Contes Russes* and *Chout*). Peasant dress, paired with masks for the various animal characters, suggested the buffoonery of crude street theatre evident in Stravinsky's music. In his AUTOBIOGRAPHY, Stravinsky praised the designs for *Renard* as one of the highlights of Larionov's career.   BARBARA SWANSON

Legacy. In legal parlance, a legacy is a tangible, quantifiable inheritance validated by law. As a metaphor for inheritance, indebtedness is far less concretely defined; Stravinsky did not make a will bequeathing his compositional identity to the composers he felt would benefit most from it, and by the time of his death he would have been well aware that the term 'Stravinskian' could be used in both positive and negative ways. On the one hand, the innovative features of his music, especially between 1911 and 1920 in The RITE OF SPRING, LES NOCES and SYMPHONIES OF WIND INSTRUMENTS, set standards widely seen as worth aspiring to; on the other hand, copying his more obvious quirks of rhythm and harmony, often in the context of a vaguely jazzy brand of NEO-CLASSICISM, began to seem too easy an option as the conventions of 1920s and 1930s MODERNISM came under critical scrutiny after 1945.

Celebrated for declaring his commitment to 'tradition' as something not inimical to innovation, Stravinsky was no less lauded for his supreme adaptability. At the time of his death, it seemed that few composers in history had travelled further, stylistically or technically, than he had over the sixty years of his career. At the same time, one of the lessons of musical history is that composers who sustained and even enhanced their prominence into old age might well lose much – if not all – of that prominence once the flow of new works had ceased and music moved on to celebrate new talents, new styles. But now that the best part of half a century has elapsed since Stravinsky's death, it certainly cannot be claimed that he has been all-but-forgotten in concert programmes and OPERA or BALLET schedules, and nor can it be conclusively demonstrated that composers have completely turned away from features plausibly definable as 'Stravinskian'.

A major reason for this is the close connection between what appears most personal to Stravinsky's music and much broader aesthetic and cultural trends in the arts since 1900, which continue to be relevant today. As far as the period between 1900 and 1970 is concerned, Stravinsky undoubtedly contributed decisively to an evolution from late Romanticism to neo-classicism that maps onto an even more fundamental evolution from early to high modernism, an evolution not grounded, as used occasionally to be asserted, in a progression from tonality to atonality, but in a process moving from a kind of tonality that was primarily diatonic to one that was crucially chromatic – extended or suspended, in Schoenbergian terms – and an approach to formal design somewhat looser, though no less coherent, than that of the classical and romantic past. Many other major composers – BARTÓK, Hindemith, PROKOFIEV and BRITTEN, for example – made similar journeys, but for reasons too complex to explore here (his closest contemporaries, Bartók, BERG and WEBERN, all died relatively young, and were denied the postwar careers in which Stravinsky cemented his pre-eminence), he had become by 1909 and remained thereafter in the forefront of contemporary composition to an even greater extent.

The strongest counterforce to Stravinskian modernism before 1950 came from the expressionist and post-expressionist qualities associated primarily with SCHOENBERG, Berg, Webern and other composers who also seemed more radically post-tonal in a commitment to the TWELVE-NOTE method that was seized on and further systematised by the post-1945 avant-garde as they attempted to sweep away what they deemed a decadent fixation on neo-classical parodies of historical styles. This dramatic clash of ideologies was at its most extreme around 1950, as the far-reaching differences between Stravinsky's The RAKE'S PROGRESS and Pierre BOULEZ's *Structures Ia* illustrate. Had Stravinsky's career come to an end at this point, his legacy, in terms of influence on composers during the years immediately after his death, could well have been very slight. As it was, however, Stravinsky's adaptation of aspects of serial technique in his compositions between 1951 and 1966, including features that even Boulez would learn from in his own later compositions, provided powerful evidence for the supreme flexibility of a language capable of combining disparate elements in ways that laid the foundations for the kind of 'steady-state' late modernism that emerged around 1980, as the more extreme avant-garde and experimental impetuses of the postwar decades ran out of steam. In particular, Stravinsky (in parallel, perhaps, with Berg) has seemed more relevant to many minimalist, post-minimalist and spectralist composers than the more intensely expressionistic heirs of Schoenbergian modernism.

A good sense of what acknowledging Stravinsky's legacy means for a composer at the present time can be found in Thomas Adès' conversations with Tom Service (2012). Adès begins in appropriately forceful terms: 'For a composer, Stravinsky is like a terminus that you have to go through to get anywhere on the train. There's no way to avoid him, and I'm fortunate in that I love everything he did and find so much to learn from.' In fact, Adès seems to learn from differences, not similarities: 'the structures in his music tends to be hard-edged, there isn't much transition, whereas … my music is always transitioning'. This seems to verge on using the opposition between classicism ('always transitioning') and modernism (as 'hard-edged') as the basis for the argument that Stravinsky teaches composers how best to find their own identity in multiplicity: 'no composer has worked through as many shifts of style as Stravinsky. So the value of that, now, as an example, is immeasurable.' Later, Adès homes in on the feeling that Stravinsky 'walked such a beautiful middle way, between borrowed surfaces and live material. Sometimes he trespasses outrageously, in both directions. He's the great example of someone for whom the style of each piece is a transparent thing that reveals the energy beneath'. And Adès piles on the paradoxes, declaring that '*Oedipus Rex* is great, to me. That is real power. But it's rather a shock, when it turns out to have so much power at the end, because you suddenly realise after all the jokes that it's deadly serious' (Adès 2012, 75–83). In this way, Stravinsky manages – as Adès aspires to manage – a modernism in which such striking oppositions are never mere contradictions.

Back in 1998, the British musicologist Jonathan Cross prefaced his book-length study of *The Stravinsky Legacy* (Cross 1998) with a warning, from the Dutch composer Louis Andriessen, that 'tracing influences can be dangerous'. Nevertheless, it is impossible to understand musical history without tracing them, however critically and sceptically. Cross' strategy – after a preliminary survey of thinking about 'Stravinsky's modernism' – is to distinguish four categories in which that modernism has proved particularly significant, first in affecting other composers during Stravinsky's lifetime, and then as evidence of his posthumous legacy. Under 'block forms' (as shown in works as different as Petrushka and Symphonies of Wind Instruments), the primary legatees are the notably diverse quintet of Varèse, Messiaen, Stockhausen, Tippett and Birtwistle. 'Structural rhythms' adds Debussy, Ives, Ligeti and Carter to the collection, with Debussy and Ives (both older than Stravinsky) representing ideas, especially about form, that had been in the air before 1905 but that Stravinsky did so much to project as essential modernist devices. 'Ritual theatres' deals even more with broader tendencies, with Berio, Boulez and Maxwell Davies added to some of those already discussed under other headings. Finally, 'minimal developments' explores what Reich, Glass, Andriessen, Adams and Torke can be said to have taken over from rhythmic and harmonic characteristics of works as well contrasted as *Petrushka* and Symphony in Three Movements, *The Rite of Spring* and Requiem Canticles.

By devoting as much space to T. W. Adorno's concentrated critique of Stravinsky's alleged failings (Adorno 1949/2006) as to Richard Taruskin's expansive appraisal of his achievements as fundamentally to do with Russian traditions (SRT), Cross is able to pinpoint very clearly how the remarkably consistent projection of these elements across sixty years of creative endeavour gave a Stravinskian (if not quite a purely Russian) slant to the entire history of musical modernism as it continues in composers of the Adams and Adès generations today. The issues involved in considering how Stravinsky actually influenced vital developments in musical composition, both during and after his lifetime, have been taken further in *Stravinsky and the Russian Period* (by van den Toorn and McGinness), whose subtitle, *Sound and Legacy of a Musical Idiom*, makes the relation to Cross' perspectives explicit. Even musicologists who would wish to argue that an adequate account of post-1900 modernism requires Debussy's, Berg's or Schoenberg's legacies to be considered in as much detail as Stravinsky's are unlikely to deny the special, and even supreme, importance of that Stravinskian bequest.   ARNOLD. WHITTALL

Thomas Adès, *Full of Noises: Conversations with Tom Service* (London: Faber and Faber, 2012).
Theodor W. Adorno, *Philosophy of New Music*, trans. and ed. Robert Hullot-Kentor (University of Minnesota Press, 2006). Originally published in German, 1949.
Jonathan Cross, *The Stravinsky Legacy* (Cambridge University Press, 1998).
Pieter C. van den Toorn and John McGinness, *Stravinsky and the Russian Period: Sound and Legacy of a Musical Idiom* (Cambridge University Press, 2012).

Leibowitz, René (born Warsaw, 17 February 1913; died Paris, 29 August 1972). Polish, naturalised French music theorist, conductor, composer and teacher. Leibowitz considered himself to be a self-taught musician, and details of his education and apprenticeship are difficult to ascertain. He came to PARIS in 1926, and in the early 1930s probably took some lessons with WEBERN in Vienna, and studied orchestration with RAVEL, as well as conducting with Pierre MONTEUX in Paris. Through meticulous analysis of the scores, and in-depth studies from 1936 onwards with Rudolf Kolisch, Erich Itor Kahn and Paul Dessau, Leibowitz acquired a profound knowledge of the music of the SECOND VIENNESE SCHOOL. As a consequence of his Jewish background, he was forced into hiding during the German occupation, and it was at this time that he wrote *Introduction à la musique de douze sons* and *Schoenberg et son école*, both books of international significance. After the liberation of Paris, Leibowitz dedicated all his resources to promoting the works of SCHOENBERG, BERG and Webern: as conductor, he organised concerts, and in 1947 a festival with the first Paris performances of Berg's *Four Songs* and Schoenberg's *Ode to Napoleon*; he gave private classes, and in numerous articles emphasised the importance of Schoenberg, advocating TWELVE-NOTE TECHNIQUE as the only viable method of composition.

Leibowitz was one of the first to call into question the achievements of Stravinsky's neo-classical period. In 1938, he judged JEU DE CARTES a nightmare without any 'pensée musicale', and the CONCERTO IN E♭: 'DUMBARTON OAKS' the result of creative impotence. When, during the Stravinsky festival in spring 1945, students of his, including Pierre BOULEZ and Serge Nigg, whistled at DANSES CONCERTANTES and furiously interrupted the FOUR NORWEGIAN MOODS, Leibowitz entered the subsequent controversy by denouncing the current situation of music in FRANCE as a grave crisis. The following year, he published a scathing commentary on Stravinsky's development. In Leibowitz' view, after the youthful promise manifested in the SCHERZO FANTASTIQUE and the remarkable though overestimated RITE OF SPRING, there had been no further progress: neglecting the demands of innovative composing, Stravinsky had chosen to return to a lifeless tonality, as well as juxtaposed and academically handled classical forms, and had thus sunk into creative atrophy – 'la misère musicale', as he characterised it.

Though informed about the Parisian controversy, in 1947 Stravinsky granted Leibowitz an interview, when the latter came to Hollywood to work with Schoenberg. According to Robert CRAFT's later account, the meeting evidently stimulated Stravinsky's interest to the extent that he subsequently ordered a copy of Schoenberg's *Models for Beginners in Composition*. Leibowitz' response was a published comparison of the development of the two composers. Praising Schoenberg's work as full of renewal, dominated by passion, boldness and risk, he described Stravinsky's recent music as frozen patterns, an ever-increasing mastery and control applied to less and less significant musical problems.

Leibowitz and Stravinsky met again in VENICE in 1956. By then, Stravinsky was working with twelve-note procedures, while Leibowitz had come under attack from a new generation, who distanced themselves from Schoenberg, postulating a more comprehensive conception of SERIALISM. Leibowitz' career now shifted towards conducting. He completed many recordings, outstanding among them a cycle of the BEETHOVEN symphonies with the Royal Philharmonic Orchestra (RPO) for RCA in 1961. In the tradition of Schoenberg and Kolisch, Leibowitz sought an analytically based interpretation and fidelity to the score, including the metronome markings. Believing that performance was re-creation, he consequently did not shrink from minimalising presumed compositional shortcomings. In his recording of the Rite of Spring, made for RCA in 1959, he chose slow tempi and tried to mitigate the perceived lack (in his view) of organic development by means of added ritardandos, as well as an emphasis on coherent structure and instrumental balance.

As a follower of Schoenberg, Leibowitz, throughout his career, continued to view Stravinsky through the prism of his own background. Leibowitz' critique, whilst of undeniable importance for a younger generation of composers, is unlikely to have had any direct effect on Stravinsky's style. Nonetheless, the evidence from the correspondence of Robert Craft is that Leibowitz was instrumental in encouraging his own interest in the music of the Second Viennese School, and to that extent may well have played an indirect role in Stravinsky's adoption of twelve-note technique in the period following the death of Schoenberg.   SUSANNE GÄRTNER

Liadov, Anatoly Konstantinovich (born St Petersburg, 29 April / 11 May 1855; died Polynovka, Novgorod district, 15/28 August 1914). Russian composer. A pupil of RIMSKY-KORSAKOV at the ST PETERSBURG CONSERVATORY, in 1878 he was appointed Professor of Elementary Harmony; then, from 1901, of Advanced Counterpoint. Alongside Rimsky-Korsakov and GLAZUNOV, he acted as musical adviser to BELYAYEV, and regularly attended Rimsky-Korsakov's Wednesday evening 'at home' gatherings.

Renowned for his facility and skill in counterpoint, Liadov wrote many examples, not just for teaching purposes but also for his own pleasure. Stravinsky owned from 1900 a copy of Liadov's pedagogical Canons (Edition Belaïeff, 1898), and recalled in his autobiography that, aged 18, even before his lessons with AKIMENKO, he 'was much drawn to the study of counterpoint'. It seems highly likely that Liadov's book would have been included in Stravinsky's studies under Akimenko, and subsequently KALAFATI, as a supplement to Rimsky-Korsakov's Practical Course in Harmony: the conductor Nikolai Malko recalls from his Conservatory student days that Lyadov 'added many supplements to [Rimsky's] course. These were always clear and always necessary. I cannot imagine how it is possible to use this textbook without Liadov's supplementary instructions.'

Stravinsky never studied under Liadov himself, yet described this laconic and modest little man to Robert CRAFT with a warmth exceptional for those Conservatory professors he had known in his youth. Stravinsky often attended concerts with Liadov, and his fondness for the professor appears to have been shared by most of Liadov's students (PROKOFIEV being a notable exception). For all his remarkable musical talent, Liadov completed very few compositions, yet his evocative orchestral works on fantastical subjects persuaded DIAGHILEV that he was ideal for composing the first fully

Russian BALLET, preferring him over Glazunov to fulfil the fairytale in dance he and BENOIS hoped to create. It seems, though, that Liadov never offered more than a vague show of interest in Diaghilev's proposal, and The FIREBIRD ultimately was passed to Stravinsky.   DANIEL JAFFÉ

Nikolai Malko, 'Liadov', in A Certain Art (New York: Morrow & Co., 1966), 33–42.
Auto; Expo; Mem; SCS; SRT

Library. Stravinsky was a voracious reader and a passionate bibliophile. He gathered books and music scores during his entire life from the whole world, and the extent of his collection astounds: his Hollywood library had around 10,000 exemplars. Stravinsky had intended to catalogue his enormous collection, but there was never time to do so (he himself could locate, in a flash, almost any volume).

Stravinsky's personal library has not been preserved in its original state. Following Vera STRAVINSKY's death, it was inherited by Robert CRAFT, who in 1990 sold many important items (approximately 700 books and 1,000 musical scores) to the PSS. Craft created a selected catalogue of this part of the collection (only 56 titles), but unfortunately it contains various inaccuracies.

Stravinsky's library is an important source, which offers new ideas about his life, work and worldview. In this regard, everything is important: the mere selection of the editions kept for many years, markings, captions and stamps, inscriptions, marginalia, newspapers tucked away in books, etc.

In order to facilitate orientation in this rich collection, it will be useful to classify its resources according to subject matter and librarianship criteria.

I. Classification According to Subject Matter

Literature in Russian, French, English.

Philosophy. Stravinsky regularly read theological and philosophical literature. In 1931, he was 'chasing' the complete works of the Russian philosopher Konstantin Leontiev, and he also possessed Rozanov's and Shestov's philosophical works. We find his marginalia in the PSS' copy of Nauka o cheloveke ('The Science of Man') by Victor Nesmelov. Some books can certainly be said to have made the composer's Neo-Thomistic reading list – for example, the copy of Jacques MARITAIN's Antimoderne (1922) with the author's inscription to Stravinsky.

Dictionaries and Encyclopedias in different languages.

Religion. In the library, we can find some evidence of Stravinsky's religious practice: a pocket-size Orthodox prayer book with his remarks, a Russian Bible with underlined verses, etc. Two books by Jacques-Bénigne Bossuet – Élévations à Dieu (the 1815 edition) and Méditations sur l'Évangile (the 1922 edition) – and Cours de religion pour des adultes by Cardinal Gasparri (1937) show his interest in the world of Catholicism (since the 1920s).

Aesthetics. In this group of volumes, a special place is occupied by Charles-Albert CINGRIA's Pétrarque (1932) – the copy with the composer's marginalia is preserved in the PSS.

Musical History. Besides the biographies of various composers, from BACH to PROKOFIEV, and historical essays, there are books on early music. Stravinsky consulted François de Lauze's *Apologie de la danse*, 1623 (London, 1952) when working on AGON.

History of Ballet. The bulk of this collection remained with Craft.

Music Theory. Stravinsky's notes in the margins of Charles-Marie Widor's *Technique de l'orchestre moderne* (1910) give testimony to a very careful reading. Stravinsky consulted Max Kuhn's *Die Verzierungs-Kunst in der Gesangs-Musik des 16–17 Jahrhunderts* (1902) when composing the *Chorale Variations on 'Vom Himmel hoch'*. Turning to dodecaphony in the 1950s, the 70-year-old master had to begin from scratch, and naturally he needed special literature on this subject. In his library in the PSS, we can find some very simple guides to dodecaphonic technique for beginners, but Stravinsky also acquired the latest basic musicological studies.

Cinema Music. On more than one occasion, Stravinsky demonstrated his desire to compose music for cinema, and he possessed a copy of Hanns Eisler's *Composing for the Films* (1947), which would have been a useful source of information for this work.

Russian Folklore. The jewels of Stravinsky's folklore collection are Ivan Sakharov's *Songs of the Russian people* (1838–9), as well as AFANASYEV's *The Slav's Poetic Outlook on Nature* (1865–9), and his *Russian Folktales* (1873). Stravinsky inherited these bibliographical rarities from his father, and brought them to SWITZERLAND in 1914.

Art and Architecture. This part of Stravinsky's collection is voluminous and represents different styles and epochs.

Books and Articles about Stravinsky and His Work. In this group of items, in particular, we can find many of the composer's critical remarks in the margins. For example, in his copy of Boris ASAFYEV's *The Book about Stravinsky*, the composer made forty-nine comments in the margins, many of them harsh.

Music Scores
Russian Music. One example of the music scores Stravinsky brought from Russia is the 1883 reprint of Daniil Kashin's *Russian Folk Songs*, which he used when working on MAVRA. His copy of Matvey Bernard`s anthology *Russian Folk Songs* was acquired in the UNITED STATES in 1942, and thematic material in the SONATA FOR TWO PIANOS can be traced to this collection.

When Stravinsky broke with the clan of RIMSKY-KORSAKOV's followers, TCHAIKOVSKY became his new idol. There are forty items in his Tchaikovsky collection in the PSS. Stravinsky also collected MUSSORGSKY's works in Lamm's (not Rimsky-Korsakov's!) editions, which reconstructed Mussorgsky's originals.

European Music of the Eighteenth–Nineteenth Centuries. In the PSS, we can find, besides Bach's works and Mozart's operas and masses, a copy of Scarlatti's Sonatas, edited by Ralph Kirkpatrick (following the original sources) with his inscription: 'For Igor Stravinsky, the composer of our time who best understands

Scarlatti'. Nevertheless, the composer, during his long life, had been used to romantic interpretations of Baroque music. When orchestrating four Preludes and Fugues from Bach's *Well-Tempered Clavier*, the 87-year-old composer reproduced in full not the 'Urtext', but Czerny's edition. Instructive piano works contain the traces of Stravinsky's efforts to develop his piano technique (*Exercises* by Czerny and Isidor Philipp).

Early Music. After moving to the United States in the 1940s–1950s, Stravinsky demonstrated great interest in the millennial musical traditions of the western church. No wonder that nearly a third of Stravinsky's musical collection in the PSS consists of medieval monody, Renaissance church and secular polyphony, and early instrumental music. Stravinsky regularly bought the newest scholarly early music editions, although he also used the earlier academic editions such as *Denkmäler deutscher Tonkunst*. Moreover, in his library we can find many non-scholarly practical editions, which are considered 'old-fashioned' from a modern point of view.

Dodecaphonic Music. Stravinsky's library contained many books on dodecaphony (*see above* 'Music Theory') – however, the most important information he could obtain was through studying serial music. So, his copy of KRENEK's *Threni*, with the author's inscription and Stravinsky's annotations, is a most interesting item with regard to the sources of Stravinsky's serial technique.

Editions of Stravinsky's Own Musical Works. Among these, there are a lot of rare early publications with Stravinsky's remarks.

II. Systematisation according to librarianship criteria
Bibliographical Rarities – for example, the lifetime edition of Lessing's *Hamburgische Dramaturgie* (1767), given to Stravinsky on his eightieth birthday by the Hamburg City Council, or *The Genuine Works of William Hogarth* (London, 1808). The first edition of Sebastien VOIROL's *Sacre du Printemps* (1913) is also an absolute rarity.

Copies with Stravinsky's Inscriptions of Ownership often help us to identify the date and place of the item's acquisition.

Items with Dedications. This group of items is a valuable source of information regarding the composer's contacts. Stravinsky possessed books and music with autographs of well-known composers (DEBUSSY, Hindemith, Krenek, etc.), writers (T. S. ELIOT, ISHERWOOD, AUDEN, REMISOFF), philosophers (Maritain), priests, artists, dancers, etc. About forty of the books in Stravinsky's library in the PSS are gifts from friends and strangers in the Soviet Union, given to the composer during his 1962 trip to the USSR.

Copies of Stravinsky's Own Literary and Musical Works with His Corrections and Notes (including many editorial proofs) allow us to observe Stravinsky in the process of his work with proofreaders, music engravers and editors.

A very important component of Stravinsky's library is the book and music copies in which the composer sketched his future works.

TATIANA BARANOVA MONIGHETTI

Tatiana Baranova Monighetti, 'Stravinsky's Russian Library', in SHW, 61–77.

Lieberson, Goddard (born Hanley, UK, 5 April 1911; died New York City, 29 May 1977). Record producer and President of Columbia Records. Lieberson was born in England but his family moved to the UNITED STATES and he studied composition at the Eastman School. He joined Columbia Records in 1938 and played an important role in the introduction of the long-playing record in 1948. In his early years at Columbia he recorded BARTÓK and SCHOENBERG performing their own works. In 1945–6, he produced Stravinsky's New York Philharmonic recordings of SCÈNES DE BALLET, FOUR NORWEGIAN MOODS, CIRCUS POLKA, ODE, The FIREBIRD, FIREWORKS and SYMPHONY IN THREE MOVEMENTS. Stravinsky became impatient when Columbia delayed publication of the *Ode* and *Circus Polka*, writing to Lieberson on 5 June 1948 to express 'utter disappointment in your failure to release my recordings', adding that 'When I signed the contract with you, I firmly believed in your enthusiasm to present to the public the genuine aspect of my compositions before those of my numerous misinterpreters who so unscrupulously cripple my works in concerts and records. Alas I was mistaken.' Lieberson replied on 15 June:

> You write as if I conduct a one man cabal against you and quite the opposite is the case. It seems to me that you have very little to complain about in regard to either me or Columbia ... Furthermore, you were at one time so incensed about our not releasing your records that you decided to sign a contract with the Victor Company, where I dare say they have agreed to record and release many more of your late works.

Lieberson's reference to Stravinsky's records made for RCA Victor in 1947–50 was a well-aimed barb: though they included recent works such as the CONCERTO IN D, ORPHEUS and MASS, the relationship with RCA floundered and, by the early 1950s, Stravinsky was back with Columbia. Under Lieberson's leadership, Columbia recorded OEDIPUS REX (Cologne Radio) in 1951, the SYMPHONY IN C (Cleveland Orchestra) and CANTATA in 1952, RAKE'S PROGRESS (Metropolitan Opera) and PULCINELLA (Cleveland Orchestra) in 1953, The SOLDIER'S TALE, OCTET FOR WIND INSTRUMENTS and SEPTET in 1954, various songs with Marni Nixon and the young Marilyn HORNE in 1955, and PERSÉPHONE in January 1957. In June 1957, Stravinsky made his first stereo recordings: AGON and CANTICUM SACRUM, and the advent of stereo gave Lieberson the opportunity to embark on a comprehensive new series billed as 'Stravinsky Conducts Stravinsky'. Most of the series is more or less as described (though *see* SSE, 420), but some performances were conducted by CRAFT. Stravinsky wrote to Lieberson about this on 1 November 1967, 'for your private and personal information'. He listed Craft's recordings and continued:

> I can see how the inclusion of these items not conducted by me blemishes the picture of a complete Stravinsky conducted by Stravinsky. But a true picture with blemishes is better than a fake. Suspicion has already circulated in the past about the actual conducting on records of some of my other late music, notably of The Flood; and we *are* guilty of some misleading in that instance in that only a few measures were conducted by me. [Craft's] performances are also mine in that they represent my wishes, and more faithfully than I am able to do myself, at my age. No deceit has been

committed or damage done thus far, and I trust none will be, but I have recently received letters asking inconvenient questions.

Almost all of the stereo 'Stravinsky Conducts Stravinsky' series was produced by John McClure (1929–2014) and the best of these records show Stravinsky's conducting at its incisive best, even if there are occasional signs of frailty in others. Lieberson's Columbia Stravinsky project remains one of the most comprehensive attempts to document a composer's performances of his own works.   NIGEL SIMEONE

Goddard Lieberson Papers, Gilmore Music Library, Yale University, Stravinsky: The Complete Columbia Album Collection (Sony Classical 88875026162, 57 discs, 2015)
Philip Stuart, Igor Stravinsky – The Composer in the Recording Studio: A Comprehensive Discography (Westport, CT: Greenwood Press, 1991).

Lifar, Serge (born Kiev, 2 April 1905; died Lausanne, 15 December 1986). Ukrainian-French dancer, choreographer and director. Lifar was the last male star of the BALLETS RUSSES and DIAGHILEV's lover. In 1928, he created the role of Apollo in BALANCHINE's APOLLON MUSAGÈTE, the second production of the BALLET (Stravinsky conducted the run). The following year, he choreographed a new version of RENARD, with added acrobats, for the company. Stravinsky already disliked Lifar, and relations soured after Diaghilev's death: in 1938, Stravinsky refused a request from Lifar to stage JEU DE CARTES, while Lifar described Stravinsky's music as 'anti-dance', and claimed it 'enfeebles dancing and weighs it down' (SSE, 99; Lifar 1938, 168).   SOPHIE REDFERN

Serge Lifar, Ballet: Traditional to Modern, trans. Cyril W. Beaumont (London: Putnam, 1938).

Literary Collaborations. While the composer's AUTOBIOGRAPHY – written together with Sergey DIAGHILEV's associate Walter Nouvel – and the publications from the American period, written under the influence of Robert CRAFT, are the most well-known books he produced in his life, they are not his only literary creations. Stravinsky's personal friendships with literati often predated collaboration and created favourable conditions for joint creative work. Some of the composer's most successful literary collaborations, with such different personalities as Stepan MITUSOV, Charles Ferdinand RAMUZ, Jean COCTEAU and Pierre SOUVTCHINSKY, started in this way.

Stravinsky's work with Stepan Mitusov (1878–1942) over the libretto of the opera The NIGHTINGALE, based on H. C. Andersen's eponymous fairytale about the superiority of natural and artistic phenomena to technical inventions, was his first full-scale literary collaboration. Mitusov, in later life a pianist and a pedagogue, was the first cousin of Elena Roerich, the wife of the artist Nicholas ROERICH. In his youth, he lived in the same house as Nikolay RIMSKY-KORSAKOV and his family. It is probably there that he met Stravinsky in the early 1900s; they also studied together at the University and took private lessons in counterpoint with Vasily Kalafati. In his youth, Mitusov was an adviser to the composer on all matters of literature and theatre, and he also had artistic talents, which later made him a close associate of Roerich's circle. Mitusov and Stravinsky worked together in 1908–9 (Act I) and again in 1913–14 (Acts II and III). The literary style of the first act, written in consultation with Vladimir Belsky, Rimsky-Korsakov's last librettist, can seem somewhat overly ornate today. In the later acts, Mitusov strove hard for compression, producing several versions for each phrase, looking for more and more succinct variants. Mitusov's approach – 'Everything I'm now writing, I'm writing for the glory of your talent' (SCS, 126) – smoothed his dealings with Stravinsky, who did not tolerate equality in such creative unions, yet relied heavily on his literary collaborators. This may explain the downplaying of the role of some of his librettists in the books written at the end of his life with Robert Craft, particularly Charles Ferdinand Ramuz, Jean Cocteau and André GIDE.

Deep in his heart, Stravinsky considered his friendship with Charles-Ferdinand Ramuz (1878–1947) as one of the highlights of his life. The same can be said of Ramuz, who spoke warmly of the composer in *Souvenirs sur Igor Stravinsky* (1929). In 1915, Ramuz was already a recognised writer in French-speaking SWITZERLAND and an active participant in the cultural renaissance of his home region, the Canton of Vaud on Lake Geneva. He was introduced to Stravinsky by Ernest ANSERMET. The bond, as Ramuz writes in his book, was complete and instantaneous. Unlike Mitusov, Ramuz had little interest in music; what fascinated him was the personality of the composer: the 'savage' and 'civilised man' who fervently loved his homeland and who was given completely to his profession despite the social conventions and the financial difficulties of exile. Starting in 1916, Ramuz collaborated with Stravinsky on Russian–French translations of almost all the Russian vocal works of Stravinsky's Swiss period, except *Podblyudnye* (Four Russian Peasant Songs). He also supplied their French titles: RENARD, Les NOCES, *Souvenirs de mon enfance, Trois Histoires pour enfants, Pribaoutki, Berceuses du chat* and *Quatre chants russes*. The composer and his librettist began by counting syllables in each line and placing word accents in order to produce a word-for-word translation, after which Ramuz worked alone to produce the final version (Ramuz 1997 (1929), 29–31). Ramuz's main task was to preserve the sonority and the imagery of Russian folk poetic texts, and he coped with the task masterfully, especially considering his total lack of knowledge of the Russian language. In 1918, Stravinsky and Ramuz created together the libretto of The SOLDIER'S TALE, a travelling theatre piece, a mixed-media project, by which they intended to earn money in Switzerland. Taking AFANASYEV's Russian folk tale 'The Runaway Soldier and the Devil' as the basis, they conflated several variants of the same tale and transferred it to contemporary Switzerland. The work was written towards the end of World War I as an echo of the war and as a Russian version of the theme of Faust: the Soldier sells his violin (that is, his soul) to the Devil in exchange for magical powers.

Jean Cocteau (1889–1963), a French Renaissance man – poet, librettist, novelist, graphic artist, playwright, film director, actor, etc. – befriended Stravinsky around 1910, when they both were starting to work for Diaghilev's 'Saisons Russes'. In 1914, Cocteau made his first unsuccessful attempt to secure Stravinsky's collaboration on a BALLET project entitled *David*. In 1918, the writer published *Le Coq et l'arlequin*, a pamphlet promoting a new school of French music at the expense of WAGNER, DEBUSSY and Stravinsky. This temporarily cooled their relationship, which regained strength again in the 1920s. In 1925, after seeing his adaptation of *Antigone*, Stravinsky asked Cocteau to write a libretto for an oratorio OEDIPUS REX after Sophocles, for subsequent translation of the text into Latin, in order to allow the composer to treat the words as a purely phonetic material in his music. The librettist worked with enthusiasm, but the first version of the libretto was not accepted by the composer who described it in *Dialogues and a Diary* as 'precisely what I did not want: a music drama in meretricious prose' (*Dial*, 22). After two drastic revisions for the sake of abbreviation, Cocteau's text was duly translated by Jean Daniélou; the original has been lost. Although Stravinsky speaks warmly about Cocteau and his libretto in his 1936 AUTOBIOGRAPHY, in *Dialogues* the composer disparages Cocteau the librettist, in particular for the interpolated synopses of the action, enunciated by 'Le Speaker' in French for the audience's benefit. The project was conceived as a surprise gift to mark the twentieth anniversary of the Saisons Russes, yet Diaghilev gave it a mixed reaction and called it 'un cadeau très macabre'.

Stravinsky's collaboration on the three-act *mélodrame* PERSÉPHONE with the French writer André Gide (1869–1951) was his first full-scale experience of French text-setting (notwithstanding the two Verlaine songs of 1910, translated by Mitusov into Russian). The collaboration, commissioned by Ida RUBINSTEIN in 1933, began enthusiastically. Being attracted to the Alexandrine metre in the first place, Stravinsky sketched sometimes directly on the text, as he did for his Russian vocal works. Gide had adapted his earlier poem about the myth of Persephone, the daughter of Demeter, who is abducted by Hades and carried to the Underworld, as a basis for his theatrical four-act play *Perséphone*. After a pre-rehearsal in January 1934, the 'total agreement' between the poet and the composer (as Gide noted previously in his diary) quickly turned into a disagreement over Stravinsky's musical treatment of Gide's text, which was metrically deconstructed in his setting and thus unintelligible to the audience. Gide thereafter avoided all the rehearsals and boycotted the première at the Palais Garnier in April 1934. Stravinsky, for his part, published a defence of his work in *Excelsior*, in which he asserted the primacy of syllables over words, yet this did not help the matter much. In *Dialogues and a Diary*, he criticised the rhythms of Gide's text as 'leaden-eared' and went so far as to suggest the commissioning of a new text in English from W. H. AUDEN (*Dial*, 37).

Stravinsky also co-operated with writers in his career as a writer of books on music. After *Autobiography* (1936), Stravinsky's second big literary project was POETICS OF MUSIC *in the Form of Six Lessons* (1962 (1939)), on which he worked together with his close friend Pierre Souvtchinsky (Pyotr Souvtchinsky) (1892–1985). The friendship with Souvtchinsky – a musician, musicologist, publisher, literary critic, politician, etc. – continued from 1922 to 1971, with a break in 1952–7. As Stravinsky recalled at the end of his life, Souvtchinsky 'always fed books to me' and 'knew me more closely than anyone else in my later years in Paris, both in the 1930s and again in the 1960s' (cited in Dufour 2006, 55). Souvtchinsky's intellectual influence on Stravinsky was huge, which is why it was deliberately and repetitively downplayed by Robert Craft after the composer's death in 1971. In 1938–9, when Stravinsky had lost his daughter, his wife and his mother in one year and had difficulties communicating with his younger son, Soulima STRAVINSKY, it was Souvtchinsky who provided the main moral support. The peak of their collaboration was the series of six lectures about the aesthetics and poetics of music, which Stravinsky had to present at Harvard University in September 1939 as a Charles Eliot Norton Chair of Poetry. Souvtchinsky wrote a detailed preliminary plan, from which Stravinsky elaborated the content of each lecture with the help of Alexis ROLAND-MANUEL (1891–1966), who was responsible for the final text, in fine literary French. The only exception was for the fifth chapter of the eventual *Poétique musicale*, 'The avatars of Russian music', whose authorship belonged to Souvtchinsky and Stravinsky only, and which was translated into French by Soulima Stravinsky.

Stravinsky's final full-scale literary collaboration, with the British poet Wystan Hugh Auden (1907–73) on the libretto of the opera The RAKE'S PROGRESS (1947–51), was as happy and harmonious as the first one with Mitusov. After several years of searching for a subject for an OPERA in English, Stravinsky turned to Auden on the advice of his neighbour in Beverly Hills, Aldous HUXLEY. The composer found his subject at the Chicago Art Institute in 1947. The Rake's Progress is the title of a series of eight paintings by the eighteenth-century artist William Hogarth, about the adventures of a hapless playboy who strays from the true path and begins to indulge in all sorts of temptations as soon as he receives his inheritance, until he ends up in a madhouse. Auden and Stravinsky had to interconnect these paintings into a narrative, to invent some new situations, and to choose or invent principal and secondary characters, which they did in the course of a week spent at Stravinsky's house in Los ANGELES in November 1947. Auden delegated part of the work of creating the final poetic text to his close friend Chester KALLMAN, without asking the composer's permission. In his very first letter to Stravinsky, Auden wrote that 'it is the librettist's job to satisfy the composer, not the other way around' (cited in Roberts 2013, 248). Although the critics did not like the characteristically distorted declamation of Stravinsky's setting and accused the composer of pastiche, this neo-classical opera has become part of the repertoire of opera houses all over the world, and remains so to this day.   MARINA LUPISHKO

Valérie Dufour, *Stravinski et ses exégètes (1910–1940)* (Brussels: Édition de l'Université de Bruxelles, 2006).
Charles-Ferdinand Ramuz, *Souvenirs sur Igor Stravinsky* (Rezé: Séquences, 1997).
Michael S. Roberts, 'Auden and post-war opera', in *W. H. Auden in Context* (Cambridge University Press, 2013), 246–54.

Lomonosov. See ORANIENBAUM

Lopokova, Lydia   (also Lopukhova, self-styled as Lopokova in the West) (born St Petersburg, 7 October 1891 OS (self-styled as 21 October NS); died Seaford, England, 8 June 1981). Russian-British dancer. Lopokova danced with the BALLETS RUSSES between 1910 and 1929. She created roles in MASSINE ballets, danced Aurora during the 1921 *Sleeping Princess* run (featuring Stravinsky orchestrations of TCHAIKOVSKY), and was a noted interpreter of the Firebird (The FIREBIRD) and the Ballerina (PETRUSHKA); it has been suggested she was the inspiration for the Ballerina. In 1916, during a company tour of Spain, it is likely she had a romance with Stravinsky. Later in life, she was involved with the emerging British BALLET scene and the Bloomsbury Group (her second husband was John Maynard Keynes).   SOPHIE REDFERN

Los Angeles. Stravinsky first visited Los Angeles in 1935 on tour, officially making California his home in June 1940 with his new bride, Vera de Bosset Sudeykina (*see* Vera STRAVINSKY); Stephen Walsh describes them as 'two more Russians in a city ... rapidly filling up with Europeans in flight' (SSE, 117)). Though Vera never embraced the Hollywood lifestyle, they resided in what her husband described as the 'hideous but lively Los Angeles conurbation' longer than anywhere else. Health and community were major draws for Stravinsky, who described LA in *Memories and Commentaries* as 'a good place to begin a new, clean-slate life'. The composer's Hollywood home became a laboratory for collaboration with artists/friends such as George BALANCHINE, and he was regularly surrounded by the likes of Nadia BOULANGER, Aldous HUXLEY, Christopher ISHERWOOD and Thomas MANN. While maintaining a relentless international touring schedule (in 1964, according to Walsh, the Stravinskys spent less than five months in their Hollywood home), for more than a quarter-century Stravinsky conducted the LA Philharmonic at the HOLLYWOOD BOWL, the Werner Janssen Symphony Orchestra, the Los Angeles Chamber Symphony Society, and at the Los Angeles Music Festival. At the Ojai Music Festival, he performed thirty-one of his compositions, and more than twice that number were performed during Lawrence MORTON's Monday Evening Concerts. By 1969, the Stravinskys were disenchanted with the west coast and a move to New York was imminent. But, in the end, Stravinsky was reluctant to pull himself away from the place he had called home for twenty-nine years. Walsh describes his trepidation at the time of the move, telling those around him that 'he did not want to leave'.   LORIN JOHNSON

Lourié, Arthur (born Propoysk, 14 May 1892; died Princeton, New Jersey, 12 October 1966). A composer and writer working after the Russian Revolution, whom Richard Taruskin considers to be 'one of the most interesting forgotten musicians of the twentieth century' (SRT, 2, 1585). Following the Russian Revolution in 1917, since his political opinions did not rest well with the new political regime, he went into self-imposed exile, and did not return from visiting Busoni in Berlin (on official business) in 1921. Lourié changed much in his life: adopting the name by which we now know him in place of his birth name – Naum Izrailevich Luria – and adding a middle name drawn from Vincent van Gogh, a painter he particularly valued; he converted from the Jewish faith of his family to Catholicism, and he moved to FRANCE, settling in PARIS in 1922.

A close friend to Stravinsky, it is likely that their first meeting was facilitated by Vera Sudeykina (later Vera STRAVINSKY) who invited Lourié for lunch in 1924 (SCS, 384). After this meeting, he became an enthusiastic supporter of Stravinsky's music and 'was eager to read proofs and make piano reductions' for him (SCS, 384). He wrote a number of articles on Stravinsky and even moved into the Stravinsky household for a period of time, to engage more closely with the composer and his family in preparing his writings. They had a disagreement sometime after 1931, and Stravinsky rarely mentioned him subsequently.

Lourié's writings respond to Stravinsky's NEO-CLASSICISM in critical detail: he noted that Stravinsky 'overcame the temptations of fetishism [*sic*] in art, as well as the individualistic conception of a self-imposed esthetic principle' (Lourié 1928, 6). The tone of his reviews and comments in this regard became more critical, and he wrote in 1929: 'In reading the score it is necessary to ignore the rhythm in order to distinguish the music beneath it. Here rhythm is driven to the maximum of its development and action; melody is totally submerged' (Lourié 1929).   HELEN JULIA MINORS

Jonathan Cross, *The Cambridge Companion to Stravinsky* (Cambridge University Press, 2003).
Arthur Lourié, 'Neogothic and neoclassic', *Modern Music*, 3 (March–April 1928).
Arthur Lourié, 'An inquiry into melody', *Modern Music*, 7.1 (December 1929), 3–11.

Lullaby, for Two Recorders Arranged in 1960 from The RAKE'S PROGRESS (1947–51) for two recorders, treble and alto. Published in 1960 (Boosey & Hawkes). Specifically, the piece is an arrangement of Anne Trulove's lullaby in the final scene of the opera (Act 3 scene 3, 'Gently, little boat'), which in the original was accompanied by two flutes. Stravinsky therefore had to reduce three parts to two in the solo verses. According to Robert CRAFT, Stravinsky made the arrangement on 15 May 1960 for the architect Perry Neuschatz, who had designed the extension to his house on North Wetherly Drive in LOS ANGELES and who was an amateur recorder-player.   JEREMY COLEMAN

SSE

Lutyens, Elisabeth (born London, 9 July 1906; died London, 14 April 1983). British composer. She had admired Stravinsky's music since her early years in PARIS, and although she did not meet him until 1954, when he visited London, her husband Edward Clark had known him since 1911. Her comment in a 1963 interview – 'music is simply organized sound, and if it is well organized it may have the power to produce emotions in the listener, but those emotions are not inherent in the music itself' (Murray Schafer 1963, 107) – comes close to Stravinsky's Apollonian affirmation. 'That is the music I like!' was Stravinsky's reported reaction to Lutyens' 6 *Tempi* when played on the piano by CRAFT in 1959. As Lutyens herself commented, 'his kindness and generosity warmed me like the sun' (Elisabeth Lutyens, *A Goldfish Bowl* (London: Cassell, 1972), 264), and the work she wrote after his death – *Requiescat* (1971) – is one of her most frankly expressive compositions.   ARNOLD WHITTALL

R. Murray Schafer, *British Composers in Interview* (London: Faber and Faber, 1963).

M

Maeterlinck, Maurice (born Ghent, 29 August 1862; died Nice, 6 May 1949). Belgian poet, dramatist and essayist, awarded the Nobel Prize in Literature in 1911. A leading figure in the Symbolist movement, Maeterlinck began as a poet (*Serres chaudes*, 1889) before turning to the theatre with strange, dream-like dramas of inaction and suggestion, the most famous of which is *Pelléas et Mélisande* (1893), set by DEBUSSY, Fauré, Sibelius and SCHOENBERG. Stravinsky's symphonic poem SCHERZO FANTASTIQUE (op. 3, 1908) was inspired by Maeterlinck's *La Vie des abeilles* (1901), a beautiful literary–scientific exploration of the life of bees, as Stravinsky told RIMSKY-KORSAKOV in a letter of 1 July 1907: 'a half-philosophical, half-imaginative work which charmed me, as they say, head over heels'. While the published score features a prefatory note, which seems to imply a programmatic structure, Stravinsky later denied any narrative link with Maeterlinck's text. DAVID EVANS

Mahler, Gustav (born Kaliště, Bohemia, 7 July 1860; died Vienna, 18 May 1911). Austrian composer and conductor. Composed mainly symphonies and *Lieder*, and served as Director of the Vienna Hofoper for ten years starting in 1897. Stravinsky often derided Mahler's work and legacy (dubbing him 'Malheur'), a view coloured to some extent by the latter's perceived influence on the SECOND VIENNESE SCHOOL. On 9 November 1907, Stravinsky attended the performance of Mahler's Fifth Symphony at the ST PETERSBURG CONSERVATORY and was reportedly impressed by the work, as well as by Mahler's conducting (*see Expo; Conv*). He was less complimentary about the Eighth Symphony (a 'German *Kolossalwerk*') when he heard it in Zurich, in December 1913, noting 'the woodenness of its absolute, unveiled platitudes'. It was a work he would be bored by again in a performance of late July 1948 at the HOLLYWOOD BOWL under Eugene Ormandy. Stravinsky always preferred Mahler's Fourth, singling it out as a favourite (*Expo*), and praised 'the lyric gift' in Mahler's songs, declaring him to be more relevant to the new music of the postwar era than his antagonist Richard STRAUSS (*Conv*). JEREMY COLEMAN

Malayev, Nikita (dates unknown). An unknown scenarist by the name of Malayev appears in descriptions of the 1937 BALLET JEU DE CARTES ('The Card Party'). Choreographed by George BALANCHINE, the ballet's trajectory is described by Charles Joseph as 'cards in a poker game led by the duplicitous Joker, who weaves his chicanery throughout three separate deals' (2011, 145). Stravinsky, an avid card player himself, told the story of its genesis inconsistently, but enjoyed describing how the idea came unexpectedly during a cab ride, prompting the composer to invite his driver for a drink. Following an unrealised request to Jean COCTEAU to provide the scenario, Stravinsky extended the invitation to Malayev, a friend of his son Soulima STRAVINSKY (and possibly Theodore as well), who was living in Marseilles. Stravinsky's motives remain mysterious, but Stephen Walsh suggests that Malayev was a talented young man with mental health issues bordering on suicidal tendencies (SSE, 53–4). Perhaps the composer was responding to filial pressure, or simply acting out of benevolence.   LORIN JOHNSON

Charles M. Joseph, Stravinsky's Ballets (New Haven and London: Yale University Press, 2011).

Mann, Thomas (born Lübeck, 6 June 1875; died Zürich, 12 Aug. 1955). German writer. Mann met Stravinsky during the latter's DIAGHILEV years, and the two reacquainted in SWITZERLAND in the 1920s. It was only after they emigrated to the UNITED STATES that they struck up a closer friendship, in LOS ANGELES, in 1943. Around the time Mann began writing his novel Doktor Faustus (23 May), his conversations with Stravinsky inevitably turned to music and, in particular, they had a long conversation about SCHOENBERG at a dinner party on 28 August (by which point Mann was working on the eighth chapter of the novel). Although its protagonist Adrian Leverkühn is more obviously identifiable with Schoenberg, notably in the use of TWELVE-NOTE technique, he resembles Stravinsky in other respects: Leverkühn shows familiarity with the Franco-Russian BALLET tradition, and his remarks on the relation between freedom and restraint in musical composition seem to ventriloquise Stravinsky's POETICS OF MUSIC (1939–40, publ. 1942).   JEREMY COLEMAN

Mariinsky Theatre, the Imperial OPERA theatre in ST PETERSBURG, is one of the oldest in RUSSIA, founded in 1783 by an Imperial decree establishing a Committee for the 'direction of theatre and music' at the Bolshoi Kamennyi theatre (now the building belongs to the ST PETERSBURG CONSERVATORY). Both of GLINKA's operas, A Life for the Tsar (1836) and Ruslan and Lyudmila (1842), were first performed there. Opera performances took place at the Bolshoi theatre until 1859, when a new opera house was built by architect Alberto Cavos and named after Empress Maria Fyodorovna, the wife of Tsar Alexander II. Until 1917, the Mariinsky Theatre functioned under the Imperial Theatre Directorate, which also controlled the Imperial theatres in Moscow. Stravinsky's father, Fyodor STRAVINSKY, made his extraordinary career as an opera singer there (first appearance in 1876, final one in 1902, as Zuniga in Carmen), so the Mariinsky Theatre was effectively a second home for Igor in his early years. He first visited the Mariinsky for a performance of A Life for the Tsar as a 10-year-old boy, on New Year's Eve 1892 (the date is established from his father's expenditure records), and then spent up to six evenings a week in his father's box watching opera and BALLET performances. As a student of RIMSKY-KORSAKOV, Stravinsky attended WAGNER's music dramas at the Mariinsky from his teacher's box. During the early years of the BALLETS RUSSES, DIAGHILEV set up an informal competition with the then Imperial Theatre Director, Vladimir Telyakovsky; many artists and painters from the Mariinsky formed the basis of Diaghilev's troupe. Mariinsky sets and costumes were reused, and its repertoire ideas often became bones of contention. The first of Stravinsky's works to be performed at the Mariinsky was The

NIGHTINGALE. The negotiations with Telyakovsky over it started as early as 1914, and the contract was officially sent to Stravinsky in CLARENS on 19 September 1915 (O.S.), but due to multiple obstacles (among which were complications with the libretto, World War I and the Russian Revolution), the première was postponed several times, and the first and only performance did not actually take place until 30 May 1918 under Albert Coates, directed by Vsevolod Meyerhold, with sets by Alexander Golovine. The State Academic Theatre of Opera and Ballet ('GATOB', as it was named from 1920; in 1935, it acquired the addition 'Kirov', after the prominent communist statesman Sergei Kirov) performed works by Stravinsky including PETRUSHKA (20 November 1920, with choreography by Léonide Leontiev after Mihkail FOKINE, sets by Alexandre BENOIS); The FIREBIRD (2 October 1921, sets by Golovine); RENARD (2 January 1927, sets by Vladimir Dmitriev); and PULCINELLA (16 May 1927, sets by Vladimir Dmitriev). The last three were choreographed by Fyodor Lopukhov.

In the era of the USSR, the music of the émigré composer was not welcome at the state-owned theatre. However, following the events of 1990–1, on 16 January 1992, the historical name of 'Mariinsky' was returned to the theatre. In the post-Soviet era, after a new staging of Petrushka (1990), Stravinsky's works acquired a prominent place in the Mariinsky repertoire under Valery Gergiev (APOLLO 1992; The Firebird 1994; The Nightingale 1995; The FAIRY'S KISS 1998; OEDIPUS REX, Les NOCES and The RITE OF SPRING 2003; and others).

ELENA VERESHCHAGINA AND TATIANA VERESHCHAGINA

Maritain, Jacques (born Paris, 18 November 1882; died Toulouse, 28 April 1973). Maritain was a French Catholic philosopher whose work engaged with many fields, including aesthetics, political theory and metaphysics. Born to a Protestant family and an agnostic as a young man, he entered the Catholic Church after a profound spiritual and existential crisis. Influenced by diverse thinkers such as Aristotle, St Thomas Aquinas and Henri Bergson, he developed a system of neo-Thomist philosophy that emphasised divine reason and transcendent order and was critical of many aspects of Western modernity.

Stravinsky read Maritain's treatise on aesthetics, Art et scolastique, in 1920 or 1921, and was intrigued by the contention that the problems of modern art could be solved by the de-individualisation of personal expression, a return to the medieval ideal of humility, and the embrace of the concept of divine order. He also heard about Maritain from Jean COCTEAU in the summer of 1925. Profoundly depressed after the death of his lover Raymond Radiguet, Cocteau had turned to Maritain for help, and as a consequence embraced Catholicism. In June of 1926, the composer finally met Maritain in person.

Maritain appears to have exerted an influence on Stravinsky's personal life and artistic work. In April of 1927, the composer returned to the Orthodox faith of his childhood. While Stravinsky denied the influence of Maritain on this return, Robert CRAFT has cast doubt on his disavowal. There are also intriguing resonances between Maritain's philosophy and the works of the composer's neo-classical period, particularly OEDIPUS REX. Stravinsky has noted that the music for Oedipus 'was composed during my strictest and most earnest period of Christian Orthodoxy', and it is perhaps possible to see the imprint of

Maritain's neo-Thomist ideas on the opera's static, monumental and deperso-
nalised character.

By the late 1920s, Stravinsky's feelings towards Maritain had become
ambivalent. In a letter to Victoria Ocampo, he described the philosopher
as 'one of those people of superior intelligence who are lacking in
humanity, and if Maritain himself does not deserve this judgement,
certainly it applies to a great deal of his work' (SPD, 632). But, in spite
of this critical assessment and growing personal distance, Maritain's
intellectual impact on Stravinsky would continue. In the Norton lectures
delivered at Harvard in 1941 (The POETICS OF MUSIC), Stravinsky elaborated
a neo-Thomist definition of the composer clearly indebted to Maritain,
and drew liberally on the philosopher's works, especially Art et scolastique.

IHOR JUNYK

Markevitch, Igor (born Kiev, 27 July 1912; died Antibes, 7 March 1983). Russian
composer and conductor, and DIAGHILEV's last protégé. Stravinsky was sceptical about the young Markevitch's gifts but heard the première of Markevitch's
Rébus on 15 December 1931, on the same programme as The RITE OF SPRING,
conducted by DÉSORMIÈRE. LIFAR described Markevitch's L'Envol d'Icare
(1933) as 'reminiscent of Stravinsky with all the defects that suggests',
a remark that probably infuriated the older Igor. Once Markevitch turned
towards conducting, he had a more cordial relationship with Stravinsky and
made several recordings including The Rite (1951 and 1959), The SOLDIER'S TALE
(with COCTEAU as the Narrator, 1962), and SYMPHONY OF PSALMS with the
Russian State Academic Choir and Orchestra, recorded in Moscow in 1962.

NIGEL SIMEONE

Markova, (Dame) Alicia (orig. Lilian Alicia Marks) (born London, 1 December 1910;
died Bath, 2 December 2004). British dancer, choreographer and teacher.
Markova, dubbed 'the child Pavlova' in Britain, joined the BALLETS RUSSES at
the age of 14. She danced the Nightingale in BALANCHINE's 1925 SONG OF THE
NIGHTINGALE and remembered Stravinsky, who called her 'little one', helping
her with the role (Joseph 2002, 65). In 1944, she was the principal in SCÈNES DE
BALLET, a ballet segment choreographed by Anton DOLIN (who also partnered
her) in Billy Rose's Broadway revue The Seven Lively Arts. The following year,
Markova created the title role in Adolph BOLM's FIREBIRD for Ballet Theatre, the
first production using Stravinsky's then newly created 1945 ballet suite.

SOPHIE REDFERN

Charles M. Joseph, Stravinsky and Balanchine: A Journey of Invention (New Haven and London:
Yale University Press, 2002).

Marsalis, Wynton: A Fiddler's Tale. Commissioned by The Chamber Music Society of
Lincoln Center (New York City) and inspired by Stravinsky's The SOLDIER'S TALE,
Wynton Marsalis' A Fiddler's Tale was premièred in April 1998. Written by
Wynton Marsalis (American trumpeter, composer and band leader, born
New Orleans, 18 October 1961) and set to a text by music critic Stanley
Crouch, the story preserves the Faustian elements of The Soldier's Tale, but
differs in its modernisation, which replaces the wartime setting of Ramuz's
drama with a contemporary one in the music business. The tale follows the

protagonist, a violinist named Beatrice Connors, as she navigates the world of popular music. Disguised as a record producer, the Devil flatters her and convinces her to part with her violin in exchange for the adulation of millions. Beatrice eventually grows weary of the hollow nature of her newfound notoriety, and after five years she longs for a return to the normalcy of her earlier life. She seemingly incapacitates the Devil in an attempt to resume her pre-fame activities, but the Devil ultimately reveals his true form and kills her.

The character's name was inspired by Beatrice Portinari, the muse of poet Dante Alighieri, while her last name 'Connors' functions as a pun (con her) that foreshadows the reason for her eventual demise. However, where Dante's Beatrice exists as a figure immediately admired by the author in The Divine Comedy and Vita Nuova, Crouch's Beatrice is an ordinary musician who is only revered after making a deal with the Devil in exchange for stardom. The narrative explores themes of fame, power and greed, and the trappings of chasing celebrity at any expense.

Marsalis' reinterpretation of Stravinsky's work preserves the original instrumentation of trumpet, clarinet, bassoon, trombone, violin, bass, percussion and narrator, and uses the same forms found in The Soldier's Tale. Elements of JAZZ permeate A Fiddler's Tale, notably in the Tango, where Marsalis inserts space for a trumpet improvisation. RICHARD DESINORD

Mass. Composed 1944–8. First performance, 27 October 1948, Teatro alla Scala, Milan. First published 1948, Boosey & Hawkes.

Text: Latin Mass.

According to Roman Vlad (1978, 157), it was during the writing of the earlier CREDO in Slavonic that Stravinsky first had the idea of setting the whole of the Mass, though he only began the setting in 1944 and did not finish it until four years later, completing in the meantime the SYMPHONY OF PSALMS and BABEL. Stravinsky's oft-quoted explanation in Expositions and Developments for the composition of his Mass was that he had been playing through some Masses by Mozart – 'rococo-operatic sweets of sin' – leading him to wish to write 'a real one' (i.e., for liturgical use). He also recorded that it was because he wanted to write a genuinely liturgical piece, but using instruments, that he set the Catholic Mass; in the RUSSIAN ORTHODOX CHURCH, the use of instruments is expressly forbidden. One must also remember, of course, Stravinsky's predilection for the Latin language itself.

The instrumentation is for wind instruments only – two oboes, cor anglais, two bassoons, two trumpets and three trombones – and the extraordinary sonority this ensemble produces in combination with the choir of men's and boys' voices is one of the most noteworthy features of the Mass. The music itself is austere and humble, but possessed of the kind of inner radiance proper to true liturgical music. The strange oscillating solos of the Gloria and Sanctus, for example, sound like refractions of Byzantine chant; the incantatory declamation of the Credo is simply a Russian Creed transplanted (as, indeed, was his earlier setting of the text); and all the movements contain memories of the Roman Catholic polyphonic repertoire all the way from the fourteenth to the sixteenth centuries, using techniques such as fauxbourdon and descant, and exploring a modal polyphonic vocabulary that subsumes dissonance into something appropriately hieratic and deliberately inexpressive. Given this, though the composer explicitly denied ever having heard the Mass by Guillaume Machaut before composing his setting, it is difficult to take this affirmation seriously.

In spite of the use of syllabic chanting in the Credo, comparable to that in the final movement of the *Symphony of Psalms*, it remains the longest movement; as Stravinsky noted, 'there is much to believe'. The Gloria and Sanctus are much more elaborate, and make use of soloists – solo alto and treble, and two solo tenors, respectively. The Kyrie and Agnus Dei are more straightforward, but the structure of the latter is interesting: the three sections of the text are given to unaccompanied choir, and separated by a repeated polyphonic verse for the orchestra. The work ends with a coda for orchestra.

Though the first performance was given in a theatre, the Mass has seen increasingly frequent performance within the context of the liturgy, choirs having become far more familiar with the idiom over the years.   IVAN MOODY

Roman Vlad, *Stravinsky* (Oxford University Press, 1978).

Massine, Léonide Fedorovich (orig. Leonid Fedorovich Miassine) (born Moscow, 27 July / 8 August 1895; died Borken, Germany, 15 March 1979). Russian dancer, choreographer and teacher. Massine was recruited for the BALLETS RUSSES as a replacement for Vaslav NIJINSKY in 1914. Like Nijinsky, he became a principal dancer, company choreographer, and DIAGHILEV's companion. He first met Stravinsky in PARIS in 1914, and in 1915 there were brief discussions about collaborating on a BALLET to be titled 'Liturgie'. It was abandoned, and while there was regular contact during World War I, they did not work together until it ended.

The year 1920 saw three Stravinsky–Massine projects produced by the Ballets Russes: The SONG OF THE NIGHTINGALE (2 February), PULCINELLA (15 May) and the first new production of The RITE OF SPRING since 1913 (14 December). For The Song of the Nightingale, Massine worked closely with designer Henri Matisse but, due to its history as an OPERA, there was limited direct collaboration with Stravinsky (he conducted the first performance). In contrast, there was a close and sometimes fraught collaboration between all involved with Pulcinella (Stravinsky, Massine and Pablo PICASSO). Problems with how the choreography related to Stravinsky's score caused Massine 'no little annoyance' (*Auto*, 83), and yet the ballet premièred to critical praise with Massine in the title role. Stravinsky and Massine also collaborated closely when the choreographer re-set The Rite (for presentation at the THÉÂTRE DES CHAMPS-ELYSÉES, the site of the 1913 première). Massine discussed the score extensively with Stravinsky and the result was, according to the composer, an improvement on Nijinsky's as it moved beyond the 'tyranny of the bar' (García-Márquez 1995, 156). In later life, plans were discussed, and there were occasional shared engagements, but they never again collaborated formally.   SOPHIE REDFERN

Vicente García-Márquez, *Massine: A Biography* (New York: Knopf, 1995).

Mavra, comic OPERA in one act to libretto by Boris KOCHNO, after Alexander PUSHKIN's poem The Little House in Kolomna. Composed July–August 1921 – 7 March 1922 (according to Robert CRAFT, overture completed in March 1924). First performance, 3 June 1922, PARIS Opéra. Conductor, Gregor

FITELBERG, staging by Bronislava NIJINSKA, sets by Léopold Survage. Published 1925, Édition Russe; 1947 (vocal score), 1969 (full score), Boosey & Hawkes. Dedicated: 'To the memory of Pushkin, Glinka and Tchaikovsky'.

Synopsis: a young maiden, Parasha, arrives home with a new cook, named Mavra, who is actually her sweetheart Hussar in disguise. The true identity of the 'cook' is revealed when he is discovered shaving.

The work was not commissioned by DIAGHILEV, but co-opted by him, probably as a favour to Kochno (for whom it was a first attempt at a libretto), and staged under the auspices of the BALLETS RUSSES. The conception of the opera is related to Stravinsky's work on the London première of TCHAIKOVSKY'S BALLET The Sleeping Beauty, as well as his brief involvement in a fashionable Russian variety show in Paris called The Bat Theatre of Moscow, and his infatuation with one of its dancers, Zhenya NIKITINA. Kochno provided the link to both of these enterprises: as the newly appointed secretary to Diaghilev he was heavily involved in the Sleeping Beauty project and could well have discussed its details with Stravinsky at the Savoy Hotel in London, where, according to Stravinsky, 'Mavra was conceived' (Expo, 81). He was also a long-term friend of Chauve-Souris' set designer Sergey Sudeykin and his wife VERA.

The Chauve-Souris cabaret programmes, with their typically 'old-Russian' flair, sentimental town romances, tzigane songs, hussar ballads and musica-lised skits based on Russian literary classics, including Pushkin, provided the necessary context for the musical forms used in Mavra.

But it is the work on The Sleeping Beauty that provided a context which would be definitive for the opera and for Stravinsky's future works. In two open letters related to Tchaikovsky, Stravinsky pledges his allegiance to the 'Latin-Slav' – that is, Europeanised strata of Russian culture – as opposed to the 'national-ethnographic element', linked with 'The FIVE' and specifically with RIMSKY-KORSAKOV. The same allegiance is affirmed in the dedication of Mavra and in an unpublished programme note to the opera, drafted in 1934. The dichotomy of 'the elements versus culture', of RUSSIAN MYTH versus a Europeanised culture, is deeply rooted in the Russian psyche. In Stravinsky's case, it was decisively resolved during this period, and would encompass the cultivated Hellenistic focus of his creativity in the years to come. This shift is the more decisive given Stravinsky's enthusiastic response to the upheavals of World War I and the Russian Revolution of February 1917. Stravinsky felt that the explosion of elemental force should have revealed to the world a new RUSSIA of 'a healthy, splendid barbarism' (as Romain ROLLAND reported in his diary, cited in SRT, 1128). When the outburst of elemental force turned out to be a catastrophe, then the aristocratic enlightened culture – fragile as it was and in reality already dissolved – became the only mainstay in art.

Stylistically, Mavra is not Tchaikovskian, more Glinkian – and still more belonging to the realm of the 'town song' or 'romance' of Pushkin's time, well known to any Russian steeped in the lyrical works of such composers as Alexander Alyabiev and Alexander Gurilyov, which provided the basis for home music-making for all classes of Russian society. The overall tonal texture, with the prevailing dominant cadences, and the melody over-saturated with leading tones, sentimental 'lyrical' sixths and 'cruel' diminished intervals ironically emphasise this stylistic model. However, it is not the functional harmony that governs the overall score, but rather the interaction of several distinct layers (the bass, the other instrumental voices and the melody), often moving in ostinati patterns, intentionally unsynchronised, so that the rare coincidence of cadential formulas in different layers strikes one as merely accidental. The opera is structured as a series of set numbers, with a full range of conventional operatic forms: arias, (love) duet and ensemble. The orchestration of *Mavra* (the scoring almost reduced to military proportions with wind instruments to the fore and limited participation by the strings), combined with its distinctive JAZZ element, were later considered by Stravinsky as among the main obstacles to the opera's reception.

Pushkin's poem is more preoccupied with its poetic style than with its innocuous plot, and the same is the case with Stravinsky's music. The question of style is first and foremost among the factors in the opera's controversial reception. Some former supporters, such as Émile VUILLERMOZ, felt themselves betrayed by what was perceived as a sudden stylistic reversal, whilst émigré critics, such as Boris de SCHLOEZER, doubted the authenticity, class origin and artistic value of its sources; others were annoyed and bored by its supposed mannerisms or 'triviality'. However, young, defiantly modern French artists, such as Jean COCTEAU, Francis POULENC and Darius MILHAUD, supported it vehemently as the harbinger of a new aesthetic and a new trend. In 1927, Arthur LOURIÉ, in a lengthy essay published in the Eurasianist periodical *Vyorsty*, attempted a radical revaluation of the opera. Focusing on the objective value of this 'unaffected work', which, in his opinion, lay 'in the method of its formal construction', as opposed to the 'rhetorical emotionalism' of Wagnerian music drama, he proclaimed *Mavra* 'a formal buttress' for Western opera, presenting 'new possibilities for the rebirth of operatic form in the West' (Lourié 2013). Hence, rather than rounding-off the Russian period, *Mavra* marks a new beginning for Stravinsky's creative work.

ELENA VERESHCHAGINA AND TATIANA VERESHCHAGINA

Arthur-Vincent Lourié, 'Mavra', in SHW, 44–52.

Mayakovsky, Vladimir (Vladimirovich) (born Bagdadi, Russian Empire (nowadays Georgia), 7/19 July 1893; died Moscow, 14 April 1930). Russian futurist poet and playwright. Stravinsky often met him during the poet's 1922 trip to the West, first in Berlin (at DIAGHILEV's, where PROKOFIEV, SOUVTCHINSKY and TCHELITCHEFF were also invited), and later in PARIS. From the latter visit survives a lively account by COCTEAU of a meeting of the three men, through which transpired the gulf that (artistically) separated him and Stravinsky from Mayakovsky. Apparently, Mayakovsky was unimpressed by Stravinsky's works and expressed his preference for Prokofiev's over Stravinsky's music. Stravinsky, for his part, questioned Mayakovsky's understanding of music, while at the same time he found him arrogant.

KATERINA LEVIDOU

Mengelberg, Willem (born Utrecht, 28 March 1871; died Zuort, Switzerland, 21 March 1951). Dutch conductor. In 1895, aged 24, Mengelberg was appointed chief conductor of the Concertgebouw Orchestra in Amsterdam, a post he held for half a century, until he was dismissed in 1945 for his collaboration with the Nazis. Mengelberg conducted The FIREBIRD in 1917, The SONG OF THE NIGHTINGALE in 1923, and the CONCERTO FOR PIANO AND WIND INSTRUMENTS with Stravinsky as soloist in 1924. In May 1925, he gave the first of many performances of the 1919 *Firebird Suite*. Stravinsky played the CAPRICCIO with Mengelberg in 1930, an unhappy experience for the composer:

> At the first rehearsal [Mengelberg] began to conduct in an impossible tempo. I said I was unable to play at that speed. Greatly flustered, he embarked on a self-justifying oration: 'Gentlemen, after fifty years as a conductor I think I may claim to be able to recognize the proper tempo of a piece of music. Monsieur Stravinsky, however, would like us to play it like this: tick, tick, tick, tick', and he cocked his forefinger in mockery of Mälzel's very useful invention. (T&C, 226–7)

Mengelberg invited Stravinsky to conduct several concerts, including THE RITE OF SPRING (28 February 1926), OEDIPUS REX and PETRUSHKA (24 April 1928), and JEU DE CARTES (28 October 1937). NIGEL SIMEONE

Messiaen, Olivier Eugène Prosper Charles (born Avignon, 10 December 1908; died Paris, 27 April 1992). French composer, organist and teacher. Messiaen first experienced Stravinsky's music when, as a student in PARIS in the 1920s, he attended a triple bill of The RITE OF SPRING, *Les* NOCES and PULCINELLA. From 1930, he embarked on a study of the *Rite*, a work that became a source of lifelong fascination, and a cornerstone of his teaching at the Paris Conservatory. Messiaen's insights into the *Rite* begin with an article in *La Révue musicale*, 'Le Rythme chez Igor Stravinsky' (1939), and reach their fullest form in the posthumous *Traité* (see also The *Technique of My Musical Language*, the recollections of Messiaen's students (Boivin 1995) and Messiaen's conversations with Claude Samuel (Samuel 1994)).

Messiaen credits Stravinsky with the invention of ametrical rhythm, attributable to rhythmic cells that are varied by the addition or subtraction of small values: such 'added values' are, of course, fundamental to Messiaen's own rhythmic style. In The *Technique of My Musical Language*, the first example in the book is from the 'Sacrificial Dance', with the 'A' cell mobile while 'B' is invariant; this is then compared with the *simhavkrīdita* from the Hindu rhythms tabulated by the thirteenth-century theorist Çarngadeva. Another example, from the repeated chords at the start of 'Augurs of Spring', shows two cells, both of which are mobile: the 'A' cell – counting forwards from each odd-numbered accent – increases, while the 'B' cell (from the second accent) decreases, giving the sequence: A2 B6 A3 B4 A5 B3. Here, as elsewhere, Messiaen's approach is severely mathematical and takes no account of the 2/4 metre that has been established by the context and the consequent syncopations. Where three cells are involved (see the start of the 'Sacrificial Dance', and in 'Glorification of the Chosen One'), Messiaen invokes the idea of rhythmic characters (*personnages*), one acting, another reacting, while the third is the observer.

If Messiaen was the first to find explanations for the rhythmic innovations in the *Rite*, he was also the first to point out Stravinsky's use of the octatonic scale; indeed, one can hear pre-echoes of Messiaen in the sound of the nocturnal prelude that opens the *Rite*'s second part, with its evocation of the magical and

241

mysterious – the octatonic scale would become mode 2 in Messiaen's 'modes of limited transposition'. The influence of the *Rite* is especially clear in Messiaen's music from the 1940s, beginning with the opening movement of *Quatuor pour la fin du Temps* (1941), the 'Liturgie de cristal', with its rhythmic layering, reminiscent of the dawn chorus that opens the *Rite* ('the awakening of nature, the scratching, gnawing, wiggling of birds and beasts', as Stravinsky described it to CRAFT), and ancestor of Messiaen's many later birdsong choruses, from *Réveil des oiseaux* (1952–3) onwards. But the work from the 1940s that comes closest to the spirit of the *Rite* is the short piano piece *Cantéyodjayâ* (1949), based on themes from the *Turangalîla-Symphonie* but the antithesis of *Turangalîla*'s juggernaut rhythms, with a Stravinskian crispness that recurs in later Messiaen in, for example, the birdsong duets of 'La Rousserolle effarvatte' (from *Catalogue d'oiseaux*, 1956–8) and *La Fauvette passer-inette* (1961). Meanwhile, Messiaen's *Trois petites liturgies* (1944) shows striking similarities with *Les Noces*, one of a handful of scores Messiaen had with him while a prisoner of war (1940–1). A fascinating study by Matthew Schellhorn has shown that the influence of *Les Noces* is so pervasive, from conception and instrumentation down to details of texture and melodic ideas, as to suggest that Messiaen was using *Les Noces* as his model.

Messiaen's admiration was confined to Stravinsky's earlier music, his later path being 'inexplicable', starting with The SOLDIER'S TALE (1918) ('ugliness for the sake of ugliness'). Stravinsky's attitude to Messiaen's music was unenthusiastic, and may have been soured by an episode in 1945 when performances in Paris of DANSES CONCERTANTES and FOUR NORWEGIAN MOODS were booed by Messiaen students (among them Pierre BOULEZ), though apparently not at Messiaen's instigation. He himself made a public apology, praising the SYMPHONY OF PSALMS, though condemning neo-classical composers who claimed to be original 'just because they have shifted a few bar lines in a Donizetti cavatina'. A photograph of a bored-looking Stravinsky at a performance of *Trois petites liturgies* in VENICE in 1957 speaks volumes.   PETER HILL

Jean Boivin, *La Classe de Messiaen* (Paris: C. Bourgois, 1995).
Olivier Messiaen, 'Le Rythme chez Igor Stravinsky', *La Revue Musical* (30 April 1939).
Olivier Messiaen, *Technique de mon langage musical* (Paris: Alphonse Leduc, 1999 [1944]).
Olivier Messiaen, *The Technique of My Musical Language*, trans. John Satterfield (Paris: Alphonse Leduc, 2001 [1956]).
Olivier Messiaen, *Traité de rythme, de couleur et d'ornithologie: en sept tomes* (Paris: Alphonse Leduc, 1994–2002).
Claude Samuel, *Music and Color: Conversations with Claude Samuel*, trans. E. Thomas Glasow (Portland: Amadeus, 1994).
Matthew Schellhorn, 'Les Noces and Trois petites Liturgies: an assessment of Stravinsky's influence on Messiaen', in Christopher Dingle and Nigel Simeone (eds.), *Olivier Messiaen: Music, Art and Literature* (Aldershot: Ashgate, 2007).

Mexico. Though Mexico was not a halt on any of Stravinsky's American tours before World War II, it became one of his most frequent destinations following his relocation to the UNITED STATES in 1939. He visited the country at least seven times between 1940 and 1961.

His first visit, from 20 July to 8 August 1940, was arranged by Carlos CHÁVEZ, who, as a conductor, had been responsible for introducing much of Stravinsky's music to the country in the 1930s. Igor and Vera STRAVINSKY, newly married, took advantage of this brief absence from the United States to regularise their status, re-entering the country formally as permanent immigrants. In Mexico City, Stravinsky conducted the FIREBIRD and PETRUSHKA suites, JEU DE CARTES, APOLLON MUSAGÈTE, and the DIVERTIMENTO from The FAIRY'S KISS. The last work was recorded for RCA Victor, but a technical fault on the recording necessitated a return trip and a second attempt the following year (14–20 July 1941). This time he augmented his repertoire with the CAPRICCIO, the SYMPHONY IN C, and the PULCINELLA SUITE. Both visits furnished excuses for social encounters with Mexican and Mexico-domiciled composers, including Manuel Ponce, Jesús Bal y Gay and Rosita García Ascot, as well as Chávez.

Stravinsky undertook further trips to Mexico City in July 1946 and February 1948, again combining conducting duties with sightseeing and socialising: a pattern that would continue for subsequent visits. Thanks to his intimacy with CRAFT from 1948 onwards, more is known of his later visits, beginning with a day trip just over the border to Tijuana on 4 September 1949, where he attended a bullfight. He returned to Mexico City in August 1960 as the prelude to a South American tour. His final two visits were undertaken the following year. On 7 April, he conducted The RITE OF SPRING at the Palacio de Bellas Artes, broadcast on television. He was back in the capital in December, where Craft conducted Stravinsky's arrangement for wind instruments of the last movement of Les CINQ DOIGTS, completed on the flight from California.

Stravinsky's Mexican sightseeing experiences reached their zenith in these 1961 visits. The April trip coincided with Easter, and Craft recalled the impressions made on them by the Good Friday ceremonies they observed in Cuernavaca and Taxco. Craft similarly recalled the gaudy Christmas lights which illuminated their December visit, while also observing Stravinsky's more spiritual response to the feast-day celebrations at the shrine of Our Lady of Guadalupe: an aspect of Mexican culture to which he was particularly attuned in the year of A SERMON, A NARRATIVE AND A PRAYER and FLOOD.

CHRIS COLLINS

Tamara Levitz, 'Igor the Angeleno: the Mexican connection', in SHW, 141–76.
SCF (94); SPD

Milhaud, Darius (born Aix-en-Provençe, 4 September 1892; died Geneva, 22 June 1974). French composer, conductor and teacher. Darius Milhaud was 21 when he heard the infamous performance of The RITE OF SPRING. In common with many other composers, he was overwhelmed by its novelty and impact and began to study polytonal combinations with Charles Koechlin. Initially, he was interested in the superimposition of chords, but by 1917 his focus shifted to the superimposition of lines/melodies. This systematic study led his early experiments with polytonality in Les Choéphores (1915), Le Retour de l'enfant prodigue (1917), Cinq Études (1920) and the Chamber Symphonies (1917–23), and informed his article 'Polytonalité et atonalité' (La Revue Musicale, 1 Feb. 1923, 29–44).

Milhaud was one of the few people who welcomed MAVRA (1922) with enthusiasm, alongside SATIE, POULENC, AURIC, COCTEAU and ANSERMET, writing in a review of the opera: 'The performance of Mavra by the Ballets Russes disconcerted the critics ... Only a handful of us musicians were overwhelmed by this work in which Stravinsky showed us an unexpected side of himself. We sensed that with *Mavra* he had embarked on a completely new path, anticipated by *Pulcinella*' (Milhaud 1982, 78).

Milhaud gave his unquestioning support for *Mavra* because he believed in the aesthetic direction that Stravinsky was taking. In a letter to Poulenc, he writes: 'I am delighted with all this, which brings us closer to Igor, who is the only man who counts really' (Poulenc 1994, 158). Although Milhaud approved of Stravinsky's deliberate shift away from RIMSKY-KORSAKOV, and his increasing emphasis on tradition, he was concerned about Stravinsky's influence on French music, particularly on Poulenc's *Les Biches*, regretting the pastiche and the 'terrible influence of Stravinsky' in a letter to Paul Collaer. Milhaud reflected on the two paths open to French composers: the new Stravinsky, and Satie. Acknowledging the positive impact of Stravinsky's latest works on the French School, he continued to regard Satie as a better model for the young French generation (Kelly 2003, 15–18).

Stravinsky and Milhaud also shared an interest in primitivism and the foregrounding of rhythm – this is most evident in Milhaud's highly original BALLET L'Homme et son désir (1918), which was inspired by watching Vaslav NIJINSKY. Milhaud shared Stravinsky's preoccupation with wind sonorities, particularly in his Chamber Symphonies. There are moments in which the impact of Stravinsky's neo-classical works is evident in Milhaud's works, particularly in the burlesque passages in *Le Pauvre Matelot* (1926) and *Esther* (1925–7), which are reminiscent of RENARD and *Mavra*.

Milhaud was part of the exodus to the UNITED STATES during World War II, settling in California in 1940, where he found himself living near both Stravinsky and SCHOENBERG. All three were part of *Genesis 1945*, which was led by the MGM composer Nathaniel Shilkret (1889–1982), and which involved several, mostly Jewish, *émigrés* from Europe. The resulting collaboration mixed popular Hollywood with the avant-garde; Milhaud was right in declaring Stravinsky's contribution, the cantata BABEL, 'the best piece of the album'.

BARBARA L. KELLY

Barbara L. Kelly, *Tradition and Style in the Works of Darius Milhaud, 1912–1939* (Ashgate: Aldershot, 2003).

Darius Milhaud, *Notes sur la musique*, ed. Jeremy Drake (Paris: Flammarion, 1982).

Francis Poulenc, *Correspondance*, ed. Myriam Chimènes (Paris: Fayard, 1994).

Mitropoulos, Dimitri (born Athens, 1 March (OS 18 February) 1896; died Milan, 2 November 1960). Greek conductor and pianist. Mitropoulos studied in Athens, Brussels and Berlin (with Busoni). He had a photographic memory and was a champion of new music but he conducted only a few works by Stravinsky. In 1943, he conducted The FIREBIRD (1919 suite) with the New York Philharmonic, of which he became Chief Conductor in 1951. He conducted PETRUSHKA in March 1951, recording it after four concert performances. At the Juilliard School on 21 May 1948, Mitropoulos conducted The SOLDIER'S TALE (privately recorded and later published). Stravinsky admitted that Mitropoulos 'could not have been very interested in my music', but greatly admired him: 'Mitropoulos was not only a freakishly gifted man, he was also gentle, humble, very generous and very kind' (T&C, 231). NIGEL SIMEONE

Mitusov, Stepan (Stepanovich) (born St Petersburg, 11/23 September 1878; died Leningrad, 25 January 1942). Russian librettist, pianist and conductor. Stravinsky met and befriended him at RIMSKY-KORSAKOV's Wednesday musical soirées. He was the librettist of The NIGHTINGALE, which is dedicated to him. Stravinsky also dedicated the first of his FOUR STUDIES, op. 7, to his friend. Importantly for their collaboration, Mitusov deemed that he should serve the composer rather than the other way round. Stravinsky's *Two Poems of Verlaine* are set to a Russian translation by Mitusov, while at the same time the latter gave the composer one of the folk tunes used in *Les Noces*. In the 1920s, he promoted Stravinsky's work as a performer.   KATERINA LEVIDOU

SCW; SRT

Modernism. Describing Stravinsky as a modernist risks evoking the mockery embedded in SCHOENBERG's text for his choral canon *Vielseitigkeit* ('Versatility') of 1925, whose reference to 'der kleine Modernsky' pokes fun at the presumed arrogance of a composer for whom being modern meant kitting himself out in a powdered wig 'just like Papa Bach'. Schoenberg seemed to be arguing that nothing was more superficially modern – modish, perhaps, rather than truly modernist, which was beyond the merely fashionable – than what Stravinsky appeared to be doing in his recent neo-classical compositions; and Schoenberg was also responding in kind to what he imagined was Stravinsky's insulting declaration, at much the same time, that 'modernists have ruined modern music ... They started out by trying to write so as to shock the bourgeoisie and finished up by pleasing the Bolsheviks' – on the grounds, a further comment suggested, that 'atonality' (and the TWELVE-NOTE method it had spawned) was equivalent to anarchy (Malkiel 1925, 9, quoted in Taruskin 2010, 678). Surely, a modern composer dedicated to the tradition-celebrating, classicising belief that, 'in borrowing a form already established and consecrated, the creative artist is not in the least restricting the manifestations of his personality. On the contrary, it is more detached, and stands out better, when it moves within the definite limits of a convention' (*Auto*, 132), could not be characterised as committed to the ruinous strategy of rejecting the old and embracing only the new?

Readers familiar with the long-standing and contentious debates around how to define modernism, as a general aesthetic concept and a specific compositional technique, will guess what comes next: the argument that, if only with hindsight, modernism in twentieth-century music, as a phase of a much longer creative enterprise, worked not by 'rejecting the old' – that unwise enterprise is better labelled 'avant-garde' – but by dramatising the irresolvable tensions between the old (containing as it did certain essential musical elements) and the new. In these terms, Schoenberg's dislike of Stravinsky's more recent music was more likely to have been rooted in its rejection of expressionism than in any anti-modernism. It is equally clear that – at least in the 1920s – Schoenberg still harboured the ambition of bringing the classical principle of organically integrated unity to bear on his new kind of totally chromatic, twelve-note harmony.

> Modernism is less a style than a search for a style in a highly individualistic sense; and indeed the style of one work is no guarantee for the next ... The

qualities we associate with painters like Matisse, Picasso and Braque, with musicians like Stravinsky and Schoenberg, novelists like Henry James, Mann . . . and Faulkner, poets like Mallarmé . . . and Stevens, with dramatists like Strindberg . . . and Wedekind, are indeed their remarkably high degree of self-signature, their quality of sustaining each work with a structure appropriate only to that work. (Bradbury and McFarland, 29)

Given its inherent diversity and instability, it is entirely appropriate that ways of aligning Stravinsky with modernism should be so well varied, ranging from passing mentions like that just quoted in sweeping generalisations about culture in modern times, to very specific and detailed interpretations of single compositions.

Tamara Levitz' *Modernist Mysteries: Perséphone* is in all probability unique as a book title in linking modernism, and 'modernist neoclassicism' (Levitz 2012, 17), with a single piece of music – without identifying the composer. Levitz' conclusion, stemming from her reading of Walter Benjamin, determinedly links BIOGRAPHY – matters to do with creative personality – with compositional character and technique. Her primary assertion is that 'if there can be said to be a single trauma that motivates the melancholia in the libretto, score, and production of *Perséphone*, it is that of social alienation' (Levitz 2012, 485), and Levitz reinforces this claim with the judgement that 'the narrative of Freudian melancholia is evident in the music's disrupted and discontinuous nature, made up of sudden temporal shifts, explosions of encrypted sonic memories, annulling of pain with nostalgic pleasure, and neo-classical borrowing' (Levitz 2012, 551). Stravinsky's innate tendency to melancholia, as Levitz diagnoses it, might also serve to stand for the pervasive tension between 'the music's disrupted and discontinuous nature' and that need to make Dionysus submit to Apollo which The POETICS OF MUSIC lectures brought down to one ultra-classical, modernism-resisting formula: 'variety is valid only as a means of attaining similarity' (*Poet*, 34). If, in his personal as well as his creative life, Stravinsky did indeed experience 'social alienation', as distinct from the 'similarity' of natural affinity with all his fellow human beings, then his embrace of modernism as defined here can indeed be interpreted as a recognition of the musical attractions of exploring just how aspirations to prioritise 'similarity' could productively co-exist with 'disrupted and discontinuous' variety.

In essence, modernism (like any other broad aesthetic category) involves an interaction between style, or mood, and structure: if the latter is encapsulated in Stravinsky's own description of OEDIPUS REX as a 'Merzbild', or collage (*Dial*, 27) – implying something opposed to the multivalent interconnectedness of true classicism – the former connected with the predominant sense of unease that matches those edgy Stravinskian rhythmic patterns and spikily dissonant harmonies that might not exclude all exuberance or comic gesturing but only very rarely, even in works with a religious, sacred emphasis, achieve some kind of other-worldly serenity. Following through such a simple oppositional concept of modernism as setting the Apollonian against the Dionysian might also be useful in its relevance to works of all periods – to PETRUSHKA as much as to SYMPHONIES OF WIND INSTRUMENTS, to *Oedipus Rex* as to ORPHEUS, to the

MASS for chorus and double wind quintet as to REQUIEM CANTICLES. Recognition of such seismic interaction underpins David Schiff's description of the SYMPHONY IN THREE MOVEMENTS as 'defying categories, it seems simultaneously Dionysian and Apollonian, experimental and primal, élite and popular, anarchic and affirmative' (emphasis added) (Schiff 2013, 197).

That such interactions pervade Stravinsky's music explains the suitability of so many of his works for presentation as ballets, as music which suggests something strongly formal and disciplined – moving 'within the limits of a convention' – yet nevertheless has the kind of sustained dynamism and poised energy that brings modernism and classicism into a special kind of confrontation. Stravinsky might have been indulging in critic-baiting posturing when he described himself as 'absolutely heartless', in connection with the 'tragic' aspect of APOLLON MUSAGÈTE (Dial, 34), but the formula signals the expressive consequences of a modernist musical language designed to create 'an equilibrium that resists fusion and synthesis' (Hyde 1996, 214). Richard Taruskin's work has shown in great detail exactly how such modernist principles emerged from and were inherent in the Russian manner that Stravinsky lived and breathed during his formative years. So potently did Stravinsky similarly persist in exploring 'the subtle play and inherent ambiguity between the tonal and the non-tonal' (or, preferably, 'post-tonal') that 'a pluralistic analytical approach' is required in order 'to unlock the mysteries and delights of works in which play with style substitutes for play within a style' (Carter 1997, 80). It needs only to be added that, in Stravinsky's beguiling modernist labyrinth, music of special emotional power is the consequence of what might so easily have turned into heartless, impersonal playfulness. Nevertheless, the true modernist's need to be uneasily detached brings us back to that possibly playful Stravinskian self-accusation of heartlessness, and his comparison with Racine's description of blissful love in Phèdre. 'The implication is that only the apparently heartless have the sympathetic detachment and artistic judgement to do justice to the tragic circumstances of humans who seem sublimely unaware of their vulnerability and mortality. Only the apparently heartless can be true artists, because true artists need to separate themselves from humanity, rather like gods' (Whittall 2003, 57).

Taruskin offers another angle on this Olympian ethos in his declaration that 'what The Rite and The Wedding have fundamentally in common is Stravinsky's lifelong antihumanism – his rejection of all "psychology"' (Taruskin 1997, 391). Nevertheless, within the capacious boundaries of musical modernism, 'antihumanism' does not result in inhuman music. As I argued in 2003,

> Just as the fact that the 'community' as represented on stage accepts the 'ceremonial murder' of the victim in The Rite of Spring 'without remorse' does not mean that everyone watching the ballet becomes anxious to restore a social order based on such 'customs', so the impact of the forces of convention affecting the bride and groom in The Wedding is as likely to prompt doubts and sympathies in audiences as any longing for an idealised past. For good or ill, present-day listeners to both works will probably sense the distance between these powerful social rites and the forces governing their own lives. (Whittall 2003a, 61)

That listeners can respond to the expressive power of Stravinsky's explicitly sacred works without necessarily subscribing to the religious beliefs they embody is another indication of the specifically modernist means he chose to employ, and which continued as late as the 'Postlude' of *Requiem Canticles*, where 'that basic sense of tension between the centrifugal and the centripetal' is shown in the way 'the horn's outlined F minor triad unfolds against the atonal processional chords' (Whittall 2003b, 56).

In 1974, Mikhail Druskin completed a pioneering study of the composer in Russian, which was widely felt to risk over-simplification, as with the claim that Stravinsky's 'ideal was ... "unstable stability", as opposed to Schoenberg's ... "stable instability"' (Druskin 1983, 122). Yet Druskin was justified in attempting to dramatise the fact that two composers, who for so long in the historiography of twentieth-century music had been cast as implacable opponents, shared a commitment to classicism-resisting aesthetics and techniques. Although 'modernism' as an open-ended concept which thrives on its inherent ambiguities and imprecision continues to provoke the most elaborate, and at times obscure, analyses of what its connotations and significance might be, its proven relevance to Stravinsky, as well as to Schoenberg and many other post-1900 composers, is an indication of its usefulness – even, perhaps, of its necessity – as a way of suggesting what Stravinskian music in all its many manifestations is actually like. ARNOLD WHITTALL

Malcolm Bradbury and James McFarland, 'The name and nature of modernism', in Malcolm Bradbury and James McFarland (eds.), *Modernism* (London: Pelican Books, 1976).

Chandler Carter, 'Stravinsky's "special sense": the rhetorical use of tonality in The Rake's Progress', *Music Theory Spectrum*, 19 (1997).

Mikhail Druskin, *Igor Stravinsky: His Personality, Works and Views*, trans. Martin Cooper (Cambridge University Press, 1983).

Martha M. Hyde, 'Neoclassic and anachronistic impulses in twentieth-century music', *Music Theory Spectrum*, 18 (1996).

Tamara Levitz, *Modernist Mysteries: Perséphone* (New York: Oxford University Press, 2012).

Henrietta Malkiel, 'Modernists have ruined modern music, Stravinsky says', *Musical America*, 10 January 1925.

David Schiff, 'Everyone's Rite (1939–46)', in Hermann Danuser and Heidy Zimmermann (eds.), *Avatar of Modernity: The Rite of Spring Reconsidered* (London: Paul Sacher Foundation / Boosey & Hawkes, 2013).

Richard Taruskin, *Music in the Early Twentieth Century* (New York: Oxford University Press, 2010).

Richard Taruskin, 'Stravinsky and the subhuman', in *Defining Russia Musically* (Princeton University Press, 1997).

Arnold Whittall, *Exploring Twentieth-Century Music: Tradition and Innovation* (Cambridge University Press, 2003a).

Arnold Whittall, 'Stravinsky in context', in Jonathan Cross (ed.), *The Cambridge Companion to Stravinsky* (Cambridge University Press, 2003b), 37-56.

Monteux, Pierre (born Paris, 4 April 1875; died Hancock, Maine, 1 July 1964). French conductor. Monteux studied the violin at the Paris Conservatory and worked for several years as a viola player, in which capacity he played Brahms in Vienna, drawing admiring comments from the composer. He conducted occasionally from 1895 onwards, securing his first appointment in 1902 as conductor for the summer season in Dieppe while continuing to work as a viola player in the Colonne Orchestra. In 1910, the orchestra was engaged to play for the BALLETS RUSSES season, and Monteux played viola in the first performances of The FIREBIRD under Pierné. The following year, Monteux conducted the world première of PETRUSHKA with the Ballets Russes. In 1912, Monteux was the conductor at the first performance of RAVEL's Daphnis et Chloé, and on 29 May 1913 he led the celebrated première of The RITE OF SPRING at the THÉÂTRE DES CHAMPS-ELYSÉES, despite having doubts beforehand about the music of 'this crazy Russian'. Monteux went on to perform the work in concert at the Casino de Paris on 5 April 1914, a performance Stravinsky attended and admired. A few weeks later, on 26 May 1914, Monteux conducted the world première of The NIGHTINGALE at the Paris Opéra. In 1919, Monteux was appointed Chief Conductor of the Boston Symphony Orchestra, but in 1924 his contract was not renewed and he began an association with the Concertgebouw Orchestra in Amsterdam, with which he conducted The Rite in 1924, Petrushka in 1925 and The Firebird (1919 Suite) in 1927, performing all three works regularly in later seasons. In 1930, he conducted FIREWORKS, and in 1933, the Suite from PULCINELLA and the CONCERTO IN D FOR VIOLIN AND ORCHESTRA (with Samuel DUSHKIN as soloist). He was appointed Chief Conductor of the San Francisco Symphony in 1935 and he worked as a guest conductor in Boston, London and elsewhere. In 1961, at the age of 86, he was appointed Principal Conductor of the London Symphony Orchestra. Monteux continued to conduct Stravinsky's pre-war ballets into the 1960s, including a performance of The Rite at the Royal Albert Hall with the LSO given in the composer's presence in 1963 to mark the fiftieth anniversary of the work's première. Monteux made several recordings of The Rite (the first in May 1929) and Petrushka (in 1930 and 1956 in Paris – the latter with Julius Katchen as the pianist – and a particularly fine version with the Boston Symphony in 1959). His other Stravinsky recordings included The Firebird 1919 Suite and a live performance from 1961 of the Symphony of Psalms. Though Monteux was interested almost exclusively in Stravinsky's earlier works, he remained fiercely loyal to them throughout his long career, earning Stravinsky's gratitude. Stravinsky wrote the GREETING PRELUDE in 1955 for Monteux's eightieth birthday, and the CANON ON A RUSSIAN POPULAR TUNE (1965) was written in memory of Monteux, though the printed score makes no mention of this. NIGEL SIMEONE

Monumentum pro Gesualdo di Venosa ad CD annum. Three madrigals recomposed for instruments. Composed February–March 1960. First performance, 27 September 1960, Venice. Conductor, Igor Stravinsky. First published 1960, Boosey & Hawkes.

I. Asciugate i begli occhi (Libro Quinto, Madrigale 14)
II. Ma tu, cagion di quella (Libro Quinto, Madrigale 18)
III. Beltà, poi che t'assenti (Libro Sesto, Madrigale 2)

According to Stravinsky, the idea of translating Gesualdo's madrigals into instrumental sounds first occurred to him in 1954. On that occasion, however, he was dissuaded by the 'uniquely vocal character' of the music. Then, in February 1960, he returned to the project, and found three madrigals that would lend themselves well to instrumental treatment. The triptych was then completed in Hollywood in March 1960 and was labelled *Monumentum pro Gesualdo di Venosa ad CD annum* (at that time, it was believed that Gesualdo was born in 1560; later, it was ascertained that the date of birth was 8 March 1566). The work was first performed on 27 September 1960 at the VENICE Biennale, in the Palazzo Ducale's Sala dello Scrutinio, by the Orchestra del Teatro La Fenice, conducted by the composer.

The *Monumentum* cannot be simply labelled as an 'instrumentation' of vocal music because Stravinsky, while complying rather faithfully with the Gesualdo original, introduced many changes, such as octave transpositions and exchanges of parts, changes in rhythm/metre, interpolations of new bars, changes in harmony, and the addition of motivic materials. All this renders the term 'recomposition', used by Stravinsky in the subtitle of the work, most appropriate. The first madrigal is the one that has undergone the most changes. The second and third madrigals, on the other hand, hardly show any significant intervention, apart from some octave transpositions. The orchestra is divided into four groups: woodwind (oboes and bassoons), horns, brass (trumpets and trombones) and strings. In the first madrigal, there are no brass instruments; in the second, no horns or strings; in the third madrigal, finally, all four groups are used, but never all together – they alternate one after the other, or join together in ever-changing combinations.

In 1960, the *Monumentum* was choreographed by George BALANCHINE for seven pairs of dancers. After 1965, this choreography was always coupled in performance with Balanchine's choreography for Stravinsky's MOVEMENTS.

MASSIMILIANO LOCANTO

Massimiliano Locanto, '"A new world of chromatic harmony polyphony": il significato della musica di Gesualdo per l'ultimo Stravinsky', in Daniela Tortora (ed.) *Gesualdo dentro il Novecento, Atti del Convegno Internazionale di studi nel quarto centenario della scomparsa di Carlo Gesualdo principe di Venosa (1566–1613)* (Naples: Edizioni del Conservatorio di Musica San Pietro a Majella, 2017), 57–88.
Colin Mason, 'Stravinsky and Gesualdo', *Tempo*, new series 55–6 (Autumn–Winter 1960), 39–48.
Claudia Vincis and Paolo Dal Molin, 'Mo(nu)mento di Carlo Gesualdo', *Acta Musicologica*, 76.2 (2004), 221–51.
Glenn Watkins, *The Gesualdo Hex: Music, Myth, and Memory* (New York: Norton, 2010).
Expo

Morges. Vaudois market town of La Côte, on the shore of Lake Geneva, between Lausanne and Geneva (SWITZERLAND), where Stravinsky lived from 1915 to 1920. Forced to stay in Switzerland at the outbreak of World War I, Stravinsky looked for a more comfortable house than the one he rented from Ernest ANSERMET in CLARENS, and finally decided to reside in Morges. There, he first lived in a suburban house, the Villa Rogivue, situated at no. 2 rue Saint-Domingue (from May 1915 to January 1917), and then in an apartment in the Maison Bornand, at no. 2 place Saint-Louis. In these two houses, Stravinsky arranged for himself a music study in the attic. Works completed during these years included The SONG OF THE NIGHTINGALE (1920), RENARD (1915–16) and PULCINELLA (1920), whilst this period also saw completion of the first version of Les NOCES (final version 1923). During the years Stravinsky spent in Morges – very difficult times in material terms, especially after the Russian

Revolution – the composer regularly encountered the conductor Ernest Ansermet and, most importantly perhaps, the writer Charles Ferdinand Ramuz, translator of *Renard* and *Les Noces*, and author of *The* Soldier's Tale (1918). In June 1920, Stravinsky and his family left Morges and Switzerland permanently, for Garches, not far from Paris, where he lived in a house provided by Coco Chanel. Ramuz remembers Stravinsky's stay in Morges in an autobiographical text entitled *Souvenirs sur Igor Strawinsky* (pp. 127–50).

STÉPHANE PÉTERMANN

C. F. Ramuz, *Souvenirs sur Igor Strawinsky*, vol. XVIII of *Œuvres complètes* (Geneva: Slatkine, 2011).
Claude Tappolet (ed.), *Correspondance Ansermet–Strawinsky (1914–1967)*, vol. I (Geneva: Georg, 1990).
Auto

Morton, Lawrence (born Duluth, 13 July 1904; died Santa Monica, 8 May 1987). Pianist, composer, impresario, music critic and close friend of Stravinsky. Morton directed the Monday Evening Concerts (formerly the Evenings on the Roof concerts) in Los Angeles from 1954 to 1971. While he first met Stravinsky in 1941, they only became close friends in the mid–late 1950s. Souvtchinsky described Morton in a letter to Stravinsky as 'a wonderful, calm person' (22 April 1960; cited in Levitz 2013, 279), and Stravinsky praised him to Souvtchinsky as 'reliable and well informed' (19 August 1961; cited in Levitz 2013, 285). Morton studied Russian in order to have a better understanding of Stravinsky, the man and his music (SSE, 655). That Souvtchinsky referred the Moscow academic M. V. Alpatov to Craft and Morton, in making arrangements for the extended celebrations for the composer's eightieth birthday in 1962, is an indicator of his importance (letter to Stravinsky, dated 19 December 1961; cited in Levitz 2013, 286–7). A number of Stravinsky's works were performed at Morton's concert series and several of the later works had their premières there. Stravinsky dedicated the Eight instrumental miniatures for 15 players to Morton in 1962, his own eightieth birthday year, and the Elegy for J. F. K. had its première as part of a Monday Evening Concert on 6 April 1964. Never managing to write the book he promised on Stravinsky, Morton nevertheless produced a number of shorter articles on aspects of his work. As someone who was close to the Stravinskys, Morton is a significant source on the composer's life, habits and health in his final years.

EDWARD CAMPBELL

SHW

Movements for piano and orchestra. Composed 1958–9. First performance, 10 January 1960, New York. Margrit Weber, piano. Conductor, Igor Stravinsky. Published 1960, Boosey & Hawkes, 'to Margrit Weber'.

(I) ♪ = 110 (II) ♩ = 52 (III) ♪ = 72 (IV) ♪ = 80 (V) ♪ = 104.

Following an idea originally proposed by Ferenc Fricsay (SSC, II, 401), *Movements* was commissioned by Swiss industrialist Karl Weber for his wife Margrit, the soloist of the première, Stravinsky conducting. Characterised by highly condensed, complex textures akin to those found in the music of the younger avant-garde, *Movements* puzzled audiences, as Stravinsky's most abstract composition to date. The composer himself drew attention to the work's novelty, calling *Movements* 'the most advanced music from the point of view of construction of anything I have composed', boasting that no analyst could figure out certain intricacies of the work's serial structure, and suggesting that 'perhaps some listeners might even detect a hint of serialism' in the rhythmic language (*Mem*, 100).

The complexity of the pitch structure stems from Stravinsky's use, for the first time, of rotational arrays, a serial device invented by Ernst KRENEK (*Lamentatio Jeremiae prophetae*, 1941–2). In his sketches, following Krenek, Stravinsky writes out each of the two halves (hexachords) of the four basic forms of the twelve-note series in the six possible order rotations. For two of these arrays, those derived from the hexachords of the prime form of the series, Stravinsky additionally transposes, as per Krenek, each rotation so that it starts on the same pitch, i.e. the first note of the original hexachord. Stravinsky then picks segments from these arrays, selectively leaping around on his charts rather than following a clear-cut path (as he would often do in later works). While the original twelve-note series remains clearly recognisable in the final score – the work begins and ends with the series and uses its basic four forms in many places – the rotational arrays obscure its identity over large stretches of the work.

Whereas tonal elements are absent to an unprecedented degree – Stravinsky speaks of a 'tendency toward anti-tonality' (*Mem*, 101) – the texture is punctuated by occasional arrivals on open fifths and fourths (e.g., first and third movement), and often features such intervals as clearly audible components in larger chromatic harmonies (e.g., second movement). The piano figures more as a chamber music partner to the orchestra than as solo virtuoso. Also new for Stravinsky is the frequent absence of an audible metric pulse, due to complex rhythmic layering. The result might allude to integral serialism, such as in STOCKHAUSEN's *Gruppen* technique, but, as the sketches document, no such procedures are actually used. As Stephanie Jordan and Julia Randel have shown, BALANCHINE's choreography of *Movements* (1963) visually brings back some of Stravinsky's obscured pulses.

The fourth of the five movements was completed last, on 30 July 1959, which date appears at the end of the published score, but Stravinsky added four short orchestral interludes by 16 August 1959. Each of these takes up the new tempo of the following piece, transitioning from a characteristic gesture of the previous movement to one typical of the next.   CHRISTOPH NEIDHÖFER

Stephanie Jordan, *Stravinsky Dances: Re-visions Across a Century* (Alton, Hampshire: Dance Books, 2007).

Christoph Neidhöfer, 'Analysearbeit im Fach Komposition/Musiktheorie über die Movements for Piano and Orchestra von Igor Strawinsky' (thesis, Musik-Akademie der Stadt Basel, 1991).

Julia Randel, 'Dancing with Stravinsky: Balanchine, *Agon*, Movements for piano and orchestra, and the language of classical ballet' (Ph.D. dissertation, Harvard University, 2004).

Joseph N. Straus, *Stravinsky's Late Music* (Cambridge University Press, 2001).

Stephen Walsh, *The Music of Stravinsky* (London: Routledge, 1988).

Music Theory. Developments in the academic discipline of music theory during Stravinsky's lifetime were as extensive and transformative as developments in compositional practice. In the 1880s, theoretical thinking about the nature of tonality and the structure and function of tonal compositions was in a phase which present-day theorists tend to regard as preliminary to the radical and intensely influential ideas of two writers whose very different perspectives on principles of compositional form and material began to emerge in the first decades of the twentieth century – Heinrich Schenker and Arnold SCHOENBERG. By the 1970s, there was a clear distinction between the kind of theoretical thinking judged to be appropriate for tonal compositions and that more pertinent to post-tonal or 'atonal' music. It was also clear by the 1970s that theory-informed analysis of Stravinsky, and many other composers active since 1900, confronted basic challenges when it came to attempting to define the technical basis of what was being analysed.

Stravinsky's music before c. 1950 evidently related to tonality without conforming in every detail to the traditional functional principles, amounting to 'common practice', in use at the time of his birth. After 1950, most of his compositions employed the TWELVE-NOTE method, yet could not be technically explained entirely by means of theories about pitch organisation that fitted with Schoenberg's concern to show the method's relevance to classical symphonic forms. Unlike Schoenberg, Stravinsky did not teach composition in academic institutions or write theoretical treatises, and although he often commented on technical and aesthetic matters, he left no systematic statements intended to guide commentators on his music. Moreover, his remarks in books and interviews suggest that his overarching 'theory of music' was crafted to discourage the kind of verbal exegesis usually deemed theoretical: for example, 'music is supra-personal and super-real and as such beyond verbal meanings and verbal descriptions' (Expo, 101). Notwithstanding such discouragement, a multitude of music specialists have acted from the sincere conviction that music as original and as important as Stravinsky's needs writing about as well as performing. And while most of such writing, beyond the biographical, falls into the categories of criticism and music history, a significant amount is both technical – concerned with materials and methods in particular compositions – and theoretical, placing those materials and methods in broader contexts according to governing theories about the nature of music, physical and aesthetic, and its compositional manifestations.

While music critics and historians writing after 1910 had no difficulty in according Stravinsky – along with (among others) Schoenberg, BARTÓK and DEBUSSY – first-rank prominence in the formal and linguistic evolution of contemporary music, pinning down precisely what was new as well as exciting about his style – that is, developing theories relevant to what made music Stravinskian – was a slow process. It was easier to jump to entirely negative conclusions from inappropriate theoretical starting points, as Schenker did in his notorious condemnation of the harmonic language of a short extract from the then-recent CONCERTO FOR PIANO AND WIND INSTRUMENTS (1923–4) as a distortion, rather than an enrichment, of masterly compositional technique (Schenker 1996).

Other early commentaries and analyses played safer in focusing on melodic and rhythmic features which highlighted Stravinsky's connections with Russian traditions, and the extent to which his art music background – in

GLINKA, TCHAIKOVSKY, MUSSORGSKY and his teacher RIMSKY-KORSAKOV, linked as these were to wider nineteenth-century methods of enriching diatonic scales with symmetrically disposed chromaticisms – reinforced important and inspiring associations between art music and FOLK MUSIC. Historians of music theory attach particular importance to the detailed rhythmic analysis of The RITE OF SPRING undertaken in 1951 by the young Pierre BOULEZ, in response to the relatively informal discussion of the work in Olivier MESSIAEN's analysis classes, simply because Boulez's concern to plot systematic schemes of interrelation and transformation between elements regarded as motivic indicated the potential for considering complex and non-traditional compositional idioms in ways that came to full fruition only when serial principles were believed to displace traditional ideas of tonal function and formal design (Boulez 1991). Nevertheless, Boulez did not set out to develop theoretical ideas and analytical techniques relevant to all aspects of Stravinsky's music; what were, essentially, still perceptions about specific stylistic details in individual works only began to acquire a more generalised, and therefore genuinely theoretical, perspective in 1960s America, when Edward T. Cone proposed a genuinely post-classical formal model of gradual movement towards integration – stratification, interlock, synthesis – rather than the classical composing out of a unity (Cone 1962), and Arthur Berger showed how the particular symmetrical features of the octatonic scale, especially with respect to pitch-centres that divided the octave into minor third (interval-class 3) steps, could explain compositional decisions on both local and larger scales (Berger 1972).

Such theorising about both form and harmonic organisation, whose relevance extended well beyond the music of Stravinsky (see MODERNISM), laid the foundations for what has since become known as an 'extended common practice', equivalent to some degree with Schoenberg's notion of 'extended tonality' (see Tymoczko 2011). The relevance of this idea has been enhanced by the tendency of composers since the 1970s to work more with post-tonal modernist techniques retaining elements of traditional tonal thinking, acknowledging the limitations of those radical avant-garde attempts to create a truly atonal music, whether twelve-note or not, that had its fullest airing in the two decades after World War II – a development which Stravinsky's later music reflects.

The productive relation between theorising about contemporary compositional techniques and the work of leading modernist composers thrived once it was no longer felt essential for such theorising to match that appropriate for classical tonal music, in which (along Schenkerian lines) a specific technical function can be attached to every pitch, however decorative or otherwise incidental. Given the iconic status of The Rite of Spring in the history of modern music, it is no surprise that this work should have featured prominently in attempts to theorise the ways in which the language of modern music differs from what came before (see, for example, Danuser and Zimmermann 2013). Equally unsurprisingly, there was little consensus between those who viewed The Rite as connected – if more by distortion than transformation – to the folk-music based materials of Russian art music as explored by Mussorgsky and Rimsky-Korsakov, among others, and those for whom it seemed to invite consideration as atonal, facilitating comparison with the no less radical works of Schoenberg, BERG and others from the same decade either side of 1913. Pitch-class set theory, and its off-shoot concerning pitch-class set genres, aspired to establish connections between pre-twelve-note, post-tonal compositions – such as Schoenberg's *Erwartung*, Berg's *Wozzeck* and *The Rite* – and actual twelve-note, serial music from after 1920, in which every pitch can be assigned an order number (rather than the functioning designation 'passing note', 'suspension', etc.) within the versions of the governing set or series in use (see, in particular, Forte 1978). In this way, a truly comprehensive theory of atonal or post-tonal structure could be placed alongside the truly comprehensive theory of tonal structure proposed by Schenker.

In practice, however, the neatness of this binary opposition between 'tonal' and 'atonal' has proved to be its own worst enemy, failing to recognise that the main point of modernism, as Schoenberg, Stravinsky and others practised it, was to acknowledge the strengths of tonally rooted classicism, but also to show how these strengths needed to be and could be supplanted in musically valid ways. So far, no school of composers has emerged using the principles of pitch-class set theory in regular and systematic fashion; nevertheless, the influence of set-theoretical ideas about the co-existence of things like ordered and unordered (that is, freely ordered) collections of pitches and/or rhythmic cells can be found in much music that belongs to the current late-modernist phase of cultural production, and here the example of Stravinsky continues to offer fruitful material for theoretical as well as analytical interpretation, not least because what once seemed to be a decisive shift in his work, from techniques that were still in some way hierarchic – governed by the properties of scales or modes with certain functional attributes, if not exactly those of diatonic classicism – to a completely anti-hierarchic (atonal) form of serialism, is no longer authoritatively seen in this way.

At the present time, analyses of modernist music, and the theories that bolster them, tend to operate with balances between fixed and free, systematic and spontaneous elements, where there is sufficient consistency to ensure coherence and sufficient freedom to ensure pleasing surprises. The interconnectedness of modernist aesthetics with theories concerning both the construction and reception (that is, perception) of Stravinsky's compositions is clear in such recent accounts as *Building Blocks: Repetition and Continuity in the Music of Stravinsky* by Gretchen Horlacher, and *Modernist Mysteries: Perséphone* by Tamara Levitz, both of which contextualise the specifics of representative compositions within wide-ranging music-theoretical or cultural-historical perspectives. In avoiding riskily deterministic concepts of pitch organisation and harmonic structuring, such accounts acknowledge, if only by default, the particular attributes of a concept of music that does not require organically interactive processes to ensure character and coherence. For example, in the SYMPHONY OF PSALMS, a work whose reliance on octatonic modality is particularly transparent, tonal centres of E, E♭, C and G are sufficiently sustained to generate connectedness over larger formal spans, even though the bar-to-bar voice-leading might not be reducible to a set of specific functional identities and procedures, beyond what is sometimes termed 'directed motion' within a context governed by the post-tonal principle of emancipated dissonance.

Yet far from such 'partial' hierarchisation being an unsatisfactory preliminary to the absolute and persuasive equalisations of a truly atonal language of music, such instances of the technique indicate that such partial hierarchisation could be as appropriate and effective in the twelve-note context of THRENI or REQUIEM CANTICLES as in the neo-classical, post-tonal world of Symphony of Psalms.

As Joseph N. Straus formulates the theoretical point: 'Stravinsky accepted ... the Schoenbergian idea that four members of the series class bound together by some musical relationships, might function as a referential norm, somewhat in the manner of a tonic region in a tonal composition' (Straus 2003, 153). In this context, the oft-quoted statement in POETICS OF MUSIC – about 'poles of attraction' that 'are no longer within the closed system which was the diatonic system' but can be brought together 'without being compelled to conform to the exigencies of tonality' (Poet, 39) – amounts to a manifesto in support of a theory of extended or suspended tonality as one possible technical equivalent of a truly modernist aesthetic of music. It is in the nature of the inherent ambivalences here that some will prefer to hear much of the music Stravinsky composed after 1950, if not after 1912, as 'atonal': certainly, it is not 'tonal' in the fully hierarchised, organicist sense expounded by Schenker. Equally certain is the judgement that Stravinsky's 'extended common practice', however thoroughly or impressionistically it is theorised, underpinned one of the most original and enduring contributions to musical composition in the twentieth century. Was Stravinsky simply wrong to declare that music was 'beyond verbal meanings and verbal descriptions'? Trying to write articles such as this one creates a certain amount of sympathy for that view, but he would surely have accepted that worthwhile music cries out to be thought about – remembered – as well as experienced emotionally; and thinking, as well as thinking about experiences, cannot not involve concepts, words. In the end, even the music can benefit – at least in theory.   ARNOLD WHITTALL

Arthur Berger, 'Problems of pitch organisation in Stravinsky', in B. Boretz and E. T. Cone (eds.), Perspectives on Schoenberg and Stravinsky (Princeton University Press, 1972), 123–54.

Pierre Boulez, 'Stravinsky remains', in Stocktakings from an Apprenticeship, trans. Stephen Walsh (Oxford: Clarendon Press, 1991).

Edward T. Cone, 'Stravinsky: the progress of a method', Perspectives of New Music, 1.1 (1962), 18–26.

Hermann Danuser and Heidy Zimmermann (eds.), Avatar of Modernity: The Rite of Spring Reconsidered (London: Paul Sacher Foundation / Boosey & Hawkes, 2013).

Allen Forte, The Harmonic Organization of The Rite of Spring (New Haven: Yale University Press, 1978).

Gretchen Horlacher, Building Blocks: Repetition and Continuity in the Music of Stravinsky (New York: Oxford University Press, 2011).

Tamara Levitz, Modernist Mysteries: Perséphone (New York: Oxford University Press, 2012).

Heinrich Schenker, 'Further considerations of the Urlinie: II (1926)', in The Masterwork in Music 2, trans. William Drabkin (Cambridge University Press, 1996).

Joseph N. Straus, 'Stravinsky the serialist', in Jonathan Cross (ed.), The Cambridge Companion to Stravinsky (Cambridge University Press, 2003).

Dmitri Tymoczko, A Geometry of Music: Harmony and Counterpoint in the Extended Common Practice (New York: Oxford University Press, 2011).

Musical Education. Stravinsky was never a conservatory student and did not receive any official musical diploma. Nevertheless, he was fortunate to study privately with one of the greatest Russian composers, Nikolay RIMSKY-KORSAKOV, who instilled in his student the highest professionalism, and transmitted to him the best traditions of the Russian nationalist school. At the same time, Stravinsky's openness to new ideas, his artistic intuition and ability to self-educate, had played a very important role in his musical formation and development.

Early Years. Although Igor's excellent musical ear showed itself very early, he was not a *Wunderkind*. His first training took the form of a few casual piano lessons in September 1891, from a temporary teacher, O. A. Petrova. In the autumn of 1893, Igor entered the ST PETERSBURG Gymnasium, where singing and elementary MUSIC THEORY were taught in the two lowest classes, and, at the same time, he began regular piano lessons with a young pianist, Alexandra Snetkova. Thanks to these lessons, at an early age Igor was able to sight-read through his father's operatic scores. His favourite occupation was also to improvise. The improvisations contributed to his better knowledge of the piano, and 'sowed the seed of musical ideas'. In 1899, Igor began more intensive piano studies with Leokadiya KASHPEROVA (she taught Stravinsky until 1901). Kashperova gave new impetus to Igor's piano playing and elevated his technique to a professional level. Nevertheless, the young composer revolted against her musical aesthetic and bad taste. For him, she was 'an excellent pianist and a blockhead'.

Music Theory Lessons: Harmony and Counterpoint. Because of his limited theoretical knowledge, Igor was unable to write down his improvisations. In 1899, he stated his intention of taking theory lessons from Rimsky-Korsakov's pupil Nikolay Tcherepnin. However, he only began to take private tuition in the theory of music in November 1901 (soon after the start of his law course), with the recently graduated Fyodor AKIMENKO. In February 1902, Akimenko was replaced by Vasily KALAFATI, who taught Igor for about two years. Both teachers were graduates of Rimsky-Korsakov's class, and were pernickety about technical precision. According to Stravinsky, their lessons covered chorale harmonisation, species counterpoint, invention, the study of BACH's instrumental works, and fugue. Igor was particularly keen on counterpoint – from about the age of 18, he began to study it alone, with no other help than an ordinary manual (*Auto*, 14). Later, he claimed that it was counterpoint that stimulated his imagination, laid the foundation of his future technique, and prepared him for study with Rimsky-Korsakov.

Rimsky-Korsakov. Stravinsky was introduced to the great composer at the rehearsal of Rimsky's opera *Sadko* in January 1901. But Stravinsky first showed Rimsky his attempts at composition not in St Petersburg, but in GERMANY, where both families were summering in 1902. In August, Igor came for five days from Berlin to Heidelberg in order to see his fellow university student Vladimir Rimsky-Korsakov, the composer's son, and to consult his father about his vocation. Rimsky-Korsakov advised him not to enter ST PETERSBURG CONSERVATORY for several reasons: (1) Igor had a lot of technical shortcomings, and was already 20 (for comparison, GLAZUNOV began to study with Rimsky at the age of 14, and PROKOFIEV became a conservatory student when he was 13); (2) Igor had to continue his university course until 1905; (3) at the Conservatory, Igor would have to undergo a standard six-year course, of which the first three years were devoted mainly to those techniques that he had been studying privately, and only in the final three years would he be let loose on free composition. Rimsky was in favour of a flexible application of this scheme, and he advised Stravinsky to continue his studies with Kalafati. He also agreed to consult with the young composer from time to time, and to take him in hand when he had acquired the necessary foundation.

Igor had the opportunity to work intensively with the Master from 16 to 19 August 1903 (29 August – 4 September) in the village of Krapachukha, where the Rimsky-Korsakovs were summering. Igor wanted to work on his new Sonata in F# Minor, for Piano, but Rimsky made him compose the first part of a sonatina, after having instructed him in the principles of the allegro of a sonata. There was also instruction in orchestration, and in the range of the instruments. Igor was to orchestrate the fragments of Rimsky's new opera (Pan Voyevoda), and then to explain the difference between his attempts and the original versions (SCS, 75–7). Rimsky taught form and orchestration together.

The consultations with the Master continued in St Petersburg in Rimsky's apartment. Following his teacher's instructions, Igor orchestrated fragments of classical music, and Rimsky explained their form and structure.

Soon, Igor became very close to the composer, his family and his circle (see Belyayev circle), but regular lessons started only in the autumn 1905, after the end of Igor's university course. In 1904, under the supervision of Rimsky-Korsakov, Stravinsky revised his Sonata in F♯ Minor. In 1905–7, he created his first work for orchestra – the Symphony in E♭ Major, treating Glazunov's Symphony in that key as a model (Rimsky himself worked in this way with Balakirev on his own Symphony following Schumann's Fourth Symphony). Stravinsky showed Rimsky-Korsakov the score of Scherzo fantastique (1908), as well as the preliminary sketches for The Nightingale. But when, in 1908, he mailed his teacher the score of the new work Fireworks, the package was returned with the note: 'Not delivered on account of the death of addressee'.

Rimsky-Korsakov was a great composer and a genial teacher and Stravinsky inherited from him high professionalism; a habit of systematic, methodical work, whatever the difficulties of mood or inspiration; a liking for order; as well as a concept of modelling. Nevertheless, with time, the pupil began to move away from the academic and conservative aesthetic of his teacher, who would oppose in principle anything new that came from France and Germany. Thus, Stravinsky was not without justification when he wrote: 'I am grateful to Rimsky for many things ... nevertheless, the most important tools of my art I had to discover for myself' (Mem, 57).

Later Years. In the 1920s, living in France, Stravinsky began his international career as a concert pianist, performing his own piano works. In 1924, before giving the Paris première of his new Concerto for Piano and Wind Instruments, he returned to apprenticeship and took private lessons from Isidor Philipp, one of the greatest representatives of the French piano school of his generation.

With regard to composition, as is well known, in the 1950s and 1960s, Stravinsky was converted to serial technique. The 70-year-old composer was forced to learn the basics and studied books on dodecaphony, as well as serial scores (*see* LIBRARY). Having accomplished the feat of self-education, he not only mastered, but also developed and renewed, serial technique.

TATIANA BARANOVA MONIGHETTI

Musical Language and Style. The origins of Stravinsky's musical language can be traced back to his apprenticeship with Nikolay RIMSKY-KORSAKOV in 1905–8. A number of essentials predate *The* FIREBIRD (1910), and may be found in the SCHERZO FANTASTIQUE (1908), a virtuoso orchestral work for which the aspiring composer gained his teacher's approval. Stravinsky inherited a two-pronged approach to musical composition: (1) Russian folk songs, modal in conception but often harmonised in a Western, quasi-tonal manner; and (2) chromatic sequences derived from symmetrical scales such as the whole-tone and the octatonic. Made up of alternating steps and half-steps (or the reverse), the octatonic scale is known in American jazz circles as the 'diminished scale'.

In Example 2a from the *Scherzo*, arpeggiated triads descend the octatonic scale's minor-third cycle in terms of E-C♯-B♭-G. The dominant sevenths of these major triads are sustained in the accompanying parts. Isolated in Example 2b, the triads and dominant sevenths yield the octatonic scale shown in Example 2c. Stems and a beam connect the roots of this vocabulary.

Example 2 (a, b and c) *Scherzo fantastique*, octatonic triads, dominant 7th chords.

octatonic scale
stemmed notes = roots of triads

The octatonic vocabulary of major and minor triads and dominant-seventh chords was called 'harmonic' by Rimsky-Korsakov; the Dorian or minor tetrachord, 'melodic'. Shown descending the octatonic scale's minor-third cycle in Example 3a are transpositions of the Dorian tetrachord. Isolated in Example 3b, these four overlapping transpositions yield the octatonic scale shown in Example 3c. Example 4a shows a form of linkage between the harmonic and the melodic: the root, seventh, and fifth of the dominant seventh (first inversion, closed position) become an incomplete or gapped Dorian tetrachord (E D (C♯) B). In turn, the Dorian tetrachord can act as a bridge between the octatonic and the Dorian mode, as shown in Example 4b.

Remarkably, the octatonic framework outlined in Examples 2, 3 and 4 would remain an integral part of Stravinsky's musical thought processes for nearly the entirety of his career. While the Dorian tetrachord would prevail in

Example 3 (a, b and c) *Scherzo fantastique*, octatonic Dorian tetrachords.

Example 4 (a and b) Dorian tetrachord.

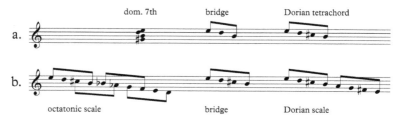

Russian-period works, melodically and as a form of linkage between the octatonic and the diatonic, the triadic perspective in Example 2 would continue in neo-classical and even early serial works.

In what would lead to the discovery of new dissonant sonorities, Stravinsky soon began superimposing the octatonic vocabulary shown in Examples 2, 3 and 4. In the second tableau of PETRUSHKA (1911), the notorious 'Petrushka chord' is one such superimposition, a stacking of the tritone-related triads rooted on C and F♯; see Example 5. Stravinsky would later claim that this *Petrushka* music of the second tableau had been 'conceived in two keys' (presumably in C major and F♯ major), a conception that would later spur the invention of concepts such as 'bitonality' and 'polytonality'. More specifically, however, it is the clashing of the two tritone-related triads, octatonically related, that determines the particular resonance of this music.

Example 5 Petrushka, second tableau, 'Petrushka chord'.

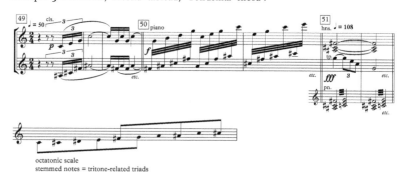

A veritable primer in the use of stratified, polyrhythmic textures, The RITE OF SPRING is no less a primer in the ways in which octatonic-related triads and Dorian tetrachords may be superimposed. Typical of the sound of The Rite is the sustained, compound chord at the beginning of the 'Ritual of Abduction'; see Example 6. In the trumpets and horns, respectively, a dominant-seventh chord rooted on E♭ is superimposed over a C major triad. The root, dominant seventh, and fifth of the E♭-dominant seventh are a continuation, registrally fixed, of the D♭-B♭-E♭-B♭ ostinato heard throughout the preceding 'Augurs of Spring'. Together with the F♯ in the timpani, the triadic configuration yields the octatonic scale shown below in Example 6. Superimposed over this octatonic component is a reiterating diatonic/modal fragment in the flutes. Contour-wise, the fragment is a fairly accurate transcription of a Lithuanian folk song drawn by the composer from a collection of such songs.

Example 6 *The Rite of Spring*, 'Ritual of Abduction', opening: superimposed triads.

Exiled in SWITZERLAND during World War I, Stravinsky turned his back part-way on this early phase of his creative life. In place of the orchestra, he began composing for small chamber ensembles, and then eventually for singers and groups that resembled peasant bands and the instrumentation of street music. In works such as RENARD (1915–16), *Les Noces* (1917–23) and The SOLDIER'S TALE (1918), he began cultivating a folk music language of his own, derived from bits and pieces of authentic Russian folk songs and popular verse.

More often than not, however, the bits and pieces of this Russian-period music were folk-like rather than folk-derived, products of what Stravinsky called a 'fabrication' – a kind of simulation of the genuine article. Open-ended melodic fragments were repeated as ostinatos or subjected to forms of metrical displacement: a fragment entering on the downbeat of a 2/4 metre might subsequently be displaced to the upbeat.

While *The Rite of Spring* is ostensibly octatonic or octatonic–diatonic, *Renard* and *Les Noces* are just the opposite. Octatonic relations intrude occasionally on an established diatonic/modal framework. In addition, the four tableaux of *Les Noces* are block structures, a formal practice typical of Stravinsky's music generally. Two or more blocks of heterogeneous material are placed in an abrupt juxtaposition with one another. In any given instance, the lengths and order of these blocks can vary from one restatement to the next, but their individual contents remain fixed. The contrasts between them are often underscored instrumentally and registrally.

Because of the high degree of symmetry entailed by the presence of the octatonic scale, interaction between it and the diatonic, modal or tonal, is inherently static. Superimposition is static as well: the art of piling one triad (or triadic part) on top of another. Superimpositions like the one in the trumpets and horns in Example 6 are 'coagulations', as Pierre Boulez described them, given that they 'annul' a sense of movement or development.

Yet those same polarised, dammed-up harmonies provide an ideal backdrop for the rhythmic invention that is often the life of Stravinsky's music. Ostinatos and stratified, polyrhythmic textures are an integral part of that invention, as is, more fundamentally, the metrical displacement of repeated motives and chords. Stravinsky spent a lifetime at the podium and at the piano attempting to demonstrate the need for a strict style in the performance of his music. In Chapter 6 of his POETICS OF MUSIC (1947), and other writings, he explained this need philosophically rather than in practical terms. Yet the musical rationale lies close to the surface. If, among other rhythmic practices, the metrical displacement of a repeated motive was to have its effect, then the beat had to be maintained evenly, with a minimum of rubato or nuance. 'My music can survive just about anything', Stravinsky reasoned, 'but wrong or uncertain tempo'.

No less a part of the rhythmic invention in Stravinsky's scores is a dry, *secco* approach to its articulation, frequent staccato doublings of legato lines, and a percussive use of the piano and string pizzicato in punctuating the accents of metrical displacement. Static harmony, displacement, a percussive articulation of displacement, and a strictly held beat to keep it all together – such, in large measure, is the nature of his musical style.

In the neo-classical works of the 1920s, 1930s and 1940s, an accommodation is sought with the tonal styles and forms of the High Baroque and classical eras. A case in point is the second movement, Andante, of the OCTET FOR WIND INSTRUMENTS (1922–3); see Example 7. The formal apparatus of this movement fits the classical model of a theme and variations, while the theme's presentation is a typical theme-and-accompaniment setting. Looking to the past as well as the future, however, the variation theme is wholly octatonic. At Rehearsal No. 25, its first phrase is transposed by a minor third, guaranteeing continued confinement to the given octatonic scale; in ascending order, A-B♭-C-C♯-D♯-E-F♯-G-(A). Beneath the octatonic theme, however, the accompaniment implies D minor (or quasi-D minor). And the tonic pitch D along with the tonic triad (D F A) lie outside the given octatonic scale. The result is a kind of static clashing or *superimposition* of the octatonic theme over its D minor accompaniment. As can be seen by the octatonic and D minor scales aligned just below the quotation in Example 7, the (A C♯ E) triad is held in common: outlined by the octatonic theme, (A C♯ E) is also the dominant within the

D minor tonality – hence the peculiarity of Stravinsky's neo-classical dominant. The two scales are brought together in the final bar by a tonic resolution on D. Although the major third, F♯, is octatonic, it relates to the D minor tonality by way of a traditional inflection, the *tierce de Picardie*.

Example 7 Octet for Wind Instruments, octatonic theme, D minor accompaniment.

All of which is not to imply that Stravinsky's neo-classical accommodations are invariably octatonic in conception. Many works, especially during the 1930s, are devoid of such complications. Yet it can often seem that the sound readily identified with his neo-classical style can be traced to the intervention of octatonic intervals in contexts which are otherwise diatonic in terms of the major and minor scales of tonality.

Shown in Example 8 is the opening of the second movement, Andante, of the SYMPHONY IN THREE MOVEMENTS (1942–5). As a form of accompaniment, the repetition of the dyad F♯/D is typically classical in origin. What happens in the lower strings in the first two bars is typical of Stravinsky, however; an F♮, pizzicato, is made to clash with the F♯ or major third of the tonic triad, (D F♯ A). Exhibited in this way is a form of 'major–minor third emphasis', according to which the minor third is brought into conflict with the major third of a tonic triad.

Example 8 Symphony in Three Movements, II, opening bars.

The rapid figuration in the flutes further along at Rehearsal No. 117 yields a pitch content of D F F♯ G♯ A B. Here, the F♮ and G♯ serve alternatively as chromatic notes to F♯ and A, respectively, the major third and fifth of the tonic triad. This is the traditional, tonal and expressive use to which these chromatic pitches are put in the music of Haydn, Mozart and BEETHOVEN.

The top stave of Example 9 can further illuminate the classical side of Stravinsky's neo-classical bargain. The three stems connected by a beam outline the tonic triad (D F♯ A); F♮, G♯ and B, forming a diminished triad, embellish the chord notes of that triad. In Stravinsky's Andante, however, with F♮ clashing with the chord note F♯, elements that might earlier have succeeded one another expressively are now statically superimposed. The origin of this superimposition may be traced to the interacting octatonic scale shown on the bottom stave in Example 9. In short, the (D F F♯ G♯ A D) content, with its symmetrically defined (D F F♯) (F F♯ A) major–minor third groupings, is as octatonic in conception as it is accountable to the D major tonality.

Example 9 D major scale and octatonic scale.

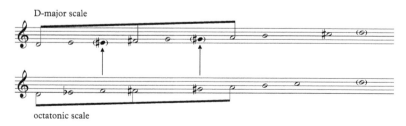

D-major scale

octatonic scale

Among the many neo-classical contexts that relate closely to the interacting circumstances sketched in Example 9, see Rehearsal Nos. 30–34 in Danses Concertantes (1942), Babel (1944), the first movement of the 'Basle' String Concerto in D (1946), and the 'Air de danse' and 'Pas des furies' in Orpheus (1947).

Stravinsky's adoption of serial, and ultimately TWELVE-NOTE, techniques during the 1950s was slow and deliberate. Inevitably, the musical language changed, even if many rhythmic phenomena, along with his method of composing with juxtaposed blocks of material, remained firmly in place: see the outer movements of Canticum sacrum (1955) and the Movements for piano and orchestra (1958–9), IV.

En route to a fully fledged twelve-note system, the serial miniatures in Agon (1953–7), the Bransle Simple, Gay and Double, are based on six-note or hexachordal rows. Although these latter are non-octatonic, they miss the octatonic by a single pitch (or interval). Often enough, Stravinsky transposes these rows in ways that extend and expose their octatonic potential.

By the early 1960s, the composer had declared himself more a serial composer than ever, and had become the inventor of new ways of creating row forms. Major works of this late period, often with liturgical or biblical texts, apply a rotation scheme to the hexachords of the twelve-note rows. In Example 10 from The Flood (1961–2), the first hexachord of this work's prime form (on top) is followed by five rotations or 'alternates'. Starting with a common set-factor, G♯, the rotation proceeds by interval order in the manner indicated by the diagonal lines: the first rotation begins with the second interval of the original hexachord, and completes its cycle upon reaching the original's first interval; the second rotation then begins with the original's third interval; and so forth. On the vertical axis in Example 10, Stravinsky reserved the six 'verticals' (as he called them), starting with the single pitch G♯, specifically for chords or 'harmonies'.

Example 10 The Flood, hexachordal rotation.

In shorter works of this period, Stravinsky confined himself to the untransposed forms of the row. Yet he seems to have regarded the hexachordal rotation scheme outlined in Example 10 as an outgrowth of compositional ends that were uniquely his.

In conclusion, melody and harmony in Stravinsky's Russian-period works are either modal, octatonic or derived from a combination of the two. Starting with *Petrushka* (1911) and *The Rite of Spring* (1913), new dissonant sonorities are created by superimposing triads and Dorian tetrachords that originate with the octatonic scale. From the 1920s to the 1940s, neo-classical works such as the second movement of the Octet marry octatonicism with high Baroque and classical tonal styles and forms. While not all neo-classical works feature an interaction of this kind, it can often seem that the sound readily identified with Stravinsky's neo-classical style can be traced to the intervention of octatonic intervals in contexts which are otherwise diatonic in terms of the major and minor scales of tonality.

With the turn to serial, and ultimately twelve-note, techniques during the 1950s, the musical language changed, even if many rhythmic phenomena, along with his method of composing with juxtaposed blocks of material, remained firmly in place. Octatonic relations are markedly present in *Agon* and in the two flanking movements of *Canticum sacrum*. By the 1960s, however, the composer had declared himself more a serial composer than ever, and had become an innovator in developing and extending the techniques of twelve-note composition. PIETER C. VAN DEN TOORN

Gretchen Horlacher, *Building Blocks: Repetition and Continuity in the Music of Stravinsky* (New York: Oxford University Press, 2011).

Pieter C. van den Toorn, *The Music of Igor Stravinsky* (New Haven: Yale University Press, 1983).

Pieter C. van den Toorn and John McGinness, *Stravinsky and the Russian Period: Sound and Legacy of a Musical Idiom* (Cambridge University Press, 2012).

Mussolini, Benito (born Predappio, 29 July 1883; died Dongo, 28 April 1945). Fascist dictator ('Duce') of ITALY between January 1925 and July 1943, and, between September 1943 and April 1945, of the Repubblica Sociale Italiana, the German puppet-regime in northern Italy. Mussolini was appointed Prime Minister in October 1922 by Victor Emmanuel III, amid a show of strength – the 'March on Rome' – by his black-shirted paramilitary followers. Unlike Hitler or Stalin, the Duce was keen to appear appreciative of musical MODERNISM. In February 1923, following the Italian première of Part I of The RITE OF SPRING, he wrote to the conductor Bernardino Molinari, 'I regret – how I regret! – missing the Stravinsky.' Stravinsky made frequent visits to fascist Italy as pianist in, and conductor of, his own works, from 1925 until 1939. There is confusion as to the number of his audiences with Mussolini, the composer's own account (in *Expo*) being characteristically untrustworthy. Meetings in February 1933 and May 1935 are well documented, but SPD also gives a date of 1930. Composer and Duce seem not to have met in March 1936: on this occasion (as on others), Stravinsky left gifts for the dictator. His notorious expressions of praise for Mussolini and fascism were made in interviews around the time of the 1935 audience. 'I don't believe anyone has a greater veneration for Mussolini than mine', Stravinsky told Alberto Gasco, music critic of the Roman daily La tribuna: 'He is the saviour of Italy and – let us hope – of Europe.' BEN EARLE

Tamara Levitz, Modernist Mysteries: Perséphone (New York: Oxford University Press, 2012), 334–6.
Fiamma Nicolodi, Musica e musicisti nel ventennio fascista (Fiesole: Discanto, 1984), 295.
Harvey Sachs, Music in Fascist Italy (London: Weidenfeld and Nicolson, 1987), 167–9.

Mussorgsky, Modest Petrovich (born Karevo, Pskov district, 9/21 March 1839; died St Petersburg, 16/28 March 1881). Russian composer. A member of the provincial landed gentry, Mussorgsky's musical talent gained him connections at a young age with leading ST PETERSBURG composers and critics, including Dargomïzhsky, BALAKIREV, BORODIN, CUI and STASOV. Mussorgsky was not the most prolific composer of the FIVE, and, after his death, RIMSKY-KORSAKOV notoriously decried the 'countless absurdities' in his harmonic voice-leading – but the influence of his operatic works and songs cannot be denied. Although Mussorgsky died before Stravinsky's birth, the young Stravinsky was well acquainted with the composer's operas through his father's appearances at the MARIINSKY THEATRE.

Stravinsky's early works composed under Rimsky-Korsakov's guidance seem like exercises in chromatic mediant relationships, interval expansion, and modal harmonies modelled on Mussorgsky. In 1909, joining an established tradition of orchestrating – and, in some cases, revising – Mussorgsky's compositions, Stravinsky provided a well-received ORCHESTRATION of Mussorgsky's 'Song of the Flea' for a 'Goethe in Music' concert in St Petersburg, sponsored by ZILOTI. DIAGHILEV also commissioned Stravinsky (later joined by RAVEL) to orchestrate and complete Mussorgsky's unfinished OPERA KHOVANSHCHINA for the 1913 season of the BALLETS RUSSES. Diaghilev positioned this project largely as an alternative to Rimsky-Korsakov's orchestration, rankling the deceased composer's family and followers in St Petersburg. Stravinsky's newly composed final chorus for the opera was arguably more faithful to Mussorgsky's original vision than Rimsky-Korsakov's bombastic ending. Perhaps the most intriguing point of influence between the composers is in their Russian text setting. Mussorgsky was renowned for his 'naturalism', exemplified by the recitatives of Boris Godunov, achieved by careful alignment of accented syllables and strong beats while grouping, or offsetting by rests, unaccented syllables on weak beats. This technique is evident in many of Stravinsky's early vocal works, notably The NIGHTINGALE (1914), although later works diverge from this manner of text setting in favour of the notorious 'floating accent'. JOHANNA FRYMOYER

Arkady Klimovitsky, 'Commentary', in Stuart Campbell (ed.), Stravinsky, Igor. Orchestrations of 'The Song of the Flea' by Modest Mussorgsky, 'The Song of the Flea' by Ludwig van Beethoven, trans. Paul Williams (Saint Petersburg: School of Music Publishing House, The Russian Institute for the History of the Arts, 2003).

Myaskovsky, Nikolay Yakovlevich (born the fortress of Novo-Georgiyevsk (now Modlin), Poland, 8/20 April 1881; died Moscow, 8 August 1950). Russian composer and teacher. One of the first Russian critics of Stravinsky's music, he compared the composer's harmonic processes with SCHOENBERG's. His early reviews fluctuated between praise and disdain, although he revered the 'extraordinary' PETRUSHKA. Stravinsky sent Myaskovsky a copy of The RITE OF

Spring, which he appears to have both admired and disliked. Although the pair were initially on friendly terms, Stravinsky's attempt to get Myaskovsky to proofread a number of his works caused great offence and resentment on the part of the latter composer. In 1927, Stravinsky called Myaskovsky 'a gifted musician' but was critical of Soviet musical life, which was 'not yet ready for me'. Myaskovsky was reportedly annoyed by these remarks, as well as by Stravinsky's considerable international fame. JOSEPH SCHULTZ

Nabokov, Nicolas (born Lyubcha, Novogrudok, Minsk region, 4/17 April 1903; died New York, 6 April 1978). Russian-born American composer, writer and administrator. From 1923 until 1928 he lived in PARIS, and, through friendship with Sergey PROKOFIEV, was introduced to DIAGHILEV's circle in October 1927, when he auditioned his cantata *Ode*. Stravinsky was present and, according to Nabokov, his enthusiasm over the score's stylistic allusions to GLINKA and other early nineteenth-century Russian composers persuaded Diaghilev to stage the work the following year. The two composers temporarily fell out over Nabokov's obituary on Diaghilev, published in the November 1929 issue of *La musique*, Stravinsky particularly angered by the claim that Diaghilev had conceived and initiated both PETRUSHKA and *Les NOCES*. Yet their relationship, once restored, became positively warm in 1930 through the coincidence of Pleyel having loaned them near-neighbouring studios (Nabokov being commissioned to write a piece for Pleyel's latest harpsichord): Stravinsky was composing the SYMPHONY OF PSALMS, and the two often lunched together, and for recreation played four-hand BACH cantatas or Handel oratorios. They fell out again, though, when Nabokov expressed dislike of Stravinsky's constant 'shadow', Arthur LOURIÉ.

Needing to improve his income, Nabokov began teaching in AMERICA in 1933, lecturing in several academic institutions until 1951 and becoming an American citizen in 1939. Through friendship with BALANCHINE, he resumed relations with Stravinsky in the spring of 1937, when the two composers attended the première of JEU DE CARTES at the Metropolitan Opera. Nabokov's article 'Stravinsky Now', published in *Partisan Review* (summer 1944 issue), won the composer's approval.

In 1945, Nabokov, with his cultural connections and his multi-lingual abilities, became coordinator of inter-allied negotiations, taking part in the denazification of GERMANY. In 1949, he joined the committee American Intellectuals for Freedom, sponsored by several leading intellectuals including Stravinsky, created to counteract the notorious Soviet-sponsored 'Cultural and Scientific Conference for World Peace' at the Waldorf-Astoria Hotel. Several Soviet commentators later claimed, erroneously, that Nabokov interrogated the script-bound SHOSTAKOVICH at that event – to demonstrate the falsity of the 'dialogue' between Soviet and American artists the conference supposedly promoted – at Stravinsky's behest. Nabokov subsequently became involved in the Congress for Cultural Freedom (CCF), an organisation sponsored – unbeknownst to himself, and indeed most of its participants – by the then recently formed CIA, which perceived the CCF's activities as a necessary riposte to the Soviet-sponsored cultural propaganda in Europe. Under CCF's auspices, Nabokov conceived and organised major cultural festivals, including ones in Paris ('Masterpieces of the Twentieth Century', May 1952 – notable for a staging of OEDIPUS REX in which both Stravinsky and Jean COCTEAU, for the first time, were involved in the actual production), Rome ('Music of Our Time', 4–15 April 1954) and Berlin (1964, for which Nabokov wrote a monograph on Stravinsky which earned the composer's approval); as major showcases for Stravinsky's music, with Stravinsky himself appearing as conductor of his own works, these all enhanced his postwar European reputation (though word reached Stravinsky after the Berlin Festival that Nabokov had made some less than flattering comments about his conducting). Nabokov also negotiated several lucrative deals for Stravinsky, including in December 1950 the conductor's fee of $20,000 for the première of The RAKE'S PROGRESS, which he secured over a luncheon meeting with Mario Labroca, head of the VENICE Biennale, and at least two major commissions: THRENI (for Radio Hamburg, getting Rolf Liebermann to agree a higher than usual fee at the composer's request) and The FLOOD (for Hamburg Staatsoper, of which Liebermann had become Director in 1959). No doubt Nabokov's influential position after the war and his sympathetic handling of Stravinsky's demand for high fees, as well as their shared Russian culture, secured him a special place in Stravinsky's affections in the last decades of his life. Robert CRAFT noted how, at Stravinsky's funeral, Nabokov took a special and symbolic place during the service, 'the only person who could have handled this', standing 'like an ambassadorial wall' between himself and Vera STRAVINSKY on one side, and, on the other, Stravinsky's children, from whom Stravinsky had been estranged in his final years. On hearing of Nabokov's death, Craft wrote: 'My Stravinsky world . . . shrinks more with this loss than with any other.'   DANIEL JAFFÉ

Vincent Giroud, *Nicolas Nabokov: A Life in Freedom and Music* (New York: Oxford University Press, 2015).

Nicolas Nabokov, *Bagázh: Memoirs of a Russian Cosmopolitan* (New York: Atheneum, 1975).

Nicolas Nabokov, *Old Friends and New Music* (London: Hamish Hamilton, 1951).

Neo-classicism. The origins of neo-classicism can be traced back to Rome in the middle of the eighteenth century, as a response to the excessive ornamentation of the Baroque and rococo, leading to a revival of interest in antiquity. Similarly, the spirit of neo-classicism prevailed among a number of composers of the early twentieth century as a reaction against the exaggerated style of nineteenth-century Romanticism. Partly due to the devastation of World War I, it is unsurprising that European composers sought refuge in the older, less emotionally charged classical ideals. Claude DEBUSSY's wartime sonatas helped to create the beginnings of the neo-classical movement – Sonata for Cello and Piano (1915), Sonata for Flute, Viola and Harp (1915) and Sonata for Violin and Piano (1916–17).

Soon after, other composers, including Stravinsky with The SOLDIER'S TALE (1917–18) and PULCINELLA (1920), continued to renew the principles of classicism, incorporating traditional musical forms and harmonic processes, and ultimately arriving at what is now known as the neo-classical movement. In The *Soldier's Tale*, Stravinsky composed a small chamber work that was easy for performers to transport to other locations, and used the opportunity to expand the dramatic role of the chorale. A few years later, in *Pulcinella* (1920), he used musical sources by Giovanni Battista PERGOLESI and other eighteenth-century composers, and collaborated with the painter Pablo PICASSO (1881–1973), who was also going through a neo-classical phase at the time.

Neo-classicism is difficult to pin down precisely when describing the works of twentieth-century composers, given the fuzzy distinction between classicism and MODERNISM in music, and in distinguishing between different adaptations of classicism in modern music. In January 1924, Stravinsky wrote 'Some ideas about my Octuor' (*The Arts*; English translation appears in *SCW*, 574–7), where he concluded: 'Form, in my music, derives from counterpoint. I consider counterpoint as the only means through which the attention of the composer is concentrated on purely musical questions. Its elements also lend themselves perfectly to an architectural construction.' Earlier in the essay, Stravinsky spoke against the freedom of interpretation in the OCTET FOR WIND INSTRUMENTS (1919–23) and other recently composed works, since their energy was already contained in the score: 'My Octuor is a musical object. This object has a form and that form is influenced by the musical matter with which it is composed.' The idea of restricting interpretation might also be related to Stravinsky's choice of wind instruments for the Octet: 'Wind instruments to me seem to be more apt to render a certain rigidity of the form I had in mind than other instruments.'

Stravinsky's desire to control the manner in which his music would be performed is also related to some of his earlier experiments with the PIANOLA. In addition to writing *Étude for Pianola* (1917), he recorded his own performance of some of his other works, for piano and also other combinations of instruments, on piano rolls as a means of preserving tempo markings and other interpretive subtleties. In the case of his CONCERTO FOR PIANO AND WIND INSTRUMENTS (1923–4; rev. 1950), the performance rights for the piano part were available exclusively to Stravinsky for several performances.

With Stravinsky's renewed interest in classicism came an interest in antiquity, specifically that of ancient Greece, and exploring the dramatic potential of a number of mythological subjects would occupy him periodically throughout the next few decades. These works would also involve collaborations with some of the key luminaries of the time – including Jean COCTEAU (OEDIPUS REX, 1926–7), Adolph BOLM (also George BALANCHINE) (APOLLON MUSAGÈTE, 1927–8), André GIDE (PERSÉPHONE, 1933), Balanchine and Isamu Noguchi (ORPHEUS, 1947–8) and Balanchine again (AGON, 1953–7).

Later in the century, figures such as Pierre BOULEZ were critical of Stravinsky's neo-classical notions of musical form, interpretation and objectivity. For example, in the essay 'Bach's Moment' (1951), Pierre Boulez writes:

Since 1920 the musical world seems to have survived on an obsession with 'classicism', an enterprise defined by two major terms: 'style' and 'objectivity'.... Without going far wrong, one could identify two effective tendencies in this 'classicism': one which aims to rediscover the total objectivity of 'pure music'; the other which, more validly, uses historical dialectic as the basis for a new 'universality of style'.... All musical activity tries to play the game under the banner of total security. Each camp calls the other romantic, a word strongly tinged with contempt in its suggestion of instability and disarray. Neoclassicists hurl anathema at dodecaphony, as an ultra-individualistic experiment, the final hypertrophy of Wagnerism; dodecaphonists, with the firm support of historical evolution, treat neo-classicism as a nostalgia for the past, and its pretended return to 'pure music' as a manifestly subjective illusion. (Boulez 1991, 1).

In a much later presentation titled 'Classique Moderne' given in 1996 (published in Danuser 1997, 306–8), Boulez would discuss the possibilities of how the 'classical' ('Classique') can interact with respect to the past, presenting three attitudes: classical as model, classical as example, or classical as reference. He argued in favour of the third, reference, as the only one of the three possibilities that allows continuing profound musical innovation/evolution/transformation, because this is the one that has a conceptual rather than a literal relationship with the past. In fact, Stravinsky (or one of his ghost writers) also raised doubt as to whether or not the term neo-classic was apropos, though long before Boulez: 'With works that are worthy of attention, and have been written under the obvious influence of the music of the past, does not the matter consist rather in a quest that probes deeper than a mere imitation of the so-called classical idiom?' ('Avertissement' ('A warning'), reprinted from The Dominant, December 1927, in SCW, 577–8).

Stravinsky and other composers moved 'back to Bach' by returning to linear musical textures – as if to celebrate the triumphs of J. S. BACH's contrapuntal style in a new way. This use of pre-existing forms would not presuppose a mere imitation of the music of the past. For example, the presence of a contrapuntal framework for each movement of SCHOENBERG's Suite for Piano, op. 25 (1921–3), the fugue in Variation E of Stravinsky's Octet, or the fugue in the second movement of SYMPHONY OF PSALMS (1929–30) does not presuppose that the listener will hear the essence of Bach in these musical compositions. In the case of the Schoenberg Suite for Piano, the structural framework would become a vehicle for his experimentation with dodecaphonic technique, whereas Stravinsky was at the crossroads between primitivism and neo-classicism. Coincidentally, in 'The problem of style', Boris de SCHLOEZER would also speak of an 'armature' ('framework'), but in regard to Stravinsky's search for a new style: 'because he has felt, profoundly, the need of a style, of a super-individual framework, Stravinsky has turned to the XVIIIth-century masters' (The Dial, 86, January–July 1929, trans. Ezra Pound).

Bach's 'continuous style', as 'the musician above all others who has so perfected that development of musical thought … in which one (musical) idea begets another' would be attributed by Schloezer as the reason why Stravinsky turned to Bach – in particular, to Bach's instrumental music. Interestingly, while Schloezer chooses Stravinsky's CONCERTINO for string quartet (1920) as an example of his 'continuous style', careful analysis of this one-movement work shows that, though it is indeed continuous, the vestiges of block form that were so characteristic of The RITE OF SPRING have now been integrated into his newly adopted 'continuous style'. He would also include a 'Russian theme' in Concertino. For the SYMPHONIES OF WIND INSTRUMENTS, written the same year, Stravinsky would incorporate Bach's continuity into his appropriation of chorale form, and simultaneously inject a sense of Russian character (the so-called 'bell motive'). Beyond Schloezer, Charles Koechlin, in his article 'Le Retour à Bach' (*Revue musicale*, 8, no. 1, 1 November 1926: 3), would encourage composers to write '*musique pure*, not pretending to signify anything. And fugues. Or rather sketches of fugues: adapted to the needs of an era where one knows the value of time.'

For CAPRICCIO (1928–9), Stravinsky acknowledged the influence of Praetorius and Weber (*Auto*, 159). Praetorius, who viewed the capriccio and fantasia forms as equivalent, defined the fugal element of a capriccio: 'when one undertakes to execute a fugue of one's choosing but dwells on it only for a short time, soon changing to another fugue' (Praetorius 2004, 38). This element would have instinctively appealed to Stravinsky, given his interest in contrapuntal structures. Regarding Weber, Stravinsky's son, Soulima STRAVINSKY, recalled, in an interview with Thor Wood, that his father heard him practising the Weber *Konzertstück* on the piano around 1928 while they were living in Voreppe, FRANCE (Wood 1977).

Tracing Stravinsky's path towards abstraction through the Bachian lands involves excerpts from several compositions, among them the last movement of the CONCERTO FOR TWO SOLO PIANOS (1932–5). As he continued to search for a new voice, Stravinsky invokes BEETHOVEN's own use of a model by Bach from the last movement of Piano Sonata No. 31 (op. 110). Other notable compositions on this path include two that have connections to Dumbarton Oaks – CONCERTO IN E♭: 'DUMBARTON OAKS' (1937–8) and SEPTET (1952–3). Stravinsky acknowledged the allusions to Bach's Brandenburg Concertos, in particular the third, in Concerto in E♭. Thematic linkages between Concerto in E♭ and Septet are also readily audible. More importantly, Stravinsky imitated Bach's contrapuntal style in the second and third movements of Septet – appropriately titled 'Passacaglia' and 'Gigue'. Bach's *Musical Offering* (BWV 1079) is likely to have influenced the framework of 'Ricercar I' and 'Ricercar II' of CANTATA (1951–2), Stravinsky probably having encountered ricercar form through the music of WEBERN, as we know that he had annotated his copy of Webern's transcription of Bach's 'Ricercar'.

In addition to the influence of Bach, Stravinsky also derived inspiration from other composers. It is commonly believed that the strongest influence for his OPERA RAKE'S PROGRESS (1947–51) was Mozart's *Così fan tutte*. His sketches for the PIANO SONATA (1924) contain an allusion to Mozart's Piano Sonata in A minor (K310). At this time in his compositional career, Stravinsky was renewing contact with Beethoven (*Auto*, 119), and the German composer's influence is apparent in the second movement of the Piano Sonata. When considering Stravinsky's reverence for Beethoven's *Thirty-three Variations on a Waltz by A. Diabelli*, op. 120 (T&C, 271), it is possible that his Adagietto might have been influenced by the thirty-first variation with the tempo marking 'Largo, molto espressivo'. A link is also commonly made between Chopin's Ballade No. 2 in F major, op. 38, and the 'Hymne' of the SERENADE IN A for piano (1925).

After completing *The Rake's Progress*, Stravinsky would embark on a path to abstraction, a shift from neo-classicism that had taken root with the

SYMPHONY IN THREE MOVEMENTS (1942–5) and BABEL (1944). As Stravinsky's compositional process would continue to evolve in his later works, where he began to echo the dodecaphonic techniques of Webern and KRENEK – in works such as CANTICUM SACRUM (1955) and THRENI (1957–8), the influence of Bach is more remote, but still present – Stravinsky indicates 'Fugato' in the sketches for VARIATIONS (ALDOUS HUXLEY IN MEMORIAM) (1963–4). His affinity for Bach continued even into the last few years of his life: he signed an arrangement of selections from Bach's *Well-Tempered Clavier* on 27 May 1969.

MAUREEN CARR

Pierre Boulez, *Stocktakings from an Apprenticeship*. Collected and presented by Paule Thévenin, trans. Stephen Walsh (Oxford: Clarendon Press, 1991).

Hermann Danuser (ed.), *Die klassizistische Moderne in der Musik des 20. Jahrhunderts, Internationale Symposium der Paul Sacher Stiftung Basel 1996* (Winterthur: Amadeus Press, 1997).

Michael Praetorius, *Syntagma musicum*, vol. III, trans. and ed. Jeffrey T. Kite-Powell (New York: Oxford University Press, 2004).

Thor Wood, interview with Soulima Stravinsky, February 1977, New York Public Library Performing Arts Division at Lincoln Center, MGZMT 5–563, accessed 23 May 2016.

Nestyev, Israel Vladimirovich (born Kerch, 4/17 April 1911; died Moscow, 9 April 1993). Soviet Russian musicologist – a noted scholar on PROKOFIEV. Lulled by what appeared to be strengthening relations between the allies after World War II, Nestyev had his first biography of Prokofiev published in the United States, so falling foul of Stalin's xenophobic postwar policy. In 1948, Nestyev was blacklisted (along with several other musicologists) by KHRENNIKOV for 'anti-patriotic, harmful activity, bent on undermining the ideological basis of Soviet music'. Nestyev henceforth presented the orthodox Soviet political and aesthetic line in his writings on music from abroad, and particularly by Stravinsky. Taking his cue from Khrennikov, Nestyev denounced Stravinsky – 'the shameless prophet of bourgeois modernism' ('Dollar cacophony' in *Izvestia*, 7 January 1951) – in several articles published in the 1950s, principally in *Sovetskaya Muzïka* where he was Deputy Editor (1954–9).

In 'Holy cacophony' (*Sovetskaya Muzïka*, February 1958), Nestyev attacked Stravinsky's TWELVE-NOTE serialism as displayed in CANTICUM SACRUM. This was partly a response to Stravinsky's dismissive comments on Soviet music in 'Answers to thirty-six questions' (posed by Robert CRAFT), first published as '35 Antworten auf 35 Fragen' in *Melos*, June 1957; then as 'Answers to 34 Questions' in *Encounter*, July 1957. (Stravinsky's 'Answers' subsequently reappeared in *Conversations with Igor Stravinsky*, published 1959, misleading some writers to assume the composer's anti-Soviet comments were in response to Nestyev's article rather than vice versa.)

When Stravinsky visited the USSR in 1962, Nestyev, who had since left *Sovetskaya Muzïka* to take a senior research position with the USSR Institute of Art History, published a long review of Stravinsky's Moscow concerts, 'Vechera Igorya Stravinskogo', in *Sovetskaya Muzïka*, December 1962: though ambivalent about ORPHEUS and ODE, he gave a warm welcome to The RITE OF SPRING, SYMPHONY IN THREE MOVEMENTS and CAPRICCIO. Without retracting his previously published comments, Nestyev conceded: 'we have not always taken the trouble to investigate his huge creative legacy, have not always managed carefully, thoughtfully to separate what was really valuable to us from all that was in decline, moribund, alien'.   DANIEL JAFFÉ

New York City Ballet. After DIAGHILEV'S BALLETS RUSSES, New York City Ballet (NYCB) became the principal exponent of Stravinsky ballets. The company grew organically from the modest AMERICAN BALLET (1935–), into Ballet Society (1946–), and then into the world-renowned troupe known today. From 1948, its home was New York's City Center, then, from 1964 until the present, the New York State Theater (now the David H. Koch Theater), at Lincoln Center. These developments were led by the American entrepreneur Lincoln KIRSTEIN, who had invited choreographer George BALANCHINE to move from Europe to develop a BALLET tradition in the US, first through the foundation of the School of American Ballet, and, later, through this series of companies. Kirstein himself remained General Director of NYCB until his retirement in 1989, whereupon he became General Director Emeritus. It is through this lineage too that Stravinsky's music was choreographed more frequently than that of any other composer (fifty-five premières in total).

Fundamentally, NYCB was George Balanchine's company: both he and Stravinsky were Russian émigrés, key contributors to the Ballets Russes, and eventually resident in the US, and they were close friends. It was only natural, therefore, for Stravinsky to be closely involved, continuing his artistic relationship with Balanchine, attending rehearsals and performances when in New York, and sometimes conducting performances there of his own work.

Important markers of Stravinsky's pre-eminence were the various festivals in his name over the years: in 1937, with the American Ballet (three ballets); after the composer's death in 1971, the most ambitious and widely acclaimed event, in 1972 (thirty-one ballets shown, twenty-two being premières); a third festival in 1982; then, after Balanchine's death in 1983, smaller festivals in 1999 and 2012.

To NYCB, Balanchine brought from Diaghilev his APOLLO (1928), and from Ballet Society, ORPHEUS (1948), returning to other scores that he had already choreographed, as well as embarking on fresh items. Many of these were to concert scores not written for dance. Beyond Balanchine's thirty-nine Stravinsky ballets, the NYCB Stravinsky story is short – a question of who used the few danceable scores that he had left untouched. Of the few who did, Jerome Robbins and John Taras stand out for undertaking a handful each. Then there are ten pieces by Peter Martins, a star dancer from the Royal Danish Ballet who joined NYCB in 1967 and was, from 1983 until 2018, ballet master and later Artistic Director. Certainly, there was an easing up of opportunity immediately after Stravinsky's death, with many new works appearing, new CHOREOGRAPHERS involved, as well as uses of Stravinsky's music that he might not have approved. Perhaps, after a while, however, the company felt that it had exhausted the Stravinsky scores that were acceptable for dance. Attention needed to turn to other composers after such an emphasis on just one. Since the millennium, there have been only two Stravinsky premières, both with choreography by Justin Peck, SCHERZO FANTASTIQUE (2016) and *Pulcinella Variations* (2017).

Long before this, however, it is important that the Stravinsky–Balanchine ballets had proved themselves central to the 'look' of NYCB, with its emblematic concentration on speed, economy, complex rhythmic values, a neo-classical tendency towards the abstract, and commitment to a contemporary American identity. A number of Stravinsky ballets (like Balanchine's AGON and MOVEMENTS and Robbins' REQUIEM CANTICLES) were dressed in practice clothes (leotards, short tunics) and made a virtue of large, sharp, athletic gesture. All these Stravinsky ballets were set to the composer's neo-classical and serial compositions. Famously, at the time of the 1982 Festival, Balanchine declared that there would be absolutely no place for settings of the Diaghilev 'Russian' ballets PETRUSHKA, The RITE OF SPRING or Les NOCES (nor were these pieces shown in 1972). Significantly, the NYCB revival of Jerome Robbins' internationally acclaimed Les Noces (1965, choreographed for American Ballet Theater) waited until after Balanchine's death.

Yet both Robbins and Taras demonstrated a narrative theatricality in their occasional contributions to the NYCB Stravinsky repertoire. Balanchine also brought them in to work alongside him in his own few dramatic explorations: Robbins for a 1970 production of The FIREBIRD (using the 1945 Suite, not the full ballet score) and the 1972 Pulcinella; Taras for PERSÉPHONE in 1982.

Robbins plays a distinctive role in the NYCB Stravinsky story. The composer was always respectful and careful to acknowledge the merit of his work; Robbins' association with Balanchine was important to him. Yet there are a surprising number of records of Robbins, or someone on his behalf, approaching the composer and being turned down, as was the case in 1960, for instance, with The Rite of Spring with the reduced ORCHESTRATION for the Royal Danish Ballet (which never happened), and a 1947 request to use Stravinsky's Orchestral Suites in a Ballet Theatre production – again dismissed, without clear reasons.

Robbins also received a rejection from the composer when he asked if he could use the SYMPHONY IN THREE MOVEMENTS in 1953. In a letter to Kirstein explaining his rejection of the idea, Stravinsky expanded, citing Robbins' now internationally celebrated The Cage (1951, to the CONCERTO IN D for strings) as the work that confirmed his unease about using his 'straight symphonic forms on the stage ... a matter of "plastic" incompatibility'. With its tale of an animal – or insect-like – tribe of women who prey on men, it is indeed astonishing that Stravinsky ever allowed his Concerto to be used in this way. He had already refused to conduct The Cage for NYCB the previous year, which would, he said, have been tantamount to 'sanctifying' the work. Still Robbins did not give up. He wrote again to Stravinsky in 1956, pressing whether he could use 'either or both' the Symphony in Three Movements and the CAPRICCIO. Instead, Balanchine eventually got both these scores, the Symphony after Stravinsky's death. Robbins' Les Noces was an exception.

The overwhelming evidence is that Balanchine and Martins as ballet masters assured the place of their own work in the repertory, to a degree far above that of their colleagues. One reason for this is quality of work, as judged by critical and audience success, but another is their power within the company hierarchy. Thirteen of the thirty-nine Balanchine works to Stravinsky still hold a regular place in the repertoire of NYCB – a number of these staged internationally – while a few others are occasionally revived or have been reconstructed. This is an outstanding statistic for any choreographer – over one-third of the Stravinsky works that he produced. There has also been no comparable composer dominance in any other ballet company. Today, this is history and Stravinsky's music maintains a heritage position within NYCB, but this is a heritage that nonetheless sustains its original dynamism, and its influence has spread to other ballet companies all over the world. STEPHANIE JORDAN

Lincoln Kirstein, *The New York City Ballet* (New York: Random House, 1973).
Nancy Reynolds, *Repertory in Review: 40 Years of the New York City Ballet* (New York: The Dial Press, 1977).

Nielsen, Carl (August) (born Sortelung, near Nørre Lyndelse, Funen, 9 June 1865; died Copenhagen, 3 October 1931). Danish composer, also conductor and violinist. Denmark's foremost composer, he wrote in almost every genre of the era and became best known for his symphonies. Nielsen took a curious interest in Stravinsky's works during the 1920s, which seemed to confirm aspects of his own still-evolving compositional style, although it remains unclear exactly which works Nielsen heard or what he really thought of them. Nielsen's Violin Concerto was programmed with excerpts from the Petrushka Suite in concert at the Danish Philharmonic Society (Dansk Filharmonisk Selskab) on 7 January 1925, with Nielsen in attendance. The two composers met later that year: on 2 December at a reception in Stravinsky's honour at the restaurant Nimb (in the Tivoli Gardens, Copenhagen), following a concert given by the Royal Danish Orchestra (Det Kongelige Kapel) which featured Stravinsky's new trio suite of The Soldier's Tale. An often-reproduced photograph shows them seated next to one another surrounded by members of the orchestra (SPD). Nielsen would complete his Sixth Symphony, 'Sinfonia semplice', ten days later, a work which bears not a few Stravinskian resemblances. JEREMY COLEMAN

Nightingale, The (Solovey; Le Rossignol). Lyrical tale in three acts. Composed in 1908–9, then in 1913–14. Libretto by Stepan Mitusov after The Nightingale by Hans Christian Andersen and the composer's indications. French version by Michel-Dimitri Calvocoressi, piano and vocal reduction by the composer, published Paris: Édition Russe de Musique / Max Eschig, 1914 (full score Édition Russe, 1923). First performance, 26 May 1914, Palais Garnier, with the choirs of the Moscow Opera and the Ballets Russes. Conductor, Pierre Monteux; staging (sets – décors) by Alexandre Benois; choreography by Boris Romanov.

(3, 3, 3, 3; 4, 4, 3, 1; timpani, percussion, piano, cel., harp, guitar and mandolin *ad. lib.*, strings)

The action in the five parts of Andersen's tale is reassembled into three acts of equal duration. The first act draws on the first part of the tale but in a highly contracted form. At night in his boat, the fisherman (tenor) delights in hearing the melodious song of the nightingale (coloratura soprano). The court arises, guided by a young cook (soprano), and persuades the bird to come to sing for the Emperor of China (bass). The second act combines and synthesises the following three parts of the tale which take place in the imperial palace. The nightingale enchants the Emperor but finds itself supplanted by a mechanical nightingale sent by the Emperor of Japan. The real nightingale takes advantage of the interest aroused by the song of the music box in order to flee, and the Emperor of China consequently banishes him. The third act corresponds to the last part of the tale. Death (contralto) comes to take the Emperor, but the nightingale returns to sing, seduces Death and sends it back to its dwelling; the Emperor who is saved wishes to thank the nightingale, who declines, preferring his freedom, but promising to return. The Emperor greets his courtesans and, while the curtain falls, one hears the voice of the fisherman enunciating the moral of the tale on a double-reed motif recalling that of the fiddle from the last song of Schubert's *Winterreise*.

The *Nightingale*, Stravinsky's first OPERA, belongs to his initial period of collaboration with the Ballets Russes, through which he became part of an epoch of profound change in the history of music. Stravinsky had met Stepan Mitusov, one of those he described as 'enlightened amateurs of the most advanced views' (*Auto*, 17), at RIMSKY-KORSAKOV's home in 1902. Mitusov was, by his own admission, a fairly lazy student. Stravinsky was at that time passionate about the creation of the review *Mir Iskoustva* by Diaghilev, and the foundation of the 'Society of Contemporary Music' by POKROVSKY, Nouvel and Nurok. It was there that he discovered the chamber music of Franck, D'Indy and Chabrier, whose comic operas he appreciated already; and Fauré, Dukas and DEBUSSY, in whom he tasted 'the awe-inspiring freedom and freshness of the métier'. He composed part of *The Nightingale* in the summer of 1908; Rimsky-Korsakov would have heard and approved some extracts from the first act at the piano just before his death. Not long afterwards, Stravinsky was caught up in the enthusiasm surrounding his first collaborations with the Ballets Russes, the ORCHESTRATION of the two piano pieces by Chopin for *Les Sylphides*, a BALLET given in the course of the 1909 season. He resumed work on *The Nightingale* during the summer of 1909, but was forced to stop once again as Diaghilev commissioned *The FIREBIRD* from him for the 1910 season at the Opéra de Paris. It is interesting to note that the atmosphere in the first scene of *The Nightingale* imitates that of the lullaby in *The Firebird*. A commission from the Free Theatre of Moscow at the end of autumn 1913 put him back on track. Stravinsky offered the first act as the complete work, but the theatre authorities refused and asked instead for three scenes. Conscious of the evolution of his musical writing since the composition of the first part, Stravinsky made a kind of prologue out of it, before producing the other two rather different acts. He composed the second at CLARENS during the winter of 1913–14, followed by the third at Leysin at the beginning of 1914. However, after the bankruptcy of the Free Theatre of Moscow, Diaghilev proposed to Stravinsky that they produce *The Nightingale* as an alternative with the Ballets Russes, since he had already engaged the singers for *The Golden Cockerel*. The composer accepted. After a concert performance at the Hôtel Continental with the composer at the piano, Diaghilev proposed an opera–ballet version of the work to the Opéra de Paris for 26 and 28 May 1914, in which the dancers mimed the roles, the Russian text being sung in the orchestral pit.

At the beginning of 1917, Diaghilev asked Stravinsky to transform his opera into a ballet – the project brought together MASSINE and Matisse – and the composer adapted the music of the second and third acts into a 'Symphonic Poem'. The SONG OF THE NIGHTINGALE was premièred in concert in Geneva by ANSERMET on 6 December 1919. While Stravinsky found that the choreographic dimension detracted from the work's refinement, it was nevertheless given as a ballet, before the triumphant performance of 2 February 1920 at the Opéra de Paris during the Ballets Russes season.

Influenced by the operas of Rimsky-Korsakov, The Nightingale displays an orchestral richness comparable to that of The RITE OF SPRING, but its vocalisations relate it to the French opera of the last third of the nineteenth century (Ambroise Thomas' Hamlet and Léo Delibes' Lakmé). MUSSORGSKY and Debussy nourished Stravinsky's harmonic inspiration – notably his use of augmented seconds, parallel intervals, pentatonic melodies – but also his orchestral means (tremolos, muted brass, doublings).

According to Stravinsky, 'the première was unsuccessful only in the sense that it failed to create a scandal ... visually ... it was the most beautiful of all my early Diaghilev works' (Mem, 132). The principal obstacle facing performance of The Nightingale is its brevity, at 45 minutes, in view of the means it requires; three scenes (décors) and lavish costumes. The opera, however, has had continuous success. It was given in London (1914 and 1919), in Rome (1916), in ST PETERSBURG in a staging by Meyerhold (1918), in Leningrad (1920), in German in Mannheim (1923), in New York and in Italian in Milan, conducted by the composer (both 1926), where the orchestral score, which was lost during one of the rehearsals, was finally recovered in an antique store where the thief tried to sell it! The work was next given in Buenos Aires and Berlin (1927), in Prague and Trieste (1935), and in Genoa (1937). After the war, there were productions in Palermo (1951), The Hague (1952), Cologne (1960), Rome (1962), Brussels (1964), Vienna and Mexico (1967), Amsterdam (1969), Cambridge (1970), London (1972) and Santa Fe (1983). Also notable, among others, were the touring productions of La Fenice of Venice, in a production by Jacques Demy (1972–6); of the Metropolitan Opera, with scenery by David Hockney (1981–7); of the THÉÂTRE DU CHÂTELET in a production by Stanislas Nordey under the direction of Pierre BOULEZ (1997); or again that of the Festival d'Aix-en-Provence in association with the opera companies of Toronto, Lyon and Amsterdam, in a production by Robert Lepage (2010–15).

CÉCILE AUZOLLE

Daniel Albright, Stravinsky: The Music Box and the Nightingale (New York: Gordon and Breach, 1989).
Igor Stravinsky, 'Le Rossignol', L'Avant-scène opéra, 174 (1995), 52–83.

Nijinska, Bronislava Fominishna (properly Nijinskaya) (born Minsk, 8 January 1891; died Los Angeles, 21 February 1972). Russian dancer, CHOREOGRAPHER and teacher. A student of Enrico CECCHETTI, Nijinska studied at the Imperial Theatre School in ST PETERSBURG and graduated into the MARIINSKY THEATRE in 1908. Like her brother Vaslav NIJINSKY, she danced with the BALLETS RUSSES from 1909. Of the Stravinsky ballets in the company's early seasons, Nijinska was an Enchanted Princess in the first production of The

FIREBIRD (1910), a Street Dancer in the first PETRUSHKA (1911), and she was Nijinsky's intended Chosen One for The RITE OF SPRING (1913) – she withdrew upon announcing her pregnancy, and Maria PILTZ created the role. In 1912, Stravinsky referred to her as 'a very great talent . . . an enchanting ballerina full worthy of her brother' (SRT, 982–3).

After a period in Petrograd (St Petersburg), where she began choreograph-ing and teaching (Serge LIFAR was a pupil), Nijinska returned to the Ballets Russes as choreographer (1921–5). In 1922, she staged the first performance of RENARD (dancing the Fox herself) and the one-act OPERA MAVRA. The following year, she choreographed her most important BALLET, the first pro-duction of Les NOCES. Stravinsky later claimed her Renard and Noces pleased him more than any other Ballets Russes production of his works (Mem, 40). In 1928, she joined the newly formed BALLETS IDA RUBINSTEIN and created The FAIRY'S KISS. In addition to Stravinsky premières, Nijinska danced the role of the Ballerina in Petrushka for the Ballets Russes, created a short duet called Jazz to Stravinsky's RAGTIME score in 1925 (Margate, UK), and, for the Teatro Colón in Buenos Aires, staged FOKINE's choreography of Petrushka and choreographed dance scenes for The NIGHTINGALE. SOPHIE REDFERN

Nijinsky, Vaslav Fomich (born possibly Kiev, ?1888–91; died London, 8 April 1950). Russian-born dancer and CHOREOGRAPHER. Nijinsky trained at the Imperial Theatre School in ST PETERSBURG, graduated into the MARIINSKY THEATRE in 1907, and was the most famous and celebrated dancer of DIAGHILEV's BALLETS RUSSES between 1909 and 1913. Also Diaghilev's lover during this period, he was a regular presence at the impresario's side and it was at a meeting with Diaghilev in 1909 that Stravinsky first encountered the dancer.

Stravinsky's earliest dealings with Diaghilev and the Ballets Russes often involved Nijinsky: the dancer starred in Les Sylphides (1909), a BALLET with a cobbled-together score of Chopin orchestrated by various composers, including Stravinsky; he performed a show piece at a Mariinsky ball in St Petersburg (20 February / 5 March 1910) to Stravinsky's orchestration of Grieg's Lyric Pieces, op. 71 No. 3, 'Kobold', and he was frequently at meetings related to the creation of The FIREBIRD (1910), though he had no direct involvement in the ballet. Nevertheless, the first major artistic venture was PETRUSHKA (1911). Nijinsky was cast as the title character and it became one of his most iconic roles. It was the only Stravinsky part he created as a dancer, and his interpretation of Mikhail FOKINE's choreography was widely lauded: Fokine claimed he never saw it bettered (Fokine 1961, 193), while Stravinsky praised Nijinsky's 'unsurpassed rendering of the role' (Auto, 34).

Their next connection was The RITE OF SPRING (1913). Nijinsky had been elevated to the position of choreographer at the Ballets Russes despite no choreographic experience (following internal disputes within the company). It took him more than 100 rehearsals to set the ballet (he turned to DALCROZE's eurhythmics) and the collaboration with Stravinsky was often fraught: the composer had strong choreographic ideas and regularly inter-vened (Marie RAMBERT remembered the composer raging when it became apparent tempos had slowed to allow for the choreography). When the ballet finally made it to the stage of the THÉÂTRE DES CHAMPS-ELYSÉES for the infamous première, Nijinsky and Stravinsky watched from the wings. The composer remembered Nijinsky standing on a chair shouting counts to the dancers.

Stravinsky's view of Nijinsky's choreography for the Rite changed dramatically over his lifetime. He defended it in 1913, claiming 'We never for a second failed to be in absolute communion of thought' (Gil Blas, 4 June 1913, in Kelly 2000, 329), and described it in a letter to Max STEINBERG as 'incomparable. With the exception of a few places everything is as I wanted it' (SPD, 102). However, by Stravinsky's 1936 autobiography, a string of criticisms (both artistic and personal) were laid at the choreographer's proverbial door: Nijinsky 'complicated and encumbered his dances beyond all reason' (Auto, 41), and 'became presumptuous, capricious, and unmanageable' (Auto, 42). The composer maintained this stance over the proceeding decades (see Mem, 37–8, and Expo, 140–3), and yet Bronislava NIJINSKA claimed that, in 1967, Stravinsky told Yuri Grigorovich: 'Of all the interpretations of Sacre that I have seen, I consider Nijinsky's the best' (Nijinska, 1981, 471).

Whatever his subsequent view, it was their last collaboration. Later in 1913, the Ballets Russes went on tour. There, without Diaghilev present, Nijinsky married and was promptly expelled from the company, with only a brief return. His dismissal compelled Stravinsky to write to Alexandre BENOIS, 'For me the hope of seeing something valuable in choreography has been removed for a long time to come' (SPD, 512). Soon the mental health problems that largely confined Nijinsky to institutions for the rest of his life became apparent. Stravinsky and Nijinsky never worked together again. As Stravinsky stated in 1936, fourteen years before Nijinsky died, 'his name belongs to history' (Auto, 42).   SOPHIE REDFERN

Richard Buckle, Nijinsky, 3rd edn (London: Weidenfeld and Nicolson, 1980).
Mikhail Fokine, Memoirs of a Ballet Master, trans. Vitale Fokine, ed. Anatole Chujoy (London: Constable, 1961).
Thomas Forrest Kelly, First Nights: Five Musical Premieres (New Haven and London: Yale University Press, 2000).
Bronislava Nijinska, Early Memoirs, trans. Irina Nijinska and Jean Rawlinson (London and Boston: Faber and Faber, 1981).

Nikitina, Yevgeniya (Zhenya/Eugénie/Génia) (born Russia, ?). Russian dancer. Classically trained Nikitina beguiled audiences at Nikita Baliyev's Le Théâtre de la Chauve-Souris, a Parisian Russian-led cabaret-cum-avant-garde-theatre which had Sergey Sudeykin and Nicolas REMISOFF as designers. Then starring as the polka-dancing title role in the Chauve-Souris's most popular entertainment, Katinka, Nikitina – memorably described by Artur Rubinstein as 'the most voluptuous blonde imaginable' (SCS, 326) – met Stravinsky in early 1921. The composer was reportedly soon besotted and they are believed to have had a brief affair. At her request for a work, Stravinsky orchestrated the polka from the THREE EASY PIECES for her, adding in a new opening and a coda referencing the music of Katinka (heard in his SUITE No. 2 for Small Orchestra).   SOPHIE REDFERN

Les Noces (Svadebka; The Wedding). A BALLET–cantata written for SATB chorus, four soloists, four pianos and percussion. Words freely adapted from a 1911 supplement to the anthology of folklore texts by Pyotr Kireyevsky (1808–56). French translation by Charles Ferdinand RAMUZ. Composed 1914–17; final ORCHESTRATION 1923. First performance, 13 June 1923, BALLETS RUSSES, Théâtre de la Gaieté Lyrique, PARIS. Conductor, Ernest ANSERMET; choreographer, Bronislava NIJINSKA. Vocal score by the composer, published 1922, J. & W. Chester; full score published 1923, J. & W. Chester (revised and corrected, ed. Margarita Mazo, 2005). Duration c. 24 min. Dedicated to S. DIAGHILEV.

"'Little Wedding'", wrote Stravinsky, 'would be the best English equivalent if "little" can be made to mean not "small" but "peasant"' (*Expo*, 114 n.1).

Conceived as early as 1912, *Les Noces* was the culmination of Stravinsky's so-called Russian period, which started with *The* FIREBIRD in 1910 and ended with MAVRA in 1922. The work's significance is reflected in its unusually long and difficult gestation. Largely composed in SWITZERLAND, the country of Stravinsky's forced exile during World War I, it was sketched following a short trip Stravinsky made to Ukraine (USTILUG and Kiev) in July 1914, with the purpose of consulting lawyers about his family property in view of the coming war (which eventually would cut Stravinsky from his home country for good). There he found the Kireyevsky volume which supplemented books by Sakharov and Tereshchenko from his father's library. The composer spent the rest of the summer in Salvan and CLARENS on Lake Geneva, choosing suitable texts for the projected work. This is when Stravinsky made his 'rejoicing discovery' (*Expo*, 121) that verbal accents were freely altered by folk singers; this discovery had a decisive impact on the emergence of his newly found stylistic idiom (Lupishko 2007). In his AUTOBIOGRAPHY, the composer suggests that *Pribaoutki* (1914), *Berceuses du chat* (1915) and *Four Russian Peasant Songs* (1914–17) were all composed after he had selected the text material for *Les Noces* (*Auto*, 54–5). The significance of these experimental vocal cycles as preparatory work for *Les Noces* – they also include *Three Children's Tales* (1915–17) and the stage work RENARD (1915–16) – is difficult to overestimate.

Stravinsky sketched a preliminary three-act scenario and finished most of the first tableau by November 1914. In February and April 1915, Diaghilev heard the first, second and some of the third tableau and hoped to stage it in Paris the following summer; however, the ongoing war and Diaghilev's hesitancy, in the circumstances given, to take a financial risk by staging another modernist ballet by Stravinsky made this project unrealisable for several years. By August 1915, two-thirds of the work was composed in short score, but soon thereafter *Les Noces* would be interrupted for several months in favour of *Renard*. Stravinsky worked on the last tableau during the summer of 1917 in Les Diablerets; later that year, Ramuz, assisted by the composer, completed the translation of the text into French. The work was completed in short score on 11 October 1917 in MORGES.

The instrumental evolution of *Les Noces* went through at least three distinct versions. The first, begun in 1917, was scored for a large chamber orchestra of some forty solo instruments (strings, woodwinds, harpsichord, cymbalom and harp). The second, dating from 1919 (tableaux 1 and 2), featured a harmonium, two cimbaloms, a pianola and percussion. Stravinsky was pleased with this version but worried that the rarity of cymbalom players and the need to synchronise the mechanical piano (pianola) with conventional instruments would make performance impractical. The final minimalist orchestration, four pianos and a percussion ensemble of six groups, 'perfectly homogeneous, perfectly impersonal, and perfectly mechanical' (Expo, 118), was not completed until the end of May 1923, within days of Les Noces' première in Paris (SCS, 365, 630 n.61).

The libretto of Les Noces, eclectically put together by the composer from about fifty geographically dispersed wedding folk song texts, mainly from Kireyevsky (1911), is a great achievement in its own right. It reflects, very selectively, the traditional order of the peasant wedding RITUAL. Stravinsky used full song texts and fragments, inserting archaisms and dialect words, onomatopoeia and excla-mations, freely modifying the shape of the texts according to his musical needs. From the same source, the composer obtained the description of the wedding ritual itself, which he inserted into Svadebka as stage directions (figures 1, 80, 81, 82, 98, 114, 126, 130, 134). The anthologies of Tereshchenko and Sakharov also contained an exposition of the peasant wedding ritual and a number of wedding folk song texts on which Stravinsky drew, relying as well on various related entries in Vladimir Dahl's Explanatory Dictionary of the Living Great Russian Language (SRT, II, 1324–54; Table IV, 1422–40).

A typical Russian folk wedding ritual, long and laborious, consists of two parts: (1) from the matchmaking ceremonies and the shaking of hands to the morning of the wedding day (the church ceremony); and (2) from the morning of the wedding day to the end of all the festivities (Birkan 1966, 242) – as much as three weeks can elapse from start to finish. Earlier drafts of Les Noces's scenario that included a more complete ritual were abandoned in favour of a succinct two-part structure that represents the events of a single wedding day. The first part comprises the first three tableaux. The first tableau shows the devichnik, a kind of bridal shower that usually takes place on the eve of the wedding; here it is mixed with the ritual of re-plaiting the bride's single braid on the morning of the wedding day into the pair of braids that married women wore arranged in a circle around the head. Tableau II, the combing and dressing of the groom and his parents' blessing, takes place at exactly the same time as the events of the first tableau. The third tableau depicts the wedding 'train' that comes from the grooms' to take the bride to church after the bride's parents, who remain at home, have blessed her. The second part consists of tableau IV that shows the krasny stol, or festive celebration at the groom's, just after the religious ceremony. The actual church ceremony is missing from the libretto, notwithstanding Stravinsky's later statement: 'Les Noces is also – per-haps even primarily – a product of the Russian church' (Expo, 115). That omission, along with the detached attitude of the author towards the subject ('with no hint of disapproval or regret' at the violent upheaval that marriage represented for the bride: Walsh 1988, 85), hints at the hidden conflict of the drama and brings to mind Viktor Shklovsky's term ostranenie ('estrangement') of 1917: a purely modernist artistic procedure of making the familiar appear strange.

Les Noces differs from Renard and the vocal cycles of the same period in that its texts are song texts, not fairytales or spoken verses such as pribaoutki.

Stravinsky could hardly have heard all these songs performed live, although he frequented southern and western parts of the Russian Empire in the 1890s–1900s and might have heard Russian, Ukrainian or Jewish wedding folk songs. Except for one peasant song (referred to as a 'factory song' in Mem, 97) at Figure 110 (bar 3), 'Ne vesyolaya da kompan'itsa' from the 1894 Istomin-Dyutsh collection of Russian folk songs, passed on to the composer by Stepan Mitusov (SRT, II, 1372), he does not cite any folk melodies. There is an adapted citation from the collection of Russian Orthodox liturgical hymns Octoechos (Figure 50, top voice), identified by Robert Craft (SRT, II, 1378). The tendency for 'progressive abstraction' (SRT, II, 1320) – which is expressed, for example, in the composer's fascination with the purely sonic side of the text material (Auto, 53), in his avoidance of portrayal of romantic feelings and in the dissociation of the four singers from individual roles – is comparable to similar processes in the contemporary Russian and European avant-garde, and anticipates Stravinsky's later NEO-CLASSICISM. Yet all the more striking is the mystical impression of déjà-vu – or, rather, déjà-entendu – made by this work on many Russian listeners, including Diaghilev, who burst into tears when he first heard it played on the piano by the composer himself (Expo, 118); Serge Lifar, who reflected on the cathartic and evocative powers of Les Noces during the musical rehearsal at Princess de Polignac's in 1923 (Lifar 2005, 419–20); and Boris de Schloezer, who called it 'the most human of all Stravinsky's works' (SCS, 366–7). Despite all Stravinsky's anti-programmatic stances in Autobiography (Auto, 53–4), what touches Russian listeners in Les Noces is the subject matter: the drama not only of the bride's destiny but of that of the peasant wedding itself – 'the apotheosis . . . of the old folk rite', destined to disappear slowly into oblivion (Belyayev 1972, 88). In Les Noces, the composer was able to plumb the deepest layers of the Russian spirit in the broadest sense of the word (including its Ukrainian and Jewish overtones), to capture its 'collective unconscious'.

In his analysis of the song texts used by Stravinsky, Rafail Birkan, relying on Asafyev (1982 (Glebov 1929)), establishes the four main genres that constitute the traditional folk wedding ritual: (1) laments; (2) the liturgical element (incantations of the saints); (3) wedding praise songs; and (4) humorous songs. Each of these genres plays its special role in the libretto. The main trajectory of the ritual itself is suggested by the progression from laments in the first part to humorous songs in the second (Birkan 1971, 172). Traditionally, different types of folk lamentations (lament, sobbing, wailing) were sung by the bride and/or by specially trained older women during the first part of the wedding only (Mazo 1990, 121–3). We observe a similar procedure in Les Noces: the first part is based on various laments of the bride and her girlfriends, as well as of the parents on both sides, and on reiterated incantations and spells – the remnants of paganism – of the Holy Virgin, God and the patron saints Luke, Cosmas and Damian. The humorous element first appears in the second tableau (Figure 41) and dominates the wedding feast in the fourth tableau.

In the music, there is a preference for archaic trichordal modal structures (a major second and a minor third within a perfect fourth), characteristic of the most ancient genres – laments and incantations. Such a structure appears first in the popevka (melodic cell) b-d-e in the initial lament of the bride, 'Kosa l'' moya', complete with the 'sobbing' grace-note f♯. This harmonic structure underlies the first tableau, shifting a major second upwards, c♯-e-f♯, in the consolation songs of the bridesmaids, 'Ne klich', ne klich', lebyodushka' (Figure 9), and reappears continuously in different places in Les Noces, e.g. in the third (Figure 65) and in the fourth tableaux (Figure 94). Descending semitones f♯-f-e, characteristic of sobbing laments and wails, are used in the bride's exclamation 'Okho-kho!' (2 bars before Figure 2) and in the refrain of the bridesmaids, 'Chesu-pochesu' (Figure 2). The harmonic basis of the groom's parents' lamentations (Figures 35–6) in the second tableau is an octatonic scale 'tone-semitone': c-d♭-e♭-e-f♯-g. The lament of both mothers at the end of the third tableau is also related to this scale (Figure 82). In the fourth tableau, the Dionysian atmosphere of the wedding feast is achieved by a constant juxtaposition of asymmetrical rhythms, vocal timbres, registers and masses of sound. The energy rises to its climax fff at the glorification of the nuptial bed at Figure 130, 'Pastel'ya moya karavatushka' (a Dorian mode based on b), and ends abruptly at the intimate address of the groom to the bride, which is based on a transposed bridal lament popevka g♯-b-c♯ (Figure 133). The only lyrical moment of the entire work, it is followed by a coda of twenty-two bars, imitative of bell-ringing.

The principle of motivic variation, related to the lexical and metrical peculiarities of the folk language, is the main method of melodic development in Les Noces. It evokes the term 'the technique of building blocks', taken from an interview given by the composer in Barcelona in 1928 (quoted in ISPS, 83). As in folklore, elements of the Russian folk language function here as a kind of oral notation of musical-rhythmic motives: words are put together each time in a slightly different order, producing semantically similar, but accentually, metrically and rhythmically different phrases and sentences (Lupishko 2013). This musical 'constructivism' (to use a term that would be coined in Moscow in 1921) was in line with the choreographic vision of it by Bronislava Nijinska who found the key to the ballet's performance at the crossroads of its archaic and modernist traits.

The younger sister of Vaslav NIJINSKY, Bronislava left the Ballets Russes at around the same time as her brother and returned to RUSSIA in 1913. In 1921, having heard of Bronislava's pedagogical success in Kiev, where she opened her own École de mouvement in 1919, Diaghilev invited her to work in Paris, where she became the only female choreographer in the history of his company. After her staging of Renard in 1922, Diaghilev invited Nijinska to put Les Noces on stage in the spring of 1922, but conflict ensued over the existing costumes and décor by Natalya GONCHAROVA, which by that time had gone through different versions and which Bronislava rejected because they were not sufficiently abstract (Ratanova 1999, 19–20). Diaghilev returned to the project in 1923, three months before the première, this time embracing Nijinska's vision of the choreography wholeheartedly and asking Stravinsky to be present at all rehearsals (the decisive argument for the impresario, says Boris KOCHNO, was Nijinska's comparison of her vision of a static ballet to Byzantine mosaics, which Diaghilev adored: Kochno 1973, 189). Nijinska the choreographer rejected elevation and soloists, and gave preference to the geometrically arranged masses of corps-de-ballet dancers, 'amazingly few movement-motives' used in different combinations (Denby 1986, 37), as well as unusual body positions such as arched arms and crossed legs as a symbolic representation of the ritual of re-plaiting of the braid. The white and brown costumes of the final minimalist version of Goncharova's designs borrowed the idea of the ballet dancers' working uniform at rehearsals. The almost empty stage, with the four pianos arranged at the four corners of it and with the schematically drawn parts of the interior – windows or the bed of the newly weds – on a light backdrop, complemented well the modernist choreography. The première of the ballet-cantata at the Théâtre de la Gaieté Lyrique in Paris on 13 June 1923 was a complete and well-deserved success, a 'perfectly well-balanced' trio of music, design and choreography (Goncharova 1979, 142).   MARINA LUPISHKO

Viktor Belyayev, Musorgskiy, Skryabin, Stravinskiy: sbornik statey (Moscow: Muzïka, 1972 (1928)), trans. into English as Igor Stravinsky's 'Les Noces': An Outline by S. W. Pring (London: Oxford University Press, 1928).

Rafail Birkan, 'O poeticheskom texte "Svadebki" Igorya Stravinskogo' ('On the poetic text of Igor Stravinsky's "Svadebka"'), in Russkaya muzïka na rubezhe XX veka ('Russian Music at the Beginning of the Twentieth Century') (Moscow and Leningrad: Muzïka, 1966), 239–51.

Rafail Birkan, 'O tematizme "Svadebki"' ('On the thematic material of "Svadebka"'), in Iz istorii muzïki XX veka ('From the Twentieth-Century Music History') (Moscow: Muzïka, 1971), 169–88.

Edwin Denby, Dance Writings (New York: Knopf, 1986).

Igor Glebov, Kniga o Stravinskom (Leningrad: Triton, 1929), Engl. trans. Richard French as Boris Asafyev, A Book about Stravinsky (Ann Arbor: UMI Research Press, 1982).

Natalya Goncharova, 'The metamorphoses of the ballet "Les noces"', Leonardo, 12 (1979), 137–43.

Pyotr Kireyevsky, Pesni, sobrannye P. V. Kireyevskim. Novaya seriya ('Songs, Collected by P. V. Kireyevsky. A New Series'), vol. I: Pesni obryadovye ('Ritual Songs'). Ed. V. F. Miller and M. N. Speransky (Moscow University, 1911).

Boris Kochno, Diaghilev et les Ballets Russes (Paris: Fayard, 1973).

Serge Lifar, Dyagilev i s Dyagilevym ('Diaghilev and with Diaghilev') (Moscow: Vagrius, 2005).

Marina Lupishko, 'The "rejoicing discovery" revisited: re-accentuation in Russian folklore and Stravinsky's music', ex tempore: A Journal of Compositional and Theoretical Research in Music, 13.2 (2007), 1–36.

Marina Lupishko, 'Stravinsky's Svadebka (1917–1923) as the quintessence of the technique of "building blocks"', in C. Flamm, H. Keazor and R. Marti (eds.,) Russian Émigré Culture: Conservatism or Evolution? (Cambridge Scholars Publishing, 2013), 179–202.

Margarita Mazo, 'Stravinsky's Les Noces and Russian village wedding ritual', Journal of American Musicological Society, 43 (1990), 99–142.

Maria Ratanova, 'Bronislava Nijinskaya – v teni legendy o brate' ('Bronislava Nijinska, in the shadow of her brother's legend'), preface to B. Nijinska, Rannie vospominaniya ('Early Memoirs'). 2 vols., vol. I (Moscow: ART, 1999), 5–61.

Stephen Walsh, The Music of Stravinsky (London: Routledge, 1988).

Nostalgia. A portmanteau word, 'nostalgia' brings together two Greek roots: nostos ('the return home') and algia ('longing'). Interestingly, although it has the appearance of a term from Greek antiquity, its origins are much more recent. It was coined by the Swiss physician Johannes Hofer in his medical dissertation of 1688. Hofer was interested in naming the melancholic homesickness displayed by Swiss soldiers fighting abroad and coined this new term because he felt it was possible 'from the force of the sound Nostalgia to define the sad mood originating from the desire for return to one's native land'.

For much of its history, nostalgia has been held in derision. Critics have often seen this fascination with the past as suspect on many different levels. They have styled it as emotionally sentimental, aesthetically kitschy and politically reactionary. This is particularly true of aesthetic philosophy during the modernist period. Key critics, such as Clement Greenberg and Theodor ADORNO, radically rejected an interest in the past and dismissed it as badly out of step with the avant-garde tendencies of the most advanced contemporary art.

In his *Philosophy of New Music*, Adorno personified these two tendencies of modern art. The drive to experimentalism and innovation he identified with SCHOENBERG, while the nostalgic reanimation of the past he associated with Stravinsky. Adorno titles his chapter on the Russian composer 'Stravinsky and restoration', a damning assessment given that the philosopher asserted that 'restoration is as much in vain in philosophy as elsewhere'.

There is some merit in Adorno's characterisation of Stravinsky as a composer turned towards the past. From the time of World War I (and arguably even earlier than that), Stravinsky's work emerged out of a deep engagement with musical and cultural history. It is possible, for example, to see The RITE OF SPRING, with its representation of pre-Christian Slavic fertility RITUAL, as a work looking back nostalgically to pre-modern times. However, because of its radical primitivist style, this work has been seen as nostalgic less often than the composer's later work.

It was in the period around World War I that Stravinsky began to explore and engage with the musical traditions of the past much more openly and explicitly (a process he later characterised as 'kleptomania'). The key work in this respect is PULCINELLA, a BALLET COLLABORATION for Sergey DIAGHILEV'S BALLETS RUSSES. Léonide MASSINE transformed a COMMEDIA DELL' ARTE play titled *The Four Identical Pulcinellas* (1700) into a ballet scenario, and Stravinsky was asked to arrange a series of fragments attributed to the eighteenth-century Neapolitan composer Giovanni Battista PERGOLESI. While he initially resisted what he saw as menial labour, this experience came to be very important to the composer.

With *Pulcinella*, Stravinsky turned quite explicitly to a kind of NEO-CLASSICISM. In this he was not alone. Modernists in many different media, many of whom participated in the cosmopolitan avant-garde community of PARIS, began to explore the possibilities of a return to classicism. In the visual arts, PICASSO returned to legible figuration and Hellenic motifs, while in literature both Guillaume Apollinaire and Jean COCTEAU penned treatises that argued for the need to return to the conventions of the classical past. In diverse works such as OEDIPUS REX, APOLLON MUSAGÈTE and PERSÉPHONE, Stravinsky explored what a return to seventeenth- and eighteenth-century neo-classicism might mean for twentieth-century music.

The critical literature on this classical turn in Stravinsky and others has been varied and contentious. As mentioned above, Adorno has been the most explicitly hostile critic. For Adorno, Stravinsky's turn back to the masters of the past appeared to be 'regression', and a capitulation to authority and order that uncomfortably echoed the totalitarian turn of the twentieth century. This is a characterisation that resonates with what the literary critic Svetlana Boym has called 'restorative nostalgia'. According to Boym:

restorative nostalgia puts emphasis on nostos and proposes to rebuild the lost home and patch up memory gaps ... restorative nostalgia manifests itself in total reconstructions of monuments of the past ... This kind of nostalgia characterizes national and nationalist revivals all over the world, which engage in the anti-modern myth-making of history by means of a return to national symbols and myths and, occasionally, through swapping conspiracy theories. (Boym 2001, 41)

With its monumentality and de-individualisation, and its use of Greek myth and Ciceronian Latin, it is perhaps possible to look at Stravinsky's *Oedipus Rex* as a manifestation of this restorative nostalgia.

However, Boym is at pains to argue that this is just one inflection of nostalgia, and not nostalgia *tout court*. In her morphology, reactionary restorative nostalgia is balanced or challenged by 'reflective nostalgia' – a much more whimsical, self-conscious and destabilising turn to the past. While restorative nostalgia is obsessed with *nostos*, reflective nostalgia 'dwells in algia, in longing and loss, the imperfect process of remembering ... [it] lingers on ruins, the patina of time and history, in the dreams of another place and another time'. This ironic nostalgia is perhaps what we see and hear in works such as *Pulcinella*. With its invocation of the carnivalesque *Commedia dell'arte* tradition, masquerade and disruption of Western classicism by eastern European musical styles, this work is anything but a pious attempt to resuscitate the culture of the past.

Far from being a naïve, or straightforwardly dubious, attempt at restoration, then, Stravinsky's forays into the past are just as divided and complex as the concept of nostalgia itself.   IHOR JUNYK

Svetlana Boym, *The Future of Nostalgia* (New York: Basic Books, 2001).

Ocampo, (Ramona) Victoria (Epifanía Rufina) (born Buenos Aires, 7 April 1890; died Buenos Aires, 27 January 1979). Essayist, translator and patron. Having been in the audience for the 1913 première of The RITE OF SPRING, Ocampo first met Stravinsky in 1932. Four years later, she invited him to ARGENTINA, leading to his first South American tour. She participated as the narrator in performances of PERSÉPHONE in Buenos Aires and in Rio de Janeiro, and again in 1939 in Florence. They remained friends, meeting socially in PARIS, New York, and again in Buenos Aires in 1960 (Stravinsky's visit to MEXICO and South America in that year having stemmed, once again, from her personal invitation). Ocampo wrote extensively about Stravinsky's music between 1927 and 1977, not least for the literary journal Sur, which she founded in 1931. She facilitated Stravinsky's career both in Argentina and farther afield; it was through her that Stravinsky first met Aldous HUXLEY in 1934.   CHRIS COLLINS

Omar Corrado, 'Victoria Ocampo y la música: una experiencia social y estética de la modernidad', Revista Musical Chilena, 61.208 (December 2007), 37–68.
Tamara Levitz, 'Igor the Angeleno: the Mexican connection', in SHW, 141–76.
Dial, 218; SSE, 42–50

Octet (Octuor) for Wind Instruments. Composed 1919–23. First performance, 18 October 1923, PARIS. Conductor, Igor Stravinsky. Published 1924, Édition Russe de Musique. Dedicated to Vera de Bosset (see Vera STRAVINSKY). Revised and corrected version, 1952, Boosey & Hawkes.

This is generally regarded as the first neo-classical work by Stravinsky. This reputation is supported by the fact that Stravinsky himself commented on it in his first theoretical manifesto ('Some ideas about my Octet') in terms of rationality and objectivity, which have subsequently become part of the history of NEO-CLASSICISM. Be that as it may, the musical qualities of the Octet, the contrapuntal density and the importance of formal and thematic construction, continue (and undeniably deepen) the direction of travel in preceding works such as SYMPHONIES OF WIND INSTRUMENTS and MAVRA. But with a structure consisting of three movements ('Sinfonia', 'Theme and variations', leading into 'Finale'), which confronts the conventions of the past without slavishly following its forms, the Octet places itself firmly at the beginning of the series of compositions in a neo-classical style.

In accordance with the pre-classical resonances of the title, the first movement 'Sinfonia' is more orientated towards the tripartite forms of instrumental music around 1750 than to classical sonata form; its tonal organisation – E♭ in the framing outer sections, and the theme of the central section heard first in

D then in A♭ – corresponds to the intervals of the initial motive of the slow introduction. In the second movement, the form evolves according to the principle of theme and variations, and it is at the same time punctuated by two returns of the first variation, a formal idea which Stravinsky would recall in the 'Passacaglia' of the Septet. The reminiscence of the Cuban tresillo rhythm at the end of the 'Finale' has the effect of the intrusion of a foreign stylistic element, having appeared thus far as an interpolation, under the form of secondary themes, in the prevailing neo-Baroque figuration, with its contrapuntal textures and motor rhythms.

Similar to the legendary genesis of The Rite of Spring, Stravinsky again links the idea of the composition and choice of instruments in his Octet to the memory of a dream: the sound of an ensemble comprising flute, clarinet, two bassoons, two trumpets and two trombones (Dial, 70). In terms of sonority, the instrumentation of the Octet assures a greater differential of timbre and dynamics than the double quartet (oboes, clarinets, bassoons and horns) favoured by Beethoven and Schubert in their wind octets. With the flexibility of register and sound quality arising from the four brass instruments (one trumpet in A, the other higher trumpet in C, and tenor and bass trombones), there would have been no problems of projection at the first performance given in the vast space of the Paris Opéra Garnier. WERNER STRINZ

Ode for orchestra. Composed 1943. First performance, 8 October 1943. Published 1947, New York and London: Associated Music Publishers and Schott. Dedication: 'in memory of Natalia Koussevitzky'.

(I) Eulogy – Lento (II) Eclogue – Con moto (III) Epitaph – Lento.

The Ode is an elegiac chant for orchestra (3.2.2.2 – 4.2.0.0 – timp. – strings) in three parts, which was written in 1943 in memory of Natalia Koussevitzky. She and her husband, the conductor Sergey Koussevitzky, had supported Stravinsky for decades and had also been co-founders of the Édition Russe de Musique, which had published works by Stravinsky from 1912. In 1942, with the death of his wife, Sergey Koussevitzky established a foundation to commission new works written in her memory. When Stravinsky received an enquiry from Koussevitsky for an orchestral work, having already written some music (for a 'hunting scene') for a film version of Jane Eyre, which was never used, he decided to incorporate it instead into the commissioned work, the Ode, where it was transformed into the central movement (Eclogue) (Boucourechliev 1987, 213).

The Eclogue is framed by two Lento movements. The work opens with the Eulogy and a quiet call from the brass before the strings go on to enunciate contrapuntal material and both elements become woven into one another. The third movement, Epitaph, continues the mood of lyrical expression, with the wind instruments shaping the melodic lines. While the bucolic and brassy 'con moto' gestures of the second movement, Eclogue, might at first seem inappropriate for a memorial composition, they recall Natalia Koussevitzky's predilection for open-air concerts in her native Russia. The première in October 1943, which was conducted by Koussevitzky himself, did not go well, with Stravinsky describing it as 'catastrophic' (SCW, 416).

FLORIAN HENRI BESTHORN

André Boucourechliev, Stravinsky, trans. Martin Cooper (London: Victor Gollancz, 1987).

Oedipus Rex. Composed 3 January 1926 – 10 May 1927; revised version 1948. First performance, 30 May 1927, PARIS, THÉÂTRE SARAH-BERNHARDT. Conductor, Igor Stravinsky. Published 1927 (vocal score: Russischer Musikverlag, Berlin), 1949 (score, revised version: Boosey & Hawkes, New York).

The oddest chapter in Stravinsky's musical biography may well be the one that surrounds the OPERA–oratorio, *Oedipus Rex* (1927). The initial spark for this venture seems to have originated with Jean COCTEAU's *Antigone*, a fairly strict reading and translation of the Sophocles play that was first staged in 1922. Intrigued by this effort, Stravinsky inquired about the possibility of undertaking a similar experiment with *Oedipus Rex*, one that would involve condensing and translating this second play into French. Long an enthusiast of the BALLETS RUSSES, Cocteau jumped at the prospect of a collaboration. (The two had been friends for a number of years.) But the task would be far from straightforward. Cocteau would oblige his friend, but it would take him three revised drafts to do so. What Stravinsky wanted was a very traditional script (hardly Cocteau's *métier*, as Stravinsky conceded at the time), something along the lines of a Handel libretto, with arias, recitatives and choruses.

Later, Stravinsky would also be asking Jean Daniélou, a Jesuit priest studying Theology at the Sorbonne, to translate Cocteau's French into Latin. (The Latin would not be a translation of the original Greek, in other words.) Infused with universality and a certain monumental character, Latin embodied gravity – or 'gravitas', to use the current term. For Catholics, Latin was the language of religious RITUAL. And for those members of his prospective audiences insufficiently familiar with either Latin or Sophocles' play (or both), Stravinsky would be providing short summaries of the action at critical points. These latter would be delivered in the vernacular (French in FRANCE) by a narrator or Speaker, who would also be appearing in evening dress. Set apart from the drama in this way, the Speaker's role is an intriguing one, even if it tired easily, as seems to have been the case for Stravinsky. The composer grew to dislike Cocteau's prose as well, which he thought haughty and pretentious. But the Speaker's interventions are indispensable, given that the music is paced by them.

The austerity of *Oedipus* as an opera was further enhanced by Stravinsky's stage directions, which left the actor/singers behind masks (as in Greek theatre), moving only with their heads and arms, and addressing the audience in an icy 'still-life' confrontation with fate. (Stravinsky's eldest son Theodore, already an aspiring artist and designer, was entrusted with the décor.) At the opening of *Oedipus*, a chorus alerts the King to the plague at Thebes. A prideful Oedipus assures the populace of his ability to uncover its cause. But a Messenger arrives to announce breathlessly that it is the King himself who has caused the catastrophe, the anger of the Gods. Unbeknownst, he has murdered his father and married his mother.

In the end, however, *Oedipus* was premièred not as an opera, but in concert form as an oratorio. Its first performance on 30 May 1927, at the THÉÂTRE SARAH-BERNHARDT in PARIS, was preceded by a trial run in the grand salon of the Princess de Polignac; in place of the orchestra, Stravinsky accompanied the singers at the piano.

This brings us to the strangest part yet of this episode. Dance-less and devoid of movement, Stravinsky's oratorio would be produced by Sergey DIAGHILEV and the Ballets Russes on a double bill that included a newly designed FIREBIRD! That such a contradiction could have been scheduled at the time seems scarcely conceivable. Not surprisingly, the audience – a dance audience on both occasions, at the avant-première and the première – reacted coolly to the new work, undoubtedly more out of bewilderment than anything else.

But the problem was that, from the start, Stravinsky had intended *Oedipus* to serve as an anniversary gift to Diaghilev on the occasion of his twentieth year in the theatre. He had sought to keep the undertaking secret for as long as possible, primarily as a means of avoiding the usual conflicts and rows. When Diaghilev learned of the project, he was not amused. 'Un cadeau très macabre', was his response: a very morbid gift.

Stravinsky once described *Oedipus* as a '*Merzbild*, put together from whatever came to hand'. Stately dotted rhythms, reminiscent of BACH, accompany Oedipus early on, while an Alberti bass heralds the entrance of the Messenger. However, from such bits and pieces of Baroque and classical cliché a unity is forged. And the glue that holds this assortment together consists often enough of features that are typical of Stravinsky's music, regardless of the stylistic orientation.

Thus, the music of the Messenger and Shepherd at Rehearsal Nos. 139–44 could have been lifted from any number of Russian-period works. A melodic fragment, modal in character, is sliced up into short segments by changing bar lines. No less typical of the composer, the shifting bar lines conceal a metrical displacement. A steady 3/4 metre could easily be inferred by the listener, according to which the main melody would be felt as falling first on and then off the crotchet beat.

The Messenger/Shepherd passages lead directly to a lengthy stratification. There are five superimposed layers, each of these consisting of the repetition of a single triad, dyad or motive that remains fixed in its register and instrumentation. The vast immobility of this passage carries a dramatic purpose. For we have arrived, following the final departure of the Messenger and Shepherd, at the high point of the opera–oratorio: Nos. 167–9 coincide with Oedipus' recognition of guilt; No. 169, the 'Lux facta est!' cadence, with his final resignation. Both musically and dramatically, then, Rehearsal Nos. 167–70 represent a period of waiting and anticipation, a pause to digest. For the main character, it is a moment of appalling humbling.

Register, instrumentation, rhythm and metre are not the only means of stasis at this point in the drama. Pitch is a means as well. The five superimposed layers, consisting, in order of appearance, of (D F A), (D F♯), B-F♯, (D F) and (F♯ B D), are all subject to the symmetries of the octatonic scale: in ascending order, D-E♭-F-F♯-G♯-A-B-C-(D).

The classical side of this neo-classical bargain makes itself felt by way of three eighteenth-century conventions: (1) the (D F♯) unit in the flutes inflects a *tierce de Picardie* in relation to the reiteration of (D F A) in the lower strings; (2) the (F♯ B D) triadic outline in Oedipus' motive is the submediant in relation to (D F♯ A); (3) the F of the (D F) unit in the clarinet clashes with B-F♯ in the timpani and with a (D F♯) in the flutes. Such clashing of major and minor thirds would become a hallmark of the composer's late neo-classical style.

PIETER C. VAN DEN TOORN

Richard Taruskin, *Russian Music at Home and Abroad* (Oakland: University of California Press, 2016).
Pieter C. van den Toorn, *The Music of Igor Stravinsky* (New Haven: Yale University Press, 1983).
Stephen Walsh, *Stravinsky: 'Oedipus Rex'* (Cambridge University Press, 1993).

Opera. As a composer of opera, Stravinsky is not to be compared with his predecessors, Massenet, Janacek, PUCCINI or STRAUSS, who were unquestionably specialists in the genre. Opera (The NIGHTINGALE, MAVRA, The RAKE'S PROGRESS) constitutes a symbolic, but not dominant, part of his compositional activity. The theatre, nevertheless, irrigates his work, something that is clearly the case with idiosyncratic productions such as RENARD (a sung and acted burlesque story), The SOLDIER'S TALE (recited, sung and acted), Les NOCES (choreographed Russian scenes with singing and music), OEDIPUS REX (a two-act opera–oratorio) or even PERSÉPHONE (a melodrama in three parts).

The world of opera was Igor Stravinsky's kindergarten. A student of the Belgian baritone Camille Everardi, his father FYODOR Stravinsky possessed a beautiful bass voice and great dramatic talent. After his first engagement at the opera in Kiev, he made his debut as Mephistopheles in Gounod's *Faust* on 30 April 1876 at the MARIINSKY THEATRE in ST PETERSBURG. He performed in a total of seventy roles; if that of Boris remained his great success, he created several parts in the operas of RIMSKY-KORSAKOV: Pan Golova in *May Night*, Prince Mstivoy in *Mlada*, Panas in *Christmas Eve*, as well as Grandfather Frost in *The Snow Maiden* (*Sniégourotchka*) in 1882, the year of Igor's birth. Fyodor Stravinsky made a good living from music and he welcomed numerous important personalities, such as César CUI, to his home. Despite his father's severity and coldness, the young Igor had access to his music library and sight-read the operas of GLINKA and Rimsky-Korsakov at the piano – notably *Christmas Eve*, which he played as a duet with his piano teacher, Leokadiya KASHPEROVA. His first musical shock was a performance of *A Life for the Tsar* at the Imperial Opera, which he already knew from the piano version; then, not long afterwards, Glinka's other masterpiece *Ruslan and Lyudmila*, which he described as 'simply mad', as well as *Boris Godunov*. He discovered the piano reductions of WAGNER's operas at the end of his adolescence and some extracts from Monteverdi's *Coronation of Poppea* in d'Indy's arrangement at the EVENINGS OF CONTEMPORARY MUSIC in St Petersburg during his university years. References to opera, notably Russian opera, appear frequently in his writings, as in his lyrical works.

Shortly after the death of his father in 1902, Stravinsky, drawn intimately by composition, became the private pupil of Rimsky-Korsakov, the tutelary figure in the development of his artistic personality. With Rimsky, he met the musical and literary youth of his generation, made friends with Stepan MITUSOV and learned from the composer of *Sadko* the techniques of Western musical composition. Under the gaze of his mentor, he orchestrated the piano parts of the operas he was completing, comparing them then with his teacher's original solutions. Not long before his death, Rimsky-Korsakov encouraged an

293

operatic project concocted by Stravinsky and Mitusov on Hans Christian Andersen's tale of *The Nightingale*. The opera *The Golden Cockerel*, which was performed in 1909, after the composer's death in June 1908, exercised a significant influence, from the point of view of timbre, on Stravinsky's first works: SCHERZO FANTASTIQUE, FIREWORKS, The FIREBIRD, PETRUSHKA, The RITE OF SPRING. Moreover, it was precisely the orchestral brilliance of these first two works that prompted DIAGHILEV to commission him to compose *The Firebird* for the 1910 season of the BALLETS RUSSES, after two probationary orchestrations of piano pieces by Chopin for the preceding season. At the end of winter 1912–13, Stravinsky, together with Maurice RAVEL, orchestrated some passages from MUSSORGSKY's KHOVANSHCHINA for Diaghilev. Surrounded by opera, how would he respond to such models?

His first opera The NIGHTINGALE is a lyrical tale in three acts which, though begun in 1908, was adjourned on account of the intense period of composition spent on Diaghilev's ballets, and was only completed finally in 1914. The nightingale appears as a metaphor for sincerity in art and human relations, and saves the Emperor from death, by virtue of his wonderful singing. The work may appear hybrid: the first act, composed initially in a truly operatic style, is considered as a prologue, while the two following acts were completed in 1913–14 for the Free Theatre of Moscow in the spirit of a large-scale BALLET ('ballet à grand spectacle'). However, the work was not performed in this institution but at the Opéra de Paris on 26 May 1914 by Diaghilev's Ballets Russes in an opera-ballet version in which the dancers mimed the roles which were sung in Russian in the orchestra pit. The style of *The Nightingale* looks back to the operas of Rimsky-Korsakov, but is equally inspired by Mussorgsky, LIADOV and DEBUSSY, and continues the research undertaken by Stravinsky in his ballets from 1910 onwards. He considered *The Nightingale* his most beautiful work from the first period of the Ballets Russes, even if it did not have the success of the preceding ballets. The three sets ('décors') and the sumptuous costumes incurred great expense despite the opera's brevity – with a duration of only 45 minutes. Stravinsky used extracts from it to fashion a symphonic poem The SONG OF THE NIGHTINGALE, which provided the musical material for a ballet that was created in 1920 by the Ballets Russes, with choreography by Léonide MASSINE.

Stravinsky's second lyrical work is *Mavra*, a short one-act opera buffa elaborated with Diaghilev in London during the summer of 1921. It tells of the deception devised by a young woman to smuggle her lover into her mother's house. In homage to PUSHKIN, Stravinsky drew on his poem *The Little House in Kolomna* and entrusted the libretto to the young Boris KOCHNO. He composed the opera in the Basque Country in the autumn and winter of 1921-2, and it is dedicated 'to the memory of Pushkin, Glinka and Tchaikovsky'. One perceives the influence of these creative figures, but also that of Dargomïzhsky. The work is conceived, in effect, as a pastiche of the Russian opera buffa of the 1830s – what the composer termed 'the old Russo-Italian opera' and for which he resuscitated the air and romance 'à l'Italienne' of the salons of the great Russian metropolises of Tsar Nicolas I, while combining them with Tzigane melodies. Stravinsky deliberately situated himself here in opposition to Wagner, and sought a sparkling and fresh alternative to the heavy 'din of the lyric drama'. The first performance of a concert version with the composer at the piano was given in PARIS as part of an evening organised by Diaghilev at the Hôtel Continental, after which the staged première took place at the Palais Garnier on 3 June 1922 under the direction of Grzegorz FITELBERG, together with Renard. The critics shunned this 'disconcerting joke' undoubtedly on the grounds of the unfavourable contrast it provided with the shimmering orchestration of The Firebird and The Rite of Spring, as well as its dated charm, which seemed at odds with the composer's scandalous reputation. Stravinsky himself considered Mavra as marking a turning-point in the evolution of his musical thought: the free appropriation of older styles.

Over a quarter of a century later, Stravinsky directed the première of his Rake's Progress at the TEATRO LA FENICE in VENICE on 11 September 1951, in a production by Carl Ebert. This opera in three acts was conceived with W. H. AUDEN from 1947, after a series of engraved reproductions of edifying paintings by William Hogarth (1732–3), retracing the fall of a young man who had too soon become the beneficiary of his paternal inheritance. The international reputation sustained by The Rake's Progress from the time of its first performance differs from the rather more subdued reception of The Nightingale and Mavra. The reason for this may pertain to the language of the libretto, English, which is more universal than Russian, and which Stravinsky polished with the help of the young Robert CRAFT, but also to the dimensions of the work, which is perfectly designed in three acts linked by three instrumental interludes. The archetypal roles, which are firmly characterised vocally, the reference to Mozart's Così fan tutte, which some think of as pastiche, as with the Faust myth, anchor The Rake's Progress in the history of opera, prefiguring the experiments of musical post-modernity, even if the spectator does not find the habitual pathos of lyric art within the work.

Finally, in 1952, Stravinsky met Dylan THOMAS, the musicality of whose verse he particularly appreciated. The two men, in response to a commission from the University of Boston, planned to write an opera on the rediscovery of language after a nuclear catastrophe, but the Welsh poet died before he could start work with the composer.

Stravinsky's three contributions to lyric art are therefore very different from one another: a flamboyantly orchestrated Russian tale, a charming humoristic bagatelle and a moral fresco conceived as a homage to the eighteenth century. However, all three bear witness to the musical preferences he affirmed throughout his career: Mozart, Glinka, Dargomïzhsky and Tchaikovsky, more than what he called the 'doctrinaire aestheticism' and 'Russisme' of the FIVE. He extolled 'the healthy tradition of dramatic art' which he recognised in opéra-comique, and in which he saw points in common with the music of Tchaikovsky: Chabrier, Gounod, Delibes, Bizet and Messager, he discovered in his youth thanks to his friend Ivan POKROVSKY. During the winter of 1922–3, he also frequented the theatre of the Trianon-Lyrique in Paris where he heard Cimarosa's The Secret Marriage, Gounod's Philémon et Baucis, La Colombe and Le Médecin malgré lui, as well as Chabrier's L'Éducation manquée. These works charmed him profoundly and he deplored the oblivion into which they had fallen and the snobbism which had led to their neglect: 'I found in them a different type of musical writing, different harmonic methods, a different melodic conception, a freer and fresher feeling for form' (*Auto*, 12).

By contrast, Stravinsky criticised Wagner explicitly. Having studied music drama and the *Gesamtkunstwerk* 'with great fervour' in his youth, he later described it as 'decadent, even pathological'. And he commends VERDI's adage 'Torniamo all'antiche e sara un progresso!', while scarcely appreciating his final operas *Othello* and *Falstaff* precisely on account of their proximity to the Wagnerian music drama. Stravinsky's paradoxical position in the world of opera lies undoubtedly in this quasi-reactionary aesthetic posture which was perceived in his own time as revolutionary. What exactly did he reproach in Wagner? The extravagance of his orchestra, that the voices disappeared within the music, the pointlessness of an artistic project tainted with religiosity. Moreover, detesting the pseudo-religious celebration of *Parsifal*, Stravinsky refused Diaghilev's request in 1914 for a theatrical parody of the orthodox liturgy with opulent costumes. He accused Wagner of having alienated the public from musical pleasure in order to lead it towards 'philosophical spec- ulation'. He abhorred his infinite melody and the system of *leitmotifs* and supported Debussy, who saw in the *Tetralogy* 'a vast musical address book'. For Stravinsky, music is unsuited to 'the expression of sentiments', to 'trans- lating dramatic situations' and 'for imitating nature'. Undoubtedly, *The Rake's Progress*, more than any other of Stravinsky's operatic realisations, is opposed point-blank to Wagner's contribution to lyric art, drawing instead on another pre-existent model: Mozartean opera. Stravinsky breaks, therefore, with the evolutionary logic that had obsessed musical circles at the turn of the nine- teenth and twentieth centuries, but which a good number of composers of opera had challenged – above all, Alban BERG. He also demonstrates by means of this atypical work that one of the pathways for modernity resides unques- tionably in the straightforward use of the past, considering, as André Boucourechliev puts it, 'history as *permanence*' and seeing 'the whole course of history as available to him' (1987, 10).

A visionary, he recognised the dramaturgical dimension of the technological innovations of his time, imagining in electronic music a possible future for the theatre: he took the example of the ghost scene in *Hamlet* which could be accompanied by 'white noise' despite the fact that the ghostly dimension of the loudspeakers seemed to him to draw more from the spiritualist 'séance' than from the art of theatre (*Mem*, 101).   CÉCILE AUZOLLE

André Boucourechliev, *Stravinsky*, trans. Martin Cooper (London: Victor Gollancz, 1987).
François Lesure (ed.), *Stravinsky: Études et témoignages* (Paris: Lattès, 1982).
Igor Strawinsky, *Poétique musicale*, J. B. Janin, ed. Roland Bourdariat. 'La Flute de Pan' Collection d'Études Musicales, 2nd edn (Paris: J. B. Janin, 1945).

Operatic Collaborations. Stravinsky's operatic activity spanned about fifty years – longer than Handel's and commensurate with VERDI's, and his techniques and strategies of collaboration varied during the course of this time. He never sought a permanent collaborator (unlike Richard STRAUSS, Verdi or even RIMSKY-KORSAKOV) or attempted to write the libretti himself (in contrast to his non-operatic works, for example *Les* NOCES), so each operatic project required an individual solution with a different collaborator. The first project,

The NIGHTINGALE, took shape wholly in the native tradition of Rimsky's circle: the author of the libretto, Stepan MITUSOV, was not only Stravinsky's fellow-student at the law faculty of the ST PETERSBURG UNIVERSITY, but also his fellow-student in the harmony class of Vasily KALAFATI, Rimsky's student and neighbour at his apartment in Zagorodny prospect, and a regular of Rimsky's musical *jours fixes*. The OPERA was influenced by Rimsky's last opera (*The Golden Cockerel*), and the initial stage of the work was completed under the auspices of Rimsky's collaborator, Vladimir Belsky, at his house. Common background facilitated communication. Mitusov was very sensitive and responsive to all the changing demands of the composer, modifying his text accordingly: in the first tableau (1907–8), he removed all the social subtext inherent in the literary source (a tale by Hans Christian Andersen) as in Rimsky's and Belsky's model (*The Golden Cockerel*); in the other two tableaux (1914), he radically reduced the words of the text, pursuing Stravinsky's new aesthetic of a 'ballet with voices'.

For The RAKE'S PROGRESS, the presumptions of collaboration changed drastically: Stravinsky did not know AUDEN previously, and approached him on the advice of his friend and neighbour Aldous HUXLEY when he decided to write an opera in English based on Hogarth's engravings, following a visit to an art exhibition in Chicago (1947). Both librettists, Auden and KALLMAN, belonged to a different generation from Stravinsky, spoke a foreign language and differed in background and even manners (see Lisa Sokolov's remarks on Auden's dirty fingernails: SSE, 211). In Stravinsky's Californian house, no appropriate bed for Auden could be found: according to Stravinsky's memories, he slept with his body on the couch and his feet, covered by a blanket pinioned with books, on a nearby chair, 'like the victim of a more humane and reasonable Procrustes' (*Mem*, 146). However, all these differences were dissolved as a consequence of mutual respect and were productively resolved during the course of the collaboration.

Between these poles of Stravinsky's operatic career were two operas of the twenties, MAVRA (1922, libretto by Boris KOCHNO) and OEDIPUS REX (1926–7, rev. 1948, libretto by COCTEAU), both presented in the Russian Seasons: although not commissioned by DIAGHILEV, both were accepted by him for staging *post-factum*. The idea of *Mavra* took shape in London during preparations for the staging of *The Sleeping Beauty*, and it was included in the PARIS season due to the absence of a choreographer for a fully fledged BALLET première. *Oedipus Rex* was kept secret from Diaghilev because it was conceived as a birthday present for the impresario ('un cadeau très macabre', as the addressee called it). In all these cases, it was the composer himself who initiated the project, and involved the librettist after having already defined the principal parameters of the proposed work. Stravinsky regarded it as 'the librettist's job to satisfy the composer, not the other way round', as Auden put it (*Mem*, 145), and Cocteau demonstrated the practical results of this relationship, reworking his drafts at least three times. Cocteau worked on the set design for *Oedipus Rex* together with Stravinsky's son Theodore, then 18 years old, but the composer himself had some clear and unusual ideas about the static theatre for which he strove (the masked faces of the chorus, the built-up costumes like boxes – thus preventing any free movement – and so on: *see Dial*, 23).

The only exception to this rule was PERSÉPHONE (1934), commissioned by Ida RUBINSTEIN, who chose the plot and the creative team, acted as producer and played the main mimetic part. This proposal was also related to a Diaghilev project, since a ballet based on the Persephone/Proserpine myth with text by André GIDE and music by Florent Schmitt was considered for the Russian Seasons as early as 1913 (a project of which Rubinstein was undoubtedly well aware). By the time of the actual composition, in 1934, however, the artistic aspirations of the prospective authors had diverged. Stravinsky later chose not to call working with Gide 'a collaboration', as there never was any 'communion' between them (*Mem*, 136, 141). They were divided not only on the issue of French prosody (which Stravinsky treated the way he treated Russian or Latin, based on 'beautiful syllables' rather than words), but on the whole approach to the material as well: the poet focused on the direct existential experience and emotional import, whilst for the composer it was the precisely calculated impersonal construction that conveyed the sacred meaning of a work of art. Annoyed by the 'incorrect' prosody, Gide did not even attend the première, based on his impressions of the private audition at Ida Rubinstein's. Others were equally disaffected due to a range of causes: shortly before the première, Jacques Copeau, the director, officially resigned because of stress caused by the general mismanagement; Kurt Jooss, the choreographer, experienced ill-will from the troupe, presumably due to prevailing Germanophobia; and Stravinsky, offended by André Barsacq's (rather than his son Theodore's) engagement as set designer without his knowledge, from that time evaded general discussion on the project, although he took an active part in the rehearsals and production.

Stravinsky always conceived collaboration broadly, and considered opera as inseparable from its theatrical incarnation. In *Memories and Commentaries*, he named the scenographer Alexandre BENOIS, with his professed penchant for 'chinoiserie', as his collaborator for The Nightingale. We also should mention Alexander Sanin, known for his extraordinary ability to direct mass scenes from the first première of the first of the Russian Seasons (*Boris Godunov*, 1908), and to whose friendly and energetic insistence (already as the director of the Free Theatre) we owe the two last tableaux of The Nightingale with their gigantic multi-personal procession. It was Sanin who co-directed the Paris première of the opera, together with Benois.

The individual contribution of each collaborator is very difficult to define precisely, since it was mostly discussed at personal meetings (for example, in Wiesbaden with Gide, when they agreed upon the three-part structure of *Perséphone*, and the role of Eumolpùs, or at Stravinsky's Californian home with Auden when the draft of The Rake's Progress was sketched, etc.). Stephen Walsh persuasively considers the introduction of The Speaker in *Oedipus Rex* as an authorial compromise for the sake of preserving the Latin text, based on indirect evidence – Cocteau's practice of translating the Greek tragedies, or the composer's irritation at the device of The Speaker, although this was voiced much later (*see Dial*, 23–5). As for *Perséphone*, on the contrary, it seems likely that the introduction of Eumolpus, in his alienating function, similar to that of the

Speaker, was the idea of the composer himself. Stravinsky named 'Mother Goose and Ugly Duchess' as Auden's contribution to the libretto of *The Rake's Progress*, but described the whole scheme of action as having been worked out by both collaborators together, step by step (*Mem*, 146). The plot was more deeply rooted in the Russian tradition than is usually assumed. *The Pilgrim's Progress* by John Bunyan, which famously served as a model *ad contrario* to Hogarth, was not only published in Russian translation as early as 1772, but served as the basis of one of the most important texts in Russian literature – the poem entitled *The Pilgrim* by Alexander PUSHKIN (1835). Fyodor Dostoyevsky drew special attention to this poem in his memorial speech honouring the poet (8 June 1880), whilst at the same time drawing attention to the link with Bunyan. Dostoyevsky considered the idea of roving, or pilgrimage, as central for Pushkin, as was the concept of 'universal responsiveness'. Dostoyevsky's memorial speech came to light again in 1921, the year of his centenary, and it struck a chord in the Russian *émigré* environment in FRANCE, with intellectual discourse focused on it. The notion of a poet as a perpetual alien, a stranger, or a pilgrim, spoke to the *émigré* self-identification, and was sensitive specifically for Stravinsky with his acute feeling of his own rootlessness – evident, for example, in his choice of texts for SYMPHONY OF PSALMS ('For I am an alien and a pilgrim in a strange land').

The Pushkin trend, by way of Dostoyevsky, with his idea of 'universal responsiveness' pointing from national to universal, defined Stravinsky's approach to *Mavra* (1922), first conceived while working on the re-orchestration of TCHAIKOVSKY's ballet *The Sleeping Beauty* for its London première. Tchaikovsky and GLINKA in music, but most of all Pushkin, embody the Europeanised cultural tendencies of Petrine RUSSIAN MYTH that opened the possibility of a breakaway from the enclosed reserve of national exoticism. For the Russian *émigré*, especially in France, the name of Pushkin functioned as a special sign, enabling him 'to find a way in the coming darkness' (Khodasevich), and Pushkin's birthday (6 June) was celebrated as the day of Russian culture. For Stravinsky, *The Sleeping Beauty* was 'the most authentic expression of the epoch in our Russian life that we call the "Petersburg period"' (as stated in Stravinsky's 'open letter' dated 1 October 1921 and published in *The Times* of London (cited in SRT, 1529)). A 'St Petersburg ballet' was linked to the quintessential ST PETERSBURG opera, *The Queen of Spades*, and through it to the literary source of the latter, Pushkin's eponymous short story. More generally, it encompassed the group of Pushkin's texts (including the literary source of *Mavra*) that Vladislav Khodasevich referred to as 'the St Petersburg novels' in his influential essay published in the periodical *Apollo* (1915). He defined their common plot as the sudden clash of an ordinary person 'with the unknown and hostile forces lying outside of the frame of action accessible to him'. The literary source of *Mavra* is included in this group based on some common structural traits, but only as a comic and travestied alternative: here, the threat to order relates only to the trickster character of the false cook, easily distinguishable and neutralised.

The other texts of the 'St Petersburg novels', however, are more relevant in relation to *The Rake's Progress*: in all of them, the main character (a pointedly unheroic figure) faces a dark and inimical force, unaware of its origin and power, with no chance to win or even come out safely, and pays for this confrontation with insanity and untimely death. Such are the fates of Evgeniy (*The Brass Monument*), Pavel (*The Lonely House on Vassilievsky Island*) and Hermann (*The Queen of Spades*), who ended his life at the Obukhov clinic – the St Petersburg equivalent to Bedlam. This madness is far removed from the edifying commonsense of the moral story: the human person, in his obvious weakness and extreme need, aroused compassion, not moral indignation. In the operatic version of *The Queen of Spades* by Tchaikovsky, the onset of madness in the main character is almost simultaneously combined with the love theme and the prayer for mercy. This very conflict, produced by the 'invasion of dark hostile forces into human life' (Khodasevich) and inherent to Pushkin's tradition, was added to the story of *The Rake's Progress* by the introduction of the character of Nick Shadow, absent from Hogarth's engravings and as little resembling Mephistopheles as Tom Rakewell resembled Faust or Don Giovanni (to name just two of the most obvious models). The common structural traits of the 'St Petersburg novels' are present in the libretto: the infernal feigning as trivial up to the moment of the final conflict, when its fearsome power is revealed suddenly; the duality of the female characters (the virginal bride embodying true love versus the sophisticated coquettish high-class lady linked with the infernal); contact with the infernal force through the garden gate (the first appearance of Nick Shadow and the triple appearance of the Stranger in *The Lonely House on Vassilievsky Island*); the card play involving cheating (*The Queen of Spades*, *The Lonely House on Vassilievsky Island*); the re-interpretation of the main character and his final heart-breaking insanity and demise. Less hardened in vice than unstable in virtue, a charming egotist, a naïve idle dreamer like Evgeniy in *The Brass Monument*, 'rake' is a frequent word in Pushkin's vocabulary, with the primary meaning of 'a careless person', almost devoid of any pejorative implications. The obvious references to Pushkin in *The Rake's Progress* (the textual quotation from his poem *A Scene from Faust* in the initial line of the third act in the draft version of the libretto, or an allusion to a 'bearded lady' from *Mavra* in the character of Baba the Turk) are just superficial examples of the continuing links to the Russian literary tradition which helped inspire Stravinsky's final opera.

ELENA VERESHCHAGINA AND TATIANA VERESHCHAGINA

Vladislav Khodasevich, *Peterburgskiye povesti Pushkina* ('Vladislav Khodasevich, Pushkin's St Petersburg Novels'), in *Apollo*, 3 (1915).
Tamara Levitz, *Modernist Mysteries: Perséphone* (New York: Oxford University Press, 2012).
Stephen Walsh, *Stravinsky: Oedipus Rex* (Cambridge University Press, 1993).

Oranienbaum (now Lomonosov), RUSSIA, is the birthplace of Igor Stravinsky – a small town on the Finnish Gulf 40 km to the west of ST PETERSBURG, built around the great Baroque palace of Peter the Great's former favourite, Prince Alexander Menshikov. In 1743, Oranienbaum became the summer residence of the future Emperor Peter III, and from 1796 it belonged to the future Tsar Alexander I: after his death, ownership passed to his brother Mikhail and his heirs. In Stravinsky's time, it became a fashionable summer resort, especially for the artistic and literary élite, including Leo Tolstoy, the poets Afanasii Fet and Fyodor Tiutchev, the Peredvizhnik painters Alexei Savrasov and Ilya Repin, and many others. The singer Daria Leonova had her dacha in Oranienbaum, and MUSSORGSKY settled there for the summer of 1880, working on KHOVANSHCHINA and *Sorotchintsy Fair*. Subsequently, Stravinsky did not remember Oranienbaum and claimed that the family never visited it after his birth, but his memory is not accurate: his younger brother Guryi was also born there (1884).

ELENA VERESHCHAGINA AND TATIANA VERESHCHAGINA

Orchestral Music. In conventionally categorised listings of Stravinsky's compositions, the pre-eminence of 'Dramatic' works is unmistakable, but the inadequacy of the most basic generic labels – OPERA, oratorio, BALLET – is no less apparent in instances such as the 'choreographic scenes' LES NOCES or the 'musical play' THE FLOOD. Similarly, although familiar titles like 'symphony' and 'concerto' appear under the heading of 'Orchestral Music', they are part of a much more diverse collection of works involving substantial groups of instruments. Several of these are either identical with or closely related to the complete ballet or opera scores, like the suites from THE FIREBIRD and PULCINELLA, the hybrid 'symphonic poem/ballet' THE SONG OF THE NIGHTINGALE, or the DIVERTIMENTO from THE FAIRY'S KISS; others, like SYMPHONIES OF WIND INSTRUMENTS and the CONCERTO IN E♭: 'DUMBARTON OAKS' for chamber orchestra, are neither for full orchestra nor – quite – CHAMBER MUSIC (especially if this implies an unconducted ensemble).

The orchestral lay-out of VARIATIONS (ALDOUS HUXLEY IN MEMORIAM) (1963–4), Stravinsky's last purely instrumental composition (apart from the 1965 CANON ON A RUSSIAN POPULAR TUNE) is as follows: two flutes, alto flute, two oboes, cor anglais, two clarinets, bass clarinet, two bassoons, four horns, three trumpets, three trombones, harp, piano and a body of thirty-six strings. This might not appear so radically different from the lay-out of the four early orchestral scores completed before his move to PARIS to find fame with the BALLETS RUSSES – SYMPHONY IN E♭ MAJOR, SCHERZO FANTASTIQUE, FIREWORKS and FUNERAL SONG (all 1905–8). Yet the transformation from a late-Romantic compositional style close to that of his Russian forebears to the intricately patterned TWELVE-NOTE counterpoints of 1965 brings with it radical changes in instrumental balance and sonority, reflecting the no less radical changes in musical form and texture that were the consequence of Stravinsky's sixty years at the forefront of mainstream modernist composition.

Stravinsky's decisive switch from symphonic to dramatic composition during the years 1908–10 confirmed his youthful genius for combining richly differentiated instrumental colours with a cogently designed formal process tied closely to the dramatic subject matter. As is well known, what appears to be the perfect match of exotic, vibrant instrumental effects (including a prominent solo piano) in PETRUSHKA stems from his original intention to compose a concertante work for piano and orchestra. Given the practical, commercial exigencies determining the activities of the Ballets Russes, it now seems remarkable that Stravinsky could get away with making such extreme demands on the abilities of conductors and orchestral players to master the innovative intricacies of *Petrushka* and THE RITE OF SPRING, and with rather fewer hours of rehearsal than the dancers; for evidence of his determination to innovate, one need look no further than his decision to allot the eerie incantation that begins The Rite to a solo bassoon in its highest register rather than to oboe or cor anglais. But with hindsight it seems inevitable that one effect of The Rite – an effect that would surely have obtained even if the outbreak of war in 1914 had not so drastically altered the cultural landscape in France – was to explode the conventional formal and musical lay-out for dance drama. Orchestrally, and in every other way, The Firebird was much closer to such nineteenth-century dance classics as Nutcracker and Coppélia than it was to The Rite. Nevertheless, in wartime, much smaller, more mobile ensembles of dancers and players were essential, underlining the decisive move away from those nineteenth-century conventions which The Rite of Spring had exploded from the inside.

After 1914, Stravinsky, like many other modernists, would tend to 'compose' his orchestras for the specific requirements of the work in question, though rarely as radically as in the definitive version of Les Noces; and even when a relatively conventional distribution of instrumental forces was part of that rethinking of tradition on which NEO-CLASSICISM relied for its effects, the differences in thematic and harmonic character between Stravinsky on the one hand and BACH, Handel, Mozart, BEETHOVEN or TCHAIKOVSKY on the other demanded equivalent contrasts in orchestral texture and colour. Indeed, Stravinsky's music tends to sound more overtly Stravinskian – more modernist – the more directly he aligns his choice of instrumental sonority with Baroque, Classical or Romantic precedent, without, at the same time, simply writing 'pure' Baroque, Classical or Romantic harmony: the use of the harpsichord in arioso-like passages in The RAKE's PROGRESS is a particularly telling example. At the other extreme, the very un-Baroque trombone and double bass writing in PULCINELLA is an equally clear instance of the composer's use of sonic parody to point up the dramatic comedy.

The sheer range of Stravinsky's instrumental imagination is encapsulated by the far-reaching contrasts between SYMPHONIES OF WIND INSTRUMENTS (1920) and APOLLON MUSAGÈTE (1927–8). The former, whose final version is laid out for twelve woodwind and eleven brass players, is one of the composer's most subtle memorials to those 'Russian traditions' so central to his development: abrasive and austere, its mosaic-like structure reinforces its ritualistic character as a tribute to that other great modernist among Stravinsky's French contemporaries, Claude DEBUSSY. A mere eight years later, Apollon Musagète is the acme of neo-classical elegance, its lay-out for a string orchestra of, Stravinsky suggested, thirty-four players ideal for the intimately lyrical character of another RITUAL, celebrating in dance the timeless virtues of Apollo and his attendant muses. Both works make sophisticated use of the contrast between soloistic and concerted writing, highlighted to a greater extent than tends to be found in pre-modernist orchestral music, and this quality carries over into those compositions whose titles and formal outlines might lead listeners to expect the closest conformity to earlier examples of symphonies or concertos.

Stravinsky's Piano Concerto (1923–4) and CONCERTO IN D FOR VIOLIN AND ORCHESTRA (1931) are both unimpeachably neo-classical, throwing up associations with Baroque, Classical and Romantic precursors in ways that make clear their distance from sources that are to be honoured rather than merely parodied. The full title of the earlier work, CONCERTO FOR PIANO AND WIND INSTRUMENTS, is not strictly accurate, since double basses and timpani are also required, but it serves to indicate that this will be music of hard edges and dramatic juxtapositions, in the tradition of the Symphonies of Wind Instruments and the recently completed OCTET FOR WIND INSTRUMENTS. At first glance, the Concerto in D for Violin and Orchestra might appear more conventional, calling for a fairly standard orchestra, including strings, and even claiming a basic tonality, as Concerto in D. Less conventionally, there are four movements, not the usual three, and all four have titles: Toccata, Aria I, Aria II and Capriccio. Here the associations are with Baroque suites in which dance-like and more reflective, lyrical movements alternate. The result is one of the most dazzling and kaleidoscopic of Stravinskian hybrids, an exuberant rethinking of concerto conventions spanning the era from Bach to Tchaikovsky, and definitive evidence of how 'reinventing the past' can be a good deal more engaging and enduring than avant-garde or experimental attempts to ignore it.

It was towards the end of his most consistently neo-classical phase that Stravinsky wrote the two orchestral works that arguably tested his capacity for rethinking and reinventing more extensively: SYMPHONY IN C (1938–40) and SYMPHONY IN THREE MOVEMENTS (1942–5). Having evoked the symphonic principle while distancing himself from its central traditions in Symphonies of Wind Instruments and SYMPHONY OF PSALMS, he now felt able to look back across more than thirty years to his own Russian apprenticeship and revert to the four-movement orchestral symphony in a key of Classical and Romantic tradition. That he did so at a time of the greatest personal and professional instability – losing close members of his family and moving from Europe to America – helps to explain why Symphony in C is the least turbulent and forceful of his major works, but it has great strengths in the unflinchingly contemporary look it takes at those musical qualities that were helping to ensure that eighteenth- and nineteenth-century symphonies remained central to Western musical experience, even to the extent of making leading moderns like Stravinsky himself seem relatively marginal. Stravinsky's gently defiant response to this reality, in Symphony in C, is perhaps clearest in the constitution, spacing and instrumentation of form-defining cadential progressions, giving aurally explicit emphasis to the distance between his own modernist idiom and a whole range of earlier harmonic models from symphonies in C, including those by Mozart, Beethoven and Bizet: music which is not only diatonic, but keeps dissonance in its pre-modernist, unemancipated place.

After this, Symphony in Three Movements seems like a deliberate Stravinskian distancing from the historical resonances so powerfully present in Symphony in C, reasserting the composer's own most characteristic stylistic and textural features in order to show their continued potential. The purely orchestrational dimension of this defiant affirmation of identity is brought into high relief towards the end of the finale, where a solo trombone and a piano initiate a raucous fugal exposition, soon joined by harp and lower strings in a Stravinskian jam session confirming the renewed flexibility and energy of such American musical institutions as Woody Herman's JAZZ band. The stimulus of American contexts also accounts for the remarkable instrumental imagination to be heard in the later ballets ORPHEUS (1947) and AGON (1953–7).

Orpheus might seem close in concept to its 'classical' precursor *Apollon Musagète*, but it is less expansively lyrical, its ambivalent expressive character embodied in the subtleties of its highly diverse instrumental textures, encapsulated in an ending where Orpheus' emblematic harp is cloaked in a softly articulated brass trio (two horns and trumpet) and a string line that opens out from two solo violins to a fully orchestrated final chord. Such instrumental refinements, playing off the flights of solo lines against the homogeneous ensembles of textures rich in doublings, recur and dominate in *Agon*. Here the abstract scenario prompts the music's suite-like sequence of movements, and the loosening of harmonic controls as Stravinsky moves closer to consistently deployed twelve-note techniques brings a new tension and transparency to the familiar ostinato figures and tightly interwoven rhythmic patterns.

The decade between *Agon* and *Variations (Aldous Huxley In Memoriam)* charts Stravinsky's increasing commitment to the kaleidoscopic textural dispersions of instrumental forces he admired in WEBERN, and such younger advocates of Webern as BOULEZ and STOCKHAUSEN. Having produced one final rethinking of the concerto principle in MOVEMENTS for piano and orchestra (1958–9), and one more 'neo-classical' recalibration of existing musical material in MONUMENTUM PRO GESUALDO (1960), he closed his orchestral account neatly enough with a glance back into his own past, taking a theme from the finale of The *Firebird* as the basis for CANON ON A RUSSIAN POPULAR TUNE (1965). Ultimately, however, it is the convincing quality of Stravinsky's evolution over time that stands out; and – appropriately – the modernist orchestral principle he pioneered and displayed in such outstanding instances as the very beginning of The *Rite of Spring*, juxtaposing collective and individual statements to maximum dramatic effect, is found at the very end of the Huxley variations, as five sharply articulated chords in the strings (twelve violins, ten violas, eight cellos) give way to a single, softly sustained G♯ in the bass clarinet. In this memorably uncompromising way, Stravinsky shows how the fundamental compositional principle of conclusive closure can be decisively rethought in his own determinedly post-classical era. ARNOLD WHITTALL

Orchestration/Instrumentation. Stravinsky, we are assured, composed at the piano. By this, we mean the second stage of composing – planning, working and writing. The conceptual stage happens anywhere – in a dream, on country walks, and so on. It's the second stage that confuses non-composers, who are inclined to ask 'How can you hear it in your head?', and 'Did it sound in performance as you expected?' Of course, Stravinsky could hear it all in his head, so why did he work at the piano? The answer is the need for a composer to place himself in the situation that is most conducive to creativity. And, for Stravinsky, this depended upon the tactile experience of hitting the keys of the piano.

An important consequence of this procedure is the way in which his treatment of the orchestra often imitates the piano – rhythmic, incisive, percussive. The piano, after all, is essentially a percussive instrument (its melodic qualities are really an illusion, despite being pursued by innumerable pianist-composers from C. P. E. Bach to RACHMANINOV). Every instrumental work by Stravinsky shows its piano origins, from the punchiness of brass to articulation for strings. Here and there, instruments would divide in order to convey a pianistic touch; a simple example is in SYMPHONY OF PSALMS at [7], where divided oboes (3 and 4) and bassoons combine legato and staccato. The CONCERTO IN D for strings has many examples of string writing that derive from piano touch.

An active and expert pianist, Stravinsky gave us a modest body of works for solo piano, ranging from the virtuosic (e.g. CONCERTO FOR TWO SOLO PIANOS) to miniatures: in addition, there are three works for solo piano and orchestra. Significantly, the piano is also an important ensemble member of the orchestra, from PETRUSHKA to SYMPHONY IN THREE MOVEMENTS. Songs with piano accompaniment fare better with piano as one of a mixture of instruments, as in the revised version of the *Three Japanese Lyrics*. Another consequence of his composing at the piano is the success of piano reductions of his orchestral scores. The piano versions of Stravinsky's works, especially THREE MOVEMENTS FROM PETRUSHKA and the duet version of *The* RITE OF SPRING, are so effective that they are established repertoire. Piano reductions of DEBUSSY and SCHOENBERG pale into insignificance by comparison.

Stravinsky's study with RIMSKY-KORSAKOV equipped him fully with orchestral 'tricks of the trade', as *The* FIREBIRD and *Petrushka* amply demonstrate. The climax of the early period, *The Rite of Spring*, repays study handsomely on every page; the sheer size of the orchestra is in line with normal practice of the time, yet the opening, scored at first for solo bassoon, at once takes us into unfamiliar territory, so eerie and cold when contrasted with the languorous flute solo (in the same pitch region) that opens Debussy's *L'Après-midi d'un faune* of two decades earlier. As *The Rite* unfolds, orchestral virtuosity comes to the fore, as in the filigree writing for flutes and clarinets in [5]–[12], with flutter-tonguing even applied to oboes (less feasible for any double-reed instrument); glissando arpeggios in harmonics for violas in the same passage; the bitonal passage that opens Part II ([79]), where a cool, sustained chord of D minor on oboes and horns provides the backing for the swaying legato writing in D♯ minor for flutes and clarinets; and the haunting moment of stillness at [87], where a six-note chord in harmonics on flutes and double basses supports the most delicate texture on the other string instruments and E♭ clarinet. In recent years, Stravinsky has become a focus of the move towards 'authenticity' in performance, and the thoroughly researched performance of *The Rite of Spring* by Les Siècles under François-Xavier Roth is a revelation. It features French woodwind, horns with piston valves rather than rotary valves, smaller brass instruments, and a string section with gut strings throughout. Quick arco/pizzicato alternations in the concluding 'Danse sacrale' have been restored, plus numerous other Ur-text details. The result offers us wonderful clarity, with no shortage of atmosphere and excitement. Above all, subtleties of the work's harmony emerge more tellingly (CD Musicales Actes ASM 15).

In the neo-classical years, orchestration was – by necessity and also by artistic desire – more economical than in the large-scale works of the Russian period. There is an emphasis on wind and brass, exclusively so in SYMPHONIES OF WIND INSTRUMENTS and the MASS, and upper strings are absent in *Symphony of Psalms*, in order to counteract any suggestion of the supposedly excessive emotion of the Romantic age. Stravinsky was conscious of attempting to capture the essence of pure compositional process, even suggesting that, if one's main impression of a piece of music is of colour and decoration rather than substance and argument, then the work is of lesser value. Smaller ensembles, sparser orchestration, and a revival of classical forms, all supported this aesthetic, and solo piano writing, for instance in the 1924 PIANO SONATA, reflects Baroque practice in its continuous textures and the manner of some of its ornamentation.

In the late 1940s, now resident in LOS ANGELES, Stravinsky prepared new versions of many of his earlier works, for several reasons: reductions in instrumentation for the sake of feasibility; revision of various details; and copyright payment, which was otherwise not forthcoming in the US. The most significant work for such treatment was *Symphonies of Wind Instruments*: performances would be more likely with the removal of alto flute and clarinet in F. The third note on trumpets 2 and 3 is corrected to C (concert B♭); in some performances of the 1920 version, it is played as a B (concert A) which does not fit the prevailing octatonic scale. The E minor passages ([15]–[26] and [29]–[37]) are adjusted to fit the pitch range of standard instruments; harmony is thus affected here and there, but it appears that the actual notes are not as vital as the *extent* of dissonance.

Stravinsky's association with Robert CRAFT led to renewed creative vigour in the composer's final years. Perhaps surprisingly, Stravinsky began to enjoy hearing Schoenberg ('Suite', op. 29), WEBERN (Quartet with saxophone, op. 22) and BOULEZ (*Structure Ia*). At first, Stravinsky's works employing aspects of serialism, with rows of four notes (in the first of the Shakespeare Songs) or five notes (IN MEMORIAM DYLAN THOMAS), feature small intervals in their melodic lines, with a clear gravitational pull towards C – more akin to Stravinsky's choral writing than to anything found in Webern. But intricate counterpoint, with wider intervals, is found increasingly as he moves towards TWELVE-NOTE rows. Fragmentary orchestral gestures, sharp contrasts and unpredictable musical discourse, as in MOVEMENTS, VARIATIONS (ALDOUS HUXLEY IN MEMORIAM) and REQUIEM CANTICLES, characterise these late works. Large orchestral forces are used sparingly, avoiding any *tutti*. In music of such novel complexity and comparative lack of tonal reference, cadences rely on texture and gesture. In this respect, the end of *Variations* is instructive: the final line reflects the rhythmic and textural pattern of bars 2–5, plus a single accented semibreve in the last bar. This note, just as at the end of Webern's op. 22, is, naturally, avoided in the previous chords – so unlike the home-coming of tonal music.

SEBASTIAN FORBES

Orlov, Alexander Alexandrovich (born Russia, 1889; died Russia, 1974). Russian dancer. Orlov trained at the Imperial Theatre School in ST PETERSBURG and danced with the BALLETS RUSSES between 1909 and 1911. He was a renowned character dancer and was cast as the Moor in the first production of PETRUSHKA (1911). As a sign of his standing, DIAGHILEV had originally intended the BALLET to première in April in Monte Carlo but the date was put back to accommodate Orlov's schedule. Alexandre BENOIS remembered him as an 'excellent artist' who created the role of the Moor 'in a masterly way' (Benois 1941, 338).

SOPHIE REDFERN

Alexandre Benois, *Reminiscences of the Russian Ballet*, trans. Mary Britnieva (London: Putnam, 1941).

Orpheus. BALLET in three scenes. Commissioned in 1946 by Lincoln KIRSTEIN's newly formed Ballet Society. Composed in 1947 in Hollywood. Choreographed by George BALANCHINE with décor by Isamu Noguchi. First performance, 28 April 1948, New York City Center of Music and Drama. Conductor, Igor Stravinsky. Published 1948, Boosey & Hawkes. The first performance prompted Morton Baum, chair of the City Center's executive committee, to invite the Ballet Society to join City Center as its resident ballet company. The fledgling troupe quickly reinstituted itself as the NEW YORK CITY BALLET, with *Orpheus* marking an early milestone in the company's young history.

The origins of this 30-minute lyrical ballet are traceable to 1928 when Kirstein first envisioned a 'second act' to Stravinsky and Balanchine's APOLLO. The Orphic myth was a topic dear to all involved parties. Kirstein and Balanchine had produced *Orpheus and Eurydice* in 1936 at The Met. Six years earlier, Balanchine prepared dances for a Parisian staging of Offenbach's *Orpheus in the Underworld*. Similarly, Stravinsky had long been attracted by the tenets of classical antiquity as expounded in such epic poems as Ovid's *Metamorphoses*.

Stravinsky himself prepared the ballet's synopsis, which appears in the published score. A weeping Orpheus laments the loss of his beloved Eurydice in the ballet's opening scene. The Angel of Death 'leads *Orpheus* to Hades' reappearing in 'the gloom of Tartarus'. In the second scene, Orpheus' 'song of consolation' moves The Furies to 'bind his eyes, and return his wife to him' as he leads her back to earth. In the pivotal pas de deux, Orpheus 'tears the bandage from his eyes', thus condemning Eurydice to Hades. The scene concludes with The Bacchantes attacking Orpheus as they 'tear him to pieces'. In the final scene, Apollo appears 'and wrests the lyre from *Orpheus* and raises his song heavenwards'.

With 'Ovid and a classical dictionary in hand', according to the composer, Balanchine and Stravinsky jointly developed the scenario during the summer of 1946. The ballet's three scenes were drafted on a few handwritten index cards now preserved at the SACHER FOUNDATION. These insightful notations reveal how thoroughly the scenario was determined before Stravinsky began composing. The precise pre-compositional timing of each discrete section of the ballet was included in the note cards. Subsequently, Stravinsky's compositional sketches disclose that Balanchine encouraged the composer to extend certain musical passages towards accommodating the envisioned choreography. Uncharacteristically, Stravinsky complied.

Orpheus stands as a model of restraint. Stravinsky subtly captures the narrative's solemnity while Balanchine's pantomimic dance appears more broadly theatrical than narrowly choreographic. There is the air of a requiem throughout, replete with both loss and the ardent hope of redemption. The music exudes a calmness, only once rising above *mezzo forte* during the dramatic Bacchantes' dismemberment of Orpheus. Otherwise, the score unfolds serenely, with little fluctuation in temper or tempo. The melodic intermingling of diatonic and modal lines creates the sense of a 'slow chant', as was the composer's stated intent. Seldom does Stravinsky employ the full complement of his orchestra. It is the lyre (harp), cast as the timeless symbol of music, dance and poetry, that predominates. Its presence is palpable from the opening scene's plaintively falling scales, meant to portray Orpheus' mournful descent into the underworld, to the final apotheosis, with Apollo offering the mystical lyre as testimony to music's eternal power. In the end, it is the ballet's quiet but compelling understatement that defines the work's elegance.

CHARLES M. JOSEPH

Maureen Carr, *Multiple Masks: Neoclassicism in Stravinsky's Works on Greek Subjects* (Lincoln and London: University of Nebraska Press, 2002).

Gretchen Horlacher, 'The futility of exhortation: pleading in Stravinsky's *Oedipus Rex* and *Orpheus*', in SHW, 79–104.

Owl and the Pussy-Cat, The, for soprano and piano. Words by Edward Lear. Composed 1965–6. First performance, 31 October 1966, LOS ANGELES, Peggy Bonini (Soprano), Ingolf Dahl (Piano). Published 1967, Boosey & Hawkes. Dedicated to Vera STRAVINSKY.

This little piece, which lasts about 2 minutes and 40 seconds, is composed to a six-stanza poem by Edward Lear, the first verse in English that Vera Stravinsky learned by heart, and it is dedicated to her. After a first performance in Los Angeles, it was subsequently performed at the 30th International Festival of Contemporary Music in VENICE on 11 September 1967.

This 'musical charm' (as Luciano Berio called it in the notes to the performance in Venice) was the last piece Stravinsky ever wrote, coming directly after he had finished the REQUIEM CANTICLES. In one of his many exchanges with Robert CRAFT, he described it as 'a musical sigh of relief, composed so rapidly after the *Requiem Canticles* – a Requiem at my age rubs close to home'. It is for soprano and piano, which plays only two lines, one or two octaves apart, throughout.

The piece is constructed on a TWELVE-NOTE row, of which only the four untransposed versions are used, with the exception of a single appearance of the inversion at the tritone in the piano to accompany the line 'And there in a wood a Piggywig stood' in the fourth stanza. There are three characters in this wonderful little poem: the owl, the pussycat and, briefly, in the middle of the fourth stanza, the 'Piggywig'. Stravinsky said that the song 'should be impersonated: a little hooted, a little meowed, a little grunted for the pig'.

KATHRYN PUFFETT

P

Page, Ruth (born Indianapolis, 22 March 1889; died Chicago, 7 April 1991). American dancer, choreographer and director. A student of Adolph Bolm and Enrico Cecchetti, Page danced with various companies during her early career (often involving Bolm). She created the role of Terpsichore in the first production of Apollon Musagète (Washington, DC, 1928). It was choreographed by Bolm, who also danced the title role. She was later involved as choreographer and dancer in a 1931 Chicago production of The Soldier's Tale, with sets by Nicolas Remisoff (designer of Bolm's Apollo). A major figure in American ballet, Page founded and led a number of companies.   SOPHIE REDFERN

Palais des Beaux-Arts (Brussels). The Palais des Beaux-Arts in Brussels was the location for the première of Stravinsky's Symphony of Psalms, for mixed chorus and orchestra, on 13 December 1930, conducted by Ernest Ansermet. The same theatre had been the venue for a staging of The Soldier's Tale on 22 December 1928, conducted by the composer.   HELEN JULIA MINORS

Paris. The story of the youthful Stravinsky's success in Paris before World War I is well known. His impact on audiences, critics and musicians has been described as transformational for contemporary music and ballet. The impresario Sergey Diaghilev was the catalyst in initiating the collaborations between the most innovative composers, choreographers and artists of the time, and was central to Stravinsky's sudden success and notoriety in Paris. The Firebird (1909–10) received its première by the Ballets Russes at the Paris Opéra on 25 June 1910. The successful collaboration of Stravinsky, Mikhail Fokine (choreography), Alexander Golovine (costumes and scenery) and Léon Bakst (costumes) brought the young composer to the attention of artistic and fashionable Parisian circles. Stravinsky began to work on Petrushka in 1910–11, with Diaghilev arranging the collaboration with Alexandre Benois, but, this time, Stravinsky was more fully involved in shaping the scenario. As Cross argues, *Petrushka* 'marks the beginning of Stravinsky as a modernist with an identity all of his own' (Cross 2015, 45). The première at the Théâtre Du Châtelet took place on 13 June 1911, with costumes by Fokine and the title role danced by Vaslav Nijinsky.

Stravinsky had already begun to work on the ballet that would make him notorious in Paris and beyond, The Rite of spring (1911–13). Despite his later claims, the collaborative drama is an essential part of the work's conception and realisation. He collaborated with Nicholas Roerich (scenario and sets) and Nijinsky (choreography). The première, on 29 May 1913 at the newly built Théâtre des Champs-Elysées, Paris, has gone down in history for having created one of the biggest musical scandals ever. The riot was due as much to the choreography as to the music: Nijinsky had chosen to choreograph every beat of the score with gestures that were deliberately disjointed, repetitive and machine-like rather than human. POULENC, MILHAUD, Koechlin and later BOULEZ were bowled over by the innovations of The Rite and spent years analysing it. T. S. ELIOT's comment was particularly apt: 'it did seem to transform the rhythm of the steppes into the scream of the motor horn, the rattle of machinery, the grind of wheels, the beating of iron and steel, the roar of the underground railway, and the other barbaric cries of modern life; and to transform these despairing noises into music' (Eliot, The Dial, October 1921).

Stravinsky completed a number of smaller works for various Parisian performances. One of these was the Three Japanese Lyrics (1912–13), which was written when Stravinsky was working with RAVEL in SWITZERLAND on MUSSORGSKY's KHOVANSHCHINA, and was inspired by SCHOENBERG's Pierrot lunaire. Ravel wrote his own songs based on the same instrumentation and tried to get all three works performed at the Société musicale indépendente in Paris, but only Stravinsky's Japanese Lyrics and Ravel's Trois Poèmes de Stéphane Mallarmé appeared on the programme of what SATIE described as 'a stupendous project for a scandalous concert' on 14 January 1914; it was a moment of European musical exchange before the outbreak of war in August. Stravinsky remained in exile in Switzerland during the war, but his impact on both mainstream and avant-garde Parisian musical life continued from a distance.

Changing Aesthetics

The armistice coincided with a palpable change in Stravinsky's musical aesthetics and a gradual distancing from his Russian heritage. On 15 May 1920, at the Paris Opéra, the Ballets Russes premièred his new ballet, PULCINELLA, which the composer famously described as 'my discovery of the past . . . the first of many love affairs in that direction' (Expo, 113). The work was shocking for being more of an arrangement of music by PERGOLESI and contemporaries, with Stravinsky only faintly appearing between the cracks in exaggerated emphasis and unexpected instrumentation. Stravinsky's homage to DEBUSSY, the Chorale from SYMPHONIES OF WIND INSTRUMENTS, which was published in a special Debussy issue of La Revue Musicale (December 1920), shows continuities with his Russian orthodox roots and a new preoccupation with wind sonorities.

Stravinsky consciously integrated himself into musical and artistic life in Paris in the postwar period. While he had been part of Ravel's artistic circle pre-war as a member of the APACHES, his attention now focused on Satie, COCTEAU and Les Six. Stravinsky's whimsical opera MAVRA (1922) was regarded as a failure by everyone apart from Satie, Cocteau, members of Les Six, Ernest ANSERMET and Jean Wiener. Indeed, former supporters, including Émile VUILLERMOZ, Ravel and the influential critic Boris de SCHLOEZER, described the work as a failure. The work demonstrates Stravinsky's new allegiance to a different Russian lineage of GLINKA and TCHAIKOVSKY, at the same time as Les Six were fashioning a French tradition less indebted to Debussy and Ravel.

Stravinsky's Octet for Wind Instruments (1923) fits more clearly with neo-classical preoccupations with form and gestures of the past, including counterpoint. Stravinsky signed an article entitled 'Some ideas about my Octuor' (1924), in which he outlined his ideas on objectivity in art: 'Music is only able to solve musical problems; and nothing else, neither the literary nor the picturesque, can be in music of any real interest' (The Arts, January 1924). Boris de Schloezer applied the term 'neoclassicism' to Stravinsky in an article of 1 February 1923 in La Revue contemporaine. Here, he pitted Stravinsky's aesthetics against Schoenberg's, linking neo-classicism with the 'stripped down style' associated with Satie and Les Six. Stravinsky's integration into French musical life was at a high point. In June that year, Les Noces received its long-awaited première at the Théâtre de la Gaieté Lyrique, Paris. Its success was huge, due to its combination of Russian-inspired exoticism and stark, postwar instrumentation of pianos and percussion. For André Coeuroy, 'Les Noces remains the most perfect attempt at synthesis of contemporary music and dance that has ever been ... achieved' (Coeuroy 1926). Stravinsky continued to dominate Parisian concert life with works such as Oedipus Rex (1926–7), Apollon Musagète (1927–8), The Fairy's Kiss (1928) and Symphony of Psalms (1930).

The Aging of Neo-classicism

Neo-classicism was now firmly associated with Stravinsky, but gradually came to signify sterility in art, thanks to entrenched debates between supporters of Schoenberg and Stravinsky – notably, Adorno, who was highly influential in questioning Stravinsky's association with modernism. Reaction came within French circles too, when Schloezer attacked Perséphone and the Concerto for Two Solo Pianos (1932–5). As Stephen Walsh asserted: 'In middle age, the great revolutionary had become an establishment icon' (SSE, 34–5). Stravinsky formally became a French citizen in 1934. However, his failure to beat Florent Schmitt to a coveted position at the Institut français in 1936 was a sign that he could never completely be accepted as French. Stravinsky embarked on a number of American tours in the late 1930s, suffered the loss of several close family members and decided to join the European exodus to the United States in 1939, but for different reasons from those of his Jewish counterparts. An almost thirty-year bond with Paris had been broken. BARBARA L. KELLY

André Coeuroy, 'Noces, musique de Stravinski', Paris-Midi, 6 June 1926.
Jonathan Cross, Igor Stravinsky (London: Reaktion Books, 2015).
Barbara L. Kelly, Music and Ultramodernism in France (Woodbridge: Boydell and Brewer, 2013).
Boris de Schloezer, 'La Musique', La Revue contemporaine (1 February 1923).

Pastorale. Vocalise (textless song) for soprano and piano. Completed on 29 October 1907 (OS), St Petersburg. The work was first performed privately two days later at one of Nikolay Rimsky-Korsakov's Wednesday soirées in St Petersburg; the first public performance took place on 27 December 1907 / 9 January 1908, at an Evenings of Contemporary Music concert in the same city, performed by Elizabeth Petrenko with the composer at the piano. Dedicated to Nadya (Nadezhda) Rimskaya-Korsakova, daughter of Nikolay, who sang the soprano part in the first few private performances. Published in

1910 (Jurgenson). The musette-like topic of the piece, written in F♯ major, belies surprising uses of chromaticism which led one audience member (Vasiliy Yastrebtsev) to describe it as 'an original song but not without strange harmonies' (quoted in SRT, 365). Stravinsky clearly retained a fondness for the work and later made several arrangements of it, including one for soprano and four woodwind instruments (oboe, cor anglais, clarinet and bassoon) in 1923 (published by Schott and first performed in Antwerp, 7 January 1924), and another for violin and piano, in collaboration with DUSHKIN in 1933 (published by Schott in 1934). *Pastorale* has been cited as 'the earliest work of his that Stravinsky continued to love and "recognize" throughout his career' (SRT, 368).

JEREMY COLEMAN

Pater noster (Otche nash). Composed 1926 (Latin version 1949). First performance, June 1937? First published 1932, Édition Russe de Musique; Latin version, first published 1949 Boosey & Hawkes. Text: Lord's Prayer.

This very brief, economical and rather severe work was originally conceived as an unaccompanied setting of the Lord's Prayer in Church Slavonic, following the composer's return to the RUSSIAN ORTHODOX CHURCH in 1926, after a long period as a non-communicant, and was adapted to Latin later. Stravinsky described it in *Memories and Commentaries* as 'a simple harmonic intonation of the words', and its simple severity places it very much at a stylistic tangent to the standard liturgical repertoire of the Russian Church at that time. Minor adjustments were made for the Latin adaptation for linguistic reasons, and the word 'Amen' was added.

IVAN MOODY

Paul Sacher Stiftung (Foundation) (PSS). Established in 1973 in Basel, Switzerland. Originally intended as a repository for SACHER's music library, the PSS has risen to become one of the world's most important music archives and international research centres. The scope of its holdings encompasses autograph manuscripts, compositional sketches, CORRESPONDENCE, films, recordings and other rare source materials. The documents of over 120 composers from both the twentieth and twenty-first centuries are represented, among them: BARTÓK, Berio, BOULEZ, Ginastera, HENZE, Ligeti, Lutoslawski, Martin, Reich and WEBERN. Notably, the Foundation houses the most comprehensive assemblage of Igor Stravinsky's vast archival materials.

A pre-eminent patron of the arts, Paul Sacher (1906–99) commissioned over 200 compositions. Formed in 1926, his Basler Kammerorchester premièred many of these new works. Sacher's friendship with Stravinsky sparked his underwriting of the composer's CONCERTO IN D (1946) and A SERMON, A NARRATIVE AND A PRAYER (1960–1). The Swiss conductor's championing of Stravinsky's music led to the Foundation's eventual acquisition of the composer's estate (*Nachlass*). Following Stravinsky's death in 1971, Sacher began collecting the composer's manuscripts – among them RENARD and PULCINELLA, as well as the APOLLON MUSAGÈTE sketchbook. In 1973, Sacher purchased the fair-copy full score of The RITE OF SPRING from Vera STRAVINSKY. Over the following decade, protracted litigation snarled the New York state courts in determining the disposition of Stravinsky's archives. Several American libraries, foundations and universities expressed interest in procuring the composer's materials. In the end, the PSS was awarded the

Nachlass in June 1983. In acquiring the enormous collection, and in accordance with explicit conditions attached to the settlement, Sacher steered the Stiftung towards facilitating modern archival studies. Operating in the newly renovated building known as Auf Burg on Basel's Münsterplatz, Sacher marshalled the requisite infrastructure, including a staff of multi-lingual specialists devoted to conserving its invaluable documents while supporting musicological research. In 1984, the Foundation mounted 'Strawinsky: Sein Nachlass. Sein Bild' at the Basel Kunstmuseum – a milestone exhibition featuring a lavish catalogue of compositional sketches, manuscripts, drawings, paintings and photographs, supplemented by several scholarly articles. Two years later, the Stravinsky Nachlass was opened to the international scholarly community.

Manuscript materials. Standing as the collection's cornerstone, the Foundation retains the composer's manuscripts extending from the early St Petersburg years to the late works of the 1960s: 390 individual folders preserve fair copies, autographs, short scores, sketchbooks, piano reductions, publishers' proofs, printed scores marked with Stravinsky's annotations, incomplete works and compositional fragments. There are 90 pages of individual sketches for the 1927–8 Apollon Musagète, tracing the BALLET's development. Over 200 sketches of the 1951 The RAKE'S PROGRESS – Stravinsky's lengthiest opus – track the transformation of both the music and libretto from as early as 1948. The composer's 1964 VARIATIONS reveal his employment of serial techniques as they unfolded in 41 pages of sketches. Examinations of other sketchbooks and revisions, drawn from virtually all of Stravinsky's works, beg an array of questions. Once the province of speculation more than judicious analysis, such source-based inquiries now suggest new perspectives that test historical assumptions.

Correspondence and Documents. Strewn through 170 boxes of letters and other documents spanning his career, Stravinsky's marginalia unveil absorbing insights. Innumerable exchanges with those inhabiting every corner of his life fill 77 boxes alone. Among the correspondents are close collaborators: ANSERMET, BALANCHINE, BENOIS, CHAGALL, COCTEAU, DIAGHILEV, NIJINSKY, RAMUZ. Although the bulk of Stravinsky's correspondence remains unpublished, Robert CRAFT released three volumes of the composer's letters between 1982 and 1985. While a useful sampling, their value is at times compromised by dubious editorial ellipses and expunctions. Another 55 boxes of annotated letters and clippings address individual compositions one-by-one. From admonishing overzealous performers to refuting misguided pundits, the composer proclaimed his convictions. Drafts of well-known writings such as the POETICS OF MUSIC convey crucial differences between the composer's initial ideas and the ghostwritten final version. Both his and Vera Stravinsky's diaries, stored in 10 boxes, offer a glimpse into their daily lives. A further 10 cartons of business ledgers and contracts betray Stravinsky's microscopic management of every composition. Text manuscripts and drafts for the popular conversation books written with Craft occupy 7 boxes (see CONVERSATIONS WITH CRAFT).

Films. Stravinsky was the subject of numerous television documentaries. The PSS retains eighty film canisters dating from the 1950s and 1960s, including documentaries produced in the UNITED STATES, Canada and Europe. The Foundation holds the huge FILM archive of British filmmaker Tony Palmer's 1982 three-hour biopic *Once at a Border*. Among these cans are noteworthy clips trimmed from rolls originally shot as part of the important 1966 CBS documentary, *Portrait of Stravinsky*. Palmer interviewed many of Stravinsky's closest colleagues from the ballet world: Geva, LIFAR, MARKOVA, RAMBERT, Danilova and Balanchine. All contribute narratives not replicated elsewhere. Informative testimony recorded in many of the film's fifty interviews was cut. Interviews with AUDEN, COPLAND, ISHERWOOD, MARKEVITCH and MONTEUX were among twenty sessions entirely excised. The Foundation retains written transcriptions of remarks found neither in the trims nor in the documentary's final version. Stravinsky's documentaries frequently perpetuate a monolithic view of the composer's carefully crafted image. Just as with the composer's unedited correspondence, it is the rich cache of such film outtakes that may project a more evenhanded image.

Photos. Beginning with early family portraits, pictures of Stravinsky are plentiful. He was endlessly photographed at the keyboard, or rehearsing, conducting, transcribing his compositions at the Pleyela onto mechanical pianola rolls (retained by the PSS), travelling extensively and conversing with the world's luminaries. Photo albums from 1914 to 1968 chronicle Stravinsky's every step. Following the composer's death, Craft and Vera Stravinsky released several of their own collections, featuring an assortment of photos taken over the course of his long career. The PSS provides access to a rich compilation of over 4,000 digitalised photographs, including numerous iconic portraits by renowned artists such as Henri Cartier-Bresson and Man Ray.

Library. Although much of Stravinsky's library is lost, the Foundation possesses several thousand of his books and scores. Some were originally part of his father's massive St Petersburg library. Others were acquired as part of the *Nachlass*. In 1990, Craft sold several boxes of Stravinsky effects to the PSS, including an additional 1,700 books and scores. The Russian section of Stravinsky's library reveals informative annotations on numerous TCHAIKOVSKY scores, as well as multiple collections of Russian folk song anthologies. As with his correspondence, the composer's off-the-record remarks are memorialised in marginalia throughout hundreds of pages. From renouncing the explications of his biographers, to notating detailed questions in such treatises as his copiously marked copy of Widor's 1910 *Technique de l'orchestre moderne*, the composer's voracious appetite for reading roused the need to voice his thoughts. He also routinely inscribed printed scores, many of which exhibit highlighted passages that caught his attention. Scholarly examination of these liberally annotated sources, ranging over music from the Renaissance to the serial scores of Webern, is essential in framing a sharper understanding of the composer's sweeping interests and influential models.

Research and Publications. The landscape of Stravinsky scholarship continues to broaden as access to the Foundation's holdings attracts international scholars. The PSS supports travel to Basel through the funding of short-term residencies. The Foundation's publications include several facsimiles exquisitely reproducing Stravinsky's compositional sketches and autograph scores. These include studies of the SYMPHONIES OF WIND INSTRUMENTS, the THREE PIECES FOR STRING QUARTET, and two separate 2013 studies of *The Rite of Spring*. An annual bulletin (*Mitteilungen der Paul Sacher Stiftung*) frequently includes selected articles on Stravinsky based upon research of the Foundation's source materials. A complete listing of published articles, exhibitions, concerts, lectures, inventories, studies and editions, and facsimiles may be explored at www.paul-sacher-stiftung. CHARLES M. JOSEPH

Pergolesi, Giovanni Battista (born Iesi, 4 Jan 1710; died Pozzuoli, 16 March 1736). Italian composer and violinist, trained in Naples and active there and in Rome. His comic intermezzo *La serva padrona* ('The Servant as Mistress') (1733) and *Stabat mater* (1736) are still frequently performed and recorded. Of the two dozen eighteenth- (and one nineteenth-) century sources employed by Stravinsky in PULCINELLA, ranging from snippets of material to complete movements, about half are by Pergolesi, mostly drawn from his operas. The published scores of the BALLET nevertheless give Pergolesi as Stravinsky's sole source in the work. The confusion doubtless stems from the mid-eighteenth-century vogue for Pergolesi, when, following his premature death, much music was misattributed to him by publishers eager for profit. BEN EARLE

Perséphone. Melodrama in three scenes, for speaker, solo tenor, chorus and orchestra, to a libretto by André GIDE loosely based on an ancient Greek hymn ascribed to Homer. Composed May 1933, Voreppe – 24 January 1934, PARIS. First performance, 30 April 1934, Ballets de Madame Ida RUBINSTEIN, Paris Opéra. Conductor, Igor Stravinsky. Published 1934, Édition Russe, Boosey & Hawkes.

Synopsis: Persephone plays with the nymphs, to whom her mother Demeter, the goddess of fertility, entrusted her. Eumolpus, the priest of the Eleusinian mysteries, warns Persephone not to look into the narcissus flower, since in its calyx the mysteries of Hades are revealed. Nevertheless, Persephone plucks the flower, sees the gloomy people of the infernal world, and feels compassion for them. In the Underworld, the shadows greet her as their Queen. Mercury offers her a pomegranate, and she bites it. In the calyx of the narcissus she sees the earthly meadows in winter and her mother grieving, and feels the pang of nostalgia. Eumolpus announces that Persephone is allowed to return temporarily to release the earth from eternal winter. Persephone reborn greets her earthly husband Triptolemus. Eumolpus enunciates the seasonal order: out of three Greek seasons, Persephone will spend two (spring and summer) with her mother, and one (winter) with Hades in the Underworld.

Perséphone was the second work commissioned by Ida Rubinstein, who chose the creative team: André Gide as poet, Jacques Copeau as director, and Kurt Jooss as overall choreographer. Copeau entrusted the sets to his collaborator André Barsacq, to the disappointment of Stravinsky, who intended this job for his son Theodore.

The subject of *Perséphone*, with a poem by Gide and music by Stravinsky, had already been considered for DIAGHILEV's Russian Seasons in 1913. For Gide, the story of Persephone was related, through a complex and intricate web of

315

intertextual links and personal connections, to very intimate experience – his honeymoon with his wife Madeleine in Sicily, where the ancient Greek cult of Persephone flourished; to his first (homo)sexual experience, which took place in Africa; to an acute feeling for natural beauty; to the specific anxiety and physical longing that he ascribed to Persephone at the moment of plucking the narcissus or biting the pomegranate. The basic concept remained intact, although his text of 1933 differs from the first drafts (1909, designed for a 'dramatic symphony' with music by Florent Schmitt; and 1913, designed for Diaghilev's ballets with the part of the naked Mercury intended for NIJINSKY), and reflects some of his later ideas (such as his idea of compassion, which leads Persephone to the Underworld to help the unhappy people there).

Not so for Stravinsky. He considered the Persephone myth not as a seasonal rite or as a paradigm of sexual longing or a (heterosexual) marriage, but as a liminal experience of life and death: 'So in the joy of spring the Greeks did not forget about death. The spring spoke to them: "hark ye mortals, this is me, I am blooming, I, Kora Persephone … !" Spring was transparent for the ancient people: it was blossoming death' (Ivanov 1904, 127). Not the seasonal fertility rite but the rite of passage between life and death (and back again) is what primarily concerned him. That accounts for the specific transparency of the orchestral and choral texture in the first two scenes, when Persephone sees through the divide between life and death, and for the unmistakable Russian Easter Hymn reference at the beginning of the third tableau (her resurrection).

From the outset, Stravinsky insisted on revealing the plot's RITUAL origin (the Eleusinian Mysteries) by introducing Eumolpus as the master of ceremony, separating the singing and miming parts and reducing the plot and characters to what was strictly necessary for the rite. Stravinsky intended the part of Eumolpus for Pierre SOUVTCHINSKY, who belonged to the closest circle of connections. To this intellectual group also belonged Albert CINGRIA, who collaborated with Stravinsky on the programme article in *Excelsior!* in which the composer made a statement on the sensitive issue of his treatment of French prosody, which aroused much critical debate and annoyed Gide to such a degree that he almost took no pains to conceal it. Gide saw his poetic text destroyed beyond recognition, distanced himself from the première and even went abroad (to Sicily) to avoid the performances. This antipathy was mutual: Stravinsky's marginalia to the libretto show the extent of their artistic differences and – most of all – his irritation with descriptions of the proposed music, which Gide included in his poetic text as author's notes.

In the article, Stravinsky argued that he was concerned with 'the beautiful strong syllables' and not with the poetical text as a whole. In fact, he did not observe the rules of French prosody: he took liberties with accentuation and made the singers pronounce silent vowels, which distorted the poetic metre. He treated the French prosody exactly as he did with Russian or Latin, concerned with the basic linguistic particles as bearers of pure immediate primary meaning, and their rhythmical interrelation as subject to musical laws only, not to those of ordinary speech. This practice of setting syllables, which Stravinsky adopted naturally and intuitively from his extensive occupation with Russian folklore and plainchant, is linked with Cingria's theory of rhythm and Souvtchinsky's notion of time.

316

Cingria's presence is perceptible in the score. At the climactic moment when Persephone bites the pomegranate, which makes her remember her mother and the earth that she left, Stravinsky employed a device very uncharacteristic of him – that of self-borrowing. He used the draft to the *Dialogue of Joy and Reason*, set to a text by Petrarch taken directly from Cingria's book on the Italian poet, which Stravinsky owned and highly appreciated. The solemn belief in music's transformative powers, turning joy into grief (and vice versa), and most beautiful and sweet at the point of death, provides the necessary extra-textual reference to Persephone's liminal experience. Stravinsky remarks in his marginalia to the libretto at this point: 'Like a cry of heart. Immense nostalgia' (Levitz 2012, 559). The open expression of emotion in this comment, as well as in the corresponding music, is extremely rare in his oeuvre.

The overall density of personal references in the score is unprecedented. Thus, the lullaby of the shadows from the second tableau, 'Sur ce lit', was initially composed for Vera de Bosset, his future wife (*see* Vera STRAVINSKY), at the moment of temporary separation, set to a poem of his own in Russian. According to Stravinsky, 'the whole of Persephone was inspired by Vera de Bosset [Sudeykina], and whatever tenderness or beauty may be found in the music is my response to those qualities in her' (Stravinsky and Craft 1962, 13, quoted in Levitz 2012, 537).

In the lullaby, Stravinsky builds the musical structure using his patent device of several ostinati complexes, interacting on distinct layers of texture and intentionally unsynchronised. There are four superimposed strati, two of which have ostinato patterns of different duration, one (on the theme of the lullaby) having twelve crotchets, and the other (the violin part) sixteen crotchets divided into groups of 3+4+5+4. These ostinati are rotated cyclically, intersecting only after the third repetition of the choral melody, creating an effect of 'weightlessness' (Carr 2005, 183–6), liminal space (Horlacher 1990, 147) and a suspension of time (Levitz 2012, 536).

Stravinsky worked freely with the text and often built musical structures not dependent on it. For example, he stated that, in the second tableau, 'the beginning must be established by the musical form so that the music is not enslaved by the dialogue' (Stravinsky's marginalia on draft 2, cited in Levitz 2012, 532). Later in the same scene, he rejected the dramatic part of Pluto (intended by Gide) on the grounds that 'the devil should not sing', and introduced a dance suite in its place, beginning with Pluto's march (with its distinct JAZZ element in the syncopated trumpet and horn), the 'infernal' sarabande (with a 'boogey-woogey' flair) and the 'celestial' one, following each other and associated with Pluto and Mercury, respectively, creating a 'neo-classical', slightly music-hall, sound.

Rubinstein and Gide polarised the critics: she for her lavish spending, outdated symbolist taste and hieratic gestures; he for his Protestant beliefs and communist sympathies. Stravinsky received a scathing critique from his old adversary, Boris de SCHLOEZER, offset by strong support from the young French camp, POULENC, LALOY, MILHAUD and others, and his syllabic approach to text-setting gained – rather unexpectedly – a warm and eloquent appreciation from Paul VALÉRY.   ELENA VERESHCHAGINA AND TATIANA VERESHCHAGINA

Maureen Carr, *Multiple Masks: Neoclassicism in Stravinsky's Works on Greek Subjects* (Lincoln: University of Nebraska Press, 2002).

Gretchen Grace Horlacher, *Superimposed Strata in the Music of Igor Stravinsky* (New Haven: Yale University, 1990).

Vyacheslav Ivanov, 'Ellinskaya religiya stradayushchego boga' ('The Hellenic religion of the suffering god'), *Novyi Put'*, 1 (1904), 110–34.

Tamara Levitz, *Modernist Mysteries: Perséphone* (New York: Oxford University Press, 2012).

Igor Stravinsky and Robert Craft, 'A quintet of dialogues', *Perspectives of New Music*, 1.2 (Autumn 1962), 7–17.

SRT

Petit Ramusianum harmonique. For speaking and singing voice(s) unaccompanied. Composed 1937, PARIS, on the occasion of the birthday of the novelist Charles Ferdinand RAMUZ (who had turned 60). The piece is Stravinsky's setting of 'three quatrains' in French by Charles-Albert CINGRIA. Cingria sent Stravinsky his text on 5 July 1937. First performance (private), 24 September 1938, in Paris at the home of Ramuz's old publisher Henri-Louis Mermod. Published 1938, in the volume *Hommage à C.-F. Ramuz* (also in Vershinina 1982).   JEREMY COLEMAN

Alexandre Blanchet and Charles Ferdinand Ramuz (eds.), *Hommage à C.-F. Ramuz* (Lausanne: V. Porchet & Cie, 1938).

I. Vershinina (ed.), *Igor Stravinsky: Vokal'naya Muzïka* ('Igor Stravinsky: Vocal Music'), vol. I (Moscow: Sovetskiy Kompozitor, 1982).

Petrushka. Composed 8 September 1910 to 26 May 1911; autograph orchestral score dated 26 January 1911 to 13/26 May 1911. First published: 1912 score and parts, 1922 4-hand piano reduction (Édition Russe de Musique). Revised version: October 1946, published 1948 (Boosey & Hawkes). First performance, 13 June 1911, PARIS, THÉÂTRE DU CHÂTELET. Conductor, Pierre MONTEUX. Choreography by Mikhail FOKINE, stage design and costumes by Alexandre BENOIS. Petrushka: Vaslav NIJINSKY; Ballerina: Tamara KARSAVINA; the Moor: Alexander ORLOV; the Magician: Enrico CECCHETTI. Four tableaux: The Shrovetide Fair – Petrushka's Room – The Moor's Room – The Shrovetide Fair (Toward Evening).

> When I was first writing Petrushka's music and did not yet think that three tableaux would grow from his little apartment, I imagined him giving a performance on the Field of Mars. Now, after our collaborative reworking, it turns out quite the opposite – that no one sees all this, that these are all just his personal sufferings, and that no one cares about them. (quoted in Wachtel 1998, 135)

Stravinsky's astonishment, expressed in a letter to Alexandre Benois in February 1911 in the midst of the work on the BALLET, reveals more than the obvious and well-known facts: that the original idea had come from the composer; that the collaboration with Benois, initiated by DIAGHILEV in autumn 1910, but starting earnestly only near the end of the year, had finally changed much of that original idea; and that the extension of the main character into a puppets' love triangle as well as its massive framing with the fairground folk scenes had transformed the nucleus (i.e. the symbolic representation of the suffering and isolated artist) into a whole complex of figures, actions and meanings. Yet exactly those 'personal sufferings' of Petrushka stood at the very beginning of Stravinsky's initial conception, sketched down in early September – namely, a *Konzertstück* for piano and orchestra, loosely conceived of as a parody of the Romantic piano concerto, heroic keyboard virtuosity now being grotesquely distorted and virtually fighting against the instrumental masses of the orchestra, itself protesting with 'sonic fisticuffs' (Stravinsky in an interview of 1928, quoted after SRT, 664). The transformation of the Romantic virtuoso into the traditional Russian puppet-booth character, who usually combined indecent, insulting mockery with a grotesque, gnome-like physical appearance, took place at a very early stage completely on Stravinsky's own initiative, possibly catalysed by the birth of his son, Soulima STRAVINSKY, in late September. But turning Petrushka, the active principle of aggression, into Pierrot, the passive principle of suffering, was the result of Diaghilev's intervention and, above all, Benois's elaboration. In European *fin-de-siècle* culture, the COMMEDIA DELL' ARTE had just been artistically ennobled, from Leoncavallo's *Pagliacci* to Russia's modernist theatre, with Vsevolod Meyerhold's anti-illusionistic staging of Blok's symbolistic *Balanganchik* ('The Showbooth', 1906) and *Sharf Kolumbiny* ('Columbine's Scarf', after Schnitzler, 1910) standing at the forefront of many other contemporary anti-naturalistic artistic models for Benois (see Andrew Wachtel, 'Petrushka in the context of Russian modernist culture', in Wachtel 1998, 1–10). The Italian characters had already been present in the harlequinades of the traditional Russian carnival theatre booths, yet this tradition, just like all the other typical carnival fairground attractions, was already extinct by 1900. To revive the non-literate, improvisatory puppet and pantomimic plays of his childhood, the boisterous carnival atmosphere, and thus the perished urban culture of folk-like customs and art forms, was the major stimulus for Benois's scenario, together with a nostalgic penchant for olden times in general, and Russia's golden past in particular. While the psychological drama of the unhappy Petrushka was rooted in Stravinsky's own imagination, Benois added the presumptuous virility of the exotic Blackmoor (a.k.a. Harlequin), the stupid superficiality of the object of desire, the Ballerina, and the demonic malignity of the old Magician (somewhere in between Pantalone and Kashchey). All of these were already pre-modelled in some of his paintings, as well as the multi-coloured spectrum of fairground visitors for the outer sections of the ballet, an ideal *mélange* of pre-modern Russian society, de-psychologised in doll's-house-like anonymity, with underlying metaphors of pre-Christian rites (i.e. pre-Petrine, pre-Western, or simply arch-Russian identity), most visibly embodied by the mummers. Benois designed the figures as well as the scenery with meticulous historical expertise, but the illusionist approach at the same time underwent stylisation. The central perspective of the fairground was framed on the proscenium by a big blue arch with inner curtain lowered for changes of scenes, emphasising the artificial nature of the play; and the almost two-dimensional flat rooms of tableaux 2 and 3 didn't allow for any spatial perception: they were instead conceived as projections of the psychograms of their inhabitants – utmost isolation and icy coldness for Petrushka, exuberance and garish colours for the Moor.

Fokine's choreography contributed enormously to the success of the ballet. He captured the folkloristic dances of the fairground scenes in a more traditional manner, but reached new heights with the foetus-like inward postures and awkward X-form jumping of Petrushka, as well as with the frivolous outward poses of the Moor and the parodistic *fouettés* of the Ballerina. Even more, Fokine was able to grasp the essence of the grotesque aspects of the music; he and Nijinsky invented new mimic and gestural elements of unprecedented expressivity, making clear that the 'real humans' on stage are not the fairground visitors, but the dolls. In creating *Petrushka*, Stravinsky was on a par with Benois, whereas Fokine now had to follow the younger composer, inverting the roles they played in FIREBIRD. Nevertheless, it is hardly possible to accept Stravinsky's later claims about his absolute dominance in the project or his disqualification of Fokine's or Benois's contributions as irrelevant or even inappropriate. Yet it is understandable that the step-by-step process of shrinking down Petrushka and his inner world within the overall design of four tableaux, as reflected in the letter cited at the outset, did concern Stravinsky quite a lot, for this was the very core of his inspiration – and now about to lose significance, or at least change perspective. Initially, the outcry of the artist-hero had been directed at his surroundings (if not provoked by them); now it had become rather a monologue of despair, hidden from all and sundry – except for the audience of the ballet. In fact, the question of perspectives is central to *Petrushka*, maybe even its main characteristic, connecting it to the modernist experiments of Meyerhold and others, even increasing the idea of a play-within-a-play by raising the number of curtains and platforms to three (main curtain, proscenium curtain, showbooth curtain), and it has been a matter of dispute between Stravinsky and Benois. On the one hand, Stravinsky wanted to eliminate the estrangement effect of the drum rolls accompanying the change of scenes, since these were contradictory to the on-stage drummers attracting the attention of the passers-by before the Magic trick. On the other hand, it was in all likelihood Stravinsky who intended Petrushka's ghost to thumb his nose from the top of the roof: not at the magician, but at the audience! The advance copy of the orchestral score from which Monteux directed the première in 1911 shows a different scenic approach, corroborated by Leonid Sabaneyev's account of the Parisian première. Here, Petrushka's ghost appeared in the opening of the curtain (that of the little show-booth), thus explicitly reflecting Meyerhold's *Balaganchik*. In the final version, Benois's stage direction speaks only of the Magician as the target of Petrushka's disdain. Yet the composer had in mind something completely different: 'His [Petrushka's] gesture is not one of triumph or protest, as is so often said, but a nose-thumbing addressed to the audience' (*Mem*, 34). In other words, the modernist demolition of the fourth wall goes back to Stravinsky, not to Benois who would have represented it *within* the reality of the play: 'I had conceived of the music in two keys in the second tableau as Petroushka's insult to the public, and I wanted the dialogue for trumpets in two keys at the end to show that his ghost is still insulting the public' (*Expo*, 136–7). Aggressivity – of the romantic piano hero, Petrushka, and his ghost – is clad in a harsh musical exterior which has become the most famous element of the ballet's music, the so-called '*Petrushka* chord', a superposition of two triads in tritone relation which can be explained either as a bitonal (or bi-scalar) combination – e.g. a discovery on the keyboard, such as suggested by the composer himself – or as an extraction of the octatonic scale which has played a pivotal role in all of Stravinsky's music up to this point, now even reaching the level of a tonality in the second tableau (see Taruskin 1987).

There has been much analytical dispute about the true nature of this signature of the main character, but seldom has the symbolic meaning been discussed. In *Firebird*, diatonicism and octatonicism stood for human vs fantastic spheres, directly prolonging the well-known Russian tradition of fairy-tale operas. In *Petrushka*, these two spheres become blurred in the melting of doll and human being, and it is exactly this synthesis which takes place in the music as well: octatonic and diatonic scales are initially diametrically opposed phenomena (orchestral accordion and fairground music vs Magic Trick), but Petrushka combines both of them, puppet and man, fantastic and real. At the end of the fourth tableau, this synthesis is ingeniously brought to fulfilment. It seems almost like the chicken-and-egg question to ask about the primacy of the octatonic or other principles: it was Stravinsky's master-stroke to achieve a fusion of the two. But his innovative creativity didn't stop here. The experimental collage techniques in the fairground scenes, ultimately fostered by Benois's pictorial fantasy and the diversity of parallel stage actions, were a means of generating musical form beyond traditional motivic–thematic developments. The bizarre dissociated pas de deux of the Moor and the Ballerina, as well as the stacking of 7/8, 3/4 and 2/4 metres (I, [3]) had no parallel in musical history (Ives apart, perhaps). The spectacular rhythmic intensity of the Dance of the Coachmen and Grooms, heightened to exuberant joyfulness in canonic combination, is generated by an unprecedented, seemingly endless pulse of regular crotchets with echoing quavers, something that reminds us of post-1945 beat music, but stands isolated in the music of Stravinsky's time. On the other hand, the 5/8 metre of the mummers with its brutal contrast of opposing instrumental forces ('sonic fisticuffs', as it were) breaks with all then-accepted principles of ballet dancing. It is a turning point in dance history, presaging the rhythmic complexities of The RITE OF SPRING. The seismographic psychological density and expressivity of Petrushka's shattered soul is musically achieved without any recourse to the emotive stereotypes which had been cultivated throughout the nineteenth century. In terms of ORCHESTRATION, the poetic idea stimulated innovative discoveries, such as the delicate and rich percussion in the Moor's dance or the 'krik Petrushki' ('Petrushka's shriek') – this was the original description of the transformed *Konzertstück*, i.e. the grotesque, mirliton-distorted voice of the show-booth puppet, which Stravinsky imitates with parallel minor seconds or tritones using the nasal timbres of clarinets, oboes and, finally, muted trumpets (in D and B♭) in the ghost scene.

The achievements of *Petrushka* are manifold. There is evidence that Stravinsky's ur-idea had been a kind of rubber-faced self-portrait, *nolens volens* symbolising the emancipation from his old surroundings, models and conventions. The ballet's core was ultimately the modernist idea of the grotesque. As such, *Petrushka* seems almost to have inspired Meyerhold's essay *Balagan* (1912), centring around the grotesque as the most important aspect of the modern theatre and claiming that 'the technique of the grotesque contains elements of the dance; only with the help of the dance is it possible to subordinate grotesque conceptions to a decorative task' (quoted in Wachtel 1988, 23). *Petrushka* could even be considered a prophetic anticipation of, if not inspiration for, Mikhail Bakhtin's famous studies on the carnival and the grotesque in his *Rabelais and His World* (written in 1940). The broader cultural reception history of *Petrushka* remains to be discovered.   CHRISTOPH FLAMM

Richard Taruskin, 'Chez Pétrouchka: harmony and tonality "chez" Stravinsky', 19th-Century Music, 10.3, special issue: Resolutions I (Spring, 1987), 265–86.

Andrew Wachtel (ed.), Petrushka: Sources and Contexts (Evanston, Ill.: Northwestern University Press, 1998).

Piano Music. It is regrettable yet perfectly understandable that those enamoured with Stravinsky's celebrated BALLET scores for DIAGHILEV and BALANCHINE, or who remain in awe of the neo-classical symphonies, may inadvertently overlook Stravinsky's contribution to twentieth-century piano literature. In such dazzling company, the solo piano music has long remained in the shadows, despite its engaging variety of musical styles. Half a century after the composer's demise, it remains under-performed and relatively unknown; it is certainly under-appreciated, for which there are several reasons. The listener's musical knowledge depends on the dissemination of repertoire, a process that is largely – in this case, quite literally – in the hands of the performer. Therein lies the problem. From the pianist's viewpoint, Stravinsky's solo works suffer from being either too ambitious for the amateur (SONATA IN F♯ MINOR, FOUR STUDIES, PIANO SONATA) or too imbued with a didactic aura for the concert artist sensitive to repertoire and reputation (TARANTELLA, VALSE POUR LES ENFANTS, LES CINQ DOIGTS). More problematic still are the works that are both technically challenging *and* idiomatically child-centred (THREE EASY PIECES, FIVE EASY PIECES). How is the dissemination of Stravinsky's piano literature via public performance even feasible when, as here in the duets, one part is so elementary that a young child can play it whilst the other part requires a professional? Furthermore, Stravinsky's writing for the piano often presents an awkwardness of a kind not encountered in other repertoire; its solution, therefore, cannot be found as a matter of course from mastering another composer's pianistic demands. Neither is the conventional route to technical excellence – via Scarlatti, Mozart, BEETHOVEN, Chopin, Schumann, Liszt, DEBUSSY, PROKOFIEV *et al.* – of much use to the pianist confronted with Stravinsky's idiosyncratic keyboard contortions, although familiarity with BACH, particularly The 48, and with Leschetizky's Method are the surest ways to prepare for those devilish neo-classical *ritornelli* (in Piano Sonata, SERENADE IN A and DUO CONCERTANT). Small wonder that Stravinsky's piano compositions are less familiar than his works for other genres when they are so rarely performed, recorded or broadcast. Yet, through their wide range of idiom and aesthetic and by revealing a subtle contribution to Stravinsky's creative path, the piano works reward both pianistic and musicological exploration.

As a reflection of this great composer's longevity, the piano literature represents seven decades of composition from the *Tarantella* fragment (1898) to TWO SKETCHES FOR A SONATA (1966), these modest works considered to be his first and last creative statements. The body of piano music composed within these experimental book-ends are neither fragments nor sketches but polished works of art with which Stravinsky supported his stylistic and aesthetic manifesto with utter sincerity, whether he was writing for virtuosi of the calibre of RUBINSTEIN (THREE MOVEMENTS FROM PETRUSHKA) or for his own children (VALSE DES FLEURS and the 'Easy' duets). Furthermore, the music that Stravinsky intended for his own performance, especially the Piano Sonata (1924) and Serenade in A (1925), holds a special place within the context of his professional re-invention as pianist-composer: in the 1920s, Stravinsky chose to proclaim his own brand of NEO-CLASSICISM from the pulpit of his pianoforte, performing his most extreme statements of Objectivity via demonstrations of pianism that have rarely been matched in terms of their demonstrative precision. In fact, for Stravinsky, the piano became more than just a musical instrument – it was an indispensable creative tool. Under his fingers, its keys became the source of music itself, his *fons et origo*, providing the sounds and intervals from which he generated his entire output. Such was his skill acquired as a pupil of RIMSKY-KORSAKOV, however, the finished result – whether instrumental, vocal, choral or orchestral – never sounds like piano music arranged for other forces. Small wonder then that Stravinsky's piano literature, formulated both *at* and *for* the very font of his creative energies, should have appeared so enigmatic to its first audiences – and often does so today.

A single incomplete sketch survives from Stravinsky's school-days. Yet, despite its fragmentary nature, the *Tarantella* (1898) is treated as a 'work' within the pages of this encyclopaedia for its historical relevance: it registers the moment when Stravinsky made the decisive step from spontaneous creation ('improvisation') to patiently crafted notation ('composition'). He was an expert at the former and a total novice at the latter: after just a few bars, the music breaks down. Yet, it was perhaps this embryonic 'failure' that prompted Stravinsky to address the minutiae, particularly the contrapuntal rigours, of music's rudiments with such enthusiasm. Furthermore, his use of five-finger patterns to articulate both the *Tarantella* melody and its accompaniment heralds a lifetime's engagement with the materials of piano technique – an absorption encouraged under the formative guidance of the pianist-composer Leokadiya KASHPEROVA (1872–1940). Most importantly, it was a premonition of Stravinsky's lifelong habit of composing at the keyboard. The piano was forever to be his preferred and trusted foundation; more specifically, pianistic materials in the form of figurations and patterns, even practice drills, were to be incorporated by the composer into his creative palette. The humble *Tarantella*, therefore, is more than a curio or an insignificant witness to Stravinsky's teenage illiteracy. It marks the spot in the sands of time when, of his own accord and without the 'benefits' of formal musical instruction, he instinctively identified the piano bench as his seat of learning.

The SCHERZO of 1902 is Stravinsky's earliest surviving compositional assignment written under the guidance of a music teacher, in this case Vasily KALAFATI (1869–1942), a former pupil of Rimsky-Korsakov. Its opening theme conceals the 3/4 metre with mischievous ingenuity, and in the coda the student attempts some ambitious contrapuntal (*stretto*) sophistication. As the music rushes headlong to the final cadence, the work seems to burst out of its pianistic confinement and demand full orchestral treatment. The following year, Stravinsky completed his first major pianistic opus. The expansive Piano Sonata in F♯ Minor (1903/4) was composed under the supervision of Rimsky himself, and demonstrates how well Stravinsky had assimilated the idiomatic traditions of his predecessors via the *Grandes sonates* of TCHAIKOVSKY and GLAZUNOV. Significantly, it is in the Scherzo movement (*Vivo*) that Stravinsky expressed himself with greatest individuality. He would soon apply his penchant for fantastical *scherzi* to the orchestral SCHERZO FANTASTIQUE (1907/8) and FIREWORKS (1908). FOUR STUDIES, op. 7 (1908) is the last solo piano work Stravinsky composed as a student of Rimsky-Korsakov. Together with *The* KING OF THE STARS (1911), these 'transcendental' études represent Stravinsky's unique testimony to the dominant presence of SCRIABIN in Russian musical life. World War I occasioned an even rarer morsel: the one-movement SOUVENIR D'UNE MARCHE BOCHE (1915) which, as its title suggests, is a dark and irreverent caricature of Teutonic militarism destined for the fund-raising, stridently anti-war, anthology *The Book of the Homeless* (1916). According to the composer's son Soulima it was improvised at the piano in MORGES on 1 September 1915, in spontaneous reaction to the German invasion of Belgium. By contrast, PIANO-RAG-MUSIC (1919) is a joyous work of extraordinary originality and demonstrates Stravinsky's excitement at hearing the novel rhythms of American popular music, increasingly to be heard in PARIS.

CHORALE (1918) was also improvised at the piano, this time as a direct response to news of the death of Claude Debussy, whom Stravinsky so admired; this *tombeau* became the foundation-stone of SYMPHONIES OF WIND INSTRUMENTS (1920). It expresses a sense of mourning, yet without indulging in any form of personal outpouring, in anticipation of the mature neo-classical monument SYMPHONY OF PSALMS (1930), which was later described by Ernest ANSERMET as 'expressing the religiosity of others'. This tendency towards emotional distancing, already apparent in the so-called 'Easy' piano duets of 1914 and 1917, would lead to the elaboration of Stravinsky's neo-classical idiom, whose sense of *objectivity* is one of its defining characteristics. *Les Cinq Doigts* (1921) were composed for Stravinsky's children and illustrate other important ingredients in the formulation of this new aesthetic: the elements of *simplicity* and *utility*. The evolution of Stravinsky's musical language towards neo-classicism (at least, its manifestation via the piano keyboard) was briefly interrupted by the arrangement of *Three Movements from Petrushka* (1921), written for the virtuoso Artur Rubinstein. Sensitive to Stravinsky's hostility towards 'interpreters', Rubinstein never recorded the work. As the pianist later complained to Alfred Cortot in 1944: 'In the music of Stravinsky one must assume the role of a sad and unquestioning servant.' This, however, was a misunderstanding. Such censure was reserved for 'interpreters' of the neo-classical repertoire, not the Russian works.

The Piano Sonata (1924) and Serenade in A (1925), together with the CONCERTO FOR TWO SOLO PIANOS (1932–5), stand at the summit of Stravinsky's neo-classical piano literature. The Sonata's first audience, at a private performance in a Warsaw hotel, reacted not altogether favourably to the music's 'unusual logic and mathematical clarity' by observing how

'Stravinsky used to walk on a rope, then a wire. Now he walks on a razor blade.' Stravinsky may well have provoked such a response by commenting, upon lifting his hands from the final chord, that 'right now [he was] struggling to create drawings at the expense of colour'. Through this allusion to the work's aural and notational austerity, the composer declared his intention to explore new paths diametrically opposed to Rimsky-Korsakov's teaching. In fact, the Sonata, whilst also containing the seeds of Stravinsky's neo-classical future, demonstrates more than any other work up to this moment his emphatic rejection of his Russian past. The final movement is a rigorously contrapuntal 'invention' replete with augmentation of the subject and, even, its simultaneous statement with the original. It presents a strangely unnerving study of repressed quasi-Baroque emotionalism tempered by an implacably extreme (icy) classicism. Prokofiev may have dismissed Stravinsky's new style as 'pockmarked Bach' but another Russian émigré, Arthur LOURIÉ, demonstrated greater understanding, possibly because he, too, was based in Paris and more open to its contemporary trends, when he wrote that Stravinsky's return to classical forms 'catalyse(d) some new ideas within him' ('catalysent en lui des idées neuves').

Stravinsky's next work for solo piano was written many years later in the UNITED STATES. TANGO for piano (1940) offers another commentary on popular dance, though, in contrast to Piano-Rag-Music, this was observed not from the perspective of a European outsider but from the composer's relocation within the Latin-American universe. In his later years, Stravinsky employed the piano in several major works, including the SYMPHONY IN THREE MOVEMENTS (1942–5) and MOVEMENTS (1958–9), yet only one further solo for piano was composed. Intriguingly, the TWO SKETCHES FOR A SONATA (1966) suggest a desire – born of personal satisfaction, perhaps – to design a unification of serial technique with a neo-classical aesthetic. Stravinsky's valedictory act of creation, therefore, may be viewed as a gesture of reconciliation and embrace – even, as Villa-Lobos expressed this, as 'a letter written for posterity without expecting a reply'. However, the Two Sketches were not to be Stravinsky's final labour of musical craft. That accolade goes to his instrumental arrangement of fugues from The Well-Tempered Clavier with which he kept his mind active in 1969 as he lay in his hospital bed in New York. En résumé, Stravinsky's long innings was defined, from start to finish, by his engagement with the life-giving properties of the piano keyboard. His regular appointment with its generative stimulus led him to believe that 'les doigts ... sont de grands inspirateurs' ('fingers are great inspirers'). This was no idle remark, but a conviction founded upon daily reassurance that composition at the piano and for the piano – above all, with the piano – could be relied upon to generate musical material suitable for all genres. The results of this stylistically varied and musically invigorating symbiosis can be grasped by whoever is drawn to the by-ways of Stravinskian literature and wishes to combine their sense of curiosity with a fearless desire for their pianism, and their powers of artistic comprehension, to be vigorously challenged.   GRAHAM GRIFFITHS

Ernest Ansermet, Les fondements de la musique dans la conscience humaine (Neuchâtel: La Baconnière, 1961).

Graham Griffiths, *Stravinsky's Piano: Genesis of a Musical Language* (Cambridge University Press, 2013).

Jarosław Iwaszkiewicz, *Wiadomosci literackie* (Warsaw), 46 (1924). In ISPS.

Joseph N. Straus, *Stravinsky's Late Music* (Cambridge University Press, 2001).

Heitor Villa-Lobos, *Villa-Lobos, sua obra*, 2nd edn (Rio de Janeiro: MEC / DAC / Museu Villa-Lobos, 1972).

Auto

Piano-Rag-Music, for piano. Completed 28 June 1919; manuscript dedicated to Artur Rubinstein. First performance, 8 November 1919, Lausanne. First published 1920, J. & W. Chester.

Piano-Rag-Music constitutes Stravinsky's final 'JAZZ'-related exploration of the years 1917–19. Although the piece was composed for Artur RUBINSTEIN, the pianist did not appreciate its merits – especially its percussive qualities – and so it was instead premièred by the Spanish pianist and harpsichordist José Iturbi, active in PARIS and later in New York. In Stravinsky's own performance, this short work lasts around 3 minutes 18 seconds.

This piece comprises a single, multi-sectioned movement, set at a brisk metronome marking of $\downarrow$ = 144. As Stephen Walsh (1993, 89) first noted, the compositional approach here is typically 'cubist', with individual elements of rag abstracted and exploited, rather than any direct evocation, although Richard Taruskin (SRT, 1479) is convinced that melodic quotation from 'some piece of Latin sheet music' is evident in the sketch material (for discussion of sketches, see Maureen Carr (2014)). In any event, the main thematic material and cellular figuration certainly derive from Stravinsky's previous 'jazz' portraits, most overtly the 'Ragtime' (and 'Tango') from The SOLDIER'S TALE.

Piano-Rag-Music presents a kaleidoscopic, fragmentary surface, commencing with very loud (*très fort*) and strident pulsating chords. Its percussive stop–start gestures are purposefully mechanistic (*excessivement court et fort; attaquez chaque fois*), with hints of Stravinsky's contemporaneous passion for the pianola and piano-roll. Exuberant, accented bursts hint at rag music 'head' motifs, the first of which (*c.* bar 18) interestingly foreshadows the opening blues-like gesture of George Gershwin's *Three Preludes* for piano (1926). This music exhibits quite a dissonant norm (acting as a cue for the set-theoretic analysis of Charles Joseph (1982)), which is contrasted by quieter, more melodic and pensive moments of focus. Amid changing metre, its rhythmic identity consists primarily of off-beat and syncopated 'maxixe' patterns: at times suggestive of jazz riffs (together with some repeated 'um-cha' figures); at other times, stuttering and close to disintegration.

Within its episodic structure are found two substantial, internal portions of unbarred music, which offer a cadenza-like semblance of improvisation. After the second portion occurs the closest thematic allusion to The *Soldier's Tale*. As the piece progresses, it accrues greater intensity and virtuosity, again featuring large, dissonant cluster chords. Finally, these insistent 'wrongnote', 'one-out' clashes become spent of their energy, and an ensuing third portion of unbarred music (*subito pp*) fades to nothing. It is as though an open window had enabled the listener to experience the piece, but that this window has now been closed.

Perhaps surprisingly, given its rhythmic complexities and unbarred portions, *Piano-Rag-Music* has nonetheless proved attractive as a choreographic
challenge, existing in various modern balletic guises. In particular, the work
has been recreated by CHOREOGRAPHERS of the NEW YORK CITY BALLET, including Todd Bolender for the Stravinsky Festival (23 June 1972) and Peter Martins
for the Stravinsky Centennial Celebration (10 June 1982).   DEBORAH MAWER

Maureen A. Carr, *After The Rite: Stravinsky's Path to Neoclassicism (1914–1925)* (New York: Oxford
University Press, 2014), 121–62.
Charles M. Joseph, 'Structural coherence in Stravinsky's Piano-Rag-Music', *Music Theory
Spectrum*, 4 (Spring 1982), 76–91.
Stephen Walsh, *The Music of Stravinsky* (London: Routledge, 1988).

Piano Sonata. Composed 1924, Biarritz, Nice: first movement, April – 21
August; second movement, completed 6 October; third movement, completed
21 October. First (private) performance, 6 November 1924, Warsaw, by the
composer. Published 1925, Russischer Musikverlag, Berlin; 1926 (ed. Albert
Spalding), Hawkes & Son, London. Dedication: 'Dediée à Madame la Princesse
Edmond de Polignac'. Order of movements: (I) $\quad = 112$ (II) *Adagietto* (III) $\quad = 112$.

The Piano Sonata was written during the summer and autumn of 1924 while
Stravinsky toured his recently premièred CONCERTO FOR PIANO AND WIND
INSTRUMENTS. Both works contributed greatly to the establishment of the
composer's new, neo-classical identity, as proclaimed in January of that year
via his manifesto 'Some ideas about my Octuor'. The Sonata presents many
archetypal neo-classical features. For example, much as in the eighteenth-
century manner, the score offers few dynamics or agogic markings; and in the
outer movements, the customary 'subjective' tempo indication in Italian is
replaced by a defiantly 'objective' metronome marking. Yet such new directions emerged from material penned six months earlier of very different origin.

1. The start of the first movement was sketched in April 1924 after the
    composer's return from a trip to Spain. There, according to Romain
    ROLLAND (1952, 852, quoted in SCS, 265), Stravinsky had been intro-
    duced to *cante jondo* by Manuel de FALLA, and had identified 'the ideal of
    music, spontaneous and "useless", a music which has no wish to express
    anything'. Although Stravinsky was later to deny any interest in Spanish
    music, it is tempting to hear a distant echo (in the opening arpeggiated
    bars) of 'the endless preliminary chords of guitar playing' and (bar 14,
    quasi trillo) 'a singer with unending breath trolling forth her long Arab
    ballad with a wealth of *fioriture*' (*Auto*, 64). If *The* RITE OF SPRING can be
    credited with elevating the parameter of rhythm to unprecedented impor-
    tance, the Sonata's equivalent achievement was to restore the dry *senza
    pedale* articulation of the *claveciniste* to the foreground of musical composi-
    tion. The musical argument of this movement is largely one of articula-
    tion, right-hand *legatissimo* versus left-hand *sempre* staccato. This is also
    a feature of the following movement.

2. The *Adagietto* presents a contrasting aspect of NEO-CLASSICISM: here,
    besides 'Couperin', there are references to the nineteenth century too,
    via 'Chopin' and 'Schubert' – though the spirit of BEETHOVEN, whose
    sonatas Stravinsky had been examining during the process of

composition, underpins the music's dark intensity. The movement vividly recalls Stravinsky's early song PASTORALE (1907), which employs a similar disposition of the hands, separating the right's florid *legato* ornamentations from the left's *secco* accompaniment.

3. Guided by contrapuntal intent, the final and most technical movement of the Sonata is a two-part invention ingeniously interwoven with compositional extensions: simultaneous augmentation (bars 19 and 117) and pedal-point (bar 128) underneath a chromatic, Bachian coda. It was precisely this kind of hard-driven neo-classical *ritornello* that provoked such hostility from Stravinsky's contemporaries, PROKOFIEV referring to such music as 'pock-marked Bach' while SCHOENBERG ridiculed 'der kleine Modernsky' in his *Drei Satiren* choruses, op. 28. Yet, whilst containing the seeds of Stravinsky's neo-classical future, the Piano Sonata demonstrates, more than any other work to date, Stravinsky's emphatic rejection of his Russian past. The view from the composer's AUTOBIOGRAPHY (1936) suggests that the Sonata represented for Stravinsky a particularly refined distillation of his neo-classical aesthetic, an extreme ideological precipice from which he would retreat in subsequent works.   GRAHAM GRIFFITHS

Graham Griffiths, *Stravinsky's Piano: Genesis of a Musical Language* (Cambridge University Press, 2013).

S. Prokofiev, *Autobiography, Articles, Reminiscences*, ed. S. Schlifstein, trans. Rose Prokofieva (Moscow: Foreign Languages Publishing House, n.d. [c. 1954]).

Romain Rolland, *Journal des années de guerre (1914–1919)* (Paris: Éditions Albin Michel, 1952).

Igor Stravinsky, 'Some ideas about my Octuor', *The Arts* (January 1924). In SCW, 574–7.

Strawinsky: Sein Nachlass. Sein Bild (Basel: Kunstmuseum Basel, Paul Sacher Stiftung, 1984).

Pianola. Stravinsky worked with the pianola between 1914 and 1930, embracing an instrument with superhuman capabilities in terms of speed, polyphony and accuracy. He was first introduced to the pianola during a visit to Aeolian Hall in London. The instrument he worked with primarily required a pianolist to operate the tempo lever with the right hand, the functions of the sustaining and una corda pedals with the left hand, and the dynamic force of the piano, favouring one half of the keyboard over the other at the E/F split above middle C, with the feet. With this much to do, interpretation on the pianist's part was inevitable. Stravinsky would eventually realise this, as we shall see below, although, ironically, he wrote in his AUTOBIOGRAPHY that he was attracted to the pianola due to its ability to eliminate interpretation. Stravinsky clearly learned much during his work with the instrument. In fact, finding various solutions to the problem of establishing dynamic relationships gave him satisfaction and led to him taking the time to make special arrangements for forty of the fifty works he released on piano rolls.

The *Étude for Pianola* is the only composition that Stravinsky wrote for this solo instrument, although a draft for the work originally incorporated other instruments as well. Once rescored for the pianola alone, it appeared in a collection of works by various composers commissioned by Edwin Evans, the British music critic. In this work, Stravinsky uses the strengths of the instrument to his advantage, with fragments of melody openly competing with one another in order to depict the streets of Madrid that he visited in 1916. It is also deliberately mechanical in sound, turning a limitation into a virtue. The *Étude* was composed in 1917, although it was only premièred in 1921. This was because of the priority given to the cutting of the rolls for PETRUSHKA and THE RITE OF SPRING. Although his contract forbade him from doing it, Stravinsky made an arrangement of the *Étude* in 1928, when it became the fourth of the FOUR STUDIES for orchestra, now entitled 'Madrid'. Stravinsky was discouraged from writing any other works for the solo pianola since he received far less than he expected for the work, and was told that he couldn't expect as much for any future composition.

While Stravinsky would never again write a piece for solo pianola after 1917, he did still envision this instrument in an ensemble. Immediately after the completion of the *Étude* in 1917, Stravinsky began the intermediate version of *Les Noces* for an ensemble of four pianolas, two cimbaloms, electric harmonium and assorted percussion. Stravinsky stopped working on this version of the score in 1919 and claimed in his *Autobiography* that he did so due to the difficulties in synchronising the mechanical instruments with the performers. This explanation may not be entirely convincing: a concert in 1924 with the singer Vera JANACÓPULOS had her sing 'Tilimbom' from the *Three Songs for Infants* accompanied by a pianola. It has been suggested that the Russian composer became disillusioned with the pianola due to the circumstances surrounding the *Étude*, as well as a letter dated 12 June 1919 – between the time Stravinsky submitted it for the piano roll to be cut, and the time he heard the work on solo pianola – from Ernest ANSERMET, describing a performance of this work. In this letter, Ansermet criticises the limitations of the instrument (while admitting that he heard the work performed on a weak instrument) as well as the intervention of the pianolist. This last point negates the entire reason Stravinsky decided to write for this instrument. Therefore, it does not seem coincidental that only weeks after receiving this letter, he abandoned the intermediate version of *Les Noces*.

In 1924, Stravinsky signed a contract with the Aeolian Company to produce rolls for the new Duo-Art pianola. This instrument was able to capture small changes in tempo and dynamics and reproduce them so that no pianolist was needed. The other advantage of this new instrument was the ability to view annotations and pictures on the piano rolls as they scrolled by. A complete set of rolls for THE FIREBIRD was released in 1929, bearing the following inscription: 'These six rolls embody an Autobiographical Sketch of the Composer's Life to the year 1910, with a Literary and Musical Analysis of THE FIRE-BIRD, and a Complete Performance of it, recorded by the Composer himself.' Edwin Evans most likely served as ghost author for the analysis in the annotations, and Stravinsky did not perform these rolls, but rather 'interpreted' them. The same is true of the piano rolls the composer published with Pleyel, which, although explicitly labelled 'adapted and performed by the composer', were subjected to a variety of transcriptional processes including hand cutting. Other rolls released in the Duo-Art series included the PIANO SONATA and the first movement of the CONCERTO FOR PIANO AND WIND INSTRUMENTS. Rolls for *Petrushka* were virtually complete but were not sent to the printer, since, unfortunately, the Aeolian Company went out of business in 1930. While the

Duo-Art pianola would have solved Stravinsky's problems with the instrument cited above, the composer was ready to move on to the next technological breakthrough that would help him eliminate interpretation: the gramophone.

MARK MCFARLAND

Rex Lawson, 'Stravinsky and the pianola', in Jann Pasler (ed.), *Confronting Stravinsky* (Berkeley and Los Angeles: University of California Press, 1986), 284–301.
Mark McFarland, 'Stravinsky and the pianola: a relationship reconsidered', *Revue de musicologie*, 97 (2011), 85–110.

Picasso, Pablo (born Málaga, Spain, 25 October 1881; died Mougins, France, 8 April 1973). One of the great artistic friendships of the twentieth century, Stravinsky's bond with the brilliant Spanish painter generated constant inspiration that fed the experimental proclivities of both men and resulted in daring innovations in art.

The two men met in Rome in April of 1917, brought together by Sergey DIAGHILEV and the BALLETS RUSSES. Picasso travelled to Italy to immerse himself in the rehearsals for *Parade* and to develop his contribution to the collaboration, while Stravinsky had been promised some conducting work in Rome, Naples and Milan. The two artists struck up an immediate friendship and spent considerable time together in Rome and Naples, exploring both the relics of the classical past and contemporary popular culture – in particular, the COMMEDIA DELL' ARTE, which would become an important motif in the work of both men in the years following the Italian journey. The carnivalesque spirit of the *commedia dell'arte* influenced their behaviour as well: apparently, after a rowdy drunken night, the pair were arrested for urinating against a wall in the Galleria and were only released when the policeman heard them referred to as 'maestri'.

This auspicious meeting also immediately influenced the artistic production of both men and inspired in them a kind of interdisciplinary experimentation. On 30 April 1917, Stravinsky used a hotel telegram to create POUR PABLO PICASSO for clarinet, which he gave to Picasso as a present. In this short, five-bar piece, Stravinsky signals his devotion to his new Spanish friend by mimicking his cubist aesthetic. Like Picasso's cubism, he emphasises the materiality of his piece, playing games with the connections between the lines on the telegram paper and the bar lines and note stems of his composition. Rhythmical and metrical games suggest the visual puns and fractured perspective of cubist visual art, while the choice of clarinet calls to mind Picasso's repeated use of this instrument in his cubist still lifes. A few days later Picasso responded in kind – creating the first of several portraits of Stravinsky. Its severe neo-classical style augurs the composer's turn back to the classical idioms of the past. However, while rooted in history, this new classicism was still modernist and would not be mistaken for the work of bygone masters, as a humorous anecdote indicates. Travelling back to SWITZERLAND on 24 April 1917, Stravinsky found that Picasso's present attracted unwanted attention from the border police. Bewildered by Picasso's stylistic deformations, the border guard insisted that the portrait was a map of secret military fortifications and that Stravinsky was a spy. It was only with the intercession of Stravinsky's friend, Lord BERNERS of the English High Commission, that the sketch was returned and the composer was allowed to go.

While these two early works are trivial, they indicate a process of collabora-tion and mutual influence that would also appear in several more significant creations. In 1919, the two artists collaborated on RAGTIME – with Picasso drawing the cover design for the composer's piano transcription of his score. Image and music echo and mimic one another. Stravinsky's exploration of syncopation and swing rhythms is picked up by Picasso, who uses a single herky-jerky line to create a picture of two musicians in motion. Further, Picasso uses musical symbols – a treble clef for the violinist and a bass clef for the banjo player – to represent the physiognomy of the two musicians. For his part, Stravinsky continues his cubist-inspired use of visual jokes, puns and multiple perspectives – for example, writing notes to appear as one pitch but sound as another (an F is given a double sharp to actually sound as a G).

But the most significant collaboration between the two artists would come the following year with their work on the Ballets Russes production PULCINELLA. This was to be a balletic interpretation of an eighteenth-century *commedia dell'arte* play, with Stravinsky orchestrating and arranging a series of musical fragments attributed to PERGOLESI. While Stravinsky was initially cool towards this idea, he was ultimately convinced, at least in part, by 'the proposal that I should work with Picasso . . . whose art was particularly near and dear to me'. The 'recollections of our walks together and the impressions of Naples we had shared . . . combined to overcome my resistance' (SCW, 286). Drawing on their shared experience of the *commedia dell'arte*, interest in classicism, and practice of collaboration and mutual influence, the two artists produced a work that would hold a significant place in both their artistic trajectories.

Like their previous collaborative work, *Pulcinella* stages a series of echoes and resonances between music and image. While both composer and painter explore the possibilities offered by a return to the idiom of classicism, both also undermine a naïve and nostalgic pastiche with a modernist focus on irony, artifice, hybridisation and destabilisation.

For Stravinsky, this was an extremely important work that helped to define the modernist classicism that would dominate his artistic production during his first period of exile after Word War I. Stravinsky would continue to explore this new fusion of classicism and MODERNISM in works such as OEDIPUS REX and APOLLON MUSAGÈTE, while Picasso figured it in works such as *Three Musicians* and *Two Women Running on the Beach*.

Picasso and Stravinsky would never be as close as they were in the period of the late 1910s and early 1920s. However, in contrast to other artistic friends, with whom Stravinsky sometimes developed volatile relations, his attitude to Picasso was always one of the deepest respect and admiration. In the later 1930s, Stravinsky acknowledged that he hadn't seen the painter for some time, but noted: 'I am a great friend of Picasso, and I admire him in all of his tendencies; he is always and consistently a great artist.'   IHOR JUNYK

Piltz, Maria Yulyevna (born Russia, 1891; died Russia, 1968) Russian dancer. Piltz joined DIAGHILEV'S BALLETS RUSSES in 1910. In 1913, she created the role of the Chosen One in the first production of The RITE OF SPRING, replacing Bronislava NIJINSKA, Vaslav NIJINSKY's intended dancer, who was pregnant. Depending on which account is read, her interpretation of the 'Sacrificial Dance' caused the audience at the première to become either louder or quieter. In the press, she was widely praised for her stamina, and the artist Valentine Gross-Hugo immortalized her portrayal of the Chosen One in a drawing printed in *Montjoie!* (June 1913).   SOPHIE REDFERN

Pitoëff, George and Ludmilla   (George born Tiflis (now Tbilisi), Georgia, 4 September 1884; died Geneva, Switzerland, 17 September 1939 / Ludmilla (*née* Smanov) born Tiflis (now Tbilisi), Georgia, 24 December 1895; died Rueil-Malmaison, Hauts-de-Seine, 15 September 1951). Georgian actors and theatre directors. The Pitoëffs directed and starred in the first production of *The Soldier's Tale* (Lausanne, 1918). Ludmilla created the role of the Princess, and George the dancing Devil (Jean VILLARD created the speaking Devil). In 1936, Stravinsky remembered it being 'good luck' that the Pitoëffs were available to work on the production and claimed to have created the dances with Ludmilla (*Auto*, 74). He later contradicted this, declaring he had mapped out the movement with author Charles Ferdinand RAMUZ (*Expo*, 95).   SOPHIE REDFERN

Poetics of Music (Poétique musicale). The *Poetics of Music in the Form of Six Lessons* constitutes the cornerstone of Stravinsky's aesthetic philosophy. The text was written in response to a March 1939 invitation from Harvard University to present a series of lectures during the 1939–40 academic year within the framework of the Charles Eliot Norton Professorship of Poetry, the first time the professorship had been granted to a musician. Harvard's invitation coincided with a very difficult period in Stravinsky's life, during which he faced the deaths of his daughter, his wife Catherine STRAVINSKY and his mother, not to mention his own HEALTH problems, for which he had been sent to a sanatorium in Sancellemoz. Stravinsky's commitments at Harvard played a decisive role in his definitive exile to the UNITED STATES.

Faced with this literary task, Stravinsky called on his friend Pierre SOUVTCHINSKY to sketch a plan for his lessons, which initially numbered eight, later reduced to six. After having outlined the lectures in April 1939, Souvtchinsky suggested that Stravinsky pursue the remaining work of writing them (in French) with ROLAND-MANUEL (Roland Alexis Manuel Lévy). This occurred in May and June of 1939. Apart from a few details, the final version of the lectures was quickly set in place and included six 'lessons'. The first, 'Getting acquainted' ('Prise de contact') was followed by 'The phenomenon of music' ('Du phénomène musical'), 'The composition of music' ('De la composition musicale'), 'Musical typology' ('Typologie musicale'), 'The avatars of Russian music' ('Les avatars de la musique russe') and 'The performance of music' ('De l'exécution'), concluding with an 'Epilogue'.

It is widely known that Stravinsky often called on collaborators to assist his writing process; determining exactly how the work of writing was divided between composer and collaborator is somewhat more complicated. In an article from the early 1980s ('Roland-Manuel and *La Poétique musicale*'), Robert CRAFT summarily reduced Stravinsky's role in the process, but in the early 2000s, new documents appeared that allowed for a fundamental revaluation of the roles of both men, to the extent that *La Poétique musicale* now represents the best-documented example of Stravinsky's many literary collaborations. Numerous stages of the text still exist. In presumed order, three documents clarify the process of Poétique's creation: a three-page plan, written in French with a few words in Russian, in the hand of Pierre Souvtchinsky; a nineteen-page development of that plan written in French and Russian, in the hand of Stravinsky (now held at the SACHER FOUNDATION in Basel); and six dossiers of drafts corresponding to the six lessons of Poétique, in French, in the hand of Roland-Manuel, also conserved in Basel. Taken together, these documents clearly illustrate the development of the text. The evidence suggests that Stravinsky asked Souvtchinsky to help him write the lectures, and that Souvtchinsky began by offering Stravinsky an outline. From that document, the composer developed a certain number of ideas and personal opinions. Roland-Manuel's manuscripts include numerous pages dictated by Stravinsky, as well as reformulations and developments of text that Roland-Manuel had written and submitted to the composer. Moving beyond the imposture implied by the approximate and inaccurate term 'ghostwriter', these exchanges are better understood as a subtle labour of collective authorship. This is why it seems more pertinent to speak in terms of 'co-authors'. From a genetic point of view, Stravinsky's process can be described as triangular: Souvtchinsky suggested the architecture of the text and set forth its main ideas; Stravinsky, an oral intermediary, was at the heart of the process, developing content and submitting it to Roland-Manuel who acted as a writer, breathing life into the text and strengthening its ideological and aesthetic impact. In total, it took the three men five months to complete the lectures, from late March to mid-August 1939. They remained true co-authors of even the final version, with their correspondence showing that they all reread, corrected and approved the published text. It may be that this circular process of authorship is also applicable to Stravinsky's numerous other writings, but this remains uncertain in the face of insufficient documentation (*see* PUBLISHED WRITINGS).

In terms of content, it should be noted that certain ideas of Poétique musicale are directly linked to one of the authors in particular. For example, the questions of time in music that had long preoccupied Souvtchinsky are also found in Poétique, with the notions of psychological time / 'temps psychologique' and ontological time / 'temps ontologique' reused word-for-word from Souvtchinsky's 'La notion de temps et la musique', published in the May–June 1939 issue of the *Revue musicale*. Generally speaking, abstract questions dealing with the ideas of musical 'speculation' / 'spéculation musicale', the search for 'the One' in the multiple / 'la recherche de l'Un à travers le multiple', and creative monism / 'monisme créateur' are all indebted to Souvtchinsky. Stravinsky had already collaborated with Souvtchinsky in late 1938, in preparation for an interview with Serge Moreux for the end of December. Many of the typically Stravinskian ideas found in this interview reappear in Poétique musicale, including the themes of listening, criticism, the avant-garde, 'musical high mathematics', speculation, technique, craft, art, inspiration, personality, individualism and taste. Of course, certain ideas relating to order in music, style, the description of compositional processes, the rejection of 'MODERNISM', and the autonomy of music in the face of the opposition between interpretation and performance had been regular leitmotifs of Stravinsky's texts since the 1920s. Other ideas can be traced to regular exchanges with Stravinsky's friends, such as

Charles-Albert CINGRIA, from whom he borrowed the notion of 'pompier-isme'. Stravinsky shared certain spiritual horizons with Roland-Manuel, a connection reflected through interest in Jacques MARITAIN's celebrated treatise Art et scolastique (Art and Scholasticism, 1920), which appears in the first lessons. Roland-Manuel may also be responsible for the influence of Paul VALÉRY. But Roland-Manuel's most remarkable contribution to Poétique musicale is his rhetorical mastery, which allowed Stravinsky to impose himself as an orator before his audience. Roland-Manuel employs all of the resources of philosophical expression in the French classical tradition: the use of aphorism; recourse to etymology; and a taste for definitions. Roland-Manuel's culture allowed him to build his demonstrations and masterfully deploy Stravinsky's thought. It should also be added that the fifth lesson, a virulent attack on the musical policies of the Soviet Union, was first written by Souvtchinsky before being translated into French by Soulima STRAVINSKY and edited by Roland-Manuel.

The Sacher Foundation also holds two typescript versions of the final text, the second of which, bearing phonetic notes for pronunciation, was used for the lectures at Harvard. This final version is identical to the first edition published by Harvard in French in 1942. A second French edition appeared in 1945 without the fifth lesson on Russian music. This censure resulted from the new political climate – since the winter of 1940, the USSR had joined the Allies. In 1947, Harvard published an English edition with a preface by Milhaud. Poétique musicale was subsequently and progressively translated into numerous other languages.   VALÉRIE DUFOUR

Robert Craft, 'Roland-Manuel and the Poetics of Music', Perspectives of New Music, 21.1–2 (1982–3), 487–505, republished as 'Roland-Manuel and La Poétique musicale' in SSC, II, 503–17.
Valérie Dufour, 'La Poétique musicale de Stravinsky: un manuscrit inédit de Pierre Souvtchinsky', Revue de musicologie, 89.2 (2003), 373–92.
Valérie Dufour, 'The Poétique musicale: a counterpoint in three voices', trans T. Levitz and B. Behrmann, in SHW, 225–54.
Igor Stravinsky, Poétique musicale (Cambridge, Mass.: Harvard University Press, 1942; new edn, ed., intro. and notes by Myriam Soumagnac (Paris: Flammarion, 2000; revised 2011).

Pokrovsky, Ivan (Vasilyevich?) (born ?, 1876; died St Petersburg, 25 October / 7 November 1906). Russian composer and pianist closely associated with the EVENINGS OF CONTEMPORARY MUSIC (ECM) – an early friend of Stravinsky's. In published conversations with Robert CRAFT, Stravinsky recalled 'a man eight years my senior' he first met in 1897, who 'was no mere amateur in music . . . for he had been a pupil of LIADOV'. In his 1936 AUTOBIOGRAPHY, Stravinsky describes Pokrovsky as a co-founder of ECM, whose enthusiasm for such French composers as Gounod, Bizet, Delibes and Chabrier was for Stravinsky an effective antidote for the academicism of RIMSKY-KORSAKOV and BELYAYEV's circle. Stravinsky told Craft: 'Pokrovsky was thin and phthisical, and he died of his disease at an early age.'

The assumption that Stravinsky's friend was Ivan Vasilyevich Pokrovsky (1876–1906) is based on an advertisement published in the newspaper Novoye vremya (20 November / 3 December 1901), announcing a forthcoming performance by 'I. V. Pokrovsky', conducting his suite The Four Seasons, on 24 November (OS); this includes the first mention in print of Stravinsky, then aged 19, who, with fellow university student Mikhail Chernov (1879–1938), was to provide accompaniment, presumably on the piano. Furthermore, an article by Yuri Verkhovsky, published in a Festschrift in honour of KARATÏGIN (1927), includes a single passing mention of 'composer I. V. Pokrovsky' as a co-founder of Evenings of Contemporary Music.

Yet by September 1904, I. V. Pokrovsky had become blind (evident from a letter from choir master and church music scholar Stepan Smolensky) and had to be supported by his wife. Meanwhile, Mikhail Kuzmin, who was involved in Evenings from October 1905 and also knew I. V. Pokrovsky, refers in his diary to a Pokrovsky (he does not mention his patronymic) who, late the following year, was on Evenings' audition panel and represented that organisation in an apparently official capacity, which appears to be in line with Stravinsky's claim that his Pokrovsky was a co-founder. Given the likelihood that Stravinsky, and certainly Kuzmin, personally knew more than one Pokrovsky, the possibility that there has been subsequent confusion between two so-named musicians cannot be ruled out on the present evidence.

DANIEL JAFFÉ

Mikhail Kuzmin, Dnevnik 1905–1907 ('Diaries 1905–1907'), ed. N. A. Bogomolov and S. V. Shumikhin (St Petersburg: Izdatelstvo Ivana Limbakha, 2000).
Maria Pavlovna Rakhmanova (ed.), Russkaya dukhovnaya muzïka v dokumentakh i materialakh ('Russian Sacred Music in Documents and Materials'), vol. VI, book 2: S. V. Smolenskiy i ego korrespondentï ('S. V. Smolenskiy and His Correspondents') (Moscow: Znak, 2010; Litres, 2017).
Auto; Expo; SRT

Pope St John XXIII (Angelo Giuseppe Roncalli, born Sotto il Monte, Italy, 25 November 1881; died Rome, 3 June 1963). Head of the Catholic Church from 1958 to his death, and canonised in 2014. As Cardinal and Patriarch of VENICE (1953–8), Angelo Roncalli gave permission to hold the world première of Stravinsky's CANTICUM SACRUM (1956) in ST MARK'S BASILICA. In doing so, Cardinal Roncalli set a precedent in staging a secular concert in a cathedral church. In Venice, Stravinsky met Cardinal Roncalli in person and was impressed by the future 'Good Pope John'. Three years later, Pope St John read in the papers that the Maestro was in Rome, invited him to the papal apartments, and honoured him with a long conversation.

Shortly before his death, Pope St John XXIII proposed to Stravinsky that he conduct a performance of his MASS at the Vatican (which did not take place) and also signed the patent making the composer a Knight Commander with Star of the Papal Order of St Sylvester. Stravinsky received the Order on the day of his concert dedicated to the Holy Father's memory in the Cathedral of St Francisco in Santa Fe (18 August 1963).

During his short pontificate, Pope St John XXIII inaugurated a new era in the history of the Catholic Church by his openness to change. He promoted a new dialogue with Protestant and Orthodox Christians, as well as with Jews and Muslims, and initiated the Second Vatican Council (1962–5). Stravinsky collected clippings from newspapers with information about Pope John's activity, kept his portrait photograph, and refused any social or professional invitations during the pontiff's illness.

TATIANA BARANOVA MONIGHETTI

Poulenc, Francis (born Paris, 7 January 1899; died Paris, 30 January 1963). French composer. As a young composer in search of a distinctive musical voice, Poulenc was deeply drawn to Stravinsky's music and ideas. He wrote in 1941: 'At the age of 20, I was absolutely crazy about Stravinsky's music. A number of my first works testify to this passionate veneration.... Now that I'm over 40 ... my fervour for Stravinsky's works remains intact, and it is still to this master that I owe some of my greatest musical joys' (Poulenc, 'Igor Strawinsky', *L'Information musicale* (3 January 1941)). Poulenc's early works reveal many traces of Stravinsky's influence and a high degree of musical and aesthetic complicity. Both composers shared a concern for wind sonorities and tonality, and were fascinated by the question of how to be modern. Poulenc's Sonata for two Clarinets (1918) immediately suggests the sound-world of Stravinsky's THREE PIECES FOR SOLO CLARINET; the two works were written in 1918, but it is unlikely that Poulenc saw Stravinsky's score. Rather, Poulenc's Sonata reveals the impact of Stravinsky's ballets in the irregular and changing bar lengths and incessant repetition of short ostinato patterns. His early wind pieces, including the Sonata for Clarinet and Bassoon (1922) and the Sonata for Trumpet, Horn and Trombone (1922) are the basis of a career-long preoccupation with wind combinations.

Stravinsky's MAVRA was a moment of revelation for Poulenc, and his letters reveal an intensification in his self-declared 'Stravinskian crisis' (Poulenc 1994, 127); *Mavra* gave him the permission he needed to write tonally and reject atonality and polytonality. In his review of *Mavra*, he asserts: 'We are in a period of standardization where all the chords appear to us on the same level. We therefore need to look for novelty in other places' (Poulenc 1922, 223).

Poulenc had his first significant success with his BALLET *Les Biches*, which received its première in Monte Carlo in January 1924 at a 'Festival français' commissioned by DIAGHILEV. The writing for wind sounds distinctly Stravinskian, suggesting the SYMPHONIES OF WIND INSTRUMENTS, but these allusions are reserved for moments of stasis and transition, where the musical action temporarily stops, before launching into a new sound-world. The most striking instances occur in the chorale-like texture at the opening of the 'Rondeau' (figure 21); the stark oboe, cor anglais and bassoon sonorities that straddle the 'Rag Mazurka' and 'Andantino'; and the short-breathed clarinet figure at the opening of the 'Petite Chanson dansée'.

Les Biches and *Mavra* also share a common source in the music of TCHAIKOVSKY. While *Mavra* captures Tchaikovsky's Russian character, Poulenc reveals a trump card: his melodic gift – and *Les Biches* is more accessible than *Mavra* because of his ability to write warm and moving melodies.

Stravinsky helped Poulenc find his own musical identity, in which sonority, tonality, melody and an awareness of artistic fashion would continue to be important for his musical sensibility. Poulenc's affinity with Stravinsky reveals the extent to which the latter was in sympathy with the musical aesthetics of post-World War I FRANCE, and the considerable role both composers played in shaping musical taste. When many had grown tired of Stravinsky's NEO-CLASSICISM, Poulenc refuted André Jolivet's claim in 1945 that French music had learned nothing from Stravinsky: 'Nothing makes me prouder than to be the friend of such a man and to acknowledge that I owe to him the clearest aspects of my musical language' (Poulenc 2011, 112).   BARBARA L. KELLY

Barbara L. Kelly, *Music and Ultra-Modernism in France* (Woodbridge: Boydell, 2013).
Hervé Lacombe, *Francis Poulenc* (Paris: Fayard, 2013).
Francis Poulenc, 'A propos de Mavra de Igor Strawinsky', *Feuilles libres* (June–July 1922), 223.
Francis Poulenc, *Correspondance*, ed. Myriam Chimènes (Paris: Fayard, 1994).
Francis Poulenc, *J'écris ce qui me chante*, ed. Nicolas Southon (Paris: Fayard, 2011).

Pour Pablo Picasso. Miniature for solo clarinet, written while Stravinsky was in Rome in the company of Pablo PICASSO, in April 1917. The piece was written directly onto a sheet of Italian telegram paper. In the booklet notes to the 2007 Naxos recording of the piece (played by the American clarinettist Charles Neidich), Robert CRAFT surmised from the mistakes in the manuscript that the piece had been written while Stravinsky and Picasso were inebriated. In fact, the unusual spellings are not all errors: the source bears the dedication 'pour Paolo Picasso', 'Paolo' being the Italian form of 'Pablo'. The dedicatee seems to have added in his own hand: 'pour la postérité' ('for posterity'). The piece changes time signature between 5/8 and 6/8 and the melody gradually rises from E to C and falls again at the end, spanning the interval of a minor sixth.
                                                                    JEREMY COLEMAN

Robert Craft, Booklet Notes to CD recording, I. Stravinsky, 'Histoire du Soldat' Suite / Renard [etc.] (cond. Craft), Stravinsky, Vol. 7, NAXOS, catalogue number 8.557505, released Jan. 2007.

Praeludium, for JAZZ ensemble. Composed 1936–7; completed 6 February 1937. First performance, 19 October 1953, LOS ANGELES. First published 1968, Boosey & Hawkes.

This briefest interwar nod to a synthesis of jazz and neo-classical style lasts under two minutes. It is scored for an ensemble broadly similar to that employed for the EBONY CONCERTO immediately after World War II: a mixture of saxophones (altos, tenor and baritone), trumpets, trombones, percussion, plus guitar and string ensemble.

Given its introductory fanfare, featuring the trumpet and snare drum, and its sheer brevity, the piece provides an attractive opener for concert programmes that seek to illustrate Stravinsky's interest in jazz, loosely defined. This miniature *Praeludium* thrives on syncopation – especially provided by incisive, punctuating brass – together with false relations and distinctive instrumental combinations and sonorities, such as the double-stopped or pizzicato strings and use of solo celesta.

The work has been recorded by the Columbia Jazz Ensemble; the original 1937 manuscript is held in the Paul SACHER STIFTUNG (Foundation) in Basel.
                                                                    DEBORAH MAWER

Prokofiev, Sergey Segeyevich (born Sontsovka, 11/23 April 1891; died Moscow, 5 March 1953). Russian composer and pianist. Stravinsky's junior by nine years, he enrolled at the ST PETERSBURG CONSERVATORY aged 13, on Alexander GLAZUNOV's urging, in 1904. Like Stravinsky, Prokofiev was involved in the EVENINGS OF CONTEMPORARY MUSIC, both as pianist and as composer, though he built an entirely positive relationship with Vyacheslav KARATÏGIN. Stravinsky and Prokofiev first shared a programme in a concert organised by Alfred Nurok in 1910, under the auspices of *Apollon* magazine, when Stravinsky played excerpts from *The* FIREBIRD (and evidently heard, or was told of, Prokofiev's disparaging comment about the music afterwards).

Though dismissive of Stravinsky's first two ballets, Prokofiev became aware of the older composer's growing success with the BALLETS RUSSES in PARIS. After his own Conservatory finals in 1914, winning the top piano prize, Prokofiev travelled to London to be introduced to DIAGHILEV and gain a BALLET commission. He subsequently met Stravinsky in 1915 when summoned to Rome by Diaghilev to discuss his ballet in progress. Stravinsky – primed by Diaghilev to join him on a charm offensive (to persuade Prokofiev to abort his first attempt at a ballet and write another one) – greeted the younger composer warmly when they were reunited in Milan. With Stravinsky, Prokofiev performed a four-hand version of *The* RITE OF SPRING, and became an enthusiastic admirer of both the *Rite* and *Pribaoutki*. Prokofiev's first completed ballet score, *Chout* (1915, revised 1920), shows Stravinsky's unmistakable influence.

They subsequently fell out in 1922 during Diaghilev's audition of Prokofiev's *Love for Three Oranges*. The argument was not simply about OPERA, which both Stravinsky and Diaghilev claimed was a moribund form, but was rooted in Prokofiev's disagreement over Stravinsky's NEO-CLASSICISM: in *Three Oranges*, Prokofiev set Carlo Gozzi's COMMEDIA DELL'ARTE drama in his own style, rather than in a neo-classical style such as Stravinsky used with his 'PERGOLESI' arrangements in PULCINELLA. Prokofiev subsequently derided Stravinsky's PIANO SONATA as 'pock-marked Bach', and APOLLON MUSAGÈTE as 'picked from the most shameful pockets: Gounod, Delibes, Wagner, even Minkus'. Their relationship was not improved by Stravinsky's close association with Arthur LOURIÉ, whom Prokofiev blamed for the destruction of several manuscripts he had left in RUSSIA, including the original version of his Piano Concerto No. 2.

Stravinsky and Prokofiev never again found common creative ground, yet their relationship eventually became cordial. Prokofiev's Violin Concerto No. 1, dismissed by Stravinsky's followers at its 1923 Paris première, was an enduring favourite of Stravinsky himself. Meanwhile, Prokofiev, self-aware enough to recognise (helped by the teachings of Christian Science) his own resentment at Stravinsky's 'disproportionate' success in Europe, noticed that Stravinsky became increasingly 'warmly affectionate and even-tempered'. Stravinsky took Prokofiev's side against Diaghilev in 1929 when the impresario – whose high-handed behaviour over *Apollon Musagète* had already irritated Stravinsky – threatened to sue Prokofiev and Païchadze (Prokofiev's and Stravinsky's publisher) for publishing *The Prodigal Son* without crediting Boris KOCHNO as co-author. That summer, Stravinsky paid a friendly visit to Prokofiev and his family, immediately before receiving the devastating news of Diaghilev's death.

Stravinsky was unsympathetic about Prokofiev's decision to uproot his family from Paris and settle in Stalinist Russia in 1936. Yet, notwithstanding his sour comment to Robert CRAFT about Prokofiev's return being 'a sacrifice to the bitch goddess, and nothing else', he confessed to having been 'touched ... very much' when he heard that a 'few weeks before [Prokofiev's] death a friend of mine in Paris received a letter from him inquiring about me'. DANIEL JAFFÉ

Daniel Jaffé, *Sergey Prokofiev* (London: Phaidon, 2007).

Sergey Prokofiev, 'Autobiography', in *Soviet Diary 1927 and Other Writings*, trans. Oleg Prokofiev (London: Faber and Faber, 1991).

Sergey Prokofiev, *Behind the Mask: Diaries 1915–1923*, trans. Anthony Phillips (London: Faber and Faber, 2008).

Sergey Prokofiev, *Prodigal Son: Diaries 1924–1933*, trans. Anthony Phillips (London: Faber and Faber, 2012).

Mem; SCS.

Published Writings. Unlike many twentieth-century composers' writings, Stravinsky's texts have little ambition to explain or theorise his compositional practice. Instead, Stravinsky preferred to discuss his works in the context of their performances and the aesthetic debates those performances raised. In total, the composer authored nine books, two of which were written in French before 1940 (*see* AUTOBIOGRAPHY and POETICS OF MUSIC), with the remaining seven published as volumes of CONVERSATIONS WITH ROBERT CRAFT. If the autobiography published in 1935 essentially sought to situate the composer's career path from its beginnings to the French musical landscape of the 1930s, *Poetics of Music*, which was originally a series of lectures given at Harvard in 1939–40, constitutes the *de-facto* aesthetic treatise of reference for Stravinsky's art. The seven books of conversations published between 1959 and 1972 contain the composer's thoughts on a variety of subjects. The two pre-1940 books present Stravinsky as the sole author, although they were both co-written in dialogue with collaborators, whereas the volumes written with CRAFT assume the place of collaboration, with double signature on their covers. Stravinsky was not a writer and, to him, literary exercise, the expression of ideas in written form, had always represented a challenge. This was due partly to questions of language, but perhaps also to a busy schedule entirely devoted to his music. This explains the relatively limited volume of his writing, as well as his frequent recourse to collaborators, who have often been too summarily designated as 'ghostwriters'. Ultimately, it was thanks to a form of midwifery subtly conducted by his interlocutors that Stravinsky managed to express his thoughts and put them into written words.

Apart from the above-cited books, Stravinsky's body of writings also includes articles published in newspapers and other periodicals, press interviews, and radio interviews prepared with pre-written scripts. Here, too, the composer probably called upon co-authors to help write his texts or prepare interviews, but he always signed his remarks alone. Sometimes he would contest the authority of certain ideas published under his name and, according to him, without his permission.

The editorial history of collections of Stravinsky's writings began with the translation, sometimes imprecise, of the many excerpts from interviews between Stravinsky and Robert Craft in *Stravinsky in Pictures and Documents* (1978) and in *Igor and Vera Stravinsky: A Photograph Album, 1921–1971* (1982). During the same period, François Lesure published a selection of six interviews in French in *Stravinsky: Études et témoignages* (1982), which was followed by Eric Walter White's monograph *Stravinsky: The Composer and His Works*, which in its 1979 edition offered the first selection of the composer's writings. In 1988, Victor Varunts published *I. Stravinsky: Publitsist i sobesednik*, a collection of annotated excerpts taken from articles and interviews, translated into Russian and covering the whole of Stravinsky's life. More recently, all of Stravinsky's writings from 1912 to 1939 (twenty-one in all), and a selection of about forty of the most pertinent interviews from the same period, were gathered and edited for the first time in French – most often their original language – in the collection *Confidences sur la musique* (2013). The body of published Stravinsky interviews has gradually grown, with various projects such as Tamara Levitz' collection of interviews in Spanish, granted between 1921 and 1949, found in *Stravinsky and His World* (2013). Surely a new volume should now be envisaged for the writings and interviews of the composer's American period.

Stravinsky's public remarks were often motivated by a desire to 're-establish the truth' and influence the direction of discussions on his music, as he was able to do as an interpreter of his own works. Without ever laying out the least theorisation or compositional system, Stravinsky progressively held forth on his choices, principles and convictions. In some cases, it is also possible to perceive the composer's desire to control the image that he projected in the public arena and to outline his place in the history of music.

In the beginning, Stravinsky's texts were rather short, with the composer preferring the form of the 'open letter' to express himself in public. In 1914, after the revival of The RITE OF SPRING, he expressed his gratitude to the musicians who played in the concert and participated in the rehabilitation of his work and reputation after the initial scandal of May 1913. Later, in 1921, he used the same format to promote DIAGHILEV's BALLETS RUSSES during the period of TCHAIKOVSKY's *The Sleeping Beauty*. During the 1920s and 1930s, Tchaikovsky would continue to represent an openly declared model in numerous texts. Along with Tchaikovsky, two other Russians, Diaghilev and PUSHKIN, held a place of privilege in Stravinsky's writings, contributing towards the edification of his artistic and literary heritage. To each, he devoted a vast textual homage in 1937.

In the 1920s, when Stravinsky's works were sometimes the object of severe criticism, the composer sought to reframe, refute and redefine the discourse on his works. In 1927, for example, he published an 'Avertissement' in which he intended to limit the usage of the term NEO-CLASSICISM. Although he resolutely renounced talking about his music in a text published in 1919, Stravinsky changed direction just a few years later. From that point onwards, he would only write three texts on his own works from his European career: the first, in 1923, was devoted to the OCTET FOR WIND INSTRUMENTS; the second, from 1934, talks about PERSÉPHONE; and the third takes the form of a lecture from 1935 ('Quelques confidences sur la musique' ('A few thoughts on music')), the only lecture he gave before Harvard, in which he discusses his works for piano. In general, during the interwar period, in both his texts and interviews, Stravinsky says very little about his music from a technical point of view. The autonomy of music and questions of a compositional level that he evokes are all themes that recur throughout his writings (order, form, inspiration, work, effort, craft, etc.). In the 1930s, many of his ideas can be found in both his articles and his books AUTOBIOGRAPHY and *Poetics of Music*, to the point that entire paragraphs were often recycled from the books to create articles or interview scripts.

Press interviews, often more spontaneous, disclosed other aspects of Stravinsky's world. One, for example, reveals his attachment to spiritual life, with Stravinsky extolling divine order and making reference to the thinking of Jacques MARITAIN, his increasingly pronounced enthusiasm for the UNITED STATES, his distrust of the radio and the passivity it inspires, and – against the background of his individual blend of personal political and religious convictions – his intense desire for order in all things: 'architecture in art is a form of order; creation is a form of protest against anarchy and oblivion' (1930, see Stravinsky 2013, 245).

When it came to writing in the private sphere, Stravinsky was far more unfettered as a correspondent. Among his published correspondence, there are two major sources: the edition of his letters with various correspondents chosen and translated into English by Robert Craft (*Stravinsky: Selected Correspondence*, 1982, 1984, 1985), and the complete edition of Stravinsky's letters with his Russian correspondents up to 1939, published in their original language by Victor Varunts as *I. F. Stravinskij. Perepiska s russkimi korrespondentami. Materiali k biografi* (1977, 2000, 2003). There are also editions of Stravinsky's exchanges with other protagonists, including RAMUZ, ANSERMET, CINGRIA, RAVEL and POULENC.   VALÉRIE DUFOUR

François Lesure (ed.), *Stravinsky: Études et témoignages* (Paris: Lattès, 1982).
CM

Publishers. Stravinsky's first publisher was M. P. Belaieff, founded in 1885. Though based in ST PETERSBURG, it used its Leipzig address as a means of securing international copyrights for Russian composers, notably RIMSKY-KORSAKOV, GLAZUNOV, LYADOV, Taneyev and SCRIABIN. The vocal score of Stravinsky's *The Faun and the Shepherdess* was published by Belaieff in 1908, with a full score following in 1913. Over the next few years, a number of Stravinsky's works were published by the Moscow firm of P. Jurgenson, the original publisher of almost all TCHAIKOVSKY's works from 1868 onwards. Jurgenson published the first editions of SCHERZO FANTASTIQUE in 1909, PASTORALE (voice and piano version) and FOUR STUDIES, op. 7, in 1910; *The* FIREBIRD and *Two Poems of Paul Verlaine* in 1911; *Two Songs*, op. 6, in 1912; *Zvezdoliki* in 1913; and the SYMPHONY IN E♭ MAJOR in 1914. Another venerable Russian firm, V. Bessel, published Stravinsky's final chorus for MUSSORGSKY's KHOVANSHCHINA in 1914.

Stravinsky's first non-Russian publisher was Schott in Mainz. On the personal recommendation of Alexander Ziloti (who conducted the earliest performances), Schott published the full score of FIREWORKS in November 1909. Despite the work's success, Schott's next Stravinsky publication was not for another twenty years, when he renewed his relationship with the firm in 1929.

Over the next two decades, Stravinsky had a number of different publishers. His most productive association was with KOUSSEVITZKY'S Édition Russe de Musique, founded in 1909 by Sergey and Natalia Koussevitzky with the aim of subsidising the propagation of new Russian music. Losses were borne by the Koussevitzkys, and all profits accrued to the composers. The venture was highly successful, both artistically and financially. To ensure better copyright protection, at least among countries that had joined the Berne Convention (the original 1887 signatories were GERMANY, FRANCE, Belgium, ITALY, Spain, SWITZERLAND, Tunisia and the United Kingdom), the firm was first legally established in Berlin as the Russischer Musikverlag, with offices in Moscow and St Petersburg, and later in PARIS, London, New York and Leipzig. The main office was moved to Paris in 1920. Stravinsky's relationship with the firm got off to a bad start when the jury that selected new pieces for publication (including, among others, SCRIABIN, RACHMANINOV, Medtner and Koussevitzky) voted to reject PETRUSHKA. The decision was overturned after Koussevitzky threatened to withdraw from the jury, and in 1912 Édition Russe published both the full score and piano duet version. The RITE OF SPRING was published in 1913 (piano duet) and 1921 (full score), and The NIGHTINGALE in 1914 (vocal score) and 1923 (full score). Other major works issued by Édition Russe after World War I included The SONG OF THE NIGHTINGALE (1921) PULCINELLA (full score only, 1924), CONCERTO FOR PIANO AND WIND INSTRUMENTS and OCTET FOR WIND INSTRUMENTS (1924), MAVRA and the PIANO SONATA (1925), SERENADE IN A (1926), SYMPHONIES OF WIND INSTRUMENTS (piano arrangement by LOURIÉ, 1926), OEDIPUS REX (vocal score, 1927), APOLLON MUSAGÈTE and The FAIRY'S KISS (1928), CAPRICCIO (1930), SYMPHONY OF PSALMS (vocal score 1930; full score 1932), PERSÉPHONE (vocal score, 1934) and a number of smaller pieces. On 1 March 1947, the catalogue of Édition Russe de Musique was purchased by Boosey & Hawkes.

While Stravinsky was in Switzerland during World War I, and the activities of Édition Russe were suspended, he had some works published by the small Geneva firm of Adolphe Henn, a publisher and concert agent whose catalogue was otherwise made up of Swiss composers. In 1917, Henn published RENARD, Pribaoutki, Berceuses du chat and the two sets of easy pieces for piano duet. At the very end of the war, Blaise Cendrars negotiated the publication of the solo piano version of RAGTIME with Éditions de La Sirène in PARIS, one of the most visually striking of Stravinsky editions with its front cover designed by PICASSO. This was La Sirène's only Stravinsky publication.

With his Russian publishers facing an uncertain future, Stravinsky wanted to find a more permanent relationship with a publisher in western Europe. Henn acted as the Geneva agent for the London firm of J. & W. Chester, originally established as a music shop in Brighton in 1874, and purchased by Otto Kling in 1915 when it moved to London. Stravinsky first contacted Kling during the war, and in November 1919 Chester came to an agreement with Henn and Stravinsky to take over the works previously published by Henn, in a deal where Stravinsky was paid 10,000 francs. In 1919, Chester also acquired pieces written during the war – notably The SOLDIER'S TALE – and the rights to Les NOCES, which was not yet finished. Chester published the vocal score in 1922 and a full score in 1923. In collaboration with Chester, Wiener Philharmonischer Verlag (a subsidiary of Universal Edition) issued 'Philharmonia' pocket scores in Vienna of Les Noces, The Soldier's Tale, RENARD, Pribaoutki, Berceuses du chat and the two Suites for small orchestra. PULCINELLA has a tangled publishing history: the vocal score was published by Chester in 1920, but apparently Kling had no interest in acquiring the performing rights to the work, and the full scores of the complete BALLET and the orchestral suite were eventually issued in 1924 by Koussevitzky's Édition Russe, which also published the various suites for violin and cello. The CONCERTINO for string quartet was rejected by Chester and was instead published by the Copenhagen firm of Wilhelm Hansen in 1923.

As noted above, Édition Russe published most of Stravinsky's music between 1921 and 1934, but in 1929 he revived the relationship with Schott in Mainz, starting with publication of the version of PASTORALE for voice and wind instruments. The *Four Russian Peasant Songs* followed in 1930, but it was the CONCERTO IN D FOR VIOLIN AND ORCHESTRA that established a significant contact with the firm. Written at the request of Willy Strecker (a director of Schott) for Samuel DUSHKIN, this was published in 1931. The other major works issued by Schott before the outbreak of World War II were the CONCERTO FOR TWO SOLO PIANOS (1936), JEU DE CARTES (1937) and CONCERTO IN E♭: 'DUMBARTON OAKS' (1938). Stravinsky and Schott appeared to be set for a fruitful partnership until war once again intervened. Stravinsky's first American publication was the TANGO for Chamber Orchestra, published by Mercury Music Corporation in 1941, but subsequently he worked with Schott's American representative, Associated Music Publishers. This relationship did not begin well: the orchestral parts for the SYMPHONY IN C prepared in 1941 were full of errors, prompting Stravinsky to write to Nadia BOULANGER about 'the idiots of Associated Music Publishers' (the score was not published until 1948, by Schott). His only realistic option was to stick with Associated Music, which published the CIRCUS POLKA (1943), DANSES CONCERTANTES, FOUR NORWEGIAN MOODS (1944), SONATA FOR TWO PIANOS, SCÈNES DE BALLET, SCHERZO À LA RUSSE, ELEGY for solo viola (or violin) (1945), SYMPHONY IN THREE MOVEMENTS (1946) and ODE (1947), the separate revision of the 'Danse sacrale' from *Le Sacre*, and the reorchestration of the 'Bluebird Pas de Deux' from TCHAIKOVSKY's *Sleeping Beauty*. All these works reverted to Schott after the war, as did the 1945 *Firebird Suite*, originally published by Leeds Music, and the *Tango* published by Mercury. The EBONY CONCERTO was published in 1946 by Charling Music, a subsidiary of Edwin H. Morris.

Shaky international copyright protection (the UNITED STATES only joined the Berne Convention in 1989, 102 years after its original signatories) and the ravages of two world wars led to a proliferation of unauthorised American editions of Stravinsky's most popular works. In 1932, Edwin Kalmus in New York issued a pirate reprint of the 1919 *Firebird Suite*, following this in 1933 with *Petrushka* and *The Rite*. In 1941, Edward B. Marks in New York produced unauthorised piano arrangements of excerpts from *The Soldier's Tale*, *The Song of the Nightingale*, *The Firebird*, *Petrushka* and *The Rite*. This was a situation that was to persist for years, and it infuriated Stravinsky, but a partial solution was soon to emerge.

Boosey & Hawkes had served as the British and American agent for Édition Russe since 1923, and in 1945 Ralph Hawkes began negotiations with Koussevitzky for the acquisition of the company. Koussevitzky was happy to sell at the right price, and Boosey & Hawkes paid dearly to conclude the deal (a figure of $300,000 is mentioned in 1946); on 1 March 1947, the entire Édition Russe catalogue was purchased by Boosey & Hawkes. On 28 December 1945, Ralph Hawkes visited Stravinsky in Beverly Hills (coincidentally on the same day that Stravinsky became an American citizen) to discuss current and future works. Some were already spoken for, such as the Symphony in Three Movements and the *Ebony Concerto*, but Hawkes was after a long-term arrangement, and in 1947 he concluded an agreement with Stravinsky offering a guaranteed annual income (initially $10,000, rising to $12,000 after two years and increasing thereafter). The CONCERTO IN D was the first new work to appear from Boosey & Hawkes (the full score was published in November 1947), and it was soon followed by other new works including ORPHEUS and MASS (1948), The RAKE'S PROGRESS (1951), and eventually the works of Stravinsky's later years.

In 1970, Harold Schonberg described Stravinsky as 'undoubtedly a millionaire' in the *New York Times*, and the composer responded ruefully in *Harper's Magazine* that 'the worst of it is that undoubtedly I *would* have been if the US and USSR had signed the Berne Convention. In that event my *Firebird* royalties alone . . . would have made up the seven-figure sum – instead of the three figures and some loose change the music actually earns for me here' (T&C, 292). Two decades earlier, facing the prospect of meagre earnings from his most famous works in the country that he had made his home, revisions of earlier pieces added significantly to Boosey's Stravinsky catalogue, ensuring copyright protection (and royalties) for pieces whose original versions were in the public domain in the United States. Some revisions were far-reaching, with changes that reflected Stravinsky's stylistic evolution (*Petrushka*; *Symphonies of Wind Instruments*) while others involved minor corrections. Boosey & Hawkes published revised versions of *Petrushka*, *Symphonies of Wind Instruments*, APOLLO (all 1947), The Rite (1948 and 1965), *Symphony of Psalms* (1948), *Capriccio* (1949), *Pulcinella* (suite 1949; complete ballet 1965) and *The Fairy's Kiss* (1950).

Boosey & Hawkes published all Stravinsky's later works, including the CANTATA (1952), SEPTET (1953), THREE SONGS FROM WILLIAM SHAKESPEARE and IN MEMORIAM DYLAN THOMAS (1954), GREETING PRELUDE, CANTICUM SACRUM and BACH–Stravinsky 'Vom Himmel hoch' (1956), AGON (1957), THRENI (1958), EPITAPHIUM (1959), MOVEMENTS, DOUBLE CANON and MONUMENTUM PRO GESUALDO (1960), A SERMON, A NARRATIVE AND A PRAYER (1961), ANTHEM (1962), The FLOOD (1963), ELEGY FOR J. F. K. (1964), ABRAHAM AND ISAAC, VARIATIONS (ALDOUS HUXLEY IN MEMORIAM) and INTROITUS (T. S. ELIOT IN MEMORIAM) (1965), REQUIEM CANTICLES and The OWL AND THE PUSSY-CAT (1967), FANFARE FOR A NEW THEATRE (1968) and the Wolf–Stravinsky Two Sacred Songs (1969). The handsome facsimile edition of the sketches for The Rite was published in 1969.

Stravinsky's relationships with publishers were often fractious, partly because he didn't trust them to treat him fairly, and partly because he wanted to exercise an unusual degree of control over the appearance of his scores. At Boosey & Hawkes, there was also his sense of rivalry with BRITTEN, who had been with the firm since signing a contract in 1935. From 1947 until 1965 (when Britten changed his publisher to Faber Music), the two composers needed to be managed tactfully, since each considered himself to have a position of special importance. Boosey & Hawkes tried to balance judiciously, even in its advertisements. The issue of *Tempo* for Summer 1951 was devoted to *The Rake's Progress*, but the back cover advertised 'Two New Operas': *The Rake's Progress* and Britten's *Billy Budd*. It was only after Stravinsky's arrival at Boosey & Hawkes that he took up poems and subjects Britten had already set: the 'Lyke Wake Dirge' is set in Britten's Serenade for Tenor, Horn and Strings (1943) and Stravinsky's Cantata (1952); Britten's *Noye's Fludde* (1958) treats the same story as *The Flood* (1961–2), as do Britten's *Canticle II* (1952) and *Abraham and Isaac* (1962–3). The original title of the *Requiem Canticles* was Sinfonia da Requiem but Stravinsky told an interviewer in 1966: 'I did not use it only because I seem to have shared too many titles and subjects with Mr. Britten already' (T&C, 98). Thanks to the emollient diplomacy of Ernst Roth (general manager 1949–64) and others, Boosey & Hawkes kept Stravinsky more contented than he had been with any of his previous publishers.   NIGEL SIMEONE

Helmut Kirchmeyer, *Kommentiertes Verzeichnis der Werke und Werkausgaben Igor Strawinskys bis 1971* (Stuttgart: Hirzel Verlag, 2002); online version (updated): www.kcatalog.org.
Helen Wallace, *Boosey & Hawkes: The Publishing Story* (London: Boosey & Hawkes, 2007).
SCW

Pulcinella. Composition completed 1920. First performance, 15 May 1920, Paris Opéra. Published 1920, J. & W. Chester (vocal score), Édition Russe de Musique / Boosey & Hawkes; 1924, Édition Russe de Musique (full score). Instrumentation: soprano, tenor, bass, piccolo, 2 flutes, 2 oboes, 2 bassoons, 2 horns in F, trumpet in C, trombone, string quintet (concertino), strings (ripieno, 4.4.4.3.3).

Movements
Overture: Allegro moderato
Serenata: Larghetto, Mentre l'erbetta (tenor)
Scherzino: Allegro
Allegro
Andantino
Allegro
Ancora poco meno: Contento forse vivere (soprano)
Allegro assai
Allegro – alla breve: Con queste paroline (bass)
Andante: Sento dire no'ncè pace (soprano, tenor and bass)
Allegro: Ncè sta quaccuna po (soprano and tenor)
Presto: Una te fallan zemprecce (tenor)
Allegro – Alla breve
Tarantella
Andantino: Se tu m'ami (soprano)
Allegro
Gavotta con due variazioni
Vivo
Tempo di minuetto: Pupillette, fiammette d'amore (soprano, tenor and bass)
Finale: Allegro assai

A BALLET with song based on the theatrical model of the COMMEDIA DELL' ARTE, produced in collaboration with the Spanish artist Pablo PICASSO, the Russian choreographer Léonide MASSINE, and the Russian impresario Sergey DIAGHILEV. *Pulcinella's* première at the PARIS Opéra was followed shortly thereafter by a performance at Covent Garden (London's Royal Opera House) on 10 June, with both conducted by Ernest ANSERMET.

The mere possibility of such a collaboration is difficult to imagine – not only given the complex personalities involved, but also because each of these luminaries was in a transition of one sort or another. For Stravinsky, 1920 represents the transition from his earlier period, often referred to as primitivism, and his turn towards surrealism and NEO-CLASSICISM. At the same time, Picasso continued to investigate cubism as he began developing his personal version of neo-classicism. Lynn Garafola has observed that 'design, in fact, now took the place of music as the center of gravity in a production', and that the artist Mikhail LARIONOV noted Diaghilev coming to understand the décor as an integral part of ballet, along with music and movement. For Garafola, 'This dramatic shift in the relationship of choreography and visual design coincided with Massine's apprenticeship and ripening artistry as a dance master. Unlike the vast majority of CHOREOGRAPHERS, who create their maiden works by imitating or reacting against choreographic models, Massine learned the rudiments of his craft from the painter's static images' (1989, 85). Yet, despite the twists and turns their own careers were taking, these visionaries were able to focus their collective energies and ensure a successful outcome for *Pulcinella*.

According to Vera STRAVINSKY and Robert CRAFT, Diaghilev began acquiring some musical sources in 1918 that would eventually become the basis for *Pulcinella*. These transcriptions of music by Gallo and others (falsely attributed to PERGOLESI) were made at the British Museum, and others were transcribed in Naples and correctly attributed to Pergolesi, but their exact chronology is uncertain (see Carr 2010). A complete list of identified sources includes works by Domenico Gallo, Carlo Ignazio Monza, Count Unico Wilhelm van Wassenaer and Giovanni Battista Pergolesi. Stravinsky's comments in *Expositions and Developments* are illuminating: '*Pulcinella* was my discovery of the past, the epiphany through which the whole of my late work became possible. It was a backward look, of course – the first of many love affairs in that direction – but it was a look in the mirror, too' (*Expo*, 113). This look backward provided him with a certain freedom to experiment with techniques that would continue to be found in his neoclassical works.

After the première in Paris, the French musicologist Louis LALOY specifically addressed Stravinsky's use of precomposed sources in a review that appeared on 17 May 1920 on the first page of *Comœdia*:

> Pergolesi's airs remain recognizable throughout, by the easy play, the smiling and languorous grace, the suave radiance. Yet they are used as themes of a burlesque symphony with the most piquant effects, by the ingenious composer whom they inspired. Did he have the right to use [these themes] in this way? Without a doubt, since his work is charming. In art, the only politics is that of results, and a masterpiece executed at the price of a slight sacrilege is no less admirable for it.

In the London première the following month, the audience was under-whelmed, though the work was nevertheless well received. Raoul de Roussy de Sales wrote:

> From the opening bars of the introduction we were all astonished at the fact that we were not more astonished. We had expected something quite different: more Stravinsky and less Pergolesi. As a matter of fact, the whole score is a kind of very curious contention between the two compo-sers, which ends, if I may say so, in the victory, or rather the vindication, of Stravinsky.... We cannot help being grateful to Stravinsky for having so skillfully thrown into relief the beauties of the old master by underlining them. (*The Chesterian*, n.s., 8 June 1920, 234–6)

However, Stravinsky did not take even a passing mention of impropriety lightly. He brushed away the controversy with a declaration of a great affection:

> No critic understood this at the time, and I was therefore attacked for being a *pasticheur*, chided for composing 'simple' music, blamed for deserting 'modernism', accused of renouncing my 'true Russian heritage'. People who had never heard of, or cared about, the originals cried 'sacrilege': 'The classics are ours. Leave the classics alone.' To them all my answer was and is the same: You 'respect', but I love. (*Expo*, 113–14)

The music of *Pulcinella* lives on both in its original format and as an orchestral suite (arranged in 1922). The PULCINELLA SUITE continues to provide the musical material for new ballets, sometimes with alternative scenarios, including a contemporary production titled *Pulcinella Variations*, choreographed by Justin Peck, the resident choreographer for the NEW YORK CITY BALLET, and premièred in 2017. Thus, the past continues to be remade, and the spirit of *Pulcinella* lives on. MAUREEN CARR

Maureen A. Carr (ed.), *Stravinsky's Pulcinella: A Facsimile of the Sketches and Sources* (Middleton, Wis.: A.-R. Editions, 2010).

Lynn Garafola, *Diaghilev's Ballets Russes* (New York and Oxford: Oxford University Press, 1989).

Pulcinella Suite. Composed c. 1922, rev. 1949). First performance, 22 December 1922, Boston Symphony Orchestra. Conductor, Pierre MONTEUX.

2202.2110, concertino strings (11111), ripieno strings (44433), duration: 22 min.

(I) Sinfonia (Overture) (II) Serenata (III) Scherzino – Allegro – Andantino (IV) Tarantella (V) Toccata (VI) Gavotta con due variazioni (VII) Vivo (VIII) Minuetto e finale.

A well-known and celebrated arrangement of the original BALLET. The vocal parts in Movements II and VIII are replaced by instruments (solo violin / oboe and brass, respectively). The work was often conducted by the composer on his concert tours; indeed, the *Pulcinella Suite* featured in Stravinsky's final concert as conductor (televised on CBC, 17 May 1967). The revision of 1949 – made, at least partially, for financial reasons – contains only superficial modifications: the addition of metronome markings and re-titling of the *Duetto* to *Vivo*. Various movements of the *Suite* were later transcribed into a series of arrange-ments for chamber ensemble (*see* SUITE ITALIENNE). JOSEPH SCHULTZ

Pushkin, Alexander (Sergeyevich) (born Moscow, 26 May / 6 June 1799; died St Petersburg, 29 January / 10 February 1837). Russian poet and writer, widely considered as the founder of modern RUSSIAN LITERATURE. Stravinsky expressed his admiration for him, although he drew on Pushkin's texts only on few occasions. The early composition exercise 'Storm Cloud' ('Tucha') survives from 1902, while his second opus, the song *The Faun and the Shepherdess*, is also based on a Pushkin text. His veneration of Pushkin notwithstanding, the only mature work that draws on him is the opera buffa MAVRA, on KOCHNO's text after the story *The Little House in Kolomna* – a work that is, moreover, dedicated to the memory of Pushkin, GLINKA and TCHAIKOVSKY. Stravinsky has also acknowledged Pushkin's influence on his APOLLO, since a couplet by the Russian poet gave rise to a Russian Alexandrine rhythm for the cello solo in the Calliope variation. In his conversations with Robert CRAFT, Stravinsky also revealed that he did not rule out the possibility that some line by Pushkin might have ended up in the libretto for *Les* NOCES, given that his source, Kireyevsky's collection of folk songs, contained some (unidentified) Pushkin verses.

An essay signed by Stravinsky also survives, titled 'Pushkin: poetry and music', published in 1940 but ghostwritten in 1937 by his son-in-law Yuri Mandelstam for the Pushkin centenary. The text sums up Stravinsky's neo-classical ideal of absolute music (the contempt of extramusical references), which he parallels to what he calls Pushkin's 'pure poetry': a disinterest in broader ideas beyond the verses. It also summarises the conviction regarding Pushkin's genuine Russianness, which unites Russian with Western cultural elements. This peculiar amalgamation of Russianness with western European culture has encouraged certain critics, notably SOUVTCHINSKY, to draw a parallel between Stravinsky and Pushkin.   KATERINA LEVIDOU

Tatiana Baranova Monighetti, 'Stravinsky's Russian library', in SHW, 61–78.
Pierre Souvtchinsky, 'Stravinsky as a Russian', *Tempo*, 81 (Summer 1967), 5–9.
Igor Stravinsky, *Pushkin: Poetry and Music*, trans. from the French manuscript by Gregory Golubeff (New York and Hollywood: Harvey Taylor, 1940).
SCW

Rachmaninov, Sergey Vasil'yevich (born Oneg, Novgorod district, 20 March / 1 April 1873; died Beverly Hills, California, 28 March 1943). Russian composer, pianist and conductor. Though, to a degree – like Stravinsky – he had inherited something of the Russian nationalist style (being initially more weighted towards BALAKIREV's work, while Stravinsky derived directly from RIMSKY-KORSAKOV), and both in their different ways admired the work of TCHAIKOVSKY, the two composers had next to no aesthetic common ground. The occasionally aired rumour that Rachmaninov advised Stravinsky on the closing 'gasp' of The RITE OF SPRING appears to have little or no foundation; yet on several occasions in the 1940s he spoke respectfully of that work, which he credited with 'solid musical merits' – an exceptional view given his general antipathy to contemporary music. As Stravinsky told Robert CRAFT, the two composers never met socially either in Russia or when near-neighbours in SWITZERLAND; yet Rachmaninov entered Stravinsky's orbit from time to time, appearing for instance as a guest at a dinner held in Stravinsky's honour at the old Steinway Hall in New York, 11 January 1925.

In the summer of 1942, both composers were living in LOS ANGELES. Rachmaninov, anxious about his daughter Tatiana's family in Europe, anticipated that Stravinsky must be equally anxious about his children, and asked Sergei Bertensson (his friend and future biographer) to sound out the Stravinskys as to whether they would welcome an invitation to dine at the Rachmaninovs' Beverly Hills home. The overture was gratefully received: over a convivial meal, the composers discussed such practical matters as royalties, concert bureaux and agents, but not a word about creative matters. Days later, Rachmaninov, recalling Stravinsky's relish of honey, personally delivered a large jarful ('a pail', Stravinsky told Craft) of the finest quality. The Stravinskys extended a return invitation. Their friendship had scarcely developed when, in February 1943, the great composer-pianist, suffering from advanced melanoma, collapsed after a recital in Knoxville; he arrived home in an ambulance, and died five weeks later. DANIEL JAFFÉ

Sergei Bertensson and Jay Leyda, *Sergei Rachmaninoff: A Lifetime in Music* (Bloomington: Indiana University Press, 2001).
Robert Cunningham, *Sergei Rachmaninoff: A Bio-Bibliography* (Westport: Greenwood Publishing Group, 2001), 12, 134.

Ragtime, for eleven instruments. Composed 1917–18; completed on Armistice Day, 11 November 1918. First performance, 8 November 1919, Lausanne (piano reduction); 27 April 1920, London (instrumental version). First published 1919, Éditions de la Sirène.

Ragtime is scored for a chamber ensemble of eleven instruments: flute, clarinet, horn, cornet, trombone, percussion, cimbalom, 2 violins, viola and double bass. The unusual inclusion of the Hungarian cimbalom accords with the composer's fascination for its rustic sonic potential in works such as RENARD (1915–16), or the original version of Les Noces (1917). Stravinsky had first heard the Roma cimbalom player Aladár Rácz at a popular bar in Geneva in 1915, while the Ragtime music relates closely to its partner piece, the 'Ragtime' dance within The SOLDIER'S TALE. As expressed in the composer's AUTOBIOGRAPHY (p. 78), these pieces constituted for him 'a composite portrait of this new dance music'. Another distinctive feature of the work lies in Stravinsky's inter-arts collaboration with Pablo PICASSO, who provided the cover of the published score as the now-so-familiar drawing of two musicians: a fiddler and a guitar-player, intricately created with a single continuous line.

Ragtime comprises a single, extended movement – lasting typically around 6 minutes – at a very swift metronome marking of $\downarrow$ = 160. Formally, it is rondo-like, with a central developmental section (c. Figure 18). An opening rag-like head motif, syncopated and dotted, has been likened by Barbara Heyman (1982, 557) to a 'harmonically out-of-focus ... caricature' of DEBUSSY's 'Golliwogg's Cake-Walk' from the Children's Corner suite. The ensuing theme, which corresponds with that in The Soldier's Tale, appears first on flute – with a blues-like gesture: D–Db–D♮, picked up by the cimbalom (Figure 1). Actual pitch 'bending' is heard in violin glissandi and, later, in the trombone (c. Figure 20).

Faithful to the letter of some rags (such as Joplin's Magnetic Rag, or Irving Berlin's early Alexander's Ragtime Band), the work adopts and resolutely maintains a regular, march-like 4/4 metre, by contrast with the irregularities and unbarred sections of the more individualized PIANO-RAG-MUSIC. Nods are made towards swinging the rhythms (Figure 1, cimbalom). Richard Taruskin (SRT, 1310) refers to this, in French Baroque parlance, as 'notes inégales' and, together with Heyman (1982, 546), makes the case for Stravinsky having heard a little relevant music, rather than having only worked from notated scores.

In typical Stravinskian fashion, there is much articulation, dynamic variation and sonic characterisation. Percussion includes side drum with/without snare, bass drum, cymbals and woodblock (tremolos). The cimbalom player is required to stifle (étouffez) the twangy timbre; strings employ harmonics, pizzicato, repeated downbows; the cornet is heard muted. Having explored these diverse effects, the piece ends with a brusque fff flourish.

The harsh verdict of Taruskin (SRT, 1310) on this Ragtime is 'flabby' and lacking in interest; however, for Heyman (1982, 556), it comes 'closest to the spirit and prototype of classic ragtime, particularly with regard to its "danceability"'. Notably, the work was choreographed in 1960 by George BALANCHINE. Heuristically, for Stravinsky it paves the way for Piano-Rag-Music.

DEBORAH MAWER

Barbara Heyman, 'Stravinsky and ragtime', Musical Quarterly, 68.4 (October 1982), 543–62.
Deborah Mawer, French Music and Jazz in Conversation: From Debussy to Brubeck (Cambridge University Press, 2014).

Rake's Progress, The. OPERA in three acts (and an epilogue). Composed between 1947 and 1951. First performance, 11 September 1951, TEATRO LA FENICE. Conductor, Igor Stravinsky, with the orchestra and choirs of La Scala, Milan. Libretto by W. H. AUDEN and Chester KALLMAN after eight engravings by William Hogarth (1733–5). Published 1951, London, Boosey & Hawkes.

Recording of the original production on 9 November 1951 – 2 CD Gala – GL 100.567

(2, 2, 2, 2; 2, 2, 0, 0; timp., harpsichord, strings).

A rare fact in the lyric universe, the libretto of *The Rake's Progress* did not derive from any literary or theatrical source. The eight engravings by the English painter William Hogarth appeared to Stravinsky as an unrelenting succession of theatrical scenes, and he conceived the opera with W. H. Auden according to the thematic and classical plan 'exposition peripeteia resolution', broken up into nine scenes and an epilogue, thus departing from the original model. More lazy than cynical, Tom Rakewell's inheritance no longer comes from his father but from a disregarded uncle, making it all the more unexpected; the misguided Sarah Young of the original is transformed into Anne Truelove, whose purity, and the unconditional power of whose love, are exalted in each act; the rich, old woman married for her money becomes a freak (the bearded lady) who is greeted with ridicule; and, finally, Tom is now sent to the asylum not to wipe out his debts but because he has gone mad. The authors also create the mephistopholean figure of Nick Shadow who addresses the spectators in the manner of a narrator, as well as Tom's three wishes. The first act oscillates between the countryside and the town. Tom Rakewell and Anne Truelove sing of their love, but Tom refuses the book-keeping job which Anne's father offers him, trusting instead in his lucky star. At this point, Nick Shadow appears and tells him of the colossal inheritance he is to receive from an unknown uncle. They return to London, where Tom is enlightened in Mother Goose's brothel. Having heard nothing of him for several months, Anne decides to rejoin him in the city. The second act takes place in Tom's house. Despite his riches, he is bored, but aspires to happiness. Nick shows him the portrait of Baba the Turk, the bearded lady and fairground attraction: would marrying her not be the proof of his complete freedom? Tom accepts. Anne rediscovers Tom but he rejects her, afraid of the dangers the city might pose to her. She assists impotently in the union of Tom and Baba, the bearded lady. As before, Tom becomes bored with Baba, rebuffs her, and is then caught up in Nick's web, fascinated by his machine for transforming stones into bread, which will make him humanity's benefactor while at the same time supporting him. The third act signals Tom's fall. His house and its contents are sold at auction. Baba renounces him and entrusts him to Anne. But Nick demands Tom's soul as payment for his services, agreeing to play cards with him as a possible means of escape. When Nick loses, he is engulfed in the shadows, but Tom remains mad. He is found ultimately in the asylum of Bedlam where Anne sings a lullaby to him before he expires. The protagonists each finally draw a moral from the story.

Stravinsky had wanted to compose an opera in English since his arrival on American soil, and the engravings of Hogarth, which he discovered at the Art Institute of Chicago appeared to him immediately as a series of operatic scenes terminating in the asylum of Bedlam. Did he know Gavin Gordon's BALLET on the same subject, which was performed to great success at Sadler's Wells Theatre in London in 1935? His North American friend Aldous HUXLEY advised him to approach the poet and man of the theatre W. H. Auden, who had already collaborated with Benjamin BRITTEN for his opera *Paul Bunyan* (1941). After a first meeting at Stravinsky's home in California during which the two men defined the outline of the work, Auden returned to New York and embarked upon the drafting of the libretto with his companion, the writer Chester Kallman, modifying some details and reconnecting the work expressly with the seventeenth- and eighteenth-century traditions of English theatre; the two librettists were also partners in the staging of the première.

Henri Barraud states that, for Stravinsky, far from being a Mozartian pastiche and the last work of what some have called his neo-classical period, *The Rake's Progress* is based on the principle of the number opera. It is consequently related to *Così fan tutte* but also to *The Marriage of Figaro*, *Don Giovanni* and even *The Magic Flute*, in terms of structure, the formation of the orchestra, the form of the arias, the recitatives accompanied by harpsichord, and Anne's psychology, which can be compared with that of Pamina. But the work alludes equally to the entire history of Italian opera – Monteverdi, Cimarosa, Donizetti, Bellini, Rossini, VERDI, while conserving a Stravinskian tone and style: fluidity, original timbral combinations, the suppleness of the vocal lines, the rejection of predictable formulas.

The Rake's Progress plunged the commentators of its time into stylistic debates which today seem outmoded, as is clear from the innumerable productions which anchor the work's post-modernity on our expectations of the great operatic repertoire. If Joseph Kerman expressed his enthusiasm for the work in 1956, André Boucourechliev, for example, who denounced its 'lofty detachment' in 1982, judged it a minor work in the operatic repertoire and in Stravinsky's output. Its remarkable history, nevertheless, has to be noted, acclaimed by the most daring opera houses and the most prestigious festivals: *The Rake's Progress* has been performed on every continent, and every season since its appearance has seen several new productions. Among others, it was mounted in 1961 at the Royal Swedish Opera in Stockholm by Ingmar Bergman; in 1972 at the Tyl Theatre in Prague, which had featured the première of *Don Giovanni* in 1787; at the Aix-en-Provence festival in 1992 and 2017; and again at the THÉÂTRE DU CHÂTELET in PARIS in a polemical staging by Peter Sellars. The first production of the work with Stravinsky conducting was recorded in its entirety, followed by several others, as well as video recordings, notably the famous Glyndebourne production given from 1975 to 1989 with sets by David Hockney, which toured in Europe and the UNITED STATES .

CÉCILE AUZOLLE

Françoise Escal, *Stravinsky et son double modèle iconographique et musical* (Paris: ENS, 1985).

Paul Griffith, *Igor Stravinsky, The Rake's Progress* (London and New York: Cambridge University Press, 1982).

Joseph Kerman, *Opera as Drama* (New York: Alfred A. Knopf, 1956).

Igor Stravinsky, 'The Rake's Progress', *L'Avant-scène opéra*, 145 (1992).

Rambert, (Dame) Marie (orig. Cyvia Rambam, then Miriam Ramberg) (born Warsaw, 20 February 1888; died London, 12 June 1982). Polish-British dancer and choreographer. Known for founding the British company that still bears her name, Rambert was engaged by the BALLETS RUSSES in 1912 to assist NIJINSKY with the preparation of the first production of The RITE OF SPRING (1913). A student, and then assistant, to Émile Jaques-Dalcroze, she brought her experience of eurhythmics to rehearsals, helping the dancers execute Nijinsky's wishes and understand the music. She was present when Stravinsky first saw the choreography, and danced in the ballet's première. Rambert considered The Rite 'musically and choreographically, a masterpiece', with only Les NOCES comparable in its power (Rambert 1972, 65).

SOPHIE REDFERN

Marie Rambert, Quicksilver: The Autobiography of Marie Rambert (London: Macmillan, 1972).

Ramuz, Charles Ferdinand (C. F.) (born Lausanne, Switzerland, 24 September 1878; died Lausanne, 23 May 1947). Writer, widely regarded as the most important of the twentieth century in French-speaking SWITZERLAND. Novelist and short-story writer, as well as essayist, poet and diarist, Ramuz was an icon for the next generation of writers in both Geneva and Lausanne, because of the great acclaim he gained from his peers. This was especially the case in FRANCE, where his works were favourably received despite considerable critical controversy with regard to stylistic issues. Ramuz made a living out of his works, publishing in Lausanne as well as in PARIS, but residing in Switzerland most of his lifetime (he lived in Paris between 1900 and 1914). Stravinsky appreciated Ramuz's sophisticated and yet simple style and his interest in the expression of popular culture. His novels are inspired by rural life and are set in the natural landscapes of the Vaud and Valais, between the lake and the mountains, and aim to explore the human experience in its greatest universality, couched in philosophical terms. To paraphrase his own words, his only subjects are love and death, approached in a style which is intentionally rugged, and that tries to achieve a kind of primitivism.

Stravinsky met Ramuz in the summer of 1915 through Ernest ANSERMET, who had been the writer's mathematics teacher in secondary school (Collège classique cantonal, Lausanne), and who was part of his intimate circle of friends. In the years during which Stravinsky lived in Switzerland, the artists became close friends and worked together on several projects, of which the most ambitious was The SOLDIER'S TALE (1918). Premièred on 28 September 1918 in Lausanne (Théâtre municipal), under the direction of Ernest Ansermet, with sets by René Auberjonois, this theatrical work was meant to provide an income for its creators, but the onset of the Spanish influenza pandemic hindered the planned tour. In addition to The Soldier's Tale, Ramuz translated into French the texts of Pribaoutki, RENARD and Les NOCES.

After Stravinsky's departure for France and then the UNITED STATES, Ramuz went on to correspond with the composer (in French), visiting him in Savoy or in Paris when he had the chance to do so, but he never collaborated with him again. The Swiss writer was seemingly upset by the perceived lack of interest on the part of Stravinsky, who was by then a world star, and he disapproved of the neo-classical manner of the composer, comparing it to the aesthetics of

Thorvaldsen (letter from Gustave Roud to Georges Nicole, 6 December 1934, in *Correspondance* 2009, 185–6). In 1929, Ramuz published an important auto-biographical text dedicated to his relationship with the composer, entitled *Souvenirs sur Igor Strawinsky*. Writing about *The Soldier's Tale*, he emphasises the bond of understanding between him and Stravinsky: 'J'étais Russe: le sujet serait russe; Strawinsky était Vaudois (en ce temps-là): la musique serait vaudoise' ('I was Russian: the subject would be Russian; Stravinsky was Vaudois (back then): the music would be Vaudois'). In AUTOBIOGRAPHY, which includes a portrait of Ramuz by Stravinsky (*Auto*, 55), the composer pays tribute to the writer and recalls their 'deep affection for each other'.

STÉPHANE PÉTERMANN

Philippe Girard and Alain Rochat, *C. F. Ramuz, Igor Strawinsky, Histoire du soldat, Chronique d'une naissance* (Geneva: Slatkine, 2007).

Stéphane Pétermann, *C. F. Ramuz: Sentir vivre et battre le mot* (Lausanne: Presses polytechniques et universitaires romandes, 'Savoir suisse', 2019).

C. F. Ramuz, *Œuvres complètes* (Geneva: Slatkine, 2005–13), especially *Souvenirs sur Igor Strawinsky*, vol. XVIII (ed. Roger Francillon and Daniel Maggetti, 2011).

Gustave Roud – Georges Nicole, Correspondance 1920–1959 (Gollion: Infolio, 2009).

Claude Tappolet (ed.), *Correspondance Ansermet–Strawinsky (1914–1967)*, vol. I (Geneva: Georg, 1990).

Ravel, (Joseph) Maurice (born Ciboure, 7 March 1875; died Paris, 28 December 1937). French composer, a brilliant orchestrator who, at the turn of the twentieth century, was part of the APACHES group of musicians, writers and artists. Stravinsky and Ravel were particularly close in 1912–14, when they both collaborated with DIAGHILEV's BALLETS RUSSES. At the première of Ravel's BALLET *Daphnis et Chloé* on 8 June 1912, they shared a box with Florent Schmitt and Maurice DELAGE; Stravinsky had previously heard a private piano performance. Ravel and Stravinsky worked together in CLARENS on a performing version of MUSSORGSKY's KHOVANSHCHINA for Diaghilev in March–April 1913.

When they were together in SWITZERLAND, Stravinsky and Ravel also discussed SCHOENBERG's *Pierrot lunaire*, resulting in the composition of Stravinsky's *Three Japanese Lyrics* and Ravel's *Trois poèmes de Mallarmé* (1913), both written for voice, two flutes, two clarinets, string quartet and piano. They were premièred on the same programme as *Pierrot lunaire* on 14 January 1914 by Jane Bathori and an ensemble conducted by Désiré-Émile Inghelbrecht. The Stravinsky texts were translated by Maurice Delage. The first of Ravel's settings, 'Soupir', is dedicated to Stravinsky, and Stravinsky's third song, 'Tsaraiuki', is dedicated to Ravel.

Critics noted common features in Ravel's and Stravinsky's works, and Ravel could be touchy about their similarities. In an interview with the *New York Times* in 1927, Ravel noted that 'Stravinsky is often considered the leader of neo-classicism, but don't forget that my String Quartet [1903] was already con-ceived in terms of four-part counterpoint, whereas Debussy's Quartet is purely harmonic in conception.' He might have added that, while Stravinsky is heralded as the originator of black-note/white-note bitonality in PETRUSHKA (1910–11), the cadenza of Ravel's piano piece *Jeux d'eau* (1901) features a similar juxtaposition.

Both Ravel and Stravinsky frequently modelled their compositions on earlier musical styles or specific works by other composers, though, whatever the context, both retained their original musical voice.   CAROLINE POTTER

Reception of Stravinsky in Russia. From the late 1930s to the late 1950s, when Stravinsky's music remained absent from Soviet music life, an entire generation grew up and perished (in World War II and during the Stalin-era repressions) without having heard the composer's work live; of those who could have heard The RITE OF SPRING in the 1920s, few lived to hear its 1959 performances by the New York Philharmonic under Leonard BERNSTEIN. Throughout the next thirty years, performances and publications were still defined by Soviet ideology, either conforming to it or compromising with it. But neither in the 1910s, nor in the 1920s, were performances of The Rite of Spring in RUSSIA comparable to the impact of NIJINSKY's BALLET in PARIS in 1913, or the performance under MONTEUX in 1914. In fact, The Rite of Spring was not perceived in Russia as a cultural turning point and this may account for the delayed acceptance by the audience at large of any form of MODERNISM – whether in ballet, the visual arts or music.

'A life without The Rite of Spring' – thus could be defined a difference between the musical and cultural consciousness of Soviet listeners behind the Iron Curtain as compared to their western counterparts (the title The Rite of Winter 1949 of a symphony by ST PETERSBURG composer Leonid Desyatnikov (1998) is symbolic). Hence the passionate desire of musicians and music lovers to reach this forbidden fruit, as attested by a passage from a letter by Leningrad students, initiated by Joseph Raiskin, and addressed to the Central Committee of the Communist Party of the Soviet Union in 1956: 'Why are we robbed of the right to hear The Rite of Spring ... ? Why can we only find out about Les Noces or Renard in the "Book about Stravinsky" by Igor Glebov [see ASAFYEV], and have difficulties borrowing it from the library? Could we return the Russian composer Stravinsky to the Soviet Union, to Russia?' In a version published in Sovetskaya Muzïka (4, 1957), this passage was deleted (Josef Raiskin's personal archive; see also RGASPI, Russian State Archive of Social-Political History). For Soviet audiences, Stravinsky was an almost mythical figure; his CONVERSATIONS WITH ROBERT CRAFT, published in Russian in 1971 as Dialogues, became a bible for several generations of readers.

There were a number of shifts in attitude towards Stravinsky in Russia, and therefore several periods in the reception history. In the first reviews, dating from 1907, critics recognised his talent, solid training, the influence of his teacher, RIMSKY-KORSAKOV (along with TCHAIKOVSKY, WAGNER and DEBUSSY), as well as his mastery of ORCHESTRATION, but failed to find lyricism, depth, melodiousness, thematic coherence, or even content, in his works. The triumph of technique over feeling, form over content, was a productive line for future criticism, which culminated in 1948.

The premières of Stravinsky's Russian ballets in Paris were reviewed in Russia mostly by ballet critics, among them Andrei Levinson, who passed a remarkable judgement on The Rite of Spring: 'I know nothing more refined than this Hottentot music' (PRK, II, 566). Music critics made their statements after the concert performances in St Petersburg and Moscow. Disappointment and scepticism regarding 'European sensations' were not uncommon in these reviews, as were negative comments directed against the status of this music within a stage production. Thus, composer Jāzeps Vītols, having deemed three fragments from PETRUSHKA a 'salade russe', continued, 'Together with the respective "hotplate", presented on stage, this "music" can pass as tolerable ... But in a concert hall, played with Glazunov's Symphony, this noise is merely tasteless, almost an insult' (PRK, II, 578). As for The Rite of Spring, what exactly listeners heard was the crucial question: according to Nikolay Myaskovsky's review, 'it would be rather brave' to pass judgement on The Rite of Spring based on Sergey KOUSSEVITZKY's performance, since many numbers 'have turned into a sonic morass' (PRK, II, 594). Discussion of Stravinsky's ballets divided Russian musicians into two camps. Among those 'contra' were Leonid Sabaneyev and Andrey Rimsky-Korsakov, the composer's son. Among those 'pro' were Vyacheslav KARATĪGIN, Vladimir Derzhanovsky and Nikolay Myaskovsky, who wrote insightful and detailed reviews and early analyses.

During the 1920s, Soviet performers compensated for what had been missed in the previous decade and quickly reacted to the Western premières. Leningrad led the way; Dmitri SHOSTAKOVICH and Maria Yudina took part in the Russian première of Les NOCES, Mikhail Druskin, a future Stravinsky scholar, played the PIANO SONATA and RENARD. In the former MARIINSKY THEATRE, Petrushka, The FIREBIRD, PULCINELLA and MAVRA were staged. The Rite of Spring was conducted by Europeans including Fritz Stiedry, Oskar Fried and Ernest ANSERMET, and Stravinsky's music was received with great enthusiasm. Regarding Stiedry's concert, Dmitri Shostakovich wrote to his friend, the pianist Lev Oborin, 'The Rite of Spring was extremely successful ... Listeners are starting to like contemporary music.' Shostakovich himself was taken aback by the 'orchestral brilliance' ('a hell of a sound') (Savenko, 'Stravinsky: the view from Russia', in SHW, 258–9). From the 1920s onwards, Stravinsky was an influence (even if hidden) on Russian composers. During this decade, though, the quantity of publications and reviews gradually declined and the quality lessened as the approaches and standards of Soviet criticism took shape. Nonetheless, in 1929, the first monograph on Stravinsky was published by Boris Asafyev (Igor Glebov).

Subsequently, Stravinsky's music quickly vanished from the stage. Rare performances were reviewed ever more infrequently. In their place appeared articles with such headlines as 'Stravinsky's ideological path' (A. Alshvang, 1934) or 'Dead music' (E. Kann, 1934), in which a more and more lengthy list of accusations was formulated. Stravinsky's music found refuge in conservatory classes and at home; Dmitri Shostakovich transcribed the SYMPHONY OF PSALMS for piano four hands to play it with his students. The process of the mythologisation of Stravinsky was probably captured by Mikhail Bulgakov's portrayal of a 'professor-psychiatrist' named Stravinsky in his novel The Master and Margarita.

Stravinsky fitted perfectly the role of the 'enemy' in the campaigns against formalism and cosmopolitanism in 1948 and 1949. Today, that collection of invectives is remarkable in its details: thus, criticising Les Noces for being 'pseudo-folk' and for 'stylisation', the composer Marian Koval (a persecutor of Shostakovich) employed the complex epithet 'frenzy-bewitching' (Sovetskaya

Muzïka, 2 (1948), 47); the scholar, Anatoly Ogolevets, forced to recant, 'acknowledged his grave fault' in 'not taking into account the barbaric sound' of The Rite of Spring (see Maksimenkov 2013, 332); the new General Secretary of the Union of Soviet Composers, Tikhon KHRENNIKOV, tried to demonstrate his awareness, describing the latest of Stravinsky's sins: 'The Apostle of reactionary force in bourgeois music, Igor Stravinsky, with the same ambivalence creates a Catholic Mass in the abstract-decadent style, as he does circus-jazz pieces' (Sovetskaya Muzïka, 1 (1948), 54). Stravinsky appeared in the film Rimsky-Korsakov (1953) as a decadent-modernist composer named Ramensky, who received the angry criticism of his teacher: 'Everything, that you have just played, is not music at all. It is a disgrace to Russian art and to art in general.'

Touring with the New York Philharmonic Orchestra in 1959, Leonard Bernstein performed The Firebird and the CONCERTO FOR PIANO AND WIND INSTRUMENTS, but most importantly The Rite of Spring, which had not been heard in its composer's motherland in thirty years. A commotion was caused by Bernstein's speech: he called The Rite of Spring a true revolution, comparing it unfavourably with the October Revolution. Bernstein's tour paved the way for Stravinsky's visit to Russia in 1962, which became an event of colossal significance. Stravinsky's arrival was like that of an extra-terrestrial being – a mythical figure given substance. Composers of all ages came out to greet him and his words passed from mouth to mouth (ironically, Stravinsky preached dodecaphony to young Soviet composers). A direct consequence of the visit was the previously delayed publication of the AUTOBIOGRAPHY in Russian (1963). The same year, the first monograph after Asafyev's was published by the notorious Boris Yarustovsky; Irina Vershinina's book on the early ballets appeared in 1967, and the firm Melodiya released records of Stravinsky's compositions. Performances were still rare, albeit given by famous musicians: Maria Yudina, Evgeniy Svetlanov, Evgeniy Mravinsky or the young conductor Igor Blazkov. In 1965, The Rite of Spring was finally premièred in Russia as a ballet; it was choreographed at the Bolshoi Theatre by Natalia Kasatkina and Vladimir Vasilev (they themselves only heard The Rite of Spring for the first time, as part of the soundtrack of Disney's Fantasia, during the course of their tour to Paris).

Stravinsky's death in 1971 partly removed certain unspoken prohibitions. Moreover, Stravinsky was officially recognised as an 'outstanding Russian composer', as signified by a decree issued by the Soviet Minister of Culture, Yekaterina Furtseva (1972), establishing a committee in charge of his creative legacy. Censors finally allowed the publication of a one-volume Russian translation of the Stravinsky and Craft conversation books, which instantly became a bibliographical gem. But when the editor of the book, Mikhail Druskin, published a concise monograph on Stravinsky in 1974, the book along with its author was put through a 'trial' at a closed meeting at the Leningrad Conservatory, in the manner of 1948–9. Performances of Stravinsky's music were still rare during this period, but the publishing houses Muzïka and Muzichna Ukraina published pirate Stravinsky scores which made them accessible to musicians across the entire Soviet Union. The next breakthrough was again The Rite of Spring: Maurice Béjart's ballet was shown on tour in Moscow (1978).

With the beginnings of *perestroika* in 1985, full access to Stravinsky's music was finally granted to performers, listeners and scholars. It was performed at an ever-increasing number of music festivals, most prominently at the 'Stars of the White Nights' under Valery Gergiev, whilst the Mariinsky Theatre was becoming accustomed to DIAGHILEV's and BALANCHINE's repertoire. Bronislava NIJINSKA's Les Noces was first staged in Russia at another ST PETERSBURG venue, the Mussorgsky Theatre, in 1995. The previous year, Dmitry Pokrovsky's ensemble performed Les Noces with folk voices, taking it back to its folklore roots. For the same ensemble, the Moscow composer Vladimir Martinov wrote his Night in Galicia (1996) and also entered into dialogue with Stravinsky, whilst the St Petersburg composer Leonid Desyatnikov fused the Russian and the neo-classical in Russian Seasons (2000), as a homage to Diaghilev and Stravinsky. Meanwhile, in 1997, Viktor Varunts published the first volume of Stravinsky's Russian CORRESPONDENCE (PRK).

After the turn of the millennium, 'Stravinsky' as a topic lost both the pathos of the fight against Soviet censorship and the euphoria of post-Soviet freedom. Instead of ideology, economics became a dominant factor, and the forbidden fruit turned out bitter. Valery Gergiev declared 2017 'a year of Stravinsky' and opened it in December 2016 with the world première (actually the second performance) of FUNERAL SONG, rediscovered in the ST PETERSBURG CONSERVATORY in 2015, but, as a whole, his own programmes that year were less significant than those of the 1990s. Not many musicians perform Stravinsky's works regularly, although exceptions include the conductors Vladimir Jurowski and Teodor Currentzis. Arguably, the most notable events occurred in the field of ballet, beginning with Vaslav Nijinsky's reconstructed The Rite of Spring, which finally arrived in Russia in 2003, in a performance at the Mariinsky Theatre. Ten years later, in 2013, the festival 'A Century of The Rite of Spring – a Century of Modernism' at the Bolshoi Theatre, curated by Pavel Gershenzon, became an important conceptual statement: ballets with choreography by Nijinsky, Béjart and Pina Bausch were presented as milestones of twentieth-century culture. For the festival, The Rite of Spring was staged by contemporary dance choreographer Tatiana Baganova. Other important Russian CHOREOGRAPHERS Alexei Ratmansky and Vyacheslav Samodurov continue Balanchine's tradition. In 2004, the complete POETICS OF MUSIC was finally released in Russian, edited and annotated by Svetlana Savenko, preceded by her own book Stravinsky's World (2001). For Russian composers in their thirties and forties, Stravinsky is still a central figure. But this generation, which was often educated and performed in, or emigrated to, Europe, is free of the old binaries of 'Soviet and anti-Soviet', or even 'Russian and Western'.

Stravinsky's apartment on Kryukov Canal in St Petersburg, where he lived for thirty years, was turned into a communal apartment during the Soviet years, but had retained its original appearance up to 2018, without having become a museum. The windows of the Stravinsky foyer in the new building of the Mariinsky Theatre look out onto it.   OLGA MANULKINA

Mikhail Druskin, *Sobranije sochinenii* ('Collected Works'), vol. IV: *Igor Stravinsky*, comp., ed. and with notes by Ludmila Kovnatskaya (St Petersburg: Kompozitor, 2009).

Leonid Maksimenkov, *Muzïka vmesto sumbura: kompozitorï i muzïkantï v strane sovetov, 1917–1991* (Moscow: Mezhdunarodnïy Fond 'Demokratiya', 2013).

Olga Manulkina, 'Leonard Bernstein's 1959 triumph in the Soviet Union', in Severine Neff, Maureen Carr and Gretchen Horlacher (eds.), with John Reef, *The Rite of Spring at 100* (Bloomington: Indiana University Press, 2017), 219–36.

Svetlana Savenko, 'The Rite of Spring in Russia', in Severine Neff, Maureen Carr and Gretchen Horlacher (eds.), with John Reef, *The Rite of Spring at 100* (Bloomington: Indiana University Press, 2017), 237–45.

Yekaterina Vlasova, *1948 god v sovetskoy muzïke* ('The Year 1948 in Soviet Music') (Moscow: Klassika-XXI, 2010).

Reiman, Elise (born Haute Terre, Indiana, ?1912–15; died Boston, 26 August 1993). American dancer and teacher. Reiman studied with Adolph BOLM and at the School of American Ballet (SAB). Connected with George BALANCHINE's companies and institutions, she danced with the AMERICAN BALLET and Ballet Society before becoming a teacher at the SAB (1945–53, 1964–93). Reiman created the role of Calliope in the first production of APOLLON MUSAGÈTE, choreographed by Bolm in 1928; she later described it as 'stilted' (Buckle 1988, 105). She also danced Terpsichore in Balanchine's first American production of the same BALLET, staged as part of the American Ballet's 1937 Stravinsky Festival (Stravinsky conducted). SOPHIE REDFERN

Richard Buckle, *George Balanchine: Ballet Master*, in collaboration with John Taras (London: Hamish Hamilton, 1988).

Reiner, Fritz (born Budapest, 19 December 1888; died New York City, 15 November 1963). Hungarian conductor. Reiner performed the CONCERTO FOR PIANO AND WIND INSTRUMENTS with Stravinsky in Cincinnati and Philadelphia in 1925, earning the composer's admiration for his 'perfect knowledge of my score'. He was Chief Conductor of the Pittsburgh Symphony 1938–48, performing The FIREBIRD, PETRUSHKA, The SONG OF THE NIGHTINGALE, PULCINELLA SUITE and the US première of the CONCERTO IN D (15 January 1948). Stravinsky admired Reiner and chose him to conduct the US première of The RAKE'S PROGRESS at the Metropolitan Opera (14 February 1953). Reiner became Music Director of the Chicago Symphony Orchestra in 1953. He conducted MAVRA, AGON and the BACH–Stravinsky 'Vom Himmel hoch' (all in 1959), and made commercial recordings of The Song of the Nightingale and The FAIRY'S KISS. Stravinsky praised Reiner for making the Chicago Symphony 'the most precise and flexible orchestra in the world' and for his technique, 'a salutary antidote to the windmill school of conducting' (T&C, 225). NIGEL SIMEONE

Kenneth Morgan, *Fritz Reiner, Maestro and Martinet* (Champaign: University of Illinois Press, 2005).

Religion. Tracing Stravinsky's spiritual trajectory is essential to understanding his work. He was baptised into the RUSSIAN ORTHODOX CHURCH, according to Stravinsky himself (in *Expositions*) merely hours after his birth, and named after the twelfth-century martyr Prince Igor of Chernigov, being baptised by full immersion and chrismated at the Nikolsky Cathedral in ST PETERSBURG on 29 July / 10 August 1882. He claimed that his parents were not particularly religious, but said also that the Church calendar was followed in the household, and detailed some memories of experiences of the Church as a child.

Stravinsky reacted against the Church as a teenager, and was a non-communicant until returning to it in April 1926. This return was not sudden, and attendance at church had been part of his life since the mid-1920s. Apart from the fact that a Russian priest, Fr Nikolay Podosenov, lived with the Stravinskys in Nice for five years, there was also the example of Jean COCTEAU's return to the Catholic faith in 1925, which Cocteau described in a letter to the neo-Thomist philosopher Jacques MARITAIN, whose acquaintance the composer made in 1929. Stravinsky must already have read Maritain's Art et scolastique (1921) by this time, and Maritain was also engaged in ecumenical discussions in Paris with the Russian religious philosopher Nikolay Berdyayev. The composer also noted that he had been reading the Gospels and other religious literature beforehand, and he wrote to DIAGHILEV on Holy Tuesday of 1926 asking forgiveness and announcing his intention to return to the Church. Another friend, the composer Arthur LOURIÉ, had converted from Judaism to Catholicism, and his wife was undergoing instruction from Maritain. While his role in Stravinsky's return to the Church is not clear, it is certainly the case that the two discussed religious matters both in person and by letter.

Remaining a communicant until 1939, Stravinsky observed in Expositions that he became so again in America, but that at the time of writing had lapsed, 'more because of laziness than of intellectual scruple – I still consider myself a Russian Orthodoxist [sic]'. He retained a strong sense of propriety, so that when Charlie Chaplin suggested, during the 1930s, a scenario for a surrealistic film project including the Crucifixion, Stravinsky was quick to dismiss it on the grounds that it was sacrilegious. He had said much the same, many years earlier, of Parsifal in his AUTOBIOGRAPHY.

Interest in questions ethical and religious never waned, and Stravinsky cultivated the company of others interested in such matters, for example W. H. AUDEN and Aldous HUXLEY when living in Hollywood.

The musical consequences of Stravinsky's return to Orthodoxy in 1926 are most evident in the three sacred choruses he began to write precisely in that year (Otche nash, Veruyu and Bogoroditse Devo, from 1926, 1932 and 1934). They stand at a decidedly oblique angle to the Russian liturgical tradition, even though it is perfectly possible to use the three pieces in a liturgical celebration. The unsentimental, 'objective' quality of these works is entirely in keeping with the composer's concerns in a more general sense, and particularly his aesthetic orientation during this period.

The composition of the SYMPHONY OF PSALMS (1930) is perhaps the most perfect example of the reconciliation of artistic originality and the simultaneous subjection of the artist to the Christian faith, dedicated as it is 'to the glory of GOD'. As well as noting the dates of the completion of the first two movements according to the ecclesiastical calendar, he gave an interview in 1930 in which he said that 'the more you cut yourself off from the canons of the Christian Church, the more you cut yourself off from the truth' (SCS, 500). As Stephen Walsh has said of the 'white ballet' APOLLON MUSAGÈTE, written in 1927–8, just after the composer's return to the Church, Stravinsky sought 'spiritual discipline and grace' (Walsh 1988, 143), and such a desire is very much related to his reading of Maritain, Bossuet and other religious philosophers; the opera–oratorio OEDIPUS REX (1927) is also not unrelated to this tendency. He met Maritain again in Chicago in 1944, at the time of his first sketches for the MASS, and, in Expositions, praises his 'intellectual clarity', something that resonates with the composer's quest to write 'very cold music, absolutely cold, that will appeal directly to the spirit' (SCW, 447).

Religious themes recurred with frequency later in the composer's life, in CANTICUM SACRUM (1955), THRENI (1957–8), A SERMON, A NARRATIVE AND A PRAYER (1960–1), the television opera The FLOOD (1961–2), ABRAHAM AND ISAAC (1962–3), INTROITUS (1965) and REQUIEM CANTICLES (1966). While The Flood and Abraham and Isaac deal with Old Testament themes, A Sermon, a Narrative and a Prayer recounts the martyrdom of St Stephen, and Canticum sacrum, in honour of St Mark, uses the Vulgate versions of both Old and New Testaments as sources. Threni sets parts of the Lamentations of Jeremiah, in Latin, and Introitus and Requiem Canticles have recourse to texts from the Latin liturgy. All of these works have a strongly RITUAL character, and are audibly descendants in this respect of the Three Sacred Choruses and the Mass. Even The Flood, while dramatic, is extremely hieratic, a feeling greatly reinforced by Stravinsky's use of a narrator and the setting of the words of God for two solo basses (in BABEL, from 1944, he had adopted a similar solution, using male choir).

After Stravinsky's death on 6 April 1971 – Holy Tuesday – there was a service in New York, but he was buried in VENICE, where, after a Roman Catholic Mass and a performance of Requiem Canticles, the full Greek Orthodox funeral service was chanted, before a waiting gondola took the coffin for burial in the Orthodox section of the cemetery of San Michele – a sequence of events neatly symbolising Stravinsky's complex and multi-faceted spiritual journey.

IVAN MOODY

Stephen Walsh, The Music of Stravinsky (London: Routledge, 1988).

Remisoff, Nicolas (also Nicolai and Nicholas) (born St Petersburg, 20 May 1887; died Riverside, California, 4 August 1975). Russian-American set designer, artist and illustrator. Associated with the Mir iskusstva group, Remisoff fled RUSSIA after the Revolution, moved to PARIS (where he designed sets for the Chauve-Souris), and then settled in America. A regular collaborator of the dancer-CHOREOGRAPHERS Adolph BOLM and Ruth PAGE, he designed the sets for the first APOLLON MUSAGÈTE, choreographed by Bolm and starring Page (Washington, DC, 1928). He also designed Bolm's 1940 FIREBIRD at the HOLLYWOOD BOWL (which Stravinsky conducted), and a 1931 production of The SOLDIER'S TALE for Page.   SOPHIE REDFERN

Renard (Baika). Composed 1915–16. First performance, 18 May 1922, Russian Ballet, Opera House, Paris. Published 1917, Ad. Henn and J. & W. Chester. Dedicated: 'Très respectueusement dédié à Madame la Princesse Edmond de Polignac'.

Instrumentation: flute (doubling piccolo), oboe (doubling cor anglais), clarinet (doubling E♭ clarinet), bassoon, 2 horns, trumpet, percussion (timpani, triangle, tambourine with bells, tambourine without bells, cylindrical drum, cymbals, bass drum), cimbalom (or piano), voices (2 tenors, 2 basses), strings.

Premièred at the Opéra in PARIS by the BALLETS RUSSES, conducted by Ernest ANSERMET, choreographed by Bronislava NIJINSKA, with scenery and costumes designed by Mikhail LARIONOV. The libretto was written by Stravinsky in collaboration with Charles Ferdinand RAMUZ from Russian folk sources collected by Alexander N. AFANASYEV.

A one-act barnyard fable of morality in which Renard the Fox tricks and captures the Cock twice, both times rescued by the Cat and the Ram. The three friends then strangle Renard and celebrate. A note at the front of the vocal score reads:

> The Play is acted by clowns, dancers or acrobats, preferably on a trestle stage placed in front of the orchestra. If performed in a theatre it should be played in front of the curtain. The actors remain on the stage all the time. They come on in view of the audience to the strains of the Little March, which serves as an introduction, and make their exit in the same way. The actors do not speak. The Singers (2 Tenors and 2 Basses) are placed in the orchestra.

This lesser-known work remains significant in the evolution of Stravinsky's compositional process, providing a glimpse into his workshop as he was endeavouring to reinvent himself after the The Rite of Spring. He was still in his Russian period and had not yet left behind his use of folk music. Where Russian folk tunes were woven into the fabric of the Rite, in Renard Stravinsky utilised a folk-music-based heterophonic technique: the repetition of short and simple melodic phrases that shifted metre almost constantly, providing a sort of off-kilter unison sound in the ensemble. In this way, it could be argued that he achieved a musical continuity that helped to unify the plot through this repetition of discrete blocks that contained a diversity of musical fragments. In future works, he developed this use of block form to include other elements – in Symphonies of Wind Instruments, Jonathan Cross describes Stravinsky's blocks as being delineated 'not only in terms of harmony, rhythm and tempo, but also by their instrumental timbre' (Cross 1998, 34). With the staging of Renard, these blocks also take on significance in the action. For example, the music that occurs immediately before the first block is at the point in the storyline where the Cock 'prepares to jump' and then 'jumps', indicated in the score as salto mortale. The music of the first block dramatises the Cock's plea for help as the Fox clutches him by the tail, creating a feeling of stasis, which is prolonged by the harmonic backdrop. At the beginning of the second block, some material from the first block is reiterated, serving as a hinge between the two blocks. The second block is more linear than blocks one and three. The plot is thickened in the third block, initiated by the C♯ that serves as a hinge from block two to three. The harmony of block one recurs in block three, this time with added notes. Stravinsky continues to unify the discrete blocks of music that he uses to dramatise the Renard storyline.

Around the same time as Stravinsky was finishing Renard, he had begun his collaboration with Charles Ferdinand Ramuz on The Soldier's Tale (1917–18). The two works share a number of qualities, from the non-traditional instrumental ensemble to the use of blocks as a compositional device, and they even share one of the distinguishing features of the opening section of Renard, a melodic and rhythmic gesture that appears to anticipate The Soldier's Tale's 'Danse du diable'. The reduction in instrumental forces, as compared with the

Rite of Spring, was unsurprising given the limitation of resources due to World War I and the Bolshevik Revolution in Russia.   MAUREEN CARR

Alexander N. Afanasyev, *Poeticheskie vozzreniya slavyan na prirodu* ('Poetic Outlooks of the Slavs on Nature'), 3 vols. (Moscow: K. Soldatenkov, 1865–9).

Alexander N. Afanasyev, *Russkie narodnye skazi* ('Russian Folk Tales'), 4 vols., 2nd edn (Moscow: K. Soldatenkov, 1873).

Jonathan Cross, *The Stravinsky Legacy* (Cambridge University Press, 1998).

Bernhard Rusam, '– *es kommt die Füchsin als Nonne verkleidet* – ': *Renard von Strawinsky* (Berlin: Weidler, 2007).

Requiem Canticles   for contralto, bass, chorus, orchestra. Composed 1965–6. First performance, 8 October 1966, McCarter Theatre, Princeton. Conductor, Robert CRAFT. Published 1967, Boosey & Hawkes, 'To the memory of Helen Buchanan Seeger'. Prelude, Exaudi, Dies irae, Tuba mirum, Interlude, Rex tremendae, Lacrimosa, Libera me, Postlude.

Stravinsky called *Requiem Canticles* (his last work with orchestra, comprising nine movements lasting just 15 minutes), a 'mini- or pocket-Requiem'. Five of the vocal movements set excerpts from the Proper of the Roman Catholic Requiem Mass – that is, the end of the Introit ('Exaudi') and six verses from the 'Dies irae' in 'Dies irae' (first two verses), 'Tuba mirum', 'Rex tremendae' and 'Lacrimosa' (last two verses). The text of the sixth vocal movement, 'Libera me', is taken from the Burial Service and is set in its entirety. An instrumental Prelude (strings only), Interlude (flutes, bassoons, horns and timpani) and Postlude (flutes, horn and pitched percussion) frame the work.

Commissioned by Princeton University alumnus Stanley J. Seeger in memory of his mother, Helen Buchanan Seeger (SSE, 498), *Requiem Canticles* was subsequently also performed at the composer's funeral in VENICE, since, as Vera STRAVINSKY relates, '*he* and *we* knew he was writing it for himself' (SCF (72), 376–7). The score abounds with tangible musical characterisations, such as in the trumpet fanfares and unsettling bassoon leaps in 'Tuba mirum'; the simultaneous congregational murmuring and singing in 'Libera me', partially inspired by VERDI's Requiem (SPD, 478); the 'chords of Death' (SCF (72), 415) in the Postlude; and the prevalence of flute sounds symbolically linked to death. To listeners at the time, the music was both 'wonderfully new' (SCF (94), 446) and immediately accessible. The latter may have had to do in part with the fact that, as Richard Taruskin has shown, features typical of Stravinsky's earlier music, such as octatonic, diatonic and symmetrical pitch collections, resurface in the serial fabric of *Requiem Canticles*.

Stravinsky uses two different TWELVE-NOTE series and their hexachordal rotational arrays. 'Exaudi', 'Rex tremendae' and 'Lacrimosa' are built from series 1 (F-G-D♯-E-F♯-C♯-B-C-D-A-G♯-A♮), the Prelude, 'Dies irae', 'Tuba mirum' and 'Libera me' from series 2 (F-C-B-A-A♯-D-C♯-D♯-G♯-F♯-E-G), whose beginning is clearly audible in the Prelude. The Interlude and Postlude use both series, which share a number of elements – for instance, the last tetrachord of series 2 is a reordered inversion of the first tetrachord of series 1. The Postlude's wide-spaced 'chords of Death', played by four flutes, piano, harp and horn, are generated from verticals of rotational arrays, while the intervening chorales of bell sounds in celesta, chimes and vibraphone over held notes in the solo horn present note-against-note combinations of two forms of each series, the only time in the work that the two series sound simultaneously for extended passages. Sustained horn pitches outline a clearly discernible arpeggiated F minor triad over the course of this final movement, harking back to the F pitch centre of the Prelude. The sombre ostinato chords of the Interlude, played by the four flutes in low register, four horns and four timpani, consist of stacked fourths and fifths simulating a dark bell sound. Other salient sustained chords characterise 'Exaudi', 'Dies irae' (with echo effect), 'Rex tremendae' – whose calming, shimmering harmonies in flutes and strings quasi-emerging from the chorus could be termed 'chords of salvation' – and 'Lacrimosa', whose sorrowful high flute harmonies over solo double bass pitted against the contralto solo sound like 'chords of tears'.

CHRISTOPH NEIDHÖFER

Claudio Spies, 'Some notes on Stravinsky's Requiem settings', in Benjamin Boretz and Edward T. Cone (eds.), *Perspectives on Schoenberg and Stravinsky* (Princeton University Press, 1968), 223–49.
Joseph N. Straus, *Stravinsky's Late Music* (Cambridge University Press, 2001).
Stephen Walsh, *The Music of Stravinsky* (London: Routledge, 1988).
SRT, II

Revised Editions: 1940s. In the 1940s, Stravinsky revised several of his earlier works – most notably his first three BALLETS RUSSES scores, as well as the SYMPHONIES OF WIND INSTRUMENTS. It has long been widely assumed that Stravinsky was simply attempting to rectify a situation in which several of his most often performed works were not covered by US copyright laws – including by far his most popular work, The FIREBIRD, which appeared to be entirely in the public domain, due to RUSSIA and subsequently the Soviet Union being non-signatories of the Berne Convention. Yet it seems that Stravinsky had no coherent plan to secure these copyrights – witness the fact that three different publishers were involved in publishing each of the revised Ballets Russes works; the coincidence of these works all being revised and published during the 1940s appears mostly due to Stravinsky acquiring American citizenship in that decade, the opportunities that followed to secure copyright being especially evident to those publishers who actively approached Stravinsky to republish those early ballets.

Even this consideration does not apply to the 1943 revision to The RITE OF SPRING, the first BALLET Stravinsky revised in that decade. He only revised the final dance, and had it published separately by an entirely different publisher (Associated Music Press) from the one that had published the entire ballet (Édition Russe de Musique) – a highly impractical arrangement from the point of view of increasing Stravinsky's royalties, since few dance companies or orchestras would be inclined to pay the two lots of hire fees necessary to perform the revised 'Danse sacrale' in the context of the entire ballet. It appears that Stravinsky's desire at that time was, in fact, simply to rewrite the ballet's most notoriously challenging section, both for players and for the conductor, based on his recent practical experience of conducting the work – not to mention all the corrections he had made to the score over the decades which had yet to be collated and published.

Late in 1943, while in Santa Barbara, Stravinsky, assisted by Nadia BOULANGER, revised 'Danse sacrale', changing details of ORCHESTRATION, and amending or correcting harmonies. The autograph copy of the revised movement that Stravinsky gave to Boulanger out of gratitude for her assistance, unusually free of annotations or corrections, is testimony to her characteristically meticulous attention to detail – with just one oversight. In making the most fundamental change to the score, amending its basic note value from a semiquaver (sixteenth) to a quaver (eighth), they failed to make the necessary change to the marked metronome speed.

Next was The FIREBIRD. In March 1945, Stravinsky was approached by Lou Levy, president of Leeds Music Corporation (LMC): aware that Stravinsky was about to gain American citizenship, Levy proposed that Stravinsky rewrite or revise his three most famous ballets, all of them still in the public domain in the UNITED STATES (save now for The Rite's reworked 'Danse sacrale'), so they could be re-copyrighted in the USA under the protection of the composer's citizenship. By early May, Stravinsky had signed a contract to revise the most popular of those ballets, The Firebird, for publication. Though Stravinsky told his son, Theodore, that he could 'at last get rid of those superfluous pantomimes willed on me by Fokine', in fact he did little more than to expand the 1919 Suite by adding just under 7 minutes of those 'superfluous pantomimes'. This was apparently at the behest of the dance critic Irving Deakin, acting as representative of Adolph BOLM and Sol Hurok, who persuaded Stravinsky to incorporate some of the pantomimes to accommodate Bolm's choreography for the Ballet Theatre's proposed 1945 staging at the New York Metropolitan. Accordingly, Stravinsky added those sections of pantomime, suitably reorchestrated to match the reduced forces used in the earlier Suite, and made some minor but effective adjustments to instrumental detail and articulation. Unfortunately, the first performance of this revised Firebird Suite was largely spoiled by the quality of the orchestral parts supplied by LMC, described by the conductor Jascha HORENSTEIN as 'simply horrible manuscripts done by non-professional copyists'. Meanwhile, with the earlier version of the Suite still available in the public domain, orchestras continued to prefer that version over the 1945 revised version.

Far more satisfactory were the new publishing arrangements with Boosey & Hawkes (B&H), the British firm having bought the entire Édition Russe de Musique (ERM) catalogue from KOUSSEVITZKY late in 1945. B&H was naturally keen to capitalise on the popular early ballets. Having discovered that many of the ERM items listed were in fact unavailable, not least due to the wartime destruction of ERM's Berlin offices, Ralph Hawkes suggested to Stravinsky that they should reprint the entire catalogue, and simultaneously establish new copyrights which, since Stravinsky had become a US citizen, would now be valid in the States. Stravinsky was contracted to revise PETRUSHKA, due to be delivered by 1 April 1946 with slightly reduced orchestration (in the event, mostly done by reducing the original quadruple woodwind scoring to triple woodwind, and reducing the original two harps to one) – a pragmatic response to the number of recent (pirated) performances which, out of necessity, used a smaller band than specified by the original score. Although Hawkes had assured Stravinsky that only the slightest amendments were necessary to secure a new copyright, Stravinsky was inspired to make a more thorough revision, retexturing and rescoring Petrushka to give it a more glittering and sharply defined sonority. He completed this on 14 October (a hitch in the finalising of the B&H contract giving licence to stretch the original deadline), and though B&H were able to continue to offer the original score for hire, Stravinsky strongly discouraged this, preferring his revised version.

The decade's last major revision was of *Symphonies of Wind Instruments*, a work hitherto only ever published by ERM as a piano reduction. Late in 1945, Stravinsky, needing a filler for a broadcast concert scheduled for January, in which he was to conduct SYMPHONY OF PSALMS, took the final chorale of *Symphonies*, as published in 1920 by the *Revue musicale*, and scored this for a wind ensemble without clarinets (matching the winds required for *Symphony of Psalms*). Then, in August 1947, he received a letter from Robert CRAFT enquiring about the possibility of getting a score of Symphonies to perform with his Chamber Arts Society in New York. In a matter of weeks, Stravinsky was writing to Ralph Hawkes of his intention to 'rewrite it [to] make it easier for performers as well as for audiences, and that without sacrificing any of my intentions'. In this form, it was first published in full score by B&H in 1952 (the original version of the score not being published until 1983 by Belwin Mills).   DANIEL JAFFÉ

Robert Craft, '"Le Sacre du printemps": the revisions', *Tempo*, 122 (Sept. 1977), 2–8.
SSC, II, III; SSE

Rhythm. In their book, *A Generative Theory of Tonal Music* (1983), Fred Lerdahl and Ray Jackendoff draw a distinction between *metre* and what they call *grouping*. Metre consists of at least two levels of pulsation, the slower one marking off the faster one into equal spans of two or three beats. The alternation between intersecting and non-intersecting beats produces the familiar tick-tock, strong-weak, down-up sensation. Beats are idealised as points in time lacking duration. By contrast, grouping, although also hierarchical in nature, consists of levels of groups; from the bottom on up, motives are followed by themes, phrases, and so forth. Groups possess duration. They can begin and end anywhere in the metrical grid, in or out of phase with the metre.

In Stravinsky's music, as in most music of the eighteenth, nineteenth and twentieth centuries, rhythm involves the interaction between these two relatively independent phenomena. Metre is entrained by the listener – it should be stressed, made physically a part of him/her. Entrainment is reflexive as well as subconscious (or preconscious). Like walking, running and dancing, metre is a kind of motor behaviour, as Justin London has described it. Once entrained, it is abandoned by the listener only in the face of 'strong contradictory evidence' – hence, with special reference to Stravinsky's music, the explosive potential of an actual disruption of the metre, the physical effect a disturbance of this kind can have on the listener. The physicality of Stravinsky's music arises accordingly, that is, from entrainment and from the challenges to and disturbances of an attuned metrical grid.

1. The temporal aspect of Stravinsky's music may be approached from three different, if overlapping, angles: metrical displacement, stratification and polyrhythm.

When a motive or chord is repeated in Stravinsky's music, it is often displaced relative to the metre. In Example 11a from the opening Allegro of

Example 11 *Renard*, opening Allegro, clarinet fragment, bars 7–13

a) score (conservative)

b) early sketch (radical)

RENARD (1915–16), the principal melody in the clarinet is introduced on the first crotchet beat of a 2/4 bar. Subsequently, a shortened version of this melody is displaced to the second crotchet beat. In terms of the minim beat or bar line, the melody falls first on and then off the beat.

Viewed psychologically, the displacement of the clarinet melody in Example 11a upsets the listener's expectations that the melody will be repeated at a metrical location that is parallel to the original. And since metrical parallelism can play an essential role in the establishment of a metre in the listener's mind, frustrating the listener's expectations in this regard can have the effect of challenging and even disrupting the metre. Challenges or metrical disturbances of this kind may be felt fairly frequently when listening to Stravinsky's music. At the salient middle range of the metrical hierarchy, metrical displacement may not be entirely unique to his music, but it is highly characteristic all the same.

Of course, the composer could have shifted the bar lines in Example 11a to allow the repetition of the clarinet melody to be aligned in a parallel fashion. This he does in Example 11b, an early sketch of this same passage in *Renard*. Here, the bar line shifts in order that the repetition of the melody might be aligned as it was initially – that is, on the downbeat. Such a motivation – one of preserving alignment against the grain of displacement – underlies much of the metrical irregularity in Stravinsky's scores.

The assumption in Example 11a is that the listener will respond *conservatively* – that is, with the metre sustained (*conserved*) and with the displacement felt accordingly. In Example 11b, however, the assumed response is *radical*. The metre is interrupted, and the melody's repetition is felt as metrically parallel.

No doubt, responses to Stravinsky's metrical displacements can be messier and a good deal less clear-cut than the notation in Examples 11a and b implies. This is because displacement is always countered by the listener's anticipation of parallelism. The two are brought into conflict – displacement and metrical parallelism – and it is their conflict that causes the listener's metrical bearings to be threatened or disturbed.

Even with highly conservative interpretations of displacement, a change in the metrical alignment of a repeated motive or chord may bring about a slight disruption of the metre. Examples 12 and 13 from The RITE OF SPRING (1913) and the SYMPHONY OF PSALMS (1930), respectively, can further illuminate this perspective. Separated by about eighteen years, the first example stems from the Russian period, the second from the neo-classical. Yet the rhythmic idea underlying these passages is very much the same: a motive is introduced and then subjected to a series of metrical displacements. In each passage, the motive enters on and off the minim beat.

The notation in Examples 12 and 13 is conservative; the listener is imagined as sustaining the metre and feeling the displacements accordingly. Crucially,

Example 12 The Rite of Spring, 'Procession of the Sage', stratification; metrical displacements of horn fragment.

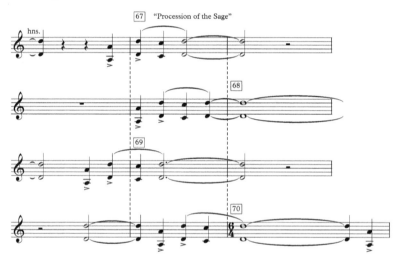

however, the repetition of the two motives is otherwise quite literal. In Example 12 from The Rite of Spring, the pitches A and D are accented while D-C-D is slurred. This articulation is retained from one repetition to the next. And while the literal nature of the repetition acts as a foil, a way of setting the displacements in relief, it also acts to refer the listener back to the fragment's original alignment. And the more that is repeated literally, the more fully aroused these conflicting expectations of metrical parallelism are likely to be.

2. The excerpts in Examples 11a and b of the opening Allegro of Renard show a stratification. The reiterating melodic fragments in the clarinet and lower strings are not varied, developed or tossed about from one instrument to the next in the manner of the classical style. Instead, they are fixed throughout in their registers and instrumentations. What counts above all in contexts of this kind is alignment. The main purpose of the basso ostinato in Example 11a is to re-enforce the 2/4 metre as a backdrop for the displacements in the clarinet melody.

Example 13 *Symphony of Psalms* (1930), III, opening bars; metrical displacements.

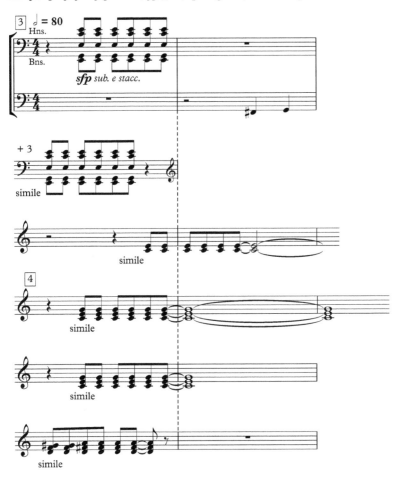

The vast majority of Stravinsky's stratifications employ an element of poly-rhythm. The displaced repetition in Example 12 from *The Rite of Spring* is part of a dense stratified texture in which – polyrhythmically and as ostinatos – motives and rhythmic patterns repeat according to varying spans or cycles. Many of the dance movements of *The Rite* are composed in this way.

All of this applies to the four tableaux of *Les Noces* (1917–23). In Example 14, the three distinct layers at Rehearsal Nos. 35–40 in the second tableau feature a vocal melody initially spanning ten crotchet beats (five 2/4 bars), an ostinato spanning a single crotchet beat (the A-B♭ reiteration in Pianos I and III), and a punctuating chord spanning three such beats. The repetition of the vocal melody is often cut short, with the initial span of ten crotchet beats undermined as a result. Yet the remaining two layers of instrumental accompaniment are true ostinatos. The invention consists of this tightly knit system of independently revolving parts, of the shifts in alignment that result from these revolving parts, and of the metrical disturbances that are brought about by these shifts in alignment.

Example 14 *Les Noces*, second tableau, lament, stratification.

Underscored by all three layers in Example 14 is the crotchet beat at 104 beats per minute. In contrast, returns to E♭, as the initial point of departure in the vocal melody, mark off the minim beat or bar line. The latter is obscured at times by the persistence of the punctuating chord and its dotted minim beat. Much of the rhythmic play of this passage rests accordingly, that is, with the 2/4 bar line established and then lost temporarily.

Possibly the earliest example of a stratified, polyrhythmic structure in Stravinsky's music appears in PETRUSHKA (1911), the opening section of the first tableau. The three separate layers shown in Example 15 include a re-iterating motive in the piccolo and oboes, a back-and-forth chordal motion in the horns, and the repetition of a Russian folk song in the lower strings. Each layer keeps to itself. Typical of stratifications generally, the layers are fixed registrally and instrumentally. And they are so rhythmically, as well. The sevens of the top layer are heard against the chordal motion in the middle one and against the groupings of two crotchet beats in the lower strings (as accented in the score).

Example 15 *Petrushka*, first tableau, stratification.

Remarkably in *Petrushka*, however, the three layers are associated with the events of a carnival. Heard simultaneously, the shouts of a carnival barker in the top layer are superimposed over the back-and-forth motion of a street accordion, and over the repetition of the folk song. For Stravinsky, the idea of a polyrhythmic stratification may have originated as a form of representation in *Petrushka*, with the composer's attempt to capture something of the bustling sound of the Shrovetide Fair at Admiralty Square in St Petersburg (c. 1830).

Stratification and polyrhythm are found in neo-classical works as well, even in Oedipus Rex (1927) and the *Symphony of Psalms*, high watermarks of this middle period. The section immediately preceding Oedipus' celebrated 'Lux facta est!' cadence at Rehearsal Nos. 166–9 is a stratification (lacking polyrhythm, however), while, in the third movement of the *Symphony of Psalms* (see Example 16), a basso ostinato spanning four crotchet beats grinds away at the 3/4 metre underscored, in turn, by the vocal parts.

Example 16 *Symphony of Psalms*, III; stratification.

In Variations (Aldous Huxley In Memoriam) (1964), a late twelve-note work, three of the variations feature a 'twelve-part polyphony', as Stravinsky called it. From one of these variations to the next, the separate rhythms of the twelve parts, along with the metrical scheme, are preserved. Unusually, however, the registers and instrumentations change. Each of the twelve layers is assigned its own series of twelve-note row-forms. Stravinsky's system of rotation is applied to the complete twelve-note row, rather than hexachordally.

3. Polyrhythm presupposes metrical displacement. To the extent that superimposed motives and rhythmic patterns repeat according to spans or cycles that vary independently of one another, they will be displaced metrically, and as each motive or pattern relates to the others. At the same time, however, displacement plain and simple is the common denominator that underlies these larger formats. This is borne out by the starting ideas of countless works and sections of works.

Spanning nearly three decades, through the neo-classical period and into the serial, Examples 17, 18 and 19 all begin with displacement. The opening idea of the Concerto in D for Violin and Orchestra (1931) enters first off, and then on the downbeat of a 2/4 bar. In Example 18 from the Symphony in Three Movements (1945), III, the G-F-G figure in the lower strings falls twice on the crotchet beat of a 4/8 bar before falling off it. In Example 19, the F♯-F figure that opens Threni (1957–8), an early twelve-note work, does much the same, falling twice on the crotchet beat and then off it. Against the grain of these displacements, fixed articulations intensify the listener's expectations of metrical parallelism.

Example 17 Concerto in D for Violin and Orchestra (1931), I, opening bars.

Example 18 Symphony in C, III, opening bars.

Example 19 Threni, opening bars.

Displacement is anti-metrical in its effect – 'contrametric', to use David Huron's term. It comes without warning, catching the listener off guard. Much of the excitement and expressive force of Stravinsky's music can be traced to rhythmic manoeuvres of this kind.

Typically, in Stravinsky's music, when a motive, chord or configuration is repeated, its alignment relative to the metre is changed. Stravinsky repeats not to vary or to develop in the manner of the classical style, but rather to displace metrically. Such displacement may occur singly or as part of a large-scale stratification or polyrhythmic texture. In the latter case, motives and rhythmic patterns, often ostinatos, are made to repeat according to varying spans or cycles. Whatever the particular case, however, displacement is often disruptive of the metre. And it may appear in all of Stravinsky, regardless of the stylistic period. PIETER C. VAN DEN TOORN

Pieter C. van den Toorn, The Music of Igor Stravinsky (New Haven: Yale University Press, 1983).
Pieter C. van den Toorn, 'The physicality of The Rite: remarks on the forces of metre and their disruption', in Severine Neff, Maureen Carr and Gretchen Horlacher (eds.), with John Reef, The Rite of Spring at 100 (Bloomington: Indiana University Press, 2017), 285–303.
Pieter C. van den Toorn and John McGinness, Stravinsky and the Russian Period: Sound and Legacy of a Musical Idiom (Cambridge University Press, 2012).

Rieti, Vittorio (born Alexandria, 28 January 1898; died New York, 19 February 1994). Jewish Italian, and later American, composer in a neo-classical idiom, who achieved notable success in BALLET music. Dividing his time between PARIS and Rome in the inter-war years, he collaborated with the BALLETS RUSSES on Barabau (1925) and Le Bal (1929), both choreographed by George BALANCHINE. He also became friendly with Stravinsky. Rieti's Second Piano Concerto (1930–7) would have been the only major work by a composer younger than himself that Stravinsky ever conducted, but the proposal, for a concert in Turin in 1938, was rejected on racial grounds. Rieti emigrated to the UNITED STATES in 1940, where the collaboration with Balanchine and friendship with Stravinsky were resumed. BEN EARLE

SSE

Rimsky-Korsakov, Nikolay Andreyevich (born Tikhvin, near Novorogod, Russia, 6/18 March 1844; died Lyubensk, 8/21 June 1908). One of the leading figures of the nationalist school of RUSSIAN COMPOSERS, a member of BALAKIREV's group The FIVE, conductor, professor of composition, harmony and ORCHESTRATION at the ST PETERSBURG CONSERVATORY (1871–1906). He employed in his works Russian folk songs, along with exotic elements (orientalism), and eschewed traditional Western compositional methods. In the 1880s, he became a leader of the BELYAYEV circle.

Rimsky-Korsakov began to play piano at 6, and started composing by the age of 10. When 18-year-old Nikolay met Balakirev, he showed him the sketches of his future First Symphony. Balakirev insisted he continue working on it under his supervision, despite Rimsky-Korsakov's only elementary knowledge of MUSIC THEORY.

When Rimsky-Korsakov became a professor at the Conservatory, he undertook a rigorous three-year programme of self-education and became a master of Western methods. He shaped several generations of Russian composers, including GLAZUNOV, LYADOV, Arensky, Stravinsky, PROKOFIEV and Grechaninov. His influence was especially important, as he served as a transitional figure between the auto-didacticism which exemplified The Five and the professionally trained composers of the next generations.

Stravinsky was a private student of Rimsky from 1902 until the death of the Master in 1908. Rimsky followed a practical method of teaching, avoiding abstract theories of composition, and this proved to be exactly what his talented and independent student needed (see MUSICAL EDUCATION). Soon, Stravinsky became very close to the teacher, his family and his circle. 'Few people can have been as close to Rimsky as I was ... for me, he was like an adopted parent' (Mem, 54). Stravinsky became a regular participant of the 'belyayevtsy' meetings in Rimsky-Korsakov's flat (appearing first on the scene in March 1903).

Rimsky attended the premières of Igor's SYMPHONY IN E♭ MAJOR and The Faun and the Shepherdess, sent him many delightful cards, and gave him the first fifty pages of the score of his OPERA The Snow Maiden. For his part, Igor assisted with the scoring of Rimsky's operas (Pan Voyevoda, The Legend of the Invisible City of Kitez), and composed a Cantata for his 60th anniversary (which has not survived); he also dedicated to his teacher the SYMPHONY IN E♭ MAJOR. After Rimsky-Korsakov's death, Stravinsky travelled from USTILUG to Lyubensk (where the composer died), then to ST PETERSBURG, and followed the coffin to the cemetery. He also created an epitaph – FUNERAL SONG for orchestra.

Rimsky-Korsakov's influence on the young composer was enormous. Stravinsky inherited from his great teacher an ideal of the strictest profession-alism, love of order, 'Apollonism', as well as some fundamental compositional methods (in particular, working with models). Nevertheless, Stravinsky's attitude to Rimsky-Korsakov was ambivalent, because of his academicism and criticism of new music, if it displayed the slightest modernist tendency.

In the years after Rimsky's death, Stravinsky began to collaborate with DIAGHILEV, at which point his music was perceived as 'too advanced' by Rimsky adherents. Igor also publicly expressed his critical attitude to Rimsky-Korsakov's editing of MUSSORGSKY's works. After the success of The FIREBIRD, and, especially, after Stravinsky's participation in Diaghilev's produc-tion of Mussorgsky's KHOVANSHCHINA, the entire Rimsky-Korsakov family turned against him. No wonder that, later, Stravinsky often allowed himself critical remarks about his teacher.   TATIANA BARANOVA MONIGHETTI

Rite of Spring, The (Le Sacre du printemps). Composed 1910[11]–13. First performance, 29 May 1913, THÉÂTRE DES CHAMPS-ÉLYSÉES, PARIS. Published 1921, Édition Russe de Musique (Russischer Musikverlag). Copyright assigned in 1947 to Boosey & Hawkes, which published an edition incorporating revisions by the composer, and a further 'new edition' in 1967, again with revisions by Stravinsky.

The Rite of Spring, third – after The FIREBIRD (1910) and PETRUSHKA (1911) – of Stravinsky's scores for the BALLETS RUSSES, received its première on 29 May 1913, a date famous for one of the most notorious scandals in musical history. What shocked the Rite's first audience has caused it to be established as an icon of MODERNISM – its exhilarating dissonances of harmony and rhythm that rise to a climax of orgiastic power all the more overwhelming for its implacable discipline. More than a century after its birth, the Rite has lost little of its influence and impact.

The Rite originated in what Stravinsky variously called a 'first thought', 'a fleeting vision' or 'a dream' that came to him in the spring of 1910. In his AUTOBIOGRAPHY (1935), Stravinsky recalled imagining a 'solemn pagan rite: sage elders, seated in a circle, watched a young girl dance herself to death. They were sacrificing her to propitiate the god of spring.' Stravinsky turned for advice to Nicholas ROERICH in view of Roerich's expertise in folk art and tradition. By the time Stravinsky left for PARIS in May, to attend final rehearsals of The Firebird, he and Roerich had devised an outline scenario and the BALLET had a working title: 'The Great Sacrifice'.

In the event, the composition of Petrushka intervened and it was not until July 1911 that Stravinsky and Roerich worked out a detailed libretto. They met at Talashkino, near Smolensk, where Roerich was designing a church in neo-medieval style for Princess Maria Tenisheva. Roerich's design for a mosaic, which survives in a sketch in the Ashmolean Museum, Oxford, showing a pipe-playing Orpheus-like figure enchanting a circle of black bears, has affinities with the opening music of the Rite. The division of the ballet into two halves, day and night, was probably Stravinsky's, the details of the sequence of rituals being by Roerich.

Stravinsky's evolving conception of the music can be seen in the facsimile volume of the sketches (Boosey & Hawkes, 1969), which contains sketches for all the sections of the Rite except the Introduction to Part 1. These reveal that the sequence of rituals and games in Part 1 was originally ordered so as to give a continuous acceleration, with the 'Ritual of Abduction' as the penultimate section, just before the solemn blessing by the Sage that releases the 'Dance of the Earth', described in Stravinsky's earliest account (December 1912) as 'the frenzied dance of the people intoxicated by the spring'. 'Spring Rounds', the third of the dances, was to have been placed second; the passage towards the end of 'The Augurs of Spring', which anticipates the melody of 'Spring Rounds', was to have acted as a transition. Part 2 was still more radically re-shaped. The sketches reveal the probability that the original sacrificial dance at the end of the ballet was to have been what is now the penultimate movement, 'Ritual Action of the Ancestors', the stuttering descent at the end representing the chosen victim's death. At some point in the late summer or early autumn of 1912, Stravinsky had second thoughts, composing a new 'Sacrificial Dance', sketched hastily straight into full score, and completed on 4/17 November 'with an unbearable toothache', and just in time for the first rehearsals with the dancers (which began in November). In the months that followed, Stravinsky re-balanced Part 2 by considerably expanding the Introduction (which began originally with the duet for two trumpets at figure 86), borrowing a succession of chords from the 'Sacrificial Dance' (figure 161) as a modulatory sequence supporting a descant that prefigures, in slow motion, the maidens' round dance, 'Mystic Circles of the Young Girls'.

The sketches also reveal the extent to which the Rite borrows from FOLK MUSIC. Stravinsky himself acknowledged only the opening bassoon solo as a folk song, but the presence of obviously copied melodies in the margins of the sketches suggests otherwise. These were traced by Lawrence MORTON to an anthology of Lithuanian folk songs assembled by Anton Juskiewicz, but the way these staid transcriptions were radically altered and enlivened by

Stravinsky suggests that the Rite may contain many more folk melodies whose source is unknown. Many of the melodies in the Rite operate within the narrow compass of perfect fourth, using the scalic intervals of tone–semitone–tone, the so-called 'minor tetrachord'. If two such tetrachords are placed a tritone apart, they form the octatonic scale, an aspect of Stravinsky's melodic and harmonic writing in the Rite that has been explored by a number of writers, notably Pieter van den Toorn and Richard Taruskin. The oft-repeated chord that opens 'The Augurs of Spring' can be analysed in octatonic terms (with E♭, D♭, B♭, G♮ and the bass F♭), and octatonic writing is evident in the quickest movements from Part 1, 'Ritual of Abduction' and 'Dance of the Earth', while a number of chord sequences in the 'Sacrificial Dance' follow an octatonic pattern (see the horns and bass trumpet at figure 144, for example). What is clear, however, is that octatonicism is part of an eclectic approach that combines with diatonic, modal or frankly dissonant writing.

Rhythmically, the Rite opposes extremes of regularity and disorder. The former is found, for example, in the repeated harmonies and ostinati of 'Augurs of Spring', and the metronomic pulsation that stalks through 'Ritual Action of the Ancestors'. The eleven chords hammered out in the bar before 'Glorification of the Chosen One' establish a pulse against which the ensuing metrical disorder may be experienced. This juggles three elements: the main idea (in 5/8 metre), a duple time 'vamp', and up-rushing scales. The shorthand used in the sketches sheds light on the closing pages of the 'Sacrificial Dance', which contain the Rite's most radical rhythmic innovations. The succession of bars of uneven lengths – commuting between units of 5, 4 or 2 semiquavers – may be understood as rhythmic 'cells', with the bars operating in pairs, with the second bar in each pair being invariant, while the first expands or contracts. Thus, the first four bars that open the final section of the 'Sacrificial Dance' (figure 186) may be tabulated as: A5–B4–A2–B4, with the numbers referring to the semiquavers in each bar. New cells are introduced from figure 192, with the final phase concerned with the increasing expansion of the 'mobile' element, leading to a climax at the furthest expansion of the cell (figure 201). Significantly, the closing pages of the 'Sacrificial Dance' make the sort of disciplined RITUAL that later would give rise to similarly memorable endings in, for example, Les NOCES, APOLLO or SYMPHONY OF PSALMS.

Stravinsky unveiled the score as it then stood (minus the final 'Sacrificial Dance') to DIAGHILEV and Pierre MONTEUX in April 1912. Monteux recalled thinking that Stravinsky was 'raving mad … The old upright piano quivered and shook as Stravinsky tried to give us an idea of his new work … I remember vividly his dynamism and his sort of ruthless impetuosity as he attacked the score.' On 9 June, Stravinsky and DEBUSSY read through the four-hand arrangement, Debussy taking the lower part. Louis LALOY, who was present, recalled that he and Debussy were 'dumbfounded, overwhelmed by this hurricane which had come from the depths of the ages, and which had taken life by the roots'. When rehearsals began, Stravinsky expressed concern about whether NIJINSKY would be able to choreograph and rehearse such a complex score when beset by a punishing schedule of performances for the Ballets Russes. Jean COCTEAU's cartoon depicting Stravinsky pulverising the piano keyboard at rehearsals while the dancers cower in a corner is confirmed by

Marie Rambert, who recalled Stravinsky's fury at arriving at a rehearsal and finding his music being played at the wrong tempo: he 'proceeded to play twice as fast as we had been doing and twice as fast as we could possibly dance'.

Cocteau also captured the scene at the première: 'the smart audience, in tails and tulle, diamonds and ospreys, were interspersed with the suits and *bandeaux* of the aesthetic crowd. The latter would applaud novelty simply to show their contempt for the people in the boxes ... The audience played the role that was written for it' (Cocteau 1921, quoted in Buckle 1971, 300). Rambert remembered that, before long, the orchestra was drowned by the commotion, and that the dancers relied on Nijinsky shouting instructions from the wings. Valentine Gross, whose sketches have proved invaluable in reconstructing Nijinsky's choreography, remembered the scene as like an earthquake: 'People shouted insults, howled and whistled ... There was slapping and even punching.' At the end of Part 1, the police were called. The hero of the hour, as Stravinsky remembered, was Monteux, who ('nerveless as a crocodile') somehow kept the orchestra together, while afterwards Diaghilev's only comment was: 'Exactly what I wanted'.

Subsequent performances of the *Rite* in 1913 passed off peacefully, and later in the summer the work was received with equanimity by London audiences, with both music and staging attracting serious critical comment, while a concert performance in Paris in 1914 was a triumph for the composer. Milestones included the 1920 revival, with new choreography by Léonide Massine, and a superb pioneering recording by the Philadelphia Orchestra under Leopold Stokowski (1930), which supersedes a spirited but untidy version under Monteux and a technically chaotic version conducted by Stravinsky himself, both issued in 1929. Also of interest is the pianola version created by Stravinsky for Pleyel (1919–22). The first fully assured recording is by the Philharmonia Orchestra conducted by Igor Markevitch (1951); other notable versions are by Stravinsky himself with the Columbia Symphony Orchestra (1960), Robert Craft conducting the USSR State Symphony Orchestra (1962), the City of Birmingham Symphony Orchestra with Simon Rattle (1987) and the Atlanta Symphony Orchestra under Yoel Levi (1991), which restores what were probably Stravinsky's original intentions with a notably fast reading of the 'Sacrificial Dance'.

Meanwhile, Stravinsky had embarked on revisions of the score – described by Louis Cyr (1983) as 'l'imbroglio presque inextricable' ('the almost inextricable tangle') – which proceeded piecemeal until 1967. Major revisions were undertaken for the first publication of the score in 1921, again in 1926 before Stravinsky conducted the *Rite* for the first time, and in 1943: these involve re-orchestration and changes to barring, especially in the 'Sacrificial Dance'. An important detail, amended in 1926, was to move the fermata in the first bar of the 'Sacrificial Dance' (where the pause was a hangover from the original ending, from before the 'Sacrificial Dance' was conceived and composed) to the third semiquaver of the bar: the effect is to make the first chord rebound from a downbeat, thus enabling the subsequent chords to be experienced as syncopations.

The great success of Diaghilev's carefully contrived public relations exercise (Buckle 1971, 299–302), especially Stravinsky's memory quoted on p. 302) for the Rite's première, rather than the intrinsic qualities of its music, have probably been the basis for the ballet's subsequent interest for ballet companies and CHOREOGRAPHERS. The work has come to stand as the token of a connection to Diaghilev's work as a whole, and as a tie to the aesthetic and cultural values of the Ballets Russes. In the decades following his death in 1929, Diaghilev was seen as the great moderniser of a classical ballet which had become old-fashioned and in need of reform, and the status of the Rite's music as a cathartic turning point in cultural aesthetics has encouraged a succession of ballet directors and ballet companies to demonstrate their engagement with modernism (which in ballet has meant dancers executing movements which lack the regularity and symmetry of older forms in the interests of new means of expression) through re-presentations and re-workings of the Rite. Recent examples have included a persuasive reconstruction of the ballet's original choreography, costumes and designs for the TV movie Riot at the Rite (2005). Although other Ballets Russes works, notably Petrushka and Les Noces, have also been recruited to the same end, the Rite has retained its pre-eminence as the flag bearer of modernism in ballet.   PETER HILL

Richard Buckle, Nijinsky (London: Weidenfeld and Nicolson, 1971).
Jean Cocteau, Cock and Harlequin, trans. Rollo H. Myers (London: Egoist Press, 1921).

Ritual and Ceremony. 'Le Sacre du Printemps is not a ballet. It is a ritual, it's an ancient rite', Prince Sergey Volkonsky stated in his review of the PARIS première (Volkonsky, 1913). However, another – although not fully impartial – reviewer, Andrey Rimsky-Korsakov, questioned the 'doubtful origin' of the rite (Rimsky-Korsakov, 1913), and had solid reasons for doing so: the existence of a seasonal spring rite performed by Slavs with a human sacrifice is not supported by any historical or ethnographical data. The rite is impossible to attribute correctly to an exact time: it contains elements of several spring rites that fill several months, from Shrovetide through Lent, Easter, Pentecost to Summer solstice (Kupala). Specific traits of a particular rite are absent, and, on the contrary, the main codes of action (the Kiss of the Earth, the sacrificial dance) are not found in any sources.

Stravinsky himself sought out Nicholas ROERICH, as his collaborator and an acknowledged expert in Slavonic antiquities, and actively participated in the construction of the libretto, drawing the material mainly from AFANASYEV's The Slav's Poetic Outlook on Nature (1865–9) (SRT, 881–9). To the list of sources named by Taruskin should be added the book Manners and Customs of the Russian People, by Alexander Tereshchenko (1848; see Baranova Monighetti 2017, 189) and The Spring Ritual Song in the West and by Slavs by Evgenii Anichkov (two vols., 1903, 1905). It was Anichkov who collated all the spring sacrificial rites that he could find, amplifying Afanasyev's list and adding animal sacrifices (immolation of a black cock on Shrovetide, etc.), whilst at the same time interrogating the concept of the sacrifice. He rejected Afanasyev's theory, based on a fertility cult, and proposed a 'scapegoat' conception: the sacrificial animal, or its substitute, accumulated collective guilt and was subject to ritual immolation, removal or purification. According to Anichkov, however, those rites, which might have involved real sacrifice in the remote past, in their present form were reduced to a game that did not imply the acute and fearful experience of a real danger as conveyed by Stravinsky's music. Dancing oneself to death as a means of sacrifice is a highly specific scenario, deriving from contemporary sources and practices. Ecstatic whirling dances (pairs, communal or individual), leading to exhaustion or fainting, or acting as a catalyst for ecstatic revelations or divinations, were part of the living religious practices of Russian peasant mystic sects, and their description was central to the majority of their ethnographic and fictional narratives (see Vereschchagina 2017, 274–6). It was widely believed that sectarian rites were seasonally conditioned and began with the adoration of the Earth, with the main annual rite (radenie) taking place at Pentecost (Mel'nikov-Pecherskii 1909, 355). This rite had a defined structure, with individual and group activities and strict functional divisions between a leader (especially female) and the rest of the participants. The individual radenie was called a 'circle' (krug) and consisted of whirling in one place for a long time, until the individual entered an altered state of consciousness, going 'beyond himself'. Divinations formed a distinct part of the rite and required specific kinetic practices (whirling, spinning, jumping) to achieve this ecstatic state (Konovalov 1908, 81–128). The types of group and individual movements were strictly codified and referred to as khozhdenie (literally, 'walking'); the term (used in the scenario of The Rite) points to its specific origin. Some types of khozhdeniia are familiar from Nijinsky's choreography: spiritual circle (a prophetess whirling in the middle of the circle of other participants moving clockwise, bouncing and jumping regularly to the beat), or wall (the men, taking each other by the hand, make up a circle round the circle of women, and run around in one direction, and the women in the opposite direction), or cross (collective crossing movements).

Thus, consistent with the doctrine of the 'creation of myth' (see Russian Myth), Stravinsky freely combines various motives of Slavonic spring rites from different locations and origins (shepherd and agrarian fertility rites, commemoration of ancestors, divination, purification) with the primary features of a contemporary peasant mystic rite, and groups them into two distinct ritual ceremonies, 'The Kiss of the Earth' and 'The Great Sacrifice', constructing a new ritual on its own artistic terms, not copying any ethnographical model.

In Les Noces, Stravinsky turned to the peasant marriage rite, which was exceptionally rich and developed in Russia, and based his scenario on ethnographically reliable sources, namely the song collections of Pyotr Kireyevsky and Ivan Sakharov, which contained texts of songs and detailed description of the ritual actions. Initially, the scenario of Les Noces included the full rite, which in real life takes several weeks, from matchmaking, with the ritual wailing of the bride, to stag and hen parties with the ritual wailing of the bride and the groom, the best man's ritual spell (exorcism), the ritual bath, through to the church wedding itself and the celebration feast. Subsequently, Stravinsky rigorously reworked the material and radically reduced the scenario, confining it to the few most important codified actions and removing duplications (for example, the ritual wailing of the bride (twice) and the groom is reduced to just one scene). Stravinsky departed from the conventional BALLET, introducing the chorus as a full participant, and originally conceived the disposition of the actors, singers and players together on stage with the pianos in the four corners, which should have created a sacred ritual space. Thus, an archaic rite converged with a radical modernist experiment.

A theatrical concept bridging archaic ritual and modernity was projected in the (unfinished) ballet 'Liturgie' (1914–15). The scenario (written by Natalya GONCHAROVA) was based not on the Christian liturgical service, but on the medieval model of a sacred mystery play, and consisted of two scenes, 'Annunciation' and 'Ascension' – the first including the Christmas, and the second the Easter, cycles – with set and costumes in Old Russian icon style with traces of the Byzantine, and the music combining Italian Gregorian with Old Russian plain chant. This combination points to the model for the ballet – two Italian sacred plays, *Annunciation* and *Ascension*, as performed to the delegates of the Council of Florence (1438–9), seen by a Russian Bishop Avraamii of Suzdal, who described them both in his enthusiastic travelogue. The project was particularly important for DIAGHILEV, considering his interest in old Russian icon-painting, stirred by the re-discovery of the 'icon Pompeii' in 1913. Just as the Russian icons proved to be a source of the most radical avant-garde visual experiments, so the sacred mystery plays seen by Avraamii and revived as a spectacle of a very special kind would have opened a new vista on theatrical history and its future direction. 'The icon-painting cubism' that Sergey Volkonsky saw in *The Rite*, is manifest in 'Liturgie', achieving its fullest expression in *Les Noces*. The unique historical situation of an Orthodox bishop commenting on the Florentine mystery plays opened the prospect of a new synthesis of Russia and Europe in the realm of art.

Not only *Les Noces*, but other folk texts of the Swiss years, especially the *Four Russian Peasant Songs*, also have their origins in ritual, above all the songs of the seasonal Christmas rites – dish-divination songs ('Shchuka', 'Puzishche', 'U Spasa v Chigisakh' and others) and carols (*Ovsen'*). The dish-divination songs are related to the Old Russian rite of divinations on the holy days after Christmas: the personal objects of the participants were laid in a dish, and then the dish was covered with a towel on which bread and salt were placed. After the first song, 'Hailing the Bread', the dish was shaken, and one object was procured from it after each subsequent song; the song was interpreted as an augury to the owner. The auguries were strictly codified and strongly differentiated: a happy or unhappy marriage; marriage with a sweetheart or a stranger – or an old man, a rich man, a poor one; richness ('Shchuka', 'Puzishche') or misery; death or travelling. The meaning of an augury could differ even within one song. For example, the song 'U Spasa v Chigisakh' meant either 'death' or 'rich wedding'. The difference, however, was conditioned not by the localisation of a song or by the overall ambivalence of the augury (as Ivan Sakharov, from whose collection Stravinsky took most of his dish-divination songs, erroneously concluded), but by the addressee of the augury: according to a Russian saying, 'For a young man – wedding, for the old one – funeral'. According to folk tradition, death and marriage are both rites of passage, and their functional meaning is equivalent. The Christmas carols (*Ovsen'*) are based on a seasonal fertility rite of blessing the house, together with the ritual sowing of the yard, and contain a ritual set of good wishes to the host; this motive of encrypted prediction is common in dish-divination songs.

The ritual, initially within a national context, preserves its importance in Stravinsky's later works, translating the national ritual code into a European one. In Perséphone, Stravinsky insisted on revealing its ritual origin, the Eleusinian Mysteries. Not the seasonal fertility rite, but the rite of passage between life and death is what primarily concerns the Russian preoccupation with this myth, in accordance with the paradigm set out by Vyacheslav Ivanov: 'The spring was transparent for the ancient people: it was blossoming death.' Transparency, as a specific characteristic of an early, pre-foliate phase of spring, when narcissi and hyacinths of the Homeric hymn are blooming, becomes characteristic of the liminal state itself, and provides the specific visual lucidity: death shines through the spring florescence; the live world is transparent and allows one to venture into the dead world, as revealed to Perséphone in the calyx of the narcissus flower. Reciprocally, the dead can peer into the live world. In spring, Perséphone returns to earth, reviving it, and, according to the myth, it is precisely in spring when she was first enraptured. Transparency is also a specific characteristic of the orchestral and choral texture of Stravinsky's score.

Acute and fearful experience of initiation is revealed in the score of The Fairy's Kiss – a ballet allegory, describing in a symbolic way the initiation rite as a consecration to artistry. In The Fairy's Kiss, the transformation of a fairytale into a myth of initiation is achieved by the use of two codes: one personal, the other theatrical, the first dating from Tchaikovsky's time, and the second from Stravinsky's formative years. The personal code is provided by the poem The Ice Maiden by Alexei Apukhtin – an intimate friend of Tchaikovsky, his fellow-student at law college and (as the family legend has it) his first (homo) sexual partner. Apukhtin set Andersen's plot as a dialogue of son and mother in the style of Goethe's Der Erlkönig; the fatal fixation on the Ice Maiden is interpreted as a story of romantic love and (at the same time) a case history of a fatal illness. The initial mood – that of a lullaby – is transferred to Stravinsky's ballet directly, defining the subtitle of the scene ('Lullaby in the Tempest') and the music, which is based on a song by Tchaikovsky to a poem by Pleshcheev describing a family scene with mother and children. The second code is the attempted transfer of Andersen's story to the theatre in the draft of a 'dreamy mystery play', Dionysus Hyperborean by Alexander Blok. Blok not only combined (by way of Nietzsche) his special, northern Dionysus with Apollo in his genre definition, but (also by way of Nietzsche) added the element of dance as well. The Maiden, whilst preserving the qualities of romantic love, also acquired the characteristics of a muse through intertextual connections with other of Blok's works written at the same time. And the main character, contaminated with Caius from another tale by Andersen, The Snow Queen, at last acquired the characteristics of a poet: his prophetic calling was to perceive the voice of eternity through the sound and fury of the time, and to create the sign of eternity from icy fragments of meaning. The moment of poetic consecration is marked as the moment of rapture from the seasonal time to the eternal land beyond time and space, a symbolic death: dying for the profane world, the poet is born for his elevated and prophetic calling. On the musical level, the liminal phase of the initiation rite as the threshold of eternity is marked by reference to the German pre-Romantics, and takes the form of a quotation from Tchaikovsky's song 'None but the lonely heart', to a Goethe poem from *Willhelm Meister*.

Another variant of rite of passage is a conversion plot, which characterises a group of works from Stravinsky's mature and late periods. They all have common motives of conscious liminality (the state on the brink of death) and of religious conversion. Liminality is often related to the motive of swelling water or flood or a quagmire (SYMPHONY OF PSALMS: 'He brought me out of a horrible pit, out of the mire and clay'; THRENI: 'Waters were flowing over my head; I said, I am cut off'); and salvation to the acquisition of a firm basis.

Ritual and ceremony may function as one of the elements of the work, not defining it as a whole – for example, 'Cortège du sage' in *The Rite of Spring*, or the procession in The NIGHTINGALE, which occupies the greater part of the second tableau. In *The Nightingale*, the procession is an element of the court ceremony of the Emperor, the meaning of which is defined by the actual political context, as well as the change of semantics of 'chinoiserie' during the formation of the OPERA and in comparison with its source. In Andersen's tale, the nationality of the mechanical bird is not specified; the introduction of a Japanese element by Stravinsky and MITUSOV at the start of the work was especially acute for Russian society, traumatised as it was by the disaster of the war with Japan (1904). In the opera, this theme receives a paradoxical shaping. At first sight, the ceremony, with its sophisticated hierarchy of costumes, supports the old European concept of immovable, frozen Chinese culture, based on the writings of Mill and Montesquieu and continued in Russia by Vissarion Belinsky (who called Slavophiles 'the Chinese' because of their opposition to progress), Mikhail Bakounine, and Vladimir Soloviev and others. However, the catastrophe of the Japanese war compelled a change of opinion: China and – especially – Japan were viewed as subject to intensive modernisation, but of a mechanical, pragmatic kind, and, in that respect, similar to European civilisation. As Dmitrii Merezhkovsky put it, 'the main "yellow danger" is not outside but inside; not that China is coming to Europe but that Europe is coming to China' (Merezhkovsky 1906, 9), i.e. Europe was itself becoming similar to China in its elimination of spiritual sources and metaphysics. The oriental exoticism of the opera, with its Chinese worldly ceremony and Japanese mechanical devices, spoke to the enlightened public (Russian as well as Parisian) not of an orientalised 'Other', but of Europeans themselves, raising the question of the dangerous reduction of the Universe to the phenomenal world, of the regrettable removal of the metaphysical dimension from the European worldview. Besides, the procession of *The Nightingale* stands in the tradition of *The Golden Cockerel*, with its pronounced satirical implications in relation to scenarios of power – that is, they both mirror the deep disillusionment with the state caused by the military disaster and the first Russian Revolution (1905). Thus, the ritual and ceremonial element is reflected in the intellectual context of the time.

Finally, in relation to ceremony, it is worth mentioning a major group formed by rites of memory, and specifically the lamentation topos. They may function as a structural element in the more developed ritual (for example, the wailing of the bride in *Les Noces*), or a musical opus (for example, the ghosts singing the funeral service ('panikhida') in *The Nightingale*; the 'Dirge' in the

Cantata), or else autonomously (Funeral Song; *Threni* as the Baroque genre of the Catholic Passion week; Requiem Canticles). They may use the old extra-musical ritual patterns (monumentum, epitaphium, elegy) or may be guided by models of various formats, styles and genres, both ancient (Monumentum pro Gesualdo) and contemporary (Elegy for J. F. K.). Rituals may be realised in the context of a national or European tradition, an example of the former occurring in the Symphonies of Wind Instruments, where, as shown by Taruskin, the Orthodox funeral service defines the musical structure of the score (SRT, II, 1487). As this brief survey of ritual and ceremony demonstrates, Stravinsky's music and thought were shaped by these concepts, in their various manifestations, from his early Russian compositions right through to the works of his final years.   ELENA VERESHCHAGINA AND TATIANA VERESHCHAGINA

Alexander Nikolaevitch Afanasyev, *Poeticheskie vozzreniya slavyan na prirodu* ('The Slav's Poetic Outlook on Nature'), 3 vols. (Moscow: Izdanie Soldatenkova, 1865–9).

Tatiana Baranova Monighetti, 'Stravinsky, Roerich and Old Slavic rituals in The Rite of Spring', in Severine Neff, Maureen Carr, Gretchen Horlacher (eds.), with John Reef, *The Rite of Spring at 100* (Bloomington: Indiana University Press, 2017), 189–99.

Vyacheslav Ivanov, 'Ellinskaya religiya stradayushchego boga' ('The Hellenic religion of the suffering god'), *Novyi Put'*, 1 (1904), 10–134.

Dmitrii Konovalov, *Religioznii ekstas v russkom misticheskom sektantstve* ('Religious Ecstasy in Russian Mystical Sectarianism') (Sergiev Posad: Tipografiia Sviato-Troitskoi Sergievoi Lavry, 1908).

Pavel Mel'nikov-Pecherskii, 'Belye golubi' ('The white doves'), in *Polnoe sobranie sochinenii* ('Complete Works') (St Petersburg: Tovarishchestvo A. F. Marks, 1909), vol. VI, 355.

Dmitrii Merezhkovsky, *Gryaduschii Ham* ('The Coming of Ham') (St Petersburg: M. V. Pirozhkov, 1906).

Andrey Rimsky-Korsakov, 'Russkie opernye i baletnye spektakli v Parizhe' ('The Russian operatic and ballet seasons in Paris'), *Russkaya Molva*, 27 June 1913, repr. in PRK, III, 572.

Alexander Tereshchenko, *Byt russkogo naroda* ('The Manners and Customs of the Russian People') (St Petersburg, 1848).

Tatiana Vereshchagina, '"The Great Sacrifice": contextualizing the dream', in Severine Neff, Maureen Carr, Gretchen Horlacher (eds.), with John Reef, *The Rite of Spring at 100* (Bloomington: Indiana University Press, 2017), 272–8.

Sergey Volkonsky, 'Russkii balet v Parizhe' ('Russian ballet in Paris'), *Apollon*, 6 (1913), 70–4), repr. in PRK, III, 572–3.

Rivière, Jacques (born Bordeaux, 15 July 1886; died Paris, 14 February 1925). In his role as a music critic for *La Nouvelle Revue Française* (NRF), one of the best-known French literary reviews, Jacques Rivière was fundamental in building the media phenomenon that grew up around Stravinsky in the 1910s. For Rivière, who was fascinated by Stravinsky, the composer formed the object of a real aesthetic quest. Among the articles in which Jacques Rivière expressed his enthusiasm for Stravinsky's music, the most enduring are his accounts of Petrushka in 1911 and, notably, *The Rite of Spring* in 1913, the literary style of which has made it an ideal text for anthologies and an excellent example of musical *ekphrasis*. In his article on *The Rite*, Rivière forgoes any reference to the picturesque, and instead describes the ballet as a work that is, at the same time, 'crude and complete, whose individual sections remain entirely primitive', evoking its 'matte-ness' (*matité*) to communicate the renunciation of all brilliance or romantic sheen ('the renunciation of sauce'). From then on, Rivière saw in Stravinsky not only a guide for the future of music, but also a symbol/icon of modernity for the arts in general, notably through the idea of devotion to the object rather than the artist's psychology. Even though Rivière continued to support Stravinsky after 1914, he was disappointed by the première of The Nightingale. In 1918, after his years as a prisoner in Germany, it was in his anti-German sentiment that he felt the most kinship with the composer:'You avenge us for any number of things, and notably for that boring and chilly rhetoric of sentiment with which Germany would like to submerge us' (letter from Rivière to Stravinsky, 29 June 1918). Stravinsky, however, was aware of Rivière's expectations and kept him at a distance: 'I'm not sure that you will share my aims' (letter from Stravinsky to Rivière, 30 June 1918). When Rivière became director of the NRF in 1919 and sought to make the review a tribune for 'the anti-impressionist, anti-symbolist, anti-Debussyste movement', he requested from Stravinsky a contribution along these lines, something to which the composer would not consent. If Rivière expressed his total faith in the paths opened by The Rite, he had little confidence in the composer's later explorations, first with the première of The Nightingale in 1914, and definitively in 1920 when he saw the work as one 'moved by suicide'. In this sense, he shared the disappointment of Boris de Schloezer who succeeded Rivière as music critic of the NRF in 1925.

VALÉRIE DUFOUR

Valérie Dufour, Stravinski et ses exégètes (1919–1940) (Brussels: Édition de l'université de Bruxelles, 2006), 137–53.

Robinson, Richard (born Edmonton, Canada, 2 June 1929; died Bakersfield, 6 September 2007). A tenor and vocal teacher who worked at Baylor University in Waco, Texas, from 1966 to 1993. He sang in the première of Stravinsky's In Memoriam Dylan Thomas, Threni and Elegy for J. F. K. Moreover, under Stravinsky's direction, he recorded a series of works for Columbia, including Perséphone and The Flood. HELEN JULIA MINORS

Anon., 'Obituary: Richard Robinson', LA Times, http://articles.latimes.com/2007/sep/13/local/me-passings13.s1 (last accessed 12 November 2018).

Roerich, Nicholas (Nikolay Konstantinovich Ryorikh (Rerikh)) (born St Petersburg, 9 October 1874; died Naggar, near Kullu, Himachal Pradesh, India, 13 December 1947). Russian painter, stage designer, theosophist, philosopher, author of numerous books, founder of many cultural institutions. Roerich graduated from the class of Arkhip Kuindzhi, the Academy of Fine Arts, in 1897, and from the faculty of law, St Petersburg University, in 1898; he also studied in Paris. A true Wagnerian in terms of his attitude towards the cultural heritage of his country and to a synthesis of the arts, Roerich was an artist-explorer and an artist-researcher, whose romantic biography reads today like a novel.

An extremely productive landscape painter, Roerich gained his reputation in the 1890s and 1900s as the most skilful interpreter of the ancient Russian pagan past. A full member of the Academy of Fine Arts, Roerich exhibited at the Academy, at the Mir iskusstva (World of Art) exhibitions (1902), at the Vienna Secession (1905) and at the Salon d'Automne in Paris (1906) under the auspices of the Russian Seasons of Sergey Diaghilev. In 1903, he became one of the leaders of the colony of artists in Talashkino, near Smolensk, the estate of Princess Maria Tenisheva, where he produced mosaics, friezes, furniture and applied art in a neo-folk style. A talented colourist, Roerich, however, never broke away from figurative art and almost always showed a preference for somewhat pompous mythological or mystical subject matters.

Roerich's charisma, broad interests, huge ambitions, tireless energy and his serious professorial manner enabled him to contribute to different spheres of Russian culture, including art pedagogy and archaeology. As a painter, Roerich was also a founding member of both 'World of Art' groups of artists, though Alexandre BENOIS was always wary of his careerism. In 1918, Roerich and his wife Elena left Russia, and lived in Scandinavia, England and the UNITED STATES until they settled in 1929 in northern India. In the 1920s, they became the founders of the theosophic movement 'Living Ethics' or 'Agni Yoga', which continues to attract huge masses of followers to these days. In the 1920s and 1930s, Roerich led two American scientific expeditions to Central Asia and was nominated twice for the Nobel Peace Prize. In 1935, he founded the Roerich Pact – an international agreement on co-operation in preservation of cultural heritage and institutions.

In 1907–15, Roerich worked as a stage designer in Russia and abroad for such famous directors as Nikolay Evreinov, Konstantin Stanislavsky and Sergey Diaghilev. Among his few productions for Diaghilev's BALLETS RUSSES, especially notable are the costumes and décor to the Polovtsian Dances from BORODIN'S OPERA *Prince Igor*, with choreography by Mikhail FOKINE (1909); excerpts from the opera *The Maiden of Pskov* by RIMSKY-KORSAKOV, retitled *Ivan Grozny*; and Stravinsky's BALLET THE RITE OF SPRING, with choreography by Vaslav NIJINSKY (1913). For the latter project, Roerich not only created the curtain, décor and costumes, but also was the co-author of the libretto and, it seems (notwithstanding the later claims of Stravinsky to the contrary), the author of the original idea. In his 1939 publication 'The origin of legends', Roerich claims that in 1910, at the request of Diaghilev, he offered Stravinsky a choice of two ideas for ballets – 'The Game of Chess', where huge hands would move large pieces on an enormous chessboard placed on the stage, and 'The Great Sacrifice', a depiction of a ritual pagan sacrifice to the Sun God Yarile in ancient Russia – and that Stravinsky chose the second (Decter 1989, 83). The initial one-tableau version of the script was created in ST PETERSBURG in 1910. Working together in Talashkino in the summer of 1911, at the estate of Princess Tenisheva with its rich collections of Russian traditional costumes and artefacts, Stravinsky and Roerich created the second version, which contained two tableaux (in their correspondence, both mentioned the ballet as 'our child'). By the autumn of 1912, Roerich had created at least three different versions of the décor of the first tableau, moving towards more colour and less detail, having probably been inspired by Stravinsky's music. Roerich's vision of ancient pagan Russia and his sketches of sets and costumes – of which Stravinsky exclaimed, 'God, I love them, it's a miracle!' in his letter to the painter of 1 December 1912 (cited in Yakovleva 1996, 48–58) – also had a profound influence on Nijinsky's ground-breaking choreography. In his writings, Roerich contrasted the 'wise primitivism' of the ancient Russian tribes with the 'wild primitivism' of the reaction of the Parisian public at the première of the ballet on the historic night of 29 May 1913 (Rerikh 1974, 361).

MARINA LUPISHKO

Jacqueline Decter, Nicholas Roerich: The Life and Art of a Russian Master (Rochester: Inner Traditions International, 1989).

John McCannon, 'Consecrated ground: sacred space in the art of Nicholas Roerich', Zimmerli Journal, 5 (Fall 2008), 84–95.

Nikolay Rerikh, Iz literaturnogo naslediya ('From the Literary Heritage') (Moscow: Iskusstvo, 1974).

Nicholas Roerich, Shambhala (New York: Nicholas Roerich Museum, 2017).

Elena Yakovleva, Teatral'no-dekoratsionnoe iskusstvo N. K. Rerikha ('N. K. Rerikh's Art for the Theatre Stage') (Samara: Agni, 1996).

Roland-Manuel, Alexis (born Paris, 22 March 1891; died Paris, 1 November 1966). Composer and music critic of Belgian origin. Roland-Manuel studied composition under Vincent D'Indy and Albert Roussel, and wrote several studies of RAVEL, his lifelong friend and teacher, to whom he was introduced by Erik SATIE. He published an insightful and positive review of Stravinsky's AUTOBIOGRAPHY in 1936, and contributed the article 'Démarche de Strawinksy' to a special edition of Revue musicale devoted to the composer in 1939. He was a key collaborator in the preparation of Poétique musicale (The POETICS OF MUSIC), Stravinsky's Harvard lectures of 1939. This series of six lectures was drafted through an intricate collaboration process between Stravinsky and Pierre SOUVTCHINSKY, who played an important role in the elaboration of the composer's aesthetic thinking. It was he who did much of the preparatory research on Soviet music, and whose interest in musical time, perception, and music as a phenonemon was a clear influence on the text. Based on extensive notes from this collaborative work, and his conversations with Stravinsky, Roland-Manuel wrote up the final version of the text, which Stravinsky then showed to his friend Paul VALÉRY for a final polishing of the French expression. As a composer, Roland-Manuel provided music for several films by the director Jean Grémillon, and from 1947 to 1961 he held the post of Professor of Aesthetics at the Paris Conservatory.

DAVID EVANS

Rolland, Romain (born Clamecy, 29 January 1866; died Vézalay, 30 December 1944). French novelist, playwright, essayist and musicologist who won the Nobel Prize for Literature in 1915. His essay Le Théâtre du peuple (1913) called for the theatre to open its doors to the masses, and made an important contribution to debates around the democratisation of the institution in FRANCE. In early 1914, Rolland asked Stravinsky to contribute to a book denouncing German barbarism, and while the composer politely declined, contesting the use of the word 'barbarian', he told Rolland that in those dark times, his article 'L'Union fait la force' had been a vital source of encouragement. Rolland protested against World War I in his pacifist manifesto Au-dessus de la mêlée (1915), calling on French and German intellectuals to make a stand. In September that year, Stravinsky met Rolland at Vevey, near Lausanne, where they discussed politics and music. According to Rolland's diary, Stravinsky sang the praises of 'the old Russian civilisation, unknown in the West, the artistic and literary monuments of the cities of the north and east', while expressing distaste for certain aspects of recent Russian BALLET, and WAGNER's *Gesamtkunstwerk*, which tended to reduce music's role to illustrating specific narrative elements. Stravinsky argued, instead, for brusque and unexpected transitions which guaranteed the sovereign role of music for its own sake. Rolland had a great musical knowledge, authoring a doctoral thesis on European OPERA pre-Lully and Scarlatti (1895), and the essay collections *Musiciens d'aujourd'hui* and *Musiciens d'autrefois* (1908), as well as an enthusiastic article on PETRUSHKA, which he heard in Geneva. Stravinsky would meet him occasionally *chez* RAMUZ, along with Paul CLAUDEL and Jules Romains, and while he had no sympathy for his writing – such as *Jean-Christophe*, a sequence of ten novels about a talented German composer living in France, or his *Vie de Beethoven* (1903) – he found him personally charming, telling Robert CRAFT, 'these books have not obstructed my feelings for the man'.

DAVID EVANS

Romanov, Boris (born St Petersburg, 22 March 1891; died New York, 30 January 1957). Russian dancer, choreographer and director. Stravinsky maintained a favourable relationship with Romanov during the ballet master's peripatetic life, which carried him from the Imperial Russian BALLET to positions in Berlin and Milan before he settled in New York. The two had joined forces early on for the BALLETS RUSSES OPERA, The NIGHTINGALE (1914), created on the heels of The RITE OF SPRING, and of which Stravinsky noted dryly that it 'was unsuccessful only in the sense that it failed to provoke a protest' (*Mem*). In what Stephen Walsh described as 'a classic World of Art approach to theatre', Romanov wove movement unconventionally throughout The *Nightingale* in a synthesis with Stravinsky's score and designs by Alexandre BENOIS. While Stravinsky reflects little on Romanov in the conversation books by CRAFT, in his AUTOBIOGRAPHY he suggests that the dance master might have replaced NIJINSKY as choreographer for The *Rite of Spring* had he been available at the time ('Romanov was busy with Florent Schmitt's *Salomé*; only Nijinsky remained').

LORIN JOHNSON

Rosbaud, Hans (born Graz, 22 July 1895; died Lugano, 29 December 1962). Austrian conductor. A devoted advocate of new music, Rosbaud became conductor of the Frankfurt Radio Symphony Orchestra in 1928 and conducted The RITE OF SPRING in 1934. After holding posts in Münster, Strasbourg and Munich, he became chief conductor of the newly established South West German Radio Orchestra in Baden-Baden in 1948. He performed many works by Stravinsky, including AGON, recorded for Véga on 8 October 1957, a few days before Stravinsky conducted the European première with the same orchestra in PARIS. Rosbaud's broadcasts of JEU DE CARTES, the Suites for small orchestra and PETRUSHKA have also been released. In June 1962, Rosbaud conducted the CAPRICCIO and *Petrushka* with the Concertgebouw Orchestra and made a fine recording of the latter piece at the same time.

NIGEL SIMEONE

Rosenthal, Manuel (born Paris, 18 June 1904; died Paris, 5 June 2003). French composer and conductor. He studied composition with RAVEL, who also arranged his conducting debut in 1928. Rosenthal became friendly with Stravinsky during the 1930s, particularly after giving The RITE OF SPRING with the Orchestre national de France in 1937. That year, Rosenthal was asked by MASSINE to arrange Offenbach's music for the BALLET *Gaîté parisienne*. When

Massine objected that the orchestrations were 'disrespectful', it was Stravinsky who urged him to accept Rosenthal's ballet, which quickly became an international success. Between January and July 1945, Rosenthal conducted a 'Festival Stravinsky' at the THÉÂTRE DES CHAMPS-ELYSÉES, a comprehensive series of seven concerts including recent pieces such as the FOUR NORWEGIAN MOODS, the performance of which was disrupted by protests and whistling by a group of MESSIAEN pupils, including BOULEZ and Serge Nigg. NIGEL SIMEONE

Rounseville, Robert (born Attleboro, 1914; died New York City, 1974). Rounseville was an established operatic tenor with a background in films, singing in the 1951 cinema production of *The Tales of Hoffmann*. He performed the lead role of Tom Rakewell in the première of *The* RAKE'S PROGRESS on 11 September 1951, under the direction of the composer at the TEATRO LA FENICE, VENICE. This performance was recorded and is available as a commercial release.

HELEN JULIA MINORS

Igor Stravinsky (2009), *Stravinsky: The Rake's Progress* (CD), Opera D'Oro, B002RCQMRY. T&C

Rubinstein, Artur (born Łódź, 28 January 1887; died Geneva, 20 December 1982). Polish-American pianist. Renowned in his later years as a leading exponent of the Romantic repertoire, at an earlier stage in his long career Rubinstein programmed a wide range of works by contemporary composers, including DEBUSSY and RAVEL. According to the colourful account in his autobiography, he first met Stravinsky in June 1914 following a performance of PETRUSHKA at the Drury Lane Theatre, London. The two struck up a friendship, and Stravinsky benefitted from Rubinstein's financial generosity during his years of penury following the Russian Revolution. In return, Rubinstein was the dedicatee of PIANO-RAG-MUSIC completed in June 1919; however, he was puzzled by the work's use of tone clusters and JAZZ rhythms and never played it. Two years later, Stravinsky was again the beneficiary of Rubinstein's patronage, in the form of a new commission with the enormous fee of $5,000. The resulting transcription, THREE MOVEMENTS FROM PETRUSHKA, in which Rubinstein collaborated, has become one of the most celebrated and demanding showpieces of the twentieth-century piano repertoire. Craft is incorrect in his assertion that Rubinstein played the transcription on only one occasion: in fact, he programmed it numerous times on both sides of the Atlantic. He and Stravinsky remained friends during the latter's years in the UNITED STATES, and Craft recounts being taken by Stravinsky to a concert at the pianist's Beverly Hills estate in 1949, when Rubinstein 'played a Mozart concerto with a small orchestra for an audience comprised almost exclusively of movie stars recognisable even without their make-up'. PETER O'HAGAN

Rubinstein, Ida Lvovna (born Kharkov, 21 September / 5 October 1885; died Vence, France, 20 September 1960). Russian dancer, actor and producer. Raised amid the wealthy and cultured families of ST PETERSBURG, Rubinstein rebelled against her background by pursuing a theatrical career. She danced with the BALLETS RUSSES (1909–11) before mounting her own productions in PARIS, much to DIAGHILEV's ire. In 1917, she approached Stravinsky about working on a hybrid theatrical work based on Shakespeare's *Anthony and Cleopatra* (with BAKST and André GIDE as potential collaborators), but the project was eventually abandoned. Over a decade later, she commissioned the BALLET *The* FAIRY'S KISS (1928) for her then newly founded company BALLETS IDA RUBINSTEIN. Choreographed by Bronislava NIJINSKA and featuring sets by Alexandre BENOIS, Rubinstein starred in the title role and Stravinsky conducted the première. Still, the ballet was not a great success; Rubinstein, known for her stage presence not her dancing ability, was poorly received.

Brief discussions about Rubinstein presenting APOLLO came to nothing, and her next Stravinsky commission was the 'melodrama' PERSÉPHONE (1934), which finally united Stravinsky and GIDE. Choreographed by Kurt Jooss, after Stravinsky had blocked Mikhail FOKINE being engaged, Rubinstein starred in the title role and was again criticised for her performance. Four years later, she attempted to bring together Stravinsky and Paul CLAUDEL for a stage work, but a subject could not be agreed. Stravinsky blamed Rubinstein and declared he had 'wasted a month for nothing' (SSC, III, 267). In 1939, Rubinstein retired from the stage.   SOPHIE REDFERN

Russia. In 1962, during a reception honouring him as a visitor to his motherland, in which he had not set foot for half a century, the 80-year-old Stravinsky exclaimed:

> A man has one birthplace, one fatherland, one country – he *can* have only one country – and the place of his birth is the most important factor in his life. I regret that circumstances separated me from my fatherland, that I did not give birth to my works there and, above all, that I was not there to help the new Soviet Union create its new music. I did not leave Russia of my own will, however, even though I disliked much in my Russia and in Russia generally. Yet the right to criticize Russia is mine, because Russia is mine and because I love it, and I do not give any foreigner that right. (SCF, 195)

This was quite a statement coming from a composer who figured, at the time, as the epitome of Cosmopolitanism, and who had for some time been expressing himself through a musical language of increasing abstraction – gradually moving away from the early modernist neo-nationalism, through the international style of NEO-CLASSICISM, to the transnational compositional method of serialism. As is evident by this declaration, Stravinsky's relationship to his motherland since he found himself living beyond its borders had been, to say the least, ambivalent. Regardless of these emotionally loaded words uttered towards the end of his life, he had resisted the strong psychological attachment to the lost homeland that frequently comes with emigration, which haunted most of his *émigré* compatriots and led them to see the preservation of their nation's culture and traditions as their sacrosanct mission. And yet one could say that, throughout his career, notwithstanding the changes in style, musical language and compositional method he employed, Stravinsky had defined his music as much against his Russian cultural background, as in conversation with western European artistic trends. It was his idiosyncratic, playful, modernist interaction with his Russian cultural heritage that initially made his name in the West, and the seeming renunciation of this background, for combined historical and aesthetic reasons starting in the 1920s (despite any lines of continuity linking his three compositional phases), that consolidated his prominent place in the western European artistic milieu.

Stravinsky's Russia was that of ST PETERSBURG, as shaped and experienced by the local intelligentsia (his father, after all, held a prominent place in the city's musical establishment, being one of the great operatic singers of his day) – although he did spend a considerable amount of time in dachas in the Russian countryside as well as USTILUG, as was the practice within the Russian gentry. At the turn of the twentieth century, the city enjoyed a rich cultural life, an international outlook and elegance, inspired by major western European capitals. As regards music specifically, the Russian capital witnessed the consolidation of Russian national music, particularly through the efforts of the circle of composers who benefitted from the patronage of Mitrofan BELYAYEV, headed by Nikolay RIMSKY-KORSAKOV, a circle to which Stravinsky himself belonged. Initially, the ideal of national music had, of course, been served by the so-called FIVE (BALAKIREV, MUSSORGSKY, BORODIN, CUI and Rimsky-Korsakov, also known as the 'Mighty Handful' or Moguchaya Kuchka), who had developed a national compositional voice that disdained conservatory training, and differentiated themselves from what could be described as the 'cosmopolitans', namely Pyotr TCHAIKOVSKY and Anton Rubinstein. Yet, by Stravinsky's time, things had radically changed. Rimsky-Korsakov, a self-taught composer himself, had accepted a post at the Conservatory and headed the new Russian school of composers, which served very different ideals from their predecessors. This new Russian school had mastered western European musical techniques to a particularly high standard, thanks to solid conservatory education, which had helped both to establish Russian national music and to institutionalise it. Indeed, their music was more academic, formulaic, resistant to modernist trends, and lacked the spontaneity of the music of the Kuchka. Thus, despite St Petersburg's otherwise international spirit, its musical scene could be described as nothing less than provincial compared to that of western European capitals. Yet, overall, turn-of-the-century St Petersburg was a haven of artistic innovation, despite (or rather because of) the reactionary political conditions that came with Nicholas II's reign – although music was slow to follow. For as long as Stravinsky was based in St Petersburg, Russian MODERNISM found its outlet primarily through the symbolist movement – FUTURISM and Acmeism, the other two prominent Russian modernist movements, would come centre stage only after the composer started spending winters in the West. Stravinsky's St Petersburg was also the base of the Mir iskusstva (World of Art) artistic group, which embraced elements of symbolism, and lay the seeds for the BALLETS RUSSES, the company that, led by Sergey DIAGHILEV, would play such a momentous part in shaping western European modernism by investing in Russia's own artistic forces and resources, and innovative recreations of its traditions. The role such an inspiring environment played in detaching Stravinsky from the safe harbours of the Belyayev circle, towards the vanguard of modernism beyond the Russian borders, can hardly be overstated.

Stravinsky was, in effect, based in Russia until 1910, when his engagements with the Ballets Russes and his aspirations for an international career drew him to western Europe – although he spent summers in Ustilug until 1914, and paid flying visits to St Petersburg around Christmas in 1910, and in 1912. SWITZERLAND became the first host country for Igor's family, followed by FRANCE, and finally, under the shadow of World War II, Stravinsky moved to the UNITED STATES. This westwards displacement was accompanied by changes in citizenship as well: skipping Swiss nationality (which he had considered taking up for some time), Stravinsky first became a French citizen (in 1934) and then an American one (in 1945), although these were choices made more for practical, rather than patriotic or aesthetic, reasons. But by the time he was prepared to change nationality, the Russia he was born and grew up in had vanished anyway.

And yet, even while in emigration, Stravinsky continued to dwell in Russia mentally for quite some time, but that was a country and nation far detached from the reality he had fled from, or from the Russia he had lived in during the first three decades of his life. It was a Russia of the past, partly (re-)discovered through quasi-ethnographic study of its folklore and traditions, and (re-)imagined primarily for the sake of western European audiences – the Russia that fed into works that belong to Stravinsky's so-called Russian compositional period. Stravinsky unearthed and resourcefully reworked in his compositions Slavic pagan, as well as more contemporary, folk and popular customs, rituals and traditions. His interest in Russia's past and more recent rural present went far beyond the mere borrowing of folk songs and tunes – which, whenever used, were not quoted as such, but would bear only a generalised stylistic identity – towards a deeper understanding (at least that was the intention) of the broader cultural context within which such songs had been used, the practices and mentalities that framed their performance. Such knowledge informed the very conception of works such as The RITE OF SPRING and Les NOCES. This approach mirrored a wider trend among the Russian artistic intelligentsia, which, since the nineteenth century, had expressed a strong interest in Russia's folk heritage. The so-called neo-nationalist artistic style, which flourished first under the patronage of Savva Mamontov and later the Princess Maria Tenisheva, fed into the aesthetic ideals of the World of Art artistic group, which recognised the latent modernist potential of antique and fabricated folk art. Through his involvement with this strand of the Russian intelligentsia, Stravinsky was encouraged to dig deep into the Slavic past and Russian folk and popular traditions, abstracting from them structural elements that could be used with modernist compositional procedures. He thus made a landmark contribution to the modernist movement overall, infusing it with momentum originating in the Russian cultural traditions, in a fashion inspired by contemporary Russian artistic creation.

As his interest in this conception of Russia started to recede, and while still in emigration, Stravinsky became re-acquainted with his motherland in yet another way: through its identification as Eurasia by the so-called Eurasianist intellectual and political movement. Eurasianism was advocated primarily in the 1920s, by eminent members of the Russian intelligentsia, who were active in various disciplines and had emigrated to various countries of western Europe after the 1917 Russian Revolution. Those intellectuals reconceptualised Russia as Eurasia – that is, a distinct geopolitical and cultural entity, a separate continent that merged European and Asian (Finno-Ugric, Tartar-Turkic and

Mongolian) features. Although the latter component was idealised, the European one was viewed through a critical lens, since Western civilisation was perceived as despotic and decadent. Eurasianism articulated millennial hopes of regeneration of the entire humankind through a cultural renaissance based on religious principles (inspired by Russian Orthodoxy) that would be realised by the Eurasian nation. Stravinsky's closest link to Eurasianism was his intimate friend Pierre SOUVTCHINSKY, a founding member of the movement. Arthur LOURIÉ, a close collaborator of his in the 1920s, who embraced Eurasianist views, is another connecting point – in fact, he wrote two major articles on Stravinsky that came out in Eurasianist publications. The aura of Eurasianist ideas, as they were articulated by Souvtchinsky and Lourié, may be felt in Stravinsky's neo-classicism, with respect, primarily, to its metaphysical aspect. More specifically, the spiritual leanings of Stravinsky's neo-classicism reverberate with ideas by Souvtchinsky and Lourié regarding what could be described as a metaphysical or sacred formalism – namely, the creation of musical forms that would express a transcendental reality rather than subjective emotions, which would thus be imbued with spiritual content. Such music would allegedly contribute to a cultural renaissance in line with Eurasianist aspirations. It is precisely this element, the religious component, that provided a link through which Stravinsky would reconnect with his motherland in the 1920s (although he had been baptised according to Russian traditions, Russian Orthodoxy became important to him only around the middle of that decade) at a time he could no longer set foot on it, and, more importantly, at a time when religion was being ostracised from Russia by the Bolsheviks. And it did so in a way that made relevant his entire neo-classical output, not only compositions with overt religious references.

Although Stravinsky's interest in religion, starting in the 1920s, was a connecting point to his motherland, it is precisely to this time that the beginning of his ambivalent attitude towards his Russian background can be traced. For instance, the renunciation of the use of original folk tunes in his works is certainly indicative of much more than an aesthetic transition from neo-nationalism to neo-classicism. The most emblematic move of distancing himself from his Russian past is probably his assertion that only one original folk tune had been used in The Rite of Spring – and this has been disproved by Richard Taruskin's enlightening identification of folk song material in this work (Taruskin 1980). The praise of pure, absolute music was the next step taken towards this end, and The Rite was again symbolically recruited for this purpose, through his assertion that he preferred it as a concert piece. In this spirit, extra-musical references in music were thus condemned and he notoriously refuted music's very ability to express anything at all. Instead, music was compared with architecture, and musical works were seen as objective constructions. Moreover, starting in the 1920s, Stravinsky abandoned Russian topics in favour of more cosmopolitan themes, and, what is more, Russian was forsaken as a language of composition – the use of Old Slavonic in three works, which were reworked in Latin in 1949, is in a sense a means of distancing and abstraction analogous to the turn to ancient Greek themes and the use of the dead language of Latin. Even MAVRA, essentially his last composition on a Russian theme and text, was a neo-classical undertaking that deconstructed and reinvented its Russian classical source in a fashion that, at the same time, enabled him to distance himself from both kuchkist nationalism and his earlier neo-nationalism. Stravinsky's second emigration, to the USA, which was eventually accompanied by the turn to the even more abstract compositional method of serialism, only intensified those tendencies and broadened the distance from Russia, literally as well as culturally.

To what extent that distance was a mental one too is a different question, and one that surfaced with Stravinsky's return to his native land (by that time renamed as the USSR) in 1962. The invitation was extended to the composer by the Soviet Union on the occasion of his eightieth birthday, when he was invited to conduct his own music, in the context of the country's increasing liberal policy – an adept propaganda move, particularly since Stravinsky's latest adopted homeland, the USA, was slow in acknowledging the importance of this birthday. Initially, Stravinsky was hesitant. For quite some time he had been critical of the Soviet regime and the lack of freedom of expression in the USSR, while in the past he had also pointed out that he would not consent to conduct his works there because the musicians were unfamiliar with the style of his music. In the end, though, he accepted the invitation, proclaiming that he thus wished to help the younger generation of musicians in his motherland. His personal CORRESPONDENCE with friends and relatives (for instance, his niece Xenya, Pierre Souvtchinsky and Maria Yudina) also played a role in his coming to terms with the idea of visiting his motherland. His trip lasted from 21 September until 11 October, and the composer was accompanied by his wife and Robert CRAFT. In Moscow (which the composer was visiting for the first time), he and Craft conducted four concerts with his music (on 26 and 28 September, and 2 and 3 October). Subsequently, they moved on to his native St Petersburg – then called Leningrad – on 4 October, where he and Craft conducted two concerts on 8 and 9 October, returning to Moscow right after the latter. The company departed from the Soviet capital on 11 October. Although, once Stravinsky found himself back in western Europe, he quickly switched back to his Western mood, the visit to the USSR had activated genuine emotional responses as intense as the statement quoted earlier, and prompted the realisation that the link to one's motherland is hard to cut. As Craft admitted, thinking in hindsight, whenever the composer could, he preferred to speak no other language than Russian all day long. Stravinsky symbolically admitted the importance of his native tongue to him – and, by extension, of Russian mentality and culture overall – in an interview to a Soviet newspaper: 'I have spoken Russian all my life, I think in Russian, my way of expressing myself (slog) is Russian. Perhaps this is not immediately apparent in my music, but it is latent there, a part of its hidden nature' (Taruskin 1980, 13). To some extent, Stravinsky was speaking on the spur of the moment. At the same time, though, he was offering a key to understanding his multi-faceted oeuvre as a single continuity, with his Russian background as a unique and single point of reference.   KATERINA LEVIDOU

Richard Taruskin, 'Russian folk melodies in The Rite of Spring', JAMS, 33.3 (Fall 1980), 501–43.
SRT

Russian Composers. Stravinsky was immersed in a musical atmosphere from childhood, and in terms of his future development as a composer, it is significant that his early experiences were dominated by the sounds of Russian music. The vocal exercises performed by his father, Fyodor STRAVINSKY, the first basso of the Imperial MARIINSKY THEATRE, formed part of the domestic background to his early years. Fyodor Stravinsky's repertoire was based on national OPERA, and Russian music had become the foundation of Igor's work, retaining its value even when Stravinsky rejected the Russian language and Russian subjects in his later compositions. Composer-compatriots played a crucial role in his creative evolution.

First and foremost among these influences was Nikolay Andreyevich RIMSKY-KORSAKOV (1844–1908). The young Stravinsky was not only his student but also an ardent admirer, literally living in the atmosphere of his music. Stravinsky imitated Rimsky-Korsakov in his early works – often unconsciously, but also at times quite deliberately and not without an element of competition. Stravinsky's fundamental connections with Rimsky-Korsakov's style were completely obvious to the first critics of his music, who perceived his early works, including The FIREBIRD, as modelled directly on his teacher. 'The sound painting of Antar and The Snow Maiden served as an ideal for Mr. Stravinsky, but he didn't go further than abject imitation' (PRK, I, 443). While this 'abject imitation' was overcome in time, certain characteristics of Rimsky's style are also noticeable in Stravinsky's more mature works. A love of unusual timbres and a taste for original scoring can be traced back to Rimsky, a great master of ORCHESTRATION. For perceptive musicians like Nikolay Myaskovsky, Stravinsky had become his teacher's true successor, as he wrote in his brilliant essay on PETRUSHKA (PRK, I, 484). In truth, the first and fourth pictures of the BALLET recall the kind of mass folk scenes that Rimsky-Korsakov created in his operas. The street songs in Petrushka also relate in part to Rimsky-Korsakov: the comic song 'Chizhik-Pyzhik' ('Siskin-Fawn'), which Tsar Dodon sings as a confession of love to Shemakha Queen in The Golden Cockerel could be considered a predecessor.

Such parallels of staging disappeared with time, but the kinship between the techniques of both composers was preserved. Thus, Stravinsky's brief motifs (popevki) came not only from folklore but also from Rimsky-Korsakov; in a similar way, the student inherited the tone–semitone scale ('Rimsky-Korsakov's scale' or the octatonic scale). However, in the case of Stravinsky, these stylistic elements became divorced from mere coincidences of plot to become universal, and we find them later in the neo-classical instrumental compositions. At the same time, the parallels in the works of the two composers took on a deeper character – among them, the archetypal motive of sacrifice, which was most important for Stravinsky, gained special significance. We can trace its roots to the beautiful, ideal, heroines of Rimsky-Korsakov's operas, perishing in a prosaic, cruel world: such idealised figures as Olga in The Maid of Pskov, Volkhovà in Sadko, Marfa in The Tsar's Bride, and especially the Snow Maiden – the predecessor of the Chosen One from The RITE OF SPRING. The latter is but the most celebrated example of the theme of sacrifice in Stravinsky's work, followed by Persephone; the Young Man in The FAIRY'S KISS; and Orpheus and the god Apollo, ascending to Parnassus to the rhythm of a funeral procession.

A deep relationship based on aesthetic principles connected Stravinsky and Rimsky-Korsakov. For both composers, the most important aspect of creativity was craftsmanship – that is, technical skills. Rimsky-Korsakov taught primarily compositional technique, which in turn was emphasised by his student. It was also no coincidence that the tone of their respective memoirs, Stravinsky's AUTOBIOGRAPHY, and Rimsky's Letopis' moyey muzïkal'noy zhizni ('Chronicle of my Musical Life'), turned out to be so similar. Both authors were focused on facts, were businesslike and avoided lyrical digressions. Finally, they shared some curious everyday ways – for example, the habit of using two pairs of glasses at the same time, which Stravinsky adopted from his teacher.

The pupil did not, however, always agree with his teacher. One of the points of contention between them related to the works of Modest Petrovich MUSSORGSKY (1839–81). While Mussorgsky had died a year before Stravinsky was born, Igor nevertheless heard a lot about him at home: Fyodor Ignatyevich was well acquainted with him and performed with him in concerts – one of his best roles was Varlaam from Boris Godunov. Stravinsky came into practical contact with Mussorgsky's music when, on behalf of Alexander ZILOTI, he orchestrated 'Mephistopheles' Song in the Cellar of Auerbach' (known as 'Song of the Flea'). When Mussorgsky's incomplete OPERA KHOVANSHCHINA was presented during the 1913 Russian Ballet season in PARIS, it had been performed heretofore only in Rimsky-Korsakov's orchestrated version. DIAGHILEV wanted to bring the opera closer to the author's intentions and suggested to Stravinsky and RAVEL that they orchestrate the episodes rejected by Rimsky. Stravinsky, like Rimsky-Korsakov before him, had to write anew the final chorus of the Old Believers' self-immolation, using Mussorgsky's sketches. The chorus became for him the first example of re-composition – that is, a piece based on someone else's material. At the same time, it was an act of creative criticism of his teacher. Both then and later, Stravinsky did not approve of Rimsky's versions of two operas by Mussorgsky: for example, he considered that Rimsky had made Boris Godunov too pompous, à la Meyerbeer, and he called it Boris Glazunov – a reference to Rimsky's former student, who was also the target of his pun. As for the music of Mussorgsky himself, Stravinsky was not in direct contact with it after Khovanshchina – the only brief exception being the piano arrangement of the chorus from the Prologue of Boris Godunov which he made for his children (MORGES, 1918). Stravinsky regarded Mussorgsky with great respect until the end of his life, and he admired his use of the orchestra, in contrast to the widespread opinion about a perceived lack of technical skill. Mussorgsky's influence was noticeable in the early period of Stravinsky's work, first of all in the manner of vocal declamation in The NIGHTINGALE (in addition, its introduction showed the direct impact of Mussorgsky's style filtered through DEBUSSY). References to Mussorgsky occurred rarely in Stravinsky's later works – however, among them is the startling example of Tiresias' solo in OEDIPUS REX: both the character and his music are an almost exact quotation from Boris Godunov (cf. rehearsal

395

number 69 in *Oedipus Rex* piano score and the beginning of the first scene (in Pimen's cell) of the first act of *Boris Godunov*).

Pyotr Il'ich TCHAIKOVSKY (1840–93) was a unique figure for Stravinsky, and he may not have spoken so enthusiastically about any other Russian composer. Traces of Tchaikovsky's influence were noticeable in Stravinsky's early compositions (SYMPHONY IN E♭ MAJOR, *The Faun and the Shepherdess*, partly *The Firebird*); however, they disappeared in *Petrushka* and *The Rite of Spring*, the works which brought Stravinsky to international prominence. Therefore, his participation in the production of *The Sleeping Beauty* by Diaghilev's BALLETS RUSSES in 1921 was perceived as a surprise, as was the performance itself. Stravinsky explained his position in an open letter to Diaghilev, published in the London newspaper *The Times* on 18 October 1921, summing up the aesthetic ideas of the Diaghilev circle, and his own views on Tchaikovsky's heritage. The polemical reference to Moguchaya Kuchka ('The Mighty Handful' or The FIVE), as opposed to the 'Russian European' Tchaikovsky, was developed later in *Autobiography* and The POETICS OF MUSIC. Defending himself against accusations of corporate solidarity in his support of Diaghilev's production, Stravinsky emphasised his creative affinity to Tchaikovsky: 'I am really one of the family.'

Stravinsky's relation to Tchaikovsky is manifest not only in individual compositions, but also in the conception of 'white ballet' and the cult of melody, developed towards the end of the 1920s. Furthermore, thematic elements derived from Tchaikovsky can be found in his works – subconscious products of an expressed kinship: examples can be found in APOLLON MUSAGÈTE, and in the finales of CONCERTO IN E♭: 'DUMBARTON OAKS', SYMPHONY IN C, etc.).

Stravinsky orchestrated two fragments of *The Sleeping Beauty* which had been cut before the première; in addition, he made an orchestral version of the coda in the final Pas de deux (No. 28) which Bronislava NIJINSKA had arranged as a Russian dance. The new orchestration of 'Aurora's Variations' (No. 15b) which, in Diaghilev's version, became a solo of the Lilac Fairy, as well as the 'Entr'acte with a violin solo' (No. 18) were generally arranged in Tchaikovsky's style, but not without significant deviations (Savenko 2001, 241–9).

In 1941, Stravinsky turned to *The Sleeping Beauty* again, and orchestrated the pas de deux 'Bluebird' for the Ballet Theater in New York. This time Stravinsky used a small symphony orchestra with piano. Nevertheless, as was the case twenty years before, he preferred more powerful sounds.

The most important product of Stravinsky's experience with Tchaikovsky's music was the ballet *The Fairy's Kiss*, commissioned and produced by Ida RUBINSTEIN's Company (1928). The initiator was Alexandre BENOIS who suggested that Stravinsky write a ballet on themes by Tchaikovsky. In a letter dated 12 December 1927, he listed fifteen piano pieces by Tchaikovsky, of which Stravinsky used seven, supplementing them with some romances. In addition, *The Fairy's Kiss* includes various allusions to Tchaikovsky's music, which, though not quotations, sometimes sound more 'authentic' than actual borrowings. That is to say, Stravinsky treated Tchaikovsky's material as his own, while at the same time avoiding sharp stylistic dissonances. It was not just the basic material which featured as a series of quotations: the fundamental concept of the ballet was in itself a quotation. In his dedication, Stravinsky spoke directly concerning the allegorical meaning of his piece: 'Like a fairy, the muse had marked out Tchaikovsky with her kiss, the seal of which lies on all the works of the great artist.' Here we can see an allusion to the idea of Fate, which is most important for Tchaikovsky. However, Fate, tragically opposed in Tchaikovsky's work to the natural human desire for happiness, became in The Fairy's Kiss divine predestination, the power of a gift, elevating the artist over his earthly destiny.

The music of Tchaikovsky featured also in Stravinsky's career as a conductor. He loved the Second Symphony most of all (conducting it often), and the String Serenade. In addition, his repertoire included the Concerto for Violin and Orchestra, the Third and Sixth Symphonies, and the Suite from the ballet The Nutcracker.

Alexander Nikolayevich SCRIABIN (1872–1915) was a dominant influence on young Russian composers at the turn of the century, who perceived his mystical philosophy and innovative musical language as a creative guide, and Stravinsky was no exception. The influence of Scriabin's piano style was noticeable in the early FOUR STUDIES, op. 7 (1908); we can hear echoes of Scriabinesque harmonies in the Firebird's dance. Even more interesting in this respect was the brief but grandiose cantata Zvezdolikiy (The KING OF THE STARS, 1912) which was completed before The Rite of Spring and dedicated to Debussy. The eschatological poem by Konstantin BALMONT, which was used for it, determined the universal scope of the sound, which undoubtedly had something in common with Scriabin's mystical opuses, especially the 'Poem of Fire' Prometheus.

Sergey Sergeyevich PROKOFIEV (1891–1953) was nearly ten years younger than Stravinsky and, in essence, belonged to another generation. They were personally acquainted and corresponded; Stravinsky's name is constantly found in Prokofiev's Diary. Prokofiev treated Stravinsky with jealous interest, first criticising and then admiring him. There were common qualities in their works – for example, an inclination towards the theatre, to sharp contrasts of character, and a love of the grotesque. However, Prokofiev's Russian style, which was formed partly under the influence of Stravinsky (as seen in the ballet Chout), turned out to be significantly different from that of his older colleague. A few years after Prokofiev's death, Stravinsky described him in the following terms: 'He had some technique and he could do certain things very well, but more than that, he had personality; one saw that in his every gesture – biological personality let us call it' (Mem, 67).   SVETLANA SAVENKO

Lawrence Morton, 'Stravinsky and Tchaikovsky: Le Baiser de la fée', in Paul Henry Lang (ed.), Stravinsky: A New Appraisal of his Work. (New York: W. W. Norton, 1963), 47–60.
Svetlana Savenko, Mir Stravinskogo ('Stravinsky's World') (Moscow: Kompozitor, 2001).
SCS; SRT

Russian Literature. Stravinsky was a zealous reader, a habit he inherited from his father. Together with this passion, he inherited part of Fyodor's sizeable library, which contained a substantial number of books on Russian literature, culture and history. Yet, the extent of his interest in and knowledge of Russian literature is not reflected in his compositions, where he did not use much of the work of Russian authors. His few settings of Russian poetry date from his so-called 'Russian' compositional period. In fact, these appear intermittently with settings of non-Russian authors (either in the original or in Russian translation).

Stravinsky's settings disclose his interest in the Russian classics, but also Russian symbolism. Being extremely familiar with Alexander PUSHKIN's work through his father – who, in fact, collected Pushkin rarities – he engaged with his texts early on in his career, in 'Storm Cloud' ('Tucha', 1902) and The Faun and the Shepherdess (1906). His opera buffa MAVRA (1922) is also based on the story The Little House in Kolomna by the great Russian poet. At the same time, he used a text by the fictitious author Kozma Prutkov for his early comic song 'Conductor and Tarantula' (1906, which is presumed lost). Prutkov, an author adored by his teacher RIMSKY-KORSAKOV as much as by Stravinsky himself, had been invented by Alexey Konstantinovich Tolstoy and his cousins Alexey, Vladimir and Alexander Zhemchuzhnikov in the 1850s. Subsequently, Stravinsky set some symbolist poetry to music, initially verses by his friend Sergey GORODETSKY (Two Songs (Romances) for mezzo soprano and piano, 1907–8), and then Konstantin BALMONT's Two Poems of Balmont (1911, rev. 1954) and KING OF THE STARS (1912).

His sparse use of Russian texts would seem to justify Stravinsky's retrospective comment that 'I was never close to any Russian literary group. The only Russian literary intellectuals I knew, Merezhkovsky and Prince Mirsky, I met in Paris' (Memories and Commentaries). The statement was made in the context of his recollections of the two symbolist poets he set to music, Gorodetsky and Balmont, and, if anything, it should alert us to the composer's anxiety of influence and the overall rhetoric that aimed to dim his Russian roots. For, although Stravinsky could by no means be deemed a symbolist, the momentous role the movement played in the cultural milieu that shaped his first artistic steps is hard to overstate, especially its influence on Diaghilev's entourage – first the Mir istkusstva (World of Art) group, and subsequently the BALLETS RUSSES. Indeed, Russian symbolism's attraction to mystical archaism, and its interest in Slavic mythology and folklore, set the background for works such as The FIREBIRD, PETRUSHKA and The RITE OF SPRING. Yet, unlike his contemporaries Sergey PROKOFIEV and Arthur LOURIÉ (both of whom set verses by Anna Akhmatova), Stravinsky did not engage with modernist texts beyond Russian symbolism. This choice cannot be attributed to a lack of interest in later literary developments (indeed, in his diaries Prokofiev records a private reading by Mayakovsky of his poetry in 1922 in Berlin, which sent Stravinsky 'into ecstasy'). In fact, although his engagement with Russian texts ended with the close of his Russian period, Stravinsky maintained an interest in Russian literature – as with literature in general – throughout his life. Even during his American years, he got hold of books by Russian and Soviet authors, often with the help of friends such as Pierre SOUVTCHINSKY and Maria Yudina, who provided him with volumes of, for example, Remizov and Pasternak.

A special chapter in Stravinsky's relationship with Russian literature is his interest in Russian folk poetry. Stravinsky familiarised himself with the genre through meticulous study of various Russian folk song collections during the years of his so-called Swiss exile – although he was probably subconsciously aware of aspects of it, having come into contact with it even earlier in his life. This contact with the folk song, as he admitted, had a momentous impact on the development of his compositional idiom overall. What attracted Stravinsky to Russian folk poetry was the realisation that the accents of the words are ignored when the verses are sung. The recognition of the musical possibilities inherent in this fact was, as he described it, one of the most rejoicing dis-coveries of his life. It should be mentioned, though, that the ensuing dissocia-tion of the sonic from the semantic aspect of words (of sound from meaning) is a feature that symbolist poets such as Gorodetsky and Balmont had already recognised and embraced in their works. The musical implications of this discovery by Stravinsky are reflected in the flexibility of stress and the element of metrical displacement that typify his works, both with and without text. And, indeed, it was a discovery with an impact on Stravinsky's aesthetics that was sufficiently profound to affect his approach to text setting and the rhyth-mic dimension of his music well beyond his Russian period. KATERINA LEVIDOU

Tatiana Baranova Monighetti, 'Stravinsky's Russian library', in SHW, 61–77.
Marina Lupishko, 'Stravinsky and Russian poetic folklore', Ex Tempore, 12.2 (Spring/Summer 2005) (www.ex-tempore.org/lupishko1/lupishkoa.htm, accessed 9 May 2018).
Sergey Prokofiev, Diaries 1915–1923: Behind the Mask, trans. Anthony Phillips (London: Faber and Faber).
Mem; SCS; SRT

Russian Musical Society (RMS), or Imperial Russian Musical Society (from 1868), was the Russian music and educational institution active from 1859 to 1917, founded by Anton Rubinstein and the Grand Duchess Yelena Pavlovna. It was sponsored by the royal family: successively Yelena Pavlovna (1860–73), Grand Duke Konstantin Nikolayevich (1873–81). and then his son Grand Duke Konstantin Konstantinovich (from 1881). The RMS had departments in several cities, including ST PETERSBURG, Moscow (founded by Nikolai Rubinstein and Prince Nikolai Trubezkoi in 1860), Voronezh, Kiev, Tiflis, Kazan, Astrakhan and elsewhere. The idea first emerged at an artistic salon hosted by Yelena Pavlovna. As stated in its charter (approved by Tsar Alexander II), the RMS strived to propagate 'the development of music education and taste and promotion of homegrown talents'. The RMS promoted both symphonic (from 1859) and chamber (from 1860) concert programmes. The first symphony concert at the RMS took place on 23 November 1859 under Anton Rubinstein, who led the symphonic programme until 1867. The public music classes there effectively laid the foundations for professional MUSICAL EDUCATION in Russia. In 1957, it was revived as the All-Russian Choir Society, and, in 1987, as the All-Russian Musical Society. Some of Stravinsky's works, among them PETRUSHKA (7 January 1915), were performed at RMS concerts. ELENA VERESHCHAGINA AND TATIANA VERESHCHAGINA

Russian Myth. In the nineteenth century, and on into the beginning of the twentieth, Russian myth was not a fixed concept or a closed system. On the contrary, it underwent intensive redefinition, re-assessment and re-invention. Reconstruction of Russian myth was closely related to the notion of nation, which in RUSSIA emerged in the early nineteenth century as part of a pan-European national discourse, and was formed by the interaction of several distinct paradigms, most notably French (Jean-Jacques Rousseau) and German (Jacob and Wilhelm Grimm, Johann Gottfried Herder, Friedrich Schlegel). These influences were somewhat fancifully intermingled and transformed. The quest for the essential Russian element was further complicated by the fact that it was to be accomplished by an enlightened élite that owed its very existence to the Petrine reforms, which aimed at 'Europeanisation' at all cost and were contrary to any 'Russianness'. The true Russia, therefore, was to be found either in pre-Petrine times or in those societal strata that evaded Europeanisation from above (that is, mostly the peasants of the central and Siberian provinces). Nonetheless, the governing status of the cultural élite was built on specifically European values and practices, and this contradiction was never resolved during Stravinsky's lifetime. The unique situation of the Russian Empire in the nineteenth century can be characterised as 'internal colonisation' (Etkind 2011, 7), as the colonisers and the colonised were separated not by sea, race or religion, but by an insurmountable cultural distance. Cultivating this cultural distance, Russia ended up 'orientalising' the peasants in its central provinces: the common Russian people were seen by the élite as both the embodiment of the national idea and, at the same time, the universal 'Other', to whom all colonial strategies were applied, ranging from violent suppression to assimilation, to ethnographical research and, finally, to guilt-driven service.

A full and systematic account of Slav mythology was produced by Alexander Nikolayevich AFANASYEV (1826–71). In his book *The Slav's Poetic Outlook on Nature* (1865–9), termed by Nikolay RIMSKY-KORSAKOV 'the pantheistic Bible of the Slavonic peoples' (SRT, 568, 880), he described the full Slavonic pantheon and calendar cycle with its rites, and interpreted it according to the methodology of the German mythological school. He researched and cited huge amounts of ethnographic material (including tales, songs, proverbs, riddles, nursery rhymes and spells), and, by analysing the metaphors, semantics and associations he found there, revealed a basic series of binary oppositions (such as light–dark, hot–cold, live–dead). In addition, he reduced the multiplicity of mythological plots to the basic myth of the union of the Sky (personified by the male God of Thunder, 'Gromovnik', and his multiple allomorphs) and the Earth. Afanasyev drew parallels between the pagan rites and beliefs of Slavs and other Indo-European peoples, and affirmed the status of the Slavic gods, granting them equality in the pantheon of Greek, German and Aryan mythology, which he envisioned as united. He maintained the idea of a 'sacred language' (as did Grimm), known to the ancient sorcerers (*veduns* and *ved'mas*) who were the first poets, and enabling them to rule the elements. The seasons, weather, nature and living space were revived in multiple images of water, forest and domestic spirits, such as *kikimora*, *leshii* or *domovoi*, and codified in a subject index – a kind of dictionary of symbols, which was added as an appendix to the third volume. A passionate collector, he published a two-volume collection of Russian folk tales (1870).

Books by Afanasyev, as well as the monumental *Explanatory Dictionary of the Living Great Russian Language* by Vladimir Dahl, were fruits of the first wave of the *narodnik* (populist) movement of the 1860s. For Stravinsky, they were basics, known from childhood: both Afanasyev's *Outlook* and the second edition of his *Russian Folktales* (1873) were in Stravinsky's US library, arriving there from his father's rich collection. Stravinsky used Afanasyev's folk tales as a source for RENARD and The SOLDIER'S TALE, and consulted Dahl's *Explanatory Dictionary* constantly, especially in the Swiss years, as shown by Richard Taruskin (SRT, 1148, 1324–49, 1422–40, 1263). Afanasyev's influence on Russian art was immense. His *Outlook* was formative for works such as Rimsky-Korsakov's *The Snow Maiden*, but for Stravinsky it belonged to the previous generation and was subsequently revised.

Mythology (specifically Slavic) was proclaimed by Alexandre BENOIS as the primary source of subject material for BALLET in his essay 'A conversation on ballet' (1908), in which he proposed The FIREBIRD as a plot, and Afanasyev's *Folktales* as its source. Yet the relation between art and myth had drastically changed since Afanasyev's time. The activities of Afanasyev and Dahl, as well as the formation of The Mighty FIVE and the foundation of arts and crafts centres in Abramtzevo and Talashkino, all took place within the prevailing European (or Petrine) myth. However, the assassination of Tsar Alexander II in the midst of his liberal reforms 'occasioned a . . . symbolic break – a blanket repudiation of the westernising tradition of the autocracy and the adoption of a new historical myth' (Wortman 2013, 146) – that is, a Russian 'national myth' (Wortman 2006, 263), focused on the pre-Petrine principality of Muscovy. *Le stile russe* became part of the official ideology from 1881 to 1917, and was boosted in various 'scenarios of power', including the programme for the coronation celebrations for the new Tsar, Alexander III, with a festive procession of the characters of popular fairytales and mythology (*bogatyri*) and state-sponsored architecture. This change of paradigm is most obvious in the presentation of the Russian Empire at the World Exhibition in PARIS (1900), in Muscovy style, with an arts and crafts section, incorporating pavilions from the exotic outposts of the Empire (far North, Siberia, Caucasus and Asia), but totally eliminating the Imperial centre of ST PETERSBURG from the exhibition. As a result, as Benois put it, 'Russia as a nation, Russia as a state was not present at the Exhibition at all.' Imposed from above, the national Russian myth ignored the enlightened intelligentsia, delegitimised the legalistic bureaucracy and, as a consequence, was rejected by the cultural élite. This rejection is reflected in the essays by DIAGHILEV and Benois published in the periodical *Mir iskusstva*, with their sophisticated critique of the old 'men of the sixties' (in Russian, *shestidesyatniki*), such as STASOV and the Peredvizhnik painters, as well as of the contemporary official Russian style (including Vasnetsov's painting and Rimsky-Korsakov's *berendei*). The disaster of the war with Japan (1904–5) stimulated a renewed search for a national identity beyond the official scenarios of power.

Russian myth had to be revived, cleansed of the official ideology and invested with modernity. The person responsible for that in the project of *The Firebird* was Aleksey Remizov, in whose two books, *Posolon'* (a seasonally based collection of tales) and *Limonar'* (a collection of mystic apocrypha), both published in 1907, the folk myth material appeared fresh and transformed, as refracted by the very special viewpoint of the author. Remizov described his methods of dealing with the folk sources in the media, referring to Vyacheslav Ivanov's doctrine of 'creation of myth' as stated in his paper 'On the Russian idea', delivered at the Russian Religious Society on 30 December 1908. Those methods were amplification (that is, enrichment of the folk material by its variants and details, without regard for ethnographical credibility) and reconstruction (that is, re-creation of a myth or a rite based on its traces or fragments, no matter how tiny).

Ivanov's doctrine of myth and myth creation was rooted in the recognition of the unique situation of the Russian Empire, where myth was to be found not in the past (in the old texts or the archaeological artefacts revealed at diggings), but in the present, i.e. in the living practice of the people, who for several centuries managed effectively to evade the civilising tendencies of the Europeanised state, and to preserve, untouched and concealed, a true archaic lifestyle, with its customs and beliefs. True mythology was revealed not in scientific research, but in the living experience of common (mostly peasant) life, existing not far from the urban centre. Myth was not an artefact but the active substratum of the everyday life of the people, subject not to research but to development, as opposed to a lethal bureaucratised ideology. In such an outlook, pagan antiquity merged with the mysticism of popular sects and traditional religious practice. National identity was envisioned in the creative union of the modern artist with the 'myth-creating spirit of the people'. Ethnographic authenticity was not required, or was even presumed dangerous, since it may divest the material of its live energy and lead to 'academic', or 'Parnassian', 'replication of a model', and not to the creation of a new – that is, true – work of art. The artist pays for this union by renunciation of a personal voice: the 'monastic art' proclaimed by Ivanov demanded 'absolute denial of everything personal and wilful', but provided instead a total 'inner, or prophetic, liberation' (Ivanov 1979, 321–4). This discourse concerning Stravinsky would be revived in twenty years by Pierre SOUVTCHINSKY and Arthur LOURIÉ, most obviously in the former's concept of ontological versus psychological time, and the latter's discussion of Stravinsky's objective 'NEO-CLASSICISM', as opposed to the psychological 'neo-Gothic' of Arnold SCHOENBERG. Rather than establishing a link between Stravinsky and the Eurasianist philosophy, it points to the common source of this discourse back in the late 1900s.

In The Firebird, 'the creation of myth' (using Ivanov's term) is evident in the scenario and in the visual plans: the plot is based on folk tales from Afanasyev's collection, but the story is told not exactly the way it is recorded in the book: it is amplified by extra details and characters, invented by the authors of the ballet (including the famous Remizov 'boliboshkas'). Stravinsky joined the project when the scenario was already completed and choreography sketched. In later projects, Stravinsky took the task of 'creation of myth' firmly in his own hands, governed not by ethnographic authenticity but by artistic choice. He used folk sources, but each time applying a different method. In Petrushka, urban lore is paraded, blatantly evident. In The Rite of Spring, on a musical level, folk sources are deliberately concealed by means of compositional technique. Stravinsky used the action code of the calendar rites based on Afanasyev's

Outlook, but reworked it freely, adding the human sacrifice (which is not documented in any sources as part of Slav calendar rites): in other words, he reconstructed a myth and a rite not supported by ethnological or historical evidence. In *Les Noces*, with its scenario fully (line by line) based on various folk texts collected by Pyotr Kireyevsky and Ivan Sakharov, the Russian myth incorporated the Orthodox religious component, which was totally absent from Afanasyev's *Outlook*, in which all the religious motives were reduced to Slav paganism. ELENA VERESHCHAGINA AND TATIANA VERESHCHAGINA

Vladimir Dahl, *Explanatory Dictionary of the Living Great Russian Language* (St Petersburg: M. O. Wolff, 1863–6).

Alexander Etkind, *Internal Colonization: Russia's Imperial Experience* (Cambridge: Polity, 2011).

Vyacheslav Ivanov, 'O Russkoi Idee' ('On the Russian idea'), in V. I. Ivanov, *Sobraniye sochinenii* (Brussels: Foyer Oriental Chrétien, 1979), vol. III, 321–38.

Richard Wortman, *Russian Monarchy: Representation and Rule. Collected Articles* (Brighton, Mass.: Academic Studies Press, 2013).

Richard Wortman, *Scenarios of Power: Myth and Ceremony in Russian Monarchy from Peter the Great to the Abdication of Nicholas II* (Princeton University Press, 2006).

Russian Orthodox Church. Stravinsky received not merely a strict religious, but also an ecclesiastical Orthodox, upbringing: 'the fasts and feasts of the Church calendar were strictly observed in our household, and I was required to attend holy services and to read the Bible' (*Expo*, 74). Nevertheless, over a period of more than two decades, he became alienated from the Church.

He returned to the Orthodox Church in Nice in 1926 under Protoiyerey Nicholay Podossenov's spiritual guardianship. Like other Russian émigrés, the Stravinskys had to make a choice between three separate jurisdictions: Archdiocese of the Russian Orthodox Church (ROC) of Constantinople; Karlovci Church (established in 1927), officially named the ROC Outside of Russia (ROCOR); The Moscow Patriarchate (utterly dependent on the communist authorities). In 1927, Podossenov – the prior of both churches in Nice (ROC) – along with his congregation, officially joined the new Karlovci jurisdiction (ROCOR), the most anti-Soviet and anti-ecumenical, and set up the Church of John the Baptist in Nice. The icons, church accessories and liturgical garments were provided by Stravinsky.

In Voreppe, Igumen Sergy, the priest of the Church of Saint Archangel Michael in Rives (ROCOR jurisdiction) became the family's spiritual mentor. During their residence in PARIS (1931–9), the Stravinskys again remained loyal to the ROCOR. They attended the Church of the Sign of the Holy Mother (Rue Odessa, 26; in the mid-1930s relocated to Rue Boileau, 32). Until 1949, the diocese was under the supervision of Protoiyerey Vassily Timofeev, who baptised Yury MANDELSTAM and married him to Mika, married Fyodor and Denise, baptised Stravinsky's granddaughter Kitty, and read the last rites over Mika, Catherine STRAVINSKY and Anna.

In the 1920s and 1930s, Stravinsky was an influential member of Russian dioceses, thanks to his fame and generous charitable donations.

Moving to the UNITED STATES in 1939, for nearly a decade Igor and Vera attended Russian churches in Hollywood, LOS ANGELES and New York. Vera Stravinsky regularly mentioned in her diary the church services they attended until 1953, at which point the Stravinskys stopped going to the Orthodox

Church, never resuming the practice. While talking about his alienation from the Church, Igor Fyodorovich always referred to being busy and in poor health. However, in a letter to his son Fyodor (10 May 1946), he voiced concern that Orthodoxy was living 'its last days . . . in those countries alien to its special spirit, structure and way of life as well as because of the complete disappearance of educated clergy' (PSS). This alienation from the Orthodox Church might also be partially explained by its intolerance to Catholicism and to any manifestations of ecumenism demonstrated by the ROCOR. Such Stravinsky works as the MASS, CANTICUM SACRUM and THRENI were totally at variance with that policy.

Nevertheless, there is some evidence of Stravinsky's continued interest in Orthodoxy in the final years of his life. His library contains an Orthodox Church Calendar for 1964, with the composer's annotations, and he created a new version of his Russian chorus Veruju ('Credo') that same year. In 1968, though very ill, he began to sketch a chorus with the Russian text of Pater noster (Otche nash). It was his last attempt to compose an independent work, returning to the text of his 1926 setting. TATIANA BARANOVA MONIGHETTI

Tatiana Baranova Monighetti, 'In between Orthodoxy and Catholicism: The problem of Stravinsky's religious identity', in Massimiliano Locanto (ed.), Igor Stravinsky: Sound and Gesture of Modernism (Brepols: Turnout, 2014), 3–29.

Russian Symphony Concerts. A Russian public concert enterprise financed by Mitrofan BELYAYEV (1836–1903) and active in ST PETERSBURG from 1885 to 1918, specifically for the advocacy and promotion of Russian contemporary music. The concerts started on 27 March 1884 (O.S.) with a public concert of Russian music given at the Petropavlovsky College under Otton Dutsh, and announced as an 'Open rehearsal of works by Glazunov'. The first official Russian Symphony Concert took place on 23 November 1885 at the hall of the Noble Assembly in St Petersburg, with a programme of BORODIN, RIMSKY-KORSAKOV, CUI, TCHAIKOVSKY and GLAZUNOV. From 1886, concerts were given six or seven times yearly and usually included the music of the Moscow school (Tchaikovsky, Taneev, Arensky), as well as the St Petersburg school (The FIVE and the Belyayev circle). In June 1889, the Belyayev concerts were presented in PARIS as part of the World Exhibition. They were unpopular because of a total lack of advertising (which was restricted due to Belyayev's specific request). After Belyayev's death, the concerts continued until 1918, and were financed from his legacy bequeathed to the Board of Trustees, including Felix Blumenfeld and Glazunov. Stravinsky's suite The Faun and the Shepherdess was first performed at a Russian Symphony Concert (1908).

ELENA VERESHCHAGINA AND TATIANA VERESHCHAGINA

Russian Vocal Music (for solo voice and piano / instrumental ensemble). An unusual feature of Stravinsky's vocal works is their multilingualism. In total, seven languages are set in his music: Russian, Latin, English, French, Italian, German and Hebrew. The appearance of a new language, as a rule, marked for Stravinsky a new stage in his stylistic evolution: this happened when Latin began to replace Russian, and it was also the case when English first appeared. At the same time, the fundamental principles of his vocal style were worked out on Russian material.

Among the first works that the 19-year-old Igor showed to his future teacher Nikolay Andreyevich RIMSKY-KORSAKOV, there was almost certainly a romance 'Storm Cloud' on PUSHKIN's verses, written in January 1902. It was first published in 1982 (Vershinina 1982, 1).

The next opus on a Pushkin text was written with a more confident hand. This was the solo cantata The Faun and the Shepherdess (1905–6), which Igor Fedorovich dedicated to his young wife Yekaterina Gavrilovna (Catherine STRAVINSKY). The cantata was performed on 14/27 April 1907 in ST PETERSBURG; critics reacted favourably to it but noted a lack of individuality in the thematic material and the colourlessness of the vocal part. The author was still too dependent on his teacher and other masters, above all TCHAIKOVSKY.

In the autumn of the same year, Stravinsky composed a short song without words, PASTORALE, for voice and piano, dedicating it to his teacher's daughter Nadezhda; she sang it for the first time with the accompaniment of the composer at a jour fixe in the house of the Rimsky-Korsakovs on 31 October /13 November 1907. This salon piece was unquestionably a creative success. Subsequently, Stravinsky arranged the Pastorale three times: for voice and a quartet of woodwinds (oboe, cor anglais, clarinet, bassoon, 1923), for violin and the same quartet, and for violin and piano (both 1933).

For evenings at the Rimsky-Korsakovs, Stravinsky also wrote his first piece based on Russian folk words – a comic song 'Kak griby na voinu sobiralis' (How the Mushrooms Prepared for War). The popular text, known in different versions, was obviously reproduced from memory by Stravinsky – that is, for him it was oral folklore. The song is based on variations of a repeating text, and the music obediently follows it, inventively emphasising humorous details. The work was not published during the composer's lifetime (see Vershinina 1982, 1).

The next vocal opus, Two Melodies, on verses by Sergey GORODETSKY, was written in USTILUG (1907–8): 'Vesna (monastyrskaya)' ('Spring (The Cloister)') and 'Rosyanka (Khlystovskaya)' ('A Song of the Dew'). Both poems were based on the stylisation of folklore motifs: maidenly love, a spell of rain, and awaiting the awakening of nature (a motif of the future RITE OF SPRING, inspired by another poem by Gorodetsky). It is obvious that Stravinsky was very attracted to the phonetics of Gorodetsky's verse, in which the words are related to each other not only in meaning, but also in sound. The composer created on this basis an impressionistic musical land-scape, with magnificent piano 'chimes' and a sweeping vocal melody.

Next appeared two 'paired' cycles – Two Poems by Paul Verlaine (1910) and Two Poems of Balmont (1911). The first cycle was perhaps the prime example of the most outright 'Debussyism' in his music. As Richard Taruskin noted, Stravinsky wrote songs not to the original text, but to the Russian translation of Stepan MITUSOV, his friend and co-author of the libretto of the OPERA The NIGHTINGALE (SRT, 655). The composer intended the Verlaine cycle for his younger brother Gury, a gifted singer, who managed to perform it twice. In 1917, Gury died at the front in Iaşi (Romania).

A year later, Stravinsky composed a cycle to words by BALMONT: 'Nezabudochka-tsvetochek' ('The Flower') and 'Golub'' ('The Dove'). The first song presented a quasi-naïve landscape sketch; mystic–erotic symbolism prevailed in the second song, close to the poetic motifs of the Khlysts – Russian sectarians, whose extreme religious practice aroused, at that time in Russian society, a burning interest. In this respect, 'The Dove' foreshadowed the cantata The KING OF THE STARS, also to the words of Balmont, completed by Stravinsky in 1912.

Stravinsky conceived his next vocal cycle as an experiment. In the Three Japanese Lyrics for soprano and chamber ensemble (1912–13), he tried to reproduce in the context of Russian translation an important feature of the Japanese language – the lack of stresses. However, other musicians doubted the success of such an approach: the musical text of the vocal part did indeed have a somewhat strange appearance. Nevertheless, in a live performance, the declamation was quite natural, thanks to the syllabic rhythm that absolutely predominated. The exotic flavour of the Japanese Lyrics can be seen in the context of a spicy orientalism, typical of art nouveau. In the Japanese Lyrics, one can see the influence of Arnold SCHOENBERG'S Pierrot lunaire, whose première Stravinsky attended whilst composing his own cycle; the score of Pierrot lunaire indirectly influenced the instrumental setting of the Japanese Lyrics (two flutes, two clarinets, pianoforte, two violins, viola, cello). Nevertheless, as for the vocal part, it is difficult to imagine anything more alien to Schoenberg's Sprechgesang than the manner of recitation proposed by Stravinsky. Three Japanese Lyrics remained an isolated episode among Stravinsky's vocal works, at least in the coming years – and even decades.

We refer specifically to vocal compositions on Russian folk texts that began to appear after The Rite of Spring and were crowned with the final version of Les NOCES. It was the Russian folk verses that allowed Stravinsky to find his own form of vocal intonation, later transferred to other languages – Latin, English and Hebrew. The variability of accent in the folklore verses – a characteristic widely recognised before Stravinsky – became in his vocal music an individual stylistic feature of the composer's technique (see FOLK MUSIC).

Three Little Songs (Souvenirs de mon enfance) for voice and piano were chronologically the first on this path (author's dating of 1906–13). The third song of the cycle 'Chicher-Yacher' is clearly the earliest, because it was used in the finale of the SYMPHONY IN Eb MAJOR (1907). Stravinsky wrote Three Little Songs for his children, and their texts belonged to the genre of oral children's folklore, which was characterised by a variety of word creation and phonetic games. So, the hero of the third song, Chicher-Yacher, was a fantastic character of unknown origin; his name did not make sense, but sounded great (such joining of words close in sound occurred in children's counting-out rhymes). The two previous songs featured birds play-acting – first a careless magpie, followed by a crow who alternately got dry, then became wet. All three songs were based on simple popevki (short diatonic motifs), imitating children's singing, but the piano accompaniment was far from elementary – it formed a dissonant harmonic counterpoint to the vocal melody. Igor Fyodorovich dedicated the songs to 6-year-old Fedik, 5-year-old Mikushka and 3-year-old Svetik (the youngest, Milène, would be born within a year). In 1929–30, Stravinsky orchestrated Three Little Songs for voice and a small orchestra.

Three Children's Tales (1917) continued this genre of folklore settings; their texts came from the collection of Afanasyev's folk tales, which were domestic reading in the young Stravinsky family. We already see Stravinsky's mature vocal style in the *Three Children's Tales*. 'Tilimbom', a song about a fire in a goat's house, extinguished by the efforts of a mutual friend, is a short rondo entirely based on a left-hand ostinato (which, by the way, anticipated the bass line of the future piece 'The Soldier's Violin' from *The Soldier's Tale*). In the right hand, there is also an ostinato, but with alternating figures, both regular and syncopated. Superimposed on this are the rhythmic patterns of the vocal part, with constant variations of motifs and shifts of accents, and reaching a climax at the end of the piece. Here is an example of 'incorrect' verbal stresses that arise due to the musical accents:Bezhit kuritsa s vedrom zalivat' koziy dom ('The hen comes running with a bucket to douse the goat shed' – SRT, 1147).

In the next song, 'Gusi-lebedi' ('The Geese and the Swans'), the very sound of the words comes to the fore. Phonetics largely determined the dialectal vernacular to which Stravinsky first turned at this time. So, in the song 'Gusi-lebedi', all the endings of the lines were sung to the 'narrow' vowel 'i', in three cases replacing the 'correct' 'e': letili – zaletili – dospili – nosila – podkhvatila – pavalila – vynosila ('(They) flew – came flying – made up – carried – picked up – threw down – took out'). On the one hand, this was an obvious imitation of the village vernacular, close to naturalism; on the other, a refined play on timbre. Similarly specific were the performance colours implied in the song: a dry piano sound, without pedal, and an open style of singing, without vibrato and with sharp dynamic contrasts. *Three Children's Tales* were created for children and, accordingly, for home performance; nevertheless, the cycle immediately reached the Russian concert stage (first performance on 23 April / 6 May 1915, Petrograd, Small Hall of the Conservatory; Zoya Lodiy and Irina Miklashevskaya). The orchestral version of 'Tilimbom' was performed under the author's baton in 1924 in Antwerp. It was slightly expanded here and sounded like a brilliant concert piece.

Two other masterpieces, *Pribaoutki* for medium voice and eight instruments (Afanasyev's Collection, 1914), and *Berceuses du chat* for medium voice and three clarinets (Collection of Pyotr Kireyevsky, 1915), were written for the concert stage. The première of both works took place on 6 June 1919 in Vienna, at a concert of the Society for Private Musical Performances (Verein für musikalische Privataufführungen), an important concert organisation headed by Schoenberg and his closest disciples. Anton WEBERN's enthusiastic response to these works has survived (letter to Alban BERG, dated 9 June 1919): 'The cradle songs are something so indescribably touching. How those three clarinets sound! And *Pribaoutki*! Ah, my friend, something quite marvellous. This realism leads us to the metaphysical' (Moldenhauer 1979, 229). PROKOFIEV, who heard *Pribaoutki* in December 1919 in New York, was also delighted and sent Stravinsky a detailed letter with comments on each of the four songs.

In the *Berceuses du chat*, a miniature cycle of no more than 5 minutes, the voice is accompanied by a rare trio of clarinettists, featuring E♭, regular and bass clarinets. In the colour of these instruments, Stravinsky probably heard something resembling a cat's purring. The melodies of *Berceuses* are akin to a homely humming for oneself: they are characterised by sparse textures and rotated mostly in a low 'lulling' register, except for the last song, which is full of life and festive in mood.

The culmination of Stravinsky's chamber vocal work on Russian texts became the *Four Russian Songs* for soprano and piano which were written in December 1918 – February 1919. Stravinsky took the words for them from the folklore collections of Pyotr Kireyevsky (the second and the third), Ivan Sakharov (the first), Tikhon Rozhdestvensky and Mikhail Uspensky (the fourth). All four songs were based on the antiphonal structure of *zapev –pripev* (chant–refrain): after an initial declamatory 'solo' follows a cantilena 'choral' response – soprano, accompanied by piano, representing both. In each refrain, the genre of the song was demonstrated: round dance ('Selezen'' ('The Drake')), counting-out rhyme ('Zapevnaya' (introductory song)), Christmastide fortune-telling ('Podlyudnaya'), prayer ('Sektantskaya' ('A Russian Spiritual')). Stravinsky emphasised vernacular and dialectal features of pronunciation; at the same time, he avoided musical quotations: as in other similar cases, they would be superfluous for him. Stravinsky widely used variation in the cycle – for example, in the first song 'Selezen'', the title word was sung in all three possible variations, with a stress on the first, second and third syllables. In 1954, Stravinsky made an arrangement of Russian songs for voice, flute, harp and guitar. In a new cycle, *Four Songs*, the following were included: 'Selezen'', 'Sektantskaya', 'Gusi–lebedi' and 'Tilimbom'.

Four Russian Songs was the quintessence of Stravinsky's Russian vocal style. Four years later, *Les Noces* appeared: it was Stravinsky's last work using Russian texts. However, the principles of treatment of the text, worked out on Russian material, were maintained in the composer's later work, and subsequently developed in the settings of other languages.   SVETLANA SAVENKO

Hans Moldenhauer in collaboration with Rosaleen Moldenhauer, *Anton von Webern: A Chronicle of His Life and Work* (New York: Alfred A. Knopf, 1979).
Svetlana Savenko, *Mir Stravinskogo* ('Stravinsky's World') (Moscow: Kompozitor, 2001).
Irina Vershinina (ed.), *Igor Stravinsky, Vokal'naya muzïka* ('Igor Stravinsky: Vocal Music'), vol. I (Moscow: Sovetskiy Kompozitor, 1982).

Russolo, Luigi (born Portogruaro, 30 April 1885; died Cerro di Laveno, near Varese, 6 February 1947). Italian futurist painter and musician (*see* FUTURISM), remembered primarily for his invention of *intonarumori* or noise-intoners, on which he performed at riotous futurist events, beginning in April 1914; and for the accompanying manifesto *L'arte dei rumori* ('The Art of Noises') (1916). Stravinsky first heard the *intonarumori* at the Coliseum in London in June 1914. At DIAGHILEV's behest, he heard them again in April 1915 at the Milan apartment of F. T. Marinetti, the leader of the futurist movement. Accounts of Stravinsky's reaction to their sound differ. But the collaboration with Russolo envisaged by Diaghilev did not occur.   BEN EARLE

SCS

Rychenberg Foundation, Winterthur, and Werner Reinhart. Werner Reinhart (1884–1951) was one of four sons of the merchant Theodor and Lilly Reinhart *née* Volkart, all of whom played an important role in SWITZERLAND's cultural life, and especially that of their hometown Winterthur. With his elder brother Georg, Werner ran the family business, Volkart Brothers, which provided the wealth facilitating his role as Maecenas. Apart from his training as a merchant, Werner also acquired proficiency as a clarinettist, enabling him to take part in concerts of the International Society of Contemporary Music (ISCM), of which he was a founding member in 1922. When, in 1918, his compatriot the French Swiss author Charles Ferdinand RAMUZ wrote to him in the name of Igor Stravinsky and the painter René Auberjonois to request support for the production of The SOLDIER'S TALE, Reinhart discovered Stravinsky, whose compositions were hitherto unknown to him, and subsequently financed the entire production. The friendship that ensued led to the dedication to Reinhart of Stravinsky's THREE PIECES FOR SOLO CLARINET. This autograph, as well as the clean copy of The Soldier's Tale, the Suite from this work for violin, clarinet and piano, the sketchbook of Les NOCES, and an autograph of the OCTET FOR WIND INSTRUMENTS were all presented to Reinhart, whose collection of music manuscripts is now owned by the Rychenberg Foundation (Rychenberg-Stiftung) and, since 1977, deposited in the Winterthur Libraries.

Werner Reinhart was for many years the treasurer of the Musikkollegium Winterthur, which was responsible for the orchestra, then called the Stadtorchester (Winterthur Symphony Orchestra), the Winterthur String Quartet, three concert series (free concerts, concerts for members of the Musikkollegium, and subscription concerts) and the music school. He often paid bills himself, enabling a golden age in Winterthur's musical past, with Hermann SCHERCHEN as main conductor. To ensure that the Musikkollegium would have sufficient funds for its various activities after his demise, he founded the Rychenberg Foundation, named after his parents' home, the Villa Rychenberg, in which he later lived and which he bequeathed to become the music school. His manuscript collection, primarily autographs of music, also contains manuscripts by Ramuz, and fourteen water colours and drawings by Auberjonois for productions of The Soldier's Tale, as well as Theodore Strawinsky's original illustrations for Les Noces and forty-nine gouaches for the 1944 Zurich staging of PETRUSHKA. Apart from those of Stravinsky, the manuscript collection of the Rychenberg Foundation consists of important autographs by Alban BERG, DEBUSSY, César Franck, Haydn, Hindemith, HONEGGER, Heinrich Kaminski, KRENEK, Mozart, Reger, Othmar Schoeck, Richard STRAUSS, WEBERN and Hugo Wolf, among many others, as well as the Rychenberg Guest Book. Werner Reinhart's letters are owned by the Musikkollegium, but housed in the Winterthur Libraries.   HARRY JOELSON

Georges Duplain, L'homme aux mains d'or: Werner Reinhart, Rilke et les créateurs de Suisse romande (Lausanne: Éditions 24 Heures, 1988).

Stadtbibliothek Winterthur (ed.), Das Rychenberger Gastbuch: Gastfreundschaft beim Musikmäzen Werner Reinhart (Zürich: Chronos Verlag, 2016).

Peter Sulzer, Zehn Komponisten um Werner Reinhart, 3 vols. (Winterthur: Stadtbibliothek, 1979–83).

S

Sacher, Paul (born Basel, 28 April 1906; died Basel, 26 May 1999). Swiss conductor and patron. Sacher felt a lifelong attachment to the music of Stravinsky, whom he considered to be the pre-eminent twentieth-century composer. In the course of his long professional career, he expressed this admiration in manifold ways, whether as conductor, as patron or as a collector of autographs.

In 1926, at the age of 20, Sacher founded the Basel Chamber Orchestra. For decades (until 1986), it served him as a vehicle for cultivating neglected classical and pre-classical repertoire and the music of his own day. Already, as a young man, before he had significant financial resources at his disposal, he successfully sought collaborations with internationally acclaimed musicians. When he first met Stravinsky in Winterthur, in March 1930, he asked the composer to take part in one of his concerts. Stravinsky's agreement led to their first and only joint appearance at a Basel concert on 2 October 1930, when Stravinsky functioned as solo pianist (in CAPRICCIO) and conductor (in APOLLON MUSAGÈTE) and Sacher performed the RAGTIME (with Aladár Rácz on cimbalom). In the decades that followed, Sacher presented a large part of Stravinsky's neo-classical, and later his dodecaphonic, compositions to audiences in Basel and in Zurich, where he regularly gave concerts with his own Collegium Musicum from 1941 to 1992. He also performed such large-scale works as OEDIPUS REX and The RAKE'S PROGRESS in his many guest appearances with various orchestras in SWITZERLAND and abroad. However, his programmes never included the ballets PETRUSHKA or The RITE OF SPRING, both of which had long been part of the concert repertoire.

In 1934, Sacher married Maja Hoffmann-Stehlin, the heiress to the Hoffmann – La Roche pharmaceutical company. Now a wealthy man, he intensified his previously modest activities as a patron. Even before the outbreak of World War II, he had commissioned three major works from Béla BARTÓK. But it was not until December 1945, after the cessation of hostilities, that he had an opportunity to contact Stravinsky, now living in Hollywood, and ask him to compose a work for the twentieth anniversary of the Basel Chamber Orchestra. The result was the CONCERTO IN D for string orchestra, premièred on 21 January 1947. In later years, Sacher frequently performed the work, and even recorded it several times. In summer 1954, he commissioned a second work from Stravinsky, which, however, proved long in the making. The composer temporised, and it was not until early 1961 that Sacher received his definitive commitment. The commission ultimately led to the cantata A SERMON, A NARRATIVE AND A PRAYER, premièred under Sacher's baton on 23 February 1962. As with the Concerto in D, the composer was not present at the première. Indeed, despite their mutual respect, the relations between the two men were never as friendly as those Sacher cultivated with many other composers he patronised, such as Arthur HONEGGER, Bohuslav Martinů, Hans Werner HENZE, Cristóbal Halffter, Pierre BOULEZ, Heinz Holliger, Luciano Berio or Wolfgang Rihm.

When commissioning new works, Sacher did not always insist on being handed the original scores. As a result, there were several striking gaps in his impressive collection of manuscripts. He began to fill those gaps in the 1970s by making purchases. At the same time, he remained on the lookout for other manuscripts from his preferred composers. In this way he acquired, in June 1973, a large number of important Stravinsky manuscripts, including not only important autograph sources for the two works he had commissioned, but also the fair copies of *The Rite of Spring*, PULCINELLA and SYMPHONIES OF WIND INSTRUMENTS, the short scores of the CONCERTO FOR PIANO AND WIND INSTRUMENTS and the CONCERTO IN D FOR VIOLIN AND ORCHESTRA, and sketches for *Apollon Musagète*. It was with these acquisitions only that Sacher became an autograph collector in the full sense, although he made his purchases not as a private individual, but in the name of his newly established foundation, the Paul SACHER STIFTUNG (Foundation). He then acquired the whole of Stravinsky's posthumous estate for his Foundation in 1983. Two years later, the Stiftung presented a cross-section of the acquired documents in an exhibition at the Basel Kunstmuseum (Art Museum) entitled 'Strawinsky: Sein Nachlass. Sein Bild' ('Stravinsky: His Estate. His Image'). Only then, in 1986, did this body of sources enter the Foundation's archive, established at Basel's Münsterplatz that same year, where they have been available for scholarly perusal ever since. FELIX MEYER

Ernst Lichtenhahn, 'Zum Wesen und zur Geschichte von Paul Sachers Kompositionsaufträgen', in *Alte und neue Musik: Das Basler Kammerorchester (Kammerchor und Kammerorchester) unter Leitung von Paul Sacher 1926–1976* (Zurich: Atlantis, 1977), 127–55, esp. 148–51.

Ulrich Mosch (ed.), *Paul Sacher – Facetten einer Musikerpersönlichkeit* (Mainz: Schott, 2006).

Albi Rosenthal, 'The Paul Sacher Foundation at the crossroads: the purchase of the Igor Stravinsky Archive', in *Paul Sacher In Memoriam* (Basel: Paul Sacher Stiftung, 2000), 37–40.

Willi Schuh, 'Kompositionsaufträge', in *Alte und neue Musik: Das Basler Kammerorchester (Kammerchor und Kammerorchester) unter Leitung von Paul Sacher 1926–1951* (Zurich: Atlantis, 1952), 41–105, esp. 96–100.

Sadoven, Hélène (born Finland, 1894; died ?). Mezzo-soprano. She performed in the role of The Neighbor at the première of Stravinsky's one-act comic OPERA MAVRA, on 3 June 1922, at the Théâtre National de l'Opéra, PARIS. She also performed the role of Jocasta in OEDIPUS REX under the direction of Stravinsky (Walsh, 1993, 70) on 30 May 1929, at the THÉÂTRE SARAH BERNHARDT in Paris.

HELEN JULIA MINORS

Stephen Walsh, *The Music of Stravinsky* (London: Routledge, 1988).

Satie, Erik (Eric Alfred Leslie) (born Honfleur, 17 May 1866; died Paris, 1 July 1925). Innovative and influential French composer. Stravinsky said of Satie:

> He was certainly the oddest person I have ever known, but the most rare and consistently witty person, too. I had a great liking for him and he

411

appreciated my friendliness, I think, and liked me in return. With his pince-nez, umbrella, and galoshes he looked like a perfect schoolmaster, but he looked just as much like one without these accoutrements.

The composers met soon after Stravinsky's arrival in PARIS. There are photographs witnessing a meeting between DEBUSSY, Stravinsky and Satie in June 1910, they had several common friends in the Paris artistic scene in World War I, and both composed for the BALLETS RUSSES.

In 1914, Edgard VARÈSE had the idea for a collaboration, conceived as a 'homage to Satie', for which he, Satie, Florent Schmitt, Stravinsky and Maurice RAVEL would contribute incidental music for a Jean COCTEAU reworking of *A Midsummer Night's Dream*. Only Satie completed music, now known as *Cinq grimaces pour 'Le Songe d'une nuit d'été'*, for this otherwise unrealised project. Satie's BALLET *Parade* surely makes a sly connection with Stravinsky's PETRUSHKA (1910–11), which was performed on the same programme as the *Parade* première on 18 May 1917. In the Acrobats' dance in *Parade*, Satie writes for bouteillophone (tuned bottles) and xylophone with no duplication of notes in their ranges, echoing Petrushka's theme which juxtaposes white and black notes, symbolising his two sides (puppet and human).

Satie wrote two articles on Stravinsky for *Vanity Fair* and *Feuilles Libres* (1922), which are very rare examples of him exploring another composer in detail, in writing that was painstakingly researched; Satie asked Stravinsky for biographical details and 'a scrap of paper which could be reproduced'. The *Feuilles Libres* article focuses on what Satie described as Stravinsky's mechanical works, in particular the *Étude for Pianola* (1917). In typically amusing fashion, Satie wrote:

> the pianola is not the same instrument as its friend the piano, with whom it has only brotherly relations. Igor Stravinsky, before anyone else, has written a work in which certain capabilities peculiar to this instrument are genuinely used. Keyboard virtuosi should know very well that they could never do what an ordinary pianola is capable of; and on the other hand, a machine could never be substituted for them.

Stravinsky made few specific comments about Satie's music, although, in conversation with Robert CRAFT, he said he disliked the 'metrically boring' *Socrate*. However, he added 'the music of Socrates' death is touching and dignifying in a unique way'.   CAROLINE POTTER

Scènes de ballet. Composed 1944. First performance (abridged version, staged, choreography by Anton DOLIN), 27 November 1944, Philadelphia. Conductor, Maurice Abravanel. Original version, 2 February 1945, New York, NYPO. Conductor, Igor Stravinsky. Published 1945, Chappell.

In 1944 Billy Rose offered Stravinsky $5,000 for a 15-minute BALLET suite to be included in his Broadway production *The Seven Lively Arts*. The result was the *Scènes de ballet*, a themeless series of eleven ballet movements lasting about 18 minutes, which Stravinsky wrote in three months. In *Dialogues*, Stravinsky wrote that it was 'a period piece, a portrait of Broadway in the last years of the war' and described it as 'featherweight and sugared', saying that his 'sweet tooth was not yet carious', but that he would 'not deprecate it, not even the second Pantomime' (which is 27 seconds long), and that all of it is 'at least well made'. In the same description, he says that the recapitulation of the fifth piece 'now sounds to me – pardon the pleonasm – [like] bad movie music: the happy homesteaders, having massacred the Indians, begin to plant their CORN'.

As he wrote the orchestral score, Ingolf DAHL arranged it at the same time for piano, and Stravinsky wrote that Rose liked the piano version but was 'dismayed' by the orchestral original. After the first night of the Philadelphia preview on 24 November, Stravinsky received a telegram from Rose: 'YOUR MUSIC GREAT SUCCESS STOP COULD BE SENSATIONAL SUCCESS IF YOU WOULD AUTHORISE ROBERT RUSSELL BENNETT RETOUCH ORCHESTRATION STOP BENNETT ORCHESTRATES EVEN THE WORKS OF COLE PORTER'. Stravinsky telegraphed back: 'SATISFIED WITH GREAT SUCCESS'. The piece was cut to a fraction of its original length when The Seven Lively Arts opened in New York. Stravinsky conducted the New York Philharmonic in the first concert performance in the winter of 1945. He conducted it also in London on 27 May 1954, at which time he was presented with the Gold Medal of the Royal Philharmonic Society of London by Sir Arthur Bliss, Master of the Queen's Musick.

The eleven movements are: 'Introduction' (Andante, in 5/8, 7/8 and 5/8), 'Danses' (Moderato, growing faster towards the end, in a variety of both quaver and crotchet metres), 'Variation' (Con moto, in 6/8 throughout), 'Pantomime' (Lento, increasing in tempo, in many metres, both crotchet and quaver), 'Pas de deux' (Adagio–Allegretto–Adagio, in alternating 3/4 (9/8) and 4/4 (12/8) in the adagio sections, and quaver metres in the allegretto), 'Pantomime' (Agitato ma tempo giusto, in 2/4 throughout), 'Variation: Dancer' (Risoluto, 4/4 throughout), 'Variation: Ballerina' (Andantino, in 3/4), 'Pantomime' (Andantino, in 3/4), 'Danses' (Con moto, in 3/8 ending with five bars of 4/8) and 'Apothéose' (Poco meno mosso, in 4/4).

The numerous completely diatonic melodies, even including the occasional pure triad, are at times almost Tchaikovskian in character, recalling that earlier homage to his great Russian predecessor, The FAIRY'S KISS. As in that work, the almost romantic melodic shapes are accompanied by contrasting ostinato figures, with frequent descending and ascending semiquaver figures. Metres are often difficult to discern, as accents at the beginnings of bars are avoided (almost obsessively, according to Eric Walter White: SCW, 421) through the use of rests on the beat and notes tied over the beat – hence the rapidly changing quaver metres are not reflected obviously in the sound of the music. In the concluding 'Apothéose' a broad melody in regular crotchets occurs entirely on afterbeats, building to a grandiose climax which is almost a parody of the ending of The FIREBIRD. This final movement was composed on the day of the liberation of PARIS, and in Dialogues Stravinsky wrote: 'I remember that I interrupted my work every few minutes to listen to the radio reports. I think my jubilation is in the music.' He wrote 'Paris n'est plus aux allemands' at the end of the score, but this was deleted when it was published.

Individual movements use the same techniques as Stravinsky's other works of this period, and quite close relationships to some of the surrounding works can be discerned. The theme of 'Pas de deux' can be seen to be related to the main subject of the opening movement of the SYMPHONY IN C, and aspects of the 'Apothéose' are recalled later in the EBONY CONCERTO. All the pieces are tonal, though, characteristically, with considerable dissonance.

KATHRYN PUFFETT

Schaeffner, André (born Paris, 7 February 1895; died Paris, 11 August 1980). French musiciologist and ethnologist who received his musical education at the Schola Cantorum, and training in anthropology at the École du Louvre. In the words of his wife, the ethnologist Denise Paulme, he was a 'musician as attentive to men as he was to instruments'. This dual education led Schaeffer to complete the first French works in ethnomusicology. His book *Origine des instruments de musique* remains a founding text of the discipline. Co-author of the first book on JAZZ written in French, with André Coeuroy in 1926, Schaeffner was also a musicologist fascinated by modern music, and the music of Stravinsky in particular. He saw Stravinsky as the starting point for musical trends that unfolded over the course of the twentieth century. In turn, Stravinsky entrusted Schaeffner with a privileged position among his French-speaking commentators. Author of a series of articles of music criticism from 1923 onwards, Schaeffner soon placed Stravinsky at the fore for his role as a mediator between Western and Eastern cultures. At first disconcerted by the composer's neo-classical turn with the première of the OCTET FOR WIND INSTRUMENTS and the abandonment of 'russisme', Schaeffner's views shifted towards the end of the 1920s, when he became a defender of Stravinsky's 'purism' and 'aesthetic of rupture'. His 'Igor Strawinsky, musicien vivant' of 1929, published in Georges Bataille's review *Documents*, in which Schaeffner describes the Stravinsky that haunted contemporary aesthetic thought ('He defeated it, illuminated it and ordered it anew'), led the composer to take an interest in the musicologist. Following their first meeting, the two men began a friendly relationship that can be seen in their CORRESPONDENCE, which lasted until the mid 1930s. Their collaboration crystallised in 1929 with one of the first books in French devoted to Stravinsky. Published in 1931 by Schaeffner (PARIS, Rieder) under the title *Strawinsky*, the book was written on the basis of interviews with the composer, and launched a practice of dialogues that would remain important to Stravinsky in most of his later writings (*see* AUTOBIOGRAPHY, POETICS OF MUSIC, and the various publications with CRAFT). At the volume's opening, Schaeffner thanks and acknowledges Stravinsky for his assistance, but the author's archives make it possible to measure the true extent of the composer's involvement in a text that can be understood as a vehicle for promoting his aesthetic point of view. Even more so, as in most of Stravinsky's public statements, Schaeffner's *Strawinsky* served to correct the views of critics and to 'set the parameters for the interpretation of Stravinskian art' (1931, p. 5). There is real reason to believe that Schaeffner's book was in this sense a response to the 1929 monograph published by Boris de SCHLOEZER, which had so strongly displeased the composer. In a later article based on Stravinsky, Schaeffner (1939) explored the conditions for objective commentary on music through musical analysis. Schaeffner wrote on Stravinsky far less frequently after World War II, but his 1971 'Au fil des esquisses du *Sacre*' remains a key essay in the Stravinskian bibliography.

VALÉRIE DUFOUR

Valérie Dufour, *Stravinski et ses exégètes (1919–1940)* (Brussels: Edition de l'université de Bruxelles, 2006), 155–75.
André Schaeffner, *Strawinsky* (Paris: Rieder, 1931).
André Schaeffner, 'Igor Stravinsky. Critique et thématique', *La Revue Musicale* (May–June 1939), 241–541.

Scherchen, Hermann (born Berlin, 21 June 1891; died Florence, 12 June 1966). German conductor. Throughout his career, Scherchen was an energetic advocate of contemporary music, ranging from the SECOND VIENNESE SCHOOL to younger composers including Nono and Xenakis. His pupils included the composer Karl Amadeus HARTMANN and the conductor Karel ANČERL. Scherchen conducted The SOLDIER'S TALE at Frankfurt on 20 June 1923 (Paul Hindemith played the violin and Carl Ebert was the Speaker), and in August that year he performed the work again at the Bauhaus Exhibition in Weimar, an occasion when Kandinsky and Klee were in the audience, as were Kurt WEILL and his teacher Busoni. At Frankfurt on 24 November 1925, Scherchen conducted the first concert performance of Les NOCES, and in 1927 he planned a Bauhaus production of the work with designs by Oskar Schlemmer (unrealised at the time). Scherchen conducted many other works by Stravinsky and gave the Frankfurt première of The RAKE'S PROGRESS in 1958. In September 1954, he recorded the complete 1911 version of PETRUSHKA and the 1919 *Firebird Suite* with the Royal Philharmonic Orchestra for Westminster, and in 1959 he recorded the PULCINELLA SUITE with the Berlin State Opera Orchestra. NIGEL SIMEONE

Kirchmeyer catalogue: www.kcatalog.org.
SCS

Scherzo for piano. Composed 1902. Published 1970 in Valeriy Smirnov, *Tvorcheskoye formirovaniye I. F. Stravinskovo* (Leningrad: Muzïka, 1970). Dedication: 'À Monsieur Nicholas Richter – témoignage d'un profond respect de la part de l'auteur'.

The *Scherzo* was the main work taken by the 20-year-old Stravinsky to his 'interview' with RIMSKY-KORSAKOV in Heidelberg in the summer of 1902, resulting in his acceptance as a private pupil. It demonstrates an aptitude for evoking compositional models: notably a Tchaikovskian lyricism in the Trio and, in the coda, contrapuntal techniques learnt from Vasily KALAFATI, which Stravinsky may also have gleaned from Rimsky's own teaching material or from GLINKA's or Lyadov's fugal experiments. Yet *Scherzo* also reveals an emergent, original voice in its tonal ambiguity, offbeat harmonisations, and impulsive cross-rhythms, which drive the work towards its strikingly abrupt conclusion. GRAHAM GRIFFITHS

Charles M. Joseph, 'Stravinsky's Piano Scherzo (1902) in perspective: a new starting point', *Musical Quarterly*, 67.1 (January 1981), 82–93.
N. A. Rimsky-Korsakov, *Practical Manual of Harmony*, ed. Nicholas Hopkins, trans. from 12th Russian edn by Joseph Achron (New York: Carl Fischer, 2005).

Scherzo à la Russe. Composed 1943–5. First performance, 5 September 1944 (version for JAZZ ensemble); 22 March 1946 (version for symphony orchestra). Published 1945, New York: Associated Music Publishers.

While the *Scherzo à la Russe* was originally intended to form part of the FILM score for *The North Star* (1943), directed by Lewis Milestone, the music for the film was finally written by Aaron COPLAND. As with the FOUR NORWEGIAN MOODS (1942), the score was simply re-orchestrated for the concert versions. Nevertheless, the *Scherzo* exists in three instrumentations: besides the orchestral version (3.2.2.2 – 4.3.3.1 – timpani, percussion, piano, harp – strings; May 1945; premièred in March 1946), a setting for jazz band was commissioned by Paul WHITEMAN, the 'King of Jazz' (premièred in September 1944). First, Stravinsky produced a version for two pianos in 1944, which is the basis for both orchestrations. In contrast to the completed scores, the sketches show that in 1943 Stravinsky conceptualised both the main section of the *Scherzo*, which is played three times without modifications, and the two trios as separate pieces with different instrumentations.

For Eric Walter White, the piece 'is closely related to the "Russian Dance" in *Petrushka*, and the 'Swiss Dances' in *The Fairy's Kiss*' (SCW, 419). Though premièred by a jazz ensemble, a certain 'Russian influence' can be found in the instrumentation: in 'Trio I', Stravinsky imitates the sound of the gusli, a form of psaltery which was one of the most characteristic instruments of Russian travelling singers (see Karlinsky 1986). Furthermore, the ORCHESTRATION of this trio with piano and harp follows the tradition of Russian 'classical' music, as, for example, in GLINKA's *Ruslan and Lyudmila* (I,1). And, of course, the title of the work reminds us of Stravinsky's origin: TCHAIKOVSKY's piano miniature, op. 1/1 of 1867, is also named *Scherzo à la Russe*.

FLORIAN HENRI BESTHORN

Simon Karlinsky, 'Igor Stravinsky and the Russian preliterate theatre', in Jann Pasler (ed.), *Confronting Stravinsky: Man, Musician, and Modernist* (Berkeley and Los Angeles: University of California Press, 1986), 3–15.

Scherzo fantastique (*Fantasticheskoye skertso*) for large orchestra, op. 3, Con moto. Composed May 1907 – April 1908, USTILUG and ST PETERSBURG (rev. 1930). First performance, 24 January / 6 February 1909, St Petersburg. Conductor, Alexander ZILOTI. Published 1909, Jurgenson. 'Dedicated to the great artist Alexander Ziloti'.

Scherzo fantastique, which Stravinsky composed while finishing his 'academic' SYMPHONY IN E♭ MAJOR, was his first experience of mastering programmatic orchestral music. Stravinsky avoided the symphonic poem genre to focus on the concept of a romantic scherzo. A subject was found in *La vie des abeilles*, a 'half-philosophical, half-imaginative' essay by Maurice MAETERLINCK. Consequently, Stravinsky named the piece *The Bees (after Maeterlinck): Fantastic Scherzo*, and he even intended to discuss 'an exact programme' with RIMSKY-KORSAKOV (PRK, I, 172). Nevertheless, by the last phase of scoring the work, he rejected the extra-musical hints in the title. From the autumn of 1907, Stravinsky's *Scherzo* was supervised by Rimsky at their regular lessons at the Zagorodnïy flat.

In June 1908, after Rimsky-Korsakov's death, the task of promoting the *Scherzo* fell to its dedicatee Alexander Ziloti. The first performance of the piece took place over six months later as part of the seventh 'Ziloti Concert' at the Assembly of Nobility, with the St Petersburg Imperial Russian Opera orchestra conducted by Ziloti. The post-première reviews ironically noted the strong influence of both Rimsky and WAGNER on the 'sparkling but empty score'; Nikolay Findeyzen even called the *Scherzo* 'venereal', drawing direct connections with the 'Venusberg' music from *Tannhäuser* (*Russian Music Newspaper*, 5, 1909; PRK, I, 449).

Stravinsky's *Scherzo* obviously continued a tradition of 'fairy' scherzos by Mendelssohn, Berlioz, Wagner and Russian composers – from GLINKA to Rimsky-Korsakov, with his *Flight of the Bumblebee*. A diligent pupil, while borrowing the colours of his teacher's decorative palette for his own 'magical' score, Stravinsky explores the principle of non-mixed timbres – as in the initial solo of trumpet *con sordino* continued by solo oboe – an exact copy of the very beginning of *The Golden Cockerel*! In an endeavour to create a dazzling, weightless 'perpetuum mobile' (Savenko 2001, 19), Stravinsky removes trombones, tuba and percussion (apart from cymbals) from the orchestra, but includes celesta, three(!) harps and piccolo clarinet in D. Starting from Rimsky's octatonic resources and Wagner's chromaticism, Stravinsky develops a more extravagant harmonic style. 'The harmony of *The Bees* will be ferocious, like a toothache, but must at once be replaced by a pleasant one, like *cocainum*', he promised Rimsky in the summer of 1907 (PRK, I, 177). But perhaps the most important achievement of the *Scherzo* concerns a new approach to melodic shapes: apart from an 'infinite' Wagnerian melody in the middle section (Moderato assai), the remainder of the thematic material is totally segmented into a series of arabesques, in a manner reminiscent of DEBUSSY. Under the influence of impressionistic impulses, Stravinsky began a fundamental reappraisal of his attitude to musical structure. And, not by chance, the *Scherzo fantastique* première marked the beginning of his acquaintance with Sergey DIAGHILEV.   NATALIA BRAGINSKAYA

Svetlana Savenko, *Mir Stravinskogo* ('Stravinsky's World') (Moscow: Kompozitor, 2001).
SCS

Schloezer, Boris de (born Vitebsk, 8 December 1881; died Paris, 7 October 1969). Philosopher, musicologist, music critic and translator, Boris de Schloezer belonged to a generation of Russian intellectuals that saw the fall of the Empire and later developed a large part of their careers within the context of FRANCE's Russian immigrant community. Schloezer studied musicology in PARIS, and sociology at the Université de Bruxelles in 1900–1, before returning to RUSSIA, where he distinguished himself as a contributor to various musical, artistic and literary reviews, participating in the major philosophical and artistic debates of Russia's pre-revolutionary period. From 1921 onwards, he pursued his career as a music and literary critic in Paris, publishing in various French and Russian reviews. He soon became a pillar of Prunières's *Revue Musicale* and the main critic of *La Nouvelle Revue Française*, periodicals with ties to Gallimard, the publisher for which Schloezer translated many masterpieces of RUSSIAN LITERATURE. In 1923, he published his first monograph devoted to his brother-in-law Alexander SCRIABIN, whose image as a 'total romantic' he opposed with the 'anti-romantic' vein of Stravinsky – this is probably the initial source of Stravinsky's general distrust of Schloezer. In 1929, Schloezer published *Igor Stravinsky*, the first book on Stravinsky written in French (Paris,

Claude Aveline) and one of the rare texts on the composer from that period not written with his involvement. Schloezer's book on Stravinsky definitively sealed the general feeling of enmity between the two men. Stravinsky's personal copy of the volume, now held at the Paul SACHER STIFTUNG, is littered with agitated annotations in the composer's hand contesting numerous points. Although convinced of Stravinsky's musical genius, Schloezer indicated his disappointment, beginning with MAVRA, which he considered a failure; it was in this context that he introduced the term 'néo-classique'. Although he showed renewed enthusiasm for a few works of the 1920s (notably LES NOCES, OEDIPUS REX and APOLLO), it was with PERSÉPHONE in 1934 that Schloezer took a stance, disqualifying as decadent all of Stravinsky's recent works, from CAPRICCIO to the SYMPHONY OF PSALMS and Perséphone (which he went so far as to call a 'cadaver'). Yet in general, and despite these disappointments, Schloezer remained convinced of Stravinsky's historical role as a composer, considering him a 'cultural phenomenon' and placing the debate on an aesthetic and phenomenological level, as is seen in his book of 1929. Schloezer was probably one of the rare minds devoted to Stravinsky's art that managed to keep their critical independence wholly intact. Schloezer was also to some extent the source of the criticisms levelled by young serialist composers against Stravinsky at the end of the 1940s.

VALÉRIE DUFOUR

Boris de Schloezer, Comprendre la musique. Contributions à la Nouvelle Revue Française et à la Revue Musicale (1921–1956), ed. Timothé Picard (Presses universitaires de Rennes, 2011).

Boris de Schloezer, Igor Stravinsky (Paris: Claude Aveline, 1929; new edn, Presses universitaires de Rennes, 2012).

Valérie Dufour, Stravinski et ses exégètes (1919–1940) (Brussels: Édition de l'université de Bruxelles, 2006), 107–34.

Schoenberg, Arnold (born Vienna, 13 September 1874; died Los Angeles, 13 July 1951). For most of the first half of the twentieth century, Igor Stravinsky and Arnold Schoenberg seemed to represent the opposite poles of contemporary music. Theodor W. ADORNO, whom no one could ever have accused of being unbiased, identified Stravinsky, in opposition to 'Schoenberg the progressive', with 'all that is destructive and regressive'. The composer Arthur LOURIÉ said that Schoenberg stood for 'neoromantic emotionalism', Stravinsky for 'classical intellectualism', and that 'these systems are diametrically opposed; one excludes the other'. Schoenberg's is 'always egocentric . . . and ends only in an affirmation of self or the personal principle', while Stravinsky's 'seeks to affirm unity and unalterable substance'. Stravinsky's biographer Roman Vlad described the popular view of Stravinsky in the first half of the century as 'the antithesis of all that Arnold Schoenberg stood for', and Schoenberg's biographer H. H. Stuckenschmidt wrote that 'Schoenberg and Stravinsky were regarded as opposites, whose points of view were irreconcilable.'

The personal relationship of the two men and their mutual knowledge of each other's music corroborated the popular view. For as long as Schoenberg lived, each seems to have carefully avoided the other and his music. The only time that Stravinsky admitted to ever having met Schoenberg was in 1912, when both PETRUSHKA and Pierrot lunaire were performed at about the same time in

Berlin, where Schoenberg was living – *Petrushka* as part of the Russian Ballet season at the Kroll Theatre, and *Pierrot lunaire* in a performance at the Choralionsaal. DIAGHILEV invited the Schoenbergs to a performance of *Petrushka*, and in turn Schoenberg invited Stravinsky and Diaghilev to a performance of *Pierrot lunaire*, giving Stravinsky a score to follow. Apparently the two composers met several times in the following week as well.

In 1913 Stravinsky called hearing *Pierrot* 'the great event of my life', and said Schoenberg was 'one of the greatest creative spirits of our era'. He referred to the music of *Pierrot* with admiration many times in future years, though he thought it would have been a much better piece without the speaker-singer, whose part in his opinion obscured the music. He once suggested that the music should be played alone, with the hearer adding the text himself if he wanted to. His references to its composer and to his knowledge of his music, however, were contradictory. In the 1920s he described Schoenberg as 'a great inventor, a harmonist who marks out new paths in that field', but continued: 'But for me Schönbergian rationalism and his aesthetic principles are unbearable.' On the same occasion, he said, 'I actually haven't the time to keep up with European musical movements: I'm too busy composing and performing my own works', yet in 1924, he said, 'I'm very interested in contemporary tendencies in the young German music and keep up with everything that goes on in this area.' In the same year, he told a reporter in Prague that he had heard nothing of Schoenberg's since 1912. In an interview in *Musical America* in 1925, he referred dismissively to those who tried to write 'the music of the future', and in his AUTOBIOGRAPHY, published in 1936, he says 'I live neither in the past nor in the future. I am in the present.'

Both Schoenberg's *Serenade* and Stravinsky's PIANO SONATA were performed at the International Society of Contemporary Music (ISCM) festival in VENICE in 1925. When Schoenberg, who was conducting his *Serenade*, over-ran his rehearsal time, Edward Dent, who was president of the Society, asked him if he thought he was the only composer in this festival. Schoenberg's answer was 'Yes'. There is no evidence that the two composers met on this occasion; nor is there any evidence that Stravinsky attended the performance of the *Serenade*. Schoenberg heard Stravinsky play his sonata, however, and walked out, later writing to WEBERN about the 'disaster of "modern music"'. Shortly after this, Schoenberg produced his *Three Satires*, op. 28, the second and third of which are aimed at Stravinsky and 'the new classicism'. Although Walsh says there is no evidence that Stravinsky knew these satires, CRAFT quotes Stravinsky as having said that, in spite of their subject, he admired their counterpoint.

After hearing Stravinsky's OEDIPUS REX at the Staatsoper in Vienna in February 1928, Schoenberg wrote in his diary that 'all Stravinsky has composed is the dislike his music is meant to inspire'. At the 1937 Venice Festival, Stravinsky's JEU DE CARTES and Schoenberg's op. 29 'Suite for 7 Instruments' were performed on consecutive days. Stravinsky was present at both performances, Schoenberg at neither.

The two men's disinclination for any contact became particularly obvious in the 1930s, when both settled in Hollywood, where they were to live a short distance away from each other for eleven years, until Schoenberg's death, without making any attempt to meet. Both attended Franz Werfel's funeral in Hollywood in 1945, where, according to Andriessen and Schönberger, Stravinsky reported seeing 'the angry, tortured, burning face of Arnold Schoenberg' and later at home referred indignantly to him, asking, 'Can you imagine someone going around shaking hands at a funeral?' A series of concerts, EVENINGS ON THE ROOF, was initiated in LOS ANGELES in 1938, and music by both Schoenberg and Stravinsky was played from time to time. Stuckenschmidt says that one could meet Stravinsky there, but that Schoenberg attended only those concerts in which his own piano music (opp. 11, 19, 25 and 33a) was played, and no others – thus implying that the two men never met there. On 7 July 1948 the Stravinskys, Schoenbergs and Thomas MANN were among a large number of guests at a dinner in honour of Alma Mahler-Werfel at the Beverly Hills Hotel, and Stravinsky was in the audience in 1949 when Schoenberg gave a speech thanking the city of Vienna for making him an honorary citizen ('a half-century too late', according to Stravinsky), but it seems doubtful that they met on either of these occasions. In spite of the apparent estrangement, however, Craft says that the first telegram to be received by Gertrud Schoenberg after her husband's death on 13 July 1951 was from Stravinsky, and that he would have liked to attend the funeral but did not do so, thinking that his presence there could only be seen as ironic.

Craft, who knew both men well and promoted and performed their music, is the source of most of what we know about Stravinsky during the years in CALIFORNIA. He claims that Schoenberg thought Stravinsky depended on formulas and 'a bag of tricks', and that Stravinsky thought Schoenberg was a slave to 'an abstract system'. In another interview from about the same time, Stravinsky said that he found 'the endless quality of atonality' repulsive.

KATHRYN PUFFETT

Scriabin, Alexander Nikolayevich (born Moscow, 25 December 1871 / 6 January 1872; died Moscow, 14/27 April 1915). Russian composer and pianist. Stravinsky's claim to Robert CRAFT that he and Scriabin 'often encountered each other [in RIMSKY-KORSAKOV's house] during my years of tutelage' was in fact impossible as Scriabin left Russia in 1904 for ITALY, SWITZERLAND and Brussels, subsequently touring the UNITED STATES until his return visit in 1909. Stravinsky met Scriabin's abandoned first wife, Vera Ivanovna, at Rimsky-Korsakov's last birthday party on 6/19 March 1908; on that occasion, she played three of her husband's *études*, which apparently prompted Stravinsky to compose his Scriabin-inspired op. 7 set.

On 27 January / 9 February 1909, Scriabin arrived in ST PETERSBURG to supervise the Russian première of *Poem of Ecstasy*, conducted by Felix Blumenfeld on 31 January / 13 February at a BELYAYEV concert. Andrey Rimsky-Korsakov, at his mother Nadezhda's prompting, invited Scriabin to his late father's house on 28 January / 10 February to introduce him to the work of the last generation of Rimsky-Korsakov pupils – STEINBERG, Stravinsky and GNESIN. According to Gnesin, Stravinsky showed Scriabin *The Faun and the Shepherdess*, rather than any of his more adventurous works – which, if true, would have been at Nadezhda Rimsky-Korsakova's behest. Yet Stravinsky's intense love of Scriabin's work held true while he composed his BALMONT setting, KING OF THE STARS – a work much indebted to Scriabin's *Prometheus* – and the The RITE OF SPRING.

He next met Scriabin, by chance, at Warsaw railway station on 9/ 22 September 1913, whence they were both travelling to Switzerland. Unable to take up Stravinsky's warm invitation to visit him in CLARENS, Scriabin invited Stravinsky to come and visit in Lausanne. This Stravinsky did on 6 October 1913, spending the afternoon delighted as Scriabin played parts of his Eighth, Ninth and Tenth Sonatas. Stravinsky was dismayed to learn, though, that Scriabin knew of the *Rite* only by reputation, and was 'amazed by all the Paris noise' as 'someone told him that I in fact am just doing the same old thing'; presumably that somebody was in fact referring to FIREBIRD (whose title character is portrayed by Scriabinesque harmonies), but Scriabin's apparent lack of awareness only reinforced Stravinsky's conviction that the celebrated composer looked upon him 'von oben bis unten' ('from above to below'). Possibly, as Richard Taruskin claims, the final straw was *Vospominaniya o Skryabine* ('Reminiscences of Scriabin') by the critic and close Scriabin-associate Leonid Sabaneyev, published on the tenth anniversary of the composer's death in 1925; in that volume, Scriabin was quoted making condescending and disparaging comments about Stravinsky's music, his most damning comments being made about *The Rite*: 'cerebral, mentalistic in the highest degree ... It's *minimum* creativity.' Yet, even before then, according to the composer George ANTHEIL, Stravinsky, after his mother Anna Stravinsky's arrival in Berlin in November 1922, was angered and almost reduced to tears by her implacable and 'inordinate admiration' of that composer. In any case, when talking to Craft a quarter-century later (*Mem*), Stravinsky gave a totally disingenuous account of his relationship to Scriabin's music, only admitting the composer's influence 'in the piano writing' of the *Four Studies*, op. 7.   DANIEL JAFFÉ

SCS; SRT

Second Viennese School. For Stravinsky's position relative to the Second Viennese School, please see the separate entries on his relationship with SCHOENBERG, BERG and WEBERN. As far as his opinion of what these composers were doing is concerned, he had little interest in either their ideas or their works in the first decades of the century, and by the 1950s, when he himself decided to compose serial music, the Second Viennese School no longer existed, all three of its most important exponents having died. In November of 1924, he told a reporter in Prague that he actually hadn't the time to keep up with European musical movements, as he was too busy composing and performing his own work, and all reports indicate that, until quite late in his life, he in fact knew almost none of the music, and had no knowledge of the compositional techniques of the Second Viennese School in the years when it was an active force.

   Probably the only time Stravinsky and Schoenberg met was in 1912, when both PETRUSHKA and *Pierrot lunaire* were being performed in Berlin, where Schoenberg lived. Apparently the two men got together several times, in what might have become a friendship, but this never happened again. Many years later, Eduard Steuermann claimed to remember a dinner at Schoenberg's house during this period, at which Stravinsky also met Berg and Webern, though in 1963 Stravinsky couldn't remember such an occasion, and Stephen Walsh has pointed out that in fact this could never have occurred, as Berg was in Vienna at this time and Webern was in Stettin. Stravinsky did meet both these men later, in the 1920s: Webern probably only once, but Berg at least twice.

Schoenberg's Verein für musikalische Privataufführungen ('Society for Private Musical Performances') presented a Stravinsky evening on 6 June 1919, in which Emmy Heim sang the *Berceuses du chat* and *Pribaoutki*. Berg was unable to attend because he was ill and had gone to his family's country house, the Berghof. Webern wrote to him about Stravinsky's songs on 9 June: 'Strawinsky was magnificent. These songs are wonderful. This music affects me unbelievably deeply. I love it especially. Something so inexpressibly moving as these cradle songs. How those three clarinets sound! And "Pribaoutki". Ah, mein Lieber, something completely magnificent. This objectivity (realism) leads into the metaphysical.' This was the only performance of these songs in the Verein, though five other works by Stravinsky were played on other occasions, and two of these were repeated several times. The FIVE EASY PIECES for Piano Duet and the THREE EASY PIECES for piano duet were both played on 9 and 16 February and 13 April 1919, with the latter repeated again on 20 September 1920. The THREE PIECES FOR STRING QUARTET were on the programme of 5 March 1920; Stravinsky's arrangement of *Petrushka: Burlesque Scenes in Four Tableaux* for piano four hands was played on 13 October 1920; and his PIANO-RAG-MUSIC was played twice, on 6 June and 31 October 1921.

In 1926 Stravinsky played his CONCERTO FOR PIANO AND WIND INSTRUMENTS at the Musikverein in Vienna. On this occasion there was a reception for Julius Bittner, the president of the ISCM, in the Hotel Imperial, and Webern, Berg and Wellesz were there. They almost certainly met Stravinsky, though there is no mention of this in either their correspondence or Vera STRAVINSKY's diary. At this time Schoenberg was no longer in Vienna, having moved to Berlin in 1925. The Verein für musikalische Privataufführungen had come to an end in late 1921.

In an interview with Robert CRAFT, undated, but presumably in the 1950s, Stravinsky is quoted as saying that 'the dodecaphonic school, for all its great merits, was obsessed by an artificial need to abnegate any suggestion of triadic "tonality" – a very difficult thing to do'. And White quotes him as saying in 1952: 'Serialism? Personally I find quite enough to do with the seven notes of the scale. Nevertheless, the serial composers are the only ones with a discipline that I respect. Whatever else serial music may be, it is certainly pure music. Only, the serialists are prisoners of the figure twelve, while I feel greater freedom with the figure seven' (SCW, 133–4).

KATHRYN PUFFETT

Septet for clarinet, horn, bassoon, piano, violin, viola, violoncello. Composed 1952–3. First performance, 23 January 1954, Washington, DC. Conductor, Igor Stravinsky. Published 1953, Boosey & Hawkes. 'Dedicated to the Dumbarton Oaks Research Library and Collection'.

(I) (no title) (II) Passacaglia (III) Gigue.

Stravinsky began the composition of the Septet in July 1952 immediately upon completion of the CANTATA, whose central movement, Ricercar II, had marked his first foray into serial composition. The three movements of the

Septet are linked via shared thematic material, with the opening of the main theme from the non-serial first movement expanded into the sixteen-note series of the partially serial Passacaglia and quasi-serial Gigue. If one senses a stylistic shift in this work, it is probably more for the increased, persistent density of the counterpoints than for the adoption of a series in the second and third movements. That series contains, in contrast to a TWELVE-NOTE row, recurring notes, and is largely diatonic with some chromaticism – as such, it is perfectly in line with Stravinsky's tonal neo-classical style. (The series contains only eight different pitch classes, ordered as E-B-A-G-F♯-G♯-C♯-B-G-F♯-G♯-G-A-C-G♯-A.) Stravinsky had recently been listening to SCHOENBERG's music, conducted by CRAFT, including the twelve-note Suite for 7 Instruments, op. 29, also a septet ending with a Gigue. But, aside from certain surface correspondences, such as the choice of an ensemble with wind and string trio plus piano, replacing Schoenberg's three clarinets with a trio of clarinet, horn and bassoon, Stravinsky's Septet bears little resemblance to Schoenberg's.

Stravinsky's first movement is in sonata form. The lively main theme in A major/minor is accompanied by motives derived from it, including augmented and inverted versions, and free material. The second-theme group, following a soft and subdued pulsating E minor triad, continues with animated counterpoint largely built from inverted, transposed or retrograded motives of the first theme and landing on a plain D major triad. The closing group introduces a comically leaping motive, which is spun out in the development section into an extended fugato. The key scheme of the recapitulation (A-E-D-C) mimics the beginning of the first-theme melody itself (a2-e2-d2-c2), which in turn makes its last fragmented and slowed-down appearance in the coda.

The serial theme of the Passacaglia, first presented in the manner of a Webernian *Klangfarbenmelodie* that moves around different instruments, remains clearly recognisable throughout the following seven of nine variations, largely because of its stable characteristic anacrusis rhythm in 3/4 time, likely modelled on that of BACH's C minor organ Passacaglia and Fugue. Each variation pairs the theme with one or several countermelodies of distinct character, many of which are built from some form of the sixteen-note series itself.

That the fugue subject of the Gigue uses the same series may not be immediately evident to a listener because the series appears in an entirely different rhythmic and melodic guise of rugged, agitated leaps and short trills. The opening three-part fugue in the strings is repeated in the piano, while over it the winds intone a second fugue with a bouncy theme based on the same series. The second half of the movement unfolds in a similar manner, starting out with the inversion of the subject, and culminating in the following double fugue on a reappearance of the opening motive from the first movement, finally revealed as the source for the series.

CHRISTOPH NEIDHÖFER

Joseph N. Straus, *Stravinsky's Late Music* (Cambridge University Press, 2001).
SSE

Serenade in A, for piano. Composed 11 April – 9 October 1925, Nice. First performance, 25 November 1925, Frankfurt, by the composer. Published 1926, Berlin: Russischer Musikverlag; (ed. Albert Spalding) London: Hawkes & Son. Dedication: 'A ma femme'.

(I) Hymne (II) Romanza (III) Rondoletto (IV) Cadenza Finala.

The Serenade in A extended the sequence of compositions, including the OCTET FOR WIND INSTRUMENTS, CONCERTO FOR PIANO AND WIND INSTRUMENTS and PIANO SONATA, through which Stravinsky established his neo-classical idiom in the early 1920s. Importantly, these works also enabled the composer's re-invention as a concert pianist, for it was from this stand-point that he announced his authority regarding the 'execution' (not interpretation) of this novel repertoire. Such was the impact of these new scores and of Stravinsky's forceful pamphleteering of them from the soap-box of his piano bench, his publishers issued an *apologia* (1925): 'It is impossible to-day ... to avoid the violent controversy to which [Stravinsky's music] has given rise, a controversy that is ... a testimony to its vitality for Stravinsky's music is so characteristic an expression of the artistic tendencies of our time.' The Serenade in A was Stravinsky's response to an invitation received, during his first American tour in early 1925, to compose a work whose every movement would fill one side of a 10-inch, 78 rpm disc. Stimulated by the restrictions of this unusual commission, Stravinsky resolved 'to imitate the *Nachtmusik* of the eighteenth century'.

1. Hymne. The serenade-like spirit of this movement, alternately radiant or reflective, suggests to some commentators a 'reference' to Chopin's F major Ballade, also written in compound duple (6/8) time. Several passages (bars 59 and 70; and in the Cadenza Finala, bar 79) provide evidence of the unusually large span of Stravinsky's hands as depicted in Picasso's 1920 portrait.

2. The Romanza, which represents the 'ceremonial homage paid by the artist to [his] guests', is a stylised minuet framed by rhetorical arabesques suggestive of the cimbalom.

3. Stravinsky described Rondoletto as offering dance music appropriate to the serenade genre by way of 'sustained and rhythmic movement'. Indeed, the music's seamless, mechanistic flow is typical of other vigorous Stravinskian *ritornelli* in the Piano Concerto, Sonata, CAPRICCIO and DUO CONCERTANT. The contrapuntal texture is reminiscent of BACH's inventions and, appropriate to this reference, the score is devoid of agogic indicators – a neo-classical practice first adopted in the Sonata. A particularly ingenious, indeed extreme, example of this occurs at the end of the Rondoletto: rather than employ the term *rallentando*, Stravinsky 'constructs' a gradual diminution of velocity (bar 118) via the systematic augmentation of note-values from semi-quavers to triplets to quavers to crochets to minims, thereby engineering a perfectly objective execution of a rallentando.

4. Cadenza Finala (*sic*) was the first movement to be composed and, according to Stravinsky, it is 'tantamount to a signature with numerous calligraphic flourishes' – a most suggestive image coming from one whose musical handwriting is amongst the most beautiful of any composer.

Stravinsky provided another clue to the work's identity: the 'in A' of the Serenade's title refers not to tonality but to the work's pitch-polarity 'on A', as it were. Imaginative instances of this aural subtlety occur at the conclusion to each movement when, via the 'play' of harmonics so quiet as to strain the listener's attention, the note 'A' is eventually revealed at the edge of silence, or *appena* ('hardly'), as this near-inaudibility is described at the very close.　　　　　　　　　　　　　　　　　　　　　　　GRAHAM GRIFFITHS

Anon. [Eric Walter White?] *Miniature Essays* (London and Geneva: J. & W. Chester, 1925).
Graham Griffiths, *Stravinsky's Piano: Genesis of a Musical Language* (Cambridge University Press, 2013).
SSC, I–III

Sermon, A Narrative and a Prayer, A. Composed 1960–1. First performance, 23 February 1962, Basel Kammerorchester, Basel. Published 1961, Boosey & Hawkes. Dedicated to Paul SACHER.

Text: New Testament, Thomas Dekker.

Described by Stravinsky as a cantata, this work, commissioned by and dedicated to Paul Sacher, is based on the life of St Stephen as recounted in the Acts of the Apostles, but also makes use of texts from the Epistles of St Paul, in the English of the Authorised Version of the Bible, and a poem by Thomas Dekker. One of the distinguishing features of the work is the use of a speaker, whose declaimed text overlaps in carefully coordinated fashion with musically intoned phrases, creating thereby a singularly RITUAL atmosphere. The musical material is derived from a TWELVE-NOTE row which Stravinsky manipulates in such a way as to provide pseudo-tonal 'anchors', consistent with his subversive use of tone rows in his late work more generally. Ritualism is emphasised by the structure: the 'Sermon' is divided in two, each part followed by the same refrain. The 'Narrative', while 'quasi-dramatic' in Stephen Walsh's phrase (SSE, 428), also makes use of techniques such as canon, ending with a coda in which all the four versions of the series are heard in combination. The final 'Prayer', to the text by Dekker, also employs canon, building up an extremely complex metrical structure, but it ends with the ritual tolling of bells (gongs, double basses, piano and harp). The work was extremely well received at its first performance in Basel, under Sacher's direction, and was encored in its entirety.　　　　　　　　　　　　　　　　　　　　　　　　　　　　IVAN MOODY

Sharaff, Irene (born Boston, 23 January 1910; died New York, 16 August 1993). An Academy Award-winning designer, Sharaff worked with Stravinsky on the 1937 JEU DE CARTES ('The Card Party'). Stravinsky had hoped his son Theodore would design the costumes, but, according to Charles Joseph in *Stravinsky and Balanchine* (2002), this was quickly blocked by the local union. On tour in New York, Stravinsky came to see how rehearsals were progressing, with Lincoln KIRSTEIN describing the composer's presence as both 'courtly' and 'terrifying', and his mortification when Stravinsky advised choreographer BALANCHINE to simplify a section (SSE, 56). Objecting even more strongly to Sharaff's costume designs (created in the style of tarot cards), Stravinsky demanded they be redone to represent modern playing cards – recognisable to all in the audience. In the end, Stravinsky conducted the première of *Jeu de* *cartes* and stated that he enjoyed Balanchine's choreography. He was apparently never satisfied by Sharaff's designs.   LORIN JOHNSON

Shostakovich, Dmitri Dmitriyevich (born St Petersburg, 12/25 September 1906; died Moscow, 9 August 1975). Leading Soviet Russian composer and pianist. Aged 13, at GLAZUNOV's encouragement, he enrolled at the ST PETERSBURG CONSERVATORY. His official teachers were Leonid Nikolayev (piano) and Maximilian STEINBERG (composition). Away from the Conservatory, he attended performances of new works by Stravinsky, Hindemith and SCHOENBERG. Stravinsky's music particularly impressed Shostakovich: his First Symphony's concertante piano part and jump-cut-like juxtapositions of musical ideas show PETRUSHKA's influence. In 1926, he was thrilled by Fritz Stiedry's 17 March performance of The RITE OF SPRING, and on 12 December was one of four pianists involved in the Russian première of Les NOCES, conducted in Leningrad by Mikhail Klimov.

Stravinsky admired Shostakovich's First Symphony, but expressed disappointment over the young composer's subsequent development. To him, *Lady Macbeth of the Mtsensk District*, which enjoyed international acclaim before being quashed in 1936 by the 28 January *Pravda* editorial 'Muddle instead of music', was 'nothing but doom and gloom ... [the] kind of tragic realism [which] would be excusable in an old man disillusioned with life'.

Meanwhile, generations of Shostakovich's students at both the Leningrad Conservatory and the Moscow Conservatory encountered SYMPHONY OF PSALMS – effectively proscribed in the USSR until Igor MARKEVITCH's performance in 1962 – in the form of their teacher's own piano duet arrangement. In 1948, following a devastating official attack on his work during the Composers' Conference chaired by Andrei Zhdanov – widely reported even outside the USSR – Shostakovich lost both his teaching posts. As part of his official rehabilitation, Shostakovich was made a delegate to the Soviet-sponsored 'Cultural and Scientific Conference for World Peace' at New York's Waldorf-Astoria Hotel in 1949. Stravinsky refused both Olin Downes' invitation to co-sign a telegram welcoming Shostakovich to the UNITED STATES, and to attend the conference to debate the Soviet composer: 'How can you talk to them?' he asked a journalist: 'There is no discussion possible with people who are not free.' At the conference, a 5,200-word speech, allegedly by Shostakovich, read aloud in English, denounced Stravinsky for 'having betrayed his native land' and 'joined the camp of reactionary modernistic musicians'. After this speech, Nicolas NABOKOV asked Shostakovich whether he agreed with the anonymous *Pravda* article which had denounced Stravinsky, Hindemith and Schoenberg: Shostakovich's cowed response to the affirmative, literally directed to the floor, told its own story.

On his 1962 visit to the USSR, Stravinsky, on arriving in Moscow, unwittingly misinformed by Pierre SOUVTCHINSKY (who had acted as mediator between Stravinsky and Soviet officials) that KHRENNIKOV had only extended the invitation to him with Shostakovich's approval, repeatedly asked where Shostakovich was. In the event, the two only met twice (Shostakovich being mostly in Leningrad when Stravinsky was in Moscow, and vice versa): first at the Metropole Hotel on 1 October, when the composers were seated either side of Yekaterina Furtseva, the Minister of Culture; the second occasion on the eve of Stravinsky's departure on 10 October, when the two were finally seated together at a banquet, held, again, at the Metropole Hotel. Shostakovich diffidently confessed to Stravinsky his huge admiration for the *Symphony of Psalms*; Stravinsky at first appeared to reciprocate by saying he shared some of Shostakovich's admiration for MAHLER, but then added that his colleague should go 'beyond' this and follow the example of Schoenberg and WEBERN.

Shostakovich thereafter was reputed to dislike Stravinsky the man, yet never lost his admiration for Stravinsky the musician. At the end of his life, he kept just two photographs under the glass on his desktop: one was a large portrait of Stravinsky, which Shostakovich put on display after the composer's death in 1971.   DANIEL JAFFÉ

Laurel E. Fay, *Shostakovich: A Life* (New York: Oxford University Press, 2000).
Tamara Levitz, 'Stravinsky's Cold War: letters 1960–63', in SHW, 273–317.
Elizabeth Wilson, *Shostakovich: A Life Remembered* (London: Faber and Faber, 2006).
SCF; SSE

Six, Les (Georges AURIC, Louis Durey, Arthur HONEGGER, Darius MILHAUD, Francis POULENC, Germaine Tailleferre). Les Six were a group of friends whose music appeared on the same programmes in PARIS from 1916: they produced only one joint publication, *L'Album des Six* for piano (1920), and this was a compilation of previously composed pieces. Jean COCTEAU, their self-styled mouthpiece, praised the simplicity and essential Frenchness of SATIE in his tract *Le Coq et l'arlequin* (1918), holding him up as an example for younger composers rather than DEBUSSY or WAGNER. Stravinsky was at the time a leading figure in the Parisian musical scene and members of Les Six moved in the same social circles as the Russian composer. Indeed, DIAGHILEV attended a concert at 6 rue Huyghens in 1918, an artists' studio used as an informal concert venue during the war years; works by the Nouveaux Jeunes (Honegger, Milhaud, Auric and Tailleferre) were frequently performed at this studio, and Poulenc and Durey soon also became associated with them.

Stravinsky was a formative influence on most of Les Six. Tailleferre and Milhaud played the piano duet version of PETRUSHKA, a revelation for Tailleferre, who was expelled from Eugène Gigout's organ class at the Paris Conservatory for her Stravinsky-influenced improvisations. Tailleferre mentions in her memoirs that she recorded a piano roll of The RITE OF SPRING with Stravinsky – for whom 'it was never loud enough' – though the roll was never released. Later, Stravinsky described her neo-classical Piano Concerto (1924), one of her finest works, as 'honest music'.

Stravinsky recommended Poulenc to Chester after seeing the *Mouvements perpétuels* for piano and *Rapsodie nègre*. The composers were also linked through the Paris-based music and book publisher La Sirène. Stravinsky's PIANO-RAG-MUSIC, published with a cover design by PICASSO, was one of their first publications; during their brief existence, they also published music by Satie and by all of Les Six except Tailleferre.

The connections between Les Six and Stravinsky (and Satie) are most clearly seen in the 1910s, in the overlap between emerging NEO-CLASSICISM, music composed for amateurs or children to play, and short, pithy character or genre pieces. Satie's sets of *Enfantines* for piano duet were composed in 1913, and Stravinsky's Five Easy Pieces for Piano Duet from 1916–17. These Stravinsky pieces were included in a Dada programme at Théâtre Michel on 6 July 1923, alongside Milhaud's 'shimmy' *Caramel mou*, Auric's *Adieu New York* and Satie's *Trois morceaux en forme de poire*.

Stravinsky's influence was most durable on Poulenc, who was the first to acknowledge his debt to the Russian composer. In 1925, Poulenc wrote a dedication: 'à vous mon cher Stravinsky à qui je dois mes plus grandes joies musicales'. The opening of Poulenc's *Gloria* (1959) strongly resembles Stravinsky's 'Hymne' from his Serenade in A (1925); there are also links between the Stravinsky movement and Poulenc's 'Hymne' for piano (1928). Poulenc went as far as to say, in an interview with his friend the actor Stéphane Audel, 'The SOUND of Stravinsky's music was so new to me that I often ask myself: "If Stravinsky hadn't existed, would I have been a composer?"'   CAROLINE POTTER

Sketches and Manuscripts (United States and Canada). The enormous number of extant musical manuscripts in Igor Stravinsky's hand demonstrate that drafting and revising with pencil or pen on paper were essential to his creative process. Indeed, these manuscripts are not only plentiful, they span nearly his entire career as a composer, documenting over fifty years of work.

The manuscripts encompass handwritten working materials from various stages in Stravinsky's compositional process. Musical ideas in their earliest forms, ranging from a few notes on a single staff to multiple bars with more complex textures, typically appear as sketches. Subsequent sketches, typically more detailed, often elaborate, expand or, occasionally, abbreviate the original notations. At a later stage in the compositional process, Stravinsky typically incorporated the revised passages into a longer, handwritten draft of a section or even of an entire movement. Among holographic materials from later stages is the short score, a complete version of the work that condenses the instrumental lines onto a limited number of staves. This short score routinely became the basis for a carefully notated full score, also handwritten, which Stravinsky would send to his publisher, who would use it in turn as the basis for the printed, published version of the work. Stravinsky's duties as a composer didn't stop at this point; once receiving the printed proofs of a composition from his publisher, he often made further changes to the work by hand. These changes ranged from corrections to the addition of newly composed music.

Furthermore, the manuscripts for Stravinsky's late, serial music also include preliminary materials that Stravinsky almost certainly constructed before he composed the earliest musical ideas for these works. The preliminary materials typically take the form of twelve-note row forms, and charts that display ordered successions of pitches derived from these rows. As he composed, Stravinsky would have referred to the rows and charts as sources for available pitch resources. In sum, from preliminary materials and fledgling ideas to handwritten annotations on printed proofs, Stravinsky's manuscripts document multiple stages in the creation of many of his works.

Stravinsky's musical manuscripts serve important roles in the study of his works and creative process. On the practical side, musicians concerned with the accuracy of a published score might consult the manuscripts for the work to investigate whether an error or unintended change might have occurred between late holographic versions and the printed score. Or historians wishing to confirm when Stravinsky composed a work might search the manuscripts of that composition for dates in the composer's hand.

Manuscripts from multiple stages of composition for a single work may allow those studying them to construct a history of a piece or movement. From musical sketches and drafts, whether contained within a bound volume – a sketchbook – or appearing as a collection of loose pages, scholars may amass the evidence necessary to deduce a plausible compositional chronology. That is, they can derive the order in which Stravinsky composed the movements of a multi-movement work, or the sequence in which he created the individual sections of a single movement. Such findings can be more than merely interesting; they can affect one's experience of a work. For example, from analysis of a published score, one might understand a specific section to be essential to the work, yet discover, upon viewing the manuscripts depicting earlier compositional stages, that this crucial passage was not part of Stravinsky's original conception of the composition. Such a finding might prompt questions that inspire reconsideration of the movement in its published form. Similarly, Stravinsky's manuscripts can also reveal the detailed history of a particular passage or section: its initial ideas and how Stravinsky transformed them during various phases of composition. Through sketches and drafts for a single passage, one can see the passage develop from its inception to its final form.

Primarily through materials, such as sketches and drafts, which document early stages of composition, manuscripts offer clues to Stravinsky's compositional procedures, the methods that he used to compose. For instance, they reveal that Stravinsky often began composition with a relatively uncomplicated version of a passage, which, during subsequent stages, became increasingly complex and irregular as he revised it. Indeed, Stravinsky seems to have maintained this particular compositional habit during virtually his entire compositional career, as illustrated by numerous manuscripts from The RITE OF SPRING through to the late, serial works of the 1960s.

Stravinsky's manuscripts are essential resources for those wishing to understand his music beyond the printed pages of the published scores. Nonetheless, even careful examination of the manuscripts cannot address two important issues: first, they cannot reveal what Stravinsky was thinking during composition or why he committed a particular musical action. That is, changes to musical material – alterations, additions and deletions – are often evident in the manuscripts, but why Stravinsky made these changes is not. Scholars can – and do – speculate regarding Stravinsky's intentions, but his manuscripts alone cannot confirm or deny such speculations. Second, the entire history of a passage, movement or work is unlikely to be represented in the manuscripts alone. Stravinsky, who is well known for composing at the piano, would probably have fashioned new ideas and revised them while at the keyboard, notating only selected versions on paper. Thus, manuscripts for a given piece may record numerous stages in the composition of a work, but it is unlikely that they exhibit all of them.

Types of archival materials other than manuscripts may have bearing on Stravinsky's compositional decisions, and thus may complement evidence provided by manuscripts. For example, contracts for commissions and correspondence with PUBLISHERS might state the required components of a work, possibly specifying, for example, the purpose of a commission, the venue or performers for the première performance, or the length of the work.

As a rule, manuscripts in individual archives in the UNITED STATES and Canada document a single stage in the composition of a work, rather than multiple stages. In this way, Stravinsky archives in the United States and Canada differ from the Stravinsky Archive at the Paul SACHER STIFTUNG (Foundation), which offers materials from numerous compositional stages for many works. An exception in the United States is the material at the Dumbarton Oaks Research Library, which includes sketches and a short score for Stravinsky's CONCERTO IN E♭: 'DUMBARTON OAKS'.

The list below provides the names of institutions in the United States and Canada that hold manuscript materials in Stravinsky's hand. Three have relatively substantial holdings; examples of items are offered for each. The other institutions typically own a single, complete manuscript or several fragmentary manuscripts for more than one work. Except for the H. Colin Slim Stravinsky Collection, all institutions noted below are located in the United States. Because no centralised catalogue exists for Stravinsky's manuscripts in the United States and Canada, the list below is undoubtedly incomplete. For the purposes of this list, printed proofs and published scores with annotations in Stravinsky's hand are considered to be manuscript holdings, along with sketches, drafts, holograph short and full scores, and other musical documents written entirely in the composer's hand.

Institutions with Substantial Holdings of Stravinsky's Manuscripts

The Juilliard School, New York. The Juilliard Manuscript Collection and the Soulima Stravinsky Collection of the Peter Jay Sharp Special Collections. Among the materials are sketches for PETRUSHKA, a signed holograph of CANTICUM SACRUM, and proofs, copyists' manuscripts, and published scores with annotations in Stravinsky's hand. Numerous items from The Juilliard Manuscript Collection are digitalised and available online.

Library of Congress, Washington, DC. Among the many materials in the collections are a holograph score of CONCERTINO, including a reduction for piano four-hands, a holograph score of APOLLON MUSAGÈTE, and printer's proofs for numerous works with annotations in Stravinsky's hand. Many items, including those in the Stravinsky/Craft Collection, are currently uncatalogued. A holograph score of Concertino is digitalised and available for viewing online.

The Morgan Library & Museum, New York. Among items in the collection are sketches and drafts of The SONG OF THE NIGHTINGALE and autograph manuscripts of SCHERZO FANTASTIQUE, Petrushka, PIANO-RAG-MUSIC, Les NOCES (including an arrangement for PIANOLA), PIANO SONATA, SONATA FOR TWO PIANOS, and arrangements for piano of The FIREBIRD and The FAIRY'S KISS.

Institutions with Smaller Holdings of Stravinsky's Musical Manuscripts

Dumbarton Oaks Research Library and Collections, Washington D.C. Rough sketches and drafts for the Concerto in E♭:'Dumbarton Oaks'.

Harvard University Library, Cambridge, Massachusetts. Incomplete materials for CANON ON A RUSSIAN POPULAR TUNE (for orchestra), SUITE NO. 2 FOR SMALL ORCHESTRA and EPITAPHIUM.

The University of British Columbia Library (H. Colin Slim Stravinsky Collection), Vancouver, Canada. Incomplete materials including sketches for Les Noces for player piano, autograph working manuscript for twenty-four bars of DIVERTIMENTO, and autograph fourteen-page transparencies of SCHERZO À LA RUSSE arranged for two pianos.

New York Public Library. Sketchbook possibly dating from 1917 with Stravinsky's transcription of a work by GLINKA, and fragments possibly for The SOLDIER'S TALE and The NIGHTINGALE.

Oberlin College Libraries, Ohio. Presentation manuscript of THRENI.

Princeton University Library, New Jersey. Autograph manuscript of the orchestral score of REQUIEM CANTICLES.

Stanford Libraries, Stanford University, California. Autograph manuscript of DANSES CONCERTANTES.

UC Berkeley Library, University of California. Holograph score of ORPHEUS.

University Library, University of Illinois at Urbana-Champaign. Manuscript score of MAVRA.

The Harry Ransom Center, The University of Texas at Austin. Signed printed piano reduction of Apollon Musagète with editorial marks in Stravinsky's hand.

LYNNE ROGERS

Charles M. Joseph, 'Stravinsky manuscripts in the Library of Congress and the Pierpont Morgan Library', The Journal of Musicology, 1.3 (July 1982), 327–37.

Sokolova, Lydia (orig. Hilda Munnings) (born Wanstead, England, 4 March 1896; died Sevenoaks, England, 5 February 1974). British dancer. Given her Russian name by DIAGHILEV, Sokolova was one of the BALLETS RUSSES' longest-serving members (1913–22, 1923–9). She danced in numerous Stravinsky premières – The RITE OF SPRING (NIJINSKY, 1913) (listed as 'Maningsowa'), the OPERA The NIGHTINGALE (Romanov, 1914) – and she created the role of Death in the first SONG OF THE NIGHTINGALE (MASSINE, 1920). She also starred in new productions of these works for the company, creating the role of the Chosen One in Massine's 1920 Rite, and Death in BALANCHINE's Song of the Nightingale in 1925. Sokolova missed the première of Les NOCES (NIJINSKA, 1923); she had rehearsed the BALLET but fell ill. SOPHIE REDFERN

Soldier's Tale, The (L'Histoire du soldat). Composed 1918. First performance, 28 September 1918, Lausanne. Conductor, Ernest Ansermet. Published 1924,

J. & W. Chester / Edition Wilhelm Hansen, London. Dedication: 'à Werner Reinhart'.

Instrumentation: violin, double bass, clarinet, bassoon, cornet (often played on trumpet), trombone and percussion; three actors (the soldier, the devil and a narrator, who also takes on the roles of minor characters), and a dancer (the princess, non-speaking).

Other versions: Piano (Grande suite), 1918; Trio for Piano, Violin and Clarinet, 1919.

Plot Summary: on the road back home, a soldier meets the devil in disguise and trades his fiddle for a book that foretells the future. His previous life in tatters, he acquires great wealth following the book's predictions. Happiness eludes him, so he returns to the road. On his adventures, he wins back his fiddle from the still-disguised devil in a musical contest, signalling his moral resurrection. The soldier recovers and marries a princess; the devil reveals himself and swears to recapture the soldier if he should leave his new kingdom. The soldier does not heed the warning and is taken by the devil for the final time.

Histoire du soldat contains the following sections:
Marche du soldat
Petits airs au bord du ruisseau
Pastorale
Marche royale
Petit concert
Tango
Valse
Ragtime
Danse du diable
Petit choral
Couplets du diable
Grand choral
Marche triomphale du diable

In 1917, Igor Stravinsky, the Swiss writer Charles Ferdinand RAMUZ (1878–1947), and some members of their circle of friends – specifically, the conductor Ernest ANSERMET (1883–1969) and the painter René Auberjonois (1872–1957) – planned an artistic collaboration that would result in a small theatre piece capable of being transported easily for performances at different locations. Werner Reinhart (1884–1951) of Winterthur provided the financial support that these struggling artists needed. Stravinsky and Ramuz developed a scenario (see AFANASYEV) that limited the number of participants to a small ensemble of seven musicians, two actors and three narrators, thus making it practical for a touring group.

In Philosophy of New Music, Theodor ADORNO refers to The Soldier's Tale as 'Stravinsky's central work' because it reflects his continued preoccupation with his past, while at the same time foreshadowing later compositional techniques. One retrospective feature involves the dramatic adaptation of a Russian folk tale. In spite of Stravinsky's tendency to muse over aspects of his Russian heritage or to use earlier compositional techniques as he was writing The Soldier's Tale, he nevertheless shaped and reshaped his musical vocabulary in a more linear fashion that prefigures his approach in later works. But the uniqueness of *The Soldier's Tale* results from the distinctive ways in which Stravinsky used musical means to illustrate the soldier's struggle between two worlds. His musical imagination is fuelled by the interaction with Ramuz, but neither collaborator overpowers the other. Since the text is narrated rather than set to music, composer and author both retain their artistic autonomy, leaving them free to experiment.

Philippe Girard makes specific note of 'Petit concert' being the central point in the score (Carr 2005, 26) – by the time that Stravinsky was working on this section, there were two strata developing in the storyline: surface-level and subliminal. As a result, certain motives in 'Petit concert' appear at the surface level, aligning themselves with events as they unfold, such as the devil falling off his chair. On a subliminal level, where the musical ideas are more deeply interwoven with the narrative, Stravinsky creates a montage that recalls past events and that foreshadows the rest of the tale, which eventually results in the triumph of the devil.   MAUREEN CARR

Theodor W. Adorno, *Philosophy of New Music*, trans. Robert Hullot-Kentor (Minneapolis: University of Minnesota Press, 2006).

Alexander N. Afanasyev, *Russkie narodnye skazi* ('Russian Folk Tales'), 4 vols., 2nd edn (Moscow: K. Soldatenkov, 1873).

Maureen A. Carr (ed.), *Stravinsky's Histoire du soldat: A Facsimile of the Sketches* (Middleton, Wis.: A.-R. Editions, 2005).

Philippe Girard and Alain Rochat, *C. F. Ramuz – Igor Stravinsky: Histoire du Soldat, Chronique d'une naissance* (Geneva: Éditions Slatkine, 2007).

Soldier's Tale Suite (L'Histoire du soldat). Concert suite of five numbers arranged in 1918–19 for violin, clarinet and piano from the original theatrical work. First performance, 8 November 1919, Lausanne Conservatory, played by E. Allegra, J. Porta and J. Iturbi. Published 1920, J. & W. Chester. Dedicated to Werner Reinhart, amateur clarinettist and Swiss patron of Stravinsky during this period. The trio suite was soon overshadowed in popularity by the arrangement of the work scored for the original instrumentation of seven players. The so-called 'grand suite' consisting of eight numbers was arranged in 1920, first performed at the Wigmore Hall, London, on 20 July 1920 under Ernest ANSERMET, and published in 1922.   JEREMY COLEMAN

Sonata in F♯ Minor, for piano. Composed 1903–4. 'Pavlovka, summer 1904'. First (private) performance 21 February 1905, at Rimsky-Korsakov's apartment, ST PETERSBURG. Published 1974, Faber Music, London (ed. Eric Walter White). Dedication: Nicholas Richter. Order of movements: (I) Allegro (II) Vivo (III) Andante (IV) Allegro.

In later life, Stravinsky may have wished his early sonata to have been 'happily lost', but there is much to admire in this compositional exercise completed under the watchful gaze of RIMSKY-KORSAKOV. As might be expected from this context, the work is bursting with a student's desire to emulate worthy stylistic models. Taruskin's account of these sets great store by TCHAIKOVSKY's *Grande sonate*, op. 37, and the Fifth Symphony, also piano sonatas by SCRIABIN (No. 3), GLAZUNOV (Nos. 1 and 2) and works by Stravinsky's former teachers of MUSIC THEORY, Fyodor AKIMENKO and Vasily KALAFATI. Two underlying purposes may be surmised here: the first was

Stravinsky's wish to demonstrate his identification with the Rimsky-Korsakov circle via an accomplished exposition of a true Belyayevtsï sense of pianism; the other was, quite possibly, to demonstrate to *himself* that, with the completion of this *echt*-Russian pianistic artwork (and, in 1907, the SYMPHONY IN E♭ MAJOR), he now had every reason to consider himself, and be considered by others, as a 'Russian composer'. A fundamental aspect of the Romantic rhetoric to which Stravinsky aspired in this work was the emotional drama of the sonata-form narrative. Stravinsky's achievement can be observed particularly well in the opening Allegro (F♯ minor, 4/4) via the lofty 'militarism' and bombast of the opening subject, ably supported by rapid octave doublings; and, by comparison, in the ardent sensibility, verging on sensuality, of the second theme (bar 33). The Vivo 'scherzo' (A major, 2/4; F major, 3/4) conveys light and flickering textures to great effect via *piano*, even *pianissimo*, dynamics at high speed. Furthermore, the fleeting moments of two-part counterpoint, some at extremely high registers, serve to establish the virtuosity not only of the pianist but also of the composer. The sustained lyricism of the Andante (D major, 6/8; G major, 2/4) and its lush textures offer a perfect vehicle for the soloist's instinct for melodic projection. Noteworthy too is Stravinsky's handling of that other trope of virtuosic guile, the inner voice – a characteristically Romantic *trompe d'oreille* also known as Thalberg's three-handed writing. The pianistic effect of the final Allegro (F♯ major, 2/4; Andante, D major, 2/4), besides its heroic and impetuous mood, is almost exclusively due to the rapid deployment of octaves whose gestural exploitation culminates (*agitato*, bar 318) in a coda of double-octave bravura cascades. The Sonata in F♯ Minor exudes that sense of improvisational *extempore* for which the young Stravinsky was famed before he addressed himself to the discipline of compositional technique. Significantly, this craft was also acquired via the imitation of a wide range of models mostly from the nineteenth century, yet also, as revealed by the frequent inclusion of contrapuntal episodes, from the eighteenth century. Thus, Stravinsky demonstrated early in his development a surprising resourcefulness and versatility to his embryonic and thoroughly cultured brand of kleptomania.   GRAHAM GRIFFITHS

Louis Andriessen and Elmer Schoenberger, *The Apollonian Clockwork: On Stravinsky*, trans. Jeff Hamburg (Amsterdam University Press; Amsterdam Academic Archive, 2006).

Graham Griffiths, *Stravinsky's Piano: Genesis of a Musical Language* (Cambridge University Press, 2013).

Kenneth Hamilton, 'The virtuoso tradition', in David Rowland (ed.), *The Cambridge Companion to the Piano* (Cambridge University Press, 1998), 57–74.

Sandra P. Rosenblum, *Performance Practices in Classic Piano Music: Their Principles and Applications* (Bloomington: Indiana University Press, 1988).

SCW

Sonata for Two Pianos. Composed 1943–4. First performance, 2 August 1944, Madison, Wisconsin: Nadia BOULANGER and Richard Johnston; 24 October 1944, Mills College, Oakland, California: Nadia Boulanger and the composer. Published 1945, Schott Musik International, Mainz. Order of movements: (I) *Moderato* (II) *Theme with Variations* (III) *Allegretto*.

The Sonata's aura of tamely harmonised Russian-ness has been traced (SRT) to its dependence on folk melodies extracted from M. V. Barnard's 1845 anthology *Pesni russkogo naroda* (*Songs of the Russian People*, repr. 1886), which

Stravinsky found in a Los Angeles bookshop in 1942. His original aim was to use this material for the soundtrack for a film, North Star. When this project was abandoned, he re-worked his sketches into Scherzo à la Russe (1943–4) and Sonata for Two Pianos, whose first movement, second theme, is modelled on Akh chto za milen'koy ('Ah, What a Handsome Lad') from Barnard's anthology. In the second movement, Theme with Variations, the notation is reminiscent of Renaissance polyphony – for example, a time-signature of 4/2 and the opening breve of Piano II's cantus firmus suggest a response to Banchieri's Canzone italiana per organo, quoted in Pétrarque (1932) by Charles-Albert Cingria, the Swiss author whose views had chimed so closely with Stravinsky's own in Duo Concertant. Variations 1 and 2 offer humorous allusions to Poulenc and J. S. Bach, respectively. Variation 3 presents a jazz-fugue interrupted by an unexpectedly po-faced tranquillo (bar 28). Variation 4 returns to the textures of the Theme via extremes of register that evoke the spacious and reverberant nave of some Italian cathedral of the composer's imagination. The final movement is formulated from arrangements of 'Ne odna v polve dorozhen'ka' ('There's More Than One Path Across the Field') and, in the Trio, 'Akh, chto èto za serdtse' ('Ah, What Kind of Heart Is This?'). GRAHAM GRIFFITHS

Song of the Nightingale, The (Pesnya Solov'ya; Chant du rossignol). Composed 1917, Morges. First performance 6 December 1919, Geneva, Orchestre de la Suisse Romande. Conductor, Ernest Ansermet. Published 1921, Édition Russe de Musique; 1947, Boosey & Hawkes. 2222.4331. Duration: 20 minutes.

Symphonic poem in three movements. Written during the first three months of 1917; completed 4 April. As The Rite of Spring had not yet been performed in Geneva, the première caused uproar. Between the first performances and the publication of the score in February 1922, Stravinsky made slight revisions. A transcription for violin and piano (1932) was produced in collaboration with the violinist Samuel Dushkin, entitled Songs of the Nightingale and Chinese March, and a transcription for piano roll was also made. A further revised version (1962) likewise contained only minor alterations. Stravinsky's piano reduction of the work gives the movements the following titles:

(I)   The Fete in the Emperor of China's Palace
(II) The Two Nightingales
(III) Illness and Recovery of the Emperor of China.

The majority of material is based on sections of Acts 2 and 3 of The Nightingale (1914), as these two acts were written concurrently some years after the first, although the 'Chant du Pêcheur' theme from Act 1 is also used. Stravinsky reduced the orchestra (omitting flute, clarinet, bassoon, trumpet, mandolin and guitar), and included cuts, re-orderings and new passages. The composer excluded or reworked the dialogue scenes from the opera, and re-orchestrated passages, given that previously vocal lines now had the potential to be extended in both range and duration. Instruments and instrumental groups were treated in a more soloistic, concertante fashion, with tuttis being largely avoided. Diaghilev requested many of these edits. The impresario had wanted to make a ballet out of The Nightingale, but Stravinsky proposed that this be done instead from the symphonic poem arrangement that he had been planning.

Despite this early attraction to the idea, he soon believed the work would function better as a 'static' concert piece. Nevertheless, a successful ballet was made and was premièred at the PARIS Opera House on 2 February 1920, with choreography by MASSINE and set designs by Matisse.   JOSEPH SCHULTZ

Souvenir d'une marche boche, for piano. Composed: 'Morges, 1 Sept. 1915'. Published 1916, Boosey & Hawkes. Facsimile in Edith Wharton (ed.), *Le Livre des sans-foyer* ('The book of the homeless') (London: Macmillan, and New York: Scribner's Sons, 1916).

This *pièce d'occasion* was Stravinsky's contribution to *Le Livre des sans-foyer*, Edith Wharton's anthology of essays, poems, drawings and musical numbers sold 'for the benefit of the American Hostels for Refugees (with the *Foyer Franco-Belge*) and of The Children of Flanders Rescue Committee'. Its distinguished pantheon of contributors included Léon BAKST, Sarah BERNHARDT, Rupert Brooke, Paul CLAUDEL, Jean COCTEAU, Joseph Conrad, John Galsworthy, Thomas Hardy, Henry James, Maurice MAETERLINCK and Claude Monet, with an Introduction by Theodore Roosevelt and an additional musical offering by Vincent d'Indy. Stravinsky's *Souvenir d'une marche boche* appears as a facsimile reproduction of the manuscript alongside a re-working of Jacques-Émile Blanche's celebrated portrait of the composer by the seashore (the figure of Stravinsky is identical, but here he is indoors, standing beside an ornamental chair). According to Soulima STRAVINSKY, his father improvised *Souvenir d'une marche boche* at the piano on 1 September 1915. Despite its title, the work does not quote a specific German march but 'refers' to the music of two German/Austrian composers for deliberate effect. The *Marche* itself presents a grotesque display of mock-militarism, featuring an impertinent parody of BEETHOVEN'S Fifth Symphony (the final movement). In complete contrast, the Trio is positively tuneful – playful even – and offers an altogether gentler portrait of the heroic spirit, intended, possibly, to 'represent' that of the Belgian nation and especially its child refugees. Glenn Watkins (2003) has suggested that the Trio owes its dotted rhythms to Schubert's stirring *marches militaires* for piano duet; he cites the last of the *Trois marches héroïques*, op. 27, D602. Watkins justifies this claim by referring to Stravinsky's apprenticeship with RIMSKY-KORSAKOV, during which, according to Stravinsky himself, he was regularly set exercises in orchestrating Schubert marches.
                                                                              GRAHAM GRIFFITHS

Graham Griffiths, *Stravinsky's Piano: Genesis of a Musical Language* (Cambridge University Press, 2013).

Glenn Watkins, *Proof through the Night: Music and the Great War* (Berkeley and Los Angeles: University of California Press, 2003).

Souvtchinsky, Pierre (Pëtr Petrovich) (born St Petersburg, 5/17 October 1892; died Paris, 24 January 1985). Musicologist, philosopher, publicist, literary and art critic, Maecenas and public figure.

Souvtchinsky and Stravinsky were closely related by friendship and creative collaboration for half a century; their communication continued intermittently from the early 1920s until the composer's death.

Souvtchinsky's family belonged to a wealthy Polish-Ukrainian aristocracy. His father was a well-born Polish nobleman, Count Piotr Szeliga-Suffczyński, engineer, chairman of the board of the Russian 'Neft' ('Mineral Oil')

Partnership. During the course of his long life, Pierre Souvtchinsky was married several times; his fourth wife, from 1933 until his death, was Marianne Lvovna Suvchinskaya, *née* Karsavina (1911–94), daughter of the famous philosopher Lev Platonovich Karsavin, and niece of a prima ballerina for the BALLETS RUSSES, Tamara Platonovna KARSAVINA.

Souvtchinsky graduated from ST PETERSBURG UNIVERSITY, played piano well (he took private lessons from Felix Blumenfeld), and trained to become an OPERA singer. In the 1910s, he entered the circle of the *Mir iskusstva* (*World of Art*), and as a result established close contact with Vsevolod Meyerhold, Sergey DIAGHILEV, Aleksey REMIZOV, and met with Alexander Blok. As a publisher, Souvtchinsky propagandised the innovative trends in Russian and European music, including the works of Stravinsky and PROKOFIEV.

In 1918, he moved to Kiev; however, during the civil war, in the autumn of 1919, he emigrated. First, he lived in Sofia, then from 1921 in Berlin; in 1925, he moved to Clamart near PARIS, then to Paris itself, where he spent the rest of his life. In Sofia, Souvtchinsky founded the Russian-Bulgarian Publishing House, which marked the beginning of the Eurasian movement. Souvtchinsky was one of the most active figures in this trend, at the heart of which was the idea of the geopolitical and ethno-cultural unity of Russia–Eurasia, opposed to European civilisation. Stravinsky and Souvtchinsky became friends in October 1922 in Berlin: communication and CORRESPONDENCE then continued intermittently until 1968 (more than 300 letters and telegrams survived – PSS; PRK, III). The Eurasian theme is not touched upon in the correspondence or other documents of Stravinsky, although the idea of a parallel between the evolution of the composer and of the Eurasian movement has been expressed by commentators including Taruskin (SRT) and Vishnevetsky (2005).

The most important episode in the history of their collaboration was associated with the creation of Stravinsky's book *The* POETICS OF MUSIC. Souvtchinsky took on the role of an intermediary between Stravinsky and the composer and music critic Alexis ROLAND-MANUEL, who became a shadow co-author of the book. Nonetheless, Souvtchinsky collaborated with Stravinsky, and his work, like that of Roland-Manuel, was paid for by the composer (Savenko 2004, 252–3). Souvtchinsky formulated the concept of musical time (*chronos*), which is set out in the second lecture with reference to his article 'The notion of time and music: reflection on the typology of musical creation' (*ReM*, 191, May–June 1939). The Russian original of the article was sent by the author to Stravinsky in December 1938 (first published in Savenko 2004, 264–74). Further, Souvtchinsky was also the author of the fifth chapter, 'The avatars of Russian music', the bulk of which he had written in Russian; its typescript is preserved in the PSS (for the first publication of the original, see Savenko 2004). The correspondence of Souvtchinsky and Stravinsky confirms Souvtchinsky's authorship (letters dated 23 and 25 May 1939). Finally, it has emerged recently that Souvtchinsky's role in the creation of the text of *The Poetics of Music* was even more significant, and in a sense fundamental, because he was responsible for the development of the plan for the entire cycle of lectures (Dufour, 2006). The lecture summary, compiled by Stravinsky himself and first published by Robert CRAFT, apparently relied on the aforementioned primary plan of Souvtchinsky.

After World War II, communication between Souvtchinsky and Stravinsky resumed by the autumn of 1946. Personal meetings occurred during Stravinsky's visits to Europe, including Paris; the rest of the time they corresponded. Souvtchinsky's new guide was the young generation of French radical composers, above all Pierre BOULEZ, with whom he became closely acquainted on the basis of a new creative activity – the concerts of the Domaine musical. However, Boulez was critical of Stravinsky's neo-classical opuses; he always preferred his works of the Russian period and, in particular, The RITE OF SPRING, to which he devoted the essay 'Stravinsky remains', published in the book *Musique russe* compiled by Souvtchinsky.

The Stravinsky–Souvtchinsky correspondence became to some extent a chronicle of the creative and private life of the composer. Stravinsky discussed with Souvtchinsky, invariably in Russian, practically everything, from everyday life and medical problems to creative events. One of the most important topics was Stravinsky's revitalisation from around 1953, with his interest in the serialist generation. Souvtchinsky played a very special role here, having become the link for Stravinsky to the new generation, especially to Boulez. Another important event for both friends was Stravinsky's return to his birthplace in the year of his eightieth birthday (1962), after almost half a century of separation. In the 1950s and 1960s, Souvtchinsky wrote several articles on Stravinsky's music, and also compiled the book *Avec Stravinsky* (Monaco: Éditions du Rocher, 1958). In 1967, the composer invited Souvtchinsky to work on his archive – in particular, for the publication of his correspondence with Ernest ANSERMET (eventually published in three volumes, 1990–2, edited by Claude Tappolet).

Souvtchinsky did not wish to write about his memories of Stravinsky: 'They would not be completely like all that was written about him, and most importantly, that he *himself* said about himself.... Let others guess and write – *who* was, this most brilliant person and musician' (Nestyev, 90–1).   SVETLANA SAVENKO

Valérie Dufour, *Stravinski et ses exégètes (1910–1940)* (Brussels: Éditions de l'Université de Bruxelles, 2006).

Izrail' Nest'yev, 'Chetïre druzhbï' (Four Friendships), *Sovetskaya Musïka*, 3 (1987), 83–93.

Svetlana Savenko (ed.), *Igor Stravinsky, Khronika. Poetika* ('Igor Stravinsky, Chronicle, Poetics') (Moscow: ROSSPEN, 2004).

Igor Vishnevetsky, *Evrasiyskoye ukloneniye v musïke 1920–1930-kh godov* ('The "Eurasianist Tendency" in the Music of the 1920s and 1930s') (Moscow: Novoye Literaturnoye Obozreniye, 2005.)

SSE

Spender, Stephen (Harold)   (born London, 28 February 1909; died London, 16 July 1995). English poet. In the 1930s, Spender was identified with the so-called 'Auden Group', a circle of young, left-wing English writers named after the poet (and eventual Stravinsky collaborator) W. H. AUDEN. While Auden and Christopher ISHERWOOD emigrated to America in 1939, Spender remained in England and grew to be an important figure in the London literary establishment. Spender became friends with Stravinsky in September 1951 and would often arrange for the composer to meet with British artists and intellectuals, including T. S. ELIOT in 1956.   MATTHEW PAUL CARLSON

Robert Craft, *Stravinsky: The Chronicle of a Friendship: Revised and Expanded Edition* (Nashville and London: Vanderbilt University Press, 1994).

Spies (Heilbronn), Claudio (born Santiago, 26 March 1925; died Sonoma, California, 2 April 2020). Composer. Spies moved from Chile to New York in 1942 to study with Nadia BOULANGER, who introduced him to Stravinsky the following year. Though based in the UNITED STATES, Spies retained connections in Chile, and helped to facilitate Stravinsky's 1960 South American tour. Subsequently, Stravinsky engaged Spies to proofread ABRAHAM AND ISAAC, VARIATIONS (ALDOUS HUXLEY IN MEMORIAM), INTROITUS and REQUIEM CANTICLES. In search of errors, Spies conducted his own analyses of the serial processes underpinning these works, which he published in a series of articles. He also published an analysis of MOVEMENTS, profiting from an alcohol-fuelled encounter in 1960 when Stravinsky showed him his working notes. He was among the select few invited to Stravinsky's funeral. CHRIS COLLINS

Claudio Spies, 'Impressions after an exhibition', *Tempo*, 102 (1972), 2–9.
Claudio Spies, 'Some notes on Stravinsky's *Abraham and Isaac*', *Perspectives of New Music*, 3.2 (Spring–Summer 1965), 104–26.
Claudio Spies, 'Some notes on Stravinsky's Requiem settings', *Perspectives of New Music*, 5.2 (Spring–Summer 1967), 98–123.
Claudio Spies, 'Some notes on Stravinsky's *Variations*', *Perspectives of New Music*, 4.1 (Autumn–Winter 1965), 62–74.

St Mark's Basilica, Venice. The city's cathedral only since 1807, this most famous of VENICE's many churches was consecrated in the late twelfth century. Originally the Doge's private chapel, it adjoins the Doge's Palace on St Mark's Square. The Byzantine structure of the basilica has been little altered since its consecration, but much of the sumptuous interior and exterior decoration – the mosaics are especially celebrated – dates from the thirteenth century onwards. The building's musical history reached its apex in the sixteenth and seventeenth centuries, when its choirmasters included Adriaan Willaert, Cipriano de Rore, Claudio Monteverdi and Francesco Cavalli, and its organists the two Gabrielis, Andrea and Giovanni. Stravinsky's connection to St Mark's is bound up with CANTICUM SACRUM. In June 1954, the composer accepted a commission from Alessandro Piovesan, Director of the Venice International Festival of Contemporary Music, for a major choral and orchestral work to be given its first performance in the basilica. Led to expect a St Mark Passion, Piovesan was bitterly disappointed when *Canticum sacrum* turned out to last just 15 minutes. Stravinsky attempted to compensate by conducting the work twice at the première (on 13 September 1956); he also conducted his recent orchestration of BACH's 'Vom Himmel hoch' variations. Though carefully conceived for performance in the building – the formal plan of the work is modelled on the five domes of St Mark's, and there are distinct echoes of Venetian Baroque church music at several points – *Canticum sacrum* did not come over well in its cavernous acoustic, nor did the Bach arrangement. BEN EARLE

SSE

St Petersburg (renamed Petrograd in 1914, Leningrad in 1924 and, once again, St Petersburg in 1991). Russian city, former Russian capital, and the largest city near Stravinsky's birthplace. Stravinsky lived there until 1910, and was profoundly marked by its artistic milieu. Most of his early works were premièred in St Petersburg, some of them at RIMSKY-KORSAKOV's Wednesday musical soirées, while at the same time he found the progressive 'Evenings of Contemporary Music' (frequented by the *Mir iskusstva* circle) particularly stimulating intellectually. More specifically, the works premièred in St Petersburg are: the SONATA IN F♯ MINOR, the Cantata for RIMSKY-KORSAKOV's sixtieth birthday, the 'Driver and the Tarantula', the SYMPHONY IN E♭ MAJOR, *The Faun and the Shepherdess*, the Two Songs, op. 6, the PASTORALE, the SCHERZO FANTASTIQUE, FIREWORKS, the FUNERAL SONG, the SUITE from *The FIREBIRD* for orchestra (1910), *Two Poems of Verlaine*, *Two Poems of Balmont*, the *Three Little Songs*, and his arrangement of the 'Song of the Flea' and the *Kobold*. During his American years, he spoke nostalgically of the city, describing it as the one dearer to his heart than any other in the world.

Stravinsky's last visit to St Petersburg was in October 1912. His next visit would be to Leningrad, as the city had been renamed, half a century later, where, on 8 and 9 October 1962, he conducted two concerts at the Great Hall of the Leningrad Philharmonie that included *Fireworks* and *The Firebird*. The programme also included *The* FAIRY'S KISS, which was conducted by CRAFT. Stravinsky enjoyed an enthusiastic reception at these concerts. On 6 October, he had visited an exhibition dedicated to him and attended a concert organised by Maria Yudina at the Union of Soviet Composers, where the OCTET FOR WIND INSTRUMENTS and the SEPTET were performed. There was a very different feel to that event. The audience being specialised (and not necessarily sympathetic to his emigration) and the repertoire much more progressive, Stravinsky found himself in a much less comfortable position; moreover, he was led to meet only a select few musicians. Nevertheless, overall during his Leningrad visit, Stravinsky did have the opportunity to interact with young Russian musicians and discuss serialism, thus fulfilling the stated main purpose of his trip to the USSR.

KATERINA LEVIDOU

Mikhail Druskin, *Igor Stravinsky: His Life, Works and Views*, trans. Martin Cooper (Cambridge University Press, 1983).
Expo; SCS; SCW; SSE

St Petersburg Conservatory. The first Russian Conservatory, initiated by Anton Rubinstein and founded by the Imperial Decree of 17/29 October 1861 as a college based on the Musical Classes of the Russian Musical Society, under the direct sponsorship of the Grand Duchess Yelena Pavlovna. The Conservatory was officially opened on 8/20 September 1862, and its first artistic director was Anton Rubinstein (1862–7 and 1887–91). Among its alumni are TCHAIKOVSKY (1865, silver medallist), Alexander GLAZUNOV, Sergey PROKOFIEV, Dmitri SHOSTAKOVICH and others. RIMSKY-KORSAKOV was on the staff of the Conservatory from 1871 and authored most of the original educational programmes, including composition, harmony and ORCHESTRATION. Stravinsky never attended Conservatory classes.

ELENA VERESHCHAGINA AND TATIANA VERESHCHAGINA

St Petersburg University. The oldest, and one of the largest, Russian federal state-owned higher education institutions, based in ST PETERSBURG. It is the successor of the Academic University, established along with the St Petersburg Academy of Sciences on 28 January 1724 (O.S.), by a decree of Peter the Great. In 1803, the educational institution at the Academy was disbanded in line with the new

Academy charter, and in the same year the Pedagogical Seminary (founded in 1783) was renamed Pedagogical College. In turn, in 1819, this became the Pedagogical Institute, before, on 20 February 1821, it was renamed yet again as the Imperial St Petersburg University, a title it retained until 1914.

The Law Faculty (up until 1833, Philosophy and Law) was among the first three faculties to be established. Its prestige had grown in the 1860s due to the legal reforms of Tsar Alexander II. Among its alumni are ROERICH (1898), DIAGHILEV (1896), BENOIS (1894), Ivan Bilibin (1900), Mikhail Vrubel (1880), Alexander Kerenski (1904) and Vladimir Lenin (1891). Stravinsky studied there in 1901–6 under the dean, David Grimm; among his fellow students was Vladimir Rimsky-Korsakov. Stravinsky passed all his exams but chose not to complete his master's thesis, and, as a consequence, did not obtain a diploma.

ELENA VERESHCHAGINA AND TATIANA VERESHCHAGINA

Stasov, Vladimir (Vasilyevich) (born St Petersburg, 2/14 January 1824; died St Petersburg, 10/23 October 1906). Russian music and art critic. He hailed the realism of Fyodor STRAVINSKY's interpretations. He fervently advocated the group of composers centred around BALAKIREV, known as the FIVE, as champions of Russianness (he actually coined the phrase 'Mighty Handful' – Moguchaya Kuchka, which literally translates as 'mighty little heap' – for them). Later, he also supported the BELYAYEV group, which included Stravinsky's teacher, RIMSKY-KORSAKOV. He thus played a momentous role in shaping the musical world in which Stravinsky grew up. Stravinsky probably first met Stasov through his father. Moreover, as part of the Rimsky-Korsakov circle, Stasov frequented the very musical soirées Stravinsky attended as a pupil, where, it seems, he had the opportunity to listen to some early music by the young composer. KATERINA LEVIDOU

SCS; SRT

Steinberg, Maximilian Oseyevich (born Vilnius, 22 June / 4 July 1883; died Leningrad, 6 December 1946). Russian composer and teacher, of Jewish heritage. A year younger than Stravinsky, he entered ST PETERSBURG UNIVERSITY in 1901, and enrolled concurrently at the ST PETERSBURG CONSERVATORY in Anatoly LIADOV's harmony class. Subsequently, he joined RIMSKY-KORSAKOV's counterpoint class in 1903, and GLAZUNOV's ORCHESTRATION class in 1904, quickly impressing both professors with his talent. Following Rimsky-Korsakov's dismissal from the Conservatory in the spring of 1905, Steinberg took classes at Rimsky's home. By 1906, Stravinsky and Steinberg ('Max') were close friends, both highly regarded among Rimsky-Korsakov's latest pupils. (Richard Taruskin's claim in his 1996 book *Stravinsky and the Russian Traditions* that Steinberg displaced Stravinsky in Rimsky-Korsakov's special favour, and that the engagement and marriage of Rimsky-Korsakov's second daughter Nadezhda ('Nadya') to Steinberg on 4/17 June 1908 represented Stravinsky's 'final humiliation', appears to be tendentious and unsupported by existing evidence.) Yet Steinberg – unlike Stravinsky – had other valuable allies within the Conservatory who continued to support his career after Rimsky-Korsakov's death. Even Stravinsky's recently acquired champion, Alexander ZILOTI, in commissioning a tribute to the late composer, turned first to Glazunov; then – when Glazunov threatened to miss the set deadline – replaced him with Steinberg, rather than Stravinsky. As Stravinsky attempted to secure a performance of his FUNERAL SONG, he confessed to his closest friend within the Rimsky-Korsakov family, Vladimir, that 'I envied Steinberg's flattering participation.'

The point where incipient resentment may have taken root, though, appears to have been when Ziloti conducted the concert suite of The FIREBIRD in ST PETERSBURG on 23 October / 5 November 1910. Though Steinberg wrote to Stravinsky that he had prevented Ziloti from cutting the Khorovod from the suite, he said nothing of his own opinion of the work, leaving Stravinsky to infer the worst from the performance's negative reviews. Their friendship was certainly further strained by Stravinsky's involvement in creating a new performing version for DIAGHILEV of MUSSORGSKY's KHOVANSHCHINA; Steinberg wrote to Stravinsky on the Rimsky-Korsakov family's behalf on 28 January / 10 February 1913 asking him to deny the rumours that he had tampered with Rimsky-Korsakov's edited version.

Still their friendship endured, and Steinberg undertook various jobs for Stravinsky, including proofreading, and obtaining some of the less standard instruments needed for The RITE OF SPRING's première. Stravinsky, no doubt enjoying his own ascendency (to judge from his patronising tone in writing to Steinberg), in turn took an interest in Steinberg's BALLET Metamorphoses, eventually persuading Diaghilev to stage the second of the ballet's three tableaux, 'Midas', in 1914 (with lacklustre choreography by FOKINE). Steinberg, arriving in Paris a fortnight before 'Midas' première, helped Stravinsky prepare the première of The NIGHTINGALE by rehearsing the singers, and spent evenings with the composer and his associates discussing works being rehearsed and the current state of music. Stravinsky was friendly until immediately after the opening night of The Nightingale, then – perhaps thrown by its disappointing reception, and quite possibly boiling over with long-concealed resentment – he suddenly became offensive. As Max reported to Nadya, matters came to a head when Igor visited him in his room and started lecturing him; Walsh speculates that Max gave as good as he got and told Stravinsky his opinion of The Rite. Whatever the content of their conversation, it ended their friendship.

They last met in PARIS in 1925, when Steinberg turned up for the première of PROKOFIEV's Second Symphony. Effectively cold-shouldered by Stravinsky, Steinberg persevered and requested tickets for PULCINELLA and The SONG OF THE NIGHTINGALE. These he received, but, at the performance of The Nightingale, found his former friend so off-hand and unwilling to find time to meet that he skipped Pulcinella and went home without seeing Stravinsky again. Steinberg continued to speak respectfully of Stravinsky, and used his music as teaching material at the St Petersburg Conservatory (where he became Director in 1934; his pupils included Dmitri SHOSTAKOVICH). Stravinsky, meanwhile, seemed incapable of mentioning Steinberg without making venomous comments, several being published before his 1962 visit to the USSR. Steinberg's widow, invited to hear Stravinsky conduct a performance of FIREWORKS (originally composed as a wedding present to the Steinbergs), refused – Robert CRAFT was told – 'because she had always known that I.S. was not fond of her husband ... or, for that matter, herself'. DANIEL JAFFÉ

Stockhausen, Karlheinz (born Mödrath, near Cologne, 22 August 1928; died Kürten, 5 December 2007). German composer and significant member of the European postwar avant-garde. In 1959, when asked by Robert CRAFT about the composition from a composer of the younger generation that had most attracted him, Stravinsky selected 'Le marteau sans maître by Pierre Boulez', going on to point out that works by radical composers such as BOULEZ and 'the young German, Stockhausen' would struggle to achieve recognition even from musicians, because of their apparent lack of roots in tradition (Conv, 127). Stockhausen's irresistible emergence as a symbol of radical innovation was clearly appreciated by Stravinsky, who only a year later responded to the same question: 'Stockhausen's Gruppen' (Mem, 118). But even if Stravinsky was aware of the extent of the rigorous compositional procedures of his works, noting that, in Gruppen, this music 'as a whole has a greater sense of movement than any of Stockhausen's other pieces', it was rather Zeitmasse – which Stravinsky knew through Boulez's performance on 26 August 1957 (SCF, 221) – that interested him the most: 'I do not think the form [of Gruppen] is more successful than that of the Zeitmasse.'

The interest was reciprocal: by that time, the music of Stravinsky was also the subject of the most respectful interest from the younger generation, and, on Stravinsky's seventieth birthday in 1952, Stockhausen wrote a highly laudatory tribute: 'Stravinsky's organisation became revolutionary with The Rite of Spring. In this, the rhythmic innovation (Erfindung) breaks with a linguistic domain which was crystallised over a period of some 600 years . . . Stravinsky's historical significance can be compared with that of Philippe de Vitry' (Stockhausen 1978, 662–3).

Although a degree of mutual respect remained, attitudes seemed nevertheless to shift in the coming years, in a manner typical of European composers: while revealing their interest in one another's music, commentaries generally finish by somehow – even if indirectly – criticising some aspects of the pieces of other composers. In the 1960s and 1970s, Stockhausen only acknowledges the work of others with accompanying criticism, whilst promoting his own compositions as the true, and indeed sole, solution for New Music. It is in this context that he characterises found or newly invented sound objects in the music of BERG, Stravinsky or VARÈSE simply as the product of collage technique, whilst his own pieces 'Mikrophonie II, Momente, Telemusik and Hymnen surpassed collage technique' by means of intermodulation and integration of distinct materials (Stockhausen 1971, 224). Such comments contrast with his earlier unstinting praise for the achievements of the Russian master: 'We have to be thankful [to Stravinsky] for so many innovations in the metric and rhythmic domain' (Stockhausen 1964, 171).

In turn, Stravinsky's generosity towards the music of Stockhausen and Boulez is not without qualification. Thus, on the one hand, he writes that the 'tempo controls . . . in the central movement of Le marteau sans maître are an important innovation', and that 'the free-but-co-ordinate cadenzas in Stockhausen's Zeitmasse . . . are also a rhythmic innovation of great value'. On the other, his reservations are also expressed in a way which compares them unfavourably to his own achievements: 'In exploring the possibilities of variable metres, young composers have contributed but little. In fact, I have seen no advance on the *The Rite of Spring*, if I may mention that work, in all the half-century since it was written' (Conv, 110). In that context, we understand Stravinsky's ironic statement after a performance of *Gruppen* in 1958 in Donaueschingen. Addressing his compliments to Stockhausen, Stravinsky humorously reacted when he saw the metronomic tempo 63.5 in the score: 'Natürlich, "Komma fünf" – der deutsche Professor' ('Of course, "point five" – the German Professor': see Kurtz 1988, 129).

FLO MENEZES

Robert Craft, *Stravinsky – Crônica de uma Amizade* (Rio de Janeiro: Difel, 2002 (1994)).
Michael Kurtz, *Stockhausen: eine Biographie* (Kassel: Bärenreiter, 1988).
Karlheinz Stockhausen, 'Beitrag zum 70. Geburtstag Strawinskys', in *Texte zur Musik*, vol. IV: 1970–1977 (Cologne: Verlag M. DuMont Schauberg, 1978), 662–3.
Karlheinz Stockhausen, 'Kadenzrhythmik im Werk Mozarts', in *Texte zu eigenen Werken, zur Kunst Anderer, Aktuelles*, vol. II (Cologne: Verlag M. DuMont Schauberg, 1964), 170–206.
Karlheinz Stockhausen, 'Kriterien', in *Texte zur Musik*, vol. III: 1963–1970 (Cologne: Verlag M. DuMont Schauberg, 1971), 222–9.

Stokowski, Leopold (born London, 18 April 1882; died Nether Wallop, Hampshire, 13 September 1977). British conductor who took US citizenship in 1915. Stravinsky wrote that 'few conductors have done as much as Stokowski to gain a hearing for new music' (T&C, 230), and this is particularly true of his enduring advocacy of Stravinsky. In 1912, he became Music Director of the Philadelphia Orchestra, and he conducted a suite from The FIREBIRD in 1917. From 1921 onwards, he played the 1919 Suite at least twenty times before 1940. Stokowski conducted The RITE OF SPRING on 3 March 1922, included it in the orchestra's first ever radio broadcast on 3 November 1929, and led the first US stage production on 11 April 1930, with the Martha Graham Ballet Company using MASSINE's 1920 choreography (Graham herself danced The Chosen One). He conducted FIREWORKS (1922), The SONG OF THE NIGHTINGALE, SYMPHONIES OF WIND INSTRUMENTS (1923), RENARD, Song of the Volga Boatmen (1924), PETRUSHKA (1927, 1935 and 1937), OEDIPUS REX, FOUR STUDIES for orchestra (1931), CONCERTO IN D FOR VIOLIN AND ORCHESTRA (with DUSHKIN) and SYMPHONY OF PSALMS (1932). After leaving Philadelphia in 1940, he conducted the SYMPHONY IN C and CIRCUS POLKA with the NBC Symphony Orchestra (1943), the CONCERTO IN D and *Petrushka* with the New York Philharmonic (1948), APOLLO with the Cleveland Orchestra (1954, 1962), MASS in Frankfurt and Santa Barbara (1955), CANTICUM SACRUM at the Empire State Music Festival in Ellenville, NY (1956 and 1957) and *Oedipus Rex* at New York City Opera (1959).

On 6 November 1922, Stokowski recorded *Fireworks* with the Philadelphia Orchestra, the first US recording of any work by Stravinsky. In 1924, he made the first of his eight recordings of the 1919 *Firebird Suite*, recording it again in 1927 and again in 1935 (both in Philadelphia), then in 1940 (with the All-American Youth Orchestra), 1942 (NBC SO), 1950 ('His' Symphony Orchestra), 1957 (Berlin Philharmonic) and 1967 (London Symphony Orchestra). His other Philadelphia recordings included The *Rite* in 1929 and an outstanding complete *Petrushka* in 1937. In 1967, in New York, he recorded The SOLDIER'S TALE with Madeleine Milhaud as the narrator (with cuts by Stokowski), the spoken roles recorded in both English and French. Stokowski was infamous for retouching scores, and all but one of his recordings of the 1919 *Firebird Suite* have a prominent tubular bell part added to the 'Infernal Dance'. In 1931, Aaron COPLAND wrote to KOUSSEVITZKY about Stokowski's Oedipus Rex in Philadelphia: 'I have wondered what Stravinsky would say . . . if he knew that Stokowski doesn't begin Oedipus as he wrote it but adds a few trumpet measures (from the second act) before the speaker appears and thereby ruins that first wonderful impact of the work'.

In January 1939, Walt Disney paid Stravinsky $6,000 for the rights to use The Rite in Fantasia (1940) and Stokowski recorded an abridged version (made by Stokowski in consultation with Disney) in April 1939. Disney's vision of 'dinosaurs, flying lizards and prehistoric monsters' was first seen by Stravinsky on 12 October 1940, a month before the first public showing. In later years he was dismissive of the film and described Stokowski's interpretation as 'execrable', but when he talked to Hindemith about Fantasia in January 1941 he was enthusiastic: Hindemith wrote to Willy Strecker saying that 'Igor appears to love it.' Whatever the composer's view, Stokowski's version of The Rite has been seen and heard by millions more people than any other recording of the work, and it undoubtedly contributed to the near-mythic status of The Rite among twentieth-century classics. NIGEL SIMEONE

Straram, Walther (Walter Marrast) (born London, 9 July 1876; died Paris, 24 November 1933). French conductor. Straram began his career as a violinist in the Orchestre Lamoureux when he was 16 years old. He assisted André Caplet at Boston Opera in 1912–14. In 1923, Straram assembled an orchestra made up of the best players in PARIS, and in 1925 this became the highly regarded Orchestre des Concerts Straram, which specialised in contemporary music. Straram conducted FIREWORKS, The SONG OF THE NIGHTINGALE, Firebird Suite, PETRUSHKA, SYMPHONIES OF WIND INSTRUMENTS and the Suites for small orchestra. On 10 February 1928, Stravinsky conducted The RITE OF SPRING with the Straram orchestra and, with them, went on to record the CAPRICCIO conducted by ANSERMET (May 1930) and the SYMPHONY OF PSALMS (February 1931). NIGEL SIMEONE

'Walther Straram (1876–1933)': www.straram.fr.

Strauss, Richard (born Munich, 11 June 1864; died Garmisch-Partenkirchen, 8 September 1949). German composer and conductor. After Strauss heard The FIREBIRD in Berlin, November 1912, he remarked condescendingly to the press, 'It's always interesting for one to hear one's imitators (Nachfolger)', and in 1914 he was no less dismissive of the works which Stravinsky presented to him, including The RITE OF SPRING (he was once overheard calling it 'more like a sacrilège du printemps'). In November 1934, as President of the Reichsmusikkammer, Strauss affirmed Stravinsky's 'pure Aryan background' while defending him against charges of cultural Bolshevism (Evans 2003). Stravinsky subsequently returned with insults about Strauss' professional manner and compositional style (Conv). In reality, he had long ago seen past the 'vulgarisms' of much of Strauss' music, praising performances of works he heard, such as Ein Heldenleben and Elektra. The latter he saw twice at Covent Garden in 1913, deeming it 'a wonderful piece'. He also praised Strauss' technical abilities as a conductor: 'his ears and his musicianship were impregnable' (Conv).   JEREMY COLEMAN

Joan Evans, 'Stravinsky's Music in Hitler's Germany', Journal of the American Musicological Society, 56.3 (Fall 2003), 525–94.
Kurt Wilhelm, Richard Strauss: An Intimate Portrait, trans. Mary Whittall (London: Thames and Hudson, 1989).

Stravinsky, Fyodor Ignatyevich (born Novïy Dvor, 8/20 June 1843; died St Petersburg, 21 November / 4 December 1902). Russian operatic bass-baritone of Polish heritage, father of Igor Stravinsky. He initially studied law, but after some success in public concerts decided to make his career in singing. He entered the St Petersburg Conservatory in 1869, studying from 1871 under Camillo Everardi. After graduating in 1873, he sang at the Kiev Opera. In that city, he met Anna Kholodovskaya – herself a competent pianist and excellent sight-reader – whom, despite her widowed mother's implacable hostility, he married in 1874. In 1876, Fyodor became a principal bass at the Mariinsky Theatre in St Petersburg, and soon was the company's most celebrated singer. Acclaimed for his superlative skill in characterisation as well as the qualities of his voice, he sang and created roles by such leading Russian opera composers as Mussorgsky, Rimsky-Korsakov, Borodin, Tchaikovsky, Serov and Anton Rubinstein, as well as excelling in the then standard repertory by Glinka, Gounod, Mozart, Verdi, Wagner and others.

Despite his success, Fyodor, as the fourth and youngest child of a once-noble but not well-to-do family, was only able to accommodate his immediate family (with four children by 1884) and their servants in a single-floor seven-room (plus kitchen) apartment in St Petersburg – extended to nine rooms in 1891, when Fyodor acquired two rooms from the neighbouring flat. When practising, Igor Stravinsky recalled, Fyodor required all his children to stay within the nursery in absolute silence. Stravinsky, though, was sufficiently intrigued by what he heard to investigate the vocal scores held in Fyodor's library, sight-reading several at the piano; in this way, he became familiar with much of his father's repertoire (he specifically recalled learning Glinka's Life for the Tsar in this way), reinforced by seeing Fyodor perform at the Mariinsky. Much of this influenced Stravinsky's earliest compositions: memories of songs and operas by Glinka, Rimsky-Korsakov and Wagner consciously or unconsciously shaped themes and harmonies in his Scherzo for piano (1902), and similarly for Mussorgsky, Serov and Borodin in How the Mushrooms Prepared for War (1904). Fyodor's extensive library reflected not only his detailed research into the background of every character he portrayed but also his interest in rare and first editions: his remarkably eclectic book collection stimulated Igor's life-long voracious reading habit.

Stravinsky had a far from easy relationship with his father, whom he (and, it also appears, many of Fyodor's colleagues) found unapproachable and with a fearful temper. Fyodor nonetheless took considerable interest in his son's musical education, finding and paying for both his piano teachers – Alexandra Snetkova and the rising young (and expensive) Leokadiya Kashperova – the former possibly, and certainly the latter, recommended to him by Nikolay Solovyov, a professor of composition at the St Petersburg

Conservatory in whose opera, *Kordeliya*, Fyodor had taken a leading role. Fyodor also paid for Stravinsky's private lessons in MUSIC THEORY with AKIMENKO, then KALAFATI, though clearly on condition that his son should pursue legal studies – as Fyodor had himself – before making a final decision whether to make music his profession. These payments Fyodor regularly recorded in meticulously neat calligraphy in his account book – as he did with all financial expenditures, along with family matters such as births, bereavements, holidays, and minutiae to do with his professional activities at the Mariinsky – so creating an invaluable resource for Stravinsky scholars.

Stravinsky's fear of his father while he was alive was such that he dutifully, if unenthusiastically, attended his law studies. Perhaps meeting Rimsky-Korsakov was a vital catalyst, but it was only after Fyodor's death from sarcoma of the spine that Stravinsky openly rebelled and demanded of his mother – unsuccessfully – that he should be immediately released from the obligation to complete his legal studies and instead be allowed to devote himself to music.

DANIEL JAFFÉ

Expo; Mem; SCS; SRT

Stravinsky, (Svyatoslav) Soulima Igorievich (born Lausanne, 23 September 1910; died Sarasota, Florida, 25 November 1994). Svetik or Nini, as his parents nicknamed him, was the third of Igor and Catherine STRAVINSKY's four children. His early years in SWITZERLAND exhibited an inclination towards painting and drawing, though he soon gravitated to the piano. Between 1913 and 1917, his exiled father composed several nostalgic pieces dedicated to his children, including numerous sets of Russian folk tales, waltzes and elementary keyboard duets. Some were manageable enough for Soulima to play. By the 1920s, his emerging skills prompted him to envision a career as a concert pianist. In September 1929, Igor wrote to Nadia BOULANGER, hoping to entrust his son's formal education to the renowned pedagogue.

Boulanger's tutelage of Soulima was enduring. Moreover, it provided her with a direct link to his father. She introduced Igor to the music of Monteverdi, which later proved influential in his own writing. She became Stravinsky's unabashed advocate, his trusted editor and meticulous proofreader for such masterworks as the SYMPHONY OF PSALMS and PERSÉPHONE. Soulima assisted Boulanger with these projects, preparing each new piano reduction. In later years, he would rework many of his father's orchestral works into idiomatically transcribed piano scores worthy of performance on their own.

Throughout the 1930s, father and son sustained a highly successful concertising partnership. Also, Soulima would help his father test, bar-by-bar, new compositional ideas demanding an extra set of hands. The CONCERTO FOR TWO SOLO PIANOS, intended as a centrepiece for their 1935 South American tour, marked an especially intense collaboration. Their 1938 recording of this 'Double Concerto' offers a window into Stravinsky's adamantly expressed views regarding the perils of interpretive excess, though Soulima contended that his father's pronouncements were not as unbending as he professed. Soulima's maturation as a pianist led to frequent performances of his father's CONCERTO FOR PIANO AND WIND INSTRUMENTS and the CAPRICCIO. Igor, now conducting regularly, cajoled his agents to engage

447

Soulima as the pianist for performances of these works under his baton. Their partnership thrived until Igor's 1939 departure for AMERICA. Soulima remained in FRANCE, playing concerts, and teaching his father's piano music in PARIS.

Immigrating to CALIFORNIA in 1948, Soulima, with his father again on the podium, performed the *Capriccio* before an audience of 8,000 at the Red Rocks Amphitheater in Colorado. Joint performances with his father at the University of Illinois in 1949 and 1950 led to Soulima's professorial appointment at the school. There he would spend the next twenty-seven years as a piano instructor. Teaching, he later admitted, opened a domain happily independent of his father. He demonstrated particular interest in the Mozart piano concerti, for which he composed several still standard cadenzas. A new collaboration with the violinist Roman Totenberg flourished, allowing Soulima to perform and record not only his father's music, but also works of SCHOENBERG, WEBERN and Dallapiccola. By the 1960s, Igor's live-in assistant, Robert CRAFT, had grown increasingly influential in shaping the composer's life. Consequently, Soulima's relationship with his father grew strained.

In 1978, Soulima retired to Sarasota, Florida. While remaining active as a pianist and editor of his father's music, he now concentrated on composition. Inevitably, Soulima would be unable to escape his father's long shadow. Nevertheless, the son's achievements attest to a diverse and significant career, even as he devotedly championed the legacy of his father's music all of his life. CHARLES M. JOSEPH

Charles M. Joseph, 'Fathers and sons: remembering Sviatoslav Soulima', in *Stravinsky Inside Out* (New Haven and London: Yale University Press, 2001), 64–99.

Stravinsky (*née* de Bosset), Vera Arturovna (born St Petersburg, 25 December 1888 / 6 January 1889 (or 1884/5: according to CRAFT, Vera admitted being 'four years older than the dates on her passport'); died New York, 17 September 1982). Russian painter and costume designer – Stravinsky's second wife. They met in PARIS in February 1921, Vera at that time married to the artist Sergey Sudeykin, and Stravinsky to his first cousin, Yekaterina (CATHERINE, *née* Nosenko; *see* Catherine STRAVINSKY). They were introduced by DIAGHILEV, having all (except Catherine) attended a Russian revue at the THÉÂTRE FEMINA in the Champs-Elysées. Afterwards they dined at an Italian restaurant, Diaghilev telling Vera: 'Igor is moody today, so please be nice to him.' Vera, in fact, found Igor lively, and she told his fortune with a pack of cards. She also presumably gave a colourful account of herself. An aspiring actress, after two unsuccessful marriages she had eloped with Sudeykin in 1913. While living in Moscow, Vera acted in films, including a version of *War and Peace* (1915). The couple also spent time in ST PETERSBURG, mixing with the leading writers and artists of the day until, after the Petrograd riots of March 1917, they fled to the Crimea. There, and in the Caucasus, Vera became active as a painter. She and Sudeykin, by then common-law husband and wife, in May 1920 took a steamer for FRANCE, their ship being attacked by pirates en route.

Stravinsky continued to see Vera in Paris (away from his family), encouraged and certainly assisted by Boris KOCHNO (Diaghilev's secretary, whom Vera first introduced to the impresario). Igor and Vera became lovers (henceforth celebrating 14 July as their 'wedding anniversary'), and spent more extensive time together in London in late October through to early November when involved in Diaghilev's production of TCHAIKOVSKY's *The Sleeping Beauty* (Vera in the mimed role of the Queen). Vera finally broke from her husband in May 1922, and, with an artist friend from Moscow, Tula Danilova, then opened a fashion shop in Deauville, 'Tula-Vera'. Vera also designed and made theatre costumes, including for the BALLETS RUSSES.

She was soon seen more regularly in Stravinsky's company, while Catherine – who had been told by Stravinsky of his relationship with Vera early in 1922 – stayed at home. Glamorous, gregarious and at ease in artistic circles, Vera was in many ways a more natural companion for Stravinsky in the chic and wealthy high-society circles he mixed in. Vera's attractiveness to Stravinsky was perhaps all the greater for being his opposite: she was tall, almost voluptuously attractive, relaxed and easily moved to laughter, while Igor was short, fussy and trim, intense and far from conventionally handsome. Those who saw them together agree they were utterly devoted to one another.

Increasingly, Vera helped Igor in dealing with the press, social and special gatherings (in a manner beyond Catherine's inclination and ability) and – over time, particularly once they had moved to the UNITED STATES – his own family. Fluent in Russian, French and German, she handled a good deal of his CORRESPONDENCE. She increasingly replaced Catherine as a sounding board for his compositions in progress, and later – Robert Craft claimed – 'played a critical role in influencing his choice of music for his concert programs, effectively countering his tendency to favour his least popular creations'.

Vera joined Igor in the States in January 1940, and they married on 9 March in Bedford, Massachussetts. From 1940 to 1969, they lived in LOS ANGELES in a home that reflected Vera's taste in painting, modern furniture and floral arrangements, while suiting Igor's passion for order. Vera resumed her painting, exhibiting widely from the early 1950s. She also became joint proprietor of a commercial art gallery, 'La Boutique', on La Cienega Boulevard near their home. DANIEL JAFFÉ

Robert Craft, *Stravinsky: Discoveries and Memories* (Franklin, TN: Naxos Books, 2013), 154–62. DB; IVSPA; SCS; SSE

Stravinsky, Yekaterina ('Katya', 'Catherine') (born 11/23 January 1881; died 2 March 1939). Stravinsky's first wife and cousin. They first met in 1890 on the USTILUG estate, where she lived with her sister Lyudmila and their widowed father Gavriyil Trofimovich Nosenko. Igor was 8, Yekaterina some 16 months older; yet, as Stravinsky recalled seventy years later, they quickly formed an emotional bond. A talented artist herself – in her late teens, Katya studied at the Académie Colarossi in PARIS – she understood and supported Igor's budding talent and growing genius in a way that his mother never did. Marriage between cousins being illegal, their low-key wedding took place in Novaya Derevnya, a village just north of ST PETERSBURG on 11 January (OS) 1906.

Katya often accompanied Igor to RIMSKY-KORSAKOV's at home gatherings, and they enjoyed reading together, including MAETERLINCK (whose *Life of The Bees* inspired SCHERZO FANTASTIQUE). Igor showed Katya virtually every musical work in progress; she in turn gave practical assistance, including making neat copies of his scores – her handwriting so similar to Igor's that (Robert CRAFT and Stephen Walsh note) specialist researchers have often misattributed the penmanship.

Katya's increasingly fragile health meant the family abandoned St Petersburg with its severe climate for summers in Ustilug from 1908 until 1913, leaving in the autumn for either SWITZERLAND or the French Riviera. Katya made all the travel arrangements; then, as they led an increasingly itinerant existence outside RUSSIA, took responsibility for the even greater operation of house moves. Her formidable organisational abilities are well documented in the CORRESPONDENCE she undertook when Igor became seriously ill in Paris, with typhoid fever, in 1913.

Whether or not Catherine (as she became known outside Russia) knew about her husband's extra-marital affairs before his involvement with Vera Sudeykina (see Vera STRAVINSKY), she undoubtedly continued to love Igor and to have faith in his genius. Nevertheless, the trauma of knowing Igor's relationship with Vera, of which Catherine was kept apprised by affectionately termed letters from Vera, sapped her happiness. According to Soulima STRAVINSKY, Catherine's return to the RUSSIAN ORTHODOX CHURCH – culminating with both Igor and Catherine receiving the sacraments in 1926 – 'replaced something that she didn't have and that her heart needed'. This, and the already very Russian atmosphere of their home life, certainly had a vital influence on Stravinsky's music.

Catherine's health continued to decline, and, after the family's move to Paris in 1933, she increasingly stayed at the sanatorium in Sancellemoz. The final catastrophe was precipitated by the arrival of a Russian charlatan who persuaded Igor that tuberculosis was not contagious. Several of the family became infected and their eldest daughter, Lyudmila ('Mika'), died late in 1938; her funeral was Catherine's last excursion before her own illness took a fatal turn. Catherine died the following spring. Even the day before her death, when Stravinsky had left the house (briefly, according to his children) to see Vera, Catherine was heard to whisper: 'Today I should have liked him to understand me as he has always understood me.'   DANIEL JAFFÉ

SCS; Sfam; SSE

Stravinsky Family. In June 1882, Fyodor Ignatyevich STRAVINSKY and his wife Anna Kirillovna (née Kholodovskaya) took up their summer residence in the district of ORANIENBAUM (now Lomonossov), a small-town holiday resort situated on the Gulf of Finland and around 30 kilometres from ST PETERSBURG, which was then fashionable with the artistic and literary intelligentsia.

Igor Fyodorovich Stravinsky was born there at midday on 17 June 1882 (5 June in the old calendar) in the Khudïntsev family dacha at 137 Swiss Street. According to the traditions of the RUSSIAN ORTHODOX CHURCH, he was baptised a few weeks later (10 August / 29 July) in St Nicholas' Cathedral in St Petersburg.

Igor was the third child in a family of four boys: Roman (born 1875), Yury (born 1878) and Gury (born 1884). Fyodor Ignatevitch and Anna Kirillovna were an integral part of the musical milieu in St Petersburg at the end of the nineteenth century. Fyodor, who was born in 1843 in the region of Minsk (Noviy Dvor), was descended from an old Polish family, the counts 'Soulima-Stravinsky'. The first part of the name was discarded in the eighteenth century, in the time of Catherine the Great, when the Soulima-Stravinsky family moved from Poland to Russia. As Fyodor's mother (Alexandra Ivanovna Skorokhodova) was Russian, he was baptised into the Orthodox Church, and it was, moreover, at this moment that the Catholic Stravinsky family became Orthodox. Fyodor studied law, and then, having become aware of his musical talents and his voice, he entered the St Petersburg Conservatory. He very quickly became famous as a bass-baritone and for his exceptional gifts as an actor, and his mastery of staging brought him great renown. He began his career as an opera singer at the Kiev Opera, where he was taken on as first bass, and it was in that city that he met Anna Kirillovna Kholodovskaya, whom he married shortly afterwards (1873). Offered a post at the Imperial Opera in St Petersburg, he signed a contract that linked him to the Mariinsky Theatre, where he made his career for twenty-five years, until his death.

Fyodor focused most particularly on the roles of Méphistopheles in Charles Gounod's opera Faust, on Farlaf in Mikhail Glinka's Ruslan and Lyudmila, and again on that of Skoula in Alexander Borodin's Prince Igor. Fyodor's success was impressive and he was sought out by the most renowned Russian composers of the time for a series of important premières: Pyotr Tchaikovsky, Nikolay Rimsky-Korsakov, César Cui, Anton Rubinstein ... he had a particular connection with Borodin, and it has been said that the choice of Igor as the first name for his son was not simple coincidence and that it was linked to the name of the eponymous hero of the famous opera of which he was very fond.

His extensive repertoire (sixty-four roles) was not limited only to Russian composers, but extended equally to French and Italian ones. The rhythm of his performances was intense and impressive. He switched from one role to another with disconcerting ease and his interpretations were widely acclaimed by the critics.

'A man without preconceptions, he set himself to rid the venerable St Petersburg stage of the dust accumulated by archaic routine, and his introduction of a lively, realistic style of acting made him a real innovator' (Sfam, 1).

He would sometimes take the young Igor with him to the theatre to watch his performances. It is in this way that Igor Stravinsky, decades later, remembered, but with a still keen emotion, having seen Tchaikovsky in the hall at a performance of Ruslan and Lyudmila. His mother, during the interval, pointed at a grey-haired man with square shoulders: Tchaikovsky, this great man who was the object of so many conversations in the family home! He wrote in his Autobiography:

> it was my good fortune to catch a glimpse in the foyer of Peter Tchaikovsky, the idol of the Russian public, whom I had never seen before and was never to see again. He had just conducted the first audition of his new symphony – the Pathetic – in St Petersburg. A fortnight later my mother took me to a concert where the same symphony was played in memory of its composer, who had been suddenly carried off by cholera ... I was far from realising at

the moment that this glimpse of the living Tchaikovsky – fleeting though it was – would become one of my most treasured memories'. (*Auto*, 7)

Fyodor, who was both very well read and cultivated, gathered a very impressive library of around 20,000 books and scores, which Igor devoured during his childhood; it would subsequently become a great source of inspiration for him – in particular, those books dedicated to folklore and to popular Russian poetry from which he would later extract the texts for RENARD and LES NOCES. His library was so well known and had such value that it was appropriated for the state by the new regime after the Revolution, and declared a 'national library': according to one anecdote, Igor's mother was named 'Librarian Stravinskaya' (*bibliotekarsha Stravinskaya*), a ploy which allowed her to remain in her apartment. The library also housed two pianos on which Fyodor and Anna played together.

Despite having grown up in this environment, immersed in music, Igor remembered 'I heard all this music only at a distance – from the nursery to which my brothers and I were relegated' (*Auto*, 5).

He feared his father's impulsive nature and violent temperament, easily irritated and only showing attention and gentleness when he (Igor) was ill, at which points he became attentive and benevolent. (It is one of the reasons Igor Stravinsky gave later for his tendency to hypochondria.)

Igor's mother, Anna Kirillovna, was the daughter of a minister of agriculture in Kiev, the city where she met Fyodor Ignatyevich, whom she married against her mother's wishes. She was 19 years of age, he 30. Anna possessed a pretty mezzo-soprano voice but did not use her voice professionally, contenting herself with singing for her own pleasure. She was a good musician. Igor was later to say: 'It was from her that I inherited the valuable ability to read orchestral scores at sight' (*Catherine & Igor Stravinsky: A Family Album*, in *Sfam*).

Even if he was closer to her than to his father, Igor nevertheless felt more of a sense of duty, rather than of tenderness, towards his mother. Their relationship was not characterised simply by the respect of a son for his mother. All his life he retained a kind of apprehension in the face of her judgement. Nadia BOULANGER recalled:

> I knew his charming old mother well who was a little astonished to have a son who was so different from herself. To see Stravinsky with his mother was one of the most moving things imaginable: standing upright, his heels touching and making this characteristic noise, pac! and they clicked. And if she did not ask him to sit down, he remained standing. He was fifty years old, glorified by all the world. But he remained standing in front of his mother, as his sons remained standing in front of him. It was both Russian tradition and the tradition of their family. (Monsaingeon 1980, 86)

Igor had no more of an affinity with his older brothers, who did not interest him particularly and who bored him more than anything. Nevertheless, he harboured a certain feeling of pride towards Roman, who was handsome and good-looking. He died prematurely in June 1897, aged 23. Yury, the second brother, who was the least close to Igor, became an engineer-architect; he remained in Russia and Igor had no further contact with him after the Russian

Revolution. He learned of his death in 1941. By contrast, he had a great and profound affection for his younger brother Gury, the only member of the family with whom he had an intimate relationship. Gury also had musical gifts, an excellent ear, a very beautiful baritone voice and the ambition, like his father, to embrace a career as an opera singer. Fate determined otherwise. Mobilised in 1914, he died of scarlet fever in 1917 at Jassy on the Romanian front. Igor, who was very affected by his death, never had the opportunity to hear his younger brother, who had made his stage debut between 1912 and 1914, just before the war, in St Petersburg.

Igor's parents did not pay particular attention to their son's musical talents. Nevertheless, Igor studied the piano from an early age, as did all children of his social status. He sometimes followed his father to the Mariinsky Theatre, situated a few steps away from their apartment (66 Kryukov Canal). It was there that he discovered Tchaikovsky's Sleeping Beauty, a discovery which sparked in him a passion for BALLET.

When he was around 15 years of age, his father obtained a free pass enabling him to attend all of the rehearsals at the Mariinsky Theatre, which became almost a second home for the young man. The artistic and creative atmosphere in which Stravinsky grew up seemed completely natural to him and, though he never spoke of the exceptional enrichment this environment provided for him, it shaped his adult personality to a great extent. He adored the city of St Petersburg, where, during the decade preceding the Bolshevik Revolution, artistic and intellectual life was intense. He later acknowledged having never again discovered such a unique place, where he felt so well.

Despite his unquestionable musical vocation, Igor's parents compelled him to study law at ST PETERSBURG UNIVERSITY. Among the students, there was a certain Vladimir Rimsky-Korsakov, the youngest son of the famous composer. The opportunity presented itself for Igor to meet the master through the intermediary of his fellow student during the summer of 1902. In December that year, Igor lost his father to cancer. He was very impressed by his father's courage in facing his illness and felt a new and unexpected affection for him. Rimsky-Korsakov, who subsequently became his ORCHESTRATION teacher, rapidly became a paternal figure for the young man. He would also be the godfather, according to the Russian custom, for his marriage to his cousin.

Igor completed his university studies in the spring of 1905 and, after spending the summer at USTILUG in Ukraine, became engaged in the autumn of that year to his first cousin, Yekaterina Gavrilovna Nosenko (Catherine's mother, Maria, being the sister of Igor's mother). Catherine and Igor first met one another as children in September 1889, thereafter spending several summers together as a family on the Nosenkos' estate.

Seventy years later, Stravinsky affirmed that he and his cousin had known from the start that they were going to marry (SCS, 43). Igor said 'we were from then until her death extremely close, and closer than lovers sometimes are, for mere lovers may be strangers though they live and love together all their lives ... Catherine was my dearest friend and playmate in Pechisky, and from then until we grew into our marriage' (Expo, 40).

453

They united their destinies privately on 24 January 1906 (11 January in the old calendar). Since imperial law forbade marriage between first cousins, the young couple found a priest, Father Afanasy Popov, to unite them secretly in the Church of the Annunciation in Novaya Derevnya to the north of St Petersburg. Rimsky-Korsakov blessed the couple and gave them an icon as a wedding present. Four children were born from their union: Theodore (1907) and Ludmila (1908) born in St Petersburg, then Svyatoslav (1910) and Maria-Milena (1914), who were born in SWITZERLAND. Igor and Catherine built a house in Ustilug, on the Nosenkos' land, and spent the summers there up to the outbreak of war.

For Igor, it was the ideal place to compose. It was in this house that he began the composition of The RITE OF SPRING, which he continued in CLARENS in Switzerland. As is well known, historic events decided that Igor would only return to Russia in 1962, invited in his eightieth year by Nikita Khrushchev (21 September – 11 October) to give a series of concerts in Moscow and Leningrad.

The Stravinskys were in the habit of leaving Russia in the early autumn – the harsh winter climate did not suit Catherine's fragile health. 'Stravinsky, like any patriarch, has made ample provision for the upkeep of a family living of a perpetual state of nomadism' (Catherine & Igor Stravinsky: A Family Album, in Sfam). Because of the war and the Bolshevik Revolution, the Stravinskys envisaged staying in Switzerland, their second homeland. It was now time for a more sedentary life, even if Igor never stopped travelling as part of his life as an artist. It was the life of a close-knit family in Switzerland, then in FRANCE, which lasted until 1938/9, a tragic period when the composer successively lost his daughter Ludmila, his wife and his mother. 'The family broke up, each one made his own life, as did Igor in marrying his second wife Vera de Bosset in the United States' (Catherine & Igor Stravinsky: A Family Album, in Sfam).

MARIE STRAVINSKY

Bruno Monsaingeon, Mademoiselle: Entretiens avec Nadia Boulanger (Paris: Van de Velde, 1980).

Suite Italienne (Pulcinella transcriptions) (Suite for Violin and Piano, after Themes, Fragments and Pieces by Giambattista Pergolesi). Completed 24 August 1925; arranged in Nice. Published 1926, Édition Russe de Musique (later Boosey & Hawkes). Dedicated to Paul Kochanski.

(I) Introduzione (II) Serenata (III) Tarantella (IV) Gavotta con due variazioni (V) Minuetto e finale.

Duration: 16 minutes.

Suite Italienne for cello and piano. Completed 1 August 1932 in collaboration with Gregor Piatigorsky. Published 1934, Édition Russe de Musique (later Boosey & Hawkes).

(I) Introduzione (II) Serenata (III) Aria (IV) Tarantella (V) Minuetto e finale.

Duration: 17 minutes.

Suite Italienne for violin and piano. Completed c. 1932 in collaboration with Samuel DUSHKIN. Published by Édition Russe de Musique (later Boosey & Hawkes).

(I) Introduzione (II) Serenata (III) Tarantella (IV) Gavotta con due variazioni (V) Scherzino (VI) Minuetto e finale.

Duration: 16 minutes.

These suites are neither identical nor merely mechanical transcriptions; as the violinist Samuel Dushkin states, Stravinsky always wanted 'to go back to the essence of the music and rewrite . . . in the spirit of the new instrument'. While the first was dedicated to and intended for Paul Kochanski, he only played it with the composer once, though he approved of the fingerings. The second and third suites bring the soloist more to the foreground as a melodic instrument. Much of the cello part of the second suite was apparently Gregor Piatigorsky's contribution, and the third was written to fill time on Stravinsky and Dushkin's joint concert tours.　　　　　JOSEPH SCHULTZ

Suite No. 1 for small orchestra. In four movements: (I) Andante (II) Napolitana (III) Española (IV) Balalaïka. Arranged between 1917 and 1925; full score completed 31 December 1925. First performance, 2 March 1926, Haarlem, Netherlands. Conductor, Igor Stravinsky. Published 1926, J. & W. Chester. The Suite is a reordered orchestral arrangement of the first four numbers of his four-hand piano collection FIVE EASY PIECES, composed in 1916–17. He had previously used the fifth and final piece of that collection for his SUITE NO. 2 (which predated Suite No. 1). These short, exotic pieces lent themselves to orchestral treatment, and the accessibility of the style is due to the pedagogical nature of the original set of piano pieces. The Suite regularly filled international concert programmes of Stravinsky's music for the next decade.　　　　　JEREMY COLEMAN

Suite No. 2 for small orchestra. In four movements: (I) March (II) Valse/Waltz (III) Polka (IV) Galop. Arranged between 1915 and 1921. First performance, 1921, as incidental dance music for the revue sketch 'Katinka (Old Polka from the 1860s)' by the Chauve-Souris company, at the THÉÂTRE DES CHAMPS-ELYSÉES. The first concert performance of the Suite took place on 25 November 1925 (Frankfurt am Main; conductor, SCHERCHEN). Published 1925, J. & W. Chester. The first three numbers of the Suite were arranged from Stravinsky's four-hand piano collection THREE EASY PIECES (Trois Pièces faciles) (1914–15), and the 'Galop' was derived from the last of his FIVE EASY PIECES (Cinq Pièces faciles) (1916–17). The commission came from ballerina Yevgeniya (Zhenya) NIKITINA, a member of the company, with whom Stravinsky later had a brief affair. The Polka (which in its original piano version had been a portrait of DIAGHILEV as a kind of circus ringmaster) became the central set piece of the sketch. The Three Easy Pieces already existed in an arrangement for chamber ensemble; for the revue, Stravinsky merely expanded the instrumentation of the first and third movements, added a 'Katinka' theme for trombone and flute as a coda to the Polka, and appended the 'Galop' as a finale. Stravinsky later recalled that 'the composition as I wrote it was given only at the first few performances' of the revue (see *Auto*) and that it wasn't long before his instrumentation was being continually rearranged for more meagre instrumental forces.　　　　　JEREMY COLEMAN

Switzerland. Born into a wealthy and Francophile social environment, Stravinsky had an intimate relationship with French-speaking Switzerland, like many other contemporary Russians belonging to the same milieu. But the choice of this country was mostly motivated by his wife's health, which led her to flee the Russian winter. In 1910, Stravinsky stayed for the first time in

Switzerland, for a few weeks. He then lived there from 1911 to 1920 (until 1914, during winter time only, and then permanently), travelling many times abroad (to RUSSIA, FRANCE, ITALY, Spain). For Stravinsky, this period is remarkable for the composition and the première of The FIREBIRD (1910), PETRUSHKA (1911), The RITE OF SPRING (1913), The SOLDIER'S TALE (1918) and PULCINELLA (1920), and, on a personal level, for the birth of his children Svyatoslav, known as Soulima STRAVINSKY (1910–94), and Milena, known as Milène (1914–2013). From 1911, Stravinsky's family spent the winter season in CLARENS (near Montreux), on the Vaudois Riviera, living successively in a boarding house, Les Tilleuls, in the hotel Le Châtelard, and in the villa La Pervenche. Its former occupant, the conductor Ernest ANSERMET, sub-let this latter residence to him. Close neighbours in Clarens, Ansermet and Stravinsky became good friends. The conductor was then the Director of the Kursaal Orchestra of Montreux, with which he gave a rendition of Stravinsky's SYMPHONY IN E♭ MAJOR, op. 1, as well as giving the composer his first opportunity to conduct an ensemble during the course of a rehearsal. In 1914, the outbreak of World War I forced the Stravinskys to remain indefinitely in Switzerland, where they stayed until 1920 (in MORGES from 1915). Cut off from his financial resources in Russia, facing difficulties in producing his works, Stravinsky was left in a difficult situation that worsened after the Russian Revolution. In Switzerland, Stravinsky established, nonetheless, close ties with artistic and intellectual figures, whose leader was the writer Charles Ferdinand RAMUZ, and with whom he worked on several projects, in particular The Soldier's Tale (1918). In AUTOBIOGRAPHY (Auto, 55), Stravinsky mentions the names of Ramuz and Ansermet, but also those of the painters René Auberjonois (1872–1957), Alexandre Cingria (1879–1945), Jean Morax (1869–1939) and Henry Bischoff (1882–1951), and of the writers Charles-Albert CINGRIA (1883–1954), René Morax (1873–1963) and Fernand Chavannes (1868–1936). However, the musical and intellectual life in PARIS being far more stimulating than the cultural milieu of French-speaking Switzerland, Stravinsky left Morges in June 1920 in order to live not far from the French capital. The ties of the Stravinsky family with Switzerland endured, nonetheless, with the eldest son, Theodore (Fyodor), marrying the Swiss-born Denise Guerzoni, and living in Geneva from 1942 onwards, becoming a Swiss citizen in 1956. In 2008, Theodore Stravinsky's granddaughter, Marie Stravinsky, founded in Geneva the Fondation Igor Stravinsky, with the aim of honouring Stravinsky's legacy and furthering knowledge of his work. In 1983, the Paul SACHER STIFTUNG (Foundation) in Basel bought Igor Stravinsky's archive for $5,250,000. Stravinsky recalls in detail his Swiss years and explains the intimate relationship he had with this country in Autobiography.   STÉPHANE PÉTERMANN

1914–1918-online. International Encyclopedia of the First World War: https://encyclopedia.1914–19 18-online.net.

Dictionnaire historique de la Suisse, www.hls-dhs-dss.ch/f/home.

C. F. Ramuz, Œuvres complètes, vol. 18, Souvenirs sur Igor Strawinsky (Geneva: Slatkine, 2011).

Claude Tappolet (ed.), Correspondance Ansermet–Strawinsky (1914–1967), vol. I (Geneva: Georg, 1990).

Symphonies of Wind Instruments (Symphonies d'instruments à vent). Composed 1920, Garches, rev. 1947. First performance 10 June 1921, Queen's Hall, London. Conductor, Sergey KOUSSEVITZKY. Published by Édition Russe de Musique and Boosey & Hawkes. Dedicated 'To the memory of Claude Debussy'.

1920: 3 flutes (3rd doubling piccolo), alto flute, 2 oboes, cor anglais, 2 clarinets in B♭, alto clarinet in F, 3 bassoons (3rd doubling contra bassoon), 4 horns, 2 trumpets in C, trumpet in A, 3 trombones, tuba.

Rev. 1947: 3 flutes, 2 oboes, cor anglais, 3 clarinets in B♭, 3 bassoons (3rd doubling contra bassoon), 4 horns, 3 trumpets in B♭, 3 trombones, tuba.

1926: Piano reduction by Arthur LOURIÉ.

Duration: 12 minutes.

Begun at Carantec. Short score completed on 2 July 1920; full score completed 30 November at Garches. Early drafts were scored for harmonium and strings, written without metre and often with altered phrasings. The Symphonies arose from a body of sketch material that also contributed to works such as the OCTET FOR WIND INSTRUMENTS, PIANO-RAG-MUSIC and the CONCERTINO; for this reason, similarities exist in the material of these works.

Henry Prunières, the Editor of the *Revue musicale*, had requested a commemorative work for his supplement issue 'Tombeau de Claude Debussy' (December 1920) as part of a collection of short pieces by various composers. Stravinsky submitted a piano work (which began life as a choral piece) published as 'Fragment des Symphonies pour instruments à vent à la mémoire de Claude Achille Debussy', written 20 June at Carantec. This was to become the final section of the Symphonies. A piano reduction of the entire work was made in 1926 by Arthur Lourié. The first performance of the *Symphonies* in the USSR in 1961 was the earliest indication of a positive shift in Soviet opinion of the composer.

Stravinsky wrote the *Symphonies* with DEBUSSY in mind, while acknowledging that its musical language was not related to the French composer's in any way. He described the work in many ways: as 'an austere ritual which is unfolded in terms of short litanies between different groups of homogenous instruments'; 'a grand chant, an objective cry of wind instruments, in place of the warm human tone of the violins'; 'tonal masses . . . sculptured in marble . . . to be regarded objectively by the ear'. Stravinsky knew that the music was difficult for an audience to appreciate immediately – as he wrote, 'I did not, and indeed I could not, count on immediate success for this work. It is devoid of all the elements which infallibly appeal to the ordinary listener and to which he is accustomed.... This music is not meant "to please" an audience or to rouse its passion.' The fact that the first performance was a 'débâcle' certainly did not help matters.

Despite the title, the *Symphonies* is not 'symphonic'; rather, Stravinsky used the term in its original meaning of the 'sounding together' of a group of instruments. There are three distinct, continuous sections, which are 'taken up in turn by each family of wind instruments'. There are only six brief musical ideas, which continually return, and nothing is developed organically or integrated. This 'mosaic-like, anti-organic form' has been called Stravinsky's most influential work from a structural point of view. Each section has a different tempo, mathematically related in the ratio 2.3.4. The use of folk-like material connects the Symphonies with the Russian period, although the radical nature of the work in general anticipates the neo-classical style.

The Symphonies was revised between 1945 and 1947. This revision has been described as 'even more direct, scanty, and stricter than the original', and as an 'entirely new version', given that parts of the score are very different from the original. The instrumentation was altered, a flute and clarinet taking the place of the alto flute and basset-horn of the original, and the scoring of the whole was revised, with oboes given a more prominent role, and clarinets and brass a less prominent role. Moreover, Stravinsky altered 'some of the pitches and the metrical structure, most of the articulation, [and] some of the rhythmic figuration'. In line with the composer's later practice, the work was also re-barred. Stravinsky reportedly revised the work to 'make it easier for performers as well as for audiences, and that without sacrificing any of my intentions'. Nevertheless, Stephen Walsh asserts that many of the errors from the original score were not corrected, and were simply carried over into the new version. The Symphonies was also transcribed (11 December 1945) for wind orchestra (without clarinets), to be performed alongside the SYMPHONY OF PSALMS for a half-hour CBS broadcast. JOSEPH SCHULTZ

Symphony in C. Composed 1938–40 ((I) composed in Paris; (II) composed in Sancellemoz; (III) composed in Cambridge, Mass.; (IV) composed in Beverly Hills, Hollywood). First performance, 7 November 1940, Chicago, Chicago Symphony Orchestra. Conductor, Igor Stravinsky. Orchestral score dated 19 August 1940. Published 1948, Schott. Commissioned to mark the fiftieth anniversary of the Chicago Symphony Orchestra.

What Stravinsky wanted to be known about the Symphony in C can be found in the 'Programme Notes' assembled by Robert CRAFT. Looking back over thirty years to 1938–9, the note begins with the stark assertion that 'the Symphony in C was composed during the most tragic year of my life' (T&C, 47): his elder daughter, Lyudmila, died of tuberculosis on 30 November 1938, and his wife Catherine STRAVINSKY from the same disease on 2 March 1939. (Stravinsky himself, and his second daughter Milène, were infected, but recovered. His mother Anna also died on 7 June 1939.) 'I survived in the weeks that followed only by working on the Symphony – which is not to say that the music exploits my grief' (T&C, 48). In complementary fashion, he also observed that 'the world events of 1939–40 did not bear tragically on my personal life, but they did disrupt the composition' (T&C, 49). Having completed the first two movements in Europe, Stravinsky composed the third and fourth movements in the UNITED STATES between April and August 1939: the first performance took place more than a year later, in Chicago on 7 November 1940, Stravinsky himself conducting.

The work was commissioned to mark the fiftieth anniversary of the Chicago Symphony Orchestra, and has seemed to some commentators to conform a little too smoothly to that implied requirement not to shock well-heeled subscribers: Stephen Walsh says that 'of all Stravinsky's 1930s scores it is the one which most obviously fits into a conventional celebration within the institutional life of a conservative culture', and 'the very character of the music ... suggests the comfortable glamour of the great symphony concert'

(Walsh 1993, 175). The upheavals recounted above, affecting not only Stravinsky's close family but his entire professional existence as war in Europe loomed, might seem sufficient explanation for music that stands back from iconoclasm. Thirty years later, the composer acknowledged that the Symphony might be neglected, 'because of the unfashionableness of its so-called neo-classicism', and consequent possible faults: 'it may be too episodic, the key-centres may be over-emphasized, and certainly there are too many ostinati', and this follows on from noting the importance of Haydn and Beethoven for the first two movements, as well as some 'Russian sentiment', or 'Tchaikovskian antecedents' in the first movement's E♭ minor episode, as well as in the introduction to the finale. Stravinsky's note even goes along with the idea that the two European movements are complemented by their American successors, since a passage in the finale 'might not have occurred to me before I had known the neon glitter of Los Angeles's boulevards from a speeding automobile' (T&C, 49–50). Most commentaries on the symphony embrace such dualities, encapsulating the essentially modernist aura of what Peter Evans calls its 'simultaneous acknowledgement and denial of classical precedent' (Evans 1974).

'Acknowledgement' involves the presence of four movements – fast, slow, fast and minuet-like in places, fast – which consistently relate to the familiar outlines of traditional symphonic forms; and the presence of tonal references centred around the fundamental C is another acknowledgement of classical precedent. 'Denial' involves much of the harmonic detail: while Stravinsky was working on the Symphony, his colleagues Pierre Souvtchinsky and Alexis Roland-Manuel were assembling materials for the Poetics of Music lectures, which speak of harmonic 'poles of attraction' which 'are no longer within the closed system which was the diatonic system', and which can be brought together 'without being compelled to conform to the exigencies of tonality' (Poet, 36–8). Even when the music is purely diatonic to C major, as with the oboe's first statement of the first movement's main theme (from bar 26) and its string accompaniment, texture, voice-leading and the role of the bass line are all at odds with traditional tonal writing, and the bold dissonances of the movement's final chords reinforce the music's distance from that tradition. The Symphony also keeps its distance from the starker adumbrations of tragedy and lament that Stravinsky had provided in The Rite of Spring and Oedipus Rex, and would again in Threni and other late works; the poised yet florid melodism of the slow movement, followed by the sprightly elegance of the third movement's dance measures might also seem to keep the focus firmly on courtly entertainment and formality. Yet there is ample drama, especially in the increasingly turbulent 'Russian' episode of the first movement, and more than a touch of melancholy reflectiveness, almost amounting to nostalgia, in the way the finale winds down to a peaceful, yet harmonically unstable, chorale.

Like Les Noces, Symphonies of Wind Instruments, Apollon Musagète and Symphony of Psalms, Symphony in C ends in a spirit of magically resonant understatement: and, of these five very different works, the three with 'symphony' in their title all treat C major in ways 'no longer within the closed system which was the diatonic system'. Preserving the concept 'symphonic' in the age

459

of modernity involved positive questioning of what the concept might mean when the primary structural and expressive force of its history before 1900 could no longer function. Naming a key, or a tonic note, in his title, which the composer did several times during his neo-classical phase, fits with the delight in pointing up the pervading musical ambivalences which came so naturally to Stravinsky. These are also a verbally prominent presence in *Poetics of Music* just at the time that the Symphony in C was giving as resourceful a compositional demonstration of ambivalence's teasing implications as could be imagined. 'Real' C major does not haunt Stravinsky's Symphony in C like an unhappy ghost from times past: it actively transforms itself into the newly flexible mode of musical expression that, by 1938, Stravinsky had triumphantly made his own.   ARNOLD WHITTALL

Peter Evans, 'Music of the European mainstream: 1940–1960', in *Oxford History of Music*, vol. X: *The Modern Age, 1890–1960* (Oxford University Press, 1974).
Stephen Walsh, *The Music of Stravinsky* (London: Routledge, 1988).

Symphony in E♭ Major for large orchestra, op. 1. Composed June 1905 – end of 1907, USTILUG – ST PETERSBURG; rev. 1913. First performance, 22 January / 4 February 1908, St Petersburg (16/29 April 1907 – movements II and III only). Conductor, Hugo Wahrlich. Published 1914, Jurgenson, with the dedication 'To my dear teacher Nikolay Andreyevich Rimsky-Korsakov'.

Order of movements: (I) Allegro moderato, E♭ (II) Scherzo. Allegretto, B♭ (III) Largo, G♯ (IV) Finale. Allegro molto, E♭.

Stravinsky was 23 years old when, having produced only one large-form composition (the four-movement PIANO SONATA in F♯ Minor) and with no orchestral experience behind him, he dared to start composing a symphony. The ambitious beginner seemed to be spurred on by the example of his then ideal – Alexander GLAZUNOV, the ST PETERSBURG wunderkind and RIMSKY-KORSAKOV's favourite, who finished his First symphony at the age of 16! Stravinsky's work on his own Symphony, op. 1, beginning in the early summer of 1905, lasted two and a half years, so that in parallel he managed to finish op. 2 (*The Faun and the Shepherdess*) and to begin op. 3 (SCHERZO FANTASTIQUE). Stravinsky received his first lessons in mastering sonata form in August 1903 from Rimsky-Korsakov, in Krapachukha, while working on 'the first part of a sonatina', as mentioned in the AUTOBIOGRAPHY. Then, from the autumn of 1905, the mentor closely followed the progress of the Symphony during their weekly meetings. Rimsky-Korsakov also took care of the performance of this first opus for his pupil. First, on 16/29 March 1907, he arranged a test run-through performance of the second and third movements, 'the only two, which yet existed in fully scored and revised form' (SCS, 103), in the course of a closed morning rehearsal of the Imperial Court Orchestra under Hugo Wahrlich at the Hall of Court Meetings. The complete Symphony was then premièred on 22 January / 4 February 1908 with the same performers, in the twenty-first programme of the Musical Novelties series. Rimsky attended both performances, sitting next to Stravinsky and carefully commenting on the details of ORCHESTRATION. The autographs of the Symphony, relating to the various stages of the compositional process, reflect Stravinsky's tireless efforts to improve the work – from the first draft score (1905), to the 'white' score

(1907) used at the première. Interestingly, there are traces of intense editorial labour in this 'final' text of the Symphony, apparently in the hand of Rimsky-Korsakov, which Stravinsky took into account in the revisions he made in 1913, prior to the work's publication. With the Symphony, this academically proficient, 'major' work, Stravinsky officially entered the musical life of the Russian capital.

Reviews of Stravinsky's first major public concert, where the Symphony was performed along with the vocal-symphonic suite *The Faun and the Shepherdess*, were mainly benevolent. The first critics unanimously noted the Scherzo as being the most successful movement of the Symphony, and praised the inventive orchestration as well as the sure formal shaping, and especially 'the cheerful, joyous turn of musical thought'. In 1912, when Stravinsky had already become a European celebrity, Nikolay Myaskovsky published a detailed analysis of the Symphony. Apart from some flaws ('pleonasms' and 'excessive mechanicalness' in the first movement), he emphasised the undoubted merits of a work which already demonstrated the genesis of its author's creative individuality (Muzïka, 91, 1912, 695–703; PRK, I, 474–7).

At the same time, the Symphony in E♭ Major is 'still very much student work' (SCS, 104), through which the young composer deliberately absorbed both the Russian and Austro-German traditions. By 1907, Stravinsky was already familiar with the symphonies of Brahms and Bruckner, as well as the music of WAGNER, whom he adored in his youth. Commenting in his *Autobiography* on the influences on his early symphony, Stravinsky named TCHAIKOVSKY, Rimsky-Korsakov and Wagner, but conceded that the decisive examples were the symphonies by Glazunov, the undisputed leader of the genre in Russia during that era (Auto, 21–2).

The 'correct' Glazunovian model, particularly the Fifth (B♭) and Eighth (E♭) symphonies, is clearly discerned in Stravinsky's Symphony, with its well-balanced structure in each of the four movements, conventional contrapuntal and motive elaboration, and 'lucid key scheme, bright, effective orchestration' (SCS, 104). The vigorous first, second and fourth movements are the most Glazunovian, whilst in the expressive Largo, Stravinsky pays a generous tribute to Tchaikovsky: Stephen Walsh hears here 'heavy echoes of the *Queen of Spades*' (SCS, 85), to which should also be added the Sixth symphony. In the second movement, reminiscences of the Scherzo from Tchaikovsky's Fourth symphony, along with traces of BORODIN and MUSSORGSKY (*Limoges Market!*) are in evidence. The impact of Wagner (*Die Meistersinger von Nürnberg*) is most direct in the festive-march episodes of the first and fourth movements. In the development section of the Finale, there is also a quasi-Brahmsian dramatic theme weaved in thirds and sixths (Figure 11) but which suddenly – in a triumph of kuchkist spirit! – is replaced by the Russian comic tune, *Chicher Yacher*, later to become the first of the *Three Little Songs* (*Souvenirs de mon enfance*). In the score of the Symphony (Figure 13), the composer subtitled the melody: 'Chicher Yacher sobiralsia na vecher' ('Chicher Yacher, He Was Going to the Feast'). Rimsky-Korsakov's presence is felt throughout the Symphony, especially in the harmonic language, and in specific thematic allusions – for example, Bobïl's motif from *The Snow Maiden* in one of the themes of the Scherzo (Figure 7). Nevertheless, there is the powerful energy of the syncopated rhythms here, by means of which Stravinsky already seemed to be attempting to escape from the fetters of 'square-cut' rhythmic patterns.

The gestation of the Symphony in E♭ Major was accompanied by a counterpoint of important events in the personal life of the maturing composer: graduation from the university, an engagement and marriage with Katya Nosenko (Catherine STRAVINSKY), and the birth of their first child Fyodor less than two months before the première in the spring of 1907. The Symphony in E♭ Major became for Stravinsky not simply 'a final examination in Rimsky-Korsakov's class' (Savenko 2001, 18), but, more importantly, marked a symbolic milestone in his gradual creative evolution. Stravinsky admitted later that the technique he had acquired in the course of composing the Symphony laid the strongest foundation for him to build upon: 'No matter what the subject may be, there is only one course for the beginner; he must at first accept a discipline imposed from without, but only as the means of obtaining freedom for, and strengthening himself in, his own method of expression' (Auto, 20).   NATALIA BRAGINSKAYA

Svetlana Savenko, Mir Stravinskogo ('Stravinsky's World') (Moscow: Kompozitor, 2001).

Symphony in Three Movements. Composed 1942–5. First performance, 24 January 1946, New York Philharmonic Orchestra, Carnegie Hall, New York. Conductor, Igor Stravinsky. Published 1946, Associated Music Publishers / Schott, New York. Dedicated to the New York Philharmonic Symphony Society.

'You have several times referred to your Symphony in Three Movements as a "war symphony". In what way is the music marked by the impression of world events?' (Dial 50). Robert CRAFT's question was obviously not irrelevant to a composition begun in 1942 and finished in 1945. But the work was even more immediately an American symphony, commissioned by the New York Philharmonic Society. Stravinsky was 57 when he left Europe for the UNITED STATES in 1939, so he was hardly likely to reinvent himself there so radically as a composer that all connections with his earlier music could be discounted. Nevertheless, Symphony in Three Movements distils and intensifies the boldly coloured and forcefully rhythmic qualities of the shorter pieces he first worked on once settled in LOS ANGELES, including TANGO for Chamber Orchestra, DANSES CONCERTANTES, CIRCUS POLKA and SCÈNES DE BALLET; and it is far from irrelevant to his wartime music that one of his first acts in CALIFORNIA, late in 1939, was to agree terms with Walt Disney for the use of The RITE OF SPRING in Fantasia (1940).

It was perhaps with all this in mind that, in the Conversations, Stravinsky emphasised the cinematic as much as the war connections, claiming that the middle movement was originally intended for the 'Apparition of the Virgin' scene in the FILM of Franz Werfel's Song of Bernadette – in the event, Stravinsky never worked on that film score – and that the middle part of the first movement 'was conceived as a series of instrumental conversations to accompany a cinematographic scene showing the Chinese people scratching and digging in the fields'. Even more explicitly, part of the third movement was 'a musical reaction to the newsreels and documentaries that I had seen of goose-stepping soldiers. The square march-beat, the brass-band instrumentation, the grotesque crescendo in the tuba – these are all related to those repellent pictures.'

After this, it might seem surprising that Stravinsky should then declare that 'the Symphony is not programmatic. Composers combine notes. That is all' (Dial, 50–2).

Although the pictorial specifics he instanced might pass the present-day listener by, reference to such contexts underlines the heterogeneous nature of a work he originally intended to be a Concerto for Orchestra, and whose sketches were headed 'Sinfonia concertante'. Yet, even if we acknowledge the appropriateness of David Schiff's description of a work that glories in 'defying categories, it seems simultaneously Dionysian and Apollonian, experimental and primal, élite and popular, anarchic and affirmative' (Schiff 2013, 197), the end-product is far from anti-symphonic. Dionysus might be more dominant over Apollo than was the case in Symphony in C, but the Symphony in Three Movements still acknowledges the classicising impetus propounded in the AUTOBIOGRAPHY and the POETICS OF MUSIC lectures. The music might even be seen as Stravinsky's response to a particular technical challenge: how to remain true to the classical element in traditional symphonic composition without writing four movements or declaring an overall tonality for the work.

The first movement is predominantly turbulent, composing out a warlike struggle between dissonantly related pitch centres, the G and A♭ that span the initial, oft-repeated flourish, standing as dominants to the more fundamental C and D♭. The movement makes an episodic yet sonata-form-evoking drama out of its progress to an uneasily quiet C major ending (not a pure triad), and the euphorically energetic third movement begins in the same harmonic region of C, though here clashing E naturals and E flats are prominent, indicating a 'flat-side' tendency driving the music towards a concluding harmonic battle, which sees the timpani hammering out Cs and Es while the rest of the orchestra enforces preparations for a final D♭-rooted chord – a full triad (to which the timpani contribute an A♭) plus an E♭. Stravinsky gave a certain emphasis to recalling the first movement's basic material in the finale, if only to point up the flexibility with which the successive stages of each, and their incremental effects on the whole, are designed; and it could also embody a not-so-implicit critique of classicism as integrated organicism, affinities with the structures of his most radical pre-neo-classical compositions – The Rite of Spring, SYMPHONIES OF WIND INSTRUMENTS – foreshadowing the mosaic-like formal designs that would accompany his adoption of TWELVE-NOTE TECHNIQUE after 1950.

The central Andante of Symphony in Three Movements also highlights clashing major and minor thirds in an octatonic context where D rather than C is the tonal centre, and the movement's initial idea contrasts these harmonic clashes with a gently lyrical melodic phrase that is, in essence, a descending D major scale. The florid solo wind writing, with prominent harp in attendance, recalls the vein of Apollonian elegance with which Stravinsky was able to broaden the notion of classicism in the direction of ancient Greek philosophy and myth. But, in Symphony in Three Movements, the whole Andante has the effect of an Interlude – a title the composer gave to the seven-bar passage linking the second movement to the third.

Keeping to the war theme in the *Conversations*, Stravinsky allowed Craft to preserve his tendency to waspish self-put-downs, suggesting that the 'final, albeit rather too commercial, D♭ sixth chord – instead of the expected C – tokens my extra exuberance in the Allied triumph' (*Dial*, 51–2). The ending is certainly as distant as can be imagined from the downbeat and often C majorish conclusions of many earlier works. In Stephen Walsh's judgement, 'the symphony finale, with its dazzling fugal and imitative exchanges, breathes a refinement that civilizes the ferocity, without in any way drawing its sting. It is neoclassicism without fancy dress and come of age' (SSE, 187). The notion of ferocious civility – in other words, of modern classicism – pinpoints the Stravinskian essence which he sustained across all his stylistic phases; it is especially potent in the Symphony in Three Movements, perhaps the least abstract of all the composer's non-theatrical concert works.

ARNOLD WHITTALL

David Schiff, 'Everyone's Rite (1939–46)', in Hermann Danuser and Heidy Zimmermann (eds.), *Avatar of Modernity: The Rite of Spring Reconsidered* (London: Paul Sacher Foundation / Boosey & Hawkes, 2013), 174–97.

Symphony of Psalms. Composed 1930, revised 1948. First performance, 13 December 1930, Société Philharmonique de Bruxelles, Palais des Beaux-Arts, Brussels. First published 1930, Édition Russe de Musique, Mixed Choir and Orchestra.

Text: Psalms 38:13–14; 39:2–4; 150.

The origin of the *Symphony of Psalms* was a commission from Sergey KOUSSEVITZKY at the end of 1929, for a symphony to celebrate the fiftieth anniversary of the foundation of the Boston Symphony Orchestra in the following year, a project initiated by Stravinsky himself earlier that year. Initially, the plan was for a purely orchestral work, but by January it had become not only choral but sacred: the composer made a note of verses 13–15 of Psalm 39 after reworking a set of earlier songs (*Souvenirs de mon enfance*), and the words of the dedication begin with the observation that it was composed 'à la gloire de DIEU': here is the real starting point of the work. Stravinsky had had the idea for a symphony based on Psalm texts for some time, as he noted in *Dialogues and a Diary*, and made this commission his opportunity.

Initial sketches for the work were made in January 1930, but the process of composition was interrupted by a series of international concert tours, and Stravinsky only returned to it in April, when he sketched out the final movement, and, after further touring and recording sessions, the rest was completed during the summer in PARIS and the resort of Charavines-les-Bains. He played it through to Koussevitzky (and Gavriyil Païchadze and Arthur LOURIÉ) in August. The title of the work took some time to be formulated exactly, and has considerable bearing on the way the composer wished the piece to be understood. Stravinsky's original idea was *Symphonie psalmodique*, which was queried by the ethnomusicologist André SCHAEFFNER. The composer then wondered in a letter to Schaeffner whether *Symphonie psalmique* would be better, but noted that:

To me the word 'psalmique' indicates only that the symphony contains some psalms sung by soloists or choirs; that is all. I was looking for a brief title which would seize the special character of my Symphony. In short, this is not a symphony into which I have put some psalms which are sung, but on the contrary, it is the singing of the psalms which I symphonize, and that is difficult to say in two words.

The text for the Symphony is composed of verses 13 and 14 of Psalm 38 (Part 1); verses 2, 3 and 4 of Psalm 39 (Part 2); and the whole of Psalm 150 (Part 3). Robert Siohan has written that 'the Symphony of Psalms gives the impression of being inspired by a harsh, strong feeling that has grown out of the anguish of mankind, punctuated by occasional lightning flashes revealing the countenance of Jehovah'. This echoes Stravinsky's own words about the work: 'The Psalms are poems of exaltation, but also of anger and judgment, and even of curses.' Thus it is that the serene calm of the last movement – one of the most extraordinary accomplishments in Western music of the twentieth century in its suspension of time in static adoration and incantatory contemplation – has been won through the rigorous contrapuntal workings of the first two, and the composer himself related this to the kind of 'apotheosis that had become a pattern in my music since the epithalamium at the end of Les Noces'. He also referred to the symbolism of the 'pyramid of fugues' in the second movement, whose canticum novum is the Alleluia which opens and closes the final movement, and the Allegro section of the third movement, a literal depiction of the chariot of Elijah ascending into heaven. Never before, Stravinsky noted, had he ever written anything quite as literal.

Stravinsky began composing the work in Slavonic, and only later changed to Latin. Though he specifically pointed out that he was not consciously aware of 'Phrygian modes, Gregorian chants, Byzantinisms' while composing, he said too that such influences may well have been present in his subconscious. These words, together with his observation that the 'Laudate Dominum' section is 'a prayer to the Russian image of the infant Christ with orb and sceptre', serve to reinforce the strong Russo-Byzantine splendour of the music, otherwise almost inexplicable since the text is in Latin and the musical processes undeniably largely Western and pseudo-Baroque in origin; Stephen Walsh has described the work as a 'gesture of solidarity with the divine order: antique songs of praise cast into the grandest of modern classical forms'.

The scoring is as important here as it is in the MASS: there are no violins or violas, so that the upper registers are entirely coloured by the woodwind and brass. (Gilbert Amy speaks persuasively of a 'ritual instrumentation' in the Symphony, an 'archetypal use of certain sonorities', as also in the Mass, THRENI and REQUIEM CANTICLES.)

It is in many ways the relationship between choir and orchestra that makes this work so radical. Stravinsky said that he wanted these two elements to be 'on an equal footing, neither outweighing the other', moving away from symphonic models of the past, yet retaining what he called the 'periodic order' of the symphony. The work is built, according to the composer, on the sequences of two minor thirds, linked by a major third, which have their origin in the motive for trumpet and harp at the beginning of the Allegro in the third movement. As with a number of other works by Stravinsky, the octatonic scale is employed during the course of the work, particularly in the first movement. This movement, appropriately described by Amy as 'litanic', is in an ambiguous E minor, and forms an extended prelude to the massive double fugue in C minor that is the second movement, whose first theme is built from the same four-note motif used in the first. The movement ends on E♭, and the third, apotheotic, movement is in C.

The revision undertaken in 1948 was mainly to correct misprints and missing indications for articulation and so on, but it also benefitted from the advice of Nadia BOULANGER, who persuaded the composer to make some alterations to the tempi for the final movement, and some of the text setting. Yet to be fully investigated is the relationship between the *Symphony of Psalms* and the *Concerto Spirituale* for choir, piano and orchestra by Arthur Lourié, written in 1929, and which may well have served as a model for Stravinsky's work; the similarities are striking.   IVAN MOODY

Gilbert Amy, 'Aspects of the religious music of Igor Stravinsky', in Jann Pasler (ed.), *Confronting Stravinsky* (Berkeley and Los Angeles: University of California Press, 1986), 195–206.
Charles M. Joseph, *Stravinsky Inside Out* (New Haven and London: Yale University Press, 2001).
Robert Siohan, *Stravinsky* (Paris, 1959).
SCS; SSC, I

T

Talich, Václav (born Kroměříž, 28 May 1883; died Beroun, 16 March 1961). Czech conductor. After studying the violin with Ševčík in Prague, Talich became leader of the Berlin Philharmonic in 1903–4 where he was inspired by Arthur Nikisch to take up conducting. He first appeared with the Czech Philharmonic in 1918 and was the orchestra's Chief Conductor from 1919 to 1941. In 1926–36, he was also Chief Conductor of the Stockholm Philharmonic. After World War II, Talich's career was disrupted by accusations of Nazi collaboration and a campaign waged by the Communist Culture Minister, Zdeněk Nejedlý. With the Czech Philharmonic, Talich conducted the Capriccio with Stravinsky as soloist (26 February 1930, at a concert for President Masaryk's eightieth birthday), as well as Fireworks, Petrushka and Pribaoutki (all in 1924) and The Rite of Spring (18 September 1926).   NIGEL SIMEONE

Yvetta Koláčková (ed.), *Česká filharmonie 100 plus 10* (Prague: Academia, 2006)

Tango for piano solo. Composed 1940, Beverly Hills. Published 1941, Mercury Music Corporation (New York) / Schott (Mainz). Transcribed for violin and piano by Samuel Dushkin in collaboration with the composer. First performance, 31 March 1941, New York, by Dushkin with Harry Kaufman. Published 2000, Schott. First ensemble arrangement scored by Felix Guenther. First performance, 10 July 1941, Philadelphia. Conductor, Benny Goodman. Published 1941, Mercury Music Corporation. Arranged by Stravinsky for nineteen instruments in 1953. First performance 19 October 1953, Los Angeles. Conductor, Robert Craft. Published 1954, Mercury Music Corporation / Schott. Arranged for two pianos by Victor Babin. Published 1962, Mercury Music Corporation / Schott.

Originally intended as a commercial 'hit song' with dance band, *Tango* first appeared as a solo piano piece after several aborted attempts at setting lyrics to the melody. Stravinsky arranged it for nineteen instruments in June–July 1953 to supplement an Evenings on the Roof concert of his so-called Jazz music. The work was transposed from D minor to E minor in part to accommodate the range of the guitar which features prominently in the arrangement.

JEREMY COLEMAN

Tansman, Alexander (born Łódź, 19 June 1897; died Paris, 15 November 1986). Polish-born composer and pianist, of Jewish heritage. Tansman lived and worked in Paris for most of his career, taking French citizenship in 1938. With the Nazi invasion, he left for America with his second wife, the pianist Colette Cras-Tansman, settling in Los Angeles in the autumn of 1941. They soon began what became an exceptionally close friendship with the

Stravinskys, Igor furthermore admiring Colette as a pianist and interpreter of his music. Tansman introduced Stravinsky to his cousin, the lawyer Aaron Sapiro, who from June 1942 became Stravinsky's attorney. Both composers were involved in Nathaniel Shilkret's *Genesis Suite* (Tansman composing 'Adam and Eve', and Stravinsky BABEL).

The Tansmans returned to Paris in 1946 where, drawing on his intimate knowledge of Stravinsky's aesthetics, Tansman wrote a study of the composer's life and works: first published in French in 1948 as *Vie et oeuvres d'Igor Stravinsky*, it then appeared the following year in a translation by Charles and Thérèse Bleefield as *Igor Stravinsky: The Man and his Music*. Besides Tansman's first-hand knowledge of the creation of *Genesis Suite*, the book provides unique insights, particularly, in the creation of the SYMPHONY IN THREE MOVEMENTS and the EBONY CONCERTO. Unfortunately, the two's friendship ended when Tansman wrote to Stravinsky on 1 June 1953 (just months after Colette's death), expressing regret that Stravinsky's CANTATA included a setting of 'Tomorrow Shall Be My Dancing Day' with its anti-Semitic verse. Stravinsky took offence, and never replied; three years later, when by chance he encountered Tansman in London during a recording session, Stravinsky refused Tansman's proffered hand of friendship. Though Tansman confessed to finding Stravinsky's work after The RAKE'S PROGRESS incomprehensible, he continued to value his earlier music as well as their past friendship. He wrote candidly yet affectionately about Stravinsky in his incomplete and posthumously published autobiography *Regards en arrière*.   DANIEL JAFFÉ

Alexander Tansman, *Regards en arrière: itinéraire d'un musicien cosmopolite au XXe siècle*, ed. Cédric Segond-Genovesi (Château-Gontier: Éditions Aedam Musicae, 2013).

Tarantella,   for piano. Composed 14 October 1898. Published 1970, in Valeriy Smirnov, *Tvorcheskoye formirovaniye I. F. Stravinskovo* (Leningrad: Muzïka, 1970). Dedication: 'Dedicated by the author to D. Rudnev'.

Stravinsky's earliest surviving 'composition' is no more than an eighteen-bar fragment, evidence of the teenage composer's attempts at notating, most probably, a favourite improvisation based upon a domestic or humorous event. The Russian musicologist Valeriy Smirnov, who discovered *Tarantella* and first presented the 'work' in 1970, attributes its pentatonic melody to the Georgian dance *lezginka*, and the left-hand fifths to GLAZUNOV'S recently premièred ballet *Raymonda* (1896/7). *Tarantella*'s greater significance may lie in its early demonstration of a *modus operandi* with which Stravinsky makes the vital creative leap from improvisation to composition, and, crucially, he uses the piano as the means of doing so.   GRAHAM GRIFFITHS

Graham Griffiths, *Stravinsky's Piano: Genesis of a Musical Language* (Cambridge University Press, 2013).

Valeriy Smirnov, *Tvorchestkoye formirovaniye I.F. Stravinskogo* ('Stravinsky's Creative Development') (Leningrad: Muzïka, 1970).

Marie Stravinsky (ed.), *Abécédaire Stravinsky* (Geneva: Éditions la Baconnière, 2018).

Tchaikovsky, Pyotr Il'ich   (born Kamsko-Votkinsk, Vyatka province, 25 April / 7 May 1840; died St Petersburg, 25 October / 6 November 1893). Russian composer; a major influence on and lifelong idol of Stravinsky. Tchaikovsky respected the musical talents of Stravinsky's father, and the former likewise 'seems always to have been lionised by the Stravinsky family' (Fyodor

468

STRAVINSKY was even a pallbearer at Tchaikovsky's funeral). Sergey DIAGHILEV, who was the fourth cousin of Stravinsky, was related to Tchaikovsky through marriage. Stravinsky saw *The Sleeping Beauty* when he was 7 or 8 and was 'enchanted' by it. He saw Tchaikovsky only once, and then at a distance, 'but his white hair, broad shoulders and plump back remained another abiding image'. The composer later called this glimpse of his hero 'one of my most treasured memories'. His death a fortnight later affected Stravinsky greatly. Later, he became acquainted with Tchaikovsky's brothers.

Diaghilev commissioned Stravinsky to arrange *The Sleeping Beauty* (and orchestrate two of its numbers) for a 1921 production, which he undertook enthusiastically. During this period, Stravinsky wrote an open letter to Diaghilev extolling the merits of both project and composer (notable at a time when Tchaikovsky was considered unfashionable). The commission also inspired the composer to write the OPERA MAVRA, dedicated to Tchaikovsky, GLINKA and PUSHKIN and utilising the vocal styles of Glinka, Dargomïzhsky and Tchaikovsky, whose combination of 'the popular element and Western musical principles' was far more appealing than the 'stale naturalism and amateurism' of the Moguchaya Kuchka. In 1941, Stravinsky adapted 'The Bluebird' (pas de deux from Act III of *The Sleeping Beauty*) for small orchestra for the Ballet Theatre in New York.

Stravinsky's most important homage to Tchaikovsky was the BALLET *The Fairy's Kiss* (1928), a work commissioned for performance on the thirty-fifth anniversary of the elder composer's death; because of this circumstance, and given that Stravinsky was free to select 'both subject and scenario', he used Tchaikovsky's music as the work's basis, and dedicated it to the composer. The ballet is an ORCHESTRATION and arrangement of a number of Tchaikovsky's songs and piano pieces, but Stravinsky altered this source material more freely than he had done in PULCINELLA (1920), adumbrating it with his own music written in the style of Tchaikovsky to create a 'collage' work (even the plot, taken from Hans Christian Andersen's *The Ice Maiden*, shares similarities with *The Sleeping Beauty*). The music fully displays Stravinsky's passion for Tchaikovsky's 'wonderful talent', although he was later to remark that it was 'saccharine salon music'.

The self-confessed compositional influence of Tchaikovsky is apparent in many of Stravinsky's works, from the early SYMPHONY IN E♭ MAJOR (1907), *The Faun and the Shepherdess* (1907) and *The* FIREBIRD (1910), to the later JEU DE CARTES (1937) and SYMPHONY IN C (1940). These influences include variation techniques and matters of orchestration. The composer particularly admired Tchaikovsky's melodies, his 'directness and good taste', and his ability to conjure a time and milieu without recourse to 'archaeological research' and 'conscious and laboured *pasticcio*'. Nevertheless, Stravinsky was also occasionally critical of the elder composer, especially his 'characteristically predictable phrase structure', and went as far as to call the *Manfred* Symphony 'the dullest piece imaginable'. In addition to this creative influence, Tchaikovsky was the only other composer whose music Stravinsky regularly conducted – indeed, he commemorated the hundredth anniversary of Tchaikovsky's birth in 1940 by conducting the Second Symphony in various performances and recordings.   JOSEPH SCHULTZ

Tchelitcheff, Pavel (born Kaluga, 21 September 1898; died Grottaferrata, nr Rome, 31 July 1957). Russian-born Surrealist painter and set designer. Stravinsky became acquainted with him in Berlin in 1922, where they would often meet with Tchelitcheff's mentor at the time, Souvtchinsky. Tchelitcheff was the set designer for Apollo (in June 1942 in Buenos Aires) and *Balustrade* (Balanchine's choreography for the Concerto in D for Violin and Orchestra in 1941), while Stravinsky stated that he would have been the ideal decorator for Perséphone. Despite his admiration for Tchelitcheff as an artist, Stravinsky found him a 'queer and difficult character', due to his superstitions and mystical leanings. Apparently, Tchelitcheff, for his part, compared the composer to a 'prancing grasshopper'. KATERINA LEVIDOU

Louis Andriessen and Elmer Schönberger, *The Apollonian Clockwork: On Stravinsky*, trans. Jeff Hamburg, preface Jonathan Cross (Amsterdam University Press, 2006).

Teatro La Fenice. Opera house in Venice, first opened in 1792, and reopened in 1837 and 2003, following devastating fires. It saw the premières of some of the most celebrated operas of Rossini, Bellini and Verdi, including the first-night flop of *La traviata* in 1853. Stravinsky first appeared on stage at La Fenice on 8 September 1925, playing his Piano Sonata. On 11 September 1934, he conducted his Capriccio there, with his son Soulima Stravinsky as piano soloist. In 1951, seventeen years later to the day, he conducted the première at La Fenice of The Rake's Progress. He would return to conduct a double bill of Oedipus Rex and The Rite of Spring on 19 September 1958. BEN EARLE

Théâtre des Champs-Elysées. Situated in an Art Deco building at 15 avenue Montaigne in Paris, the Théâtre des Champs-Elysées was founded by journalist Gabriel Astruc, designed by Auguste Perret and opened in 1913. For Stephen Walsh, it demonstrated Astruc's 'confidence in art' and was 'an expression of the contemporary spirit' (SCS, 201). The opening gala concert, on 2 April 1913, consisted of a French musical feast, with two orchestral symphonic poems, Claude Debussy's *Prélude à l'après-midi d'un faune* and Paul Dukas's *L'apprenti sorcier*, followed by Gabriel Fauré's *La naissance de Vénus*, Vincent d'Indy's *Le camp de Wallenstein* and Camille Saint-Saëns's *Phaeton*.

In its opening year, the theatre housed the Ballets Russes in what was the company's fifth season, and its staging of the première of Stravinsky's seminal The Rite of Spring on 29 May 1913 brought it widespread attention. The theatre had received some positive reactions regarding its acoustics and Ravel wrote to Stravinsky, who was working on *The Rite* in Clarens, to inform him that 'the acoustics . . . are so perfect that you can even hear the refinement of Berlioz's harmonies' (SCS, 201). Significantly, the season had opened on 15 May 1913 with a restaging of Stravinsky's Firebird and the première of Debussy's *Jeux*.

Stravinsky's music returned to this theatre, with the composer as conductor, for a Gala revival of *Les Noces* in 1924, and the theatre was later used in the film *Coco Chanel and Igor Stravinsky* (2009), directed by Jan Kounen. HELEN JULIA MINORS

Nigel Simeone, *Paris: A Musical Gazetteer* (New Haven: Yale University Press, 2000).

Théâtre du Châtelet. Situated at the Place du Châtelet in Paris, this was one of two theatres planned by Baron Haussmann, who was chosen by Napoleon III to manage the regeneration of the city. Designed by architect Gabriel Davioud and opened in 1862, the theatre was originally intended to seat 3,000 spectators, but now seats 2,500, since its refurbishment in 1989. The Ballets Russes held a number of premières there in 1909, 1911, 1912 and 1917, including Stravinsky's Petrushka (13 June 1911) and Satie's *Parade* (18 May 1917). Prior to this, Stravinsky orchestrated two movements from *Les Sylphides* for Diaghilev, which were staged at the theatre on 2 June 1909. It was also host to performances by Vaslav Nijinsky, in the title role in *Petrushka*, as well as to productions by established choreographers and dancers, including Anna Pavlova, and Tamara Karsavina.   HELEN JULIA MINORS

Nigel Simeone, *Paris: A Musical Gazetteer* (New Haven: Yale University Press, 2000). SCW.

Théâtre Femina. Situated at no. 90 on the Champs-Elysées, Paris, this theatre had a particular clientele, not least because, much like the Savoy Theatre in London, it was housed inside a hotel – in this case, the Hôtel Femina. The theatre, which consisted of a large room with proscenium stage, opened in 1907, and from 1911 onwards focused on operetta and other light repertoire, before closing in 1929. As Taruskin outlines (SRT, II, 1539–41), this theatre attracted Russian artists of all kinds, as well as the general public. It came to public attention in 1921, as it hosted a variety show entitled 'Le Théâtre de la Chauve-Souris à Moscou' ('The Bat Theatre of Moscow'), which had its origins in songs sung in the cellar of the Moscow Art Theatre. The presence of this theatre in Paris gives testimony to the growing Russian artistic activity during the time of Stravinsky's collaborative work in the city. Notable were the décor and set designs by Diaghilev's long-time friend Sergey Sudeykin (1882–1946), the same designer as for Florent Schmitt's *Le tragédie de Salomé* (1913), a work which was subsequently dedicated to Stravinsky. Diaghilev, who was invited to the rehearsal of this new production by Sudeykin, brought Stravinsky with him.   HELEN JULIA MINORS

Philippe Chauveau, *Les Théâtres parisiens disparus, 1402–1986* (Paris: Éditions de l'Amandier, 1999).

Théâtre Sarah Bernhardt. This theatre, which opened in 1862 as the Théâtre Lyrique Impérial, was renamed many times, its seventh title – Théâtre Sarah Bernhardt – being given in 1898 when the celebrated French actress Sarah Bernhardt began her two-decade career producing new works there. The origins of the theatre are significant as it was one of two nineteenth-century theatres built by Baron Haussmann (the other being the famous Théâtre du Châtelet). It housed a number of premières for the Ballets Russes, including Stravinsky's Oedipus Rex conducted by the composer on 30 May 1927. Other premières by the company included Satie's *Mercure* (1 June 1927) and both Prokofiev's *Le Pas d'acier* (7 June 1927) and *Le fils prodigue* (21 May 1929). It was also the venue for the European première of Stravinsky's Apollon Musagète (12 June 1928).   HELEN JULIA MINORS

Roger Nichols, *The Harlequin Years: Music in Paris 1917–1929* (London: Thames and Hudson, 2002).
Nigel Simeone, *Paris: A Musical Gazetteer* (New Haven: Yale University Press, 2000).

Thomas, Dylan (Marlais) (born Swansea, 27 October 1914; died New York, 9 November 1953). Welsh poet. While negotiating a new OPERA commission in 1953, Stravinsky invited Thomas to prepare the libretto. On 22 May, they met in Boston, where Thomas proposed a post-apocalyptic scenario involving a new Adam and Eve. However, before Thomas could complete the libretto, he died prematurely as a result of his struggles with alcoholism and diabetes. The following year, Stravinsky composed IN MEMORIAM DYLAN THOMAS, a setting of Thomas' most famous poem, the villanelle 'Do Not Go Gentle into that Good Night', for tenor and chamber ensemble.   MATTHEW PAUL CARLSON

SSE

Thomson, Virgil (born Kansas City, 25 November 1896; died New York City, 30 September 1989). American composer and critic. He met Stravinsky while studying with Nadia BOULANGER in 1921 in PARIS. His musical style, much influenced by that of SATIE and French NEO-CLASSICISM, was of no interest to Stravinsky, but they nevertheless got on well together, and the Russian composer had no doubts about Thomson's critical influence. While he wrote for various publications, his criticism is best known from his time as chief music critic of the *New York Herald Tribune* (1940–54). In 'The Official Stravinsky' (1936), he referred to the composer's AUTOBIOGRAPHY as 'brief and smug' and as inducing the feeling that 'Mr. Stravinsky has just swallowed the canary and doesn't mind our knowing it' (Kostelanetz 2002, 104). On the question of composition, he found it 'strange that [Stravinsky] should continually pose himself such limited problems, that he should never for once really want to do something large and easy. But restriction is apparently of his nature.' He wrote of Stravinsky in 1966 as 'a major modern force' from 1910 onwards, and as 'the most admired living composer', while reflecting waspishly on the unusual literary relationship linking Stravinsky and CRAFT.   EDWARD CAMPBELL

Richard Kostelanetz (ed.), *Virgil Thomson: A Reader: Selected Writings, 1924–1984* (Abingdon: Routledge, 2002).
Virgil Thomson, '"Craft-Igor" and the whole Stravinsky', review of *Stravinsky: The Composer and His Works* by Eric Walter White, *The New Yorker*, 15 December 1966.

Three Easy Pieces for piano duet 'left hand easy' (1914–15). Composed: (I + II) September – 30 November 1914, CLARENS (III) 6 March 1915, Château d'Oex. First (public) performance 22 April 1918, Lausanne, Conservatoire: N. Rossi and Ernest ANSERMET (with the FIVE EASY PIECES); 8 November 1919, Lausanne, José Iturbi and the composer. Published 1917, Ad. Henn, Geneva and J. & W. Chester Ltd, London. Dedication: (I) Alfredo CASELLA (II) Erik SATIE (III) Sergey DIAGHILEV.

(I) March (II) Waltz (III) Polka.

Although these didactic and entertaining duets were written essentially for Stravinsky's children, they also represent a significant stylistic landmark by revealing the composer's shift from Russian to international genres. In a letter to ANSERMET, Stravinsky referred to these pieces as 'music-hall numbers', with

DIAGHILEV portrayed (in the 'Polka') 'as a circus ring-master ... cracking his whip and urging on a rider on horseback'. The manuscript of the March is illustrated with a cartoon showing cannons firing the letters of CASELLA's name. The pianist of the 'easy' *seconda* part must demonstrate a surprising level of musicality via shifting time-signatures (March) and *colla parte* accompaniment (Waltz: Trio) and must execute subtleties of articulation appropriate to each movement.   GRAHAM GRIFFITHS

Graham Griffiths, *Stravinsky's Piano: Genesis of a Musical Language* (Cambridge University Press, 2013).

Three Movements from Petrushka. Transcription of the BALLET score by the composer for piano solo. Composed August–September 1921, Anglet. First performance (subtitled 'Sonata'), 26 December 1922, PARIS, THÉÂTRE DES CHAMPS-ELYSÉES; Jean Wiener. Published 1922, Russischer Musikverlag, later Hawkes & Son (London). Dedication: Artur RUBINSTEIN.

(I) Russian Dance (II) In Petrushka's Cell (III) The Shrovetide Fair.

Despite Stravinsky's triumphs with the BALLETS RUSSES, the end of World War I found the composer's family in a state of considerable hardship. The combined upheavals of war in Europe and revolution in Russia had caused fees to be unpaid and royalties not to be honoured. When news of the Stravinskys' dire situation reached Ernest ANSERMET, he wrote to Manuel de FALLA who approached Artur RUBINSTEIN, who, to his eternal credit, sent (as Stravinsky was later to recall) 'the generous sum of 5,000 francs'. The *Three Movements from Petrushka* might be said, then, to have been born out of an act of considerable kindness. In return, Stravinsky offered to write Rubinstein 'a sonata' derived from the PETRUSHKA score. The opportunity arose in 1921 when the two collaborated over the summer to create a work of such virtuosity that it would forever prove too great a challenge for Stravinsky himself.

1. The first movement features the music of the 'Russian Dance' for three puppets, which concludes the ballet's opening tableau. It is typical of the work's exuberant variety of pianistic styles: from the NOSTALGIA of virtuosity reflecting the twilight of the long nineteenth century, to the innovation of ostinati heralding MODERNISM's dawn. The impact of Stravinsky's *burlesque* depends to a large degree upon the alchemy that results from the juxtaposition of these stylistic extremes.

2. The second movement may be viewed as personifying the whole work, for it was the first music that Stravinsky composed as 'a sort of *Konzertstück*' before conceiving of the ballet. For this reason, the performer of In Petrushka's Cell may feel with some justification that (s)he is engaging with Stravinsky's original instrumental scenario. This sense of authenticity is enhanced at the moment of placing one's hands on the keys, black-and-white, in the perfectly pianistic realisation of the famed *Petrushka*-chord (bar 8).

3. The music of the final movement is largely taken from the fourth tableau. It depicts the *mêlée* in the street as the crowds are entertained by the Wet-

Nurses (bar 35), by the Gypsies and a Rake Vendor (bar 107), and by the Coachmen (bar 168). At the entrance of the Masqueraders (bar 286), the Shrove-Tide Fair reaches its exuberant climax. (This piano version omits the ballet's grim, though haunting, *dénouement*.) By 1935, Stravinsky had not only overlooked Rubinstein's role in the work's creation but also, in full neo-classical stride, denied that the work was a transcription at all. Rather, it had been conceived as an 'exclusively musical work' for which the dramatic action of the ballet was irrelevant. Upon hearing *Three Movements*, however, there can be little doubt that the ill-fated puppet had a mischievous, pianistic soul. GRAHAM GRIFFITHS

Graham Griffiths, Stravinsky's Piano: *Genesis of a Musical Language* (Cambridge University Press, 2013).
Igor Stravinsky, 'Quelques Confidences sur la musique', Conférence de M. Igor Strawinsky faite le 21 novembre 1935, in SCW, 581–5.
Auto; SPD

Three Pieces for Solo Clarinet. Composed October–November 1918, for Werner Reinhart. First performance, 8 November 1919, Lausanne. First published 1920, J. & W. Chester. Dedicated to Werner Reinhart.

As noted on the score, these three study-like miniatures are preferably to be performed on a clarinet in A. Reinhart, the dedicatee, was an arts patron-cum-amateur clarinettist, and Stravinsky's work constituted a thank-you present to him, completed shortly after The Soldier's Tale (the first production of which he sponsored).

The first piece, *Sempre p e molto tranquillo* (MM $\downarrow$ = 52), has a hypnotic quality, with rotating motivic lines articulated by breath marks, based in the low 'chalumeau' register; its often irregular metre (2/4, 5/8, 7/8) creates an improvisatory character, closing on an extended pause. By contrast, the second number explores a far wider registral palette and dynamic range (*mf*, with a central *pp* portion), at a fast tempo of $\downarrow$ = 168. In common with Piano-Rag-Music, an improvisatory sense is maximised by the removal of bar-lines. This music is intricate and melismatic, utilising many grace notes within smooth arpeggiated and scalic figurations; three- and two-note rhythmic groupings of semiquavers and quavers predominate. The finale ($\downarrow$ = 160) is distinguished by a constant *forte* dynamic, while combining the variable metre and rhythmic diminution of the preceding pieces. Incisive and insistent, with much accentuation in the clarinet's upper register, it thrives on repeated pitch cells, with the thematic material loosely derived from the 'Ragtime' of The Soldier's Tale. A strident *ff* burst of sound ends on an ascending octave gesture. DEBORAH MAWER

Three Pieces for String Quartet. Composed 1914. First performance, 13 May 1915, PARIS; Yvonne Astruc, Darius MILHAUD (violins), Jurgensen Delgrange (viola), Félix Delgrange (cello). Revised version, 1918. Published 1922, Éditions Russes de la Musique / Boosey & Hawkes.

The Three Pieces for String Quartet, dedicated to Ernest ANSERMET, were written in 1914 at the request of the Flonzaley Quartet, to be performed on their tour of Europe and North America the following year, and were first performed by that group on 8 November 1915 in Chicago. When they were later performed in New York City, they were given the title 'Grotesques'. Coming only a year after the notorious RITE OF SPRING performance in Paris, these little pieces, which last altogether about 8 minutes, represent, along with several other works of the same time, an enormous retrenchment: a great economy of forces and of length. They were not published until 1922, by which time, however, they had already been orchestrated on their way to becoming the first three of FOUR STUDIES for orchestra, which included also the ORCHESTRATION of a study for PIANOLA (player piano) written in 1917. When these four pieces were published together in 1930, they were entitled 'Danse', 'Excentrique', 'Cantique' and 'Madrid'. The subsequent reappearance of music in new guises was to be a hallmark of Stravinsky; not only did these three pieces have an afterlife, Walsh tells us that the first had been composed originally as a piano duet.

White calls these 'contrasting studies in popular, fantastic and liturgical moods'. Although the three pieces have many characteristics in common – polytonality, the use of ostinato and a predominance of minor seconds and minor ninths, a great variety of playing instructions for all the instruments – their 'moods' could hardly be more different from each other.

Walsh describes the first as toying with the possibility of a musical machine, a dance for clockwork musicians. The motoric effect is emphasised with the utmost economy of means, only nine different pitches being employed during the course of the piece – each instrument being confined to the repetition of between two and four notes – and the metres restricted to a repeated three-bar sequence: 3/4, 2/4, 2/4. The viola part is essentially a sustained pedal consisting of a minor ninth interval. This rigorous design allows for no development or variation, no modulation or change of colour or speed, and the independent role of each instrument is emphasised by the sharply differentiated contrasts of timbre.

The second piece, which is indeed 'excentrique', is unlike the first in almost every way. It is made up of many short sections, most of which repeat with some variation but not in any regular order, and there are many and irregular changes of tempo and metre. Some sections are static ostinatos; others are sudden leaps or arpeggios; still others are sharp pizzicato notes or staccato notes with grace notes. The music leaps excitedly all over the place, using a great variety of playing techniques, including one in which the upper three instruments are to be held upright like a cello. Stravinsky said that this piece was inspired by his seeing the dwarf clown 'Little Tich' in London in 1914.

The third of these pieces could hardly be a greater contrast to the second – or the first. It is entirely homophonic in the manner of a chorale, but, after two bars of introduction, it is structured as an antiphon of twenty-four bars (abababa), which is followed by an eleven-bar period of contrasting material and a six-bar ending that refers back to the introduction. The first, second and fourth *a* sections of the antiphon are all five bars long and very similar, using only three notes, C, D and E♭, in a melody that begins like the 'Dies irae', played by violin I and doubled consistently by violin II a perfect fourth below. The third *a* section expands the melody to include F and G, and the distance between the two violins is varied at several points, with their coming together on the same note on three occasions. The fourth a section consists of only the first three bars of the first a section, but these are repeated exactly. While the violins move in parallel fourths throughout the a sections, the distance of viola and cello from the melody changes constantly, although the chords of section a1 are exactly repeated in section a4. The three short b sections are identical.

Stravinsky later said of the third piece, 'the last 20 bars are some of my best music of that time'. White sees material from these pieces as germinal to themes in later compositions: the violin I theme of No. 1 is extended in the main theme of the last movement of the SYMPHONY IN C; a phrase in No. 2 is repeated almost verbatim in the fugue of the SYMPHONY OF PSALMS; and the introduction of No. 3 is more fully worked out in the coda of the SYMPHONIES OF WIND INSTRUMENTS (SCW, 234). KATHRYN PUFFETT

Three Songs from William Shakespeare for mezzo-soprano, flute, clarinet, viola. Composed 1953. First performance, 8 March 1954, LOS ANGELES. Conductor, Robert CRAFT. Published 1954, Boosey & Hawkes. 'Dedicated to Evenings on the Roof (Los Angeles)'. (I) 'Musick to heare' (Sonnet 8) (II) 'Full fadom five' (*The Tempest*, Act I, Scene 2) (III) 'When Daisies Pied' (*Love's Labour's Lost*, Act V, Scene 2).

Stravinsky continued his exploration of serialism, after the CANTATA (1951–2) and SEPTET (1952–3), in this set of songs on texts by Shakespeare. As in the Cantata, but unlike in the Septet whose movements are linked via shared pitch structures, each piece is developed from a different material. The musical characters of the three songs are as diverse as the chosen texts.

The first song opens with a serenade-style flute melody accompanied by a mixture of pizzicato, staccato and legato gestures in the clarinet and viola that move up and down diatonically between C and G. The opening flute line and the rest of the song (except for the diatonic final bars in clarinet and viola) are built entirely from different transformations of the four-note motive B-G-A-B♭, used as a series. Through mostly transposition and inversion of this series, which contains both the major and minor third (B/B♭) of an otherwise diatonic pitch segment, Stravinsky creates an overall chromatic texture with striking local diatonic flavour. The song is replete with text painting, including a digressing permutation of serial order at 'offend thine eare', portraying the discomfort experienced by the protagonist of the sonnet as he listens to music he would otherwise enjoy, due to his rejection of the harmony of married life (invoked by arrivals on consonant open fifths).

The source pitch material of the second song is presented at the outset via a text metaphor. Bell-like melodic and harmonic fourths and fifths taken from the cycle C-F-B♭-E♭-A♭-D♭-G♭-C♭ refer to the measured depth in the opening line of 'Full fadom five thy Father lies' from Ariel's song on the whereabouts of the presumed-drowned king. The voice intones this text line on the seven notes between F and C♭ from the cycle of fourths/fifths, which corresponds to a diatonic scale (G♭ major or E♭ minor). On the second line of text, these pitches are reordered into a seven-note series, e♭1-d♭2-g♭1-f1-b♭1-c♭2-a♭1, with the neighbouring b♭1-c♭2 repeated for the purpose of word painting (on 'Corrall'), accompanied and followed by various transformations and free motivic material derived from the series, using similar rhythms. As in the first song, such serial operations generate chromaticism while maintaining local diatonic character. Following intensified semitonal sigh motives (after 'knell'), the song concludes with an evocation of bell sounds.

The last movement portrays the plenitude of floral colours and the mocking cuckoo calls in Shakespeare's song by means of chromatically embellished diatonic modes with an emphasis on shimmering open-fifth sonorities. Aside from local pitch palindromes in the voice (reminiscent of bars 2–6 of the previous song), the movement does not allude to serial procedures.   CHRISTOPH NEIDHÖFER

David Carson Berry, 'The roles of invariance and analogy in the linear design of Stravinsky's Musick to Heare', Gamut: The Online Journal of the Music Theory Society of the Mid-Atlantic, I.1 (2008), https://trace.tennessee.edu/gamut/vol1/iss1/1.
Joseph N. Straus, Stravinsky's Late Music (Cambridge University Press, 2001).

Threni: id est lamentationes Jeremiae prophetae. Composed 1957–8. First performance, 23 September 1958, VENICE. Conductor, Stravinsky. Published 1958, Boosey & Hawkes. Dedicated to North German Radio. This was Stravinsky's first entirely TWELVE-NOTE composition, and, at approximately 35 minutes, the longest he ever composed. The Latin text is excerpted from chapters 1, 3 and 5 of the Book of Lamentations. It is scored for SATB chorus and six soloists (soprano, alto, two tenors and two basses), and full orchestra augmented by piano, celesta, harp, tam-tam, sarrusophone and fluegelhorn; however, the ensemble never plays tutti.

Threni is in three sections (*De Elegia Prima, De Elegia Tertia* and *De Elegia Quinta*), the first two multiply subdivided. The work begins with a brief duet for female soloists, 'Incipit lamentatio Jeremiae Prophetae', followed by an elaborate rondo-like setting consisting of verses prefaced by choral presentations of letters of the Hebrew alphabet (Aleph, Beth, He, Caph and Resh), three statements of a ritornello (featuring tenor solo and fluegelhorn), and two canonic tenor duets. By combining blocks of literally repeated material with similar, but varied sections, Stravinsky constructs a highly coherent but strongly variegated succession of textures.

De Elegia Tertia is in three sections: *Querimonia* ('Complaint'), *Sensus Spei* ('Perceiving Hope') and *Solacium* ('Compensation'). In *Querimonia*, Hebrew letter names, sung by the chorus with sparse orchestral accompaniment, provide punctuation, with each letter sung three times. The solo *basso profondo* first performs without accompaniment, but is then joined by a tenor soloist for a brief canon. In the subsequent verses, additional male soloists join to sing canons in three, and then four, voices. *Sensus Spei* brings a faster tempo and denser textures, including sustained notes in woodwinds and brass. This is the longest and most dramatic section of the piece. Especially lovely are the eight-voice settings of the words *'Perii'* ('I am cut off') and *'Ne timeas'* ('Fear not'). Soprano and alto soloists sing the first verse of the *Solacium* with light woodwind accompaniment; tenor and bass soloists sing the second verse with four horns. The third and fourth verses add the full chorus to the four soloists, but the orchestra is silent except during the Hebrew letters. *De Elegia Quinta* begins with a brief duet for the bass soloists. All six vocal soloists are joined by the full chorus in this short and lightly scored final movement.

Like ABRAHAM AND ISAAC, Threni is an austere and solemn work. Its beauty may not be readily evident to some listeners. Yet in this important work Stravinsky refined and consolidated his personal method of composing twelve-note music. Significantly, Stravinsky knew Ernst KRENEK's Lamentatio Jeremiae prophetae (1941), and he adopted Krenek's procedure of hexachordal rotation – first used in that work – which was to play an important role in nearly all of Stravinsky's later works. In part, this explains why Stravinsky's late music sounds so different from twelve-note compositions by SCHOENBERG, BERG and WEBERN.   DAVID H. SMYTH

David Smyth, 'Stravinsky as serialist: the sketches for Threni', Music Theory Spectrum, 22.2 (Fall 2000), 205–24.
Joseph N. Straus, Stravinsky's Late Music (Cambridge University Press, 2001).

Timofeyev, Grigory Nikolayevich (born Yaroslavl, 4/16 June 1866; died on a train to Voronezh, 18 March 1919). Russian music critic and lexicographer – the first to write an encyclopedia entry on Stravinsky. A regular music critic for Rech' in 1906–17, he covered Stravinsky's earliest public appearances as a composer in ST PETERSBURG, reviewing the EVENINGS OF CONTEMPORARY MUSIC concert of 27 December 1907 / 9 January 1908, which featured Stravinsky's songs 'Vesna' (setting GORODETSKY) and the vocalise PASTORALE; then the Court Orchestra concert of 22 January / 4 February 1908 in which Stravinsky's SYMPHONY IN E♭ MAJOR received its first complete performance, alongside The Faun and the Shepherdess. Timofeyev criticised Stravinsky's music for being too derivative, yet, apparently on the strength of these two performances, invited Stravinsky to submit a résumé (the earliest account written by the composer of his early life and musical education) which Timofeyev then used as the basis for a biographical entry published in the Bol'shaya entsiklopediya (St Petersburg, 1909). Timofeyev published a more enthusiastic review of FUNERAL SONG in Vestnik Yevropï (5, 1909). He also wrote Stravinsky's first press notice to appear outside RUSSIA, 'Les Nouveautés de la musique russe', published in Revue musicale SIM 5 (Paris, 1909).   DANIEL JAFFÉ

Tippett, Michael (born London, 2 January 1905; died London, 8 January 1998). British composer. In his autobiography, he described early encounters with Stravinsky's music, hearing the composer 'play his Capriccio for piano and orchestra, returning somewhat later to conduct his CONCERTO IN D FOR VIOLIN AND ORCHESTRA and to give recitals with Samuel Dushkin: his hard-edged, percussive playing in the Petrushka excerpts made a particular impact on me' (Tippett 1991, 18). Tippett was responsible for the British première of the CONCERTO IN E♭: 'DUMBARTON OAKS' at Morley College in 1943, conducted by Walter Goehr; Les Noces was also performed there, and Tippett gave a radio talk on the work, later published. In his earlier compositions, culminating in The Midsummer Marriage, completed in 1952, Tippett (a friend of Eric Walter White) was especially stimulated by Stravinskian interactions between the Dionysian and the Apollonian in an essentially neo-classical context. Later, he claimed that his change to a more expressionistic post-tonal style in his second OPERA, King Priam (1958–61), was influenced by AGON, from which he learned 'how to deploy an operatic orchestra in an entirely new way – treating solo instruments as equals both within the ensemble and against the voices on stage' (Tippett

478

1991, 226). For Tippett, Stravinsky's 'great quality lies in the strength of passion of the two sides of his nature. He had on the one hand the gift of immediately arresting and dynamic invention – on the other he had an equally extreme intellectual passion for order' (1995, 50). ARNOLD WHITTALL

Michael Tippett, 'Stravinsky and Les Noces', in Meirion Bowen (ed.), Tippett on Music (Oxford: Clarendon Press, 1995).

Michael Tippett, Those Twentieth Century Blues: An Autobiography (London: Hutchinson, 1991).

Twelve-Note Technique / Serialism. Any composer who celebrates imitative textures, reveres canonic and fugal writing, and pursues rigorous motivic transformation might be said to be a 'serial' composer of a sort, since such writing preserves a series of notes or intervals. By this reckoning, Machaut, Josquin, BACH and Haydn could be called by the name, and so could Stravinsky, from his earliest works onwards. The first four notes of The FIREBIRD occur in transposed, inverted and retrograde orderings throughout the BALLET, wherein Stravinsky also makes extensive use of chains of alternating major and minor thirds. Throughout his career, Stravinsky employed series of notes and intervals of varying lengths: he was always a 'serial' composer to some degree.

Today, 'serialism' is generally understood to be the invention of Arnold SCHOENBERG (1874–1951). Like Stravinsky, Schoenberg began his career writing tonal music. Later, after exploring free atonality, he began using note rows of varying length and make-up, but ultimately (in the 1920s) he used rows consisting of all twelve notes of the chromatic scale. Schoenberg and Stravinsky were never on friendly terms, even after both immigrated to the UNITED STATES and became residents of LOS ANGELES. Theodor ADORNO's influential book Philosophy of New Music (1949) located the two composers in a highly charged polar opposition: Schoenberg the progressive versus Stravinsky the regressive. Many subscribed to the view that these two were the modern counterparts of the infamous WAGNER versus Brahms rivalry of the previous century. The musical world was shocked – some were horrified – when, shortly after Schoenberg's death, Stravinsky took up serial composition in earnest.

In Stravinsky's Late Music (2001), Joseph Straus provides a detailed account of Stravinsky's change of course, tracing the influences of Robert CRAFT, Arnold Schoenberg, Anton WEBERN, Ernst KRENEK, Pierre BOULEZ and Milton Babbitt, while insisting that, in the end, Stravinsky was no slavish imitator. Stravinsky invented his own highly personal versions of serial techniques to create powerful works that scarcely resemble those of Schoenberg or younger composers. Straus also argues that, in the late works, Stravinsky generally de-emphasises the musical devices and techniques he favoured in his earlier works (particularly the interaction of diatonic and octatonic pitch collections, as detailed in the writings of van den Toorn and Taruskin), with the result that his late music is truly fresh and essentially different from his own earlier compositions. But Stravinsky's conversion was a complex process, and it is important to acknowledge continuities, habits and proclivities that persisted as he accomplished the change.

In a famous passage from Themes and Episodes, Stravinsky said he experienced a crisis as he outgrew the 'special incubator in which I wrote The Rake's Progress' (T&E, 23). The contract for that work (signed in January 1947) enabled him to concentrate his efforts for several years almost exclusively on composing his last and longest OPERA, rather than seeking out commissions and conducting jobs. At precisely this juncture, Robert Craft became Stravinsky's personal assistant. One of his early assignments was to write liner notes for the first recording of Stravinsky's MASS (begun in 1944, completed in 1947). Craft's efforts to describe Stravinsky's pitch structures, cadences and (notably) some 'tricky canons' in the 'Agnus Dei' were derided by a *Los Angeles Times* critic as 'superintellectual gymnastics'. The canons involve imitative statements of series of pitches that are distributed among the choral parts, rather than presented as a theme in a single voice. Stravinsky would use this technique in many of his later serial compositions. The important point is that he composed these canons before he met Craft, and indeed before he climbed into the 'incubator'.

Other scholars have pointed out instances of serial pitch ordering in works written before Schoenberg's death. In a 1962 article for *Music Review*, for example, Donald Johns discussed 'An early serial idea of Stravinsky', noting his use of a long string of notes (mostly diatonic and replete with many repetitions) in the second movement of the SONATA FOR TWO PIANOS (1943–4). Johns did not remark upon Stravinsky's use of partial statements of the series, which foreshadows his use of the same technique in CANTICUM SACRUM, THRENI and other later works. Such truncation allows Stravinsky to secure the effect of centricity, granting some degree of priority to a particular note, even in highly chromatic and otherwise atonal passages.

In his late years, Stravinsky often carried with him pocket scores of BEETHOVEN's last string quartets. In *Dialogues*, he singles out the *Grosse Fuge*, calling it 'a miracle ... contemporary forever ... It is pure interval music, this fugue, and I love it beyond any other' (*Dial*, 124). At the age of 80, Stravinsky recognised the profound relationship between the strictures of fugal composition and those of a modern serialist. Doubtless, Stravinsky was proud of the double fugue in the second movement of his SYMPHONY OF PSALMS (1930). Analysts have observed occurrences of the 'B-A-C-H' motive (B♭, A, C, B♮) therein. This cipher is used extensively in Schoenberg's *Variations for Orchestra* (1929) – although Stravinsky did not know it – and also occurs in the Prelude to the graveyard scene in the final act of THE RAKE'S PROGRESS, and in a number of note rows upon which Stravinsky's late works are based.

The composer was deeply touched when Ernst Krenek presented him, on his eightieth birthday, with a canon with a Latin text spelling out an acrostic of Stravinsky's name using exactly eighty words (SSC, II, 334–5). Krenek's *Lamentatio Jeremiae prophetae* (1941), which is based on the Bible's most extensive acrostic text (the twenty-two letters of the Hebrew alphabet occur in succession in verses of the first and third chapters of Lamentations), obviously sparked Stravinsky's interest in setting portions of the same text in *Threni* (1957–8), his first entirely twelve-note composition. Furthermore, as Straus demonstrates, Stravinsky made a close study of Krenek's serial charts, annotating the rotational operations Krenek developed. Stravinsky would employ modifications of this rotational technique in most of his late works.

As they forged their individual compositional paths, Stravinsky and Schoenberg both remained faithful to their roots and reverent towards past masters. As much as we treasure their bold inventiveness, we should acknowledge their deep connections to the past.

The Works of Stravinsky's 'Serial' Period

The twenty compositions Stravinsky completed between 1951 and 1966 may be divided into two general groups: smaller and larger. Among the former, the THREE SONGS FROM WILLIAM SHAKESPEARE (1953), IN MEMORIAM DYLAN THOMAS (1954) and ELEGY FOR J. F. K. (1964) are perhaps the most interesting, in that they movingly set texts of great power with accompaniment by sparse, colourful instrumental ensembles. EPITAPHIUM (1959) for flute, clarinet and harp is a brief funeral tribute to Prince Max Egon von Fürstenberg. The FANFARE FOR A NEW THEATRE (1964) is a very short twelve-note duet for two trumpets, dedicated to Lincoln KIRSTEIN and George BALANCHINE. The DOUBLE CANON (1959) for string quartet is another tiny gem, and the ANTHEM (1961–2) – an *a cappella* setting of 'The Dove Descending' from T. S. ELIOT's *Four Quartets* – is again as sonically lovely as its verses are profound. INTROITUS (1965) – an especially solemn work for male chorus, solo viola and double bass, harp, and percussion – is dedicated to the memory of Eliot. The OWL AND THE PUSSY-CAT (1966) is a whimsical romp, honouring VERA STRAVINSKY's affection for the Lear poem, which she used to practise her English.

The larger works range from extended chamber works to settings for large orchestra. One prominent group uses sacred (mostly biblical) texts: the CANTATA (1951–2) is in a large, seven-part form, with three statements of a 'Dirge' that functions like a rondo refrain. The five-part form of *Canticum sacrum* (1955), dedicated to the city of VENICE (where Stravinsky is buried beside DIAGHILEV), features symmetries some say resemble those of ST MARK'S BASILICA, where it was first performed. The short, sparse tenor solo 'Surge, aquilo' from this work, based on verses from the Song of Songs, was Stravinsky's first entirely twelve-note movement. The final sonority provides an excellent illustration of how row truncation can reinforce pitch centricity: the final perfect fifth (A supporting E) affirms the considerable emphasis that has accrued to A as a quasi-tonic throughout. This is achieved by omitting the last two notes of an inverted statement of the row. *Threni* (1957–8) was, as noted above, his first entirely twelve-note score, and his longest; it, too, was first performed in Venice. As noted earlier, Stravinsky makes extensive use of rotated statements of the series in this work, as well as occasional truncations and omissions. A SERMON, A NARRATIVE AND A PRAYER (1960–1) is a chamber cantata based mainly on New Testament verses. The following year, Stravinsky composed a musical play, *The* FLOOD (1961–2), first presented on television. The story of Noah was interrupted by advertisements for Prell shampoo, among other secular commodities. Far more serious is the setting of another text about a testing of faith, ABRAHAM AND ISAAC (1962–3), for baritone solo and chamber orchestra. The text is in Hebrew, and the work is dedicated to the people of Israel. Stravinsky's sublime REQUIEM CANTICLES (1965–6), his last major composition, is clearly a funeral Mass for himself, again cast in a symmetrical, multi-movement design. The work is based on two different twelve-note rows; in some movements, both are used. It is a tribute to Stravinsky's consummate skill that the result of his most highly refined compositional technique yielded some of the loveliest music he ever produced. One encounters here rhythms as lively as any he ever wrote for dancing, as well as vivid orchestral colourings of spectacular delicacy.

The remaining works of larger dimensions are for instruments only. The SEPTET (1952–3) is for three winds, piano and three strings. Its three movements use traditional forms (sonata, *passacaglia* and *gigue*), and it is the last Stravinsky work to employ a key signature. It is partly based on note rows of varying lengths, carefully constructed to promote unity among the three movements, all of which display a notable allegiance to the note A. The composer's sketches include even more self-analysis than is printed in the score – showing, for example, how he carefully extracted all of the major and minor triads that can be formed from the unordered eight-note 'rows' that are used in the final movement (see the violin part at R27). AGON (1953–7) is a pivotal work, as might be expected from one of such long gestation. This 'contest' for twelve dancers is the best-known of Stravinsky's late works, for it is regularly performed by the NEW YORK CITY BALLET. Lightly but beautifully scored, it provides multiple rewards for the ears as well as the eyes. The overall form again features a *ritornello* (first named 'prelude', with later iterations labelled 'interlude'), serving to punctuate four groups of three dances. Stravinsky's evident delight in play with numbers parallels his joyful explorations of musical palindromes, canons and other such devices throughout the work. Quite notable is a gentle but compelling alternation between passages of smooth diatonicism and some much more dissonant chromatic writing. With familiarity, one accepts the contrast as readily as one does in *The Firebird*. MOVEMENTS (1958–9) for piano and orchestra is a virtuosic display of compositional technique, in five sections (movements) separated by brief interludes during which the piano does not play. In just under 10 minutes, one hears an astonishingly light and nimble progression of sound characters on parade. Not surprisingly, George Balanchine choreographed the work for the New York City Ballet in 1963. Stravinsky's VARIATIONS (1963–4) for large orchestra are dedicated to the memory of Aldous Huxley. The density and complexity of the music, which lasts under 5 minutes, is breathtaking. Not only are all of the pitches derived from a twelve-note row, but several sections are based on a succession of 4- plus 3- plus 5-quaver bars (equalling twelve). The first is scored for twelve solo violins, the second for ten solo violas, and the last for twelve winds; these combinations create extraordinary colours. The variations pose a steep challenge for listeners, but, for those with patience and determination, the piece will repay repeated hearing. Harp and piano are used in tandem throughout, with no other percussion. Even so, parts of the work dance vigorously.

In sum, Stravinsky was, from his early years, enamoured of constructive devices and techniques that became the foundation for his later adoption of serialism. His late music, like that of Beethoven and Schoenberg, can thus function as a lens through which to view his earlier works. Of course, some prefer the perspective of a chronological account, tracing the 'progress of a method' (to use Edward T. Cone's phrase) or setting down a series of 'firsts' (as does Straus on p. 4). Stravinsky's music after *The Rake's Progress* remains the work of one of the most fecund and persistently inventive musical minds in all history. A fuller appreciation of these remarkable creations will require going beyond a preoccupation with charts and plans that reveal arcane manipulations of pitch structures. Stravinsky's textures, rhythms and tone colours are, if anything, more dazzling than ever in his late music, and careful attention to them may indeed provide a more effective and enjoyable way to approach his last works.   DAVID H. SMYTH

Theodor W. Adorno, *Philosophy of New Music*, trans. and ed. Robert Hullot-Kentor (Minneapolis: University of Minnesota Press, 2006). Originally published in German, 1949.

Edward T. Cone, 'Stravinsky: the progress of a method', *Perspectives of New Music*, 1.1 (1962), 18–26.

Donald Johns, 'An early serial idea of Stravinsky', *Music Review*, 23.4 (1962), 305–13.

David Smyth, 'Stravinsky as serialist: reading the early serial sketches', *Perspectives of New Music*, 37.2 (Summer 1999), 117–46.

Joseph N. Straus, *Stravinsky's Late Music* (Cambridge University Press, 2001).

Susannah Tucker, 'Stravinsky and his sketches: the composing of *Agon* and other serial works of the 1950s' (Ph.D. dissertation, Oxford University, 1992).

Pieter C. van den Toorn, *The Music of Igor Stravinsky* (New Haven: Yale University Press, 1983).

SRT

Two Sketches for a Sonata, for Piano. Composed 1966. First performance, 3 February 1973. Unpublished. The manuscript score, signed 'IStr.1966', is held at the Paul SACHER STIFTUNG (Foundation).

If one is to consider the TARANTELLA fragment of 1898 fit for inclusion in the *Cambridge Stravinsky Encyclopedia*, then there can be no doubt that the fully completed *Two Sketches for a Sonata*, composed in Stravinsky's late, serial idiom, must also be included. Each apophthegmatic 'movement' consists of just a single, unbarred line, whose total duration in performance is less than 1 intensely experienced minute. The first *Sketch* presents a sustained, gently oscillating texture characterised by linear and vertical use of the major and minor ninth. The second *Sketch* suggests a faster tempo, being more rhythmically defined and characterised by short decisive gestures (punctuated by rests) which, in combination, invite the performer to prioritise the music's inherent contrasts of articulation. Stravinsky's workings reveal his TWELVE-NOTE row to be formed from two hexachords a tritone apart, the first *Sketch* opening with a statement of this in the composer's favoured retrograde-inversion. The score's lack of markings – nothing to indicate tempo, dynamics or 'expression' – is taken to an extreme more neutral, even, than in the PIANO SONATA (1924). When such notational 'objectivity' is considered alongside the title's reference to a proposed 'sonata', one might imagine that, in his eighty-sixth year, Stravinsky wished to reconcile present serial interests with past neo-classical concerns. As if to support this reading, the *Two Sketches* eventually arrive at the note A, in unison and with a resonant 'effect' created by the lowest A played staccato. Not only is this strongly reminiscent of the SERENADE IN A of four decades earlier, and its *jeu acoustique* 'on A' at the conclusion to each movement, one is also reminded (Straus, 2001) of the idyllic scenes in Act 1 of THE RAKE'S PROGRESS. There, the pitch-centre 'A' is associated with Anne's garden, where 'love alone reigns'. Who can tell the reasoning behind Stravinsky's selection of this same note to bring closure to what he might well have anticipated was his final creative act, for, to borrow one of his most celebrated *mots justes*: 'In order to create there must be a dynamic force, and what force is more potent than love?'   GRAHAM GRIFFITHS

Robin Maconie, *Experiencing Stravinsky: A Listener's Companion* (Lanham, MD: Scarecrow Press, 2013).

Joseph N. Straus, *Stravinsky's Late Music* (Cambridge University Press, 2001).

United States of America. Igor Stravinsky had hoped to travel to the United States for the BALLETS RUSSES' American tour in 1916 and was disheartened when excluded from Sergey DIAGHILEV's plans. During his years living in Europe following the outbreak of World War I and the Russian Revolution, he imagined the United States as a land of economic prosperity, drawn by what he perceived as a progressive community of artists. While completing Les NOCES in PARIS in 1923, he attempted to arrange a tour with Leopold STOKOWSKI and the Philadelphia Orchestra, but his first US tour was not realised until 1925. In December, he sailed on the SS *Paris* from Le Havre for New York, a piano installed in his cabin the only solace for the bumpy eight-day voyage.

The New York public was well aware of the 43-year-old composer's creative powers upon his arrival (The RITE OF SPRING was introduced to Americans in 1922 and had been performed not long before in New York). Within a few days, Stravinsky made his debut at Carnegie Hall with the New York Philharmonic, conducting The *Firebird Suite*, SCHERZO FANTASTIQUE, FIREWORKS, PULCINELLA and The SONG OF THE NIGHTINGALE (only *Scherzo* was a New York première). Following visits to Philadelphia, Cleveland, Chicago, Detroit and Cincinnati, Stravinsky returned home to Europe with a substantial sum of money. But his impressions were contradictory; reporters were told of his fascination with the fast pace of American life, yet behind closed doors, as Stephen Walsh notes, he described the people themselves as 'dull and dreary' (SCS, 407–8). In the decade between visits to America, Stravinsky became a French citizen, intent on remaining in Europe.

His second US tour in 1935 was motivated by diminishing performance opportunities in a volatile Europe. Crisscrossing the USA by train for sixteen weeks, Stravinsky's itinerary included appearances in mid-western cities and eventually landed him in CALIFORNIA, where an old acquaintance from RUSSIA (Alexis Kall) invited him to stay at his home in LOS ANGELES. Thus, a powerful connection between the *émigré* community of his past with the city of angels was made. In southern California, Stravinsky established a relationship with the LA Philharmonic, and doors were opened to exotic commercial ventures in the FILM industry (including a collaboration with Charlie Chaplin, ultimately leading nowhere). Yet the trip seems to have yielded only positive impressions.

Once back in FRANCE, performance opportunities became increasingly bleak, coupled with the family's growing HEALTH costs (his wife, Katya (Catherine STRAVINSKY), and daughter, Mika, were both undergoing treatment for tuberculosis). His mistress and future second wife, Vera Sudeykina (*see* Vera STRAVINSKY), and his mother both received his financial assistance. The need to leave Europe could not have felt more pressing; the Nazis had just occupied the Rhineland in the spring, and fear and hunger besieged Paris. Stravinsky planned a return to the USA as soon as possible, but awaited a concrete offer.

A BALLET commission for the newly minted AMERICAN BALLET, the brain-child of Lincoln KIRSTEIN, appeared at just the right time, requiring travel to New York in 1936 for the première of JEU DE CARTES. Stravinsky made his North American conducting debut with The Rite of Spring and appeared for the first time in Canada. Curious projects sprang up within his busy touring schedule, including the creation of PRAELUDIUM, for JAZZ ensemble, a response to American jazz that Walsh describes as 'a ragbag of things heard in Manhattan bars and clubs' (SSE, 58). The composer began dreaming about a new symphony, influenced in part by impressions of American life, which Walsh suggests would become his SYMPHONY IN C. Following his tour of the west coast, Stravinsky returned to New York for the première of Jeu de cartes with a diagnosis of tuberculosis. Coughing fits had begun in Los Angeles while rehearsing in the chilly, barn-like Shrine Auditorium and, while confined to bed rest, he stubbornly coached the ballet's rehearsal pianist from his hotel room. Jeu opened to a full house at the Met on 27 April 1937, marking a potent chemistry between choreographer George BALANCHINE and Stravinsky, and launching a creative alliance that would endure for the remainder of his life. He returned to Europe in May, newly invigorated and taking with him a commission for a chamber work, CONCERTO IN E♭: 'DUMBARTON OAKS'.

The next couple of years would be some of the most challenging and traumatic for the composer. In quick succession, Stravinsky lost both his wife and daughter to tuberculosis, followed by the death of his mother. In a matter of months, Britain and France declared war on GERMANY and little remained to keep him in Europe (Walsh records his lament: 'my family is destroyed – I no longer have anything to do in Paris' (SSE, 89)).

Through his long-time friend and colleague, Nadia BOULANGER, Stravinsky received an invitation in 1939 to give a series of public lectures (POETICS OF MUSIC) and master classes at Harvard University. In September, he headed once more to America, aboard the Manhattan, unsure of when Vera would join him and how long he would stay. Between lectures, he performed widely in the Midwest and on both US coasts, visiting Los Angeles for a meeting with Walt Disney to discuss the animated film Fantasia. Vera finally joined her husband-to-be in January 1940; between concerts and lectures, they were married on 9 March 1940 in a Harvard professor's home. Weighing a return to a war-torn Europe against a promising new life in America, the couple began the process of applying for US citizenship. California, with its restorative climate, seemed the place to begin a fresh new chapter. In May, the newlyweds arrived by train in Los Angeles ('like refugees', according to Vera). Walsh describes how the couple would continue to track advances of Allied troops from their new home, with coloured pins on maps (SSE, 155). It would be five years before Igor and Vera would take their formal oaths as US citizens.

In the summer of 1940, Stravinsky made his debut at the HOLLYWOOD BOWL conducting Firebird. Although Stravinsky's national and international touring continued, his investment in the creative landscape of LA grew exponentially. During his years living there, he appeared numerous times with the LA

Philharmonic and at the Hollywood Bowl, beginning with an all-Stravinsky programme at the Philharmonic Auditorium in 1941. He also conducted the Werner Janssen Symphony Orchestra, the Los Angeles Chamber Symphony Society, and at the Los Angeles Music Festival (premièring Agon in 1957). The Ojai Festival also had a long-standing relationship with Stravinsky, as did Monday Evening concerts which presented seventy-two performances of fifty-eight of his compositions.

The Stravinskys' home at 1260 North Wetherly Drive in West Hollywood became the central meeting ground for friends, collaborators and family, and he spent long, undisturbed hours in his studio in the company of two service-able upright pianos, a clutter of pencils on his desk and Russian icons on the walls. Visitors included Thomas Mann, Artur Rubinstein, Aldous Huxley and Christopher Isherwood. Fellow émigré composer Sergey Rachmaninov (who was briefly Stravinsky's Beverly Hills neighbour) even brought a jar of honey to his doorstep. This would be the Stravinskys' place of respite for the next twenty-three years, which the composer described, according to long-time friend and colleague Lawrence Morton, as 'my last, longest, happiest, and I should hope – final home'. While both Igor and Vera appreciated the Mediterranean climate of southern California, Vera grew to dislike the monotony of suburbia. Yet she happily took the job of family taxi driver, delivering her husband around town in their used Dodge. (In 1950, the couple travelled by car across the entire USA, depositing Stravinsky in New York just in time to conduct yet another Firebird.) By 1944, Stravinsky was introduced to Robert Craft, a Juilliard student whose tenacity and intellectual prowess brought him into their life as a respected colleague, loyal interpreter of Stravinsky's work and indispensable personal assistant. National and international touring was a constant – their east-coast second home of New York allowed easy access to Europe and a lifeline to old friends from his Diaghilev days, such as Tchelitcheff or Léger.

Stravinsky's artistic life in America moved in two opposing directions: ongoing requests for celebrity appearances at performances of the Firebird or Petrushka standing in stark contrast to the composer's desire for adventure and risk. Reluctant to dwell in the past, his current creative preoccupations were what mattered most to him at any given time. Though his American life could not help but provide fuel for new creative ventures, he dodged suggestions of specific cultural or historic references in his music. He reminded his audience in the conversation books with Craft that 'composers combine notes. That is all. How and in what form the things of this world are impressed upon their music is not for them to say.' Yet, when reflecting in Themes and Conclusions on his Symphony in C, which premièred in Chicago in 1940 and which was conceived at least in part during his American years, he observed that ideas may otherwise 'not have come to my ears in Europe . . . before I had known the neon glitter of Los Angeles's boulevards from a speeding automobile'.

Projects in America went far beyond the concert hall and encompassed Broadway, film and even television. At dinners and special events, the Stravinskys were absorbed into a celebrity pool that included Marlene Dietrich, Cecil B. DeMille, Hedda Hopper and Max Steiner, a network that allowed for commercial opportunities that might never have presented themselves in Europe. More than one Hollywood producer approached Stravinsky to compose for movies, and he was offered substantial sums of money simply to lend his name to existing film scores (business practices which generally caused the composer to shy away from the silver screen). Other ventures outside the concert hall included SCÈNES DE BALLET for Broadway producer Billy Rose's The Seven Lively Arts. Stravinsky's fascination with text and music led to the production of the opera The RAKE'S PROGRESS with poet W. H. AUDEN, created mostly in Hollywood prior to its VENICE première. An attempted collaboration with Dylan THOMAS evaporated with the poet's untimely death, to Stravinsky's great dismay.

Perhaps even greater was Stravinsky's passion for writing music for dance, a seed planted early by Diaghilev in Paris and which resulted in an explosion of commissions for the Ballets Russes and the Ballet Theatre, as well as the American Ballet (later the NEW YORK CITY BALLET). Choreographer and fellow Russian émigré George Balanchine remained the primary muse and catalyst. Together they pioneered Balustrade (1941) for de Basil's Original Ballet Russe, DANSES CONCERTANTES (1944) for the Ballet Russe de Monte Carlo, ORPHEUS (1948) for Ballet Society, and Agon (1957) for the New York City Ballet – many of the scenes animated through conversations in Stravinsky's Beverly Hills home. The two even collaborated for television in 1962 for a CBS production, The FLOOD, a hybrid work with a biblical storyline that, to Stravinsky's chagrin, was received negatively by the critics.

Even as an American citizen, Stravinsky's identity remained devoutly Russian. Though reluctant to associate with the government of the Soviet Union following his immigration to America, he accepted an invitation to return to his country of birth in 1962 and, upon landing in Moscow, remarked 'my whole makeup is Russian. Perhaps in my music it's not at once obvious, but it's there in the background, in its hidden nature' (SSE, 463). His return to Russia came on the heels of a disappointing eightieth birthday year in his adopted country, where few organised concert celebrations had left him feeling neglected (notwithstanding a dinner with the Kennedys at the White House).

Even in his seventies, Stravinsky continued to reinvent himself in ways that took critics by surprise. His 1955 CANTICUM SACRUM, created while confined to his Hollywood study for six months, re-launched him as a trailblazer in the eyes of many European critics. By the 1960s, while a relentless schedule had taken a toll on his health, he refused to rest on bygone glories and his 1966 REQUIEM CANTICLES earned him a standing ovation at the première. Previously eschewing the associations of personal events in his music, with Requiem Stravinsky created a patchwork of remembrances of close friends who had passed away during its composition. On 27 April 1969, he made his last appearance in public during an Homage concert at New York State University, Stony Brook. The necessity of advanced medical care dictated a final move to New York, where he died on 6 April 1971. Though his niece Xenya pleaded for his final resting place to be in Russia, Vera chose the island of San Michele in Venice, setting aside her husband's fear of water (never a strong swimmer,

Stravinsky previously avoided visiting Diaghilev's grave located on the very same island (SSE, 273)). A burial in Los Angeles was out of the question – Vera felt her husband had already been forgotten there. Perhaps Stravinsky's adopted home, though a catalyst for so much that was reimagined in his life and art, was never intended to replace memories.   LORIN JOHNSON

Ustilug, Russian Empire (now Ukraine). Dates of Stravinsky's visits: 1890–1914. A small town in the Volyn region in Ukraine, close to the Polish border, where Stravinsky's maternal uncle-in-law (and future father-in-law) Gavriyil Trofimovich Nosenko (1832–97) had his country seat, consisting of a house, a distillery and land. Stravinsky first visited Ustilug with his mother Anna in 1890, regularly spent his summer there with his brother Gury, and first met his future wife Yekaterina (Catherine STRAVINSKY) there. Ustilug remained his favourite working-place until 1914, and sixteen of his works were conceived there, either fully or partially, including the SYMPHONY IN E♭ MAJOR, SCHERZO FANTASTIQUE, FIREWORKS, The NIGHTINGALE and The RITE OF SPRING (according to Dialogues, the opening bassoon solo was conceived there). The house of Gavriyil Nosenko, and Igor's house built according to his own design (although heavily reconstructed), still remain. A Stravinsky Museum was opened there in 1990.   ELENA VERESHCHAGINA AND TATIANA VERESHCHAGINA

Valéry, Paul (born Sète, 30 October 1871; died Paris, 20 July 1945). French poet, essayist and polymath fascinated by the process of composition and the ability of the conscious mind to observe itself in action. Valéry is well known for his Monsieur Teste character, a fierce intellect devoted to self-examination, and for fifty years' worth of notebooks (*Cahiers*) unintended for publication, containing wide-ranging reflections on art, science, mathematics, philosophy and the interaction between mind, body and world. Valéry produced some major poems, neo-classical in form and style, which BOULEZ claimed had a profound influence on Stravinsky. These include the dramatic monologue 'La Jeune Parque', a reflection on self-consciousness with a structure, Valéry told André GIDE, modelled on the recitative style of Gluck or WAGNER. Stravinsky read *Monsieur Teste* before 1914, and after he met Valéry in the early 1920s, they remained 'ever after natural friends'; in *Portraits mémoires*, Stravinsky recalls, 'we saw each other so regularly that we might be thought to have formed a "circle"'. The composer found his friend 'a deep source of intellectual and moral support' on two important occasions. Valéry helped with details of French expression in Stravinsky's Harvard lectures of 1939, *Poétique musicale* (The POETICS OF MUSIC), and intervened when Gide, 'horrified by the discrepancies between my music and his', complained that Stravinsky mangled his text in PERSÉPHONE. According to Stravinsky, Valéry 'affirmed the musician's prerogative to treat loose and formless prosodies (such as Gide's) according to his musical ideas, even if the latter lead to "distortion" of phrasing or to breaking up, for purposes of syllabification, of the words themselves'. Valéry attended the performances, and after the première wrote Stravinsky a famous, oft-quoted letter: 'the divine detachment of your work touched me … What I have sometimes searched for in the ways of poetry, you pursue and join in your art. The point is, to attain purity through the will' (2 May 1934). In 1959, sensitive to the mystic resonances in Valéry's writing, Stravinsky wrote, 'The Valéry who most interests me at present is one whose very existence most critics would deny: the religious. Valéry's nature *was* in some way religious, no matter how essentially non-religious his writings.'   DAVID EVANS

Valse des fleurs, for piano duet.   Composed 30 September 1914, CLARENS. First performance, 26 February 1949, New York, Soulima STRAVINSKY and Beveridge Webster. Published 1983, facsimile, in Robert CRAFT, *A Stravinsky Scrapbook 1940–1971* (London: Thames and Hudson).

Considered the earliest of Stravinsky's 'easy' duets, the *Valse des fleurs* certainly earns the subtitle '*Elementary seconda*' due to its forty statements of the one unchanging C major pattern. The work's greater subtlety lies in the *prima* part, which evokes the running quavers and gentle syncopation of the homonymous waltz in *The Nutcracker* (1892). Situated midway between other works with Tchaikovskian associations (the SONATA IN F♯ MINOR and MAVRA), the *Valse des fleurs* carries the seed of Stravinsky's evolving interest in a *style dépouillé* whose 'simplicity' will deflect his post-RITE OF SPRING music away from Russian associations towards an internationalist neo-classical aesthetic.

GRAHAM GRIFFITHS

Graham Griffiths, *Stravinsky's Piano: Genesis of a Musical Language* (Cambridge University Press, 2013).
ASS; SSC, I

Valse pour les enfants, for Piano. Composed December 1916 – January 1917. First performance, May 1922 (by the composer in the offices of *Le Figaro*). Published 21 May 1922, *Le Figaro*, PARIS). Dedication: 'Une valse pour les petits lecteurs du Figaro' ('A Waltz for the Little Readers of *Le Figaro*').

Valse pour les enfants shares its two-patterned *ostinato* accompaniment with two other waltzes: 'Waltz' (THREE EASY PIECES, 1914) and 'Valse' (*The* SOLDIER'S TALE, 1918), thus neatly illustrating Stravinsky's progression towards NEO-CLASSICISM via the by-ways of popular dance. A more significant indicator of Stravinsky's stylistic transformation was his private protest at the newspaper caption (published with the score in 1922) which stated that the piece had been 'improvisée au *Figaro*'. This provoked Stravinsky to append a banner headline to his original manuscript: 'Not improvised in the least, but quite thoroughly composed!' – emphatic confirmation that he now disassociated himself from music-by-impulse in favour of music-by-craft, as in this charming and artful creation ('construction') of apparent artlessness.

GRAHAM GRIFFITHS

Graham Griffiths, *Stravinsky's Piano: Genesis of a Musical Language* (Cambridge University Press, 2013).

Varèse, Edgard (born Paris, 22 December 1883; died New York City, 6 November 1965). French-American modernist composer who, after studies in PARIS with d'Indy, Rousel and Widor, as well as encouragement from Romain ROLLAND and DEBUSSY, moved to Berlin in 1907, where he came under the influence of Richard STRAUSS and Ferruccio Busoni. He emigrated to New York in 1915, where he was to spend most of the rest of his life. Consequently, while Europeans have often considered him an American composer, North Americans viewed him as a European.

While Varèse claimed that he had been present at the Paris première of Stravinsky's The RITE OF SPRING in 1913, it seems that he first heard the work in a concert performance in Paris in the spring of 1914 (Zimmerman, in Meyer and Zimmerman 2006, 164). Though he downplayed the importance of the work for his own development, commentators have highlighted clear correspondences between aspects of the *Rite* ('Danse sacrale' and the 'Danses des adolescentes') and Varèse's *Amériques* (1918–22; rev. 1927), though he could only have known Stravinsky's piece in piano reduction at the time (Zimmermann, in Meyer and Zimmermann 2006, 164). While his aesthetic shared something with Stravinsky's description of his OCTET FOR WIND

INSTRUMENTS, as a musical object, comprising form and matter, Varèse consistently rejected any kind of NEO-CLASSICISM.

In *Memories and Commentaries*, while claiming never to have heard *Amériques* or *Arcana*, Stravinsky noted that 'they look as though the shadow of *Le Sacre* had fallen over them'. He continued: 'I do know and greatly admire *Ionisation*, *Octandre*, *Density* 21.5, and *Intégrales*, and I consider Varèse's present activity – tape recording the sound of New York City – of the highest value and not merely as documentation, but as material of art' (*Mem*, 102–3). Prompted by CRAFT, Stravinsky expressed himself at greater length in *Dialogues*, where he highlighted Varèse's pursuit of 'pure sound', an arena beyond the realm of 'twelve-tones' (*Dial*, 109).

Stravinsky recognised something of his own three great Russian ballets in Varèse's *Arcana*, going so far as to pinpont distinct moments of similarity (*Dial*, 110–12), and he suggested that Varèse's 'motorized metrical scheme' may also have been in his debt. He lauded the exploration of 'live instrumental music and electronically recorded sound' in *Déserts*, and praised Varèse's use of dynamics as an element of form, as well as his writing for percussion and wind instruments: 'I love the guiro, the gongs, the anvils of *Ionisation*; the thundering metal sheets, the lathes, the claves of *Déserts*; the parabolas of siren music that make *Amériques* sound like an old-fashioned air-raid', concluding that 'the best things in his music – the first seven measures from No. 16 in *Arcana*, the whole of *Déserts* – are among the better things in contemporary music' (*Dial*, 112).   EDWARD CAMPBELL

Felix Meyer and Heidy Zimmermann (eds.), *Edgard Varèse: Composer, Sound Sculptor, Visionary* (Woodbridge, Suffolk: The Boydell Press, 2006).

Variations (Aldous Huxley In Memoriam), for orchestra. Composed 1963–4. First performance, 17 April 1965, Chicago. Conductor, Robert CRAFT. Published, 1965, Boosey & Hawkes.

Stravinsky began working on the *Variations* at Santa Fe in July 1963, and completed the score in LOS ANGELES on 28 October 1964. He had already drafted some sections of the work when he found out that Aldous HUXLEY, to whom he had been very close in the Californian years, had passed away on 22 November 1963 (the same day as Kennedy's assassination). Therefore, he decided to dedicate the composition to the memory of his friend.

The term 'Variations' is not used in the sense of the classical form, since what is continuously 'varied' is not a 'theme' but the physiognomy of a TWELVE-NOTE row. The transformations which the series undergoes are based on the most complex techniques that Stravinsky had devised since MOVEMENTS (1958–9), such as the rotational arrays and the vertical reading of the serial matrixes. Despite the seemingly rigorous nature of these procedures, however, Stravinsky maintained that the original row had come to mind as a concrete melody and not as an abstract sequence of pitches.

The work is conceived as a single movement made up of eleven sections – some consisting of two or three subsections – each marked by a tempo indication. Sections 2, 4 and 10 are identical with respect to texture – twelve-part polyphony – rhythmic structure and tempo, thus serving as a sort of refrain. In each of these, the single polyphonic parts feature a different combination of serial segments and instrumental layout. Section 9 is a three-part *fugato*.

One of the most striking aspects of the score is the ORCHESTRATION, which is based on the contrast between instrumental families and solo parts. In some sections, there is a continuous unfolding of contrasting instrumental colours – something that Stravinsky compared to SCHOENBERG's *Klangfarbenmelodie*. Each twelve-part polyphonic refrain, on the contrary, is entirely entrusted to a single timbre, resulting from a dense intertwining of very similar-sounding instruments (1st refrain: twelve solo violins; 2nd refrain: ten violas + two double basses; 3rd refrain: twelve wind instruments) within a narrow tessitura.

In *Variations* – as in many other compositions after *Movements* – the static, repetitive and regularly pulsed musical time which characterised Stravinsky's previous 'styles' is much less evident. The typical Stravinskian ostinatos almost completely disappear here. Throughout the score, a basic pulse (set at a metronome rate of 80) is always present, but is frequently not clearly distinguishable, due to the highly intricate rhythm, which makes extensive use of irrational subdivisions.

Stravinsky strongly emphasised the innovative and 'advanced' aspects of the work. In a programme note – which was most likely written by Robert Craft – published in *Themes and Episodes* and (in an expanded version) in *Themes and Conclusions*, he maintained that 'the [first] twelve-part variation ... is probably the most difficult music to analyse aurally in its entirety I have ever composed'. Nonetheless, while in the USA the score was admired (and analysed) by composers and music theorists such as Milton Babbitt and Claudio SPIES, the reception by the European musical avant-garde was generally cool. One may take as typical the judgement expressed in an interview (published in *Melos* in 1967) by Pierre BOULEZ, who, while recognising that the score was an admirable one for a composer of Stravinsky's age, maintained that 'there was nothing new there that Webern had not already done'.

In 1966, the score was choreographed by George BALANCHINE (*Variations*, premièred 31 March). In this version, the music was performed three times, first with a *corps* of twelve females, then with six males, and finally with a solo danced by Susanne Farrell. Another version of the choreography, this time conceived only as a solo for Farrell, was created by Balanchine for the 1982 Stravinsky Centennial Celebration.   MASSIMILIANO LOCANTO

Jerome Kohl, 'Exposition in Stravinsky's orchestral Variations', *Perspectives of New Music*, 18.1/2 (Fall/Winter 1979 and Spring/Summer 1980), 391–405.

Massimiliano Locanto, 'Choreomusicology beyond "formalism": a gestural analysis of *Variations for orchestra* (Stravinsky–Balanchine, 1982)', in Patrizia Veroli and Gianfranco Vinay (eds.), *Music-Dance: Sound and Motion in Contemporary Discourse* (London: Routledge, 2018), 35–56.

Paul Schuyler Phillips, 'The enigma of "Variations": a study of Stravinsky's final work for orchestra', *Music Analysis*, 3.1 (March 1984), 69–89.

Claudio Spies, 'Notes on Stravinsky's Variations', *Perspectives of New Music*, 4.1 (1965), 62–74.

Venice, Venice Festival. Italian city built in a lagoon at the north-western extreme of the Adriatic Sea, and celebrated not just for its watery beauty, but also for its rich cultural heritage in the fields of painting, theatre and architecture, as well as music. On 15 April 1971, Stravinsky's funeral was held in the church of Santi

Giovanni e Paolo. The composer was then buried on the cemetery island of San Michele, not far from the grave of Sergey DIAGHILEV, who had died in Venice in 1929. Stravinsky had not asked to be buried in Venice, but had been a frequent visitor to the city, which maintained its musical traditions in the twentieth century by way of its principal OPERA house, the TEATRO LA FENICE, and, from 1930, the International Festival of Contemporary Music. The Festival, launched by MUSSOLINI'S regime as an offshoot of the more famous art festival, the Biennale (founded 1895), was designed to act as an international showcase for fascism's commitment to the latest trends in music. It quickly attracted the most celebrated names in contemporary composition, including Stravinsky, who appeared at the third Festival in 1934, conducting his CAPRICCIO, with his son Soulima STRAVINSKY as soloist. He returned for the fifth Festival in 1937, conducting JEU DE CARTES. After World War II, the Festival hosted four Stravinsky world premières: The RAKE'S PROGRESS (La Fenice, 1951), CANTICUM SACRUM (ST MARK'S BASILICA, 1956), THRENI (Scuola Grande di San Rocco, 1958) and MONUMENTUM PRO GESUALDO (Doge's Palace, 1960). The composer conducted on each occasion.   BEN EARLE

SSE

Verdi, Giuseppe (born Roncole, near Bussetto, 9 or 10 October 1813; died Milan, 27 January 1901). The pre-eminent Italian composer of the latter half of the nineteenth century, many of whose operas remain fixtures of the international repertory. Stravinsky's enthusiasm for Verdi, especially for his middle-period operas, dates from the 1920s. It is polemically linked to the denigration of WAGNER. Indeed, until his last years, when he changed his mind on the issue, Stravinsky regarded the later Verdi as ruined by Wagner's influence. Echoes of Verdi's style are evident in OEDIPUS REX, as Stravinsky himself acknowledged, and have also been detected in CONCERTO IN E♭: 'DUMBARTON OAKS', The RAKE'S PROGRESS and REQUIEM CANTICLES.   BEN EARLE

Massimiliano Locanto, 'Obiter dicta: l'immagine di Verdi negli scritti di Stravinskij', in Lorenzo Frassà and Michaela Niccolai (eds.), Verdi Reception (Turnhout: Brepols, 2013), 195–216.

Verlaine, Paul (born Metz, 30 March 1844; died Paris, 8 January 1896). French poet who, with Charles Baudelaire, Arthur Rimbaud and Stéphane Mallarmé, is seen as an important precursor to French symbolist literature of the 1880s, and provided crucial inspiration for the Moscow Symbolists led by Valery Bryusov and Konstantin BALMONT in the 1890s. Notorious for an eventful life marked by alcoholism, a violent temper, fifteen months in prison and a love affair with Rimbaud, Verlaine was elected Prince des Poètes by fellow Parisian authors in 1894. Especially influential were the slim volume Romances sans paroles (1873–4), which explores subtle shades of feeling with reference to both music and painting, his studies of 'cursed poets' in Les Poètes maudits (1884), as well as the poem 'Art poétique' (Jadis et naguère, 1885), which begins 'De la musique avant toute chose' ('Music above all'). Stravinsky set two poems by Verlaine (op. 9, 1910), dedicated to his younger brother Gury, both relatively slow and in B♭ minor, for baritone and piano, arranged for baritone and orchestra in 1951. The texts are typical of the impressionist Verlaine, painting vignettes of melancholy and ecstasy in brief poems of short lines. 'Un grand sommeil noir' (*Sagesse*, 1881) describes the loss of desire, culminating in the image of the poet as a cradle, rocked silently in an empty vault. 'La Lune blanche' (*La Bonne Chanson*, 1870), also set by Gabriel Fauré in the nine-song cycle *La Bonne Chanson* (op. 61, 1894), describes 'l'heure exquise', an exquisite moment of nocturnal calm shared by two lovers in the moonlit woods.   DAVID EVANS

Villard, Jean ('Gilles') (born Montreux, Switzerland, 2 June 1895; died Saint-Saphorin, Switzerland, 26 March 1982). Swiss poet, actor, singer, comedian and cabaret owner. Later known as the songwriter behind the Édith Piaf hit 'Les Trois Cloches', Villard created the spoken part of the Devil in the first production of The SOLDIER'S TALE (Lausanne, 1918); the danced Devil was performed by George PITOËFF. Stravinsky was present at rehearsals and Villard vividly remembered the composer at the piano, 'unrestrained, hammering the keys with nervous hands and sustaining his dynamism with an improbable number of kirschs' (SCS, 290).   SOPHIE REDFERN

Voirol, Sebastien (pseudonym of Gustaf-Henrik Lundqvist) (born 1870; died Lausanne, 16 November 1930). French writer of Swedish origin, and brother-in-law of August Perret (the architect of the THÉÂTRE DES CHAMPS-ELYSÉES). Voirol belonged to Parisian avant-garde circles and promoted all the latest trends – cubism, surrealism, FUTURISM, etc. He collaborated with Henry-Martin Barzun and Riciotto Canudo and was close to Apollinaire, Picabia, Severini, Brâncusi, etc.

In November 1913, Voirol gave Stravinsky a copy of his new play entitled *Le Sacre du Printemps* – a verbal version of the BALLET, based on its scenario and dedicated to NIJINSKY and Stravinsky. The work was published by the author as a facsimile of the manuscript (written in green, purple, blue and red ink) limited to fourteen copies (one of which is preserved in the PSS). It was performed at the Théâtre des Champs-Elysées on 3 June 1917 with staging by Mme Lara, and décor by Atelier Martin. In the same year, the author published the second edition of his work (limited to twenty-five copies), supplemented by his own portrait by BAKST, a facsimile of a page of Stravinsky's manuscript, and a watercolour drawing most likely by Paul Poiré.

The text of the play should be recited by a chorus and several protagonists (as in ancient Greek drama). In addition to the Elders, Old Woman and the Chosen One ('L'Adolescente à la tresse en diadème'), Voirol introduced several new characters, including 'Le jeune homme pâle' ('the pale young man'), who is in love with the Chosen One. The play ends with a protest by the Young Man against cruel ancient law. The literary style is close to symbolism, but at the same time demonstrates an avant-garde principle of 'simultanism' (invented by Barzun in poetry): some fragments of the text should be performed simultaneously by the different groups of chorus or characters. According to Barzun and Voirol, this principle corresponded to Stravinsky's polyrhythm and polytonality in The RITE OF SPRING.   TATIANA BARANOVA MONIGHETTI

Vuillermoz, Émile(-Jean-Joseph) (born Lyon, 23 May 1878; died Paris, 2 March 1960). French music critic. Very prolific, he published thousands of texts on music in numerous journals and newspapers between 1899 and 1960. He was also active as a record, radio, cinema, theatre and literary critic, as well as a columnist. Former student in composition at the Paris Conservatory, Vuillermoz was a fervent supporter of Gabriel Fauré, Claude DEBUSSY and Maurice RAVEL, and one of the founding members of the Société musicale indépendante (SMI) in 1910. With other musician and artist friends, he was part of a group called the APACHES, which met from the turn of the century until 1914; Stravinsky occasionally joined them from 1910 onwards – some letters from Stravinsky to Vuillermoz attest their cordial relationship during those years. It was in this context that Vuillermoz witnessed some informal performances of parts of The RITE OF SPRING, which he referred to in his first biographical article on the composer published in the Revue musicale SIM in May 1912. In this text, the critic lauded Stravinsky's 'machinist' style.

Vuillermoz enthusiastically received The FIREBIRD, PETRUSHKA, The Rite of Spring and The NIGHTINGALE, as well as the Three Japanese Lyrics performed at the SMI in January 1914, The SOLDIER'S TALE and Les NOCES, which he considered as an aesthetic extension of The Rite of Spring. In the 1920s, Vuillermoz was a fierce opponent of a type of music that he perceived as anti-Debussyist. However, he had a favourable opinion of PULCINELLA. Later, without ever denying Stravinsky's importance, he vigorously rejected most of the composer's works, from MAVRA to THRENI, with the exception of JEU DE CARTES, which enchanted Vuillermoz as he believed that Stravinsky had abandoned 'his sterile research of neo-classicism, to immerse himself once again in a living, colourful, luminous and dynamic art'.

In his Histoire de la musique (1949), Vuillermoz insisted on the composer's versatility, whose 'bold experiences ... are not all absolute successes but are always interesting', and stated that, because of his 'protean genius', Stravinsky did not produce a 'stravinskyist' style.

MARIE-PIER LEDUC

É. Vuillermoz, 'Igor Strawinsky', Revue musicale SIM, 8.5 (15 May 1912), 15–21.
É. Vuillermoz, 'La musique. Révélations à Venise', Candide (7 October 1937), 17.
É. Vuillermoz, Histoire de la musique (Paris: Fayard, 1949).

496

Wagner, (Wilhelm) Richard (born Leipzig, 22 May 1813; died Venice, 13 February 1883). German composer and poet of predominantly stage works; also conductor and critic. Born a year before Wagner's death, Stravinsky belonged to an artistic era in which Wagner's legacy exerted a near-ubiquitous influence. In his early teens, he was an enthusiastic student of Wagner's works, and his interest developed under RIMSKY-KORSAKOV when he attended performances of The Ring of the Nibelung in ST PETERSBURG from 1906 onwards (see SRT, 247–8). In summer 1912, DIAGHILEV persuaded Stravinsky to join him at Bayreuth to see Parsifal (the performance took place on 20 August). Stravinsky later claimed to have been appalled by the pseudo-religious atmosphere of the whole thing (*see* Auto) and repudiated the Wagner tradition from this time, proclaiming himself 'Wagner's Antichrist', despite the influence of so-called 'Gesamtkunstwerk' among Diaghilev's circle (Craft 1982). In fact, Stravinsky was more enamoured of Parsifal than such accounts suggest, and, indeed, the Bayreuth performance, which interrupted work on The RITE OF SPRING, may have confirmed many of the central features of that work: Wagner's final OPERA is at any rate a striking depiction of RITUAL sacrifice of a female (Kundry) rendered by means of a 'static' musical score. Stravinsky's offhand, ironic anti-Wagnerian asides hardened into official polemic in such writings as the Poétique musicale (POETICS OF MUSIC, 1942), conceived and written in part by Pierre SOUVTCHINSKY (Dufour 2003): here, Wagner is contrasted unfavourably with Giuseppe VERDI as a destroyer of melodic form, and denounced for imposing the 'tyranny' of music drama which has 'smothered [music] under literary flowers'. In a subtler argumentation, the author of Poétique musicale also suggested that Wagner's music exemplified what he termed 'psychological time', as opposed to 'ontological time', meaning subjective temporal experience at odds with the 'chronometrical' time supposedly espoused by Stravinsky. The Russian composer's long-term attachment to purely instrumental forms was in itself a refutation of 'music drama', and the operas he produced clearly posed historical alternatives to the Wagnerian model: e.g., MAVRA (in the 'Russo-Italian tradition') and The RAKE'S PROGRESS ('in the mould of an eighteenth-century "number" opera').   JEREMY COLEMAN

Robert Craft, 'My life with Stravinsky', The New York Review of Books (10 June 1982), 6–10.
Valérie Dufour, 'La "Poétique musicale" de Stravinsky: Un manuscrit inédit de Souvtchinsky', Revue de musicologie, 89.2 (2003), 373–92.
Arnold Whittall, 'Stravinsky and music drama', Music & Letters, 50.1, (Jan. 1969), 63–7.
SRT

Walter, Bruno (Bruno Schlesinger) (born Berlin, 15 September 1876; died Beverly Hills, 17 February 1962). German conductor. Walter studied composition before becoming a conductor, working closely with MAHLER in Hamburg and Vienna. Before 1939, he held major posts in Munich, Berlin, Leipzig and Vienna, leaving Austria in 1939 to settle in the USA. He conducted the CONCERTO FOR PIANO AND WIND INSTRUMENTS in PARIS (20 May 1928), with Stravinsky as the soloist. Stravinsky described the experience as 'a pleasure altogether unanticipated ... My scrambled meters gave him no trouble at all and he conducted the Concerto as well as any conductor with whom I played it' (*Saturday Review*, 31 March 1962). NIGEL SIMEONE

Webern, Anton von (born Vienna, 3 December 1883; died Mittersill, 15 September 1945). Webern's admiration for Stravinsky is evident in an ecstatic letter he wrote to BERG after a Stravinsky evening at the Verein für musikalische Privataufführungen in 1919 (see a quotation from this letter in the entry for the SECOND VIENNESE SCHOOL). Stravinsky's admiration of Webern, however, came very late in life – even later than his respect for the music of SCHOENBERG and Berg.

Stravinsky was never as enthusiastic about Webern's music as he was about Berg's. CRAFT quotes him as saying:

> Webern seems to put a low premium on the listener's sense of involvement. Not only is his music wholly unrhetorical but it does not invite participation in the argument of its own creation as, say, Beethoven's does, with its second subjects, fugal episodes, developments of subsidiary parts, its schematic elaboration and integration. Instead, each opus offers itself only as a whole, a unity to be contemplated. It is essentially static, therefore, and thus the cost in subjectivity is high. (T&C, 93)

This remark about the lack of second subjects, etc., makes one wonder whether Stravinsky – or Craft – really understood how Webern's music was organised. But, in spite of his questioning the degree of interaction involved in listening to Webern, Stravinsky also said, rather curiously, 'He brings a new and intensely individual voice to music, and he has a power to move' (T&C, 96). In a more critical attitude, he said that Webern 'seems to have been obsessed with the device of the silent or "suspended" beat, with the note on the anacrusis' (T&C, 94), and that:

> those dying-away, *molto ritenuto e molto espressivo* phrase endings have become a little tiresome; and the touch of cuteness in some of the vocal music: the too-frisky piano figure introducing 'Wie bin ich froh!', for instance; the 'Glück' at the end of the Chinese choruses (in which the *chinoiserie* is also less subtle than in the early Li-Tai-Po song); and that wretched 'Bienchen' in *Gleich und Gleich* (did Webern know Hugo Wolf's setting of this poem?), which should have been a large wasp with a good sting. But these are minor objections, arising from simple conflicts of temperament. (T&C, 93)

Somewhat surprisingly, in light of the remarks just quoted, for the tenth anniversary of Webern's death, Stravinsky wrote a eulogy for *Die Reihe* 2 that reads:

The 15th of September 1945, the day of Anton Webern's death, should be a day of mourning for any receptive musician. We must hail not only this great composer but also a real hero. Doomed to a total failure in a deaf world of ignorance and indifference he inexorably kept on cutting out his diamonds, his dazzling diamonds, the mines of which he had such a perfect knowledge.

– and in April 1955 Stravinsky and Craft visited Webern's grave at Mittersill.

The two men seem to have met only once, at a reception in Vienna in 1926, and it is very unlikely that they would have become friends, even if they had had the chance. Stravinsky once said of the mountains, which were all-important to Webern: 'They tell me nothing.'   KATHRYN PUFFETT

Igor Stravinsky, *Die Reihe 2. Anton Webern* (Theodore Presser Co. in association with Universal Edition; original German edn, Universal Edition, 1955; English edn, 1958, 2nd rev. edn, 1959), p. vii.

Weill, Kurt (Julian) (born Dessau, 2 March 1900; died New York, 3 April 1950). German composer and critic. Best known for his collaborations with Bertolt Brecht, he emigrated to the USA in 1935 and naturalised as a US citizen in 1943. As Theodor W. ADORNO first noted, the parody-laden surrealist techniques of Weill's celebrated *Dreigroschenoper* (1928) had a precedent in Stravinsky's THE SOLDIER'S TALE, a work of music theatre that for Adorno exemplified 'the best, radical Stravinsky'. Weill attended the German première of *Die Geschichte vom Soldaten* (Werner Reinhart's translation) in Frankfurt, June 1923. He was so impressed that he declared it an 'intergenre (*Zwischengattung*) most assured of a future' which could even 'form the basis of a certain type of new opera'. Indeed, the work directly inspired Weill's conception of music theatre combining different styles and genres, including spoken narration, and was a source for Weill's trademark use of popular idioms: ragtime, foxtrot and – above all – tango. Stravinsky's comparatively austere OEDIPUS REX (1927) was no less important a model, leading Weill to write his radio cantatas *Das Berliner Requiem* (1928) and *Der Lindberghflug* (1929).   JEREMY COLEMAN

Theodor W. Adorno, 'Zur Musik der Dreigroschenoper', in David Drew (ed.), *Über Kurt Weill* (Frankfurt: Suhrkamp, 1975), 39–44.

Kurt Weill, 'Die neue Oper', *Der neue Weg*, 60.2 (1926), 24–5, repr. in Kurt Weill, *Musik und Musikalisches Theater: Gesammelte Schriften*, ed. Stephen Hinton and Jürgen Schebera (Mainz: Schott, 2000), 42–5.

Western Classical Tradition. With his three most famous ballets, presented by DIAGHILEV'S BALLETS RUSSES in PARIS – The FIREBIRD (1910), PETRUSHKA (1911) and The RITE OF SPRING (1913) – Stravinsky secured international recognition. Together with DEBUSSY, he was regarded as a leading composer of the French avant-garde. French, rather than Russian?

Although geographically separated, FRANCE and RUSSIA had enjoyed a cultural liaison for some time. The upper classes in Russia thought and spoke in French, whilst Russian music was often performed in Paris, to great acclaim. Nationalism in music is often regarded as a means by which a composer can assert national confidence and identity through reference to

FOLK MUSIC, an increasingly endangered species towards the end of the nine-teenth century. However, following the unification of GERMANY in 1871 and its consequent rise in power, France felt strongly allied to Russia, not only in music. Such a link seems to have been fuelled and enhanced by the French press, thus adding a political dimension to nationalism.

Nineteenth-century Russian music had often taken account of western European stylistic developments, but the later years of the century saw a break away from this approach in the more radical music of BORODIN and MUSSORGSKY. For the young Stravinsky, the stylistic spectrum was wide. His earliest works sometimes reflect TCHAIKOVSKY (The Faun and the Shepherdess, op. 2), or even Schumann and STRAUSS (SYMPHONY IN E♭ MAJOR, op. 1), before a more obviously Russian idiom developed. The orchestral richness and orientalism of his teacher RIMSKY-KORSAKOV add a further spectrum of influ-ences, and the occasional use of what we now know as the octatonic scale, in Mussorgsky and Rimsky-Korsakov in Russia, and Debussy and RAVEL in France, indicates a technical connection between the two traditions; as demon-strated by Pieter van den Toorn, and subsequently by other scholars, Stravinsky's music is saturated with octatonicism.

In a wider European context, the years leading up to World War I witnessed an unprecedented rate of discovery and change, affecting every level of human endeavour – science and technology, social hierarchy, art in all its forms – in ways that were uncomfortable at the time and unpredictable in their conse-quences. Monarchies fell, social norms crumbled and everything seemed, in retrospect, to be heading inexorably to the horrors of war. It would have been odd if music did not reflect this. Yet, just a little earlier, complete mastery of nineteenth-century style was in evidence. Beautifully crafted works such as SCHOENBERG's D Major String Quartet, SCRIABIN's Piano Concerto and Stravinsky's PIANO SONATA IN F♯ MINOR and Symphony in E♭ Major, give no hint of impending revolution. Soon, leading composers of the time experi-enced an irresistible creative urge which they could not fully control or explain. Stravinsky admitted as much when reflecting on the process of composing The Rite of Spring. The famously riotous response at its première in May 1913 was not an isolated occurrence; Schoenberg faced a similar experience when con-ducting a concert of new music in Berlin in 1910. Many decades later, BOULEZ pronounced 1912 as the Golden Year of the century's musical creativity, citing The Rite of Spring (the composition of which was mainly completed in 1912), Schoenberg's Pierrot lunaire, Debussy's Jeux and BERG's Altenberglieder.

In the context of Western European culture, Stravinsky sometimes retained more of his Russian heritage than perhaps even he was aware of at the time. He once declared that the only Russian tune in The Rite of Spring is the opening bassoon solo, which is a variation of an ancient chant. However, it has since been revealed that the work has numerous melodies from Russian and Lithuanian folk song, recalled from the composer's early childhood – perhaps subconsciously. In some works that appeared immediately after the war, Stravinsky's Russian heritage appears equally clearly, perhaps as a natural expression of NOSTALGIA for a now-lost country. Among these are Les NOCES, which, in its final version, accompanies four vocal soloists and choir with four pianos and much percussion – a far cry from the rich ORCHESTRATION of his pre-war music. Furthermore, the composer admitted that the disconnection of characters (bride, groom, etc.) from particular voices is a distinctly Russian element of the work which would be hard for Western audiences to appreciate.

Russian RITUAL appears to dominate SYMPHONIES OF WIND INSTRUMENTS, which pursues a mosaic pattern of events, switching suddenly from one musical idea to another. Nevertheless, overall coherence is arguably present, by two means. As regards pitch references, the opening has G as its tonal centre, with high D above. The work proceeds via extended passages based in E minor, and eventually descends to C, concluding when all notes that don't belong to C major are eliminated and the opening high D is restored to its original register in the final chord. In addition, three speeds are cleverly linked, in strict ratios, an idea which Elliott CARTER developed more fully later in the century. One feels a distinct Russianness in works in which he chose to write in Latin – the opera-oratorio OEDIPUS REX and the choral-orchestral SYMPHONY OF PSALMS. To Stravinsky, Latin was timeless, ritualistic, 'monumental'. In *Oedipus*, action is often restricted, following the manner of ancient Greek tragedy in which dramatic turning-points are reported rather than presented on stage. Melody is often minimal, here and in *Symphony of Psalms*, and the serene ending of the latter's final movement ([22]–[28]) arguably contains his finest example of ostinato technique. A repeating bass of four minims, in 3/2 time, recurs every four bars, while the choir has phrases in six-bar units – in this way, a straight repeat only occurs after twelve bars. The result is a remarkably effective sense of eternity.

To what extent did Stravinsky embrace the neo-classical aesthetic, so prominent in the 1920s and 1930s? In some respects, certain elements in the works of the war years anticipate the stylistic changes of the succeeding decades. The SOLDIER'S TALE is a unique work, which highlights the dilemma of re-creating theatre in a war-torn Europe, with its small number of players and dancers; it also reveals the composer's widening of stylistic resources, including Viennese waltz, ragtime and JAZZ. In the Paris of the 1920s, this was not so out of place, but Stravinsky was a leader in incorporating styles foreign to the norm of Western heritage: non-Russian perhaps in one sense, but, with its biting textures and bold contrasts, not one bar could have been written by anyone else. During the three decades after the composition of *Les Noces*, he produced a succession of instrumental works, each in three or four separate movements, alluding to the sonata principle and culminating in two more symphonies. On the other hand, a sense of irony is never far away, as though a fundamentally Russian ingredient is essential. Is the SYMPHONY IN THREE MOVEMENTS a genuine symphony, or is it BALLET music? To some critics, for instance Robert Simpson (1967, 11–12), the Symphony in Three Movements is best heard as a ballet – 'It is no symphony', he wrote, with reference to a concept which he regarded as more mosaic and episodic than structural and organic. Yet, in the outer movements at least, the rhythmic energy carries the listener along most persuasively. And if 'Western' coherence is sought, it can be found. This symphony is as much 'in C' as his other symphony of that period, entitled 'SYMPHONY IN C'. But the opening of the first movement, based on G (as dominant) soon superimposes D♭ tonality; with great excitement, the final movement ends in D♭, perhaps fulfilling a gesture initiated early in the first movement. To take another example, the first movement of the CONCERTO IN E♭: 'DUMBARTON OAKS' for chamber orchestra presents us with a clear E♭ tonality, with intrusions of the note D. D rises in importance, as the tonal centre of the subsidiary material ([7]–[11]), and the final chord of that movement retains a D in what is otherwise a clear E♭ chord. The seeming simplicity of certain other works of the period was a surprise to many, who wondered what had happened to the revolutionary spirit of The Rite. The ballet PULCINELLA defied expectations and was not the only work to be clearly reflective of eighteenth-century style, whilst the climax of the period is the beautifully crafted OPERA The RAKE'S PROGRESS – a 'final gasp of neoclassicism', as one critic put it. On the surface, Stravinsky is clearly harking back to a Western classical ideal, with a complex, love-triangle story delivered in arias and recitatives, all couched in music that is remarkably easy to grasp when compared to the pioneering outlook of his earlier and later works. Tonal centres are readily discernible, rhythmic patterns are more continuous, and spontaneous energy conveys the impression of power in reserve. Yet a certain Russian distancing prevails: we are onlookers, no more emotionally involved in the destinies of the opera's main characters than we are sympathetic to the fate of the sacrificial virgin in The Rite, or joyful at the spectacle of bride and groom in Les Noces.

His output of the 1950s and 1960s is notable for his adoption of some aspects of serial method, encouraged by Robert CRAFT. Progressive composers forty years younger than Stravinsky, in Europe and the USA, were engaged in a renewal of the language of music in the wake of World War II, and it is remarkable how Stravinsky was able to contribute to this move. A guiding spirit was the music of WEBERN, but if direct imitation was tempting, it proved unwise (and indeed impossible). Serial purists were ready to criticise Stravinsky for not aiming at an atonal equilibrium and for allowing perfect fourths and fifths to dominate the texture. However, Stravinsky was writing Stravinsky, not effecting a reconciliation with the Schoenberg school. Thus, tonal references in late Stravinsky are frequent, with, especially, a leaning towards C major – black and white notes clashing and resolving to C. This is most obvious in IN MEMORIAM DYLAN THOMAS, but arguably it is also present in the simplest section of MOVEMENTS for piano and orchestra – movement 4; see the end of pages 11, 12 and 13. Here, the twelve-note row itself is an example of interlocking perfect fourths and fifths. A further example of Stravinsky's individual approach to serialism can be seen in the word-painting that occurs in the third of the Shakespeare Songs, where black notes find contrast in four bars of white notes for the text 'And Ladies smockes all silver white, Do paint the Medowes with delight'. In 'Musicke to heare', the first of this set of songs, the introduction finds the four-note row, on flute, accompanied by a dislocated five-note scale of C major, on clarinet and viola; and every cadence suggests a planned progress towards C, despite the serial elements present throughout the song – see bars 8, 21, 34 and 50.

Indeed, throughout his career, Stravinsky was adept at selecting aspects of Western European musical vocabulary, carefully modified to suit his creative aims. Without wholly abandoning its Russian origins, the music of Stravinsky stands as a supreme icon of Western European culture.   SEBASTIAN FORBES

Robert Simpson, The Symphony, vol. II: Elgar to the Present Day (London: Pelican, 1967).

Whiteman, Paul Samuel (born Denver, Colorado, 28 March 1890; died Doylestown, Pennsylvania, 29 December 1967).

Paul Whiteman was dubbed the 'King of Jazz', according to the broad definition of JAZZ that applied within the early 1920s. His main claim to fame was as the bandleader who commissioned George Gershwin's *Rhapsody in Blue* (1924), billed as 'An experiment in modern music'. Whiteman's symphonic jazz orchestra provided a slick and commercially successful – essentially white – concert-hall translation of African-American jazz and blues. His association with Stravinsky was occasioned by the composer's reworking of SCHERZO À LA RUSSE (1943–4). Originally intended for FILM use, Stravinsky re-orchestrated the *Scherzo* for jazz band, construing it for Paul Whiteman's Band (a large ensemble featuring six saxophones, wind, brass, percussion and strings), although this 4-minute work was in fact premièred in 1944 by Blue Network radio. Parallels exist here with another (rather unsuccessful) arrangement by Stravinsky of part of MAVRA, for the Jack Hylton Orchestra, which premièred at the Paris Opéra in February 1931.   DEBORAH MAWER

$$\boxed{Z}$$

Ziloti (Siloti), Alexander Il'yich (born near Kharkov, 27 September / 9 October 1863; died New York, 8 December 1945). Russian pianist and conductor. In 1903, he launched the Ziloti Concerts in St Petersburg, involving the Mariinsky Theatre orchestra, mainly held at the 1,400-seat Hall of the Assembly of the Nobility. Ziloti's seasons presented the capital's best-performed and most enterprising programmes, eclipsing the more conservative Belyayev-sponsored Russian Symphony Concerts. Ziloti himself conducted dozens of first Russian performances and world premières including – of major consequence to the composer – two of Stravinsky's works.

Through Ziloti's concerts, Stravinsky first heard Dukas' *Sorcerer's Apprentice* (its St Petersburg première on 16/29 October 1904), Debussy's *Nocturnes* (15/ 28 December 1907, its first Russian performance – without its final movement) and Ravel's *Rapsodie espagnole* (3/16 January 1909), all of which influenced the young composer's growing orchestral mastery. Ziloti's first direct involvement with Stravinsky appears to have been in 1907, when he fruitlessly recommended *The Faun and the Shepherdess* to the publisher Julius Zimmerman. When Stravinsky showed Ziloti Scherzo fantastique early in 1908, the pianist-conductor wrote immediately to the publisher Jürgenson urging him to accept this 'superb piece' – a suggestion taken up within a month. Ziloti also scheduled its première for 24 January / 6 February 1909; Stravinsky, in gratitude, dedicated the work to Ziloti. Given Ziloti's enthusiastic support, Stravinsky naturally approached him to perform Funeral Song, but Ziloti had already commissioned Glazunov to write a piece in Rimsky-Korsakov's memory, and could not programme two funeral works. Nonetheless, the *Scherzo fantastique* première was a triumph and something of a landmark for both Ziloti and the composer – Stravinsky being called to the stage, and Ziloti receiving a long, standing ovation at the end of the concert; Ziloti's biographer Charles Barber describes the concert (which also included the Russian première of Elgar's First Symphony) as 'the breakthrough' which saved Ziloti's concert series from financial disaster. It was also the concert in which Sergey Diaghilev first heard and was impressed by Stravinsky's work, leading to the composer's career-changing work for the Ballets Russes. Ziloti naturally followed that success by conducting the première of Stravinsky's Fireworks (9/ 22 January 1910), which he again commended to a publisher – on this occasion Schott, with whom Ziloti negotiated on Stravinsky's behalf a fee of 200 marks.

Prior to this, early in May 1909, Ziloti commissioned Stravinsky to orchestrate Beethoven and Mussorgsky's settings of the 'Song of the Flea' for a concert on the theme of Faust, held on 28 November / 11 December that year. Almost eleven months later, at the same venue, Ziloti conducted the first Russian performance of music from The FIREBIRD in the form of a suite he premièred on 23 October / 5 November 1910: though the music offended a large section of the audience, who left during the performance, it was warmly reviewed by KARATÏGIN in both *Apollon* and *Otkliki khudozhestvennoy zhizni*.

Stravinsky had one last practical encounter with Ziloti when, in October 1921, at Diaghilev's request, he orchestrated two numbers omitted from the original production of Tchaikovsky's *Sleeping Beauty*, using as his source Ziloti's piano reduction of the score.   DANIEL JAFFÉ

Charles Barber, *Lost in the Stars: The Forgotten Musical Life of Alexander Siloti* (Lanham: Scarecrow Press, 2002).
SCS; SRT

Appendix 1　Musical Works

Compiled by Daniel Jaffé

The following worklist is especially indebted to Eric Walter White's 'Register of Works', published in SCW (1979); in preparation of this list of 'Musical Works', information from White's 'Register' has been updated, amended, added to and elaborated in the light of research by such scholars as Robert CRAFT, Helmut Kirchmeyer, Christian Goubault (Igor Stravinsky, 1991), Richard Taruskin and Stephen Walsh, as well as amendments and corrections being made by the present author after consulting primary and contemporary sources, referenced where appropriate.

Although no attempt has been made to include all Stravinsky's musical sketches, all known and identifiable discrete compositions – whether or not completed, or even if not readily available – are listed, including brief musical salutations Stravinsky composed from time to time as personal tokens or gifts for friends and colleagues. Several such pieces, many not included in any previously published worklist, have been identified primarily through the Inventare der Paul Sacher Stiftung, 5: Igor Strawinsky (Amadeus, 1989), as well as other publications detailed within the present worklist.

For details beyond the scope of this present list, Eric Walter White's 'Register of Works' may be referred to through the 'W' numbers, while the 'K' catalogue numbers refer to the catalogue created by Stravinsky scholar Helmut Kirchmeyer, readily available online at www.kcatalog.org; still being updated according to ongoing research as this book goes to press, each entry on this site includes a good deal of information concerning errors in the published scores, the nature of each revision or edition of a particular work, and, where possible, a detailed outline as to the genesis of each work.

To aid cross-referencing, each work referred to is identified by a reference number which begins with the ordinal number found in the first column of the table. For example, 26: W22/K16 refers to Three Japanese Lyrics, listed at No. 26 in the first column of the table, and catalogued respectively in White's Register of Works at No. 22, and in Kirchmeyer's catalogue at No. 16.

Stravinsky Worklist

W	K	Title	First Performance	Publication	Remarks
1	N1	Tarantella, for piano, incomplete			Written October 1898 (St Petersburg); ms, 'dedicated' to A. Kudnev. Now held at St Petersburg State Public Library.
2	N3	Tucha ('The Storm Cloud'), romance for voice and piano (text by A. Pushkin)		Sovetskiy Kompozitor, in Igor' Stravinsky Vokal'naya Muzïka, vol. I, 1982; Faber and Faber, 1986	1902
3	N2	Scherzo for piano		Facsimile in V. Smirnov, Tvorcheskoye Formirovaniye I. F. Stravinskovo, Leningrad: Muzïka, 1970; Faber and Faber, 1973	1902; discovered among Nikolay Richter's papers in the 1960s
4	1	Piano Sonata, F# Minor	9/22 February 1905 at Nikolay Rimsky-Korsakov's home by Nikolay Richter	Faber and Faber, 1974	1903–4
5	N4	Cantata (for Rimsky-Korsakov's sixtieth birthday), for chorus and piano (?), lost	St Petersburg, 6/19 March 1904		c. 1903–4
6	N5	How the Mushrooms Prepared for War (Kak gribï na voynu sobiralis), song for bass and piano (text by 'Koz'ma Prutkov')		Boosey & Hawkes, 1979	1904 (St Petersburg)

(cont.)

	W	K	Title	First Performance	Publication	Remarks
7	7	N6	Song settings of poems by 'Koz'ma Prutkov', including 'Konduktor i tarantul' ('The Driver and the Tarantula'), lost	Possibly by Stravinsky at Nikolay Rimsky-Korsakov's home on the composer's fifty-ninth birthday (6/19 March 1903)		c. 1903; 'Konduktor i tarantul' possibly added 1906
8	8	2	The Faun and the Shepherdess (Favn' i pastushka; Faune et bergère) (text by A. Pushkin), suite for mezzo-soprano and orchestra, op. 2	St Petersburg, 14/27 April 1907 (private); 22 January / 4 February 1908 (public), both cond. Hugo Wahrlich	M. P. Belaïeff, 1908 (vocal score), 1913 (full score); Boosey & Hawkes, 1964	1905–6 (Imatra, St Petersburg); dedicated to Yekaterina Gabrielovna Stravinsky
9	9	3	Symphony in E♭ for orchestra, op. 1	St Petersburg, ?16/29 April 1907 (Scherzo – and possibly Largo – only); 22 January / 4 February 1908 (complete), both cond. Wahrlich; second revised version: Montreux, 2 April 1914, cond. Ernest Ansermet	Jurgenson, 1914; Forberg, 1964	1905; revised 1907 (Ustilug); dedicated to 'my dear teacher N. A. Rimsky-Korsakov'; post-1908 revisions presumably prior to 1914 publication.
10a	10	6	Pastorale, vocalise for soprano and piano	St Petersburg, 27 December 1907 / 9 January 1908, Yelizaveta Petrenko (soprano), either Mladen Iovanovich or Stravinsky (piano)	Jurgenson, 1910; Chester	1907 (Ustilug); dedicated 'A M-lle Nadiejda Rimsky-Korsakov'
10b	10	6	Pastorale – arr. for soprano, oboe, cor anglais, clarinet and bassoon	Antwerp, 7 January 1924, Vera Janacopoulos, cond. Stravinsky	Schott	Arranged for Vera Janacopoulos, 1923 (Biarritz)

10c	10	Pastorale – extended version for violin, oboe, cor anglais, clarinet and bassoon		Schott, 1934	Arranged with Samuel Dushkin's assistance, 1933
10d	10	Pastorale – extended version for violin and piano		Schott, 1934	Piano part a reduction of arrangement for Samuel Dushkin, 1933
11	11	Two Songs for mezzo-soprano and piano, op. 6 (texts by Gorodetsky)	No. 1 only: St Petersburg, 27 December 1907 / 9 January 1908. Yelizaveta Petrenko (soprano), Mladen Iovanovich or Stravinsky (piano); both songs: 24 February / 9 March 1909, Anna Zherebtsova (mezzo-soprano), Mikhail Bikhter	Jurgenson, 1912 or 1913	'Spring': 1907 (St Petersburg, Ustilug); 'A Song of the Dew': 1908 (Ustilug)
12	12	Scherzo fantastique (for large orchestra), op. 3	St Petersburg, 24 January / 6 February 1909, cond. Alexander Ziloti	Jurgenson, 1909; Schott	May 1907 – April 1908 (Ustilug, St Petersburg); dedicated to Ziloti
13	13	Fireworks for orchestra, op. 4	St Petersburg, 9/22 January 1910, cond. Ziloti	Schott, 1910	May/June 1908 (Ustilug); orchestration revised May 1909
14	14	Funeral Song (Pogrebal'naya pesn') for orchestra, op. 5	St Petersburg, 17/30 January 1909, cond. Felix Blumenfeld	Boosey & Hawkes, 2017	1908; lost after première, then rediscovered 2015
15	15	Four Studies for piano, op. 7		Jurgenson, 1910; Anton J. Benjamin	June/July 1908 (Ustilug)

(cont.)

	W	K	Title	First Performance	Publication	Remarks
16	B.II	N8	Chopin: Nocturne in A♭, op. 32/2; Grand Valse brillante in E♭, op. 18 – arr. for orchestra for the ballet Les Sylphides	Paris, 2 June 1909, cond. Nikolay Tcherepnin	Boosey & Hawkes: Grand Valse, 1997; Nocturne, 2002	1909
17	B.III:i	N9	Beethoven: Flohlied, op. 75/3 – arr. for bass voice and large orchestra	St Petersburg, 28 November / 11 December 1909, cond. Ziloti	Sovetskiy Kompozitor, in Igor' Stravinsky Vokal' naya Muzïka, vol. II, 1928; Boosey & Hawkes	1909
18	B.III:ii	N10	Mussorgsky: 'Song of the Flea' ('Pesnya Mefistofelya o blokhe') – arr. for bass and orchestra	St Petersburg, 28 November / 11 December 1909, cond. Ziloti	Sovetskiy Kompozitor, in Igor' Stravinsky Vokal' naya Muzïka, vol. II, 1928; Boosey & Hawkes	1909
19	B.I	N7	Grieg: Kobold, op. 71/3 – arr. for orchestra, lost	St Petersburg, Mariinsky Theatre, 20 February / 5 March 1910 (Paris, 19 May 1909, the date given by White, Goubault and Kirchmeyer, was the première of Le Festin – but see Remarks); as part of Les Orientales: Paris, Théâtre National de l'Opéra, 25 June 1910, cond. Gabriel Pierné		c. 1909. Though some sources claim it was arranged for the ballet divertissement Le Festin, it appears to have been first used as a solo vehicle for Nijinsky. After its St Petersburg première, Kobold was incorporated in the ballet divertissement Les Orientales
20a	16	10	The Firebird (Zhar'ptitsa), fairy story ballet in two scenes	Paris, Opéra, 25 June 1910, cond. Pierné	Jurgenson, 1912; Schott	1909–10 (St Petersburg)
20b	16	10	The Firebird – Suite for Orchestra	St Petersburg, 23 October / 5 November 1910, cond. Ziloti	Jurgenson, 1912	1910

			Title	Performance	Publisher	Notes
2oc	16	–	The Firebird – Berceuse, for orchestra	Bordeaux, 8 February 1914, cond. Stravinsky	Jurgenson, 1912	Wind section reduced from original score
2od	16	10	The Firebird – Suite for Orchestra	Geneva, 12 April 1919, cond. Ansermet	Chester, 1920	1919 (Morges) – arr. for a smaller orchestra than original ballet
2oe	16	10	The Firebird – Prelude, Ronde, arr. for violin and piano		Schott, 1929	Dedicated to Paul Kochanski (who made transcription with amendments by Stravinsky), 1926
2of	16	10	The Firebird – Berceuse, arr. for violin and piano		Schott, 1929	Dedicated to Paul Kochanski (who made transcription with amendments by Stravinsky), 1926
2og	16	10	The Firebird – Berceuse, arr. for violin and piano	Possibly 13 March 1936, London (BBC broadcast), Dushkin and Stravinsky	Schott, 1932	Arranged in collaboration with Samuel Dushkin, 1931–2
2oh	16	10	The Firebird – Scherzo, arr. for violin and piano		Schott, 1933	Arranged in collaboration with Samuel Dushkin, 1932
2oi	16	10	The Firebird – Suite for Orchestra	New York, 24 October 1945, Horenstein	New York: Leeds Music Co., 1946	1945, using same size orchestra as 1919 suite, plus snare drum
21a	17	11	Two Poems of Verlaine, for baritone and piano, op. 9	St Petersburg, 13/26 January 1911, Gualter Bossé (bass)	Jurgenson, 1911; Boosey & Hawkes, 1954	August 1910 (La Baule, Brittany); dedicated 'A mon frère Goury'
21b	17	11	Two Poems of Verlaine, arr. baritone and chamber orchestra		Boosey & Hawkes, 1952–3	1910 (La Baule), 1951–2

(cont.)

W		K	Title	First Performance	Publication	Remarks
22a	18	12	Petrushka, burlesque in four scenes	Original ballet: Paris, Châtelet, 13 June 1911, cond. Pierre Monteux; concert version: Paris, 1 March 1914, cond. Monteux	Édition Russe, 1912	1910–11, dedicated to Alexandre Benois; concert ending added Berlin, 1911
22b	18	12	Three Movements from Petrushka, for piano	Paris, 26 December 1922, Jean Wiener (piano)	Édition Russe, 1922; Boosey & Hawkes, 1947	Written for Artur Rubinstein, 1921
22c	18	12	Danse russe, for violin and piano	Berlin, 28 October 1932, Dushkin	Édition Russe, 1932	Transcribed in collaboration with Samuel Dushkin, 1932
22d	18	12	Petrushka, burlesque in four scenes (fully revised 1946 version)	First and Fourth tableaux only: Boston, 22 February 1946, cond. Stravinsky; revised ballet: Chicago, 23 October 1954, cond. Stravinsky	Boosey & Hawkes, 1948; 1971 (fully corrected version)	October 1946 (Hollywood)
23a	19	13	Two Poems of Balmont, for soprano or tenor and piano	St Petersburg, 28 November / 11 December 1912, Sandra (Aleksandra Aleksandrovna) Belling (soprano), Ernst Belling (piano)	Édition Russe, 1912; Boosey & Hawkes	1911 (Ustilug); No. 1 dedicated 'to my mother'; No. 2 'To my sister-in-law Lyudmila Belyankin'
23b	19	13	Two poems of Balmont, arr. for soprano or tenor, two flutes, two clarinets, piano and string quartet	Los Angeles, 29 November 1954, Bonnie Murray (soprano), cond. Ingolf Dahl	Boosey & Hawkes, 1955	1954; instrumentation the same as for 26: W22/K16
24	20	14	Zvezdoliky (Le Roi des étoiles; The King of the Stars), for male chorus and orchestra (text by Balmont)	Brussels, 19 April 1939, cond. Franz André	Jurgenson, 1913	1911–12 (Ustilug); dedicated to Claude Debussy

			Work	Premiere	Publication	Date / notes
25a	15	21	Le Sacre du printemps (Vesna svyashchennaya; The Rite of Spring), scenes of pagan Russia in two parts	Paris, Champs-Elysées, 29 May 1913, cond. Pierre Monteux	Édition Russe, 1913 (piano duet), 1921 (full score); Boosey & Hawkes, 1948	1911–13 (Ustilug, Clarens); dedicated to Nicholas Roerich
25b	–	–	Le Sacre du printemps – concert version of prelude to Part II (with reduced wind sections)	Geneva, Victoria Hall, 5 February 1923, cond. Ansermet		1922 (Paris); created at Ernest Ansermet's request
25c	15	21	The Rite of Spring – revised and rescored 'Sacrificial Dance'		'Sacrificial Dance' only: AMP, 1945; complete ballet: Boosey & Hawkes, 1965 (with revised 'Sacrificial Dance')	1943 (Santa Barbara)
26	16	22	Three Japanese Lyrics, for soprano, two flutes, two clarinets, piano and string quartet (text Japanese, trans. A. Brandt)	Paris, 14 January 1914, Galina Nikitina (soprano), cond. Désiré-Émile Inghelbrecht	Édition Russe, 1913	1912–13 (Ustilug, Clarens)
27	17	23	Three Little Songs (Souvenirs de mon enfance), for voice and piano (text Russian folk poems)	Petrograd, 23 April / 6 May 1915, Zoya Lodi (soprano) and Irina Miklashevskaya (piano)	Édition Russe, 1914	c. 1906; rev. 1913 (Clarens)
28	N11	B.IV	Mussorgsky/Stravinsky: Khovanshchina – aria of Shaklovitiy and final chorus	Paris, 16 or 18 June 1913 (on the intended day of the première, 5 May, Diaghilev substituted the Rimsky ending, postponing use of Stravinsky's ending until later in the run).	Vocal score of final chorus: Bessel, 1914	1913 (Clarens)

(cont.)

W	K	Title	First Performance	Publication	Remarks
29	18	The Nightingale (Solovey; Le Rossignol), musical fairytale in three acts (libretto: Stepan Mitusov, after Andersen)	Paris, Opéra, 26 May 1914, cond. Monteux	Édition Russe, 1923	1908–9 (Ustilug), 1913–14 (Clarens, Leysin)
30	19	Three Pieces, for String Quartet	1914 version: Paris, (?13 or 19)* May 1915, Yvonne Astruc, Darius Milhaud, Arthur Honneger?**and Félix Delgrange; 1918 version: London, 13 February 1919, Philharmonic Quartet * Uncertainty due to indecipherable handwritten date in letter by Alfredo Casella. ** Listed by Goubault (p. 174) but unconfirmed by other sources.	Édition Russe, 1922	1914 (No. 1, 26 April, Leysin; Nos. 2 & 3, July, Salvan); rev. 1918 (Morges), and September 1921 (Anglet). See also 73: W38(A)/K51
31	20	Pribaoutki, for male voice and eight instruments (text by Afanasyev)	London, 22 February 1918, Olga Haley, cond. Eugene Goossens	Henn, 1917	1914 (Salvan)
32	N12	Valse des fleurs, for piano duet	New York, 1949, Chamber Art Society	Facsimile in R. Craft, A Stravinsky Scrapbook 1940–1971, London, Thames and Hudson, 1983: 146–7; Boosey & Hawkes, 1997	1914 (Clarens)

			Title	Premiere	Publication	Notes
33a	28	21	Three Easy Pieces for piano duet	Paris, 9 February 1918, Juliette Meerovitch and Alfredo Casella	Henn, 1917; Chester	1914–15 (Clarens); 'March' dedicated to Alfredo Casella; 'Waltz' to Erik Satie; 'Polka' to Sergey Diaghilev
33b	28	21	'Marche' (No. 1 from Three Easy Pieces), for twelve instruments		Unpublished	1915; ms held in PSS
33c	28	21	'Polka' (No. 3 from Three Easy Pieces), for cimbalom		Facsimile in Feuilles musicales, Lausanne, March–April 1962	1915; transposed a tone lower from original to fit range of cimbalom
34	29	N14	Souvenir d'une marche boche, for piano		In E. Wharton, ed., The Book of the Homeless, London: Macmillan; New York: Scribners Sons, 1916	1 September 1915 (Morges)
35	-	N13	Liadov: Prelude, op. 11 – arr. for orchestra		Unpublished	1915: according to Christian Goubault, this was orchestrated for the ballet Contes Russes; ms held at Paris National Library
36	30	22	Berceuses du chat, for contralto and three clarinets (text: Russian folk poems)	Paris, 20 November 1918, Pierre Bertin	Henn, 1917	1915–16 (Clarens, Château d'Oex, Morges)
37	31	23	Renard (Baika), burlesque in song and dance, for two tenors, two basses and small orchestra (libretto: Stravinsky, after Afanasyev)	Paris, Opéra, 18 May 1922, cond. Ansermet	Henn, 1917	1915–16 (Château d'Oex, Morges)

(cont.)

W		K	Title	First Performance	Publication	Remarks
38a	35	28	Four Russian Peasant Songs (Podblyudnïye), for female voices (text: Russian folk poems)	Geneva, 1917, cond. Vasily Kibalchich	Schott, 1930	1914–17 (Morges, Clarens)
38b	35	28	Four Russian Peasant Songs, arr. for female voices and four horns	Los Angeles, 11 October 1954, cond. Robert Craft	Chester, 1958	1954 (Hollywood)
39	34	N16	Valse pour les enfants, for piano		Le Figaro, Paris, 21 May 1922	1916/1917 (Morges); dedicated 'Pour les petits lecteurs du Figaro'
40a	33	24	Three Children's Tales (Tri Detskiye pesenki, Trois Histoires pour enfants), for voice and piano (texts: Russian folk poems)		Chester, 1920	1916–17; see also 53c: W43(A)
40b	33	24	'Tilimbom' (extended version from Three Children's Tales), for voice and orchestra	Antwerp, 7 January 1924, Janacopoulos, cond. Stravinsky	Chester, 1927	December 1923 (Biarritz)
41	B.V	N15	Song of the Volga Boatmen, arr. for wind and percussion	Rome, 9 April 1917, cond. Ansermet	Chester, 1920	1917; written for Diaghilev's Ballets Russes to replace the Imperial Russian National Anthem
42	32	25	Five Easy Pieces, for Piano Duet	Paris, 9 February 1918, Meerovitch and Casella	Henn, 1917	1916–17

				Premiere	Publication	Date (place)
43	36	N17	Canons, for two horns, lost			1917; written, according to R. Craft, for a Dr Roux in Switzerland, himself an amateur horn player, who requested a new composition instead of payment for removing Lyudmila Stravinsky's appendix
44a	37	40	Les Noces (Svadebka; The Wedding), Russian choreographic scenes – first draft for voices and large mixed ensemble			1914–17 (Clarens, Château d'Oex, Morges, Les Diablerets)
44b	37	40	Les Noces – intermediate draft (scenes 1 & 2 only) for voices, harmonium, two cimbaloms, pianola and percussion			1919 (Morges)
44c	37	40	Les Noces – final version for solo voices, chorus, 4 pianos and percussion	Paris, Gaité Lyrique, 13 June 1923, cond. Ansermet	Vocal score: Chester, 1922; full score, c. 1923	1921–3 (Garches, Anglet, Biarritz, Monte-Carlo)
45a	24(A)	26	The Song of the Nightingale (Le Chant du rossignol), symphonic poem and ballet in one act for orchestra (arr. from The Nightingale, Acts II–III)	Concert: Geneva, 6 December 1919, cond. Ansermet; staged: Paris, Opéra, 2 February 1920, Ansermet	Édition Russe, 1921; Boosey & Hawkes, 1947	1917 (Morges)

(cont.)

W	K	Title	First Performance	Publication	Remarks
45b	24(A)	'chant du rossignol' and 'Marche chinoise', for violin and piano		Édition Russe, 1934	Transcribed in collaboration with Samuel Dushkin, 1932 (Voreppe)
46	38	Étude for pianola		Piano roll: Aeolian (No. T967B), 1921	1917 (Morges, Les Diablerets); dedicated to Madame Eugenia Errazuriz
47	97	Berceuse, for voice and piano (text: Stravinsky)		Expositions and Developments (UK edition), Faber, 1962: 150–1	1917 (Morges), composed for his daughter Lyudmila
48	N19	'Lied ohne Namen', for two bassoons	London, Queen Elizabeth Hall, 30 October 1979, John Price and Joanna Graham	In SSC, I, Faber, 1982: 410; Boosey and Hawkes 1997	1916–18 (title added in 1949)
49	N18	Mussorgsky: Boris Godunov – opening chorus, arr. for piano		Boosey & Hawkes, 1997	1918 (Morges)
50a	29	The Soldier's Tale (L'Histoire du soldat), to be read, played and danced, in two parts, for seven players (libretto: Charles Ferdinand Ramuz)	Lausanne, Théâtre Municipal, 28 September 1918, cond. Ansermet	Chester, 1924	1918 (Morges)
50b	29	The Soldier's Tale – Suite, for violin, clarinet and piano	Lausanne, 8 November 1919, José Porta (violin), Edmond Allegra (clarinet), José Iturbi (piano)	Chester, 1920	1918–19 (Morges)
50c	29	The Soldier's Tale – Suite, for seven players	London, Wigmore Hall, 20 April 1920, cond. Ansermet	Chester, 1922	1920 (Morges)
51a	30	Ragtime, for eleven instruments	London, Aeolian Hall, 27 April 1920, cond. Arthur Bliss	Chester, 1920	1917–18 (Morges); dedicated to Madame Eugenia Errazuriz

			Title	First performance	Publisher	Composition date
51b	42		Ragtime – piano reduction	Lausanne, 8 November 1919, Edmond Allegra	Éditions de la Sirène, Paris, 1919 (notable for Picasso's specially drawn cover); Chester	1917–18 (Morges)
52	45		Three Pieces for Solo Clarinet		Chester, 1920	1918 (Morges)
53a	43		Four Russian Songs, for voice and piano (text: Russian folk poems)	Geneva, 17 March 1919, Tatyana Tatyanova (soprano)	Nos. 3 and 4 only: Le Revue Romande, 15 September 1919; Chester, 1920	1918–19 (Morges); dedicated to Mme and M. Maja and Bela Strozzi-Pečić
53b	-		'Sektantskaya' (No. 4 from Four Russian Songs), for voice, flute and cimbalom		Facsimile in SSC, I, 427–9.	February–March 1919
53c	43(A)		Four Songs, for voice, flute, harp and guitar	Los Angeles, 21 February 1955, Marni Nixon, cond. Robert Craft	Chester, 1955	Instrumental versions of Nos. 1 and 4 of Four Russian Songs and Nos. 1 and 2 of Three Children's Tales (1954).
54	44		Piano-Rag Music, for piano solo	Lausanne, 8 November 1919, José Iturbi	Chester, 1920	1918–19 (Morges); commissioned by Artur Rubinstein
55	B.VII	N20	Rouget de Lisle: La Marseillaise, arr. solo violin	London, Queen Elizabeth Hall, 13 November 1979, Kyung Wha Chung	Boosey & Hawkes, 1997	1 January 1919 (Morges)
56a	46		Pulcinella, ballet in one act (music after Pergolesi and others) for solo voices and chamber orchestra	Paris, Opéra, 15 May 1920, cond. Ansermet	Vocal score: Chester, 1920; full score: Édition Russe, 1924	1919–20 (Morges)

(cont.)

	W	K	Title	First Performance	Publication	Remarks
56b	46	34	Pulcinella – Suite, for chamber orchestra	Boston, 22 December 1922, cond. Monteux	Édition Russe, 1924; Boosey & Hawkes	1920–2 (Morges, Biarritz)
56c	46	34	Pulcinella – Suite, for violin and piano	Private: Winterthur, 12 November 1925, Alma Moodie (violin) and Igor Stravinsky (piano); public: Frankfurt, 25 November 1925, same performers	Édition Russe, 1926; Boosey & Hawkes	August 1925 (Nice); arranged for Paul Kochanski
56d	46	34	Suite italienne, for violin and piano	Berlin, 28 October 1932, Samuel Dushkin (violin) and Igor Stravinsky (piano)	Édition Russe, 1934; Boosey & Hawkes	1932; arranged for Dushkin
56e	46	34	Suite italienne, for cello and piano		Édition Russe, 1934; Boosey & Hawkes	1932; arranged by Stravinsky and Gregor Piatigorsky
57a	47	35	Concertino, for string quartet	New York, 23 November 1920, Flonzaley Quartet	Hansen, 1923	1920 (Carantec, Garches)
57b	47	35	Concertino, arr. piano duet		Hansen, 1923	Possibly 1920
57c	47	35	Concertino, arr. twelve instruments	Los Angeles, 11 November 1952, cond. Stravinsky	Hansen, 1953	1952
58a	48	-	Fragment des Symphonies pour instruments à vent, à la mémoire de C. A. Debussy (chorale)		Piano reduction: Debussy memorial supplement to La Revue Musicale, December 1920	1920; commissioned by Henry Prunières, this chorale became the closing section of Symphonies (K36)
58b	48	36	Symphonies d'instruments à vent (for twenty-four instruments)	London, Queen's Hall, 10 June 1921, cond. Koussevitzky	Piano reduction (by A Lourié): Édition Russe, 1926; full score: Belwin Mills, 1983; Boosey & Hawkes, 2001	1920; dedicated 'à la mémoire de Claude Debussy'

			Title	Premiere	Publication	Notes
58c	-		Chorale, for wind ensemble (without clarinets)	New York, 30 January 1946, cond. Stravinsky	Unpublished	1945; Stravinsky scored the chorale, as published in *Revue musicale* 1920, as a filler for a broadcast concert including Symphony of Psalms – hence omitting clarinets
58d	48	36	Symphonies of Wind Instruments (for twenty-three instruments) (revised 1947 version)	New York, 31 January 1948, cond. Ansermet	Boosey & Hawkes, 1952; corrected edition, 2001	1947
59	32(B)	38	Suite No. 2, for small orchestra	Paris, 1921 (exact date unknown)	Chester, 1925	Arrangement of *Three Easy Pieces* (33a: W28/K21), and 'Galop' from *Five Easy Pieces* (42: W32/K25), 1915–21; orchestrated for the Théâtre de la Chauve-Souris, Paris
60	49	37	Les Cinq Doigts (The Five Fingers), for piano	Paris, 15 December 1921, Jean Wiener	Chester, 1922	Completed 18 February 1921 (Garches)
61	B.VIII	N21	Tchaikovsky: The Sleeping Beauty – orchestration of 'Variation d'Aurore' and Entr'acte preceding finale Act II	London, Alhambra, 2 November 1921, cond. Gregor Fitelberg	Boosey & Hawkes, 1981	April–September 1921
62	49(A)	37	Eight Instrumental Miniatures for 15 players	Los Angeles, 26 March 1962 (1–4 only), cond. Robert Craft; Toronto, 29 April 1962 (complete), cond. Stravinsky	Chester, 1963	1962 (Hollywood); dedicated to Lawrence Morton

(cont.)

	W	K	Title	First Performance	Publication	Remarks
63a	50	39	*Mavra*, *opéra bouffe* in one act (libretto: B. Kochno after Pushkin)	Paris, Opéra, 3 June 1922, cond. Gregor Fitelberg	Édition Russe, 1925; Boosey & Hawkes	1921–2 (Anglet, Biarritz, Paris)
63b	–	39	'Chanson de Paracha' ('Russian Maiden's Song'), for soprano and orchestra	Paris, 7 November 1923	Édition Russe, 1925; Boosey & Hawkes, 1948	1922–3 (Biarritz); rev. piano version 1947 (for Vera Bryner)
63c	50	39	'Chanson Russe', for violin and piano		Édition Russe, 1938; Boosey & Hawkes	Arranged by Dushkin and Stravinsky, April 1937 (New York)
64	51	41	Octet for Wind Instruments	Paris, 18 October 1923, cond. Stravinsky	Édition Russe, 1924; Boosey & Hawkes 1952	1922–3 (Biarritz, Paris)
65	52	42	Concerto, for piano and wind instruments	Paris, 22 May 1924, Stravinsky (piano), cond. Koussevitzky	Two-piano reduction: Édition Russe, 1924; full score: 1936; Boosey & Hawkes (1950), with minor revisions/corrections.	1923–4; dedicated 'à Madame Nathalie Koussevitzky'
66	53	43	Piano Sonata	Donaueschingen Festival, 26 July 1925*, Felix Petyrek *Date as reported in *The Musical Times*, 1 September 1925: 844	Édition Russe, 1925; Boosey & Hawkes	1924 (Biarritz, Nice)
67	54	44	Serenade in A, for piano	Frankfurt am Main, 24 November 1925, Stravinsky	Édition Russe, 1926; Boosey & Hawkes	11 April – 9 October 1925 (Nice); dedicated 'to my wife'
68	32(A)	45	Suite No. 1, for small orchestra (arr. of *Five Easy Pieces* Nos. 1–4, 42: W32/K25)	Haarlem, 2 March 1926, cond. Stravinsky	Chester, 1926	1925 (Nice)
69a	55	46	Our Father (*Otche nash*), SATB choir (Slavonic text)	Paris, Salle Gaveau, 18 May 1934, cond. Stravinsky	Édition Russe, 1932; Boosey & Hawkes	July 1926 (Paris)

69b	55	Pater noster, SATB choir (Latin text) – revised version of Otche nash		Boosey & Hawkes, 1949	March 1949
70	56	Oedipus Rex, opera-oratorio in two acts (libretto: Jean Cocteau, Jean Daniélou)	Concert performance: Paris, Théâtre Sarah-Bernhardt, 30 May 1927, cond. Stravinsky; first stage performance: Vienna, Staatsoper, 23 February 1928, cond. Franz Schalk	Vocal score: Édition Russe, 1927; full score: Boosey & Hawkes, 1949	1926–7 (Nice); concert ending to Jocasta's aria, October 1948
71	57	Apollon Musagète, ballet in two scenes, for string orchestra	Washington, Library of Congress, 27 April 1928, cond. Hans Kindler	Édition Russe, 1928; Boosey & Hawkes	1927–8 (Nice)
72a	58	The Fairy's Kiss (Le Baiser de la fée), ballet in four scenes for orchestra (music after Tchaikovsky)	Paris, Salle Garnier, Opéra, 27 November 1928, cond. Stravinsky	Piano score only: Édition Russe, 1928	April–October 1928 (Talloires, Nice)
72b	58(A)	Divertimento, for violin and piano	Strasbourg, 12 December 1934, Dushkin (violin), Stravinsky (piano)	Édition Russe, 1934	Arr. with Dushkin, 1928–33 (Fontainebleau)
72c	58(A)	Divertimento, for orchestra	Paris, Salle Pleyel, 4 November 1934, cond. Stravinsky	Édition Russe, 1938	1928–34
72d	58	Ballad, for violin and piano		Boosey & Hawkes, 1951	Arr. with Jeanne Gautier, 1947
72e	58(A)	Divertimento, for orchestra – revised		Boosey & Hawkes, 1950	1949
72f	58	The Fairy's Kiss (Le Baiser de la fée), ballet in four scenes – revised		Boosey & Hawkes, 1952	1950

(cont.)

W	K	Title	First Performance	Publication	Remarks
73	38(A)	Four Studies for orchestra (arr. Three Pieces, for String Quartet, 30: W25/K19, and Étude for pianola, W38/K27)	No. 4 only: Paris, 16 November 1928, cond. Stravinsky; complete: Berlin, 7 November 1930, cond. Ansermet	Édition Russe, 1930; Boosey & Hawkes	Nos. 1–3: 1914–18 (Morges); completed: 1928 (Nice)
74	59	*Capriccio for Piano and Orchestra*	Paris, 6 December 1929, Igor Stravinsky (piano), cond. Ansermet	Édition Russe, 1930; Boosey & Hawkes	1928–9 (Nice, Echarvines)
75	–	*Church Prayer* (Iže Cheruvimy) for sopranos, incomplete			1930; ms held in PSS
76	60	*Symphony of Psalms*, for chorus and orchestra	Brussels, 13 December 1930, cond. Ansermet; US première: Boston, 19 December 1930, cond. Koussevitzky	Vocal score: Édition Russe, 1930; full score, 1931; Boosey & Hawkes (1948), with minor revisions/ corrections	1930 (Nice, Echarvines); commissioned by Koussevitzky for fiftieth anniversary of Boston Symphony Orchestra
77	61	Concerto in D, for violin and orchestra	Berlin, 23 October 1931, Samuel Dushkin (violin), cond. Stravinsky	Schott, 1931	1931 (Nice, Voreppe); dedicated to Dushkin
78	62	*Duo Concertant* for Violin and Piano	Broadcast: Berlin, 28 October 1932, Dushkin, Stravinsky	Édition Russe, 1933; Boosey & Hawkes	1931–32 (Voreppe)
79	–	*Dialogue de la joye et de la raison*, for two singers and keyboard instrument (text: Petrarch, trans. Charles-Albert Cingria), incomplete		Facsimile in SSC, I, 371–8	1933
80a	55	'Creed' ('Simvol' Veri') for SATB choir (Slavonic text)	Paris, Salle Gaveau, 18 May 1934, cond. Stravinsky	Édition Russe, 1933; Boosey & Hawkes	12 August 1932 (Voreppe)
80b	55	'Credo' – version of 'Creed'		Boosey & Hawkes, 1949	February 1949

			Title	Premiere	Publisher	Date
8oc	63	55	'Creed' – revised version with Slavonic text		Boosey & Hawkes, 1966	May 1964
81	64	56	Perséphone, melodrama in three scenes, for speaker, solo tenor, chorus and orchestra (text: André Gide)	Paris, Opéra, 30 April 1934, cond. Stravinsky	Édition Russe, 1934; Boosey & Hawkes	1933–4
82a	65	57	Ave Maria (Bogoroditse devo), for SATB chorus (Slavonic text)	Paris, Salle Gaveau, 18 May 1934, cond. Stravinsky	Édition Russe, 1934; Boosey & Hawkes, 1967	1934
82b	65	57	Ave Maria – version with Latin text		Boosey & Hawkes, 1949	1949
83	66	58	Concerto for Two Solo Pianos	Paris, Salle Gaveau, 21 November 1935, Igor and Soulima Stravinsky	Schott, 1936	1931–5 (Voreppe, Paris)
84	67	59	Jeu de cartes, ballet in three deals	New York, 27 April 1937, cond. Stravinsky	Schott, 1937	1935–6 (Paris)
85	68	82	Praeludium, for jazz ensemble (1937; subsequently revised in 1953; adding celesta, guitar and strings)	Revised version: Los Angeles, 19 October 1953, cond. Robert Craft	Revised version: Boosey & Hawkes, 1968	1936–7 (Paris, New York); revised 1953
86	69	N24	Petit Ramusianum harmonique, for speaking and singing voice unaccompanied (text: Charles-Albert Cingria)	Paris, 24 September 1938 (private performance)	In Hommage à C.-F. Ramuz (Lausanne: Porchet, 1938); I. Vershinina (ed.), Igor Stravinsky: Vokal'naya Muzïka ('Igor Stravinsky: Vocal Music'), vol. I (Moscow: Sovetskiy Kompozitor, 1982)	1937, written to celebrate Ramuz's sixtieth birthday

(cont.)

W	K	Title	First Performance	Publication	Remarks
87	70	Concerto in E♭ ('Dumbarton Oaks'), for chamber orchestra	Washington, DC, 8 May 1938, Nadia Boulanger	Schott, 1938	1937–8 (Châteaux de Montoux, Paris)
88	71	Symphony in C, for orchestra	Chicago, 7 November 1940, cond. Stravinsky	Schott, 1948	1938–40 (I: Paris; II: Sancellemoz; III: Cambridge, Mass.; IV: Beverley Hills, Hollywood)
89	–	'To Mister Paul', vocal piece (text: Stravinsky)		Unpublished	1940; for Paul Sachs; ms held in PSS
90a	72	Tango, for piano	Arr. Dushkin for violin and piano: New York, 31 March 1941	Mercury, 1941	1940 (Hollywood); originally planned for voice and instruments
90b	72	Tango – arr. for instrumental ensemble	Los Angeles, 19 October 1953, cond. Robert Craft	Mercury, 1954	1953; transposed a tone higher from original (D minor to E minor)
91	73	Danses concertantes, for chamber orchestra	Los Angeles, 8 February 1942, cond. Stravinsky	AMP, 1943; Schott	1940–2 (Hollywood)
92	B.VIII	Tchaikovsky: The Sleeping Beauty – arr. 'Bluebird' pas-de-deux Act III for small orchestra	New York, February 1941	Schott, 1953	1941, commissioned by Lucia Chase
93	B.IX	J. S. Smith: The Star-Spangled Banner, arr. for chorus and orchestra	Los Angeles, 14 October 1941, cond. James Sample	Mercury, 1941	1941
94a	74	Circus Polka, for piano	New York, 9 April 1942, cond. Merle Evans	AMP, 1942; Raksin arr: AMP, 1948	1941–2 (Hollywood); subsequently arr. David Raksin for circus band, 1942

94b	74	64	Circus Polka, for orchestra	Cambridge, Mass., 13 January 1944, cond. Stravinsky	AMP, 1944; Schott	1942
95	75	65	Four Norwegian Moods, for orchestra	Cambridge, Mass., 13 January 1944, cond. Stravinsky	AMP, 1944; Schott	1942 (Hollywood)
96	76	66	Ode, elegiac chant in three parts for orchestra	Boston, 8 October 1943, cond. Koussevitzky	AMP/Schott, 1947	1943 (Hollywood); dedicated to the memory of Natalie Koussevitzky
97	80	67	Sonata for Two Pianos	Madison, Wisconsin, 2 August 1944, Nadia Boulanger and Richard Johnston	AMP/Chappell, 1945	1943–4
98	77	68	Babel (part of collaborative Genesis Suite), for narrator (male), male chorus and orchestra	Los Angeles, 18 November 1945, cond. Werner Janssen	Schott, 1953	1944 (Hollywood)
99a	78	70	Scherzo à la Russe – original version for jazz band	Blue Network Radio, 5 September 1944, Paul Whiteman Band	Chappell, 1949	1944 (Hollywood)
99b	-	70	Scherzo à la Russe – for two pianos	Oakland, Mills College, 25 October 1944, Nadia Boulanger, Igor Stravinsky	AMP, 1945; Schott	1943/4
99c	78	70	Scherzo à la Russe – symphonic version	San Francisco, 22 March 1946, cond. Igor Stravinsky	Chappell, 1945	1945 (Hollywood)
100	79	69	Scènes de ballet, for orchestra	Philadelphia, 27 November 1944, cond. Maurice Abravanel	Chappell, 1945	1944 (Hollywood)

(cont.)

	W	K	Title	First Performance	Publication	Remarks
101	81	72	Elegy for solo viola (or violin)	Los Angeles, 11 February 1945, Germain Prévost	Chappell, 1945	1944 (Hollywood); written for Germain Prévost
102	82	73	Symphony in Three Movements	New York, Carnegie Hall, 24 January 1946, cond. Stravinsky	AMP/Schott, 1946	1942–5; dedicated to the New York Philharmonic Symphony Society
103	-	N28	'Welcome Richard', for singer (text: Stravinsky)		Unpublished	1945; for Richard Rodzinski; ms held in PSS
104	83	74	Ebony Concerto, for clarinet and jazz ensemble	New York, Carnegie Hall, 25 March 1946, Woody Herman's Band, cond. Walter Hendl	Charling, 1946; Edwin H. Morris / Boosey & Hawkes	1945 (Hollywood); dedicated to Woody Herman
105	84	75	Concerto in D ('Basler Concerto'), for string orchestra	Basel, 27 January 1947, cond. Paul Sacher	Boosey & Hawkes, 1947	1946 (Hollywood); 'Dedié à la Basler Kammerorchester et son chef Paul Sacher'. This was the first of Stravinsky's scores to be published by Boosey & Hawkes
106	-	N29	Balanchine/Stravinsky: Birthday Chorale		Dance Index, 1982	1946; Balanchine composed a Russian acrostic on the name 'Igor' for Stravinsky's sixty-fourth birthday, which Stravinsky promptly harmonised.
107	85	71	Hommage à Nadia Boulanger ('Petit Canon pour la fête de Nadia Boulanger'), for two tenors (text: Jean de Meung)		In Clifford Caesar, Igor Stravinsky: A Complete Catalogue, Boosey & Hawkes / San Francisco Press, 1982: 8	1947 (Hollywood); ms held in PSS

108	86		Orpheus (Orphée), ballet in three scenes	New York, 28 April 1948, cond. Stravinsky	Boosey & Hawkes, 1948	1947 (Hollywood)
109	87		Mass, for mixed chorus and double wind quintet	Milan, Teatro alla Scala, 27 October 1948, cond. Ansermet	Boosey & Hawkes, 1948	Kyrie and Gloria: 1944 (Hollywood); the rest: December 1947 – March 1948 (Hollywood)
110	88		The Rake's Progress, opera in three acts (libretto: W. H. Auden and C. Kallman)	Venice, 11 September 1951, cond. Stravinsky	Boosey & Hawkes, 1951	1947–51 (Hollywood)
111	-	N30	Happy Birthday..., two-voice arr. by Stravinsky		Unpublished	1951; written for seventy-fifth birthday of Mary Curtis Zimbalist (founder of the Curtis Institute); ms held in PSS
112	89		Cantata, for soprano, tenor, female chorus and small instrumental ensemble (texts: anon., fifteenth–sixteenth centuries, English)	Los Angeles, 11 November 1952, cond. Stravinsky	Boosey & Hawkes, 1952	April 1951 – August 1952 (Hollywood); dedicated to the Los Angeles Chamber Symphony Society
113	-	N32	Chorale Theme for improvisation on organ		Facsimile in SSC, I, 251	January 1952 (Hollywood); written at the request of Bernard Gavoty for the use of Marcel Dupré, then the organist at Saint-Sulpice, Paris
114	90		Septet, for clarinet, horn, bassoon and piano quartet	Washington, DC, 23 January 1954, cond. Stravinsky	Boosey & Hawkes, 1953	July 1952 – February 1953; dedicated to the Dumbarton Oaks Research Library and Collection

(cont.)

W	K	Title	First Performance	Publication	Remarks
115	91	Three Songs from William Shakespeare, for mezzo-soprano, flute, clarinet and viola	Los Angeles, 8 March 1954, cond. Robert Craft	Boosey & Hawkes, 1954	1953; dedicated to 'Evenings on the Roof'
116	N33	'Succès, triomphe au Roi David, mon cher Milhaud', for singer (text: Stravinsky)		Unpublished	1954; the title of this short congratulatory piece alludes to Trois Psaumes de David, op. 339 by Darius Milhaud; ms held in PSS
117	92	In Memoriam Dylan Thomas, for tenor, string quartet and four trombones	Los Angeles, 20 September 1954, Richard Robinson (tenor), cond. Robert Craft	Boosey & Hawkes, 1954	1954
118	93	Greeting Prelude ('for the eightieth birthday of Pierre Monteux'), for orchestra	Boston, 4 April 1955, cond. Charles Munch	Boosey & Hawkes, 1956	1955 (Hollywood)
119	–	12-note Note to Laurence Morton, musical sketch		Facsimile in Jann Pasler (ed.) Confronting Stravinsky: Man, Musician, and Modernist, University of California Press, 1986: 343	9 September 1955
120	94	Canticum sacrum ad honorem Sancti Marci Nominis, for tenor and baritone soloists, chorus and orchestra (texts: Vulgate, from Deuteronomy, Psalms, Song of Solomon, St Mark's Gospel and First Epistle of St John)	St Mark's Basilica, Venice, 13 September 1956, cond. Stravinsky	Boosey & Hawkes, 1956	1955

121	B.X	87	J. S. Bach: Chorale-Variations on 'Vom Himmel hoch', arr. chorus and orchestra	Ojai, California, 27 May 1956, cond. Robert Craft	Boosey & Hawkes, 1956	1955–6 (New York, Hollywood); dedicated to Robert Craft
122		95	Agon, ballet for twelve dancers	Concert: Los Angeles, 17 June 1957, cond. Robert Craft; staged: New York, 1 December 1957, cond. Robert Irving	Boosey & Hawkes, 1957	1953–7; dedicated to Lincoln Kirstein and George Balanchine
123		N31	To Paul Hindemith, vocal piece (text: Stravinsky)		Unpublished	1957 (Kirchmeyer gives the date as 1951, but the later date published in the Paul Sacher inventory seems more plausible: Craft's diary records that the two composers dined that year in Munich on 30 September – the piece may have been written then)
124		–	Message to Ingolf Dahl, for two singers		Unpublished	1957; ms held in PSS
125		96	Threni: id est lamentationes Jeremiae prophetae, for soloists, mixed chorus and orchestra (text: Vulgate Lamentations)	Sala della Scuola Grande di San Rocco, Venice, 23 September 1958, cond. Stravinsky	Boosey & Hawkes, 1958	1957–8
126		–	To Robert and Beatrice Cunningham, for singer		Unpublished	8 June 1958 (Beatrice was sister of Lawrence Morton); ms held in PSS

(cont.)

W	K	Title	First Performance	Publication	Remarks
127	B.XI	93	Gesualdo: Tres sacrae cantiones ('Da pacem Domine', 'Assumpta est Maria', 'Illumina nos'), completed for six, six and seven voices	'Assumpta est Maria' only: New York, 10 January 1960	Boosey & Hawkes: 'Illumina nos', 1957; complete, 1960	1957–9
128	97	91	Movements, for piano and orchestra	New York, 10 January 1960, Margrit Weber (piano), cond. Stravinsky	Boosey & Hawkes, 1960	1958–9; dedicated to Margrit Weber
129	98	90	Epitaphium für das Grabmal des Prinzen Max Egon zu Fürstenberg, for flute, clarinet and harp	Donaueschingen Festival, 17 October 1959	Boosey & Hawkes, 1959	1959
130	99	92	Double Canon for String Quartet	New York, 20 December 1959	Boosey & Hawkes, 1960	1959; 'Raoul Dufy in Memoriam'
131	B.XII	94	Monumentum pro Gesualdo di Venosa ad CD Annum, three Gesualdo motets recomposed for instruments	Venice, 27 September 1960	Boosey & Hawkes, 1960	1960
132	100	95	A Sermon, a Narrative and a Prayer, cantata for alto and tenor, speaker, chorus and orchestra (texts from Epistles of St Paul, and Acts of the Apostles (Authorized Version), and by Thomas Dekker)	Basel, 23 February 1962, Basler Kammerorchester, cond. Paul Sacher	Boosey & Hawkes, 1961	1960–1 (Hollywood); dedicated to Paul Sacher

			Title	Premiere	Publisher	Date / Notes
133	101	96	Anthem: 'The Dove Descending Breaks the Air', for chorus a cappella (text by T. S. Eliot)	Los Angeles, 19 February 1962, cond. Robert Craft	In *Expositions and Developments*, Faber and Faber, 1962; Boosey & Hawkes, 1962	1961–2 (Hollywood)
134	102	98	*The Flood*, musical play for solo speakers and singers, chorus and orchestra (text by Robert Craft, after Genesis (Authorized Version) and the York and Chester Miracle Plays)	CBS TV (USA), 14 June 1962, cond. Stravinsky and Robert Craft; first public performance: Santa Fe, 21 August 1962; first live staged performance: Staatsoper, Hamburg, 30 April 1963	Boosey & Hawkes, 1963	1961–2
135	-		To Anton Hartmann, in two voice parts		Unpublished	1962; ms held in PSS
136	103	101	*Abraham and Isaac*, sacred ballad for baritone and chamber orchestra (text from Genesis – in Hebrew)	Jerusalem, 23 August 1964, Ephraim Biran, cond. Robert Craft	Boosey & Hawkes, 1965	1962–3; dedicated to the people of the State of Israel
137	B.XIII	99	Sibelius: *Canzonetta*, op. 62a, arr. for eight instruments	Los Angeles, 30 September 1963, cond. Robert Craft; Finnish Broadcasting Company, 22 March 1964	Brietkopf & Härtel, 1964	1963; after Stravinsky had been awarded the Wihuri–Sibelius Prize
138	104	100	*Elegy for J. F. K.*, for baritone and three clarinets (text by W. H. Auden)	Los Angeles, 6 April 1964, cond. Robert Craft	Boosey & Hawkes, 1964	March 1964 (Hollywood)
139	105	102	*Fanfare for a New Theatre*, for two trumpets	New York State Theater, Lincoln Center, 19 April 1964	Boosey & Hawkes, 1968	1964 (Hollywood); dedicated 'to Lincoln [Kirstein] and George [Balanchine]'
140	106	103	*Variations (Aldous Huxley in Memoriam)*, for orchestra	Chicago, 17 April 1965, cond. Robert Craft	Boosey & Hawkes, 1965	1963–4 (Santa Fe, Hollywood)

	W	K	Title	First Performance	Publication	Remarks
141	–	–	For Lucia Chase and the Ballet Theater, for singer (text: Stravinsky)		Unpublished	1965, celebrating the twenty-fifth anniversary of the American Ballet Theater; ms held in PSS
142	107	104	Introitus (T. S. Eliot in memoriam), for male chorus, harp, piano, two timpani, two tam-tams, solo viola and double bass (text from 'Requiem aeternam')	Chicago, 17 April 1965, cond. Robert Craft	Boosey & Hawkes, 1965	1965 (Hollywood)
143	16(A)	105	Canon on a Russian Popular Tune, concert introduction or encore for orchestra	Toronto, 16 December 1965, cond. Robert Craft	Boosey & Hawkes, 1973	1965
144	108	106	Requiem Canticles, for contralto and bass soloists, chorus and orchestra (text from 'Missa pro defunctis')	Princeton University, 8 October 1966, cond. Robert Craft	Boosey & Hawkes, 1967	1965–6 (Hollywood); dedicated to the memory of Helen Buchanan Seeger
145	109	107	The Owl and the Pussy-Cat, for soprano and piano (text by Edward Lear)	Los Angeles, 31 October 1966, Peggy Bonini (soprano), Ingolf Dahl (piano)	Boosey & Hawkes 1967	1965–6; dedicated 'to Vera'
146	B.XIV	108	Hugo Wolf: Two Sacred Songs (from Spanisches Liederbuch), arr. for mezzo-soprano and three clarinets in A, two horns in F, and string quintet	Los Angeles, 6 September 1968, Christina Krooskos, cond. Robert Craft	Boosey & Hawkes, 1969	1968 (San Francisco)

| 147 | - | 110 | J. S. Bach: Preludes and Fugues from *Das wohltemperierte Klavier*, in E minor, C# minor, B minor (Book I) and F major (Book II) arr. for woodwind and strings | No. 1 only: San Diego, 13 September 1982; Neuchâtel, 18 January 2005 | Unpublished | 1969 (Hollywood, New York) |
| 148 | - | 109 | Sketches for a Piano Sonata | Columbia University, 3 February 1973, Madeleine Malraux | | 1966–71 |

Appendix 2   Selected Audio Recordings Made by Igor Stravinsky

During the modern period, an increasing number of creative figures and technologies become integral to the production of any one recorded 'performance', however disseminated. The more agencies involved, the more removed have modern recordings become from the intimacy, flaws and individualised sounds of the earliest equivalents. The would-be listener to Stravinsky's music is confronted with a bewildering profusion – too great for a contribution of this scope to do justice to (let alone explore the notion that modern recordings offer 'more of the same'). This discussion focuses on selected recordings, contrasting historical materials with more recent readings of a limited number of Stravinsky's works. Performers of all stripes are bound to reckon with the monolithic legacy of Stravinsky's recording career. Two projects are referential for any and all subsequent performances and recordings. One is the complete set of recordings of large ensemble works led by Stravinsky and latterly Robert Craft (Columbia Symphony 2015), and the other *Stravinsky: The Recorded Legacy* (Sony Classical 1991).

The Soldier's Tale. Stravinsky recorded The Soldier's Tale three times, in 1932 (Paris), 1954 (New York) and 1962 (Los Angeles). The first performance betrays his significant shortcomings as a conductor: tempi are often too fast, and in the 'Ragtime' (from the *Three Dances*), rhythmic imprecision is compounded by a chaotic ensemble. Swing is haphazard rather than assured and the instruments' timbres and attacks are highly differentiated from one another: the bassoon reedy, the clarinet piercing, and the bright trombone belligerent. This causes problems of intonation, compounded by the minimal use of vibrato consistent with contemporary preferences. By 1954, earlier rhythmic inconsistencies have been resolved: now clean and incisive, timbres retain an appropriate character (the violin in 'Ragtime' avoids being too polished and projects some 'rough edges' redolent of the fiddle). The 1954 recording was made in the United States, and Robert Philip draws attention to its 'mellow' tone and, concomitantly, less distinctive instrumental ensemble (Philip 2004, 135). The recording and rehearsal process under Stravinsky can be glimpsed on the Columbia Records-produced film (*A Recording Session with a Composer: Igor Stravinsky*, 1955), as can his curious conducting style, fists closed and with a cigarette (lit whilst beating time!) in lieu of a baton.

The 1962 recording recalls the precariousness of the earliest, taking the 'Ragtime' briskly and foregrounding the violin's slightly scratchy timbre, but the wind instruments' rounded tones are more akin to those of 1954. All three of Stravinsky's recordings contrast sharply with that by Gerard Schwarz and the Los Angeles Chamber Orchestra (released in 1984). The 'Ragtime' section is polished (one might say, too polished): the violin's virtuosic facility might be applied with equal vigour to any page of animated repertory, thus undermining anything distinctively 'Stravinskian' – or, indeed, stylistically 'Ragtime' (Van Gansbeke 2012).

The Firebird. Unlike The RITE OF SPRING, The Firebird was a critical success when it premièred in 1910 as part of the BALLETS RUSSES season at the THÉÂTRE DES CHAMPS-ELYSÉES. Within a year, Stravinsky had produced a concert suite, revising it again in 1919 and 1945 (probably, in part, to renew copyright permissions). Towards the end of Stravinsky's life, Eric Walter White speculated that The Firebird 'suffers occasionally from an excess of expressiveness ... Such effusiveness must have become increasingly embarrassing to Stravinsky as time went on; but on various occasions he did his best to adjust matters by producing shorter suites for concert performance' (SCW, 188–9).

Ironically, as Stravinsky's recordings were purged of expansive, romantic gestures (e.g., the 1961 recording of the original BALLET and the final commercial recording of the 1945 Suite, made in 1967), other readings sought the 'Russianness' evinced by the earliest Firebird performances. Valery Gergiev's interpretation of the 1910 ballet with the Kirov Opera Orchestra takes some creative risks but, in doing so, arguably draws out sonic elements more compatible with earlier twentieth-century performance practices ('vitalism'). The introduction ('Kashchey's Garden') is notably slower than either Stravinsky's tempo indication or his own recordings, but the ensuing thematic development is fast and raw. By contrast, the middle of the work lacks momentum. In the 'Infernal Dance', Gergiev's ensemble sounds more 'Russian' and rough-hewn in tone than even Stravinsky's 1928 offering, which prioritises gestural expression over detail, resulting in scrappiness, especially in the brass. Gergiev privileges the theatre of the piece over the geometric clarity of rhythmic detail that characterises Stravinsky's 1961 recording.

The 1929 Recordings of The Rite of Spring. Similar comparisons between the theatre and concert 'faces' of a piece apply, of course, to the Rite. All recorded within a single year (1929), the recordings by Stravinsky, MONTEUX and STOKOWSKI are a fascinating study of their conductors' respective conceptions. Monteux's performance with the Orchestre Symphonique de Paris retains the nuances, lilts and rubati essential when conducting music for dancers, accommodating their more complex steps with physically achievable tempi. Stokowski, conductor of the American première of the concert version in 1922 (Philadelphia Orchestra), directed the first fully staged American performance within a year, with choreography by Léonide MASSINE. His approach – particularly the 'Sacrificial Dance' – might be described as Wagnerian, imagining the 'total work of art'. He allows space for expansive espressivo excursions, particularly in string melodies. In Monteux's and, especially, Stravinsky's offerings, the introduction to the Second Part ('The Sacrifice') prefigures the 'magical realism' of the second movement of György Ligeti's Violin Concerto (1989–92), with its folk tunes, string harmonics and otherworldly ocarinas. In Stokowski's recording, however, string melodies evoke Romantic tragedy, aided by some exaggerated portamenti. Stokowski's underpinning of the violin solo in high harmonics with a rich alto flute timbre (at R83) misses the truly mysterious sound that Stravinsky achieves at that moment by bringing out the violin, consigning the rest of the accompaniment to a softer dynamic. At the same juncture, Monteux's and Stravinsky's strings indulge in post-Romantic expression and *portamento* at odds with performances typically heard today. A tiny detail underlines the Wagnerian element in Stokowski's approach: at R85, where there is little going on save the lower strings playing *pp senza sord.*, the conductor elicits a clear slide between the two pitches, according significantly more 'space' and grandeur to the gesture than the context warrants.

Surprisingly, considering the emphasis placed on the score's rhythmic character, all three recordings apply *accelerandi* at phrase endings to a greater or lesser extent, whether by design or habit; given tempi already too fast for the ensemble to cope with, this increases the impression of instability, which is also evident in Stravinsky's 1928 recording of The Firebird Suite. Monteux's 'Sacrificial Dance' is taken much faster than Stravinsky's, but, despite some jumbling of sound, the phrasing is more focused. A few bars before, the straight-toned delivery of the bass clarinet usefully illustrates the differentiated timbre discussed elsewhere.

Both European recordings are strikingly different in another essential aspect: Monteux effectively negotiates the frequent changes of mood – by turns, angular, mysterious, lyrical and powerful – by treating contrasts as opportunities for gestural shaping through expressive *rubato* and tempo shifts. By comparison, Stravinsky's reading appears stilted at the junctures between sections and contrasted textures. At sixteen years' distance from the première, the two are essentially conducting different works: for Monteux, the legacy of the ballet's choreography remains in the 'concert' performance, whereas Stravinsky has already internalised the work as a concert piece. His 'sectionalised' reading of the work in 1929 can be taken as evidence that he already wished to focus on formal and tempo relationships rather than the ballet's original narrative.

Stravinsky 1960. Much of the recorded history of the Rite after 1960 owes something to Stravinsky's 'definitive' recording for Columbia (Fink 1999, 331). Here, a concern for 'geometric' relationships between long-range tempi has precedence over any local *rubato*, and the ensemble's precision consigns the stumblings of 1929 to the past. From the bassoon's opening strains, it is clear the composer has re-imagined the Rite: sonorities are mellifluous and blended (this is a North American orchestra) and the performance's energy arises from its rhythmic incisiveness. This recording showcases the first generation of musicians for whom the Rite has become part of the canon, no longer the most avant-garde repertoire they have encountered. This poses the question whether it loses something essential, which – in spite of their obvious shortcomings – the earliest recordings preserve: danger. By 1960, however, Stravinsky's view of the work is vested in its tempo relationships. Here may reside the difference to which he referred between an 'authentic' reading of the origins of the work and problematic ones in which 'the music is alien to the culture of its performers' (Dial). The composer criticises Herbert von Karajan's 1964 account (Berlin

Philharmonic) for being 'too polished, a pet savage rather than a real one. The *sostenuto* style is a principal fault.' He argues that 'there are simply no regions for soul-searching in *The Rite of Spring*' (Dial, 89–90).

Stravinsky's notorious pronouncements against 'interpreting' his works are a threat to any quest for originality by modern-day performers and listeners, who are further stymied – potentially at least – by the authority of the written document (Ur-text) post-1945, and achieve accuracy at the expense of imaginative risk-taking (see Philip 2004, 137).

An effective way forward is presented by Simon Rattle: leading von Karajan's former orchestra, he establishes live recording as the standard for much of its repertoire under his tenure. His 2013 release consists not of a single live recording but of several concert performances, with a preliminary studio take in rehearsal; this is obviously useful for patching in excerpts as needed. The work's conclusion offers a real test of the impact of any recording. From R192 onwards, Stravinsky (1960) is loud and brutal (none of the 1929 recordings convey this passage nearly as emphatically). Rattle, though also powerful, introduces a greater degree of dynamic shift between the brass, wind and strings' ascending two-note figure and the horns' intervening material. Different again is another centenary recording: in Tugan Sokhiev's 2013 account, the string/wind/brass gesture is delivered with such violence that it 'cracks' and leaps out of the texture in complete dynamic contrast with the material between each iteration. One could never accuse the sound world thus conjured up of being 'alien to the culture of its performers', as it harks back to the instrumental colours of early recordings of *The Soldier's Tale*. Sokhiev's *Firebird* (part of the same release) is similarly 'unfiltered'.

These more recent recordings should counter any concerns of 'loss of character', and yet their special elements are only fully brought into relief by comparison with the earliest exemplars. Students of 21st-century conducting and performance are learning pieces at nearly 100 years' distance from some of the examples discussed here, but the value of returning to those original efforts in support of personal authenticity cannot be overstated.

LOIS FITCH

Berliner Philharmoniker. 2013. *The Rite of Spring*. Cond. Simon Rattle. Comp. Igor Stravinsky.

Columbia Records. 1955. *Columbia Records Presents a Recording Session with a Composer: Igor Stravinsky*. Accessed 30 November 2018. www.youtube.com/watch?v=9MWHO_y2Fu4.

Columbia Symphony Orchestra. 1961. *Three Favourite Ballets: Stravinsky Conducts Firebird, Petrushka, The Rite of Spring*. Cond. Igor Stravinsky. Comp. Igor Stravinsky. M3S 705.

Columbia Symphony Orchestra [and other ensembles]. 2015. *The Complete Columbia Album Collection*. Conds. Igor Stravinsky and Robert Craft. Comp. Igor Stravinsky.

Kirov Orchestra. 1998. *The Firebird*. Cond. Valery Gergiev. Comp. Igor Stravinsky.

Orchestre national du Capitole de Toulouse. 2013. *Stravinsky: The Firebird; The Rite of Spring*. Cond. Tugan Sokhiev. Comp. Igor Stravinsky.

Sony Classical. 1991. *Stravinsky: The Recorded Legacy*. Comp. Igor Stravinsky. SX22K46290.

Robert Fink, "'Rigoroso ($\flat$ = 126)': 'The Rite of Spring' and the forging of a modernist performing style', *Journal of the American Musicological Society*, 52.9 (1999), 299–362. doi:10.2307/832000.

Robert Philip, *Performing Music in the Age of Recording* (New Haven and London: Yale University Press, 2004).

Brett Van Gansbeke, 2012. *The Orchestral Bassoon*. Accessed 28 November 2018. www .orchestralbassoon.com/stravinsky-soldiers-tale-part.

NB. A number of historical recordings were accessed via YouTube and/or Spotify. The recordings are not otherwise widely available. Due to the frequent removal and re-uploading of YouTube materials, the references are not given here. However, the recordings referred to are always identifiable and can often be found on YouTube, Spotify, iTunes or elsewhere on the web, or as part of special releases (for example Sony Classical. 2013. *Stravinsky: Le Sacre du Printemps 10 Reference Recordings*. Comp. Igor Stravinsky. 88725461742.)

Select Bibliography

Writings, Conversations and Other Texts by Igor Stravinsky

Stravinsky, Igor, *Stravinsky: An Autobiography* (New York: Simon and Schuster, 1936).

Stravinsky, Igor, *Poetics of Music in the Form of Six Lessons*. Trans. Arthur Knodel and Ingolf Dahl (Cambridge, Mass.: Harvard University Press, 1947).

Stravinsky, Igor, *Chroniques de ma vie* (Paris: Éditions Denoël, 1962).

Stravinsky, Igor, *Themes and Conclusions* (London: Faber and Faber, 1972).

Stravinski, Igor, *Confidences sur la musique: Propos recueillis (1912–1939)*. Texts and interviews selected, edited and annotated by Valérie Dufour (Arles: Actes Sud, 2013).

Stravinsky, Igor, and Robert Craft, *Conversations with Igor Stravinsky* (London: Faber and Faber, 1959).

Stravinsky, Igor, and Robert Craft, *Memories and Commentaries* (London: Faber and Faber, 1960).

Stravinsky, Igor, and Robert Craft, *Expositions and Developments* (London: Faber and Faber, 1962).

Stravinsky, Igor, and Robert Craft, *Themes and Episodes* (New York: Knopf, 1967).

Stravinsky, Igor, and Robert Craft, *Dialogues and a Diary* (London: Faber and Faber, 1968).

Stravinsky, Igor, and Robert Craft, *Retrospectives and Conclusions* (New York: Knopf, 1969).

Stravinsky, Igor, and Robert Craft, *Memories and Commentaries: New One-volume Edition* (London: Faber and Faber, 2002).

Stravinsky's Published Correspondence

Craft, Robert (ed.), *Stravinsky: Selected Correspondence*, 3 vols. (London: Faber and Faber, 1982, 1984, 1985).

Tappolet, Claude (ed.), *Correspondance Ansermet–Strawinsky (1914–1967)*, vol. III (Geneva: Georg, 1992).

Varunts, Viktor (ed.), *I. F. Stravinsky: Perepiska s russkimi korrespondentami. Materiali k biografi*, 3 vols. (Moscow: Kompozitor, 1997, 2000, 2003).

Varunts, Viktor (ed.). *I. Stravinsky: Publitsist i sobesednik* (Moscow: Sovetskiy Kompozitor, 1988).

Walzer, Pierre-Olivier (ed.), *Charles-Albert Cingria: Correspondance avec Igor Strawinski* (Lausanne: Éditions L'Age d'Homme, 2001).

Writings by Robert Craft and Members of the Stravinsky Family

Craft, Robert, A Stravinsky Scrapbook 1940–1971 (London: Thames and Hudson, 1983).

Craft, Robert, Stravinsky: Chronicle of a Friendship, revised and expanded edn (Nashville and London: Vanderbilt University Press, 1994).

Craft, Robert, Stravinsky: The Chronicle of a Friendship 1948–1971 (London: Gollancz, 1972).

Craft, Robert (ed.), Dearest Bubushkin: The Correspondence of Vera and Igor Stravinsky, 1921–1954, with Excerpts from Vera Stravinsky's Diaries, 1922–1971, trans. Lucia Davidova (London: Thames and Hudson, 1985).

Stravinskaya, K. Yu., O. I. F. Stravinskom i evo blizkikh (Leningrad: Muzïka, 1978).

Stravinsky, Vera, and Robert Craft, Stravinsky in Pictures and Documents (New York: Simon and Schuster, 1978).

Stravinsky, Vera, Rita McCaffrey and Robert Craft, Igor and Vera Stravinsky: A Photograph Album, 1921 to 1971 (London: Thames and Hudson, 1982).

Strawinsky, Theodore, and Denise Strawinsky, Stravinsky: A Family Chronicle 1906–1940, trans. Stephen Walsh (London : Schirmer, 2004); edited translation of T. and D. Strawinsky, Au cœur du foyer (Bourg-la-Reine: Zurfluh, 1998), which incorporated a revised text from Theodore Strawinsky, Catherine & Igor Stravinsky: A Family Album (London: Boosey & Hawkes, 1973).

Books on Stravinsky

Andriessen, Louis, and Elmer Schönberger, The Apollonian Clockwork: On Stravinsky, trans. Jeff Hamburg (Amsterdam University Press; Amsterdam Academic Archive, 2006).

Boucourechliev, André, Stravinsky, trans. Martin Cooper (London: Victor Gollancz, 1987).

Carr, Maureen A., After the Rite: Stravinsky's Path to Neoclassicism (1914–1925) (New York: Oxford University Press, 2014).

Carr, Maureen A., Multiple Masks: Neoclassicism in Stravinsky's Works on Greek Subjects (Lincoln and London: University of Nebraska Press, 2002).

Carr, Maureen A. (ed.), Stravinsky's Histoire du soldat: A Facsimile of the Sketches (Middleton, Wis.: A.-R. Editions, 2005).

Carr, Maureen A. (ed.), Stravinsky's Pulcinella: A Facsimile of the Sketches and Sources (Middleton, Wis.: A.-R. Editions, 2010).

Cross, Jonathan. Igor Stravinsky. (London: Reaktion Books, 2015).

Cross, Jonathan, The Stravinsky Legacy (Cambridge University Press, 1998).

Cross, Jonathan (ed.), The Cambridge Companion to Stravinsky (Cambridge University Press, 2003).

Druskin, Mikhail, Igor Stravinsky: His Life, Works and Views, trans. Martin Cooper (Cambridge University Press, 1983).

Dufour, Valérie, Stravinski et ses exégètes (1910–1940) (Brussels: Edition de l'Université de Bruxelles, 2006).

Francis, Kimberley A., *Nadia Boulanger and the Stravinskys: A Selected Correspondence* (University of Rochester Press, 2018).

Francis, Kimberley A., *Teaching Stravinsky: Nadia Boulanger and the Consecration of a Modernist Icon* (New York: Oxford University Press, 2015).

Griffiths, Graham, *Stravinsky's Piano: Genesis of a Musical Language* (Cambridge University Press, 2013).

Hill, Peter, *Stravinsky: The Rite of Spring* (Cambridge University Press, 2000).

Horgan, Paul, *Encounters with Stravinsky: A Personal Record* (New York: Farrar, Straus and Giroux, 1972).

Horlacher, Gretchen G., *Building Blocks: Repetition and Continuity in the Music of Stravinsky* (New York: Oxford University Press, 2011).

Jaffé, Daniel, *Historical Dictionary of Russian Music* (Lanham: Scarecrow Press, 2012).

Jordan, Stephanie, *Stravinsky Dances: Re-visions Across a Century* (Alton, Hampshire: Dance Books, 2007).

Joseph, Charles M., *Stravinsky Inside Out* (New Haven and London: Yale University Press, 2001).

Joseph, Charles M., *Stravinsky and Balanchine: A Journey of Invention* (New Haven and London: Yale University Press, 2002).

Joseph, Charles M., *Stravinsky's Ballets* (New Haven and London: Yale University Press, 2011).

Lesure, François (ed.), *Stravinsky: Études et témoignages* (Paris: Lattès, 1982).

Levitz, Tamara, *Modernist Mysteries: Perséphone* (New York: Oxford University Press, 2012).

Levitz, Tamara (ed.), *Stravinsky and His World* (Princeton University Press, 2013).

Libman, Lillian, *And Music at the Close: Stravinsky's Last Years* (London: Macmillan, 1972).

Maconie, Robin, *Experiencing Stravinsky: A Listener's Companion* (Lanham, MD: Scarecrow Press, 2013).

Neff, Severine, Maureen Carr and Gretchen Horlacher (eds.), with John Reef, *The Rite of Spring at 100* (Bloomington: Indiana University Press, 2017).

Pasler, Jann (ed.), *Confronting Stravinsky: Man, Musician, and Modernist* (Berkeley and Los Angeles: University of California Press, 1986).

Slim, H. Colin, *Stravinsky in the Americas: Transatlantic Tours and Domestic Excursions from Wartime Los Angeles (1925–1945)* (Oakland: University of California Press, 2019).

Straus, Joseph N., *Stravinsky's Late Music* (Cambridge University Press, 2001).

Taruskin, Richard, *Defining Russia Musically* (Princeton University Press, 1997).

Taruskin, Richard, *Russian Music at Home and Abroad* (Oakland: University of California Press, 2016).

Taruskin, Richard, *Stravinsky and the Russian Traditions: A Biography of the Works through Mavra*, 2 vols. (Berkeley and Los Angeles: University of California Press, 1996).

van den Toorn, Pieter C., *The Music of Igor Stravinsky* (New Haven: Yale University Press, 1983).

van den Toorn, Pieter C., and John McGinness, *Stravinsky and the Russian Period: Sound and Legacy of a Musical Idiom* (Cambridge University Press, 2012).

Walsh, Stephen, *The Music of Stravinsky* (London: Routledge, 1988).

Walsh, Stephen, *Stravinsky, A Creative Spring: Russia and France 1882–1934* (New York: Knopf, 1999; London: Jonathan Cape, 2000).

Walsh, Stephen, *Stravinsky, The Second Exile: France and America 1934–1971* (New York: Knopf, 2006; London: Jonathan Cape, 2006).

White, Eric Walter, *Stravinsky: The Composer and His Works*, 2nd edn (London and Boston: Faber and Faber, 1979).

Index

RUSSIAN VOCAL MUSIC, Stravinsky's, 404–8
Russolo, Luigi, 202, 408
   A Meeting of Motor-car and Aeroplanes, 182
   The Art of Noises, 182, 408
RYCHENBERG FOUNDATION, The, 408–9

Sabaneyev, Leonid, 356, 421
SACHER, Paul, 2, 86, 96, 97, 115, 118, 121,
   223, 307, 333, 334, 337, 411, 418,
   430, 456, 483
SACHER STIFTUNG/FOUNDATION, Paul, 73,
   90, 108, 120, 410–11, 425
Sachs, Arthur, 119
SADOVEN, Hélène, 411
Saint-John Perse, 120
Sakharov, Ivan, 171, 379, 380, 403, 408
   Songs of the Russian People, 224
Samodurov, Vyacheslav, 358
Sancellemoz, 452
Sanin, Alexander, 39, 121, 298
Sapiro, Aaron, 468
Sargent, Malcolm, 120
Sartre, Jean-Paul, 74, 184
SATIE, Erik, 14, 120, 140, 243, 244, 310, 311,
   386, 411–12, 427, 472, 478
   Cinq grimaces pour 'Le Songe d'une nuit
     d'été', 412
   Enfantines, 428
   Mercure, 471
   Parade, 17, 99, 101, 140, 412, 471. See also
     COCTEAU, Jean
   Socrate, 412
   Trois Morceaux en forme de poire, 428
Sauguet, Henri, 141
Scarlatti, Domenico
   Sonatas, 224
SCÈNES DE BALLET, 3, 33, 38, 43, 44, 94, 112,
   126, 138, 142, 226, 236, 412–14, 488
SCHAEFFNER, André, 110, 120, 177,
   414–15, 464
Schenker, Heinrich, 111, 266
SCHERCHEN, Hermann, 8, 120, 185, 194, 409,
   415, 455
SCHERZO, 323, 415, 454
SCHERZO À LA RUSSE, 156, 203, 415–16, 431,
   435, 503
SCHERZO FANTASTIQUE, 34, 38, 54, 60, 111, 158,
   160, 163, 164, 221, 233, 258, 259,
   275, 294, 324, 416–17, 430, 440,
   460, 504
Schlegel, Friedrich, 400
Schlemmer, Oskar, 415
SCHLOEZER, Boris de, 61, 96, 120, 240, 272,
   284, 310, 311, 317, 384, 414, 417–18
   neo-classicism, 418
Schmitt, Florent, 11, 138, 143, 177, 298, 311,
   316, 354, 412
   Le tragédie de Salomé, 387, 471
Schneiderhan, Wolfgang, 8
SCHOENBERG, Arnold, 3–4, 14, 26, 56, 57, 64,
   67, 75, 82, 89, 118, 135, 207, 211, 218,

   220, 221, 222, 226, 233, 234, 245,
   248, 266, 267, 287, 311, 402, 418–20,
   425, 428, 454, 478, 493, 498, 500
   atonality, 4
   De profundis, 1
   Erwartung, op. 17, 57, 266
   Models for Beginners in Composition,
     221
   Moses und Aron, 57
   Pierrot lunaire, op. 21, 82, 310, 354, 406,
     418, 500
   Serenade, 419
   String Quartet in D Major, 500
   Suite, op. 29, 84, 306, 419, 423
   Suite for Piano, op. 25, 272
   Three Satires, op. 28, 26, 328, 419
   twelve-note composition, 4
   Wind Quintet, op. 26, 84
Schoenberg, Gertrud, 420
Schoenberg's Variations for Orchestra, op.
   31, 425
School of American Ballet. See New York:
   NEW YORK CITY BALLET
Schott Music, 9
Schubert, Franz, 165, 290
   Trois Marches héroïques, op. 27, D 602,
     436
Schumann, Robert, 208, 500
SCRIABIN, Alexander, 7, 78, 117, 120, 176,
   189, 207, 212, 324, 342, 397, 417,
   420–1
   Piano Concerto, 500
   Piano Sonata No. 3, 433
   The Poem of Ecstasy, 163, 420
   Prometheus, 163, 420
SECOND VIENNESE SCHOOL, 128, 221, 233,
   415, 421–2
Sellars, Peter, 352
SEPTET, 64, 84, 113, 226, 273, 290, 422–3,
   425, 440, 476
SERENADE IN A, 62, 98, 111, 273, 322, 323,
   324, 424–5, 428, 483
serialism, 30, 59, 66, 75, 84, 90, 101, 104,
   125, 129, 168, 170, 175, 192, 196, 199,
   215, 219, 221, 252, 258, 260, 306,
   325, 411, 422–3, 425, 428, 439, 440,
   476, 483, 502
SERMON, A NARRATIVE AND A PRAYER, A, 90, 159,
   174, 202, 410, 411, 425
Sert, José-Maria, 141
Sert, Misia, 119, 158
Sessions, Roger, 175
Severini, Gino, 127
Shapero, Harold, 120
SHARAFF, Irene, 16, 42, 127, 425–6
Shazar, Zalman, 201
Shchukin, Sergey, 190
Sheppard, John, 90
Shestakova, Lyudmila, 65
Shilkret, Nathaniel, 26, 89, 244
   Genesis Suite, 468

Printed in the USA
CPSIA information can be obtained
at www.ICGtesting.com
CBHW071744200824
13480CB00005B/211

9 781316 506202